Small Fruit Crop Management

GENE J. GALLETTA, EDITOR

USDA-ARS, Fruit Lab, PSI, BARC
Beltsville, Maryland

DAVID G. HIMELRICK, EDITOR

Department of Horticulture
Auburn University
Auburn, Alabama

LYNDA CHANDLER, ILLUSTRATOR

Temple Terrace, Florida

PRENTICE HALL
ENGLEWOOD CLIFFS, NEW JERSEY 07632

Library of Congress Cataloging-in-Publication Data

Small fruit crop management / Gene J. Galletta, editor, David G.
  Himelrick, editor, Lynda Chandler, illustrator.
    p.   cm.
    Bibliography: p.
    Includes index.
    ISBN 0-13-814609-8
    1. Berries. 2. Grapes. 3. Kiwifruit. 4. Fruit-culture.
I. Galletta, Gene J.   II. Himelrick, David Glenn
III. Chandler, Lynda E.
SB381.S62   1989
634.7--dc20   89-3937
                                      CIP

Editorial/production supervision and
  interior design: Marcia Krefetz
Cover design: Wanda Lubelska Design
Manufacturing buyer: Laura Crossland

© 1990 by Prentice-Hall, Inc.
A Division of Simon & Schuster
Englewood Cliffs, New Jersey 07632

Printed in the United States of America
10 9 8 7 6 5 4 3 2 1

ISBN 0-13-814609-8

Prentice-Hall International (UK) Limited, *London*
Prentice-Hall of Australia Pty. Limited, *Sydney*
Prentice-Hall Canada Inc., *Toronto*
Prentice-Hall Hispanoamericana, S.A., *Mexico*
Prentice-Hall of India Private Limited, *New Delhi*
Prentice-Hall of Japan, Inc., *Tokyo*
Simon & Schuster Asia Pte. Ltd., *Singapore*
Editora Prentice-Hall do Brasil, Ltda., *Rio de Janeiro*

Contents

2 FACTORS THAT INFLUENCE SMALL FRUIT PRODUCTION

14

3 STRAWBERRY MANAGEMENT   83

Contents

8 CRANBERRY MANAGEMENT 354

Preface

One of the first service projects undertaken by the Viticulture and Small Fruit Working Group of the American Society for Horticultural Science in the late 1970's was to study the need for a proposed comprehensive and up-to-date small fruit culture textbook. The feasibility committee, consisting of R. S. Bringhurst (California), G. Cahoon (Ohio), J. W. Courter (Illinois), R. G. Hill Jr. (Ohio), W. B. Nesbitt (North Carolina), E. Pierson (Nebraska), and G. J. Galletta (Maryland), Chairman, found that the need for such a text was real. The proposed readers would be college and junior college students, agribusiness people, county extension personnel, farmers, interested amateurs, and professional horticulturists.

Following a charge by the Working Group in 1981 to plan such a book, the committee prepared an outline of the book, suggested authors, and established the following book development rationale:

1. No prior reader knowledge of nonarboreal fruit crops would be assumed.
2. Basic botanical composition (plant habit), relationships, developmental pat-

terns, and environmental responses of the major temperate zone fruit crops would be thoroughly described and illustrated.

3. The principal cultural systems in use and some major variations would be outlined and related to the botanical structure, peculiarities, and responsiveness of each plant species.

4. Although this would be principally an American text and reference book, contributions by knowledgable individuals would be solicited from any place in the world where each crop or subject was important.

5. It was hoped that this information and form of presentation would stimulate future perceptive students of these crops to develop improved and more efficient cultural systems.

G. Galletta was appointed Editor, and he solicited authors, secured an illustrator, prepared chapter outlines, devised manuscript and citation formats, prepared a book prospectus, submitted same to publishers, and negotiated a contract with Prentice-Hall. Progress was slow due to other job pressures of the Editor and authors, deaths, retirements, and personnel realignments. In 1986, Galletta asked D. G. Himelrick to help him finish the book. Himelrick worked with the authors, illustrator, and publisher to secure revised and updated manuscripts and illustrations. He also had the manuscript committed to word processing disks. Both editors have contributed considerable original material to the text and illustrations. Although a number of colleagues have reviewed portions of the manuscript and used same in teaching, none have read the entire manuscript. The editors together made the final (painful but necessary) condensation and choice of illustrations. Responsiblity for factual errors, omissions, or oversimplifications rests with the editors, who hope that the increased experience and knowledge gained during the protracted preparation period will be reflected by more comprehensive subject coverage and a longer useful life for this work.

The book has three major sections. Chapters 1 and 2 are introduction and background knowledge necessary for small fruit culture. The temperate-zone small fruit crops are introduced and characterized, and their uses, growth patterns, world production, and factors that must be considered and understood for successful small fruit production are discussed. In Chapters 3 through 11 the domestication, history, taxonomic, and economic botany and management possibilities for the principal small fruit genera is presented. The crops are arranged in this general order: perennial herbs, biennial-caned trailing to erect shrubs, perennial-caned shrubs and related woody rhizomatous colonies and evergreen trailing vines, freestanding bushes and tall shrubs, and deciduous supported vines. Chapters 12 through 14 concentrate on the fruit product — its maturation, quality considerations, harvesting, handling and shelf-life preservation and extension, marketing preparation, marketing options, business management decisions, and economic outlooks.

The book is suitable for a three-hour, semester long college course in its entirety. For shorter course offerings in America, we would suggest covering Chapters 1 through 3, 4 or 5, 7 or 8, 10, 12, and 13 or 14, depending on the crops of interest in your area. Of course, there are many other possibilities, and the extensive reference and suggested reading lists should challenge the serious student.

ACKNOWLEDGMENTS

The editors are indebted for the encouragement, assistance, and patience of the following during the preparation of this manuscript: Dr. Miklos Faust and other USDA colleagues; the Cornell Cooperative Extension Service; illustrator Lynda Chandler; our secretaries and assistants, Joyce Mason, Mary Ann Town, Mary Van Buren, Vivian Davis, and Steven Spell; the several editors, their assistants, and the staff at Prentice Hall who worked with us; the American Society for Horticultural Science Headquarters staff; the "3 Bob"; our colleagues of the Viticulture and Small Fruit Working Group; our authors and chapter reviewers; Rosanne Galletta for copy editing; and finally, our wives, Nada and Kathy.

G. J. Galletta
D. G. Himelrick

Contributors

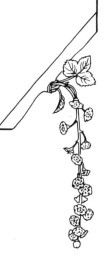

Dr. M. Ahmedullah (Pomologist – Grape Physiology)
Department of Horticulture
Washington State University
Pullman, WA 99164

Dr. Walter E. Ballinger* (Postharvest Physiologist – Blueberries and Grapes)
Department of Horticultural Sciences
North Carolina State University
Raleigh, NC 27650

Dr. Royce S. Bringhurst* (Pomologist–Geneticist, Strawberry Improvement)
Department of Pomology
University of California
Davis, CA 95616

Mrs. Lynda Chandler (Illustrator-Horticulturist)
326 Bahamas Avenue South
Temple Terrace, FL 33617

Dr. J. W. Courter (Extension Specialist — Direct Marketing of Horticultural Crops)
Dixon Springs Agricultural Center
Department of Horticulture
University of Illinois
Simpson, IL 62985

Dr. Perry C. Crandall* (Physiologist — Raspberry and Strawberry Culture)
Washington State University
Southwestern Washington Research Unit
1919 N.E. 78th Street
Vancouver, WA 98665

Dr. Malcolm N. Dana* (Pomologist-Teacher, Small Fruit Culture)
Department of Horticulture
University of Wisconsin
Madison, WI 53706

Dr. Hugh A. Daubeny (Geneticist — Raspberry and Strawberry Breeding)
Agriculture Canada Research Station
6660 N. W. Marine Drive
Vancouver, British Columbia
Canada V6T 1X2

Dr. Paul Eck (Physiologist — Blueberry and Cranberry Culture)
Department of Horticulture and Forestry
Rutgers University
New Brunswick, NJ 08903

Dr. A. R. Ferguson (Physiologist-Botanist, Kiwifruit)
Division of Horticulture and Processing
DSIR, Private Bag
Auckland, New Zealand

Dr. Richard C. Funt (Pomologist — Extension, Fruit Crops Production Economics)
Department of Horticulture
Ohio State University
Columbus, OH 43210

Dr. Gene J. Galletta (Geneticist–Pomologist, Small Fruit Improvement)
Fruit Lab, USDA, ARS
BARC West
Beltsville, MD 20705

Dr. Robert E. Gough (Botanist–Pomologist, Highbush Blueberry and Culture)
Department of Plant and Soil Science
University of Rhode Island
Kingston, RI 02881

Dr. Ivan V. Hall* (Botanist–Physiologist, Blueberry Ecology, Physiology, and
    Culture)
Agriculture Canada
Agricultural Research Station
Kentville, Nova Scotia B4N 1J5
Canada

Dr. Laszlo Harmat (Pomologist, Ribes Culture)
Pomology Research Institute
4244 Ujfeherto, Hungary

Dr. David G. Himelrick (Physiologist–Pomologist)
Department of Horticulture
Auburn University
Auburn, Alabama 36849

Dr. R. Brian How* (Economist — Marketing of Agricultural Products)
Department of Agricultural Economics
Cornell University
Ithaca, NY 14853

Dr. Fenton E. Larsen (Pomologist — Rootstocks, Defoliation, and Nursery Prob-
    lems)
Department of Horticulture/Landscape Architecture
Washington State University
Pullman, WA 99164

Dr. James N. Moore (Pomologist — Fruit Crops Breeding)
Department of Horticulture and Forestry
University of Arkansas
Fayetteville, AR 72701

Dr. Justin R. Morris (Postharvest Physiologist — Raw Product Quality and Grape Processing)
Department of Horticulture & Food Science
University of Arkansas
Fayetteville, AR 72701

Dr. Aldar Porpaczy (Pomologist — Ribes Breeding)
Pomology Research Institute
9431 Fertod, Hungary

Dr. Marvin Pritts (Pomologist — Extension, Small Fruit Physiology and Culture)
Department of Pomology
Cornell University
Ithaca, NY 14853

Dr. Robert M. Skirvin (Pomologist — Fruit Crop Tissue Culture)
Department of Horticulture
University of Illinois
Urbana, IL 61803

Dr. Sara E. Spayd (Food Scientist Postharvest Physiologist — Processed Fruit, Wine, and Grape Quality)
Washington State University
Irrigation Agriculture Research and Extension Center
Prosser, WA 99350

Dr. James M. Spiers (Physiologist — Small Fruit Nuturition and Physiology)
Box 287
USDA, Small Fruit Research Station
Poplarville, MS 39470

Dr. Elden J. Stang (Physiologist — Fruit Physiology, Cranberry Management)
Department of Horticulture
University of Wisconsin
Madison, WI 53706

This book is dedicated to the present, but especially to the retired and deceased small fruit, viticulture, and pomology researchers and teachers, to whom we owe so much. We hope that this contribution is some small repayment for their keen interest in the subject, and their influence on us.

The Editors and Contributors
of *Small Fruit Crop Management*

* = retired.

Chapter 1

The Small Fruit Crops

G. J. GALLETTA
D. G. HIMELRICK

DISTINGUISHING THE SMALL FRUIT CROPS

Since prehistoric times, humankind, and members of many animal species, have been attracted to plants bearing edible berries. In the generic sense, berries are pulpy, usually edible fruits of rounded shape and small size, irrespective of their structure. Botanically, a berry is a simple fruit, derived from ovarian floral tissue only, in which the fruit wall or pericarp has a uniformly pulpy or fleshy consistency. Berry-like fruits have long been and are still gathered from the wild. Small fruit plants adapted to temperate regions have been cultivated for only the last two to four centuries, the most recent domestication being that of the highbush blueberry, *Vaccinium corymbosum* L. (Coville, 1937). The exception is the grapevine *(Vitis vinifera* L.), which was cultivated in Egypt 5000 to 6000 years ago (Snyder, 1937).

Cultural Rationale

Small fruit plants are grown for many reasons. The fruits themselves are highly prized for their varying shapes, textures, flavors, and colors. Consumption of small fruits, either fresh or processed, alone or in combination with other foods or beverages, seems to enhance one's sense of well-being. In medieval times, dried strawberry plants (including fruits) were used to cure depressive illnesses. European artists of the same period used the strawberry to symbolize perfect righteousness, eternal salvation, noble thought, and modesty (Darrow, 1966; Bruggman, 1966).

Small fruit plants are highly decorative, in both the vegetative or the flowering and fruiting stages. Although some of the plants are large shrubs, they can easily be pruned and trained to a more manageable size. Small fruit plantings can be made in very small areas, or can be used to screen or border unsightly areas. Intensive culture of small fruits can lead to high yields and profits from modest land areas. Harvesting of most small fruit crops is straightforward because large volumes of fruit are borne within easy reach of the picker or the harvesting machine. The versatile cultural methods and uses of these attractive and nutritious fruits continue to increase their popularity.

Small Fruit Crop Characteristics

The temperate-zone small fruit plant species are all *dicotyledonous angiosperms* (flowering plants with netted-veined leaves that bear two modified storage or "seed leaves"—the cotyledons—on their embryos). The small fruits are all *perennial* plants which are *usually woody*. In nature they colonize new areas through seed dispersal by birds and other animals. They often spread within an area by some form of vegetative (asexual) reproduction of a seedling mother plant, such as runnering (strawberry), rooting of prostrate aboveground or partially covered stems (cranberries, grapes), budding of horizontal underground stems (lowbush blueberries), sprouting of root buds—"suckers" (red raspberries and many blackberries), rooting of specialized stem tips that touch the soil (black raspberries), or rooting of new peripheral shoots originating at the stem–root transition area—the shrub "crown"—to form a thicket (Juneberries, gooseberries, currants, and some rabbiteye blueberries).

Small fruit plants vary in growth habit from creeping vines (cranberry) and climbing vines (grape) through low-growing herbaceous or woody colonies (strawberry and lowbush blueberry) and multistemmed thickets or hedges (raspberry and blackberry) to freestanding erect shrubs (highbush blueberry).

Small fruits are *genetically heterozygous* (contain many dissimilar pairs of character determinants or genes); hence they do not reproduce individuals from seed that are very similar to (almost exactly like) the seed parent. The small fruits are thus characterized as *"not coming true from seed"*, and valuable individuals must be propagated from nonsexual plant parts *(vegetative reproduction)*.

These plants are grouped because they all bear *fruit of small to moderate size.* The fruit is borne either singly or in clusters, on flowering branches or shoots growing from axillary buds which usually develop between the leaf base and the stem on young, new growth. Most temperate-zone small fruit species develop flowering shoots from buds produced the preceding season. To develop normally, the buds usually require a chilling period, such as that provided by cool winter temperatures. Many tropical and subtropical plants and temperate-zone annual species produce flowers from current-season buds. Certain strawberries and raspberries may also flower on current-season growth and are termed "everbearing" and "fall-fruiting", respectively.

Small fruit plants are generally *grown on their own roots*. Exceptions are *vinifera* grapes and certain gooseberries which are grafted onto rootstock selections that tolerate certain soil situations or parasites, or which permit the development of a tree-like form to facilitate mechanical harvesting. The small to moderate adult size of small fruit plants adapts them for intensive culture in which thousands of individual plants are grown on 1 hectare (approximately 2.5 acres).

In summary, the small fruit plants are predominantly woody perennial dicot angiosperms which are usually vegetatively propagated; grown on their own roots; bear small to moderate-sized fruit on herbs, vines, or shrubs; and are densely planted and intensively cultivated on modest-sized land areas. They are cultured for their botanical true or accessory fruits, which are usually used as desserts, or in beverages and flavored products.

However, modern cultural methods and newer cultivars (cultivated varieties) are making the classical distinctions between the tree and small fruit crops less obvious. Use of tissue culture methods of propagation makes it possible in many circumstances for normally grafted tree fruits to be grown on their own roots. Use of dwarf or spur-type trees and close-spaced and trellised orchards reduces the plant size and increases the number of trees planted per unit area to a point where they are comparable to the small fruits in size and appearance. Indeed, vigorous bush fruit cultivars are larger plants than genetic dwarf peaches or apples grown on very dwarfing rootstocks such as 'Malling IX'. Similarly, hybridization and selection within small fruit species has produced strawberries as large as plums, and blueberries and grapes as large as cherries. Additionally, there are small fruit shrubs such as sparkleberry *(Vaccinium arboreum* Marsh) which have a strong tendency toward the monostem or tree-like character. Many of the newer small fruit cultivars also have fruit flesh of the same firm consistency as the stone fruits *(Prunus* spp.), rendering the old British term 'soft fruits' less appropriate. Similarly, the notoriously short shelf life of many small fruit species has been lengthened by appropriate breeding and selection techniques. Thus the small fruit plant classification is an arbitrary, but useful grouping.

Cultivated and Potentially Useful Small Fruit Species

The principal plant genera cultivated for their berry-like fruit in temperate climates are *Vitis* (grapes), *Fragaria* (strawberries), *Rubus* (raspberries, blackberries, loganberries, etc.), *Ribes* (currants and gooseberries), and *Vaccinium* (blueberries, bilberries, whortleberries, cranberries, etc.). Recently, the genus *Actinidia* (kiwifruit or Chinese gooseberry) has become extensively cultivated in New Zealand, parts of Europe, and the United States.

Temperate genera cultivated regionally include *Amelanchier* (June- or serviceberries or saskatoons), and *Sambucus* (elderberries). Some improved selections have been named of the American cranberrybush *(Viburnum trilobum* Marsh), of the Tara or wild fig *(Actinidia arguta* Miq.), and of the bush honeysuckle *(Lonicera* spp.). Small fruit genera considered worthy of investigation and possible domestication in North America are *Shepherdia argentea* Nutt (buffalo berry, rabbit berry, or Nebraska currant), *Berberis* (barberries), *Mahonia, Gaulteria* (wintergreen or checkerberry) and *Eleagnus* (goumi). Other small fruit species that have shown promise for domestication in Europe and parts of Asia are lingonberry *(Vaccinium vitisidaea),* the bilberries *(Vaccinium myrtillus* and *V. uliginosum), Actinidia chinensis* (smooth-skinned species), and the arctic raspberries *Rubus arcticus* spp. *arcticus* and the hybrid allfieldberry *(Rubus arcticus* L. subsp. × *stellarcticus).* This by no means exhausts the list of potentially useful temperate small fruit species. Berry breeders have been incorporating useful germplasm into already improved genera by using both domestic and foreign species as parents, especially those from Asia and the Pacific islands. By so doing, people living in the northern, middle, and southern latitudes of the temperate zones should be able to enjoy locally grown fruits of each of the principal small fruit genera in the future. Additionally, temperate-zone plant culture is being adapted to subtropical and tropical regions. Table 1–1 summarizes the plant habit and climatic and site adaptation necessary for the principal temperate cultivated small fruit crops.

SPECIFIC USES OF SMALL FRUIT PLANTS

Traditional uses of small fruit plants have ranged from consumption of fresh fruit, and plant extractions for medicinal uses and dyestuffs, to being a component of a wide variety of processed foods and beverages. Additionally, the plants have provided aesthetic ornamental appeal in garden plantings. Few people are acquainted with the versatile and diverse manner in which small fruits can be used.

Food and Beverage Uses

Uses for fresh fruit include eating out of hand as a snack food or dessert; as toppings or fillings with cereals, ice cream, pastries, and so on; as garnishes for meat and vegetable dishes and iced beverages; and in salads.

Processed fruit uses include expressed juice from single species or in blends; fermented or extracted juice of fruit for making wines, brandies, teas, and liqueurs; cooked as jams and jellies; made into compotes and concentrates, toppings, syrups, or purees for mixing with other products, such as yogurt, sherberts, ice cream, sorbets, fruit bars, candies, processed snacks, and pastries; extracted for flavors and colors; and canned, dried, frozen, or freeze-dried for later use.

Dietary benefits from the small fruits are similar to those of many of the tree

TABLE 1-1 CULTIVATED TEMPERATE SMALL (SOFT) FRUIT CROPS OF THE WORLD

COMMON NAME	SCIENTIFIC NAME[a]	PLANT HABIT	CLIMATIC ADAPTATION	SITE CONSIDERATIONS
Garden strawberry	*Fragaria x ananassa* and *Fragaria* spp.	Stoloniferous perennial herbs	Basically cool temperate	Well drained, light for early production, heavy for maximum production
Alpine strawberry Wood strawberry Musky (Hautbois) strawberry	*F. vesca* var. *semperflorens* *F. vesca* var. *sylvestris* *F. moschata*	Stoloniferous perennial herbs	Basically cool temperate	As above + garden borders or forcing
Red raspberry (European) Red raspberry (American) Black raspberry (eastern North American) Purple raspberry	*Rubus idaeus vulgatus* *R. idaeus strigosus* *R. occidentalis* *R. neglectus* (*occidentalis x strigosus*)	Suckering shrubs, biennial top, perennial root	Basically cool temperate	Medium to light soils; good fertility and drainage; sensitive to nematodes, root diseases, and virus concentrations
Erect thorny blackberries (American)	*Rubus* species hybrids, including elements of *R. alleghe-niensis, frondosus, pergratus, argutus,* etc.	Suckering shrubs, biennial tops, perennial roots	Warm temperate	Choose warmer, more protected sites that are well drained—soil and air—and free of crown gall
Semierect thorny blackberries (European) Semierect thornless blackberries (American)	*Rubus* species hybrids, including elements of *R. procerus, rusticanus, thysiger,* etc. Species hybrids among American and European thorny species but including *R. rusticanus* var. *inermis*			
Himalaya Evergreen	*R. procerus* *R. laciniatus*			
Dewberries (trailing) Eastern U.S. Southeastern U.S. Western U.S.	*R. baileyanus* *R. trivialis* *R. ursinus* and *macropetalus*	Trailing shrubs, biennial tops, perennial roots	Warm temperate	Choose warmer, more protected sites that are well drained—soil and air—and free of crown gall

TABLE 1-1 CONTINUED

COMMON NAME	SCIENTIFIC NAME[a]	PLANT HABIT	CLIMATIC ADAPTATION	SITE CONSIDERATIONS
Raspberry– blackberry hybrids	*R. loganobaccus*			
Red and white currant	*Ribes sativum*	Shrubs, perennial roots and tops	Cold temperate	Loam soils, moisture retentive but well drained, cooler sites with best air drainage, somewhat shade tolerant but not heat tolerant
Black currant (European)	*R. nigrum*			
European gooseberry	*R. grossularia*			
American gooseberry	*R. hirtellum*			
Lowbush blueberry	Principally *Vaccinium angustifolium*, with mixtures of *V. angustifolium* var. *nigrum, V. boreale,* and *V. myrtilloides*	Rhizomatous low shrubs, perennial	Cool to cold temperate	Acidic and often exposed sites, variable moisture requirements, woodlot or bog natural populations tended and harvested
Highbush blueberry	Hybrids of *V. corymbosum, australe, angustifolium,* etc.	Perennial shrubs	Cool to warm temperate	Acidic, organic sands with good drainage and aeration, and permanent but moderate soil moisture
Rabbiteye blueberry	*V. ashei*	Large perennial shrubs	Warm temperate	Acidic organic or mineral soils without undue moisture stress; will tolerate higher pH and drier soils than highbush—bloom too early on lowland soils
Cranberry	*Vaccinium macrocarpon*	Perennial creeping evergreen vine with upright stems	Cool temperate	Same soils as highbush blueberry, needs adequate water source for periodic flooding
Elderberry	*Sambucus canadensis*	Tall deciduous shrubs, stoloniferous	Warm to cool	Tolerant to variable soil moisture and type, best on fertile silt loams
Highbush cranberry	*Viburnum trilobum*	Tall, spreading shrubs	Cool temperate	Best adapted to cool, moist and fertile soils; tolerant of partial shade

Common name	Scientific name[a]	Growth habit	Climate	Notes
Juneberry	*Amelanchier alnifolia*	Stoloniferous shrub	Cool temperate	Broadly adapted but needs good soil drainage
European grape	*Vitis vinifera*	Perennial woody deciduous climbing vines	Warm temperate	Warm, dry climate needed; sightly acid to neutral well-drained soils, need nematode- and phylloxera-resistant rootstocks
Muscadine grape	*V. rotundifolia*	Perennial woody deciduous climbing vines	Warm temperate	Tolerates heat and humidity, own-rooted
American bunch grape	*V. labrusca* plus other principally American *Vitis* species	Perennial woody deciduous climbing vines	Cool to warm temperate	Own-rooted, tolerate cooler soils and temperatures
French-American grapes	*V. vinifera* – various American species	Perennial woody deciduous climbing vines	Cool to warm temperate	Own-rooted; similar to American types for site requirements
Kiwifruit	*Actinidia deliciosa*	Rampant long-lived perennial vines	Warm temperate	Best on deep, porous soils; heavy water requirement, susceptible to frost and wind damage, 220-day growing season

[a]Taxonomic authorities omitted for conciseness; see appropriate chapters.

fruits and vegetables. They are good-to-excellent sources of vitamins (especially vitamin C), minerals, organic acids, easy-to-digest carbohydrates, fiber, and water. Other benefits of small fruits range from the very high vitamin C and digestive enzyme content of kiwifruit to the beneficial acidifying effects of cranberry juice on the urinary tract. Additionally, small fruit crops act as stimulants to the digestive tract. *USDA Agricultural Handbook 8–9* (USDA, 1982) gives extensive listings of the nutritional value of specific food crops, including the small fruits.

Additional Uses

Since small fruit plants have aesthetic appeal throughout the year, they may be grown in a number of ornamental landscape situations. Most strawberries, many blueberries, and some raspberries and blackberries can be grown successfully in containers on patios. Shy-running strawberries, low-growing blueberries, and dwarf brambles make fine border plants. Strawberries, grapes, cranberries, creeping blueberries, and trailing brambles can be trained to make appealing hanging baskets.

The taller-growing bushes of blueberries, currants, elderberries, highbush cranberries, and blackberries can be used as single or grouped specimen plants, or trained as hedges, or used as living fences or screens to create a private outdoor sitting area. Raspberries and the small fruit vine crops can be trained along fences. Many of the bush types, as well as the brambles, grapes, and kiwifruit can be espaliered (flat plane or fan-cultured) along a wall, fence, or on an arbor or pergola. Lower-growing bush fruits can be grouped with nonfruiting ornamental plants. An obvious example would be blueberry and/or cranberry in an Ericaceous group setting which might include *Clethra, Azalea, Rhododendron,* and so on. There are a number of ornamental blueberry cultivars, such as 'Johnblue' (fine-leaved *Vaccinium darrowi* selection), 'Bloodstone', 'Ornablue', and 'Tophat', which would be useful in such arrangements. Similarly, Alpine strawberries might border a grouping of taller summer- and fall-flowering herbaceous perennial plants.

People desiring to attract wildlife, especially birds, should consider including small fruit plants in their landscaping plans. Netting may be necessary to exclude birds from plants that are intended for harvest.

Cut flowering branches of the small fruit plants can add much to spring and summer flower arrangements. Similarly, cut dormant canes of grapes, and possibly thornless blackberries, can be used to fashion wreaths, and cut dormant branches of bush fruits can add height or interest to dried flower arrangements.

GROWTH PATTERNS OF THE SMALL FRUITS

Since reproductive structures (fruits) are the desired product of the small fruit plants, and since they are perennial plants, it is necessary to grow the plants to full vegetative and reproductive maturity. This implies the development of reproductive sites on the vegetative body, and the accumulation of reserve carbohydrates and plant hormones that stimulate flower bud initiation. The initiated flower buds must then develop into flowers, be fertilized, and develop into mature marketable fruits.

Fortunately, a mature fruit plant, well-tended and healthy, will produce one or more crops of fruit each year for many years.

To better understand successful management techniques for these crop plants, it is useful to consider that they develop in two overlapping cycles, successively and simultaneously. Figure 1-1 represents the two cycles, the maturation cycle and the seasonal cycle. The field maturation period (from planting of the juvenile propagule to full cropping levels) in the small fruits varies from just over 1 year for most strawberries to 8 or 9 years for kiwifruit. However, fruit production in certain strawberries may begin in the planting year (1 year after propagation) or in as little as 2 to 4 years for the woody bush and vine fruits.

The maturation cycle is represented in Fig. 1-1 by three widely separated stages. Drawing A represents the original planting stock: pruned to a small size, usually entirely vegetative, and freshly transplanted. Drawing B represents a plant that has undergone considerable vegetative growth and limited development of sexual structures (flower buds). At this intermediate point the original plant body is still a large part of the plant. By the fully mature stage the original plant body has been largely overgrown and crowded out by new plant parts (drawing C) and may have been pruned out as being too weak. Sexual structures and sites are now very numerous and dispersed all over the supporting stems (canes). The planting cycle may be reinitiated from either the intermediate or fully mature stages by rooting of stem cuttings in this instance. (In Fig. 1-1 a highbush blueberry was selected for illustration since the vegetative and flower buds are separated in this species.)

Drawings D_1 to D_4 (Fig. 1-1) illustrate the seasonal development along one mature shoot of a blueberry plant. In D_1 the dormant shoot shows prominent flower and leaf buds which expand (drawing D_2) into flower clusters and leafy shoots, respectively. By midsummer (drawing D_3) the flower clusters have been pollinated and mature into fruit clusters. The leafy shoots have completed one flush of growth and may be starting a second flush from the penultimate bud. Axillary buds are becoming visible at the leaf petiole bases along the length of the first flush. At the end of the growing season (drawing D_4), peduncles of the fruit clusters and fruit pedicels or pedicel scars may persist on the old, dried fruiting shoots. A few leaves may have persisted on the vegetative shoots. Axillary buds along the vegetative shoots will have matured into either flower or leaf buds, which will expand during the next growing season into fruit-bearing or leaf-bearing shoots, respectively.

This seasonal cycle may continue indefinitely as long as the supporting branch remains healthy and new vegetative growth is made each year. In practice, older canes are removed after several years to make room for younger and more vigorous renewal canes.

Figure 1-1 could be repeated, listing management steps to be executed by the grower or his or her agents between the cycle stages instead of plant development phases. The relative emphases to be placed on the different operations could also be indicated. Obviously, those operations that will result in good plant survival and the rapid establishment of a large vegetative structure are most important in the interval from planting to intermediate maturity. Those operations leading to a mature plant body able to support an optimum number of fruiting sites and structures should be emphasized during the final maturation period. Operations that ensure continued

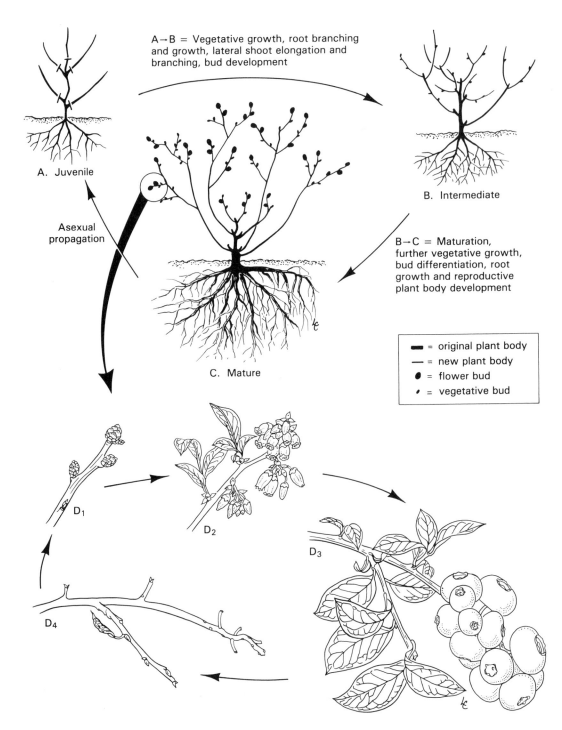

A→B = Vegetative growth, root branching and growth, lateral shoot elongation and branching, bud development

A. Juvenile

B. Intermediate

Asexual propagation

B→C = Maturation, further vegetative growth, bud differentiation, root growth and reproductive plant body development

C. Mature

= original plant body
— = new plant body
= flower bud
= vegetative bud

D₁

D₂

D₃

D₄

FIGURE 1-1 General developmental cycle of a small fruit plant.

development of fruiting sites and maximum fruit production should receive highest priority when the plant is fully mature.

Recently, Abbott and Gough (1987) characterized the root growth of three highbush blueberry cultivars over three growing seasons, and correlated root growth with shoot growth, soil temperature, and seasonal development of highbush blueberries. Their results (Fig. 1-2) add another dimension to our understanding of the seasonal cycle in mature small fruit plants. They conclude that the growth rate of unsuberized white roots in mulched, mature highbush blueberry plants was limited by soil temperatures outside the range 57.2 to 64.4°F (14 to 18°C), and that root and shoot growth are not antagonistic in blueberries, but follow the same general patterns, with reduced growth during fruit maturation and harvest.

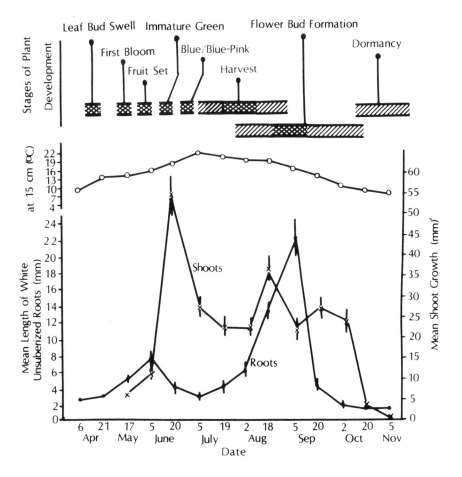

FIGURE 1-2 Elongation of white unsuberized roots in relation to shoot growth, soil temperature, and stage development of highbush blueberry plants. Vertical lines represent SE. SE < 1 are not plotted. Hatching indicates beginning and ending stage, crosshatching indicates peak period of stage. [After Abbott and Gough (1987).]

The most definitive source of world agricultural statistics are the production year-books of the Food and Agricultural Organization (FAO) of the United Nations. The editors of these yearbooks caution, however, that their figures are incomplete in many instances, and that they reflect only agricultural products and volumes that are sold and transported to the consumer.

The FAO editors' point about incomplete production data is especially applicable to many of the small fruits and vegetables. Sizable acreages of strawberries and bush berries are grown for direct on-farm or local market sales. Galletta (1980) found that more than half of the strawberries grown in the eastern United States were not reported in USDA Crop Reporting Board Statistics because they were not marketed through customary wholesale and retail channels. Crops such as blueberries, cranberries, and kiwifruit have been produced principally in limited areas within the United States and New Zealand, respectively, until quite recently. Production figures for such crops are generally recorded by commodity marketing associations or by states or provinces in which such production takes place.

Extent and Location of, and Trends in Small Fruit Production

World fruit production is reported by the FAO (1985) in the following categories: total, apples, citrus fruits, bananas, and grapes. The Old World or European grape *(Vitis vinifera)* is one of the earliest domesticated and most widely grown crops. Grapes account for 20% of the world's marketed fruit and nut (pomological) crops. The three next-oldest berry crops (strawberries, raspberries, and currants) combined account for an additional 1% of the recorded marketed fruit and nut crops sales.

Grapes have traditionally been marketed and consumed in the fresh, fermented, and dried states. In 1985, 49.6% of the grapes were marketed fresh, 48.6% fermented, and 1.8% dried. Table and wine grape production is concentrated in the developed countries, especially in Europe; raisin production is concentrated in Asia, Europe, and North America, and is split evenly between developed and undeveloped areas. Grape production as a whole has declined slightly, with wine production in Europe and the larger producing areas declining over the last 5 to 6 years. Table grape and raisin production has remained stable or increased slightly in the same period. Remarkable grape yields per unit of land area have been achieved in South Africa, Australia, and the United States.

Small fruit production is concentrated in the developed countries and in the areas where these crops originated or were domesticated (grapes: Near East and Europe; strawberries: Europe and North America; raspberries and currants: Europe). However, excellent production areas for these crops exist at some distance from the centers of origin or areas of domestication. Examples include New Zealand for kiwifruit, California for strawberries and grapes, and British Columbia and Scotland for red raspberries.

In general, small fruit production is gaining in popularity and becoming gradually but continually more dispersed. Total fruit and nut production for the period 1980 to 1985 increased moderately. With the continuing emphasis on balancing and diversifying human diets for improved health, fruit culture in general, and small fruit culture in particular should continue to grow in the foreseeable future, barring environmental catastrophes or global political conflicts.

REFERENCES

ABBOTT, J. D., AND R. E. GOUGH. 1987. Seasonal development of highbush blueberry roots under sawdust mulch. J. Am. Soc. Hortic. Sci. 112:60–62.

BRUGGMAN, M. W. 1966. The strawberry in religious paintings of the 1400's. In G. M. Darrow (ed.). The strawberry. Holt, Rinehart and Winston, New York.

COVILLE, F. V. 1937. Improving the wild blueberry. p. 559–574. In U.S. Dep. Agric. Yearb.

DARROW, G. M. 1966. The strawberry (history, breeding and physiology). Holt, Rinehart and Winston, New York.

Food and Agricultural Organization of the United Nations. 1985. FAO production yearbook. Vol. 39. United Nations, New York.

GALLETTA, G. J. 1980. Strawberry production trends in eastern USA. p. 1–11. In N. F. Childers (ed.). The strawberry: cultivars to marketing. Horticultural Publications, Gainesville, Fla.

SNYDER, E. 1937. Grape development and improvement. p. 631–664. In U.S. Dep. Agric. Yearb.

United States Department of Agriculture. 1982. Composition of foods. U.S. Dep. Agric. Agric. Handb. 8–9.

Chapter 2

Factors That Influence Small Fruit Production

D. G. HIMELRICK
G. J. GALLETTA

INTRODUCTION

Historically, the major advantages of commercial-scale small fruit culture have been the relative ease of establishing plantings, the short time from planting to economic return, and the facility to shift plantings to newer cultivars or to exit the business. Junebearing (short-day) strawberry production is a good example of these advantages because growers secure returns in the year after planting, and a successful planting may profitably be renewed for a number of seasons. However, intensive strawberry culture such as the annual production systems employed in California and Florida using plastic-covered raised beds on fumigated soil, with high-density plant spacing, drip irrigation, and special fertilization methods, is very expensive. Similarly, trellising requirements of grapes, kiwifruit, and many brambles requires special knowledge and additional capital investment, even though such plantings may be profitable and productive for decades. Also, full economic production of most of the small fruit crops (bushes and vines) is not realized until 3 to 6 years after planting.

PLANTING CONSIDERATIONS

There are a number of very important preplanting decisions that must be made to ensure success in small fruit management. One logical ordering of these considerations follows:

1. Small fruit *crops* (species) to be grown
2. *Economic investment* (land, equipment, supplies, planting stock, etc.) needed and *potential returns*
3. *Marketing outlets* to be served (processing, pick-your-own, roadside, wholesale, etc.)
4. Selection of proper *cultivars* for regional adaption and chosen market outlets
5. *Site selection* (preparation and modification needs, soil drainage and fertility, topography, cropping history, prevailing climate, potential pest problems, proximity to transportation and market outlets, type of community, etc.)
6. *Management personnel* (background and experience of operators, numbers and types of seasonal or permanent laborers, supervisors, etc.)

Deciding which small fruit crop(s) to grow is the first step toward the realization of a productive small fruit planting. This fundamental decision should be preceded by extensive background research into the economics, cultural feasibility, marketing options, and practical chances for success. The choice(s) of small fruit crop species to be grown will influence many of the other considerations listed above.

Economic investment in land, cultural and transportation equipment, storage facilities, supplies, planting stock, labor, marketing expenses, insurance, and family income can be substantial. Potential growers should solicit crop production cost analyses from state extension specialists, county agents, researchers, consultants, or experienced growers. If loans are to be obtained, a financial business plan and potential budget will need to be prepared. The economic investment and the potential returns of a particular crop should be compared to that of other farming alternatives or investment options. Farming must be viewed as a business with sound financial management practiced in all aspects of the operation. Chapter 14 contains detailed useful information on the economics of small fruit production.

The choice of a marketing outlet will dictate or limit other planning considerations, such as the size of the planting, cultivar selection, plant spacing, row orientation, road location, parking needs, equipment, and storage facilities. Pick-your-own (PYO) marketing (customer on-farm harvesting) generally requires a wider range of cultivars, easy public access to the planting itself, adequate parking adjacent to the planting, traffic control for check-out accountability, and special attention to appearance and upkeep. Pick-your-own marketing also requires extensive public contact, along with good management and interpersonal skills.

On-farm or roadside marketing requires picking labor and on-site grading and storage facilities. A well-traveled location or easily directed access to the roadside facility and a wide range of cultivars are needed. Closed containers offered for sale must comply with USDA grades.

Wholesale marketing through local and national produce marketing channels is common because greater volumes of fruit can be sold. Wholesale marketing requires more picking labor, an ample supply of bulk containers, and loaders and field trailer equipment to move fruit from the planting to the packhouse or central loading point. It also requires a distribution or processing facility to accept your fruit and provide minimum acceptable standards for packaging or processing. Additional packing and brokerage fees will be incurred with wholesale marketing. Small fruit marketing and distribution channels are discussed further in Chapter 13.

Proper cultivar selection should include adaptation to a particular geographic region or planting site. Extensive background research and consultation is critical to correct cultivar choice. For example, in a typical strawberry yield trial the highest-yielding cultivars often have double the production of the lower-yielding selections. Many cultivars are excellent for pick-your-own operations but may be totally useless for shipping. Some cultivars are well suited for processing, while others do not produce an acceptable product. Having more than one marketing outlet is good insurance and provides for better cash flow and the opportunity to market the entire crop. Not all fruit may be of suitable appearance or quality for the fresh market. In seedless table grape vines only 50 to 75% of the clusters may be suitable for fresh market table grapes. Growing a cultivar whose remaining fruit clusters are suitable for wine or juice production would be an important economic consideration.

Land ownership can be an obstacle to proper site selection. Persons who already own property may be reluctant to purchase more land, even if their current property is less than desirable for small fruit production. Planting on a marginal site is poor economics when the high cost of establishment, frequent replanting, and decreased productivity is considered.

Soil characteristics, freedom from frost, and previous cropping history are key criteria in the selection of a future planting site. A soil with good internal drainage is important for optimum production of small fruit crops. Many small fruit crops are susceptible to "wet feet" symptoms as a result of prolonged root exposure to waterlogged soils. Soils with a moderate water-holding capacity and good internal drainage are ideal for most situations. The water-holding capacity of a particular soil is also important in evaluating the need for supplemental irrigation. Availability, quantity, and quality of the local water supply must be considered where supplemental irrigation is anticipated.

Since cold air flows downhill and accumulates in low areas, sites higher in elevation than the surrounding terrain should be considered for planting. Airflow barriers such as a continuous woodline should be modified to create openings, allowing cold air to leave the site. Weather records and recording thermometers to evaluate winter temperatures and spring frost hazard potential for future planting sites will provide valuable information.

In considering the previous cropping history of a property, complete site preparation of new land may present problems different from those of a replant situation. For example, many small fruit crops are susceptible to the verticillium wilt fungus found in many soils. In replant situations, these small fruit crops should not be planted where verticillium-susceptible crop plants have been grown during the past 3 years. Such crops include tomatoes, peppers, eggplant, potatoes, strawberries, and raspberries. In fallow land weeds such as nightshade, ground cherry, horse nettle, lamb's-quarters, pigweed, and cocklebur are verticillium susceptible. In particular sections of the country, other soilborne diseases may be a problem, such as cotton root rot following cotton and oak root rot on land recently cleared of hardwood trees. Nematodes may be at high enough levels to need preplanting fumigation, particularly on sandier soils following crops such as tobacco.

Replanted land may have high residual levels of herbicide in the soil. Specific insect and disease pests may be present at levels that are tolerable by well-established mature plants, but may severely restrict the growth of young plants. In some cases the soil may be excessively compacted, or large amounts of salts may have accumulated from past fertilization and irrigation practices.

Topographical elements such as the degree of slope, and potentially wet, low-frost-pocket, and erosion areas must all be evaluated. The slope may dictate the method used in setting the plants, and whether straight rows or contour planting should be employed. Additional considerations, such as the potential for wildlife damage, water and power availability, and the personality of the neighbors who surround the farm should all be reviewed before any major investment is made.

A site selected for a small fruit planting is likely to need modification prior to planting to overcome factors unfavorable for small fruit production. These include weeds, nematodes, soil pathogens, poor drainage, low organic matter, and improper soil pH and nutrient status. Once the plants are in the ground, it may be nearly impossible to reduce populations of harmful organisms or correct certain nutrient deficiencies. A critical year in fruit production is the one prior to planting. During the summer before planting, attention should be given to bringing the perennial weeds under control. Many weeds, such as brambles, honeysuckle, quackgrass, and Johnsongrass, are much easier to control before planting than after establishment. Deep plowing may be useful to break up impervious subsurface hardpan layers. Systematic tiling or grading and leveling are frequently required to improve drainage. Cover-crop incorporation will increase the organic matter content of a soil, improve the tilth, or add nutrients to the soil. Certain cover crops also help reduce the number of harmful nematodes. Creeping red fescue, Kentucky tall fescue, and perennial ryegrass have all been shown to suppress nematode development. Cover crops are recommended during the year prior to planting after perennial weeds have been eliminated. Nematode tests should be made to determine the need for fumigation. Many growers routinely fumigate for weed, disease, and nematode control.

Conditions are generally most suitable for fumigation in late summer or early fall. Some deep-rooted cover crops may aid in penetrating impervious soil hardpan layers.

It is important to have the soil analyzed and adjusted according to the test results. A soil test will report the pH, the cation-exchange capacity (a measure of the resistance of the soil to changes in pH and its potential for holding nutrient elements), and amounts of various nutrients present in the soil. Collect enough soil samples to provide uniformity for the site. If obvious differences exist in the soil type across the site, individual soil samples should be taken to reflect these differences. Soil samples should be taken to a depth of at least 12 in. (31 cm). If liming is necessary, it should be done well in advance of planting, along with the incorporation of other plant nutrients, such as phosphorus and potassium, as indicated by the soil test results.

Anyone contemplating small fruit production should consider the abilities and limitations of the personnel involved in the management of the operation. The background and experience of the operators will greatly influence the ease of operation, the need for outside consultation, and the potential for effective problem solving. A small fruit farm is a complex operation requiring a variety of supervisory, labor, bookkeeping, and financial management personnel. The need for seasonal labor and management staff availability must be considered well in advance of the need.

ECOLOGICAL EFFECTS ON PLANT ADAPTATION

The planting location (site) influence on plant growth and productivity originates from three basic site components: **soil, climate,** and **other living organisms** (biotic component).

The *soil* is the root-anchoring medium and is the principal reservoir of water, nutrients, and solar heat. Soil porosity is critical in maintaining proper air and moisture-containing areas for root penetration, aeration, and nutrition, and for nutrient uptake. The soil structure largely determines its water- and nutrient-holding capacity and how much of its native mineral content is retained. The chemical soil reaction (degree of acidity or alkalinity) determines nutrient uptake rates and interactions, and which soil microorganisms and weed seeds can persist and thrive. The organic matter fraction of the soil aids its workability (tilth) and drainage and helps to hold water and plant nutrients. These physical and chemical soil properties which affect plant growth are also influenced by the slope, elevation, and previous plant cover of the soil.

Critical factors of the *climate* that influence plant growth are **temperature, precipitation, solar radiation,** and **air movement and content.** *Temperature* limits determine when plant metabolism (at the cellular level) and growth and development (at the tissue and organ levels) start and stop and the rate(s) at which metabolism and development progress. Temperature levels set the length of the growing season, and cumulative higher or lower temperatures are necessary to trigger such phenomena as bud and leaf expansion, flower opening, and onset of fruiting. Cumulative temperatures also influence the development of the pathogenic and beneficial organisms living with the fruit plants. In our temperate-zone plants, such development stage stimulation is often jointly initiated by light and temperature regimes acting together. Extreme temperatures injure plants or critical plant parts such as flower buds. The normal seasonal extreme temperatures determine which plants will grow and thrive in a given location.

Precipitation is the original source of the universal biological solvent, water. No plant growth or development takes place in the absence of water. Water is a component of both living cells and tissues and of the fluids that nourish them and transport their products and by-products. Too little or too much water is injurious to plants. Ideally, water should be distributed over both the growing season and the dormant season for perennial plants. Of course, more water is needed in times of high plant activity, high temperatures, or heavy air movement. The effect of the moisture content in the air (relative humidity) on plant growth and development is poorly understood or often overlooked. Plants grow more rapidly, or at least accumulate more photosynthates, when relative humidities are high because fewer manufactured plant products are lost through respiration and transpiration. Many plant disease spores germinate and are transported better in periods of high relative humidity, thus increasing disease incidence and severity. However, fruit maturation is often favored by low moisture levels. Color, flavor, and epidermal ("skin") integrity are favored by cool night temperatures, sunny days, and low humidity. These conditions also minimize fruit-rotting-organism development.

Solar radiation is the ultimate source of light and heat for our planet. Light duration, wavelength, intensity, and level are all important to certain phases of small fruit plant development. These light effects vary with species, genotype (or cultivar) within species, at different temperatures, and even for different propagation modes.

Atmospheric *carbon dioxide* is the principal carbon source of the light-mediated process of photosynthesis, wherein plant sugars are manufactured. Atmospheric *nitrogen* can also be washed into soils during violent summer rains. Particles of air *contaminants* have been particularly injurious to plants such as grapes. Continued heavy *winds* can stunt or dwarf plant growth and break off young or heavily laden branches. Fruit set can be reduced by strong spring winds (drying out of flower anthers and stigmas). However, moderate winds can reduce the risk of spring temperature inversions and subsequent spring frost.

The *biotic component* of a site consists of those animal, other plant, or microorganism remains, eggs, seeds, or spores in the soil at planting time, and those that invade or infest the planting during the subsequent period of small fruit culture. Such extraneous plants, animals, and microorganisms may be inconsequential to, competitive with, mutually beneficial with, or injurious to the small fruit crop plants.

Weeds usually compete with crop plants for water, nutrients, air, and light, especially when small fruits are being established or in periods when the fruit plants are growing slowly or are fruiting heavily. At certain periods in the growing season, however, a light weed cover can hold soil, slow down plant growth and aid in fall acclimation, or can serve to trap snow around the fruit planting. Insects may eat plant parts, colonize them for egg laying or overwintering, suck plant juices, act as virus vectors, or control troublesome insects. Mites have most of the same functions as insects. Soilborne or aerial fungi and bacteria may be beneficial or pathogenic, the latter either killing or weakening the plant, unless the pathogenicity is mild. Similarly, systemic viruses and virus-like particles can cause disease, weaken plants, or be neutral. Burrowing animals and nematodes are frequently injurious to plant roots. Browsing animals may severely injure or eat fruit, flower buds, and tender shoots and foliage. Birds are severe fruit-eating pests, particularly of blueberries, grapes, and brambles.

CLIMATIC INFLUENCES AND SITE SELECTION

The combination of external or extrinsic conditions that surround a plant directly affects its growth and development and determines its suitability for production in a given area. Weather is the state of the atmosphere at a given time and place, described by specific variables such as temperature, moisture, wind velocity, atmospheric pressure, and degree of sunshine or cloud cover. Climate may be viewed as the meteorological conditions, including temperature, precipitation, wind, humidity, sunshine, evaporation, cloudiness, and other factors, that characteristically prevail in a particular region. The climate of a locale is the long-term normal weather for that location for a given day of the year or over a specified interval of time such as a month, a season, or a year. This composite of general weather conditions of a particular region or place averaged over a number of years has a profound influence in determining which plants can be grown and the best methods and timings to achieve satisfactory results with them. The production of temperate-zone fruit crops is limited by the climate of a particular geographical region.

The geographical location of these farms pragmatically reflects the importance of climate and site selection in the production of small fruit crops. The concentration of farms in specific areas reflects the successful adaption of certain fruit crops to the modified weather conditions of these macroclimates. Figures 2–1, 2–2, and 2–3 indicate the location of particular small fruit crops in the United States: grapes, strawberries, and other berries (raspberries, blackberries, blueberries, cranberries, etc.), respectively.

Latitude

Temperature is inversely correlated with latitude. The farther from the equator, the cooler the average annual temperature becomes, because the sun's rays strike the earth more directly near the equator and are consequently filtered and scattered by less atmosphere. As the depth of the atmosphere increases, the amount of solar energy reaching the earth decreases due to additional absorption, reflection, and scattering by the atmosphere. The temperature differences between regions associated with latitude are caused largely by differences in insolation (radiation received from the sun), which in turn is dependent on both daylength and the angle of the sun

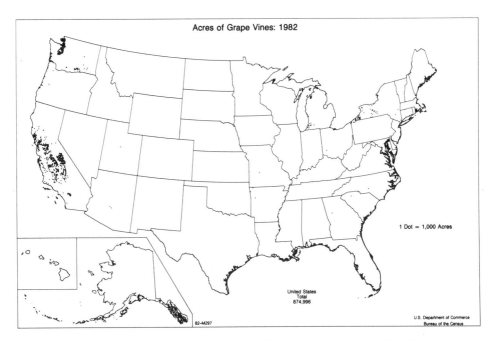

FIGURE 2-1 Geographical location of grape acreage in the United States. (From U.S. Department of Commerce, Bureau of the Census.)

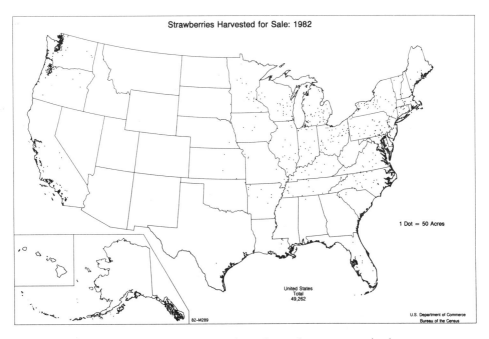

FIGURE 2-2 Geographical location of strawberry acreage in the United States. (From U.S. Department of Commerce, Bureau of the Census.)

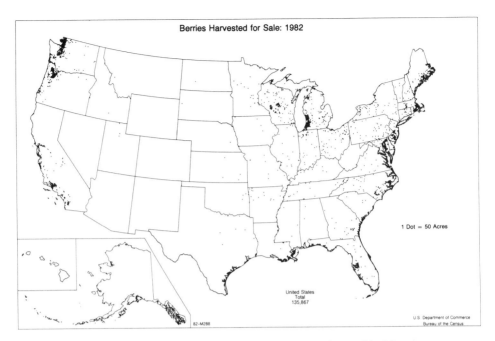

FIGURE 2-3 Geographical location of berry (raspberry, blackberry, blueberry, cranberry, etc.) acreage in the United States. (From U.S. Department of Commerce, Bureau of the Census.)

(Halfacre and Barden, 1979). Table 2-1 illustrates the effect of latitude on temperature means and ranges. The mean annual temperatures for both summer and winter decrease with increasing northern latitude. Additionally, the temperature ranges that fruit plants must tolerate increase with increasing latitude.

Latitude also directly affects the length of daylight or photoperiod that plants will experience at various times during the growing season. Daylength increases with increasing northern latitude during the summer months. Plants growing in more northern latitudes will have longer daylengths, although the light intensities will decrease because the maximum angle of the sun will be less. For example, on June 21 the maximum sun angle for Miami, Florida (28° latitude) is 87° above the horizon. For the same date, Los Angeles (latitude 34°) has a maximum sun angle of 79°, and New York City (latitude 40°) has a maximum angle of 74°.

Continentality and Sources of Moisture

Land and water surfaces react differently to the incoming rays of the sun. In general, land surfaces are heated rapidly by solar insolation; but the heat does not penetrate deeply, so land surfaces also cool rapidly. On the other hand, water warms up slowly, holds a much larger quantity of heat than the land surface, and cools slowly.

The effects of distance from a water source are that the interiors of continents tend to be drier and hotter in summer and colder in winter than the coastal areas;

TABLE 2-1 EFFECT OF LATITUDE ON TEMPERATURES IN VARIOUS CITIES OF SIMILAR
LONGITUDE AND ELEVATION

LOCATION	DEGREES NORTH LATITUDE	TEMPERATURE (°F)			
		Mean Annual	Mean January	Mean July	Range Jan.–July
Brownsville, Tex.	25°54′	74	61	84	23
Fort Worth, Tex.	32°50′	66	46	85	39
Oklahoma City, Okla.	35°24′	60	37	83	46
Lincoln, Nebr.	40°49′	53	25	79	54
Huron, S.D.	44°23′	46	14	75	61
Fargo, N.D.	46°54′	41	7	71	64
International Falls, Minn.	48°34′	36	3	66	63

there are also greater differences between daily maximum and minimum temperature. There are many exceptions to these generalized effects of continentality. The
exceptions, such as dry coastal areas and moist interiors, result from the effects of
other climate controls superimposed on the continentality effect (Baldwin, 1973).

Ocean Currents

Well-established ocean currents have a great effect on the climates of coastal areas.

Mountain Barriers

Not only do mountain ranges have colder temperature conditions at higher elevations, but they also act as barriers to block the flow of prevailing winds and the
movement of storms. Also, air flowing upward on the slopes of a mountain barrier
tends to drop much of its moisture on the windward side of the range. This is the
reason for the deserts that lie to the east of many of the west coast mountain ranges.

Elevation (Altitude)

Temperature in the atmosphere decreases with increasing elevation or altitude. The
average decrease in temperature is approximately 3.3 to 3.6°F for every 1000 ft of
elevation, or for each increase in elevation of 100 m the mean temperatures decline is
about 0.6°C.

Altitude and latitude work in tandem. According to Hopkin's bioclimatic law,
a specific biological phenomenon occurs 4 days later and the temperature becomes
1°F colder for each degree of north latitude or each 400-ft rise in elevation. In
southern latitudes, altitude can serve to approximate the cooler growing conditions
of more northerly sites. In so doing it may become a method of enhancing quality in
some crops such as wine grapes. In the northern reaches of temperate fruit growing,
altitude serves to accentuate the effects of latitude and in so doing, is more of a
limiting factor.

There is not a great deal of information in the literature concerning the effects
of planting site altitude on small fruit crops. However, several studies have made

mention of orchard altitude. One of the first of these was by Phillips in 1922, in which he studied the effects of climatic conditions on bloom and ripening dates of several species of fruit trees. He suggested that epochs in fruit-bearing trees were retarded in their development by one day for each 101-ft (31-m) increase in altitude. This was a broad statement that covered both blooming and ripening dates of five fruit crops: apples, peaches, cherries, pears, and plums. In 1956, Dragavcev conducted a more specific study which dealt exclusively with the retardation of fruit ripening in relation to increasing altitude. He reported that apples were delayed in their ripening by about 4.1 days for each 100-m increase in altitude (1.25 days per 100 ft). He also made the observation that the retarding effect of altitude was increased at higher altitudes. In other words, at altitudes between 700 and 1400 m (2300 to 4600 ft) there was a 3.5-day delay in ripening for each 100-m increase (1.1 days per 100 ft); whereas between 1400 and 1680 m (4600 to 5500 ft) the delay was 5.7 days for each 100-m increase (1.74 days per 100 ft).

Climatic Subdivisions

Climatologists recognize three levels of climate. *Macroclimate* is the climate of a large general region such as the Pacific coast, the Rocky Mountains, or New England. Macroclimatic regional divisions may also be found within a state, such as the distinction in climate between eastern and western Washington. The macroclimate of a region may be deduced from records of regional weather recording stations. Such records describe the distribution and level of rainfall, temperature, solar radiation, humidity, windspeed, evaporation, and other characteristics. Climatic patterns deduced from a central recording station can be representative of areas many miles in extent. Some specific examples of macroclimates might be the Napa Valley of California or the Finger Lakes of New York.

Mesoclimates (topoclimates) represent climatic variation within a region. Mesoclimate is site climate and is exemplified by a specific area such as the Carneros area in the Napa Valley or the western slope above Seneca Lake in the Finger Lakes. Mesoclimates are localized areas where values of some parameters, such as radiation or temperature, are affected by topography characteristics such as slope or aspect. Mesoclimates are normally representative of distances less than 1 mile, depending on the topography.

Microclimate is the climate around and within the plant canopy. The climate within a plant canopy can be very different from that measured just above the canopy, due to attenuation of climatic elements by canopy components. Microclimates change over distances of centimeters. It is the climate within a particular field, orchard, or vineyard that is modified by the site and the fact that plant cover is present.

Regional Adaptation

The continental United States can be generally divided into 10 regional climates (Fig. 2-4):

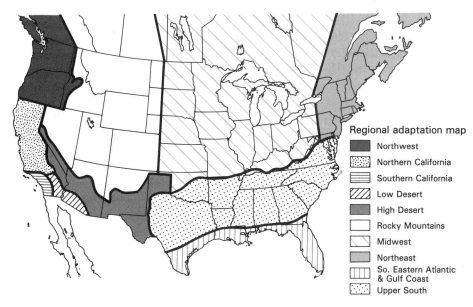

FIGURE 2-4 Regional adaptation map showing 10 general climatic zones for the United States and Southern Canada.

1. *Pacific Northwest.* The cool moist climates typified by the cities of Portland and Seattle are strongly influenced by the Pacific Ocean. Soils are generally acid. High elevation areas east of the Cascade Mountain Range begin to resemble the Rocky Mountain region.

2. *Northern California.* This diverse climate region is influenced by proximity to the Pacific Ocean. Inland areas have warm summers and cool winters. Coastal areas are milder in summer and winter.

3. *Southern California.* High summer temperatures, mild winters, and low annual rainfall characterize this area. It differs greatly from areas along the Gulf coast that are in the same USDA (U.S. Department of Agriculture) hardiness zones. Soils are often alkaline.

4. *Low Desert.* This region is typified by the cities of Palm Springs, California, and Phoenix and Tucson, Arizona. Soils are often alkaline. Very hot summers with strong winds and high light intensity are common. Winters are mild; low temperatures depend on the elevation.

5. *High Desert.* This represents a wide range of mostly high-elevation areas with hot summers, cold winters, and low annual rainfall. Soils are often alkaline.

6. *Rocky Mountains.* Generally, these are high elevation areas with abundant winter snowfall and short summers. Lower-elevation areas, such as Denver, Colorado, and Salt Lake City, Utah, can grow the widest range of plant material.

7. *Midwest.* This region includes the dry, windy climates of the Great Plains and

moisture areas around the Great Lakes. Climates change drastically over short distances around the Great Lakes relative to their proximity to water.

8. *Northeast*. Winters here are generally milder than in the midwest due to the moderating effect of the Atlantic Ocean. However, high-elevation areas can be very cold. Soils are typically acid.

9. *Southeastern Atlantic and Gulf Coast*. This is a narrow strip of land with mild winters and hot, humid summers. Annual rainfall is high and is dispersed evenly throughout the year.

10. *Upper South*. This zone is made up of many different climates influenced by elevation, latitude, and proximity to the Atlantic Ocean. Its northern, southern, and eastern boundaries are a transition to adjacent regions.

Table 2-2 compares the annual climates of 14 cities located near major fruit growing areas in the United States. The effect of latitude, elevation, and proximity to large bodies of water or mountain ranges can be observed in terms of normal daily temperatures, precipitation, and sunshine percentage.

Temperature

Temperature is undoubtedly the single most important limiting factor in temperate-zone fruit production. Factors such as length of frost-free growing season, heat unit accumulation during the growing season, maximum growing season temperatures, and minimum winter temperatures are important climatic considerations in site selection.

The variation in temperature can be extreme even within the conterminous United States. The highest air temperature observed was 134°F (57°C) recorded at Greenland Ranch in Death Valley, California. The lowest recorded temperature was −69.7°F (−56.5°C), which occurred at Rogers Pass, Montana. By definition, the freeze-free growing period is between the dates of the last 32°F temperature in spring and the first 32°F temperature in autumn, and is usually referred to as the growing season. Temperatures, however, may drop to freezing or below at the ground surface because of radiation loss on clear, calm, nights even when the official low temperature measured in the shelter 4 ft (1.2 m) above the ground is as high as 10°F (5.6°C) above freezing.

Frost-Free Days

The length of the frost-free or freeze-free period is most important for long-season fruit crops such as apples, grapes, everbearing strawberries, and fall-fruiting raspberries. For example, the average minimum number of frost-free days that are recommended for potential sites for American-type grapes are 165 days—for even the earliest-maturing varieties. For *vinifera* grapes, the frost-free vegetative period should be greater than 180 days. The map in Fig. 2-5 is divided into seven zones, which are approximations of the length of the frost-free period for the United States and southern Canada. More detailed maps are available for each state which

TABLE 2-2 ANNUAL CLIMATE OF 14 MAJOR CITIES IN THE UNITED STATES LOCATED NEAR MAJOR FRUIT GROWING AREAS

	Elevation (ft)	Extreme Low Temp. (°F)	Normal Daily Temp. Maximum Jan.	Maximum July	Minimum Jan.	Minimum July	Mean Jan.	Mean July	Growing Season Last Spring Frost	First Fall Frost	Frost-Free Days	Heat-Degree Days (Base 50°F) Apr. 1 to Oct. 31	Percent Relative Humidity (July) A.M.	P.M.	Precipitation (inches) Apr. to Sept.	Percentage of Possible Sunshine July
Fort Smith, Ark.	447	−10	50	94	28	71	39	82	Mar. 26	Nov. 4	223	4830	88	55	25.3	72
Fresno, Calif.	328	19	55	98	36	63	45	81	Feb. 15	Nov. 27	285	4951	62	22	2.2	96
San Francisco, Calif.	130	20	55	70	41	54	48	63	Jan. 7	Dec. 29	356	1910	86	60	3.3	66
Denver, Colo.	5283	−30	43	88	16	59	30	67	May 3	Oct. 16	166	2558	68	34	11.5	72
Orlando, Fla.	108	20	71	90	50	73	60	81	Jan. 31	Dec. 17	319	6150	90	59	36.1	62
Caribou, Maine	624	−41	20	76	2	54	11	65	May 19	Sept. 21	125	1279	83	58	23.3	64
Grand Rapids, Mich.	784	−21	30	83	16	60	23	72	Apr. 23	Oct. 30	190	2408	82	55	23.0	61
Trenton, N.J.	56	−14	39	85	25	67	32	76	Apr. 4	Nov. 8	218	3392	70	51	24.8	62
Buffalo, N.Y.	705	−20	30	80	18	61	24	70	Apr. 30	Oct. 25	179	2307	79	55	22.1	68
Raleigh, N.C.	434	−1	51	88	30	67	41	78	Mar. 24	Nov. 11	237	4159	90	59	25.1	61
Salem, Oreg.	195	−12	45	82	32	51	39	67	Apr. 14	Oct. 27	197	1627	85	40	11.6	70
Dallas, Tex.	481	4	56	96	34	74	45	85	Mar. 18	Nov. 12	239	5811	80	49	20.0	81
Seattle, Wash.	386	0	43	75	33	54	38	65	Feb. 2	Nov. 30	280	1927	81	49	13.4	63
Yakima, Wash.	1061	−25	36	88	19	53	28	71	Apr. 21	Oct. 15	177	2197	68	25	28.8	85

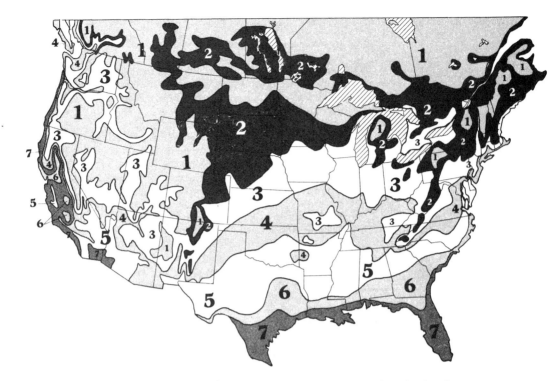

FIGURE 2-5 Map of the United States and southern Canada showing seven growing season zone approximations. The approximate number of days in the frost-free period for each zone is as follows: 1, 30–120; 2, 120–150; 3, 150–180; 4, 180–210; 5, 210–240; 6, 240–270; 7, 270–365. (Courtesy of Rodale's *Organic Gardening.*)

illustrate the effect of mesoclimates on the average length of the growing season. Figure 2-6 shows detailed frost-free maps for New York and Washington. Note the effect of Lakes Erie and Ontario and the Hudson River in New York and the Pacific Ocean in Washington on increasing the number of freeze-free days of sites in close proximity to these bodies of water. The topographic effect of the Adirondack Mountains of New York and the Cascade and Olympic Mountains of Washington is also evident in the growing-season configurations.

Since topography, terrain features, and elevation are important factors in the occurrence of freezing temperatures, caution is recommended in the interpretation of growing-season maps in hilly areas. Higher elevations, northerly facing slopes, deep valleys, and areas of poor air drainage are subject to late spring and early fall frosts and hence will have a shorter freeze-free season.

Average freeze-free periods and frost dates are simply the probability that freezes will occur on a given date 50% of the time. Variation from this average can be significant. Table 2-3 shows the probability of spring and fall freezes of 32°F (0°C) and 28°F (−2°C) and the freeze-free period for Lambertville, New Jersey. The probability range for a 32°F frost can vary as much as 16 days later in the spring

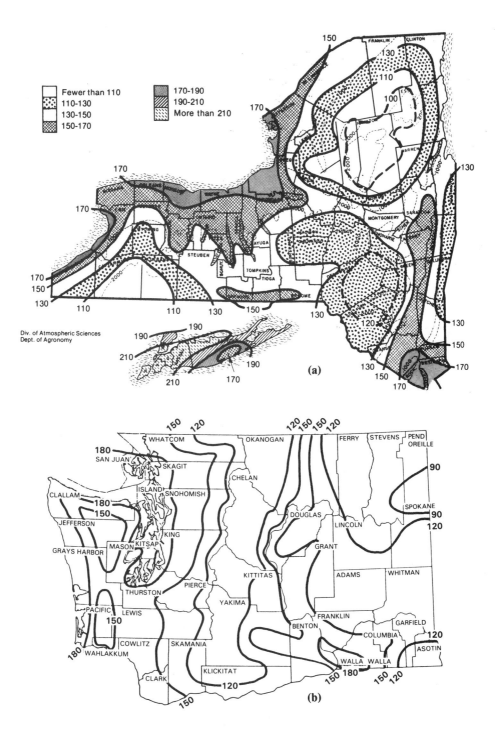

FIGURE 2–6 Maps of (a) New York and (b) Washington showing average length of days in the freeze-free growing season.

Climatic Influences and Site Selection

TABLE 2-3 DATA FROM LAMBERTVILLE, NEW JERSEY, SHOWING THE PROBABILITY OF SPRING AND FALL FREEZES AND THE FREEZE-FREE PERIOD

TEMPERATURE (°F)	PROBABILITY OF A LATER DATE IN SPRING (%)								
	90	80	70	60	50[a]	40	30	20	10
Spring Freeze Dates (month/day)									
32	4/11	4/17	4/21	4/24	4/28	5/01	5/04	5/08	5/14
28	3/28	4/02	4/05	4/08	4/11	4/14	4/17	4/20	4/25
Fall Freeze Dates (month/day)									
32	9/30	10/05	10/09	10/12	10/15	10/17	10/21	10/24	10/29
28	10/17	10/22	10/25	10/28	10/31	11/02	11/05	11/09	11/13
Freeze-Free Period (days)									
32	194	185	179	174	169	164	159	153	145
28	221	214	210	206	202	198	194	189	183

Source: Local climatological data, NOAA.

[a]These are the dates normally reported as the average frost dates 32°F.

and 15 days earlier in the fall than the average date. The freeze-free period can also vary from 194 days to 145 days compared to the average 169 day freeze-free period.

Heat Units

Growth, development, and maturation of small fruits is influenced by such factors as size of crop, cultural practices, and weather conditions—especially temperature. Temperature variations between seasons will therefore influence the accuracy of predictions of maturity based on days from full bloom to harvest. Winkler (1948) determined the heat units requirements to mature several varieties of California table grapes. Similar computations, attempting to relate total heat unit requirements for 'Concord' grape maturation in Michigan, did not yield satisfactory results (Van Den Brink, 1974). However, modified heat unit methods, at a base temperature 50°F (10°C), were developed that quite accurately forecast the optimum maturity date for commercial crop harvest of 'Concord'. Morris et al. (1980) found that using degree-day accumulations and effective heat unit summations did not prove to be methods superior to use of the number of days for predicting grape maturation. This observation is supported by the research of Tukey (1942), who found the average number of days from bloom to harvest to be relatively accurate in predicting the harvest of such perennials as cherry, peach, pear, and apple.

Cumulative Growing Degree Days

The use of growing degree days is a means by which plant growth can be related to the air temperature. In general, the rate of plant growth increases as seasonal temperatures increase or warm.

On each day of the growing season the air temperature normally increases during the daylight hours to a maximum in the afternoon and cools during the night hours to a minimum value shortly before sunrise. Thus, for each 24-hour day, there is a maximum (high) and a minimum (low) temperature. The arithmetical average of these two values is designated as the mean temperature for the day, or the daily mean temperature.

So-called *cool-season crops* such as peas grow when the daily mean temperature in the spring has warmed to a level of 40°F (4°C). Some growth can also be seen under cool early season temperatures for small fruit crops such as strawberries. On the other hand, *warm-season crops,* such as grapes, require a daily mean temperature of at least 50°F (10°C) before growth will occur. Such temperature levels are referred to as a base or threshold temperature.

The concept of the growing degree day involves determination of the number of degrees Fahrenheit by which the daily mean temperature on a given day exceeds an appropriate base temperature. Each degree in excess is called a *growing degree day.* The greater the daily excess, or number of growing degree days, the warmer was the day's weather, and presumably, the greater was the rate of crop growth. The growing degree days are determined in this manner for each day and accumulated from the beginning to the conclusion of the growing period of a given crop. The result is the number of accumulative growing degree days for a specific growing season. Such data for a large number of growing seasons are summarized to obtain the expected accumulative growing degree days.

A daily mean temperature of 50°F is used as the base for calculating the daily quota of growing degree days for temperate fruit crops. Calculation is made as follows: First, note the maximum (high) and minimum (low) temperatures for the 24-hour calendar day; then average the two numbers to obtain the daily mean temperature. A maximum of 80°F and a minimum of 62°F would yield an average (daily mean) temperature of 71°F. Subtracting the base temperature of 50°F yields an excess of 21 degrees, or 21 growing degree days for that day. Similar calculations can be made using a base of 10 degrees on the Celsius scale:

$$\text{daily growing degree days (GDDs)} = \frac{\text{daily max. temp. (°F)} + \text{daily min. temp. (°F)}}{2} - 50$$

The temperature extremes (high and low) are recorded for each day of the growing season from the initial date after the last 32°F recording in the spring to the date prior to the first 32°F recording in the fall. By adding together the growing degree days for each day in this period, the accumulative or total for the frost-free growing season is obtained. On days when the daily mean temperature is 50°F or colder, there is no excess of degrees, and the number of growing degree days is taken as zero or none. Average cumulative growing degree days determined in this manner for a base temperature of 50°F are shown in Figure 2-7 for New York and Washington.

Less precise heat-degree-day accumulations may also be determined by the use of mean monthly temperatures. For example, the mean monthly temperature for Mansfield, Ohio, during July is 72°F (22°C). The heat summation for the month would be 72 − 50 = 22 x 31 days = a heat summation of 682 degree days.

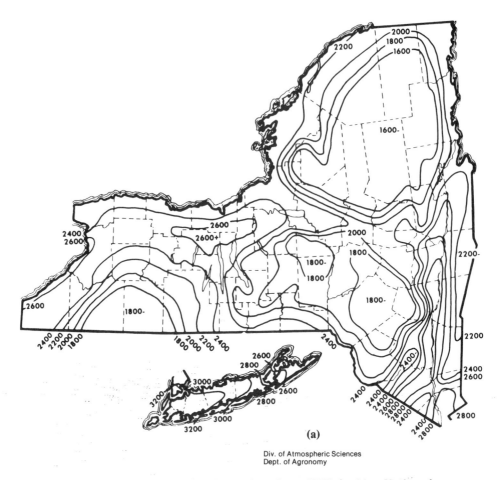

Div. of Atmospheric Sciences
Dept. of Agronomy

FIGURE 2-7 Average growing degree days (base 50°F) for New York and Washington (1 April to 31 October) states. [(a) From Northeast Regional Climate Center, Department of Agronomy, Cornell University; (b) from Washington State University.] Note that the marginal figures for Washington State (b) have to be multiplied by 100 to be comparable to those in New York (a).

In selecting the best-adapted cultivars for a given area, the interactions of both frost-free growing period and growing degree days should be considered. For example, the growing season for Seattle in western Washington is 255 days, while Prosser in eastern Washington has a growing season of 157 days. However, Prosser has 2427 accumulated heat units, while Seattle has only 1882 accumulated growing degree days during the growing season. Some fruit cultivars that mature in Prosser will not mature in Seattle with only 1882 heat units, even though it has a growing season that is 98 days longer. The primary reasons for the difference is the modifying effect of the Pacific Ocean on temperatures and the fact that Prosser has more sunny days. Seattle averages only 65% of the sunshine possible for the area, while localities in eastern Washington such as Walla Walla average 85% of the possible

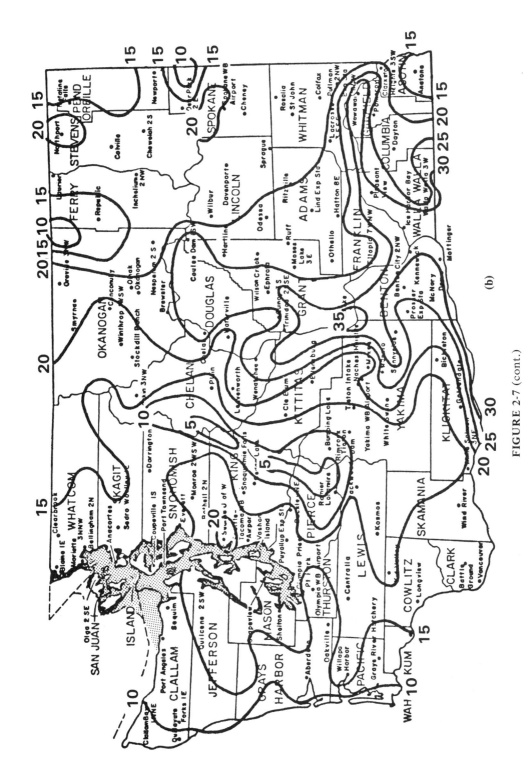

FIGURE 2-7 (cont.)

(b)

33

sunshine. Locations that collect higher percentages of the maximum amount of possible sunshine from sunrise to sunset generally have relatively clear sky conditions. In this case, Seattle averages only 10 clear days in July, while Walla Walla averages 21.

The prediction of maturity and average harvest dates of most temperate-zone fruit crops is closely related to accumulated heat units during the growing season. For example, a wide range of heat unit requirements can be observed among American-type grape cultivars. One of the lowest heat unit requirements for maturity is displayed by the cultivar 'Beta', which requires only 1450 heat units, while other late-season cultivars such as 'Catawba' may require 2500 growing degree days.

Cold Hardiness

Cold hardiness is the ability of a plant to resist injury during exposure to low temperature. The geographical suitability of temperate-zone fruit crop culture is also critically limited by the winter hardiness of various cultivars. One of the most recognized systems of hardiness zone classification has been established by the USDA. It classifies North America into 10 hardiness zones based on 10°F (5.6°C) increments of average annual minimum temperatures (Fig. 2-8). This classification may no longer be a reliable planting guide in many parts of the United States. The climate in North America has been growing colder. More than 60% of the National Weather Service's stations have reported record low temperatures for the past 20 years, and almost half have recorded all-time lows since 1973. These changes have prompted a redrawing of the boundaries of the hardiness zones.

The two hardiness-zone maps most commonly used today were developed by the Arnold Arboretum of Boston and the United States Department of Agriculture (USDA). The USDA map was issued in 1960, and the Arnold Arboretum map was last updated in 1967. The two maps are similar, but they do not use the same temperature ranges to divide different zones. New maps produced by Meteorological Evaluation Services have 10 zones reflecting the same temperature ranges appearing on the Arnold Arboretum map. In the first map (Fig. 2-9), hardiness-zone divisions are based on average minimum annual temperatures for the 10-year period from 1974 to 1983. In the second map (Fig. 2-10), zone divisions are based on the coldest temperatures ever recorded at those weather stations.

The most significant differences between the old and revised hardiness-zone maps can be found in the southeast and the west. For example, virtually all of Florida used to be in zone 9, but now the northern part has been reclassified as zone 8, reflecting the hard freezes that have hit the state's citrus orchards in recent years.

Growers who live on hills or mountains who plan to use hardiness-zone maps as planting guides should remember that most of the National Weather Service stations are located in major cities or suburban settings. The temperatures observed at these locations do not generally represent the temperatures measured in elevated terrain such as the Adirondack Mountains in New York or the Rockies in the west. Such major topographic features are not accounted for in the current revisions of the hardiness maps. Corrections to the zone for a particular location in a mountainous region can be made by applying the rule of thumb that the minimum

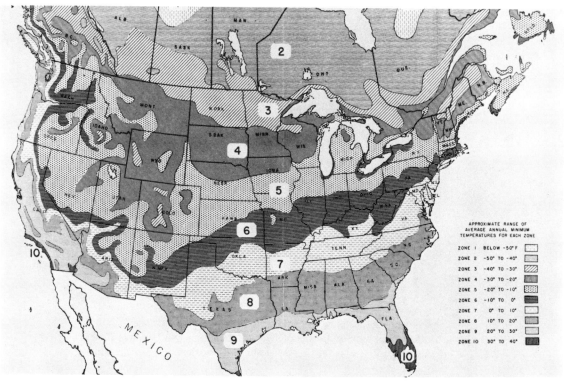

FIGURE 2-8 Plant hardiness zones of the United States and southern Canada, showing average annual minimum temperatures. (From U.S. Department of Agriculture.)

temperature will decrease by 3°F for each 1000 ft of elevation above the nearby National Weather Service station. Mesoclimates and microclimates within these zones can substantially change the expected minimum winter temperatures. The best method of site selection includes consultation of local weather records as well as data collection from strategically placed thermometers or thermographs on the proposed planting site.

Cold hardiness among small fruit species shows considerable variation. Muscadine grape cultivars are best adapted to the southeastern and Gulf states, where winter temperatures seldom fall below 10°F ($-12°C$). Conversely, most highbush blueberry cultivars can tolerate winter temperatures of up to southern Maine and central Michigan but are generally winter-killed at temperatures lower than $-20°F$ ($-29°C$).

Cold hardiness of fruit crops also varies among individual plant parts. Damage may occur to buds, shoot tips, canes, crowns, trunks, or root systems. In perennial woody species such as grapes and blueberries the hardiest tissue is the xylem or wood and the phloem or bark. The least hardy tissues are the ovaries of the flower buds and the cambium (the area of cell division between the xylem and phloem). Different amounts of damage can occur to these plant parts, depending on when the stress occurs. In general, the aboveground portion of the plant is less

Climatic Influences and Site Selection

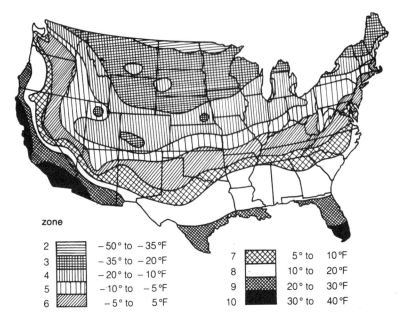

zone		
2		−50° to −35°F
3		−35° to −20°F
4		−20° to −10°F
5		−10° to −5°F
6		−5° to 5°F
7		5° to 10°F
8		10° to 20°F
9		20° to 30°F
10		30° to 40°F

FIGURE 2-9 Hardiness zones based on 1974–1983 average minimum winter temperatures. Limits of average minimum temperatures for each zone. (Country Journal © June 1986 by Historical Times, Inc. Harrisburg, PA.)

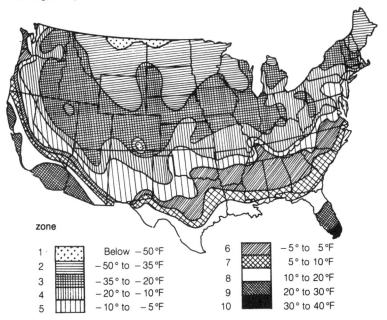

zone		
1		Below −50°F
2		−50° to −35°F
3		−35° to −20°F
4		−20° to −10°F
5		−10° to −5°F
6		−5° to 5°F
7		5° to 10°F
8		10° to 20°F
9		20° to 30°F
10		30° to 40°F

FIGURE 2-10 Hardiness zones based on extreme minimum temperatures. Limits of extreme minimum temperatures for each zone. (Country Journal © June 1986 by Historical Times, Inc. Harrisburg, PA.)

protected from severe winter temperatures and has the greatest potential to sustain winter injury. Soil, grass sod, mulch, or cover crop help to reduce cold penetration and protect root systems from cold damage. The penetration of cold to the root zone is less in moist, heavier clay-type soils than in lighter, more open, drier soils. Winter snow cover provides excellent protection for crowns and root systems of temperate fruit crops. Cold damage is normally reduced in winters with a good ground cover of snow, compared to years where snowfall is light and the ground remains clear for much of the time. The natural insulating value of snow appears to increase temperatures about 2°F (1.1°C) per inch (2.5 cm) of snow depth. Table 2-4 describes one set of temperature measurements showing the insulating quality of snow.

Cold tolerance of fruit crops is also related to the physiological state of the plant and the preconditioning that it has received prior to the cold temperatures. Acclimation is a hardening-off process by which fruit crops gain an increased ability to withstand cold winter temperatures. The changes in many perennial plant species fall into a three-stage process. The plant begins early acclimation in response to shortening daylength. Additional acclimation occurs in response to frosty autumn nights. The final stage occurs in response to temperatures below 32°F (0°C) in which parts of the plant remain in a constantly frozen state. It is during this final state that fruit buds reach their maximum hardiness level. If the ambient air temperature rises above 32°F (0°C) and the tissues thaw, some deacclimation or dehardening will occur. It appears that peach and grape buds may deharden at a rate of 1°F (0.56°C) per hour, but they will reharden at only 1°F (0.56°C) per day.

Frost and Freezes

Cold or freeze damaging temperatures range from the 53°F (12°C) temperature that causes damage to bananas to around 15°F (−9°C) necessary to kill unprotected strawberry crowns, down to −31°F (−35°C) that will cause the death of well-hardened highbush blueberry stems. The main factors involved in producing freeze injury to fruit crops are the degree of low temperature, duration of low temperature, and prefreeze environmental conditions. Stages of growth or dormancy determine what degree of low temperature and duration can be tolerated. A combination of vigorous plant growth or active metabolism and a warm prefeeze weather environment presents a very favorable situation for damage from freezing temperatures.

TABLE 2-4 INSULATING VALUE OF 9 in. (23 cm) OF SNOW[a]

	TEMPERATURE [°F (°C)]	
Air	−14	(−26)
Snow surface	−1	(−18)
3-in. (7.6-cm) depth	16	(−9)
6-in. (15-cm) depth	22	(−6)
9-in. (23-cm) depth (soil surface)	28	(−2)

Source: Rutgers Cooperative Extension.

[a]Measurements were conducted in January in New Jersey.

Frost is defined as the process by which ice crystals are deposited on an exposed surface. This is the result of the temperature of the exposed surface falling to the dew-point temperature of the air. The dew point is simply the temperature at which condensation occurs in that particular air mass, or the temperature that a surface would have to reach to form dew. In fact, frost is simply frozen dew. Instead of the moisture (water vapor) in the air condensing out of the air as a liquid, it goes directly from the water-vapor state to solid ice crystals.

In many cases the terms 'frost' and 'freeze' are used interchangeably, although they may be classified as two distinct phenomena. *Freezes* are cold-weather conditions of relatively long duration, during which the water in organic material is frozen, resulting in severe damage to the tissues of the organism. An *advective* or windborne freeze occurs when a large cold air mass moves into an area bringing freezing temperatures. Wind speeds are usually above 3 to 5 mph (5 to 8 km/h) and clouds may be present. The thickness of the cold air layer ranges from 500 to 5000 ft (153 to 1530 m) or more. Attempts to protect crops by modifying the environment are very limited in effect under these conditions.

Frosts are cold-weather conditions of relatively short duration during which organic materials may be damaged by exposure to surrounding air temperatures lower than 32°F (0°C). A radiation frost occurs when the surrounding air is nearly still or has only calm winds (less than 5 mph, 8 km/h), and when the sky is clear or there is a large hole in the cloud cover allowing heat to escape. These conditions often allow a temperature inversion to develop. Inversions exist when the atmosphere becomes layered with a warmer air mass above a cooler air mass between it and the ground. These conditions are also commonly called 'atmospheric' or 'thermal' inversions. There are two basic inversion conditions of significance to growers. Low ceiling inversions exist when the air above the plant is considerably warmer than the air below plant-top level; heated ground air will rise to the level of the overhead air, which is warmer than the ground air. High ceiling inversions exist when overhead air is only a few degrees warmer than the air below plant-top level; thus heated ground air will rise by convection much farther, to meet air of similar temperature (Valli, 1971). The performance of heaters, wind machines, and sprinklers is much more effective when a low ceiling inversion exists.

Frost/Freeze Protection

Critical temperatures. The key to successful frost protection is knowing when to start. The consequences of error are excessively high-operation costs on the one hand, and crop injury on the other. The basis for determining when to start is the critical temperature.

The *critical temperature* is the temperature that the buds, flowers, or fruits will endure for 30 minutes or less without injury. Because of the complex nature of the problem, published critical temperatures are often conservative, especially before full bloom. They usually are too high, to protect unusually tender tissues. As a result, frost protection equipment often is operated unnecessarily. However, buds or flowers may become more tender than normal and losses may be sustained at temperatures above those shown in published literature. Other factors may contribute to deviations from expected performance. Thermometers may be inaccurate or improperly exposed, and tissue temperatures may differ from air temperature. Tables 2-5 and 2-6 show the critical temperature for grapes and strawberries at various stages of development and for various environmental conditions.

Phillips et al. (1962) suggest critical temperatures for four stages of strawberries based on observations and opinions as follows: tight bud 22°F (−5.5°C); balloon bud 28°F (−2.2°C); full bloom 31°F (−0.5°C); and green fruit 28°F (−2.2°C). Boyce and Strater (1984) presented T_{50} values (the temperature that killed 50% of the samples) for five stages of bud development. Immature berries had a T_{50} of 24.3°F (−4.3°C); open blossoms 23.2°F (−4.9°C); emerging primary buds 24.8°F (−4.0°C); buds on expanded truss 22.3°F (−5.4°C); and unopened buds with petals visible 22.3°F (−5.4°C). A range of 5.4°F (3°C) was observed by Ourecky and Reich (1976) in flower frost tolerance in 21 cultivars of strawberry.

Not all blossoms or buds are injured at the same temperatures. Several explanations can be offered to account for the observed tolerances, such as differences in frost tolerance and stage of development, temperature variations due to

TABLE 2-5 ESTIMATED CRITICAL TEMPERATURES [°F (°C)] OF DEVELOPING CONCORD GRAPEVINE BUDS AT DIFFERENT STAGES OF DEVELOPMENT[a]

| | BUD SURFACE MOISTURE STATUS | |
STAGE OF DEVELOPMENT	Wet	Dry
Scale-crack	22 (−5.6)	15 (−9.4)
First-swell	24 (−4.4)	18 (−7.8)
Full-swell	26 (−3.3)	19 (−7.2)
Burst	26 (−3.3)	21 (−6.1)
Exposed shoot	27 (−2.8)	

Source: Johnson and Howell (1981).

[a]Values are LT_{50}, where 50% of the growing buds were killed.

TABLE 2-6 CRITICAL TEMPERATURES (AIR) FOR STRAWBERRY BUDS, FLOWER, AND FRUIT[a]

BUDS EMERGE	BUDS CLOSED	FLOWER OPEN	SMALL GREEN FRUIT
10°F	22 to 27°F	30°F	28°F
−12.2°C	−5.6 to −2.8°C	−1.1°C	−2.2°C

Source: Funt et al. (1985).

[a]Duration of temperature for damage can be 20 minutes to 2 hours, depending on wind, humidity, and cultivar.

Climatic Influences and Site Selection

location, foliage cover or mulch, cultivar differences, and the influence of super-cooling. A number of factors influence the degree of injury inflicted on a plant by low temperatures. These are:

1. The stage of development of the fruit crop
2. Preceding temperatures
3. The amount of leaf cover over the blossom or fruit
4. The severity and duration of the freeze
5. The wind speed and the cloud cover
6. Wetness or surface moisture

Site selection.   The best method of frost/freeze protection is good site selection. Microclimate monitoring may be used to evaluate a site not yet committed to production. Temperature surveys should be made on lands contemplated for new plantings. Well-distributed temperature recordings should be made throughout the site for at least one season, and preferably two, prior to planting.

Species and cultivar considerations.   It is important to recognize that there is substantial variation between different types of fruit in their susceptibility to frost/freeze damage. In the case of tree fruits, apricots flower and develop very early, while peaches, cherries, and pears are somewhat later, and apples are delayed even further. The same is true for small fruit crops, with strawberries and gooseberries commonly flowering before the danger of frost has passed. In contrast, muscadine grapes are one of the latest southern fruit plants to bud-out in the spring. Bud swell and the commencement of growth can also vary dramatically among related species. For example, the French American hybrid grape cultivar 'Baco Noir' may begin growth 2 weeks earlier than a *vinifera* cultivar such as 'Chardonnay'. Additional differences in tenderness and cold hardiness also exist between small fruit crops and should be considered in site selection. For example, in areas where cold damage is common, growers should carefully select cold hardy cultivars such as the 'Beta' grape, 'Northland' blueberry, or 'Kent' strawberry.

Cultural practices.   Plants themselves can influence air stagnation and frost hazard. For instance, if branches extend so far out that they join or interlock with branches of other plants, natural air drainage is reduced. Hedgerow plantings, especially, present a problem. Whenever soil erosion is not a problem, plantings should run downhill with the slope to allow air to drain freely. When planting, it may be advisable to leave an air drainage channel in draws rather than continuing the plants across the draw. Draws clogged with trees and woody shrubs can retard cold air drainage and should be kept open as part of annual pruning chores.

Sandy and coarse-textured soils have a higher frost hazard than do finer-textured soils. Their greater pore space caused by the larger particle size means that they store less heat. Sandy soils also have a lower water-holding capacity and tend to dry out faster. This shortens the life of increased protection resulting from moistened soil compared to heavier soils.

Soil stores solar heat during the day and releases it through radiation at night. Heat comes from both the backlog of heat stored in the subsoil and the more recent heat stored in the surface soil. Most of the heat is exchanged from the surface 6 in. (15 cm). For this to be an effective source of heat, certain conditions must be met.

1. *The soil must be moist.* Dry soil contains a large amount of air, a poor conductor of heat. In dry soil only the surface warms during the day, and this heat is lost quickly during the night. A moist soil stores more heat and also conducts heat better. Table 2-7 shows the heat reflectivity under various floor management options. A wet soil will release about 2½ times as much heat as dry soil.

2. *The soil must be firm.* Any soil cultivation will tend to warm the soil earlier than undisturbed soil, advance bud break, and increase the potential for low-temperature damage. After the initial stimulation, newly worked soils tend to be cold in terms of stored heat. They contain more air space than a firm soil, so can neither store nor conduct much heat. After cultivation, soils should be firmed by rainfall or irrigation. Firming newly cultivated soil by cultipacking or rolling may also be helpful.

3. *The soil must be bare.* The presence of cover crops, weeds, organic mulches, or trash on the soil surface is detrimental. The presence of such matter insulates the soil surface so that it cannot absorb or give up heat readily. Low-mowed ground covers are not as insulating as taller plants. By far the warmest conditions are favored by a bare soil surface.

The most successful frost/freeze protection strategy would include preparation of the site so that the floor is a good thermal conductor. The ideal situation would be a smooth, bare, moist, firm soil. Other preparations aimed at retaining natural plant and ground warmth along with facilitating good air movement through the planting will also aid in minimizing the frost/freeze hazard. Assuming that plants are properly pruned and that rows are laid out parallel to nocturnal air drift will be of benefit. Nocturnal drift is often exactly the opposite of prevailing daytime wind direction. Finally, sites in potential frost areas that see the maximum amount of sunlight during the day, such as southern or western slopes, will have a greater opportunity to absorb and reradiate thermal energy.

TABLE 2-7 COMPARISON OF MINIMUM TEMPERATURES OF SOIL SURFACES UNDER VARIOUS TYPES OF FLOOR MANAGEMENT PRACTICES.[a]

Bare, firm moist ground	Warmest
Shredded cover crop, moist ground	½°F colder
Low cover crop, moist ground	1–3°F colder
Dry, firm ground	2°F colder
Freshly disked ground	2°F colder
Higher cover crop	2–4°F colder
In some instances where high cover crop restricts air drainage	6–8°F colder

[a]Listed in order of increasing hazard.

Climatic Influences and Site Selection

Frost protection devices. There are several basic frost protection methods or devices commonly used to protect horticultural crops. These frost protection techniques include the following: (1) heaters, (2) wind machines, (3) low-level and sprinkler irrigation, (4) fog, and (5) the use of these systems in combination. For the small fruit crops, sprinkler irrigation is generally considered the superior method.

Chilling Requirement

Most deciduous fruit crops require a period of cold temperature below 45°F (7°C) during the winter to induce dormancy and to promote satisfactory fruit and shoot development in the spring. The length of cold period required, or chilling requirement, has been established for most fruits, but can vary dramatically between species. Different wild species within a fruit type may also vary widely. The wild blackberries of Vermont, for example, would probably need considerably more chilling on the average than would blackberries of Texas. Table 2-8 shows the approximate chilling requirement of common small fruit crops.

Temperate fruit crops respond to extended periods of short daylengths and cold temperatures by becoming dormant. In the most general sense, dormancy is best exemplified by the absence of growth. It has been suggested recently that plant dormancy regulation may be controlled in three manners:

1. *Eco-dormancy*: regulated by environmental factors such as temperature extremes, nutrient deficiencies, and water stress.
2. *Ecto-dormancy*: regulated by *physiological factors within the plant but outside the affected structure* (buds, etc.); controlled by such influences as apical dominance and photoperiod.

TABLE 2-8 APPROXIMATE NUMBER OF CHILLING HOURS REQUIRED TO BREAK WINTER REST FOR VARIOUS TEMPERATE SMALL FRUIT CROPS BETWEEN 30 AND 45°F (0 AND 7°C)

SMALL FRUIT	HOURS OF CHILLING
Grapes	
vinifera	100–400
labrusca	1200–1500
Strawberry	200–300
Blueberry	
Rabbiteye	200–500
Highbush	650–850
Blackberry	
Thorny	200–600
Thornless	700–1100
Raspberry	800–1700
Currant	800–1500
Gooseberry	800–1500
Kiwifruit	500–600
Cranberry	2000

3. *Endo-dormancy*: regulated by *internal physiological factors inside the affected structure*; controlled by factors such as the chilling response and photoperiod (Lang et al., 1985). Dormancy has also been commonly subdivided into rest and quiescence.

   (a) *Rest* is the condition during which growth will not occur despite the presence of favorable environmental conditions. In this case, the buds are dormant because of internal physiological blocks (usually levels of natural plant chemical products) that prevent growth. This is the state that is directly influenced by chilling temperatures.

   (b) *Quiescence* is the failure to grow because of unfavorable environmental conditions such as cold temperatures or drought.

The temperatures that are most efficient in meeting the chilling requirements of plants are between 37 and 50°F (3 and 10°C), with the most commonly accepted chilling temperature range being between 32 and 45°F (0 and 7°C). Temperatures above 59°F (15°C) will reverse the chilling process, with freezing or near-freezing temperatures being ineffectual in chilling unit accumulation. Each fruit species, and often cultivars within species, have varying temperature ranges for effective chilling, partial chilling, and dehardening.

Topography

The fact that cold air is heavier than warm air and flows to lower elevations should be taken into consideration when establishing fruit plantings. As a general rule, a site that is higher than the immediate or adjacent areas is less subject to freezes. This is especially important during radiation-type freezes (clear skies and calm winds) when the coldest air is found at or near the ground level. With the colder air flowing to the lower elevations, the air that is lost from the higher elevations is then replaced by warmer air from above the earth's surface. The end result is that the warmest air is found at the higher elevations and on slopes rather than in the lower areas. The foregoing conditions occur during radiation-type freezes. With advection-type freezes, crops on higher locations may frequently suffer more damage than those at lower locations.

Cold air movement during radiational cooling fosters the emergence of *thermal belts* along valley slopes, as illustrated in Fig. 2-11. During the night they develop individual air circulations between the air that is cooled on the slopes and the reservoirs of warm air above the valley floor. Gradually, downward-moving cold air sinks into the valley, lifting warm air above it and creating a warm thermal belt along the midsection of the slope. It is this mesoclimatic (topoclimate) factor that makes certain slopes good sites for fruit plantings. Valleys and other depressions tend to collect cold air drainage and become frost pockets. Downward-moving air currents can also be dammed behind topographic or vegetative barriers or settle into depressions in the land surface, leading to the formation of cold islands, frost holes, cold air pools, and frost hollows. A good general rule is that at night concave land surfaces are cold and convex surfaces are warm.

Topographic orientation (i.e., aspect or compass direction toward which a site

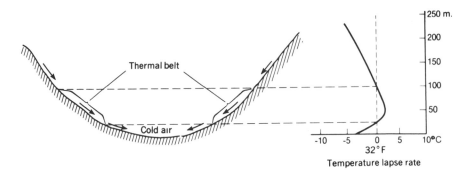

FIGURE 2-11 Microclimate created by sloping terrain: the thermal belt. (From Howard J. Critchfield, *General Climatology,* 3rd ed., © 1974, p. 270. Adapted by permission of Prentice-Hall, Inc., Englewood Cliffs, N.J.)

faces) is a critical determinant of radiation interception, temperature, and consequently, soil moisture regimes and growing season length. There is a complex slope–aspect interaction. The amount of solar radiation and heat are dependent on the latitude, declination of the sun, altitude of the sun, angle of the slope, and the direction it faces.

Slopes facing toward the sun (southeast to southwest) have warmer climates than slopes facing away from the sun, and sun-facing slopes have higher minimum temperatures 5 to 8°F (9 to 14°C) warmer during the spring and fall. These temperature differences lead to longer growing seasons of up to 30 days, soil temperature differences of 7°F (13°C), and moisture regimes that range from cool and moist to hot and dry.

Greatest differences in microclimates are found to be between north and northeast and south to southwest exposures instead of between directly north or south exposures. North-facing slopes have cool temperatures, which often retard shoot development in the spring enough to reduce frost damage; south slopes tend to warm up faster in the spring, stimulating bud burst and shoot elongation before all frost hazard has past. West slopes have the limitation of being exposed to prevailing winds during warm growing seasons causing shoot damage or drying injury.

Effect of Water

Large bodies of open water substantially moderate the climate of the surrounding area. Water has the ability to absorb and release heat slowly across the growing season. This useful property of water is due to its high specific heat. *Specific heat* is the number of calories of heat required to change the temperature of 1 g of a substance by 1°C. Materials with a high specific heat show relatively small changes in temperature in response to a given amount of heat energy. For example, the specific heat (cal/g per degree celsius) of water is 1.00, while ice is 0.50 and steam is 0.48. Other environmental substances have very low specific heats, such as air = 0.24 and sand = 0.20.

High-Temperature Stress

Air temperatures ranging from 77 to 86°F (25 to 30°C) are considered optimum for the growth of most temperate-zone fruit crops. Leaf temperatures higher than 86°F (30°C) can cause internal water deficiencies, sunburn damage, dehydration of fruit, and reduced growth rate. High temperatures can result in bleaching of chlorophyll from leaves, leaf tissue necrosis, phloem and cambium death, and fruit scalds. Additionally, high temperatures can decrease the acid content and increase the pH levels of fruit as well as inhibiting color formation and causing uneven ripening.

Excessive temperatures usually occur when plant parts are exposed to very high light intensities and radiant heating becomes a severe problem, or when soil temperatures increase markedly. Dissipation of radiant energy is usually dependent on cooling by evaporation of water and by conduction to the atmosphere. Nevertheless, leaves in full sunlight may experience a 18 to 27°F (10 to 15°C) rise over ambient temperatures, and some fruit tissues with relatively small surface-to-volume ratio may have temperatures 54°F (30°C) above ambient.

Temperature influences the rates of photosynthesis, respiration, and other metabolic processes. Day/night temperatures affect the balance between yield, growth, and fruit quality. Many species have particular temperature requirements for flower initiation, blooming, fruit set, and fruit growth and development, with unusual temperatures resulting in abnormal or malformed flowers or fruit.

High temperatures play a role in color development and maturity of the fruit. Grape cultivars such as 'Concord', 'Cardinal', 'Tokay', and 'Emperor' do not color well at very high temperatures. If these varieties were grown in a cool region, they would develop adequate coloring. Night temperatures are more important than daytime temperatures. The differential of the two temperatures is also important. A large temperature differential can partially overcome the effects of high temperature. For example, 'Exotic' and 'Ribier' grapes have been shown to be more tolerant of high temperatures. The greater the complexity of the color compounds, which are composed of anthocyanins, the more tolerant to higher temperatures is the cultivar.

A sudden rise in temperature during maturation may cause sunburn of the fruit. This can be recognized by browning, shriveling, and eventually a drying of the affected grapes or the entire cluster. Overcropped vines appear to be more sensitive to sunburning. Vines that are receiving adequate irrigation and are properly trellised for needed shade will withstand damage due to a sudden temperature change better than will those that are water stressed, exposed to direct sunlight, or both.

Temperature plays a major role in the respiration of organic acids in fruits. As the temperature increases, the rate at which the acid is respired increases. For each 5.6°F (10°C) rise in temperature, the rate of respiration doubles. A cultivar will be higher in acid (at the same sugar level) when grown in a cool region versus a warm one. Varieties with high acid content can be grown successfully in warm areas.

Transpiration Rate

The factors influencing the rate of transpiration include two principal groups: environmental factors and morphological factors. The former include conditions external to the plant, whereas morphological factors include structural features and habits of growth of the plant, sometimes referred to as internal factors. The important environmental factors that influence transpiration are (1) relatively humidity of the atmosphere, (2) air movement (windspeed), (3) air and plant temperature, (4) light intensity, and (5) soil conditions (water available to plant).

Relative humidity is the ratio between the actual weight of moisture and the total amount of water that can be held by a unit volume of air at a specific temperature and pressure expressed as a percentage.

Relative humidity is a percentage value that expresses the ratio between the actual amount of water vapor in the air and the amount of water vapor the air could hold at the given temperature. The higher the temperature, the more water vapor the air can hold. For each 1°F that air temperatures are increased, a 2% drop in relative humidity can be expected. If the air is holding one-half as much water vapor as it could hold, the relative humidity is 50%. If the air is cooled to saturation (100% relative humidity), fog or dew can form, depending on wind conditions and other factors. Early morning fog is dissipated by rising temperatures. The relative humidity of fog is 100%, but as temperature increases, the capacity of the air to hold more water vapor also increases, the relative humidity decreases to less than 100%, and the fog evaporates.

An increase of 20°F (11°C) usually doubles the capacity of air to hold water vapor; consequently, when air temperature increases 20°F (11°C), an existing 100% relative humidity will decrease to 50%. In general, relative humidities are lower during the afternoon when the air temperature reaches its daily maximum, and higher in the early morning when the minimum temperature for the day occurs (Baldwin, 1973).

Relative humidity is important in relation to the incidence of foliar disease and transpiration from plant tissues. Disease related to high humidity in the macroclimate of a given area such as the southeastern United States, or within a microclimate such as the canopy of a grapevine, can be a serious problem for fruit growers. Excellent reviews of the effects of atmospheric humidity on horticultural crops can be found in Lipton et al. (1978) and Grange and Hand (1987).

Soil Flooding

When a soil is flooded, gas exchange between the soil and air is drastically reduced. Shortly after a soil is inundated, microorganisms consume practically all the oxygen in the water and soil. However, poor soil aeration is not limited to flooded soils, but is a problem with many fine-textured soils. Such soils contain little air, and gas exchange between them and the atmosphere is very slow.

Poor soil aeration and deoxygenation of the rooting medium associated with flooding induces a number of changes in the soil and in plants that usually adversely influence growth. A wide variety of toxic compounds accumulate in waterlogged soils. The absence of oxygen at once triggers a sequence of chemical and biochemical reduction reactions in the soil. Some of these reduced components (NO_2^-, Mn^{2+}, Fe^{2+}, and S^-) as well as microbial metabolites can sometimes accumulate to concentrations that are injurious to root metabolism. An aerobic metabolism within oxygen-deficient roots may also give rise to products that are potentially injurious to metabolism if they accumulate to abnormally large concentrations. Leaching and denitrification under flooded soil conditions may also deplete soil nitrogen.

Shortly after they are flooded, plants exhibit sequential changes in metabolism and physiological processes. Reduced water absorption and closure of stomata leading to a lowered rate of photosynthesis are among the earliest plant responses to flooding. Subsequent changes include decreased permeability of roots; reduced mineral uptake; alterations in growth–hormone balances; leaf epinasty, chlorosis, and abscissions; and arrested vegetative and reproductive growth. Morphological changes include hypertrophy of the lenticils as well as formation of special tissues.

Waterlogging of soil is not restricted to areas of heavy rainfall but also occurs periodically in arid regions that are irrigated. Under certain conditions the flooding of soil by irrigation adversely affects plants by decreasing soil aeration and causing erosion and salt problems.

Flood tolerance varies widely among plant species and cultivars. The relative flooding tolerance of small fruit crops follows: most tolerant to slow or imperfect drainage — elderberry, gooseberry, cranberry, grape, and blueberry; relatively intolerant — black currant, kiwifruit, strawberry, blackberry, and raspberry.

Drainage of Agricultural Land

The methods used for land drainage may be classified in two broad categories:

1. *Surface drainage.* Land surfaces are reshaped as necessary to eliminate ponding and establish slopes sufficient to induce gravitational flow overland and through channels to an outlet. Surface drainage may be divided into works that (a) remove water directly from land by land smoothing, land grading, beddings, and ditching; and (b) divert and exclude water from land by diversion ditches, dikes, and floodways.

2. *Subsurface drainage.* Ditches and buried drains are installed within the soil profile to collect and convey excess groundwater to a gravity or pumped outlet. The drop in pressure resulting from discharge induces the flow of excess groundwater through the soil into the drains. Interceptor drains are used to prevent entry on the land when groundwater moves laterally. Drains are oriented approximately at right angles to the direction of groundwater flow. Relief drains are used when land surfaces are nearly flat, flow velocities low, or interception of groundwater ineffective. Drains are commonly (but not necessarily always) oriented approximately parallel with the direction of groundwater flow.

Climatic Influences and Site Selection

Irrigation

Small fruit crops benefit from supplemental irrigation in most areas of the country. Vegetative growth, fruit size, and quality all respond to soil water applications. Avoidance of physiological disorders and the uniform production of fruit can also result from proper irrigation. Good soil moisture promotes improved vegetative growth on young plants as well as encouraging good flower bud development for subsequent fruit production.

In addition to supplying water during periods of drought and water stress, irrigation systems may also provide many fringe benefits. Irrigation is being used successfully in many parts of the country to prevent or reduce crop losses from spring frost and freezing weather. There are two ways in which irrigation can be used to achieve this: (1) by delaying bloom through evaporative cooling, and (2) by adding heat to prevent the freezing of blossoms or other plant parts.

Irrigation can be used to improve both yields and quality of some crops by reducing the temperature on hot days. Irrigation systems may also be used for the chemical applications. Soluble and emulsifiable chemicals such as fertilizers, herbicides, and other pesticides can be applied through irrigation systems. There are several advantages to the irrigation application of chemicals: (1) savings in labor and equipment costs, (2) more uniform applications of fertilizers and herbicides, and (3) more efficient uptake of fertilizers by the plants.

The harvest dates of some crops can be controlled by the use of irrigation. This is especially important with such crops as high-value fruits, vegetables, and flowers. It enables growers to market them when you can get the best prices. Harvest-date control is accomplished by using irrigation to assure prompt bud break or germination and steady growth throughout the growing season. Limiting the amount of water at the right time for some crops will cause the plants to mature earlier. Limiting the amount of water for certain other crops will delay their maturity.

Properly timed irrigations can be used to disrupt the feeding or life cycles of certain insect and mite pests of fruit crops. Such applications require an understanding of the biology and dynamics of the insect and mite populations to be controlled.

Irrigation Methods

There are four basic methods of applying water: (1) sprinkler, (2) surface, (3) trickle, and (4) subsurface.

With the *sprinkler method* water is sprayed through the air and falls to the ground like rain. This is accomplished by using either one or more rotation sprinklers or spray nozzles/or perforated pipe. The water is sprayed into the air, broken up into various-sized droplets, and distributed over the ground.

In the *surface method,* water is applied to the soil at the ground level. It flows by gravity over the surface of the field. This is accomplished in two ways. For close-growing crops — ones that are sown, drilled, or sodded — the entire field is flooded.

For row crops or crops in beds, the water is directed down furrows between the rows.

Trickle irrigation is a system for supplying filtered water directly onto or below the soil surface. Water is carried through an extensive pipe network to each plant. The outlet device that emits water onto or into the soil is called an *emitter*. After leaving the emitter, water is distributed to a *wetted zone* by its normal movement through the soil.

Below-surface irrigation is classified into (1) subirrigation, and (2) subsurface irrigation.

With the *subirrigation* method, water is supplied to the root zone by artificially regulating the groundwater table elevation. In subirrigation, check dams and gates are used to maintain the water level in the soil from open ditches or from jointed or perforated pipe. The water is held just below the root zone 12 to 36 in. (30 to 91 cm). Water moves into the root zone by capillary action. Water moves from the surface of wet soil particles to drier soil particles because of surface attraction forces. This attraction may be upward, sideways, or downward, depending on where the drier soil is located.

With deep-rooted crops such as citrus trees, the water level may be raised periodically to near the surface for irrigation. Then it is lowered to provide for root development.

In *subsurface irrigation,* water is applied below the surface by porous or perforated plastic pipe. This method of applying water is somewhat similar to trickle irrigation. Instead of the pipe being placed on top of the ground, it is 'planted' under the row in the root zone.

Factors Determining Irrigation Method

Land slope. If the land is level, or it can be made level without too much expense, any of the four irrigation methods can be used. If the land is sloping, choices may be limited to using the sprinkler or trickle method. With the trickle method, emitter discharge rates can be matched to soil intake rates. Uniform pressure distribution can be obtained through pressure regulation and lateral arrangement. Some types of surface and subsurface systems can also be used on sloping land, but most of these systems require land leveling or benching.

Intake rate. You must know the water intake rate of your soil (how fast it can absorb water) to determine the maximum rate at which you can apply irrigation water so that surface puddling and runoff will not occur. Several conditions affect the intake rate of the soil. Two of the more important ones are texture (size of the soil particles) (Table 2-9) and surface sealing due to compaction and salts. The larger the soil particles and the farther apart they are, the faster the intake rate. In addition, slope, crop cover, and tillage conditions will also affect the water intake rate.

If your soil has a low water intake rate [0.5 in. (13 mm) per hour or less], you can use the sprinkler, surface, or trickle method. If your soil has a high water intake

TABLE 2-9 INTAKE RATES AND AVAILABLE WATER-HOLDING CAPACITIES OF SOILS WITH DIFFERENT TEXTURES

SOIL TEXTURE	INTAKE RATE (in./hr)	AVAILABLE WATER-HOLDING CAPACITY (in./ft)
Sand	1.0–5.0	0.5–0.7
Sandy loam	0.7–1.0	0.8–1.4
Loam	0.6–1.0	1.0–1.8
Silt loam	0.5–1.0	1.2–1.8
Clay loam	0.3–0.8	1.3–2.1
Clay	0.1–0.5	1.4–2.4

rate [3.0 in. (76 mm) per hour or more], you may be limited to the use of the sprinkler, trickle, or subsurface method. With high intake rates, it is usually impractical to try to apply water by the surface method. You will have too much water absorbed at the head of the irrigated area and not enough delivered to the opposite or lower end. You can correct this condition by shortening the length of run. But you will reach a point when the length of run may be too short to be practical.

If your soil has a moderate water intake rate [0.5 to 3.0 in. (13 to 76 mm) per hour], you can use any of the four methods. Your system must be designed to apply water according to the intake rate of your soil.

Water-holding capacity. The *water-holding capacity* of soil is the amount of water it will hold after the free water has been drained away by gravity. The water-holding capacity of a soil depends largely on its texture (Table 2-9).

All the water a soil will hold is not available equally to plants. As the plant roots remove available water following an irrigation, the remaining water is bound more tightly to the soil—thus is less available to the plants.

The water-holding capacity does not affect the method of irrigation. It does, however, determine the frequency of irrigation and the amount of water applied per irrigation. This means that if you have a coarse-textured soil, your irrigation system must be designed to apply water more frequently than if you have a fine-textured soil. You must be able to irrigate the entire field before the water content of the soil drops too low. Otherwise, your crop may not reach its maximum potential.

Water tolerance of crops. If you grow crops that are likely to develop fungi or disease under high moisture conditions, you may have difficulty with the sprinkler method. The presence of water around the leaves or fruit from sprinkler irrigation tends to promote some diseases. This is seldom a serious problem, however.

If you grow crops that cannot tolerate having their roots stand under water for several hours, you may not be able to use the surface method of application. The reason is that with some types of surface systems and soil conditions, the water must remain on the field for several hours (2 to 24 hours, depending on the soil intake rate) before it can penetrate into the root zone. In this time, the plants may become damaged. Root diseases are more likely to occur with surface systems than with sprinkler systems.

Wind action.   Wind action may affect the water application efficiency of the sprinkler and surface methods. Strong wind action will distort the water distribution pattern to the extent that you may get very little water on the windward side (direction from which the wind is blowing) of the sprinkler and get too much water on the other side.

Wind affects the distribution pattern whether the rate of application is high or low. High winds will sometimes affect the application efficiency of surface irrigation. This is particularly true on large, unplanted level areas.

Irrigation Scheduling

Irrigation scheduling allows an irrigator to supply water in a timely manner and in sufficient amounts to alleviate soil moisture shortages. Many parameters or factors, all interacting with one another, must be considered in arriving at a workable and efficient irrigation schedule.

Soil, plant, climate, and management are important. Important soil factors include texture, depth, structure, salinity, the presence of root-restricting barriers, aeration, surface and internal drainage, available water-holding capacity, and water table depth. Important plant factors include the kind of crop, rooting characteristics, and drought tolerance, and the growth stage(s) most affected by shortages of soil moisture. Climatic factors of importance are precipitation, solar radiation, daylength, air temperature, wind, and relative humidity.

Management factors are those that can be changed by the farm operator and include virtually all farming practices that affect crop growth. Examples are fertility regime, pruning, plant population, and row spacing. When developing an irrigation schedule for an entire farm, the irrigator must consider how much water is available in relation to the number of acres of land requiring irrigation during peak water-use periods. Two approaches can be taken: (1) plant only the acres for which water is available to meet peak demand, or (2) plant a calculated excessive number of acres and store water in the root zone for a planned deficit irrigation schedule during the period of peak demand. The crop mix on the farm is also an important consideration because some crops use less water during certain months than others do. Furthermore, some crops require smaller but more frequent irrigations.

The discussion above would suggest that irrigating soils correctly requires a high level of management. One of the most difficult irrigation management decisions involves the actual scheduling of individual water applications. The application of too little water at one time or applying it too infrequently results in plant water stress, which reduces crop yields. On the other hand, applying too much irrigation water is wasteful and leaches mobile fertilizer nutrients below the rooting zone. In some areas applying too much irrigation water raises the water table and many drown the crop.

SOILS

Soil Surveys

Soil surveys should be the first source of information about the properties of soils for fruit crops. Detailed soil maps and descriptions of the soils are available for most counties from the district (county) office of the Soil Conservation Service or the Cooperative Extension Service. Unpublished soil maps and descriptions can also be obtained from the Soil Conservation Service offices. Soil maps are made by digging many soil pits and auger corings in agricultural areas. Digging a pit can be a valuable means of thoroughly evaluating the soil characteristics of a particular site.

Most fields contain several different soils, and it is valuable to rate the soils for fruit crops to determine the most efficient cropping systems. Some soil characteristics that should be considered in evaluating a site include drainage class, depth to water table, water-holding capacity, slope, rooting depth, trafficability, permeability, erosion, stoniness and rockiness, pH, texture, and elevation. Table 2-10 summarizes the physical and chemical properties of soils as they are affected by soil texture.

Soil Drainage

The ability of a soil to drain excess water from the entire soil profile, yet hold sufficient water for normal plant growth is known as *soil drainage.* Soils are classified into drainage groups by their moisture status during the growing season. The moisture status during the growing season is determined either by observing the soil moisture conditions over a period of years or by measuring the soil depth to

TABLE 2-10 PHYSICAL AND CHEMICAL PROPERTIES OF SOIL AS INFLUENCED BY SOIL TEXTURE

	SOIL TEXTURE CLASS			
SOIL PROPERTY	Sand	Silt	Clay	Loam[a]
Water infiltration (permeability)	Good (fast)	Medium (moderate)	Poor (slow)	Medium (moderate)
Water-holding capacity	Poor (low)	Medium (moderate)	Good (high)	Medium (moderate)
Drainage	Excellent	Good	Poor	Good
Erodibility	Easy	Moderate	Difficult	Moderate
Aeration	Excellent	Good	Poor	Good
Cation exchange	Poor (low)	Medium	Good (high)	Medium
Tillage (workability)	Good (easy)	Medium (moderate)	Poor (difficult)	Medium (moderate)
Root penetration	Good	Medium	Poor	Medium
Spring temperature	Warms fast	Warms moderately	Warms slowly	Warms moderately

[a]Loam soils may vary substantially in their soil properties, depending on the actual proportion of sand, silt, and clay particles that are present.

color mottling. Mottling is a color change in response to soil drainage. Soils that are well drained have uniformly bright colors, such as brown, yellow, red, or combinations of these colors. The surface soils may have these bright colors, yet be darkened by organic matter. Surface and subsurface soils may also inherit darker colors from gray-black or black shales present in the parent material. Uniform light gray colors in the profile indicate prolonged saturation with water. If the surface soil is light gray, water stands on or near the surface for prolonged periods during the summer. If there are alternating periods when the soil is saturated and is not saturated with water at a particular depth, some of the bright brown or yellow colors change to gray spots or mottles. The depth to this color change determines the soil drainage group or class.

Soil Composition

Every soil consists of mineral and organic matter, water, air, and living organisms. The approximate volume composition of a representative silt loam surface soil in optimum condition for plant growth would be close to the following estimates. It would contain about 50% pore space, which can be occupied by air and water. At optimum moisture for plant growth this pore space would be roughly divided between 25% air space and 25% water space. The proportion of air and water is subject to great fluctuations under natural conditions, depending on the weather and other factors. The solid space is made up of about 45% mineral matter and 5% organic matter in our representative soil.

Soil Type

Most agricultural soils contain less than 20% organic matter and are classified as *mineral soils*. These soils are further classified based on their soil textural class name. Soils that contain 20 to 65% organic matter are called *muck soils*. Soils containing over 65% organic matter are classified as *peat soils*.

Soil Texture

Soil texture refers to the relative proportion of particles of various sizes in a given soil. Soil particle size include: clay (less than 0.002 mm), silt (0.002 to 0.05 mm), sand (0.05 to 2 mm), and gravel (larger than 2 mm). For example, a loam-textured soil consists of about 35 to 45% sand, 35 to 45% silt, and 10 to 25% clay.

Soil Moisture

Soil moisture is classified in several different ways and is characterized by certain soil moisture constants. *Field capacity* is the percentage of water remaining in a soil 2 or 3 days after having been saturated and after free drainage has practically ceased. *Permanent wilting point* or *wilting coefficient* is the percent of soil moisture at which a wilted plant will not recovery turgidity in a saturated atmosphere of 100% relative humidity. This is the lower limit of the available water, which has a soil moisture tension of about 15 atm (15 bar). The *available water* is that percent which remains in a given soil after it has drained to field capacity but before it reaches the permanent wilting point.

Soil Chemistry

Nutrient-supplying power is defined as the capacity of a soil, both topsoil and subsoil, to provide nutrients for crop needs. Within the topsoil, both mineral composition and organic matter affect nutrient content. The very smallest soil particles are called *colloids*. Colloids are primarily responsible for the chemical reactivity of soils. Soil colloids are derived from clays. Each colloid (clay and organic) has a net negative (−) charge. The negatively charged colloids attract cations (positively electrically charged elements, e.g., Ca^{2+}) and hold them much like a magnet holds small pieces of metal.

This characteristic of colloids explains why nitrate nitrogen (NO_3^-) is more easily leached from the soil than is ammonium nitrogen (NH_4^+). Like soil colloids, nitrate has a weak negative charge. So nitrate is not held by the soil but remains as a free ion in soil water to be leached through the soil profile in some soils and under some rainfall conditions.

Cation-exchange capacity. Cations held on the soil colloid are exchangeable and can be replaced by other cations. Calcium can be exchanged for hydrogen and/or potassium or vice versa. The total number of exchangeable cations a soil can hold (the amount of its negative charge) is called its *cation-exchange-capacity* (CEC). The higher a soil's CEC, the more cations it can retain.

Soils differ in their capacities to hold exchangeable K^+ and other cations. The CEC depends on amounts and kinds of clay and organic matter present. For example, a high-clay soil can hold more exchangeable cations than can a low-clay soil. Also, CEC increases as organic matter increases.

The CEC of a soil is expressed in terms of milligram equivalents per 100 g of soil and is written as milliequivalents (mEq per 100 g). Clay minerals usually range from 10 to 150 mEq per 100 g in CEC values. Organic matter ranges from 200 to 400 mEq per 100 g.

Aside from applying proper amounts of lime and fertilizer to maintain soil pH and base exchange cations, it is important that calcium, magnesium and potassium be supplied in the proper balance. Although a rather wide range is generally acceptable, the balance usually falls within this range: calcium 70 to 75%; magnesium, 10 to 15%; and potassium, 2 to 5%. Where the balance between calcium and magnesium may fall out of the desired range, limestone recommendations will call for a low- or high-magnesium limestone (calcitic or dolomitic).

Soil Organic Matter

Soil organic matter (OM) consists of plant and animal residues in various stages of decay. The decomposition of soil OM serves to improve both the physical and chemical condition of the soil. OM also serves as a source of energy for soil microorganisms as well as a source of supply for plant nutrients. The bacteria which are feeding on the OM produce complex carbohydrates that cement soil particles together in aggregates and improve soil structure. The penetration of roots is improved by good structure brought about by this decomposition. Improved soil structure also facilitates the entrance and percolation of water through the soil and thus helps to reduce soil erosion. The water-holding capacity of sandy soils is increased by the incorporation of OM, while resulting aggregation in heavy soils may improve drainage. OM holds nutrient elements and protects against loss of minerals by leaching until they are released by the action of microorganisms. Acids produced in the decomposition of OM may help make mineral nutrients in the soil available to plants. Organic matter contains about 5% total nitrogen, so it serves as a storehouse for reserve nitrogen. But nitrogen in organic matter is in organic compounds and not immediately available for plant use.

Soil Testing

There are several basic objectives associated with soil testing. They include determination of proper fertilizer applications, estimation of nutrient needs in advance of a crop, and evaluation of the existence and/or seriousness of any deficiency or toxicity for various crops. The two basic objectives for soil testing are diagnosis to correct nutrient deficiencies, and diagnosis to avoid nutrient excesses. During the development of soil testing over the past few decades, the former objective was foremost. Only recently has the latter objective been recognized as highly important.

Soil test results from different laboratories will vary in the method of reporting results and the number and type of tests reported. Typically, a soil pH value will be given, with a buffer pH also commonly reported. Closely associated with the pH test is the exchangeable acidity, which is normally reported only on soils below pH of 6.0. Exchangeable acidity is reported as mEq per 100 g of soil. Cation-exchange capacity (CEC) may also be reported as mEq per 100 g, along with the percent base saturation of potassium, magnesium, calcium, and possibly mEq per 100 g of sodium.

The lime recommendation will be based on these values, in addition to the measurement of exchangeable calcium (Ca), magnesium (Mg), and potassium (K), which are normally reported in pounds per acre. Liming rates may be given in terms of effective neutralizing value, calcium carbonate equivalent, or a lime test index of limestone, and may require an additional conversion table for interpretation. Available phosphorus (P) is also reported in terms of pounds per acre.

In some areas of the country where soils are naturally calcareous, a lime test to determine the amount of solid lime in the soil may be reported. Electrical conductivity, exchangeable sodium percentage (ESP), or soluble salt concentrations may also be reported for alkaline soils.

Other elements, such as iron (Fe), aluminum (Al), manganese (Mn), sulfur (S), zinc (Zn), boron (B), copper (Cu), NO_3-nitrogen, and NH_4-nitrogen, may also be reported as pounds per acre or parts per million (ppm). These are typically done only as special tests and may cost extra. The percent organic matter (OM) may also be a useful analysis.

Interpretation of soil test results will vary from region to region, as will the standard values and optimum ranges for various constituents of the soil test. Suggested nutrient ranges, ratios, and needs will also depend on the proposed crop to be grown.

Soil Acidity and Liming

The common measurement for soil acidity is the pH scale, a measurement of the free hydrogen ions in the soil solution. The pH scale ranges from 0 at the extremely acid end to 14 at the strongly alkaline end, with 7 being neutral. It is important to note that the pH scale is a logarithmic one, which means that a change of 1 unit actually represents a 10-times multiplier. So a pH of 6 is 10 times more acid (with 10 times more free hydrogen ions) than a soil with a pH of 7. Similarly, a soil with a pH of 5 is 10 times more acid than a soil with a soil at pH 6, and 100 times more acid than pH 7. This explains why a ton or two of lime per acre may boost a soil with a pH of 6 up to a 6.5 range, while several tons may be needed to move a soil from a pH of 5 up to 6.

Soil tests commonly report both a simple soil pH value and a buffer pH value. The soil pH is obtained by adding distilled water to soil and reading the pH value. This pH value is the acidity of the root environment (i.e., the pH to which the plants are exposed). The soil pH measurement is an intensity measurement such as temperature. Temperature in degrees Fahrenheit or Celsius tells how cold or hot it is but not how much heat will be needed to change the temperature a certain number of degrees. A measurement in BTU's tells us how much heat is required to raise the temperature a certain number of degrees. Similarly, the buffer pH tells how much limestone is required to raise the pH from its present level to a neutral pH of 6.8 to 7.0. If the soil pH is greater than 7.0, no limestone is needed and the buffer pH is meaningless.

Calcium chloride solution may be used instead of distilled water to overcome the background effects of salt in the soil. In this case the background salt matrix desorbs iron and aluminum, which hydrolyzes water and lowers the pH. $CaCl_2$ measurements are usually 0.5 pH unit lower than H_2O.

Although soil pH is an excellent single indicator of soil acidity, it does not determine lime requirement. Lime requirement is the amount of good-quality agricultural limestone needed to establish the desired pH range for the cropping system being used. When pH is measured in the laboratory, only 'active' acidity is determined. 'Potential' acidity must also be considered. Some method of relating a change in soil pH to the addition of a known amount of acid or base is necessary. Such a method is called *lime requirement determination*.

The lime requirement of a soil is related not only to the pH of that soil, but also to its buffer or cation-exchange capacity. Total amounts of clay and organic matter in a soil, as well as the kind of clay, will determine how strongly soils are buffered—how strongly they resist a pH change. Buffering capacity increases with the amounts of clay and organic matter. Such soils require more lime to increase pH than do soils with a lower buffer capacity. Sandy soils, with small amounts of clay and organic matter, are weakly buffered. So they require less lime to change the pH.

Benefits from liming. The major reason for liming acid soils is to prevent them from becoming acid enough to reduce crop yields. Liming has several beneficial effects:

1. It reduces acidity and provides a more favorable environment for the growth of soil microorganisms. This is important, especially for nitrogen fixation by legumes and for nitrification of ammonium to nitrate and for the transformation of phosphorus and sulfur.

2. Lime increases the availability of phosphorus, especially in soils containing large amounts of iron and aluminum. The solubility of iron and aluminum phosphates increases as acidity is reduced and may reach toxic levels. Figure 2–12 illustrates the influence of pH on the availability of plant nutrients in mineral soils.

3. Liming decreases potassium losses caused by leaching and increases potassium availability.

MINERAL SOILS

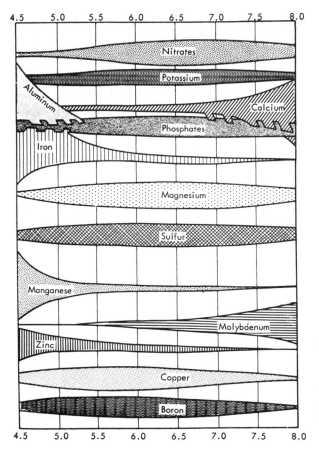

FIGURE 2–12 The relationship between soil pH and relative plant nutrient availability. (the wider the bar, the greater the plant availability). (From *Soils Handbook,* Kentucky Agr. Exp. Sta., Misc. Publ. 383, 1970, p. 28.)

4. Lime supplies calcium and magnesium, nutrients essential for plant growth.

5. Adding calcium improves the structure of acid clay soils by causing clay particles to aggregate.

6. Increasing the soil pH results in the precipitation of toxic aluminum, manganese, and similar elements.

7. Liming increases the effectiveness of some important herbicides and may also influence some insecticides and nematicides.

Critical pH values.   Each fruit crop has its own relative tolerance to various soil pH ranges. There are optimum pH values found within broader acceptable ranges (Table 2-11). Soil pH values above or below certain critical levels will cause noticeable restricted growth, visible deficiency symptoms, and reduced productivity.

Selecting liming materials.   When selecting a suitable liming material, consider the need for magnesium, desired rate of pH change, materials available, and relative neutralizing value.

Table 2-12 gives general lime recommendations based on soil texture class. Accurate lime recommendations require laboratory analysis of a particular soil in order to determine the cation-exchange capacity (exchange acidity), organic matter, percent base saturation, and other constituents.

In the case of acid-loving crops such as blueberries, the soil pH may need to be lowered. In this situation the use of agricultural grade sulfur is recommended as a soil amendment. One year is required for bacteria to oxidize sulfur and lower the soil pH. No more than 400 lb of sulfur should be used on established blueberry plantings in 1 year. Table 2-13 gives the approximate quantities required to change the soil pH of various soil types and initial acidity levels.

TABLE 2-11   SOIL pH RANGES FOR SMALL FRUIT CROPS

CROP	OPTIMUM	DESIRABLE RANGE
Blueberry		
Highbush	4.5	4.0–5.2
Lowbush	4.5	4.3–5.0
Rabbiteye	4.5	4.2–5.5
Cranberry	4.5	3.5–6.0
Raspberry	6.5	5.4–7.0
Strawberry	6.2	5.0–6.5
Blackberry	6.2	4.5–7.5
Grape		
vinifera	6.5	5.5–7.0
Hybird	6.0	5.0–7.0
American	6.0	4.0–7.0
Muscadine	6.0	5.5–7.0
Black currant	6.5	6.0–7.0
Red currant	6.5	5.5–7.0
Kiwifruit	6.5	5.0–6.5

TABLE 2-12 PREPLANT LIME RECOMMENDATIONS TO RAISE SOIL pH TO 6.5 (TONS OF 100% ENV LIME NEEDED PER ACRE)[a]

	SOIL TYPE		
CURRENT pH	Sand	Loam	Clay
4.4	3.9	6.7	10.4
4.6	3.8	6.6	10.3
4.8	3.7	6.5	10.1
5.0	3.6	6.3	9.8
5.2	3.4	5.9	9.2
5.4	2.7	4.7	7.2
5.6	2.2	3.8	5.9
5.8	1.8	3.1	4.8
6.0	1.3	2.3	3.5

[a]The number obtained from the table assumes the lime to be 100% effective at neutralizing the acid in the soil. To find the actual amount to apply, this number must be divided by the actual lime score of the lime purchased. If a grower finds a lime source that the dealer says is 60% ENV, he or she must apply the recommended number divided by 60. For example, 6.3/0.60 = 10.5 tons per acre.

TABLE 2-13 PREPLANT SULFUR RECOMMENDATIONS TO LOWER SOIL pH TO 4.5 (POUNDS OF SULFUR NEEDED PER ACRE)[a]

	SOIL TYPE		
CURRENT pH	Sand	Loam	Clay
4.5	0	0	0
5.0	175	530	800
5.5	350	1050	1600
6.0	530	1540	2310
6.5	660	2020	3030
7.0	840	2555	3830
7.5	1000	3040	4560

[a]Aluminum sulfate can be substituted at six times the suggested rates.

PLANTING STOCK

In the interactive scheme leading to profitable small fruit culture we have stressed that

preplanning + site preparation + skillful plantation management + intellegent marketing
= profitable small fruit culture

If the preplanning process is sound and leads to suitable capital and management team accumulation, and correct species and site selection, then

planting stock + environmental influences + management practices = realized marketable yield

The importance of high-quality planting stock cannot be overemphasized. No combination of favorable environmental circumstances and consistently good management can overcome the handicap of the wrong cultivar or poorly grown or diseased nursery stock. Quality nursery stock must be true to name, well grown, and balanced in root and top growth, vigorous, and free of diseases and pests. It costs more to purchase guaranteed and certified planting stock from a reputable nursery, but the higher price is a wise investment in this instance. A consideration of the nature, improvement, and selection of small fruit cultivars, and their propagation and nursery production methodology follows.

Propagation and Nursery Practices

Sexual propagation of these small fruit crops by seeds is not used to any extent by nurseries because each new plant would be genetically different from the next (i.e., they do not "come true" from seed). To produce genetically identical true-to-type plants, some form of asexual propagation must be employed. Plants of cultivars that are reproduced in this manner (clones) are genetically similar and therefore are also phenotypically (in outward appearance) similar in their growth and fruiting responses and fruit characteristics.

Propagation methods.   The principal vegetative (asexual) methods used in propagation of small fruit crops are illustrated in Fig. 2-13, which shows a hypothetical small fruit mother plant bearing all the types of plant structures used in propagation. The point of detachment, the type and appearance of the plant part (propagule), and the finished propagule ready for field transplanting are also illustrated. The methods are described below.

In the use of *cuttings,* a plant part (root, stem, leaf bud, or leaf) is detached from the mother plant and incubated in a rooting medium under high humidity or placed prior to the dormant season directly in a well-prepared nursery row. Successful stem and leaf and bud cuttings will initiate adventitious roots. Successful root cuttings will initiate adventitious sprouts. Leaf cuttings must initiate both new roots and a new growing point.

In *layering,* a plant stem is induced to form adventitious roots by covering it with a moist soil medium while the stem is still attached to the mother plant. The rooted, or layered, stem is then detached and transplanted. Layering may be accomplished by burying a stem tip, mounding soil around a number of stems, or burying the entire stem (or alternating adjacent stem segments) in a trench.

Division of specialized plant structures from the mother plant often provides new plants. The divided or separated daughter plant may already be rooted, or the roots may be induced. Small fruit division examples are *runnering* in strawberries, where aboveground prostrate stems called *stolons* or *runners* form plants at alternate nodes; *crown division* in strawberries, where shortened stems called *crowns* are separated when a number of them have been produced by the same mother plant; and *suckering* in blackberries and red raspberries, where horizontal underground rhizomes bud and root.

In *grafting,* a dormant bud or stem section (the top or *scion*) of one plant is inserted and attached onto a rooted or unrooted stem of a second plant (the

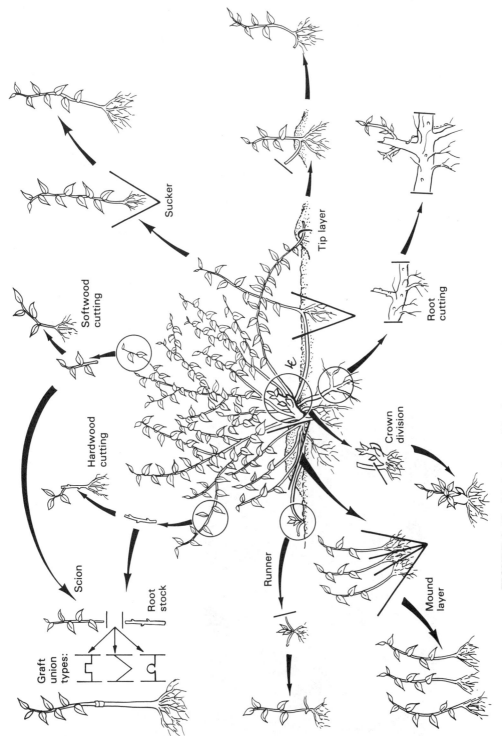

FIGURE 2-13 Methods used in the propagation of small fruit crops.

Softwood cutting

Sucker

Hardwood cutting

Scion

Root stock

Graft union types:

Runner

Mound layer

Tip layer

Crown division

Root cutting

rootstock or understock). There are a variety of grafting and budding methods (Hartmann and Kester, 1983). Grafting may be done indoors, on a greenhouse bench, in a nursery row, or on established plants in the field.

Micropropagation ("tissue culture") is a very specialized and aseptic modification of the cutting method where a minute piece of the mother plant (explant) is established *in vitro* (stage I) on a sterile plant nutrient medium and grown under a standardized light and temperature regime. The established explants are aseptically transferred to, and grown in, a nutrient medium containing elevated levels of cytokinin hormones (stage II), which causes a lateral branching or plantlet proliferation without rooting. Proliferated plantlets may then either be rooted in high-humidity chambers on a rooting medium or transferred aseptically to another nutrient-medium-filled jar, which contains heightened levels of auxin hormones (stage III) to induce rooting (Fig. 2-14). Rooted plantlets are then acclimated to normal atmosphere indoor conditions and planted in containers of sterile soil-substitute media (stage IV) to be grown to field-transplanting size.

The two principal uses of tissue culture systems are the rapid mass propagation of clones (which allows new cultivars to be introduced more quickly and provides large inventories of older, popular cultivars), and the production of virus- and disease-free plant stocks (specific pathogen-tested clones). *In vitro* culture systems also have the potential for convenient distant shipment of propagation material and the long-term storage of clonal material (repositories and germplasm banks). The use of apical meristem shoot tip culture is the primary method of eliminating viruses from stock plants and their progeny. This technology has greatly improved the quality of planting stock that is available to the small fruit grower.

FIGURE 2-14 Virus-free black currant plants produced by embryoid development in tissue culture.

Small Fruit Cultivars

The term *cultivar,* a contraction of "cultivated variety", is used in scientific literature to distinguish cultivated varieties from *botanical varieties* (*var.*). Botanical varieties are naturally occurring variant forms in a wild plant species. The less precise older term, *variety,* is still used in nursery catalogs and by producers, agricultural business people, and the general public. A cultivar is a plant type, within a particular cultivated species, that can be distinguished from other plant types by one or more characters.

Clonal nature of small fruit cultivars.   With the exception of Alpine strawberries, small fruit cultivars are *clones.* That means that all the plants of a cultivated small fruit variety, such as 'Concord' grape, which do or did exist, trace back through generations of vegetative (asexual) reproduction to the single outstanding vine found and named by Ephriam Bull of Massachusetts (Hedrick, 1908). Vegetative propagation almost always results in new plants which possess the same characteristics as the mother plant from which they were separated. This ensures the stability and uniformity of the cultivar.

Origins of small fruit cultivars.   Small fruit cultivars have originated from the selection and propagation of *superior individual plants in wild* (or collected) *natural populations* (e.g., 'McFarland' cranberry or 'Rubel' blueberry). They have originated also as *chance seedlings* in garden cultivar plantings ('Loganberry'), or as *sports* or *mutants* from previously existing cultivars ('Thornless Evergreen' blackberry). More recently introduced small fruit cultivars have resulted from *selection and propagation of superior seedlings* in progenies *from controlled hybridizations* (cross-pollinations) among chosen parent clones ('Tioga' strawberry). Such small fruit breeding is carried out by private citizens, scientists working for plant improvement or seed companies, and scientists working in state (provincial) or federal laboratories.

Small fruit improvement.   Continued plant improvement and 'variety testing' is necessary for the general health and growth of established and beginning small fruit industries. This is so because, like people, no single cultivated plant variety is perfect or adapted to all areas. Also, popular cultivars may encounter serious new disease or environmental problems, which may render them less suitable for culture.

Successful plant improvement programs usually follow most of the following general steps:

1. *Definition of aims.* The several objectives of the breeding program are devised, including the industry and geographic area to be served and the use(s) for which the product is to be improved.

2. *Base population evaluation.* This includes collecting, growing together, and evaluating the performance of a large and diverse group of foreign and

domestic cultivars, breeding selections, and native (wild) plant introductions of the species to be improved.

3. *Parent selection.* Clones are selected from the base population, which possess a number of desirable characteristics to serve as parents of the next generation—the expectation is that the parent clones will transmit the valuable characters to a large proportion of the hybrid seedlings.

4. *Making controlled pollinations.* This involves planning the pollinations, propagating parent plants, bringing desired males and females into as nearly simultaneous bloom as possible, and executing the desired pollinations without contamination from unwanted pollen.

5. *Seed collection.* This involves harvesting fruit from successful pollinations; separation of seed from fruit; and cleaning, drying, storing, and cataloging of seed.

6. *Seed germination.* This includes seed treatments which will aid germination, media and location preparation, seed sowing, and care.

7. *Seedling preparation.* Germinated seedlings are screened to identify certain useful seedlings such as thornless or disease-resistant types, and desired vigorous seedlings are grown to field-transplanting size.

8. *Field evaluation.* Transplanted seedlings are evaluated for plant habit, vigor, disease tolerance, and flower and fruit characters—the best seedlings are selected and vegetatively propagated.

9. *Selection testing.* New selections are compared with previous selections, and with standard and new cultivars for plant and fruit production performance. The worth of a new selection is judged by how it compares to cultivars and selections within the same ripening class. Better selections are again propagated for further testing.

10. *Advanced selection testing.* Better selections are tested in one or more locations in replicated trials which help to compare good selections against named cultivars and to predict whether the results may be repeatable over many years and locations. The most promising selections are compared with standard cultivars at a number of locations to detect the range of adaptation of the potential new cultivars.

11. *Introduction.* True-to-type disease-free stocks of new cultivars are provided to propagators to increase for introduction. Facts about the origin, performance, plant availability, and introduction rationale are prepared. Introduction announcements and publicity follow. The introducing breeder is usually required to save supporting documentation about and foundation stock of the new cultivar if the cultivar was produced with public funds.

The entire breeding cycle may take 10 to 20 years initially, and 7 to 15 years for older small-fruit-breeding programs to go from cross to introduction. It is relatively quick and easy to detect promising candidates. Determining their consistency of performance and their true potential value is difficult and time consuming.

Small fruit cultivar commercial characteristics. New, inexperienced, or marginal small fruit producers judge the worth of a cultivar in terms of yield per acre, reasoning "the more yield, the more profit". This criterion lacks sophistication in modern competitive agriculture. To be most profitable, a modern cultivar must have the following characteristics: planting stock availability, easy to grow, consistently high marketable yield, high product consumer appeal, durable handling qualities, and multiple uses. Each of these general judgment criteria has a number of components, which form the bases for breeder, evaluator, nurseryman, grower, produce handler, and consumer opinions about different cultivars.

Planting stock availability depends largely on the ability of the cultivar to produce ample supplies of plant material suitable for vegetative reproduction, and high vegetative propagation success under varying environmental situations. These consistent and easily propagated plants make it profitable for the nursery owner to carry these cultivars, and they can be offered to the public at lower plant costs (example: 'Earliglow' strawberry).

Cultivars that are easy to grow are those tolerant to disease, pest, and soil or climatic stresses and pressures. They require lower grower inputs, but respond readily to increased care (examples: 'Bluecrop' and 'Tifblue' blueberries, 'Concord' grape, 'Allstar' strawberry).

Consistent high marketable yield is related to general vigor and health, good vegetative plant body development, consistent flower bud initiation, high flower number and/or high fruit set, large fruit size and/or many fruits, and tolerance to fruit rots (examples: 'Honeoye' and 'Chandler' strawberries, 'Thompson Seedless' grape).

Product consumer appeal is related to fruit *appearance* (symmetry; shape; size; color; "skin" gloss, soundness; peduncle, pedicel, or calyx appearance), *flavor* (texture, color, size, sweetness, acidity, aromatic compounds, associated pleasant or off-flavors, balance), *durability* (shelf life), and *usefulness* (does it meet the need for which it was purchased? will it meet other needs?) (examples: 'Raritan' strawberry, 'Hayward' kiwifruit, 'Marion' blackberry, 'Haida' raspberry).

Durable handling qualities include fruit 'skin' integrity, rot resistance, firm fruit flesh, and appearance retention (examples: 'Earliglow' and 'Pajaro' strawberries, 'Hull Thornless' and 'Chester Thornless' blackberries).

Multiple-use cultivars can be cooked, preserved, frozen, eaten fresh, baked, or perhaps juiced or dried. (A prime example is 'Thompson Seedless' grape. Other examples are 'Earliglow' and 'Sparkle' strawberries, 'Royalty' raspberry, and 'Rubel' and 'Jersey' blueberries.)

Cultivar selection difficulties are amply illustrated by strawberry cultivar and selection evaluation reported in recent volumes of *Advance in Strawberry Production,* the research journal of the North American Strawberry Growers Association. Galletta et al. (1982) and Hancock et al. (1982) commented on the variation in strawberry clone performance over different growing seasons on the same farm (but in different fields) in Maryland and Michigan, respectively. In the Maryland study yields were reduced, the ripening season was compressed, but fruit size was stable in a warm moist spring as contrasted with an earlier 'normal' spring. The clones, which had all originated in Maryland, did not shift with respect to each other with the season variation. In the Michigan test, cultivar yield shifts over three harvest seasons reflected the production stability and adaptation of clones originated at many different North American locales.

Reports by Galletta and Swartz (1984) and Sanford and Reich (1985) for Maryland and New York, respectively, indicate many of the expanded criteria used by breeders in selecting new cultivars and comparing new cultivars to older ones to assess breeding progress. Of interest is the observation that 'Allstar' and 'Lester' strawberries, which originated in Maryland, retained their fruit size, appearance, and sweetness when grown in New York, but had lower yields than they did in Maryland.

A particularly thorough variety trial over a 3-year period was reported by Kaps et al. (1987) for southwest Missouri. Data included total and marketable yield, maturity season, peak harvest, mean fruit size and seasonal mean size for the third harvest season, plant vigor and row fill percentage, and reactions to four naturally occurring leaf diseases. Only fruit-quality parameters were missing. Interestingly, the most promising cultivars and their state of origin were: early — 'Earliglow' (Maryland); early midseason — 'Honeoye' (New York), 'Redcoat' (Canada), 'Redchief' (Maryland); late midseason — 'Allstar' (Maryland), 'Arking' (Arkansas), 'Canoga' (New York); late — 'Delite' (Illinois). This indicates rather broad tolerance of many eastern U.S. clones to the continental temperatures of this south central location.

In what amounted to a high-alkaline soil stress test in Colorado, seven Junebearing and five multiple cropping clones were compared by Renquist and Hughes (1985). All the multiple croppers showed iron chlorosis. Six of the seven Junebearers had acceptable yields. Three of the Junebearers showed insignificant or only slight symptoms of iron chlorosis — 'Guardian' (from the east), 'Delite' (from the midwest), and 'Shuksan' (from the west). These results could not have been predicted. They demonstrate the importance of securing reliable and complete local information about a cultivar and comparing it with information about the cultivar from its area of origin before trying to grow it.

PEST CONTROL IN SMALL FRUIT PLANTINGS

Weeds*

Perhaps the single most difficult task of the small fruit grower is weed control. Economic losses attributed to weeds are considered to be greater than losses caused by insect or disease damage. For strawberries alone, losses are estimated to be 25% of the potential crop (Chandler, 1979). In addition to competing directly with crops for water, nutrients, and light, weeds can serve as hosts for insects, diseases, and nematodes. Flowering weeds can also compete with crops for pollinating insects.

Each grower experiences a different degree and type of weed pressure, so there is no single answer to the problems created by the opportunistic behavior of weed

*Much of this section was contributed by Marvin Pritts of Cornell University.

species. It is not practical to pull weeds in large plantings by hand, nor is a complete reliance on chemicals a sound management strategy. For example, more than 55 weed species are now resistant to at least one class of herbicide, and this number is expected to increase rapidly.

Weed control is especially difficult in small fruit plantings for several reasons. First, small fruit crops are relatively small or slow growing and are not good competitors against rapidly growing weed species. Second, the perennial nature of small fruit crops excludes some very effective methods of weed control, such as annual plowing or fumigation. Third, small fruits are considered minor crops of high value, so many chemical companies are not willing to label a product with high associated risk and low volume returns to the company. Although many products exist which will control weed growth, most are not available for use by the small fruit grower. For these reasons, the successful grower must have an integrated program that uses several strategies and tools for managing pest populations.

Types of weeds. Weeds are classified into three general categories: annuals, biennials, and perennials. Control methods will differ for the three types.

1. *Annuals.* An annual plant is one whose seed germinates and completes its life cycle during one year by producing a new crop of seed. Annual weeds are generally easy to control, but they produce many seeds and are persistent. Examples of summer annuals whose seeds normally germinate in the spring include foxtails, crabgrass, lamb's-quarter, smartweed, and ragweed. A winter annual is one whose seed germinates in the fall and completes its growth by the next fall. Examples of winter annuals include annual bluegrass, shepherd's purse, and chickweed.

2. *Biennials.* A biennial plant completes its life cycle during two growing seasons. Seeds of biennial plants germinate in the spring and grow vegetatively through the first summer. The following spring, after a winter chilling period, the plants flower and seeds develop and mature by the end of the second summer. This category includes weeds such as wild carrot, mullen, and burdock. Biennials often have a fleshy tap root, which makes them difficult to control and often requires the use of a systemic herbicide.

3. *Perennials.* Perennial plants can live indefinitely, although the tops may die down in winter. Once established, a perennial weed will grow for many seasons and may be difficult to control. This group is most difficult to control because they may propagate by various methods, such as seeds, rhizomes, bulbs, and other vegetative means. They often have good food reserves, which makes them difficult to eliminate. The use of systemic herbicides is often required. Examples of this category include quackgrass, plantain, bindweed, dandelion, and nutgrass.

General categories of herbicides

1. *Contact*: a herbicide that causes localized injury to plant tissue where contact occurs. Examples: Gramoxone, Dinitros.

2. *Translocated (systemic)*: a herbicide that is moved within the plant. The term is frequently used in a more restrictive sense to refer to herbicides that are applied to the foliage and move downward through the plant to underground parts. Examples: Roundup, 2,4-D.

3. *Soil active (residual)*: a herbicide that persists in the soil and injures or kills germinating weed seedlings over a relatively short period of time. Most of our preemergence herbicides are of this type. Examples: Karmex, Simazine, Surflan.

Modes of activity of herbicides

1. *Preemergence*: must be applied to the soil prior to the emergence of weeds that are to be controlled. This type of herbicide has the ability to control weeds only before or soon after they emerge.

2. *Postemergence*: may be applied after the emergence of weeds that are to be controlled. These herbicides control established weeds to varying degrees.

Strategies for weed control

1. *Eliminate all weeds before planting.* A key to successful small fruit growing is the elimination of perennial weeds the year before the plants are set. This can be accomplished in several ways. One could repeatedly cultivate an area for an extended period of time to force weeds to expend all their stored energy on regrowth. A heavy sheet of black plastic over the area to be planted will also eliminate most weeds if left in place for one season. A nonselective herbicide (e.g., glyphosate) could be applied to the planting area one year before planting, causing all plants to die within 3 weeks of application. The area can then be tilled and a cover crop could be planted. The cover crop will help prevent weed-seed germination for the remainder of the year, help to control soil erosion, and add organic matter to the soil when it is plowed under the spring before planting. Systemic herbicides such as glyphosate are particularly effective because the material kills the root system, which then eliminates the possibility of regrowth.

Crop rotation incorporates many of these principles. Corn, for example, quickly develops a canopy that retards the growth of all but the most persistent weeds. The practice of cultivating corn periodically also destroys many young weeds. In addition, herbicides used on corn are effective against many of the broadleaf perennial weeds which are problems in small fruit plantings. If crop rotation is practiced, one should test for herbicide carryover before planting small fruits.

There are several fumigants that will kill weed seeds if used at high rates before planting, and will provide additional benefits, such as control of nematodes, soil insects, and disease: methyl bromide + chloropicrin, dichloropropene-dichloropropane combinations, methyldithiocarbamate, and methylisocyanate. Soil must be properly prepared before fumigation. It should be friable and moist with no clods, there should be no plant residues, and soil temperatures should range between

50 and 68°F (10 and 20°C). Soil fumigation is costly, but most experienced growers are convinced of its worth.

2. *Prevent weeds from becoming established after planting.* Organic mulches not only inhibit seed germination, but gradually improve soil structure and conserve moisture. Straw is an excellent mulch for strawberries and raspberries, sawdust works well on blueberries, and wood chips or pine needles are good for grapes. Black plastic works for short periods but is not yet practical as long-term mulch for perennial crops.

Cover crops can be used to prevent weed establishment after planting. When managed properly, the competitive ability of the cover crop is directed against encroaching weeds, while interference with crop growth is minimized. Cover crops can also be used to regulate nutrient levels and promote the hardening process in woody plants.

One should keep surrounding fields mowed to prevent weeds from flowering and releasing seeds into the planted area. If weed seeds are present in a planted area, preemergent herbicides can be used. These herbicides cause mortality of germinating seedlings, and thus prevent weed establishment. If mulches or herbicides are not used, one should regularly cultivate the weed-free area around the plants no deeper than 2 inches (5 cm). The root systems of small fruit crops are usually very shallow, and deep cultivation can cause considerable damage.

3. *Remove established weeds when they appear.* Hand weeding is unavoidable for the small fruit grower. One should regularly pull weeds that become established so that they will not develop an extensive tap root or flower. Cultivation will also help eliminate established weeds. There are a few herbicides that can be used in small fruit plantings to kill or retard the growth of established weeds.

Considerations for selecting chemical weed control materials

Label. Not all chemicals that are effective at controlling problem weeds in small fruits are labeled for use. Chemical companies often consider small-acreage, high-value crops to be of high risk and not worth the cost of pursuing a label. In addition, pesticide regulation is under state control, so a chemical that may be legal to use in one state might not be labeled in adjacent states. It is important to consult individual state recommendations for small fruit production before using any herbicide.

Selectivity. Most chemical herbicides are selective and work only on specific classes and developmental stages of plants. Some are active on grasses but not broadleaf plants, while others affect seed germination but not growth or related processes. Because of this selectivity, a grower can manage weed populations by applying the proper rate of chemical at the appropriate time. An effective herbicide can be selected only if the identities of weeds in the planting are known.

Preemergent grass herbicides are most effective when applied soon after soil has settled around transplants, or in late fall or early spring in established plantings before weed emergence. These chemicals work best if incorporated into the potential root zone of germinating weeds immediately after application. Incorporation can be achieved by rainfall, irrigation, or shallow cultivation.

Herbicides such as chloroxuron, dichlobenil, simazine, and terbacil are effective in preventing germination of broadleaf weeds. Timing of application is similar to that of preemergent grass herbicides. Dichlobenil and terbacil are common to both groups; however, they are expensive and 'hot' and allow little room for applicator error. Many growers elect to use a mixture of grass and broadleaf herbicides, such as oryzalin and simazine, for broad-spectrum control.

A few chemicals have been developed to kill established plants. Fluazifop and sethoxydim may be used in nonbearing plantings to control grasses between the height of 2 and 8 in. (5 to 21 cm). The chemical 2,4-D amine may be used on Junebearing strawberries to control established broadleaf weeds. Terbacil, dichlobenil, and chloroxuron also have limited postemergent activity on specific pests. Glyphosate is a systemic herbicide and may be used in vineyards between leaf drop and the end of bloom. Gramoxone will burn the tops of perennial weeds in established plantings but will not prevent regrowth from the intact root system.

It is difficult to control established broadleaf weeds in established crops chemically because of similarities in growth habit and biochemistry. The number of preemergent grass herbicides available to the grower is much greater than the number of postemergent broadleaf herbicides. This observation should reinforce the desire to eliminate weeds before planting the crop.

Effects of herbicides on crop growth. Chemicals must be applied at the proper time or directed at a specific location to be effective. For example, 2,4-D permits some broadleaf weed control in strawberries if it is applied when weeds are actively growing; however, floral development in strawberry is impaired if applications occur during periods of flower bud initiation. Similarly, misdirected sprays of gramoxone can cause considerable phytotoxicity in crops.

Plant age also influences susceptibility to herbicide injury. A newly established planting of brambles, for example, may not be tolerant of dichlobenil. Many herbicides, both pre- and postemergent, are safe only for use on established plantings.

Propagation method has been found to influence sensitivity to preemergent herbicides during the planting year (May et al., 1987). For example, tissue-cultured raspberries exhibit phytotoxicity to herbicides considered safe for use with conventionally propagated nursery stock. Cultivars also exhibit differential sensitivity to herbicides (Masiunas and Weller 1986). For example, 'Guardian', 'MicMac', 'Tribute', and 'Tristar' strawberries are reportedly sensitive to terbacil, while 'Royalty' raspberry is sensitive to simazine.

Herbicides such as terbacil have relatively narrow ranges of effectiveness, above which crop phytotoxicity occurs. It is important that growers use application devices that have been properly calibrated and deliver a uniform rate of chemical.

Environmental effects on herbicide activity. Temperature can influence the activity of certain herbicides. Dichlobenil will begin to volatilize when temperature exceeds 50°F (10°C), and this could result in crop damage with little residual effect during weed-seed germination. This chemical should be applied only during late fall or early spring. Other herbicides work only when weed species are actively growing, and cool temperatures may reduce effectiveness.

Excessive moisture can reduce the effectiveness of many preemergent herbicides by moving the chemical below the zone of active root growth. Rainfall can also be detrimental to the activity of foliar-absorbed herbicides such as glyphosate if it occurs too soon after application. Lack of rainfall can reduce the activity of preemergent herbicides, notably napropamide, or it can reduce plant vigor, which causes loss of efficacy in postemergent herbicides such as fluazifop.

Soil type also influences activity and herbicide mobility. Molecules of simazine tend to adsorb to clay particles, requiring higher rates of application in clay soils compared to sandy soils. Soil organic matter has much the same influence. Terbacil, for example, is unsafe to use on low-organic-matter soils, and oryzalin is ineffective on high-organic-matter soils.

These examples serve to reinforce the need to read the product label carefully and consider integrated approaches to weed management. The successful grower must use a combination of biological, mechanical, and chemical tools to maintain pest populations at an acceptably low level.

Plant Diseases

There are numerous diseases that attack the small fruit crops and cause damage ranging from cosmetic to plant death. The causal organisms of the common small fruit diseases are fungi, bacteria, mycoplasmas, and viruses. The fungal diseases are by far the most common plant pathogens of small fruit crops. Fungi can attack virtually all plant parts. Examples of small fruit fungus diseases are strawberry gray mold on flowers and fruits, blueberry twig and cane blight, powdery mildew of grape leaves, stem canker of blueberries, and verticillium wilt of raspberry and strawberry roots.

Bacterial diseases range from those of relatively minor importance such as angular leaf spot in strawberry to those causing serious economic losses, such as crown gall in raspberries and grapes. There are also highly modified bacteria known as rickettsia-like organisms. The devastating soilborne Pierce's disease, which limits grape production along the Gulf coast, is a representative of this group of organisms.

Mycoplasmas consist of a membrane enclosing a living protoplasm which may vary in shape during the life of the organism. With mycoplasma infections, the accompanying loss of productivity can also be of direct concern, as in the stunt disease of blueberries, which is vectored by the sharp-nosed leafhopper.

Virus diseases can also cause loss of productivity and dramatically reduce the life of the planting. Symptoms of a single virus are often latent (the infected plant showing no symptoms). Such plants may exhibit lack of vigor, slight stunting, or reduction in yields. The most common vectors for the transmission of viruses and mycoplasmas from infected to healthy plants are sucking insects such as aphids and leafhoppers, along with nematodes (Fig. 2-15). Examples of insect-transmitted virus diseases are raspberry mosaic and blueberry shoestring virus. Virus diseases trans-

FIGURE 2-15 Tomato ringspot virus is transmitted by soil nematodes. It causes a general weakening of the plants, crumbly fruits, and yellow or light-green ringspot symptoms on newly infected leaves. The fruit shown on the left is from healthy red raspberry plants, while the crumbly fruits on the right are from infected plants.

mitted by nematodes are exemplified by fanleaf in grapes and necrotic ringspot in blueberries. Raspberry bushy dwarf disease is transmitted in virus-infected pollen, which is transferred by bees during pollination.

Control methods. Professional pathologists, entomologists, and farm consultants stress the importance of understanding the life cycles of potentially damaging crop pests. Control of these pests by various methods is most effectively targeted at the one or more vulnerable points in the life cycle.

Sanitation. Keeping the site clean and free of sources of inoculum can be of primary importance in effective disease control. New plantings should always be established with quality planting stock from reputable nurseries. All plant material should be free of insect and disease contamination and should be virus-indexed whenever possible.

Methods such as rogueing and destroying diseased plants within a field as well as removing other host plants from adjacent areas are effective in preventing the spread of disease. For example, virus-infected blueberry plants should be removed whenever they are discovered, and the diseased plants burned or buried. Isolating crop plants from sources of potential infection such as wild species growing in close proximity can be a practical means of disease prevention. For instance, the removal of wild brambles from areas surrounding a raspberry planting is an important measure in preventing the spread of virus diseases from wild plants by insects.

Removing and destroying prunings that harbor diseases and insects is a sound cultural practice. The use of cultivation to bury diseased plant material may also be a useful technique, as in the case of mummy berries in blueberries. The removal of diseased fruit from the plant during harvest can be important in minimizing future infections. This can be particularly important in crops such as strawberries, which ripen over an extended period and require multiple harvests.

Washing and sanitizing tractor implements and pruning equipment can help to prevent the transfer of disease between plants, especially from established to younger fields on the same farm. Other practices, such as avoiding travel in the planting while the plants are wet or timing irrigations to allow for rapid drying of the foliage, can also be useful. In some cases, filtration of irrigation water may also aid in disease control.

Site selection and modification.   Selection of a planting site with good air movement and adequate internal soil water drainage will facilitate disease control in the planting. Selecting a site and planting scheme that takes advantage of natural air movement patterns can help prevent infections by encouraging quick drying of the plant foliage and fruit after wetting periods. The construction of efficient surface and subsurface water drainage systems can help to prevent and limit the spread of soilborne disease. An often overlooked technique is the establishment of drainage furrows or shallow ditches along the edge(s) of a planted field to divert drainage or runoff water from topographically adjoining and more elevated areas, even those that are meadow strips or unplanted. The use of raised-bed plantings can be useful in avoiding infestations of root diseases such as *Phytophthora* root rot in raspberries or red stele in strawberries.

Sites that minimize plant stress can contribute indirectly to disease prevention by maintaining a healthy, moderately vigorous, winter-hardy plant. For example, winter injury to grapevines that are growing in low cold pockets within a vineyard will ultimately lead to the development of crown gall growth at the point of bark splitting. Modifying the vigor of plants by judicious fertilizer application may also help to minimize growth patterns which increase the disease susceptibility of a plant. The use of excessive nitrogen fertilization in strawberries may lead to soft, disease-susceptible berries, while high nitrogen in grapes may cause excessive foliage development. Dense canopies cause higher humidity levels around the fruit, along with slower drying conditions after wetting periods, which both contribute to disease infections.

Chemical control.   Chemical control of plant diseases can involve natural products such as sulfur or copper and lime applied as sprays or dusts. Additional chemical control is provided by a wide range of complex organic pesticides. The vast majority of pesticides must be used on a protectant basis and be applied before infection has occurred. In addition to these preventive sprays, some fungicides possess postinfection or "kickback" activity and can be used for a limited time after infection has occurred. Several fungicides have eradicant properties and may be used to 'burn out' infections or overwintering inoculum. Some pesticides have a systemic activity which allows them to be translocated some distance within the plant from the point of surface contact.

Soil fumigation chemical control is typically a broad-spectrum treatment for many soilborne pests, such as diseases, insects, nematodes, and weed seeds. These chemicals are injected into the soil, where they volatilize into a gas that kills many of the soilborne pests.

Disease-resistant cultivars.   One important disease control strategy involves the planting of disease-resistant cultivars such as those resistant to red stele root rot in strawberries or to stem canker in blueberries. In an area where the red stele fungus is known to exist in the soil and a strawberry cultivar for early production is desired, the choice of a resistant cultivar such as 'Earliglow' would be much better than the choice of a susceptible cultivar such as 'Earlidawn'. In areas where blueberry stem canker is a problem, resistant cultivars such as 'Harrison' and 'Bluechip' would be a better choice than 'Blueray' or 'Bluecrop' as a midseason-ripening highbush cultivar.

In other instances there is simply a degree of susceptibility. If a grower planned to produce a French-American hybrid grape for red wine production in a relatively wet area of the country, the choice of cultivar might dramatically affect the success of the spray program. In this instance, planting 'Baco Noir' instead of 'Chancellor' would significantly reduce downy mildew problems in the vineyard.

Insects and Arthropods

Insects and arthropods damage plants in a number of ways. They may actually eat and remove plant parts or interfere with the development of other plant parts. Strawberry fruits tunneled into by sap beetles or small slugs are rendered unsalable. Blossom pedicels of strawberries into which a strawberry weevil (clipper) has oviposited and has partially detached will not develop further. Unfortunately, these are often the earliest flowers, which bear the largest fruit, commanding the highest prices. Some insect larvae chew on the root system or burrow into crowns or canes. In either case the nutrient and water-gathering capacity and the plant's transport system has been reduced, resulting in growth reduction or death, in extreme cases.

Sucking insects make sting-like wounds into which plant toxins and disease-causing organisms can be introduced, and from which plant juices and nutrients can be extracted. When populations of sucking insects or mites build up, host plants are visibly dwarfed and weakened.

Insect-resistant cultivars. Various small fruit breeding programs have attempted to incorporate observed insect and mite resistance into selected small fruit cultivars. Resistance to these pests can be assessed by evaluating leaf damage symptoms or by determining the insect or mite populations that are supported on particular cultivars. When such resistance can be shown to be a genetically heritable trait, it can be used in the breeding and selection of resistant cultivars. In the case of strawberries, the inheritance of resistance to twospotted spider mites has been evaluated in several breeding programs. Immunity to the aphid vector of raspberry mosaic virus complex, resistance to the aphid vector of raspberry leaf curl, and resistance to the raspberry fruit worm has been combined into the germplasm of the 'Royalty' raspberry. The natural differences in insect resistance (tolerance) between cultivars or species is exemplified by the range of susceptibility to the grape phylloxera (root louse). American types such as 'Concord' experience little difficulty with this insect, while *vinifera* types such as 'Chardonnay' may be totally destroyed by the insect. As a result of this difference, the use of phylloxera-resistant rootstocks on *vinifera* cultivars is a standard cultural practice in much of the world.

Site selection and modification. Sites that are isolated or located away from traditional areas of large plantings of a particular crop may be less prone to attack by specific crop pests. For example, an insect such as the blueberry leafminer is only sporadic in the wild, but can be found in abundance in many cultivated fields. In this case, migration between fields in areas of intensive cultivation is much more likely than if a new planting were established in a nontraditional growing locality. A different situation exists for many insects in other crops, such as the berry moth in grapes. This insect typically migrates into vineyards from wild grapevines located in adjacent woodlands. Insect-vectored virus diseases of brambles are also influenced by the location of the planting and the presence of wild brambles near the site. Destroying the native species in the area can help to reduce insect populations and the sources of viruses and other pathogens.

Biological and chemical control. Normally the most effective control strategy is that of directly targeting the pathogen and/or vector. In this situation we can take advantage of biological controls such as the use of *Bacillus thurengiensis* bacteria to control feeding larvae or milky spore to control Japanese beetles. Other biological control measures include the use of natural predators and diseases that attack economically important small fruit insects and mites. A classic example is the Lady beetle and its larvae, which feed on aphids.

A recent area of promise for insect control is the use of insect growth regulators which interfere with the insect's development. Insect pheromones (sex attractants) can also be used to lure insects to traps, or to confuse the males and thus make the location of and mating with females difficult. Another technique that has been explored is the release of sterile male insects into the area to interrupt the breeding cycle.

The most common insect control involves the use of chemical pesticides. Chemical effectiveness can be greatly enhanced by timely scouting of plantings to enable insecticide application to be made at the most appropriately vulnerable points in the insect life cycle.

Nematodes

Nematodes are tiny nonsegmented roundworms (eelworms) that attack and feed either on the surface or interior of the roots of crop plants. The characteristic root appearances following nematode infestations, such as root knot, cyst, lesion, and stubby root, are commonly used to suggest which of the parasitic nematode genera are involved in the infestation. While feeding, nematodes may inadvertently introduce disease organisms or toxins into the root system of the plant, in addition to the physical damage visited on the host root system.

Leaving the land fallow and planting crop species that are resistant to specific nematodes may be of use in reducing the populations at a given site. In many situations it is economically impractical to leave the land without crops for a sufficient length of time. Other measures include chemical control by the application of a variety of soil fumigants.

Additional control measures include the use of tolerant or resistant genotypes and species of small fruit crops. Experiments investigating the relative resistance of red raspberry genotypes to root lesion nematodes have shown a notable degree of difference (Vrain and Daubeny, 1986). Cultivars such as 'Latham' and 'Nootka' supported low numbers, while 'Chilcotin' supported high numbers of nematodes. The use of nematode-resistant cultivars as rootstocks is also an effective method of increasing the tolerance of a crop to this pest. Using nematode-resistant rootstocks in grape production, such as SO 4 or Dogridge, has become a standard practice where susceptible cultivars are grown. Nematodes may also act as vectors for the spread of disease. The complex interactions in the disease cycle may involve a control strategy of the nematode vectors, such as the use of 039–16 and 043–43 grape rootstocks, which are immune to feeding by the *Xiphenema index* nematode. In this example we are ultimately concerned with controlling the fan leaf virus, which is transmitted by the feeding of the nematode vector.

Other Animal Pests

Selective foliage and young shoot browsing by deer, geese, domestic livestock, and occasionally rabbits may set growth back in dry springs or summers. Swelling flower buds of highbush blueberries and other fruit crops in early spring can be particularly appealing to deer and related mammals. Damage is often most severe in fields near wooded areas.

Root and lower cane or rhizome feeding is usually a late winter phenomenon involving voles, mice, rabbits, gophers, and other burrowing animals. Damage is most severe when small fruit plantings are located near woods, next to orchards, or when plantings are sodded and/or mulched.

Fruit damage and outright losses can be formidable, since birds, deer, bears, squirrels, raccoons, and other animals are very fond of berry crops. Fruit loss is most severe in small, home, or isolated small fruit plantings.

Control measures for animal damage take basically four forms: *exclusion, repulsion, diversion,* or *capture.* Exclusion devices include fencing, netting, and growing plants inside animal-proof structures. Repulsion techniques include noise-makers or firearms, visual scare devices, and chemical or animal product repellents. Diversion includes planting of more attractive crops for the animals near your own, and erecting paths, shrub, or ditch barriers that may divert animals from entering your planting. Capture may involve lures and traps, with captured animals either relocated or eliminated. There are also animal and nature lovers who plant more of a given crop than they need so as to share some with the animals. This practice is more common in rural settings.

REFERENCES

ALLEY, C. J., AND A. T. KAYAMA. 1978. Vine bleeding delays growth of T-budded grapevines. Calif. Agric. 32:6.

BALDWIN, J. L. 1973. Climates of the United States. NOAA, U.S. Department of Commerce, Washington, D.C.

BOXUS, P., C. DAMIANO, AND E. BRASSEUR. 1984. Strawberry. p. 453–486. In P. V. Ammirato et al. (eds.). Handbook of plant cell culture. Vol. 3. Macmillan, New York.

BOYCE, B. R., AND J. B. STRATER. 1984. Comparison of frost injury in strawberry buds, blossoms, and immature fruit. Adv. Strawberry Prod. 3:8–10.

BROOME, O. C., AND R. H. ZIMMERMAN. 1978. In vitro propagation of blackberry. HortScience 13:151–153.

CHANDLER, J. M. 1979. Estimated losses of crops to weeds. In D. Pimentel (ed.). CRC handbook of pest management in agriculture. Vol. III. p. 95–109. CRC Press, Boca Raton, Fla.

COHEN, D., AND D. ELLIOTT. 1979. Micropropagation methods for blueberries and tamarillos. Proc. Int. Plant. Prop. Soc. 29:177–179.

COUVILLON, G. A., AND F. A. POKORNY. 1968. Photoperiod, indolebutyric acid, and type of cutting wood as factors in rooting of rabbiteye blueberry (Vaccinium ashei Reade), cv. Woodward. HortScience 3:74–75.

DRAGAVCEV, A. P. 1956. On the question of the retardation of fruit ripening in connection with increasing altitude. Bot. Zh. 41:416–417.

DURNER, E. F., J. A. BARDEN, D. G. HIMELRICK, AND E. B. POLING. 1984. Photoperiod and temperature effects on flowering and runner development in day-neutral, Junebearing and everbearing strawberries. J. Am. Soc. Hortic. Sci. 109:396–400.

FISHER, D. D. 1962. Heat units and number of days required to mature some pome and stone fruits in various areas of North America. Proc. Am. Soc. Hortic. Sci. 80:114–124.

FUNT, R. C. ET AL., 1985. Ohio strawberry production, management and marketing manual. Ohio State Univ. Bull. 436.

GALLETTA, G. J., AND A. S. FISH, JR. 1971. Interspecific blueberry grafting: a way to extend Vaccinium culture to different soils. J. Am. Soc. Hortic. Sci. 96:294–298.

GALLETTA, G. J., AND H. J. SWARTZ. 1984. 1983 evaluation of promising strawberry selections and cultivars at Beltsville, Maryland. Adv. Strawberry Prod. 3:20–22.

GALLETTA, G. J., A. D. DRAPER, AND H. J. SWARTZ. 1982. Seasonal variation in potential cultivar evaluation trials. Adv. Strawberry Prod. 2:17–21.

GRANGE, R. L., AND D. W. HAND. 1987. A review of the effects of atmospheric humidity on the growth of horticultural crops. J. Hortic. Sci. 62:125–134.

HALFACRE, R. G., AND J. A. BARDEN. 1979. Horticulture. McGraw-Hill, New York.

HANCOCK, J.F., H. C. PRICE, AND A. A. HAFER. 1982. Strawberry cultivar trials at Michigan State University, 1974–1980. Adv. Strawberry Prod. 2:19–20.

HARADA, H. 1975. In vitro culture of actinidia chinensis Pl. as a technique for vegetative multiplication. J. Hortic. Sci. 50:81–83.

HARMON, F. N. 1943. Influence of indolebutyric acid on the rooting of grape cuttings. Proc. Am. Soc. Hortic. Sci. 42:383–388.

HARMON, F. N. 1954. A modified procedure for greenwood grafting of vinifera grapes. Proc. Am. Soc. Hortic. Sci. 64:255–258.

HARMON, F. N., AND J. H. WEINBERGER. 1959. Effects of storage and stratification on germination of vinifera grape seeds. Proc. Am. Soc. Hortic. Sci. 73:147–150.

HARMON, F. N., AND J. H. WEINBERGER. 1963. Bench grafting trials with Thompson seedless grapes on various rootstocks. Proc. Am. Soc. Hortic. Sci. 83:379–383.

References

HARTMANN, H. T., AND D. E. KESTER. 1983. Plant propagation principles and practices. Prentice-Hall, Englewood Cliffs, N.J.

HEDRICK, H. P., 1908. The grapes of New York. N.Y. State Agric. Exp. Stn. Rep. 1907.

HEYDECKER, W., AND M. MARSTON. 1968. Quantitative studies on the regeneration of raspberries from root cuttings. Hortic. Res. 8:142–146.

JOHNSON, D. E., AND G. S. HOWELL. 1981. Factors influencing critical temperatures for spring freeze damage to developing primary shoots on Concord grapevine. Am. J. Enol. Vitic. 32:144–149.

KAPS, M. L., M. B. ODNEAL, AND J. F. MOORE, JR. 1987. Strawberry cultivar evaluation in the Missouri Ozark region. Adv. Strawberry Prod. 6:36–40.

KENDER, W. J. 1965. Some factors affecting the propagation of lowbush blueberries by softwood cuttings. Proc. Am. Soc. Hortic. Sci. 86:301–306.

KOZLOWSKI, T. T. 1984. Flooding and plant growth. Academic Press, Orlando, Fla.

KRAFT, S. E. 1976. Environmental factors influencing the production of wine grapes in commercial Finger Lake vineyards. M.S. Thesis, Cornell University, Ithaca, N.Y.

KRUL, W. R., AND G. H. MOBRAY. 1985. Grapes. p. 396–434. In W. R. Sharp et al. (eds.). Handbook of plant cell culture. Vol. 2. Macmillan, New York.

LANG, G. A., J. D. EARLY, G. C. MARTIN, AND R. L. DARNELL. 1987. Endo-, para-, and ecodormancy: physiological terminology and classification for dormancy research. Hort-Science 22:371–377.

LAWSON, H. M., AND J. S. WISEMAN. 1976a. Weed competition in spring-planted strawberries. Weed Res. 16:345–354.

LAWSON, H. M., AND J. S. WISEMAN. 1976b. Weed competition in spring-planted raspberries. Weed. Res. 16:155–162.

LEAR, B., AND L. LIDER. 1959. Eradication of root-knot nematodes from grapevine rootings by hot water. Plant Dis. Rep. 43:314–317.

LIDER, L. 1963. Field budding and the care of the budded grapevine. Calif. Agric. Ext. Ser. Leafl. 153.

LIPTON, W. J., ET AL. 1978. Relative humidity: physical realities and horticultural implications. HortScience 13:551–574.

LYRENE, P. M. 1980. Micropropagation of rabbiteye blueberries. HortScience 15:80–81.

MAAS, J. L., AND H. M. CATHEY. 1987. Photomorphogenic responses of strawberry to photoperiodic and photosynthetic radiation. J. Am. Soc. Hortic. Sci. 112:125–130.

MASIUNAS, J. B., AND S. C. WELLER. 1986. Strawberry cultivar response to postplant applications of terbacil. HortScience 21:1147–1149.

MAY, G., M. PRITTS, AND J. NEAL. 1987. Herbicide studies with raspberries. Proc. N.Y. Hortic. Soc. 132.

MORRIS, J. R., D. L. CAWTHON, S. E. SPAYD, R. D. MAY, AND D. R. BRYAN. 1980. Prediction of 'Concord' grape maturation and sources of error. J. Am. Soc. Hortic. Sci. 105:313–318.

NEUBERGER, H., AND J. CAHIR. 1969. Principles of climatology. Holt, Rinehart and Winston, New York.

NICOLL, M. F., AND G. J. GALLETTA. 1987. Variation in growth and flowering habits of Junebearing and everbearing strawberries. J. Am. Soc. Hortic. Sci. 112:872–880.

OURECKY, D. K., AND J. E. REICH. 1976. Frost tolerance in strawberry cultivars. HortScience 11:413–414.

PHILLIPS, H. A. 1922. Effect of climatic conditions on the blooming and ripening dates of fruit trees. Cornell Univ. Agric. Exp. Stn. Memo. 59:1377–1416.

PHILLIPS, E. L., M. D. MAGNUSON, A. H. JONES, A. VAN DOREN, E. L. PROBSTING, AND P. C. CRANDALL. 1962. Washington state freeze circular. Wash. State Univ. Agric. Exp. Stn. Circ. 400.

RAKE, B. A. 1954. The propagation of gooseberries. I. Some factors influencing the rooting of hardwood cuttings. Ann. Rep. Long Ashton Res. Stn. 1953, p. 79–88.

RENQUIST, A. R., AND H. G. HUGHES. 1985. Strawberry cultivar evaluation in Colorado: 1982–1984. Adv. Strawberry Prod. 4:53–55.

SANFORD, J. C., AND J. E. REICH. 1985. Breeding progress in strawberry cultivars adapted to the northeastern United States. Adv. Strawberry Prod. 4:39–44.

SCOTT, D. H., AND A. D. DRAPER. 1967. Light in relation to seed germination of blueberries, strawberries and *Rubus*. HortScience 2:107–108.

SCOTT, D. H., AND D. P. INK. 1948. Germination of strawberry seed as affected by scarification treatment with sulfuric acid. Proc. Am. Soc. Hortic. Sci. 51:299–300.

SMAGULA, J. M., AND P. M. LYRENE. 1984. Blueberry, p. 383–401. In P. V. Ammirato et al. (eds.). Handbook of plant cell culture. Vol. 3. Macmillan, New York.

SMITH, S. H., R. E. HILTON, AND N. W. FRAZIER. 1970. Meristem culture for elimination of strawberry viruses. Calif. Agric. 24:8–10.

TORRE, L. C., AND B. H. BARRITT. 1979. Red raspberry establishment from root cuttings. J. Am. Soc. Hortic. Sci. 104:28–31.

TUKEY, L. D. 1942. Time interval between full bloom and fruit maturity for several varieties of pears, apples, and cherries. Proc. Am. Soc. Hortic. Sci. 40:133–140.

TURNER, J. H. 1980. Planning for an irrigation system. American Association for Vocational Instructional Materials, Athens, Ga.

VALLI, V. J. 1971. Basic principles of freeze occurrence and prevention of freeze damage to crops. Spot Heaters Inc., Sunnyside, Wash.

VAN DER BRINK, C. 1974. Predicting harvest date of the 'Concord' grape crop in southwest Michigan. HortScience 9:206–208.

VRAIN, T. C., AND H. A. DAUBENY. 1986. Relative resistance of red raspberry and related genotypes to the root lesion nematode. HortScience 21:1435–1437.

WINKLER, A. J. 1948. Maturity tests for table grapes: the relation of heat summation to time of maturating and palatability. Proc. Am. Soc. Hortic. Sci. 51:295–298.

ZIMMERMAN, R. H., G. J. GALLETTA, AND O. C. BROOME. 1980. Propagation of thornless blackberry by one-node cuttings. J. Am. Soc. Hortic. Sci. 105:405–407.

SUGGESTED READING

Weeds

ANDERSON, W. P. 1983. Weed science principles. West, St. Paul, Minn.

BESTE, C. E., AND N. E. HUMBURG. 1985. Herbicide handbook of the Weed Science Society of America. Weed Science Society, Champaign, Ill.

CRAFTS, A. S. 1975. Modern weed control. University of California Press, Berkeley.

GUPTA, O. P., AND P. S. LAMBA. 1977. Modern weed science. Scholarly, St. Clair Shores, Mich.

KING, R. D. 1985. Farmers weed control handbook. Doane, St. Louis, Mo.

MUENSCHER, W. C. 1980. Weeds. Comstock, Ithaca, N.Y.

ROSS, M., AND C. LEMBI. 1985. Applied weed science. Burgess, Edina, Minn.

Insects

DAVIDSON, R. H., AND W. F. LYON. 1987 Insect pests of farm, garden, and orchard. Wiley, New York.

ELZINGA, R. J. 1981. Fundamentals of entomology. Prentice-Hall, Englewood Cliffs, N.J.

EVANS, H. E., ET AL. 1984. Insect biology: a textbook of entomology. Addison-Wesley, Reading, Mass.

PFADT, R. E. 1985. Fundamentals of applied entomology. Macmillian, New York.

PYENSON, L. L., AND H. E. BARKE. 1981. Manual for entomology and plant pathology. AVI, Wesport, Conn.

ROMOSER, W. S. 1981. The science of entomology. Macmillan, New York.

ROSS, H. H., ET AL. 1982. A textbook of entomology. Wiley, New York.

WILSON, M. C., ET AL. 1984. Practical insect pest management: fundamentals of applied entomology. Waveland Press, Prospect Heights, Ill.

Diseases

AGRIOS, G. N. 1988. Plant pathology. Academic Press, San Diego, Calif.

BOS, L. 1985. Introduction to plant virology. Halsted Press, New York.

COOK, R. J., ET AL. 1988. Annual review of pytopathology. Annual Reviews, Palo Alto, Calif.

CONVERSE, R. H. (ED.). 1988. Virus diseases of small fruits. U.S. Dep. Agric. Handb. 631.

FRY, W. E. 1982. Principles of plant disease management. Academic Press, New York.

HORST, R. K. 1978. Westcott's plant disease handbook. Van Nostrand Reinhold, New York.

INGHAM, D. S., AND P. H. WILLIAMS. 1988. Advances in plant pathology. Academic Press, New York.

LUCAS, G. B., AND C. L. CAMPBELL. 1985. Introduction to plant diseases: identification and management. AVI, Wesport, Conn.

ROBERTS, D. A., AND C. W. BOOTHROYD. 1984. Fundamentals of plant pathology. W. H. Freeman, San Francisco.

Soils and Nutrition

BRADY, N. C. 1974. The nature and property of soils. Macmillan, New York.

N. F. CHILDERS. 1966. Nutrition of fruit crops. Horticultural Publications, Rutgers University, New Brunswick, N.J.

JONES, U. S. 1982. Fertilizers and soil fertility. Prentice-Hall, Englewood Cliffs, N.J.

DONAHUE, R. L. ET AL. 1983. Soils: an introduction to soils and plant growth. Prentice-Hall, Englewood Cliffs, N.J.

Plant Propagation

DIRR, M. A., AND C. W. HEUSER. 1987. The reference manual of woody plant propagation. Varsity Press, Athens, Ga.

HARTMANN, H. T., AND D. E. KESTER. 1983. Plant propagation principles and practices. Prentice-Hall, Englewood Cliffs, N.J.

MACDONALD, B. 1986. Practical woody plant propagation for nursery growers. Timber Press, Portland, Oreg.

Fruit Breeding

JANICK, J., AND J. N. MOORE (EDS.). 1975. Advances in fruit breeding. Purdue University Press, West Lafayette, Ind.

MOORE, J. N., AND J. JANICK (EDS.). 1983. Methods in fruit breeding. Purdue University Press, West Lafayette, Ind.

General Small Fruit References

CHILDERS, N. F. 1983. Modern fruit science. Horticultural Publications, Gainesville, Fla.

FERGUSON, B. 1987. All about growing fruits, berries and nuts. Ortho Books, San Francisco.

JACKSON, D. 1986. Temperate and subtropical fruit production. Butterworth, Stoneham, Mass.

MCEACHERN, G. R. 1978. Growing fruits, berries and nuts in the South. Gulf, Houston.

RYUGO, K. 1988 Fruit culture. Wiley, New York.

SHOEMAKER, J. S. 1978. Small fruit culture. AVI, Westport, Conn.

TURNER, D., AND K. MUIR. 1985. Handbook of soft fruit growing. Longwood, Wolfeboro, N.H.

WALHEIM, L., AND R. L. STEBBINS. 1981. Western fruit, berries and nuts. H. P. Books, Tucson, Ariz.

WESTWOOD, M. N. 1978. Temperate-zone pomology. W. H. Freeman, San Francisco.

Climate

ANON. 1968. Climatic atlas of the United States. Environmental Science Services Administration. U.S. Department of Commerce, Washington, D.C.

ANON. 1974. Climates of the states. Vols. 1 and 2. Water Information Center, Port Washington, N.Y.

ANON. 1984. Comparative climatic data for the United States. NOAA, Ashville, N.C.

CHANG, J. 1968. Climate and agriculture. Aldine, Chicago.

GEIGER, R. 1965. The climate near the ground. Harvard University Press, Cambridge, Mass.

NEUBERGER, H., AND J. CAHIR. 1969. Principles of climatology. Holt, Rinehart and Winston, New York.

OLIVER, J. E. 1973. Climate and man's environment. 1973. Wiley, New York.

ROSENBERG, N. J., B. L. BLAD, AND S. B. VERMA. 1983. Microclimate: the biological environment. Wiley, New York.

RUFFNER, J. A. 1980. Climates of the states. Vols. 1 and 2. Gale Research Co., Detroit, Mich.

SEEMAN, J., Y. I. CHIRKOV, J. LOMAS, AND B. PRIMAULT. 1979. Agrometeorology. Springer-Verlag, New York.

Chapter 3

Strawberry Management

G. J. GALLETTA
R. S. BRINGHURST

INTRODUCTION

"The strawberry is a delectable fruit, highly prized by almost everyone" wrote Norman Childers (1980) in his foreword to *The Strawberry,* the proceedings of the National Strawberry Conference in Saint Louis, Missouri. Childers continued: "Even though strawberries are a relatively minor crop in the USA . . . they comprise a very important living for thousands of growers. Worldwide, the strawberry is found in every country from the arctic to the tropics. It is more widely distributed than any other fruit, including the grape". These observations allude to the nearly universal appeal of strawberry fruits to the human senses of smell, sight, and taste; the very broad environmental tolerance of the plant, which permits considerable variation and flexibility in cultural systems; and the high profit levels that can be realized by the knowledgeable strawberry grower.

CULTIVATED TYPES

Fruit has been gathered from natural stands of all of the world's strawberry species, and plants from all of them have been transplanted to garden culture at one time or another. Since the advent of the modern garden strawberry (*Fragaria x ananassa* Duch.) in the eighteenth century, strawberry culture has become increasingly limited to clones of this species hybrid. However, the unique aromas and flavors of the Wood (*F. vesca*) and Musky (*F. moschata*) strawberries account for their continued but limited culture today (Fig. 3-1).

Wood and Alpine Strawberries

The soft and small but aromatic-fruited wood strawberry (*fraise des bois—Fragaria vesca* L.) is the most widely distributed of the world's strawberry species, being found throughout Europe, northern Asia, North America, and northern Africa (Reed, 1966). It is a diverse species known in many forms or botanical varieties. Some of its variants are found at higher elevations in the mountains of the West Indies, Central and South America, and some of the Pacific islands.

The Wood strawberry was probably gathered in Europe in recent prehistoric time, but it was definitely known by the Romans, some of whom (like the Roman Senator Cato, 234–149 B.C.) may have cultured plants in their gardens (Lee, 1966; Wilhelm and Sagen, 1974). Romans like the first-century poet Ovid knew the Wood strawberry in the two major forms that have survived to this day: the compact continuously flowering Alpine (*F. montana fraga*) strawberry (Fig. 3-2), some of which produced runners also; and the wood strawberry, which was a slight plant, spread by runners and which flowered only occasionally (the *F. mollia fraga* or soft strawberry) (Wilhelm and Sagen, 1974).

There are medical references to the use of strawberry leaves in the thirteenth century (Lee, 1966). Extensive culture of Wood and Alpine strawberries began in the fourteenth century in Europe, and these were the principal strawberries of commerce until the nineteenth century. During the sixteenth century the strawberry became a common garden plant, both as an ornament and a table delicacy. Euro-

FIGURE 3-1 Potted greenhouse specimen plants of *Fragaria vesca* (left) and *Fragaria virginiana* (right) used as sensitive virus indicator clones. (From O. Mageau, U.S. Department of Agriculture.)

FIGURE 3-2 Portion of a field plot of modern Alpine strawberry cultivar, 'Baron Solemacher,' in flower and fruit. Cultural system illustrated is single hill, raised bed, with straw mulch between the rows. (From O. Mageau, U.S. Department of Agriculture.)

peans of this time cultivated both white- and red-fruited forms. The everbearing Alpine form (*F. vesca semperflorens*), although known, was not cultivated until the eighteenth century (Lee, 1966).

Musky (Hautbois, Hautboy) Strawberries

The Musky species of strawberry (*F. moschata* Duch. = *F. elatior* Ehrh.) is a native of forests and tall grass country, usually in shaded areas, through Europe east into Russia and Siberia. This strawberry is vigorous with prominently veined leaves. It typically bears its flowers well above the leaves, and its fruit is slightly larger than that of *F. vesca,* is variable in color from light red to dull brownish or purplish red, bears raised achenes, and has an aromatic, strongly vinous flavor much like that of Muscat grapes (Reed, 1966).

Also known as the Bohemian, Capron, or Capiton berry, a white large-fruited type was brought into cultivation by the Flemish Belgians about the middle of the sixteenth century. The white Capiton clone was cultured extensively in England, where it was also forced for out-of-season production. Red-fruited forms of the Capiton berry were discovered in Bohemia, and their culture quickly spread to England, Italy, and much of Europe in the seventeenth century. Selections of the red-fruited class of Capiton strawberries became the Hautbois or Moschata strawberries of the eighteenth century. Unfortunately, the exceptionally aromatic Hautbois clones of this period passed out of existence, but the species and much of its variability was preserved in botanical gardens (Wilhelm and Sagen, 1974).

Modern Garden (Cultivated) Strawberries

In 1766, a classic book (*Histoire naturelle des fraises*) detailing all that was known about strawberries at that time, was published in Paris, France. It was the result of several years of strawberry research by its young author, Antoine Nicholas Duchesne (age 19), a student of the noted French botanist, Bernard de Jussieu, of King Louis XIV's Trianon Garden at Versailles. Duchesne concluded that the new, large-fruited hermaphroditic "pineapple" strawberry, *F. ananassa,* was a hybrid between the Scarlet strawberry (*F. virginiana*) and the Frutillar (Chilean or *F. chiloensis*) (Fig. 3-3).

The Scarlet or Virginia strawberry (*Fragaria virginiana* Duch.) is one of the three variable octoploid strawberry species of North America. The Scarlet is the meadow strawberry of eastern North America, spreading from Louisiana and Georgia north to Hudson Bay and the plains states of the United States and Canada (Reed 1966; Scott and Lawrence, 1975). The Virginia strawberry was introduced several times from eastern North America to France, England, Holland, and Sweden in the period 1534 to 1857 (Wilhelm and Sagen, 1974). From the botanical garden at Paris specimen plants were distributed additionally to Belgium, Germany, Switzerland, and Italy. The traits for which this species was admired were its large fruit size (three to four times that of the native European species), its earlier and longer fruiting period, and its sweetness and strong, distinctive fragrance. Although some of the early forms of the Virginian in Europe were greenish in color, except on the side exposed to the sun, the classic bright scarlet fruit color that we know as typical of the species was represented in other accessions.

Although described in botanical catalogs since 1597 for the green form, and since 1613 for the large red-fruited Canadian type, it was not until superior seedlings or clones became known, such as the 'Scarlet Virginia' described by the English

FIGURE 3-3 Top: Parent species of modern cultivated strawberries; left, *F. chiloensis;* right, *F. virginiana. Bottom:* left to right, North American and South American *F. chiloensis,* cultivated *F.* x *ananassa* in center, eastern, and western U.S. types of *F. virginiana.* (From O. Mageau, U.S. Department of Agriculture.)

botanists Robert Morison (1672) and John Ray (1686), that Scarlets became widely cultured in English gardens (Wilhelm and Sagen, 1974). Attempts by English gardeners to raise new varieties of *F. virginiana* from seed increased the known varieties of Scarlets from 3 to 26 by 1824 (Lee, 1966), and the Scarlet varieties were popular English garden strawberries of the late eighteenth and early nineteenth centuries.

The Chilean or beach strawberry (*F. chiloensis* Duch.) is another of the New World octoploid strawberries. In North America it is confined to beaches stretching from Alaska to near Santa Barbara, California (Reed, 1966). In South America, *F. chiloensis* is abundant along the beaches and inland in coastal Chile, in the Andes mountains from near Concepcion south to below Coyhaique, on the eastern slopes in Argentina and on mountain tops in Hawaii.

The natives of Chile both gathered from the wild and cultivated superior types of the Chilean strawberry prior to the Spanish conquest in the mid-sixteenth century (Lee, 1966). The Spanish appreciated the size and flavor of the Fruitilla or Chili, and distributed plants to Peru in 1557. Fruitillas cultivated in the area around Concepcion, Chile, were highly praised by visiting clergymen in 1646 and 1709. The cultivated Chile of Concepcion was exported to France by Lt. Colonel Amedee Francois Frezier (Fraser) in 1714 (Lee, 1966; Wilhelm and Sagen, 1974). Frezier was an intelligence officer for Louis XIV of France. He posed as a merchant while spying on and mapping Spanish holdings along the coasts of Peru and Chile during the period June 1712 to February 1714 (Lee, 1966).

Frezier arrived in Marseilles in August of 1714 with five living plants of the Chilean strawberry from Concepcion. Two of these he gave to Roux de Vallone, the ship's cargomaster, who had authorized the supply of water that kept the plants alive on the 6-month journey from Chile. Of the remaining three, Frezier kept one plant, gave one to botanist Antoine Jussieu to culture in the King's Garden in Paris, and gave the last one to his superior at Brest, Peletier de Souzy (Lee, 1966). From Paris the Chilean strawberry was distributed to botanical and horticultural gardens in Holland, England, Belgium, and Germany. It proved vigorous but unfruitful and not hardy in most European locations, except in the Brest area of Brittany.

In Brest, and especially the nearby community of Plougastel, farmers learned that the sterility of the Chili could be overcome by interplanting pollinators of the Hautbois and Virginian strawberries in among the Chilis. The famous "Plougastel" strawberry of Brittany evolved from being pure *F. chiloensis* fruit in 1750 to being hybrid seedlings from *F. chiloensis* × *virginiana* natural pollinations, to being seedlings from hybrids, or *F. ananassa,* much as we know it today (Wilhelm and Sagen, 1974).

The significance of Frezier's introduction of the Chilean strawberry from Concepcion is fourfold: (1) the Concepcion Chili became the type specimen for the botanical species *F. chiloensis;* (2) as a highly selected and improved type of *F. chiloensis,* it proved an admirable female parent of the hybrid strawberries (the Pines or Pineapples), which were the progenitors of the modern cultivated strawberry; (3) Frezier's plants, being female, led Duchesne to conclude that the Chili strawberry, like the Capiton, had separate sexes in nature and needed cross-pollination to be fruitful; and (4) that the new hermaphroditic Pine strawberries could indeed arise as hybrid seedlings from Chilean strawberries pollinated by

Virginian (Scarlet) strawberries. Subsequently, *F. chiloensis* plants and seeds from other parts of South America, North America, and Hawaii were exported to Europe, the United States, and other strawberry production centers and used in breeding.

Pine (short for "Pineapple") strawberries suddenly appeared in English gardens during the middle of the eighteenth century, usually from Dutch seed or plant sources (Wilhelm and Sagen, 1974). The plants had fruit with a unique pineapple-like fragrance and flavor; large hermaphroditic (bisexual) flowers; large fruit with the seed embedded in the flesh; a large, many-lobed flower calyx; and leaves that were large, oval, crenate (scalloped at the margins), and prominently veined.

Private citizens were the first to try to improve the cultivated strawberry, starting in 1817 with Thomas A. Knight of England (Scott and Lawrence, 1975; Lee, 1966, Wilhelm and Sagen, 1974). Notable early cultivars grown from seed of either hybridized or open pollinated cultivars include the English cultivars 'Downton' (1817), 'Elton' (1828), 'Keens Imperial' (1814), 'Keens Seedling' (1821), 'Jucunda' (1854), 'Sir Joseph Paxton' (1862), 'Noble' (1884), and 'Royal Sovereign' (1892); and the American cultivars 'Hovey' (1834), 'Wilson' (1851), 'Neunan' (1868), 'Crescent' (1873), and 'Sharpless' (1872) (Darrow, 1966; Lee, 1966).

In the United States, a group of particularly valuable cultivars, grown in the first half of the twentieth century, have been important contributors to the strawberry germplasm of today (Darrow, 1966). They are 'Marshall' (chance seedling—Massachusetts, 1890), 'Klondike' (private hybrid, 1901), 'Missionary' (chance seedling—Virginia, 1900), 'Dunlap' (private hybrid, 1900), 'Howard 17' (private hybrid, 1915), 'Aberdeen' (private hybrid, 1910), 'Blakemore' (USDA hybrid, 1929), 'Fairfax' (USDA hybrid, 1933), 'Aroma' (private hybrid, 1891), and 'Nick Ohmer' (private hybrid, 1898). Many of the modern American cultivars have North American *F. chiloensis* and different clones of *F. virginiana* that were not transported to Europe in their backgrounds. Some recent cultivars also possess germplasm from the third North American octoploid species, *F. ovalis* (*F. virginiana glauca* Staudt), the variable Rocky Mountain strawberry. Although it has been possible to introgress germplasm from some of the diploid species into the cultivated strawberry experimentally, named strawberry cultivars are derived almost exclusively from *F. chiloensis, F. virginiana,* and to a lesser extent, *F. ovalis.*

RELATED GERMPLASM AND UTILITY

Botanical Relationships

Strawberries (genus *Fragaria*) are dicotyledonous angiosperms in the rose family (leaves alternate, stipulate; flowers bisexual). The large and very diverse rose family (Rosaceae) includes many fruit and flowering plants highly prized by human beings, such as apples, peaches, raspberries, blackberries, and roses. Flowers in the rose family have one of three structural types. Plant species within the family are classified according to flower type and plant habit. Strawberries are in the rose family tribe Roseae (or Potentilleae), in which flower ovaries are superior, fruits indehiscent, ovaries become an achene, pistils are more than one, achenes are more than one, leaves are compound, pistils are borne on a flat or convex receptacle, calyx lobes have five alternate bractlets, styles are deciduous from the achene, receptacles are conic and fleshy, plants are herbs, and leaves are tri-foliate. Close botanical relatives of strawberries are *Potentilla* (five-finger or cinquefoil), *Geum* (old man's whiskers), *Fallugia* (Apache plume), *Cowania* (cliff rose), *Rubus* (raspberries and blackberries), *Rosa* (roses), and *Duchesnea* (mock strawberry).

Description and Species

Jepson (1951) characterizes the genus *Fragaria* as follows: 'Perennial herbs, the leaves and flowers in a basal tuft, giving off prostrate stems or runners. Leave 3-foliate, with membranous stipules and cuneate-obovate serrate leaflets. Flowers white, borne in cymes on a naked scape. Calyx persistent, bearing 5 bractlets alternate with the calyx lobes. Petals obovate, short-clawed. Stamens about 20. Pistils numerous, distinct, borne on an elevated convex receptacle; styles lateral. Fruit berry-like, formed of the enlarged succulent receptacle which bears the minute seed-like achenes. (Name in reference to the fragrance of the berry)'.

The genus *Fragaria* could be considered as a section of the much larger and older genus *Potentilla,* to which it is closely related and from which it was probably derived. *Fragaria* (basic chromosome number $= x = 7$) contains a complete polyploid series ranging from diploid ($2n$ or somatic chromosome number $= 14$) to octoploid ($2n = 56$). The origin of the polyploids is not known, but they could have arisen from functioning unreduced gametes (a process already observed in nature as leading to the evolution of the next ploidy level — $10x$ or decaploid, $2n = 70$). The known living strawberry species are listed in Table 3–1 with abbreviated natural distributions and fruit characteristics.

Species Relationships

There are a number of ways to determine the origin of polyploid strawberry species. Scott and Lawrence (1975) reviewed several lines of evidence. Islam's study (1961) of a haploid *F. vesca* showed largely univalent (unpaired, random disjunction to poles) behavior of the seven chromosomes of the basic set. The widely distributed normal diploid *F. vesca* can then be said to have two uniform basic chromosome sets (*genomes*), which can be designated "AA" or "2A", where A = one genome of seven chromosomes. Dowrick and Williams (1959) attempted intercrosses of the five diploid species *F. vesca, F. viridis, F. nubicola, F. nipponica,* and *F. nilgerrensis. F. vesca* and *F. viridis* were interfertile and showed some crossing success with the asiatic diploids; *F. viridis* showed more genetic affinity to the asiatic species than did *F. vesca. F. nilgerrensis* was relatively isolated from most of the other species. *F. viridis* and *nipponica* were interfertile in either direction, as were *F. nubicola* and *F. nipponica.* This suggests either that the extant diploid species are polyphyletic (are descended from different ancestral species) in part, or that the present species have diverged further (established reproductive isolating barriers) after descending from a common ancestor. There is merit in both arguments.

TABLE 3-1 WORLD SPECIES OF *FRAGARIA* (STRAWBERRY)[a]

SPECIES	NATIVE AREA	FRUIT CHARACTERS
Diploids (2*n* = 14)		
F. vesca L.[b]	Circumpolar	Long ovate–variable, bright red, raised seeds, very aromatic, very soft flesh
F. viridis Duch.	Europe to eastern to central Asia	Small, firm, pink-red, aromatic, seeds set in pits
F. nilgerrensis Schlect	Southeast Asia	Small, round, pink, tasteless to unpleasant, many seeded–sunken
F. daltoniana J. Gay	Himalayas, 10,000–15,000 ft	Elongate-ovoid, bright red, tasteless
F. nubicola Lindl ex. Lacaita	Himalayas, 5,000–13,000 ft	Resembles *vesca*
F. iinumae Makino	Japan, mountains	Ovoid, 1½ cm long, achenes sunken, resembles *F. daltoniana*
F. nipponica	Japan	—
Tetraploids (2*n* = 28)		
F. moupinensis (Franch.) Card.	Tibet, China	Small, similar to *nilgerrensis*
F. orientalis Losink	Siberia, Korea	Soft, conical to round, slight aroma, seeds sunken
Hexaploids (2*n* = 42)		
F. moschata Duch.[b]	Northern Europe to Siberia	Light to dark dull purplish red, soft, irregular to ovoid, musky or vinous, aromatic, raised achenes, strongly reflexed calyx
Octoploids (2*n* = 56)		
F. virginiana Duch.[b]	Eastern North America	Twice the size of *vesca,* soft, light to deep red or scarlet, white flesh, tart, aromatic, sunken seeds, subglobose to ovoid
F. chiloensis (L.) Duch.[b]	Pacific beaches of North America, Chile, Argentina, Hawaii	Dull red brown, white flesh, mild, firm, round to oblate, small to large, achenes raised or sunken
F. ovalis (Lehn.) Rydb.[b] (*F. virginiana glauca* Staudt)	Rocky Mountains to west coast	Round, pink, small, flavorful
F. mandschurica Staudt[c]	Manchuria	G. Staudt, 1959
F. inturupensis Staudt[c]	Island North of Japan	G. Staudt, 1973
F. x ananassa Duch.[b,d]	Cultivated	Large, red, variable in all traits

Source: Adapted from Reed (1966); Scott and Lawrence (1975).

[a] Many of these species contain variants that have been given species rank by other authors.

[b] Cultivated forms of these species exist.

[c] 1959: 9th Int. Bot. Congr. Proc. 2:377; 1973: Willldenowia 7:104.

[d] Contains germplasm from *F. virginiana, chiloensis,* and *ovalis.*

Fadeeva (1966) extended this type of crossing study to include three octoploid, a hexaploid, and a natural and induced tetraploid species. The American and cultivated octoploids were interfertile and showed some affinity with *F. vesca*. Staudt deduced (1967, 1968) from a study of sex types in 3*x*, 4*x*, 5*x*, and 6*x* plants derived from *F. vesca* (2*x*), *F. viridis* (2*x*) and *F. orientalis* (4*x*) that *F. vesca* genomes are the basic genetic units in tetraploid and hexaploid species. For example, the sex expression of *F. moschata* (6*x*) was similar to that of a doubled triploid from a *vesca* × *orientalis* cross. Senanayake and Bringhurst (1967), from a cytological analysis of natural pentaploid hybrids, deduced that two genome (B) pairs in *F. virginiana* and *F. chiloensis* are homologous, and that these octoploid species share a common genome (A) with *F. vesca*. They proposed the genome formula for octoploid strawberries (including cultivated) as AAA'A'BBBB.

Fruit Uses

Strawberries are principally used as fresh fruit. They are also used in processed forms such as cooked and sweetened preserves, jams or jellies, and frozen whole berries or sweetened juice extracts or flavorings, then used in making a variety of other processed products. Nutritionally, strawberries are valued as a low-calorie carbohydrate and a high source of vitamin C and fiber.

Fresh uses for strawberry fruits seem limited only by the imagination of the consumer. For the true strawberry fancier, strawberry fruit may just be capped, washed, and eaten alone, or whole or sliced with sugar and/or cream or milk or in a wine-flavored syrup. Washed strawberries with the stems attached may be dipped into powdered sugar, chocolate, or cream cheese dips. As toppings, whole or sliced and sweetened berries are put on cereals, cakes, puddings, ice cream, and so on. Whole, sliced, or lightly crushed berries may be used in dairy, carbonated soft drinks, fruit punch, or alcoholic beverages. In the United States glazed fresh strawberries are used as a pie filling in prebaked pie shells by at least one major restaurant chain. Berries used as toppings may also be used as a "mixed-in" ingredient in cake batters, puddings, gelatin salads, and milk shakes.

A favorite U.S. dessert is *strawberry shortcake*. The original rural American recipe called for homemade drop or rolled biscuits sliced in half. The bottom biscuit half was topped with sweetened sliced strawberries. The top biscuit half was placed over the dressed lower half, and was itself topped with whole or sweetened sliced strawberries. The entire strawberry-filled and strawberry-topped biscuit in a bowl was then covered with whipped cream or whole milk.

Often overlooked as fresh strawberry uses are the combination and garnish options. Fresh strawberries offer a tart and colorful component when blended with stone, pome, and tropical fruits, with other berries, or with melons. Particularly appealing combinations are strawberries with peaches and/or bananas, with honeydew, and with a citrus salad. Fresh whole or sliced strawberries make an excellent peripheral or top garnish for cheese plates, meat roasts, egg or poultry dishes, and for certain vegetable dishes such as potato salad.

Strawberry preserves, jams, and jellies are a very popular type of processed strawberry. They need no refrigeration until opened, make an excellent export product, and will last as long as the container is intact and the added preservative sugar persists. Mashing berries together with sugar and pectin as in jamming is one of the few ways that strawberries can be cooked successfully. Cooking whole berries in a sugar syrup as in canning makes a poor product because of losses of color, flavor, and texture during heating. Quick frozen whole, sliced, or pureed strawberries are the most common processed strawberry marketing outlet. Strawberry juice is sometimes blended with that of other fruits. Processed strawberries are common components and flavorings of milk products, especially yogurt. Processed berries are also used in baked products, cereals, ice creams, sherbets and ices, fruit bars and powdered drink mixes, candies, and so on.

Fermented strawberry juice does not make very acceptable wines because the finished color is a sickly amber, the wine does not age well, much natural flavor is lost, and undesirable off-flavors frequently occur. However, some strawberry-flavored liqueurs are reasonably good.

BOTANY

Although strawberry species and clones vary superficially to substantially in plant appearance and structure, certain organizational features of all strawberries are common. These were listed in the botanical relationships and *Fragaria* taxonomic description portions of the previous section. The appearance, development, soil, climate, and disease reaction patterns of strawberries that follow are largely those of the highly heterozygous polyploid species hybrid, the garden strawberry (*Fragaria* × *ananassa*).

Morphology of the Plant

Darrow (1966), Dana (1980), Guttridge (1985), and Avigdori-Avidov (1986) summarize their own work and that of many others concerning the structure, growth, and flowering of the strawberry plant. Included with the text are excellent schematic diagrams, drawings, and photographs in the Darrow book.

Crown. Although the strawberry may appear to be an acaulescent (stemless, with leaves and flowers arising from a basal tuft) perennial herb, it is neither stemless nor truly herbaceous. The strawberry stem is compressed into a rosetted "crown" about 1 inch (2.5 cm) long, which is covered on the outside by overlapping leaf bases (*stipules*). The crown produces leaves at very close intervals along the stem axis, flowers at the terminal position on the stem axis (is determinate), and roots from the base of the crown. The aboveground habit of the strawberry plant is represented in drawing A of Fig. 3–4, which shows a 'Tristar' strawberry plant growing, fruiting, flowering, and runnering in the late fall. The runner (stolon) is the type of "long shoot" and the flower and fruit cluster one type of "short shoot"

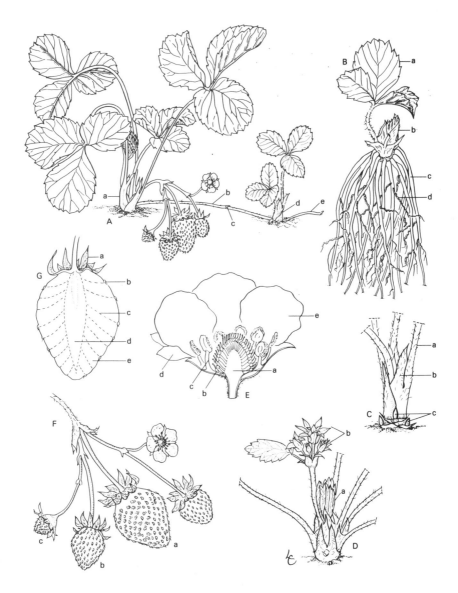

FIGURE 3-4 Strawberry morhology. A, plant habit: a, crown and leaf bases; b, stolon (runner); c, first (blind) runner node; d, daughter plant; e, secondary runner. B. planting stock-dormant: a, old leaf from previous season; b, crown; c, primary root; d, secondary root. C. dormant crown (partially dissected): a, base of old leaf petiole; b, stipule (sheath) at base of old leaf; c, axillary buds (reproductive or vegetative). D. crown base-post planting expansion: a, new leaf expanding; b, expanding inflorescence. E. flower-longitudinal section: a, receptacle; b, pistil and fruit wall; c, anther; d, sepal; e, petal. F. fruit cluster: a, primary fruit; b, secondary fruit; c, tertiary fruit. G. fruit-longitudinal section: a, cap (calyx); b, seed (achene); c, vascular bundle; d, pith; e, receptacle (cortex).

produced by the strawberry, which two branching types, as Guttridge indicates, the strawberry forms in common with other rose family genera.

The strawberry crown bears, in the axil between each leaf and the crown, buds or axillary meristems. Figure 3–4, drawing C, shows a crown with several leaf bases removed to expose the axillary buds. These *axillary buds,* responding to the prevailing environment and nutrition level, determine the subsequent development of the strawberry plant. Axillary buds may remain dormant or may expand to become *runners* or *branch crowns.* The crown terminal bud usually contains five to seven developing leaves, enclosed within the stipules of the last emerged leaf. When the terminal meristem becomes an inflorescence, vegetative crown extension is continued by the uppermost axillary bud. The continuing vegetative crown growth displaces the inflorescence of the original terminal axis off to one side. Axillary buds may also form *inflorescences* (flowering branches) at the terminus of the shoot after initiating two- to four-leaf primordia.

Internally, the crown is composed of a central *pith;* a *vascular cylinder* made up of a network of anastomosing vascular bundles and traces to the leaf petioles, buds, roots, and flower stalks; a largely parenchymatous and shallow *cortical area;* and the *epidermis.* As the crown ages (usually near the end of the first growing season or in the dormant season) lignification of certain vascular elements during and following lateral crown growth produces a distinctly hard and 'woody' tissue in the crown. Old woody crowns can be seen in eroded areas of a field planting, in the center of the root system of "mother" nursery plants during cleaning and grading, and in potted plants that have remained in the pot too long. The functional roots, leaves, and other organs all originate above the older woody portion of the crown, making the old crown resemble a deciduous tree scaffold branch, or a small fruit bush cane. Thus some consider the strawberry plant during its entire life as a short-lived woody perennial, with essentially the same physiological responses to environmental conditioning as deciduous fruit trees, vines, or shrubs.

Runners. *Runners or stolons* (Fig. 3–4, drawing A) are prostrate two-noded stems, originating from the axillary buds of the crown. A vigorous plant may expand 10 to 15 runners or "runner strings" in the course of the growing season. Along the runners, over 100 daughter plants may eventually root from one mother plant during the season. The first runner of the season usually originates from the axil of the first new leaf initiated on the crown in the spring, rather than the first leaf to expand in the spring, which was initiated the previous fall. The first internode of the runner elongates for several inches and ceases growth with the bract and an axillary bud (often called the "blind" node). This first or blind node grows out another prostrate and elongated branch runner or stem internode identical to the original runner from which it arose. This runner from the first node ends in a second node that has a bract and axillary bud. A succession of very short internodes are developed at the second node. The nodes terminating these very short internodes produce leaves and more axillary buds, which form a *daughter plant,* thus terminating the original runner after apparently two nodes. The first axillary bud of the daughter plant may produce another stolon, with two nodes and another daughter plant to form a runner chain. The runnering process is continued from successive daughter plants until environmental factors become limiting for further extension of runners.

The first or "blind" runner node may produce a runner and daughter plant if the second internode is damaged or destroyed. The blind node can also be induced to grow following hormone application or if apical dominance is disturbed. A daughter plant initiates "peg roots" at the second node of the runner by the time the first leaf has emerged at the third node (second daughter plant node). Under optimum conditions a daughter plant could survive if runner support were interrupted after 2 to 3 weeks. Runner production is very variable from clone to clone. Most strawberry cultivars produce enough runners under good nursery growing conditions that runner plant production is still the principal asexual propagation method for strawberries (Fig. 3–5).

Leaves. *Leaves* of the strawberry (Fig. 3–4, drawing A) are compound pinnate and *trifoliolate,* consisting of three *leaflets* (each leaflet has its own little stem or *petiolule*) attached to the main leaf stem (*petiole*) which is enlarged at the base to form a winged *stipule* that wraps around the crown. Leaflets vary in shape from wedge (widest at the top) to obovate (widest near the top). The leaflet blades (*laminae*) often are held flat when young. As they age, leaflet margins frequently curl up or down characteristically for each clone and may appear oval or round. Leaflet margins bear characteristic serrations. Upper leaflet surfaces have characteristic colors varying from light yellow-green to very dark green. Lower leaf surfaces are often a waxy very light green with prominent veins. All leaf and petiole surfaces have amounts and types of hairiness that again are characteristic of clone and plant age.

FIGURE 3–5 Variation in quantity and time of runner production in short-day (Junebearing) strawberry clones. (From O. Mageau, U.S. Department of Agriculture.)

Leaves are arranged in a tight 2/5 spiral around the crown, each sixth leaf located above the first. Leaves vary in "normal" plastochron interval (time elapsed between successive leaf emergence) from 8 to 12 days. The plastochron interval varies with temperature, being more rapid in spring and summer than in fall. Leaves of *F. chiloensis* are evergreen; those of *F. virginiana* are killed by severe frosts. Hybrid cultivars are intermediate in leaf persistence through the winter. Leaf unfolding in the spring may be accomplished in as little as 2 to 3 weeks in warm weather. A terminal vegetative bud usually has 5 to 10 unexpanded leaf primordia. Individual leaves may live from 1 to 3 months and vary widely in leaf thickness, leaf area, and cuticle thickness. Having considerable stomata and large internal cell areas exposed to air space within the leaf (Darrow, 1966), strawberry leaves are capable of very heavy water use, wilting, and leaf and feeder root death in warm, dry periods.

Roots.   *Roots* of the strawberry arise adventitiously from the base of new leaves along the crown. Roots will not emerge, however, unless in contact with and/ or partially covered by moist soil. It is all too common to see runner plants with emerged root tips not rooting because the soil is too dry or the tips are pointing away from the soil. Consecutive new roots of strawberry originate in a definite pattern around the crown and higher up on the crown than the older roots, following the pattern of leaf formation along the crown. Again, the new roots, originating above the older roots on the crown, must be in contact with soil to elongate and grow successfully. A dormant nursery plant showing the primary root system and a few lateral roots is represented in Fig. 3–4, drawing B. Primary roots normally live for a year, but they may die in a few weeks in stressful or disease-prone environments, or persist for several years in very sandy situations, such as the *F. chiloensis* on the Pacific coast beaches. Modern cultivated strawberries, having more *F. virginiana* than *F. chiloensis* germplasm in their backgrounds, tend to have the many, short-lived primary root pattern of the *F. virginiana*. Usually 20 to 35, but as many as 100 or more primary roots and thousands of lateral second-, third-, and higher-order branch rootlets make up the root system of a mature strawberry plant.

The primary roots are usually the soil-penetrating roots. The smaller, much branched secondary roots are feeder, soil-binding, and exploring roots. The generally fibrous appearance of the strawberry root system results from the combination of a large number of small rootlets branching from a relatively large number of primary roots. The visible parts of a root are the root tip, the white rootlet behind the tip, and the suberized and darkened older and thicker portion of the root. The root tip is the actively growing part of the root. The white rootlets absorb most of the water and nutrients directly. The older, nonwhite root portion absorbs some water but is mostly conductive. The central vascular cylinder (the stele) of the strawberry root is noteworthy. Its color and consistency are often used as indicators of root and plant health. Even when outer root tissues are badly discolored and partially decomposed, a healthy stele will appear like a flexible white or ivory-colored intact string.

Root system size depends on how the natural vigor of each clone is expressed and how the plant is grown. Some strawberries (e.g., 'Earliglow') make many daughter plants, each with a relatively small root system, as in matted row culture of mother and daughter plants. Other strawberry cultivars (e.g., 'Titan') make relatively few runner plants, and each plant has a large root system and a number of branch crowns. Several studies have shown that although strawberry roots may penetrate soils to a depth of 40 to 42 in. (100 to 105 cm), 50 to 90% of the root system is usually confined to the upper 6 in. (15 cm) of soil, and 25 to 50% of the roots to the upper 3 in. (7.5 cm). Root penetration is usually greater on lighter (more porous or sandier) soils or on well-prepared soils than on less porous or more poorly prepared soils.

Flower stalks (inflorescences) and flowers.   Figure 3-4 depicts a young inflorescence expanding from the crown (drawing D), a longitudinal section through a hermaphroditic (bisexual) flower (drawing E), and a ripening fruit cluster (truss) with an opened flower remaining (drawing F). The illustrated expanding and expanded inflorescences are relatively small and uncomplicated. Drawings D and F show the principal parts of the strawberry flower stalk or inflorescence. The naked (leafless) inflorescence arising from a seemingly stemless plant such as the strawberry is sometimes called a *scape*. The principal thick stem of the inflorescence to the point of first branching is known as the *peduncle*. Stems leading from the peduncle branch point (node) to the second subsequent branching points (nodes) are *inflorescence branches*. The stem supporting each individual flower, and later berry, is called a *pedicel*. The strawberry inflorescence is also known morphologically as "basically a *dichasial cyme*, but very variable in detailed structure" (Guttridge, 1985). A *dichasium* is a determinate cluster of flowers that arises from a common peduncle by dichotomous branching immediately beneath the terminal flower. Since this dichotomous branching or "forking" of the flower stem continues for two, three, or four cycles behind each group of terminal flowers initiated, the strawberry flower stalk is a type of *compound dichasium*. A *cyme* is a type of dichasium in which some of the secondary branches have been lost, the remaining flower stems are of different lengths and the flower cluster is more or less flat-topped or convex (the flowers being borne in a bunch at about the same height).

Darrow (1929) first indicated the complexity of strawberry inflorescence types and their subsequent effects on berry development in his pioneering study of strawberry flower counts and inflorescence habits in a number of hybrid and species clones. He also characterized the nature of the inflorescence. Darrow felt that the strawberry inflorescence peduncle and pedicels were continuations of the vegetative stem and its branches. He noted that at each node of the inflorescence a bract replaced the subtending leaf, and the bud in the axil of each bract may develop into a branch of the inflorescence. The bract subtending the entire inflorescence is larger than subsequent bracts and may be almost the size of a true leaf, although variable in parts from one to three. A typical inflorescence axis has three internodes—two long internodes on each side of a very short internode, each subtended by a bract. The very short internode with two bracts close together makes it "appear that two opposite branches emerge from the same point and that there are three branches at each node just as there are three leaflets to each typical leaf."

Considerable variation in inflorescence types was found within and among six principal cultivars, species hybrids, and a species representative examined in detail by Darrow (1929). In a perfectly filled and matured strawberry fruit cluster with all branches present after four successive orders of branching, one would expect to find one large primary berry (from the first initiated terminal flower), two secondaries of medium-large size, four tertiary berries of medium size, eight small quaternary berries, and 16 very small quinary fruits—a total of 31 fruits. Darrow found a variation of from 1 to 39 flowers per cluster in the clones he examined. Inflorescence types within a clone varied from 29 types in 397 inflorescences for 'Klondike' to 124 types in 536 clusters for 'Dunlap'. Cluster-type criteria were branching point (basal versus high), number of major branches, and rebranching patterns (number and symmetry of flowers per major branch). Darrow noted that the second- and third-order fruits produced on basal branched inflorescences could be as large as primary fruits in some clones, whereas secondaries and tertiaries were often considerably smaller than primaries when borne on high branched crowns.

In a complete and perfect flower (Fig. 3–4, drawing E) all four floral whorls and both male and female sexual parts are present. The floral axis of the strawberry flower is swollen at the tip of the pedicel to form a *receptacle*. Into this swollen tip, hundreds of *pistils* are inserted spirally around the receptacle with the *ovaries* embedded in the receptacle and connected to it by a vascular trace. The pistil *styles* and *stigmas* are pointed away from the receptacle. The aggregated pistils and the receptacle constitute the female portion of the flower. Outside of and surrounding the receptacle and pistils are a double ring of 20 to 35 *stamens,* each of which consist of a short stalk or *filament* to which the *anther* or pollen producing floral part is attached. The stamens are the male parts of the flower. When the anther is ripe, it splits along a longitudinal suture, and mature pollen grains exude from the opening, to be picked up by wind or insects. Outside the rings of stamens are usually five separated white *petals,* which make up the *corolla.* The corolla offers protection to the sexual parts of the flower when closed, and when open attracts animals with color, scent, and sugary nectar secretions from glands at the base of the petals. The outer floral ring is the *calyx,* made up of one or two rings of five *sepals* each. The principal function of the calyx is flower protection in the bud stage, and some fruit protection in early developmental stages.

The successively initiated flowers are progressively smaller and have fewer pistils. Resulting fruits from later-initiated flowers are also smaller; hence fruit size is said to depend on the number of pistils on a receptacle (which can vary from about 500 on a large primary flower to 50 or less on a very small quaternary or quinary flower). This view is a bit too simple, since pedicel size and hence water supply also decrease in successively initiated flowers. Completeness of pollination and fertilization, internal hormonal levels, receptacle epidermis elasticity, receptacle cell number and enlargement potential, and nutrient and water supply are all factors in ultimate fruit size, in addition to floral pistil number and inflorescence position. Development of strawberry flowers normally proceeds from outside to inside, so that the floral parts originate in this order—sepals, petals, stamens, pistils.

Plants of some strawberry species are dioecious, including the parent species of the cultivated strawberry. They have male (staminate) or female (pistillate) flowers only on separate plants. In these instances female plants must be interplanted with male or perfect-flowerd plants to produce fruit. However, even in species where the sexes are borne on separate plants, some males produce some perfect flowers and produce a little fruit. There are also some hermaphroditic or perfect-flowered individuals in natural populations. Practically all cultivars originated through hybridization and human selection since the mid-nineteenth century have been chosen with perfect flowers, hoping to effect self-fertilization. Occasionally, sterile or partially sterile individual plants are found which produce no fruit or no late fruit even though the blossoms appear bisexual. Even among perfect-flowered cultivars, there are seasonal and locational differences in flower and pollen productions, degree of fertilization, and fruit set.

Fruit. *Strawberry fruit* (Fig. 3–4, drawings F and G) development starts with the transfer of pollen from the anthers to the collective stigmas of the same or other flowers. When the anther ruptures, there is enough force to throw some pollen grains onto nearby pistils. Early pollen is wet and sticky, later pollen is lighter and dry. Later pollinations are achieved by wind and insect transfer. Pollen on each stigma germinates, nuclei within the pollen grain grow down the style and fertilize certain cells in the *ovule* within each *ovary* to form an *embryo* and a nourishing *endosperm* tissue. This fertilization initiates the growth of the embryo into a hard seed within a hard indehiscent fruit called an *achene*. These dried one-seeded fruits are the true "fruit" of the strawberry, which we call the "seeds" of the fruit. The developing achene produces a hormone that causes a small portion of the receptacle around it to enlarge and ripen. A maximum number of ovules must be fertilized to assure maximum achene development and the growth stimulation of the entire receptacle surface. The "berry" that we eat includes the ripened receptacle (swollen specialized stem tissue), the hard achenes (true fruits and seeds), and any remaining dried styles (the tiny pieces of "straw" on the periphery of the berry). Usually not eaten are the *cap* (enlarged and matured floral calyx), any dried stamens adhering to the cap, and the *stem* (the enlarged and mature flower pedicel). The longitudinal section drawing (G of Fig. 3–4) illustrates the edible portions of the strawberry "fruit", the interior fleshy *pith,* the *ring* of *vascular bundles* with traces leading to the achenes, the fleshy *cortex* outside the ring, and the *epidermis* ("skin"), which bears a few hairs and the superficial *"seeds".*

From pollination to berry ripening takes 20 to 50 days, depending on cultivar, prevalent temperatures, pollen availability, berry size, and regularity of fertilization. Large-fruited primary berries ripening in the spring, when lower temperatures prevail and less good pollen is available, are often irregular in shape and ripen in about 30 days. Main crop berries, which are smaller, open their flowers when good pollen is more abundant, and develop during higher temperatures, are more regular in shape and ripen in 20 to 23 days. Conversely, everbearing fruit ripening during high summer temperatures ripens quickly in 20 to 30 days but is often small and irregular because viable pollen is limiting, and high temperatures put stress on a limited root system. In the fall when temperatures are cooler and good pollen is more abundant, ripening is slower (35 to 50 days), but the fruit is larger, more regular in shape, and of better quality.

Strawberry planting stocks are generally either dried and cleaned *"seed"* (the achenes from the "fruit" surface), or *runner* daughter *plants* dug and transplanted immediately, planted following a few days to a few weeks of refrigerated storage, or planted following a period of extended cold storage at slightly subfreezing temperatures.

Seeds are used to grow plants of diploid Wood or Alpine (*F. vesca*) strawberry cultivars, which show very little variation ("come true") when grown from seed. Seeds are also used to reproduce populations of wild strawberries native to areas distant from the growing locale. And, of course, seeds from controlled pollinations are germinated in strawberry breeding programs to produce progenies of known parentage for artificial selection.

Strawberry seed may be sown directly following extraction from the fruit if it is not permitted to dry and the germinating temperatures are kept in the range 75 to 55°F (23.9 to 12.8°C). Dried seed usually germinates more rapidly and uniformly if it has been scarified for 10 to 20 minutes with concentrated sulfuric acid or after-ripened [stratified moist and refrigerated at 35 to 40°F (1.7 to 4.4°C)] for 2 ½ to 3 months prior to sowing. Seed germination is best when seed is sown, *uncovered,* on the surface of fine-milled sphagnum moss. Germination of unstratified seed takes 10 to 90 days; of pretreated seed, 6 to 40 days.

The first sign of germination is the emergence of the tiny white radicle (root) from the seed coat. If the sphagnum surface is kept moist, the radicle will turn and penetrate the sphagnum within a few days. After rooting the seed will be lifted and the seedling stem will expand to permit the two seed leaves (cotyledons) to be exposed. In a few more days, the seedling growing point will resume growth and the first leaf (usually lobed, but with only one blade) will emerge. As growth continues, the stem thickens and a series of very small but increasingly larger three-parted leaves emerge. The seedlings can be transplanted with care from the seeding tray to soil mixes in pots or flats from the cotyledon stage on, but transplanting is more successful after 6 to 8 weeks when the seedlings have two to three true leaves and a multiple-branched root system. Seedlings are grown an additional 6 to 8 weeks in the soil mixture to field transplanting size. By then, vigorous seedlings will have 6 to 10 leaves, a crown as thick as a lead pencil, and a branched root system that would fill a 2 ½ to 3 in. (6.4 to 7.6 cm) pot or cell.

Runner plants from the first and second seasonal runner cycles (first and second daughter plants), having developed earlier, will have larger and thicker crowns, larger and better developed root systems, more leaves, and more flower bud primordia than later-developing runner plants. These earlier runner plants are preferred for late summer and fall planting because they have higher transplanting survival, and start to grow and produce fruit earlier. However, third- and later-cycle runner plants may be well rooted and grow to suitable transplanting size during protracted mild fall weather when the soil retains sufficient moisture and temperatures remain above 45 to 50°F (7.5 to 10°C).

The commercial strawberry runner plant is produced from superior, selected, and tested clones that have been named (cultivars). They usually have been grown from disease-free, true-to-type mother plants by professional nursery personnel under state agency supervision and prescribed sanitary field conditions. The nursery plant will have developed from the mother plant during one growing season. As such, it will consist of a thick crown(s) containing a number of leaf and flower stalk promordia, several full-sized leaves (or leaf petioles and stipules if dormant and trimmed), and an extensive root system (trimmed or not).

Field-transplanted seedlings or runner plants, in response to lengthening periods of daylight and increasing temperatures, will first establish root–soil contact, and then show a top growth pattern that is characteristic for the seedling or cultivar. Short-day seedlings will not bear any flowers or fruit in the season of planting. Short-day runner plants will expand the leaf primordia and then the inflorescence primordia already formed in the crown. In some circumstances, growers will harvest the fruit from flowers initiated in the nursery. If this is done, runner emergence is delayed until later fruit in the cluster is ripening, and the vegetative growth is reduced until the crop is harvested. In most instances, nursery-initiated flowers are removed to promote vegetative growth. In some cultural systems, runners are also removed. Runner removal promotes the formation of branch or multiple crowns, and also of more runners.

Characteristic top-growth season patterns for cultivars and seedlings may vary to include:

1. Large-leafed *tall* plants with an *"open"* habit. These tall plants may vary in runnering from none to many, but usually have a moderate number of daughter plants and relatively few leaves per plant. Some of the daughter plants, and often the mother "large, open" plant, will develop a branch crown late in the season.

2. *Medium*-sized *compact* plants having a medium to large number of smaller leaves. Frequently, these compact plants will be sparse runner makers and will produce several branch crowns instead. Runnering may be copious on some of these *medium compact* plants.

3. *Small* plants varying in leaf number, branch crown formation, and runnering ability. Some small plants quickly produce a great many runners and daughter plants, and rapidly fill up and overreach the allotted planting area. Usually, smaller, free-runnering types produce no or few branch crowns in the planting year.

Obviously, there are also plant habits intermediate to the above.

Late in the season some compact medium plants may bear one to several small flower clusters. These flowering plants may prove to be two- or repeat-croppers in some seasons, or weak day-neutrals, a type of everbearer. Some small plants produce flowers very soon after setting. Later, they will produce branch crowns which flower also, and some runner plants, which may also flower through the late summer and fall. This last type is a strong expression of the multiple-cropping or everbearing habit. Strong day-neutrals usually do not produce as many runners as do single-cropping types.

Leaves produced later in the growing season tend to be shorter and smaller. As leaves get older, their petioles bend over until the leaflets touch the ground and flatten. Continued runner production widens the plant bed and makes it more dense. Late in the season runner, leaf and crown production slows down, and older leaves turn yellow or yellow-orange to red or red-purple. If the leaves are killed by frost, they become brown, and the later leaves fall over the crown area, affording a degree of winter protection.

In the second and later years, leaf, flower, and runner emergence patterns are similar to those of the planting year (expansion of crown leaf primordia followed by flower stalk primordia expansion), except that fruit recovery rather than vegetative production techniques is emphasized. Guttridge (1985) indicates that inflorescences emerge from the bud, on the average, after five to six leaves have emerged. The flowers in a cluster open in the same sequence in which they were initiated — from primary to quaternary. The crown has by now resumed growth and is producing new leaves. Flower anthesis (pollen shedding) occurs after about two more leaves have emerged, and fruit ripening after three more leaves have emerged.

It was thought that top and root growth took place alternately, as in many of the tree fruit crops. Although top vegetative growth is slowed considerably during fruit ripening and very warm periods (over 85°F or about 30°C), root growth need not stop in shaded or otherwise temperature-moderated soils. A nurseryman observed that soil temperatures in uncovered sandy soil can be 105°F (40.5°C) when air temperatures are 85 to 90°F (29.4 to 32.2°C), and that runner production and top growth ceased then (P. C. Massey, personal communication). Swartz found (Galletta et al., 1981) that fruit size of 'Tribute' and 'Tristar' strawberries was related inversely to temperatures in the root zone 6 weeks previous (when the inflorescences were still in the crown or just emerging). These observations suggest that root and top growth in the strawberry take place together, but that the root is the more sensitive partner to environmental stress, and perhaps the most limiting plant part in growth and development.

Environmental Interactions

In strawberry culture, the desired objective is the maximum production of fruit suitable for the selected market(s) at (a) preselected delivery time(s). Since strawberry flower bud initiation terminates the growth of the particular stem axis upon which it occurs, the salable product is harvested at the end of the vegetative cycle that produced it. However, the extended normally biennial fruit development period, the sympodial branching habit of the rosetted rootstock or crown, the perennial nature of the plant, and the continual and subtle interactions between the plant and its environment make the strawberry a challenging crop to produce.

The biennial fruit development period is a common feature of perennial plants, wherein flower buds initiated in one growing season expand and form fruit in the following growing season. The grower thus has the added cost and concern of winter protection and at least an additional 6 months of culture. The sympodial growth habit of the crown refers to the shunting aside of the crown axis ending in a floral primordium, and the continuation of crown growth by the next lower bud(s).

This permits a crown to develop several branch crowns and inflorescences. The grower must then be concerned with balancing top and root growth, vegetative and reproductive development, and development within and among crowns. Growth balancing becomes more critical if the planting is intended for fruiting several times instead of just once.

The grower must successfully manipulate various physical and chemical properties of the soil medium; optimize and modify the growth influencing climatic features light, temperature, precipitation, and air movement; and control neighboring biotic populations to achieve suitable plant and fruit growth and development. To add to the challenge, environmental stimuli influence the strawberry in concert, rather than singly.

Soil needs. The critical limiting features of strawberry root systems are typically shallow soil penetration; very fine, delicate, and short-lived feeder roots; and sensitivity to water-saturated soil, to high salt levels, and to nematodes, certain root fungi, and soil insects. These strawberry root concerns should be addressed in choosing and preparing a planting site because the establishment of a strong, healthy root system is an important prerequisite for good plant top vegetative development and flower and fruit production.

Soil features desirable for strawberry culture are:

Good internal drainage	Even contour
Good moisture retention	Ease of working (tilth)
Water availability	Temperature (moderate)
Soil depth	Modest salt levels
Humus (organic matter)	Freedom from noxious weeds
Freedom from nematodes	Freedom from insects and soil disease
Native fertility	organisms

It is necessary to remember that the strawberry root system consists of two types of roots, which vary in structure, function, longevity, and stress reaction (White, 1927; Darrow, 1966; Wilhelm and Nelson, 1970, 1980). White noted the presence of large, adventive roots which differentiated slowly from the crown, and fibrous branch roots, which differentiate rapidly from the large roots. The stout, adventive roots have been called primary, structural, or "peg" roots by other authors; the branch roots or rootlets are also known as secondary, lateral, feeder, or "white" roots.

Wilhelm and Nelson (1970), from their developmental and anatomical studies of strawberry roots in fumigated California soils, reported a number of significant findings which influence strawberry culture [summarized by Wilhelm and Nelson (1980)]. They include the following:

1. Root system penetration may improve to 6 to 8 ft (1.8 to 2.4 m), and be abundantly branched, consisting of perennial structural roots and their major branches, and fasicles (many-branched) of *transient* feeder rootlets.
2. Structural roots conduct absorbed water and nutrients upward and elaborated

foods downward, and store food reserves as starch. Spring growth and flowering is heavily dependent on these stored reserves.

3. Feeder rootlets have no cambia, are composed only of primary tissues, have a life expectancy of a few days to a few weeks, and are concerned primarily with water and nutrient absorption.

4. The strawberry root rarely has true root hairs, but the many-branched feeder rootlet fasicles appear like hairs. Dead fasicles are constantly replaced by new rootlets, often at the same site. *Thus the plant can mine the same soil area repeatedly* for water and nutrients.

5. Root and feeder rootlet growth occurs primarily during nonfruiting and vegetative dormancy periods. Late and heavy-cropping depletes stored reserves and may inhibit rootlet regeneration in the dormant period.

6. Roots depend on soil oxygen. Feeder rootlets, especially, do not tolerate drastic soil water content and oxygen-level variation. Soil waterlogging, especially if prolonged, will kill rootlets immediately or up to several months later, depending on the duration of standing soil water, and on temperatures following the waterlogged period. Waterlogging also favors the development of, and invasion by, root-damaging fungi.

The significance of these findings should not be altered by culture on nonfumigated or less deep soils of other textures. We would expect the root development pattern to be the same and to vary in degree rather than in kind.

Since strawberry culture is successful on a broad variety of mineral soil types, and over a wide range of soil reactions (pH 4 to 8.5), and in view of the root habit and development patterns noted above, *critical soil factors* would seem to be soil porosity, water relationships and availability, depth, tilth, freedom from noxious pests, and native and potential fertility, in that order.

Strawberry plant root size is pretty well established within 2 to 3 months of the first growing season. Thereafter, extensive top growth minimizes root expansion. It is critical to maintain soil aeration to keep the feeder roots alive and functional through the season. (Eastern U.S. growers are familiar with the growth spurts following shallow tillages early in the life of a planting.) The repeated assertion that best growth and yield is attained on *deep, fertile sandy loams* indicates that the slightly larger than medium pore space of these soils affords the best compromise between water retention capacity and rapid internal drainage.

Sandy loams usually have a large enough clay and organic matter fraction that water and nutrient retention is good and that the soil works easily and should not compact badly. The many sandy loam or loam soils available in nonarid growing regions usually have a soil reaction on the slightly acid side and within the optimum range (pH 5 to 7) for strawberry culture. Sandy loams also respond better to soil fumigation, adapt better to frequent harvest and irrigation schedules, accumulate less salt over the life of the planting, and have fewer minor element problems than do other soil types (Welch et al. 1982).

It is usually pointed out that the largest and latest production of berries is from plants grown on cool, heavy, fertile soils, but that the drainage of these soils is poor and compaction may be a problem. Heavy soils can be used by planting on raised beds, using an organic or synthetic mulch, choosing a cultivar that will tolerate clayey, moist soils, reducing tractor passage, applying chemicals through the irrigation system, subsoiling, and so on.

Similarly, the earliest and most profitable berries are grown on light sandy soils, but they tend to be infertile and subject to drought stress. These weaknesses can be reduced by soil-building programs to incorporate more organic matter, increased nutrition, cultivar choice, preplanting fumigation, supplemental irrigation, and so on.

Gently sloped sites are preferred to either steep or flat sites, because of improved soil and air drainage. Southern and western exposures of sloping sites warm more quickly in the spring, and plants start earlier than those on northern and eastern exposures, which retain more moisture, are cooler, and start plant growth later. On any soil type it may be wiser to either avoid or try to level low spots that might accumulate water and disease organisms.

The water supply should provide 10 to 50 gal/min per acre of good-quality water for strawberries, preferably toward the upper end of the range to avoid the necessity for a reservoir (Welch et al., 1982). Laboratory testing of the water should indicate low amounts of sodium, chloride, and boron. If irrigation water contains more than 700 to 900 ppm total salts, special care may be required in applying the water to prevent salt from accumulating to toxic levels. Drip irrigation, although expensive to install, may effect considerable savings in water use. Drip irrigation may be beneficial where water supplies are marginal or expensive, and where soils have a high salt content, low infiltration rate, or poor drainage.

Certainly soils with hardpans should be avoided unless the hardpans can be broken up or penetrated prior to planting. When possible, soils shallower than 8 in. (20 cm) should not be planted to strawberries. Depths of 12 to 36 in. (30.5 to 91 cm) or more are preferred, particularly if the soil preparation can be thorough enough that the strawberry roots can penetrate and ramify the entire area. One of the advantages of ridged bed culture is the thorough soil preparation, which ensures that strawberry roots will have at least 10 in. (25.4 cm) of fine, aerated soil through which to grow.

Modification of the strawberry planting site 1 to 3 years prior to strawberry planting is often recommended. This permits the establishment of crop rotations and cultural practices that will reduce nematode, weed, insect, and disease populations in the soil. Planting of strawberries after strawberries, nightshade family vegetables (*Verticillium*), corn (crown borer), sods (grubs), or soybeans (*Sclerotium*) is not advised without intervening soil fumigation.

Climatic influences.   The strawberry is very responsive to environmental stimuli, which may alter its normal developmental patterns. The principal climatic influences upon strawberry fruit yield, plant growth, and formation of runner plants were identified previously as *temperature, precipitation, light,* and *air.* Aspects of each climatic factor that influenced fruit crop growth were discussed thoroughly in Chapter 2. It was noted that the climatic factors usually interacted in influencing plant growth, but that one factor was usually dominant in triggering a given plant response. However, the effect of the dominant factor in eliciting that plant response may be shown to vary with plant species, cultivar within species, growing season, time within the growing season, and growing locale.

Growth-response relationships. There are basically three commercial strawberry plant products. In order of increasing complexity, they are nursery stock or runner plants (RP), fruit quantity or yield (Y), and fruit yield possessing certain desirable fruit qualities (YQ) for certain market outlets. Each of these plant end products is the result of a sequence of plant organ developments resulting from (1) the massing of a critical level of usable nutrient or elaborated plant product reserves, (2) an environmental triggering stimulus, and (3) the period necessary for development. Since most internal plant processes are chemical or physical in nature, the rate of development to a recognizable plant response is temperature conditioned. Development also depends on having at least threshold levels of soil moisture, atmospheric and dissolved soil oxygen, atmospheric carbon, and dissolved soil inorganic plant nutrients. Sunlight provides heat energy and emission spectral wavelengths, without which such processes as photosynthesis and photoperiodic responses would not occur.

As an example of product *component analysis,* let us trace the chain of events that produces high fruit yields in strawberry. In its simplest form, fruit yield (Y) = fruit number (N) by average fruit size (S):

$$Y = N \times S \qquad (1)$$

This relationship is basically true whether the yield is measured by volume or by weight, from plant areas, single plants, or plant crowns within a single plant.

Fruit number (N) depends on the number of fruit set (or developed) (Fs) from each inflorescence (Infl), by the number of inflorescenses (#Infl) and the size of the inflorescences (Infl. Sz), or by the total number of flowers (#Fl), giving

$$N = Fs \times (\#Infl \times Infl. \ Sz) \qquad (2)$$

but #Fl = #Infl × Infl. Sz; hence

$$N = Fs \times \#Fl \qquad (2a)$$

Also, fruit size (S) = number of achenes = position in inflorescence (Pos) by inflorescence branching pattern (Br) by completeness of pollination and fertilization (Fert). A substitute expression for fruit size would be

$$S = Pos \times Br \times Fert \qquad (3)$$

Hence a more complete expression for fruit yield would be the substitute

$$Y = (Fs \times \#Fl) \ (Pos \times Br \times Fert) \qquad (4)$$

all implied in expression (1). Note that the total number of inflorescences and flowers may be negatively related to the size and set of fruit (as one increases, the other decreases). Similarly, fertilization and fruit set are not fully independent processes.

Fruit is borne at *flower initiation sites* suitably dispersed around the *bearing area* on a structurally supportive *plant body*. In strawberries the supportive and bearing areas are telescoped into the primary and branch crowns. The potential flower initiation sites (FIS) are the primary and axillary buds or *meristems* at each node along each crown. Thus crowns (C) times expanded leaves on each crown (L) minus runners (R), which are expanded vegetative structures and no longer potential floral sites, should roughly equal the potential flower initiation sites. Only the unexpanded leaves will not be included.

$$FIS = (C \times L) - R \qquad (5)$$

Presumably, the more crowns and leaves and the fewer runners present on a plant at the end of the growing season, the more flowers and inflorescences will be present on that strawberry plant the following spring. However, the only buds that will produce flowers are those that are on crowns which become the terminal growing axis (terminalization or T), and in which the terminal bud differentiates into a floral axis (the process of flower bud initiation = FBI). Further, only those initiated inflorescences that expand or develop (FBD = flower bud development) the following spring are counted as the number of flowers (#F1) in expression (2a). Expression (2a) can now be expanded to show the dependency of one plant response to another:

$$N = Fs \times (FBD \times FBI \times T \times FIS) \qquad (6)$$

The photosynthetic surface (plant volume or leaf area = leaf # × average leaf size); the reserve storage capacity (crown # × crown dia.) and the land area fill (# plants or crowns/unit area) of the plant should also relate to the plant yield. In various experiments all of these factors have been positively correlated with yield (as one increases, so does the other). However, many of the experiments have demonstrated the law of diminishing returns. At some point the plants got too large, too crowded, or too vegetative, and flowering and fruiting declined. In some plants branching and flowering were very prolific, and flower set and fruit size were both poor. Thus yield predictability varies for each clone, growing locale, and cultural system. Consistently high yielding strawberry cultivars seem to take different paths to success. An overall yield formula should take into account the following factors:

$$Y = PS \times RC \times BA \times PN \times FIS \times \#Fl \times N \times S \qquad (7)$$

where Y = total fruit yield

PS = plant fill, probably in crowns/unit area, with an estimate of crown size

RC = root capacity in terms of a size × uptake index

BA = bearing area, probably easiest measured by plant volume or its components

PN = net photosynthesis, which accounts for both total carbohydrate production rate and the energy lost in respiration

FIS = potential initiation sites measure by relationship (5)

#Fl = realized floral potential count − inflor.# × size, or just flower #

N = realized fruit set or number of developed fruit

S = average fruit size of the entire crop, as determined by a sample from each harvest

Thus the total fruit yield is dependent on the maturation and functioning of every organ of the strawberry plant. And the extent of maturation and functioning realized by each organ in sequence depends on the changing environments in which they develop.

Runner plant production (RP) depends on the initial number of crowns planted, the number of axillary meristem sites produced (leaves × crowns again), the number of axillary buds that expand as primary runners, the number of primary runners that produce first daughter plants, the number of first daughter plants that produce runners and second daughter plants, and so on.

The yield of fruit having certain qualities such as shipping merit (attractiveness, good size, color, firmness, skin texture and gloss, etc.) is determined by grading the total yield into its utility classes. The knowledgeable grower may shift the proportion of the crop into one market class or another by appropriate cultural and harvesting emphases.

Examples of experiments that sought strawberry growth response correlations (yield components and others) are:

1. Nicoll and Galletta (1987), studying everbearing and Junebearing strawberry growth and fruiting in growth chamber and greenhouse tests, found:
    a. Dry weight of reproductive organs (a *yield* measure) *positively correlated* with number of inflorescences, fruits, leaves, and crowns, but *negatively correlated* with weight of roots or runners, total or average leaf area or leaf petiole length, or plant volume (size).
    b. *Plant volume* (a vigor measurement) was *positively related* to leaf, crown, root, and runner dry weights and leaf area and petiole length, but *negatively related* to crown number, reproductive dry weight, fruit number, and inflorescence number.
    c. *Inflorescence number* related positively with leaf and crown number and crown size, but negatively to runner weight, leaf size, and plant size.
    d. *Fruit number* related positively to number of inflorescences, leaves, and crowns, but negatively to root and runner weight, leaf area and size, leaf petiole length, and plant size.

2. Swartz et al. (1982), studying the effect of crown density per unit area in matted row culture for four cultivars, two seasons, two bed heights, and two bed widths, and using the general yield formula

$$\frac{\text{yield}}{\text{acre}} = \frac{\text{plants}}{\text{acre}} \times \frac{\text{crowns}}{\text{plant}} \times \frac{\text{trusses}}{\text{crown}} \times \frac{\text{flowers}}{\text{truss}} \times \% \text{ fruit set} \times \text{fruit weight}$$

found:
    a. Cultivars showed not only inherent yield differences in both seasons, but differences in yield components as well. The superior yield of 'Earliglow' over 'Redchief' in 1980 traced to larger fruit size and more crowns despite

féwer trusses per crown. In 1981, 'Allstar's' yield superiority over 'Earli-glow' traced to larger fruit size, but 'Allstar' outyielded 'Guardian' because of improved fruit set.

b. Bed height did not influence yield; the superior yield of narrow 12 in. (30 cm) over wide 24 in. (61 cm) bed widths was not traceable to crown density, flower truss number, flower truss size, fruit set, or fruit size.

c. At lower crown densities there are more fruits per crown because of more inflorescences per crown, and in some years, increased fruit set.

d. Highest fruit yields per crown occur at the lowest crown densities due to more and larger fruits, but maximum yields per unit area occur at medium crown densities per unit area.

e. Percent fruit set decreases as the number of flowers, inflorescences, or crowns/unit area increases. The crown contribution to fruit set is less important.

f. Fruit size also decreases as the number of inflorescences, crowns, flowers, or fruits per unit area increases. The fruit crowding effect was striking in both years; the crowding effects of the other organs was significant in one out of two years.

3. Popenoe and Swartz (1985), studying the yield components response of two cultivars in four or five cultural systems over a 2-year period, found:

a. One cultivar ('Redchief') yielded very well when summer planted; the other ('Allstar') did not.

b. For spring-planted trials, yields were better in the first year but not the second in the very closely spaced single-hill system known as a *ribbon row*. The increased ribbon row yields in the first year were attributed to an increase in crown number and leaf area.

c. Type of soil fumigation, bed height, and type of irrigation did not influence yields, but soil type did. Deeper (24 in. or 61 cm), heavier (more than 30% clay) soils outyielded shallow (6 in. or 15 cm), lighter soils (less than 20% clay) by 50%. "Raised beds were slightly more productive in heavier, more poorly drained soils."

These studies, among many, may serve to illustrate the complex interactions of strawberry cultivars in yield response to soil, season, locale, and cultural system variation. It is important to note that *the net effect of a yield component in the same cultivar varies as the environment in which the cultivar is grown changes.*

Climatic influences on strawberry growth responses.

Root Growth. The effects of constant root temperatures on plant part composition and mineral nutrition of strawberries were studied independently by Roberts and Kenworthy (1956) in Michigan and Proebsting (1957) in California. 'Robinson', a berry adapted to the north, was grown at 10°F (18°C) root temperature increments from 45 to 75°F (7.2 to 23.9°C). Root growth (dry weight) was good over the entire root temperature range but was a little heavier at the lower temperatures (45 and 55°F) than at the higher temperatures, especially when soil nutrients were higher. Leaf weight (dry) and total plant dry weight were heavier with each increase in root temperature and reached maximum levels at the highest root temperature (75°F). Leaf potassium accumulated with increasing root temperature. There was no change in either root or leaf accumulation of other mineral elements or protein content associated with change in root temperature.

'Lassen' and 'Shasta', adapted to warmer climates, were grown at root temperatures ranging from 45 to 90°F (7.2 to 32.2°C). Temperatures above 90°F had previously been found unsuitable. Dry weight partioning of plants grown at the six different root temperatures led to the following observations. Total plant growth dropped at the extremes, was satisfactory when roots were in the 55 to 85°F (12.8 to 29.4°C) range for 'Shasta' and 45 to 85°F (7.2 to 29.4°C) range for 'Lassen'. Optimum total growth was made at root temperatures of 75°F (23.9°C). Root growth for both varieties was heaviest at root temperatures of 45 to 65°F and optimum at 55°F. Crown growth was optimum at soil temperatures of 65°F for 'Shasta' and 45°F for 'Lassen'. Runners developed only at soil temperatures ranging from 65 to 90°F (18.3 to 32.2°C) and were optimum at 75°F. Fruit developed only at the lower soil temperatures (45 to 55°F, 7.2 to 12.8°C) and was optimum at 45°F. Leaves and petioles grew best at soil temperatures of from 55 to 85°F, optimizing at 75°F. Root temperatures had little effect on nitrogen accumulation in the major plant organs. Root potassium declined with increasing root temperature. Leaf and runner potassium peaked at soil temperatures of 65°F; root potassium levels varied with cultivar; and crown potassium increased and fruit potassium decreased with increasing temperatures.

In summary, root growth is best at cool (55°F, 12.8°C), crown growth at moderate (65°F, 18.3°C), leaf growth at moderately warm (75°F, 23.8°C), and fruit development at quite cool (45°F, 7.2°C) root temperatures. The relationship of nutrient element accumulation and root temperature varies with the nutrient being considered, the plant part analyzed, and the cultivar.

Crown and Leaf Growth. Crown and leaf growth occur over a very wide range of air temperatures, from just above freezing to about 95°F (35°C). Growth is more rapid as temperature and daylength (photoperiod) increase, up to a point, leaf growth being optimum between 68 and 79°F (20 to 26°C) and averaging 73°F (22.8°C) (Darrow, 1936). Leaf petiole length is particularly sensitive to temperature and photoperiod effects (Guttridge, 1985). Leaf elongation was increased by higher irrigation level and by growth under black plastic mulch (Renquist et al., 1982). Both higher irrigation and mulch increased soil temperatures in the upper 7.9 in. (20 cm). Leaf area increased and leaf emergence rate decreased in older runner plants of three Junebearing cultivars (Jahn and Dana, 1970). Leaf area and petiole length increases due to long days are normally followed by shorter and smaller leaves in late summer and fall (Darrow, 1966). This size reduction can be overcome or lessened by runner removal or deblossoming in June- or everbearers (Darrow, 1966; Jahn and Dana, 1966; Forney and Breen, 1985). Deblossoming of the everbearing clone 'Brighton' also caused crown, leaf, and root dry weight increases, increased starch content of crowns, petioles, and roots, but decreased net photosynthesis (Forney and Breen, 1985).

Crown branching of Junebearing strawberries normally occurs after runnering, when the daylength becomes too short for runner formation (average of 10 hours) (Darrow and Waldo, 1934). Runner removal increases and may hasten branch crown development. Everbearers, Alpine strawberries, and Junebearers that are inherently poor runner producers produce many more branch crowns than runnering Junebearers do in a growing season.

The *rest period* (quiescence or ectodormancy) in the strawberry is caused by repeated short days and is conditioned by low temperatures (Darrow and Waldo, 1934). The inductive short-day period is thought to be 4 to 6 weeks (Guttridge, 1985). Darrow and Waldo (1934) felt that strawberry clones have a characteristic temperature–daylength response which determines their regional adaptation. "Southern varieties grow under short days at relatively low-growing temperatures and need little rest or no dormant period. Northern varieties grow very little under short days and, if first exposed to short daily light periods, require a low-temperature dormant period to break their rest period". An important feature of the "prerest" period is that top-growth reduction produces an excess of carbohydrates and other reserves, which are stored in various tissues of the crown, the petioles, and the primary roots, mainly as starch. Simple starch detection tests have been devised to determine when nursery plants are dormant enough to dig.

Darrow and Waldo (1934) considered that all varieties would respond to a period of freezing or subfreezing temperatures to break the rest period. They felt that additional daylength treatments would partially break the rest in some cultivars but not in others. The cumulative period of low temperature needed to break the rest is called the *chilling requirement*. We now know that effective chilling temperatures may range from about 30 to 50°F (−1 to 10°C), with all temperatures in the range not being as effective as others. Each species has its own temperature range pattern for chilling requirement. The strawberry pattern has not been completely elaborated, but temperatures of 28.4 to 43.7°F (−2 to 6.5°C) seem effective, 49 to 50°F (9.5 to 10°C) less effective, and 57.2°F (14°C) ineffective (Guttridge, 1985).

Cold Hardiness. In the dormant period, the lowest temperature that crowns can experience without exhibiting immediate, partial, or delayed injury is important in determining the northern limits of the plant's adaptation. Species and cultivars of strawberries vary from very tender such as the 'Ambato' *F. chiloensis,* which is killed in Maryland, to clones such as 'Dunlap', 'Ogallala', and 'Fort Laramie', which will tolerate −40 to −50°F (−40 to −45.6°C). Crowns of many cultivars will be injured at temperatures of 20 to 25°F (−6.6 to −3.9°C) and killed outright at 10 to 15°F (−12.2 to −9.4°C). These facts led to the practice of applying a winter mulch for winter protection after the plants have hardened. By the time autumn temperatures of 20°F (−6.6°C) have been reached, plants are considered to have hardened and mulch application to be safe. Crowns can also be injured by low temperatures in the late winter and early spring when the chilling requirement has been met. Such late injury can be particularly severe if sudden low temperatures follow a mild period. For this reason the winter mulch is retained until growth has just started under the mulch.

However, hardy clones such as 'Catskill' can sustain cold damage under certain conditions, even though well hardened and fully dormant. Boyce and Smith (1967), using artificial freezing of dormant 'Catskill' crown sections and electrolytic injury evaluation, showed that injury increased (1) as freezing rates increased, (2) the longer the crowns remained frozen, and (3) with repeated freezing and thawing. Thawing rates increased injury only when they were very rapid. Plants that had started growing quickly lost their resistance to low temperatures.

Marini and Boyce (1979) demonstrated that exposure of acclimated (hardened) 'Catskill' plants to sublethal low temperatures resulted in a variety of anomalous growth patterns and visible crown tissue browning. In this test potted plants were frozen slowly at temperatures of 32 to −4°F (0 to −20°C), thawed for 24 hours, returned to cold storage for a month, and then brought into a greenhouse for growth and fruiting. All plants survived the 0 and −4°C (24.8°F) temperatures; all plants were killed at −4°F (−20°C). The sublethal temperatures were 17.6°F (−8°C), 10.4°F (−12°C), and 3.2°F (−16°C), with 50% of the plants calculated killed at 9.5°F (−12.5°C). Plants frozen at the sublethal temperatures exhibited late leaf emergence, early runner emergence, slightly narrower leaves, more deformed leaves, less leaf dry weight on nonfruiting plants, considerably reduced numbers of flowering plants, and fewer blossoms per plant.

Runner Production. Runner production is decidedly favored by long days and high temperatures. If a clone produces any runners at all, it will do so under longer days and higher temperatures, as demonstrated elegantly by Darrow (1936) and by Durner et al. (1984). Darrow's greenhouse study compared a number of cultivars grown under natural short days beginning in September with a 16-hour day at 70°F (21.1°C), 60°F (15.5°C), or 55°F (12.8°C) temperatures. Runnering only took place at 70°F (not lower). In the Durner et al. studies, runnering at a constant 70°F yielded an average 2.0, 1.2, and 0.4 runners per plant for long-day, night-interruption, and short-day photoperiods, respectively. Junebearing (JB) plants (Fig. 3–5) produced no runners under short days until average daily temperatures were 75.2°F (24°C) and many more runners at an average 82.4°F (28°C). Everbearers (EB) and day-neutrals (DN) produced equal numbers of runners under short days across temperature regimes averaging 60.8°to 82.4°F (16 to 28°C). Plants of all flowering habit classes (JB, EB, and DN) produced runners at all four temperature regimes (averaging 16, 20, 24, and 28°C) when grown under simulated long days (9 hours + 3 hour night interruption). Runner production was generally best at the higher temperatures.

In many experimental and commercial strawberry plant or fruit production situations, plant establishment, runner expansion, and daughter plant production have been increased and accomplished earlier by judicious supplemental water and nutrient applications. Rates and timing of water and fertilizer applications vary markedly with production region, planting time, cultural system, and cultivar.

Flowering and Fruiting. Flowering and fruiting in strawberries are very complex processes, dependent on a series of growth steps that establish and develop a plant body, along which potential flowering sites are produced. The conversion of these buds from vegetative to floral stem tips (flower bud initiation) depends on an intricate control system involving photoperiod and temperature. Strawberry cultivars fall into one of three classes with respect to flower initiation and development. They generally flower and fruit *once, twice,* or *more than two times* per year.

The vast majority of strawberry cultivars are 'single croppers', also known as 'Junebearers' or 'short-day' or 'noneverbearing' types. Single-cropping temperate-zone strawberries are called *facultative short-day plants.* They require daylengths shorter than about 14 hours or temperatures less than about 59°F (15°C) for flower induction (Guttridge, 1985). Flower *induction* occurs in the leaf upon exposure to a repeated photoperiod and/or temperature, which causes production of a flower bud. Flower *initiation* is the set of physical and chemical changes that occur in the bud upon receipt of the floral stimulus from the leaf. Flower *differentiation* is the actual development of floral organs, flowers, and an inflorescence within the bud. Flower *development* is the visible expansion of the flower cluster out of the bud. In practice, induction, initiation, and differentiation (the microscopic within leaf and bud events) are referred to as flower bud initiation (FBI) and the visible flower cluster emergence from the bud as flower bud development (FBD). Pomologists often use the less precise terms "fruit bud" development, initiation, and so on.

In areas such as Norway, flower induction occurs in August at latitudes of up to 69°N, when the natural daylength exceeds 21 hours (Heide, 1977). In cultivars such as 'Zefyr' and 'Glima', which are adapted to Norway, temperature becomes the dominant determinant; and temperatures less than 64.4°F (18°C) are necessary to induce flowering at 24 hours of daylight. In cultivars such as the old 'Missionary', widely grown in the southern United States and in Central America, photoperiod becomes the dominant factor. In Maryland, 'Missionary' needed 10- or 12-hour photoperiods in 1928 to produce flower clusters in 1929. The normal photoperiod in 1928 under hot summer conditions produced no flowers. In the following year (1930) 'Missionary' plants produced an average of 71, 54, and 24 flowers per plant from 1929 summer inductive daylengths of 10, 12, and 'normal' (14 to 15 hours) (Darrow and Waldo, 1934). Darrow and Waldo (1934) also pointed out: (1) that flower bud formation takes place when daylength is too short for branch crown formation; and (b) that over 80 cultivars and species with a partial rest period continued flowering or fruiting in the greenhouse until July or August of the next year, but that the same 80 clones formed no flowers after they had experienced a complete rest period.

Single-cropping strawberries vary widely in the minimum number of short-day *photoinductive cycles* (day–night combinations) necessary to induce flowering. The minimum number varies between 7 and 14, but can be as much as 23 cycles (Guttridge, 1985). The critical photoperiod to induce flowers varies at temperatures above 59°F (15°C), various laboratory studies suggesting that it lay between 12 and 16, 12 and 14, 11 and 14, 11 and 15, 13 and 15, and 13 and 16 hours. The optimal daylength for flower induction is probably between 8 and 11 hours. Outdoor critical inductive photoperiod in September in northern temperate climates is suggested to have a threshold of 14 hours (Guttridge, 1985).

Most single-cropping (noneverbearing) strawberries can be made to reflower more or less continuously (appear like everbearers) if grown under low or cool temperatures. Junebearers are grown like everbearers in climates having mild winters (such as California and Florida).

Flower induction can be inhibited by gibberellic acid (GA) treatments, as well as by growing the strawberry plants under long days or high temperatures, or by interrupting the dark period with a 1 to 3 hour night interruption or by completely chilling the plant. Successful night interruption treatments in Junebearing strawberries indicate that floral induction is controlled by a long dark period rather than by a short light period (Borthwick and Parker, 1952). Interestingly, if flower bud differentiation in a nursery has occurred prior to digging, partial chilling or GA application may increase emerged inflorescence branch length and initiate more rapid emergence from the bud. Theoretically, flower bud initiation may be aided by minimizing water and nutrient supplies at the appropriate time, if sufficient plant growth had been made up until then. Practically, in a field production situation, the timing and the intensity of the water and nutrient deprivation would be difficult unless weather and growth patterns could be carefully monitored with modern electronic sensing, recording, and data accumulation devices.

Darrow (1966) points out that the strawberry harvest period lengthens as one proceeds from higher latitudes toward the equator. Part of this increase in harvest season is due to an extended period of mild inductive temperatures and photoperiods in the fall in more southern latitudes. Additionally, there are three temperature zones in the southeastern United States and in California where (1) flower bud initiation continues through the winter, (2) flower bud initiation occurs each fall and each spring, and (3) flower bud initiation occurs each fall and in some springs. (These three zones roughly correspond to USDA hardiness zones 10 [average minimum winter temperatures 30 to 40°F (-1 to 4.4°C), 9 (average winter minimum 20 to 30°F (-6.6 to -1°C)), and 8 (average winter minimum 10 to 20°F (-12.2 to -6.6°C)], respectively.) Spring-initiated fruit can be recognized as large primaries ripening at the end of the harvest season and known as a 'crown crop'. In areas such as the Coastal Plain of the Carolinas, there is not a temporal separation between the 'crown' and the fall-initiated crop. Darrow concludes that the temperature-sensitive strawberry clones adapted to the mildest areas, if grown under short days and cool temperature, as in the Central American highlands, would be everbearing (flower and fruit continuously).

Everbearing is the other general strawberry flowering habit class. Additionally, clones regularly bearing more than one crop a year have been called perpetuals, four-seasons, rebloomers, remontants, and most recently "day-neutrals". None of these terms accurately describes this category of plants. In the generally three wild species sources of the everbearing trait *F. vesca, F. virginiana,* or *F. virginiana glauca*), the everbearing clones are native to the northern or elevated ranges of their natural distributions.

In the diploid wood strawberry, everbearing and runnerless traits are controlled by a single recessive Mendelian gene each. The Alpine cultivars of today are homozygous recessive individuals for each character, and they breed true. Expression of the everbearing character in Alpines is direct. They either do or do not bloom continuously; there are no intermediate situations.

Cultivated octoploid everbearers, in contrast, have always displayed variation in the expression of the summer- and fall-fruiting character. Some everbearers produce a spring and fall crop only, much like the two-cropping Junebearers. Others may produce a midsummer crop only, a sporadic summer and a good fall crop, a reasonable but cyclic summer and fall crop, a cyclic late summer and heavy fall crop, or a small but steady supply of fruit through the growing season. Bringhurst, who introduced the *F. virginiana glauca* source of the everbearing habit into cultivated strawberries, recognized two "strengths" of day neutrality. He called them "weak" or "strong day-neutrals" depending on the proportion of daughter plants bearing flowers in the summer nursery. Older everbearers had been classed as facultative long-day plants.

Many people (Durner et al., 1984) feel that Junebearing, everbearing, and day-neutral clones represent three distinct classes on the basis of short-day promotion of Junebearing, long-day promotion of everbearing, and no day-neutral difference in flowering associated with photoperiod. However, their temperature × photoperiod trials indicate similar flower development patterns for temperature and photoperiod for all three types. The major difference is a descending order of temperature sensitivity as one progresses from JB to EB to DN. Indeed, the simulated long-day (NI) flower production enhancement was most striking in day-neutrals. Nicoll and Galletta (1987), using Durner's maximum discriminatory temperature regime, tested the validity of variable summer-fruiting field-classified clones in a growth chamber and a greenhouse test. Tested clones included strong, weak, and very weak ("reverted") day-neutrals, and older everbearing and Junebearing types. The older everbearers and the weak day-neutrals had similar growth habits and induced as many or more flowers as did the strong day-neutrals, but did not mature as many fruits as the strong-day neutrals or have as high a reproductive effort. The very weak day-neutrals were large plants that behaved essentially like Junebearers.

In a phytotron test with SD versus NI, six light-level treatments, and Alpine seedlings compared with representatives of the previous field classes, Nicoll (1984) found NI enhancement of flower production in some weak and some strong day-neutrals, but not in others. Alpine was insensitive to photoperiod, and produced considerably more flowers than did the strongest day-neutral. Consideration of Durner et al.'s findings and their own led Nicoll and Galletta (1987) to agree with Darrow's conclusion (1966) that strawberry flowering ranges in a continuous gradation from obligate single-cropping ('Fairfax') to facultative short-day through the various degrees of everbearing or day-neutral to the most continuous Alpine. They proposed three morphologically recognizable expression stages of the everbearing habit: weak, intermediate, and strong day-neutral, and characterized them. Better descriptive terms might be single-cropping, double-cropping, and multiple-cropping, with intermediate forms such as single-cropping (two-crop tendency).

Vegetative environmental responses of all flowering habit classes of strawberries are the same but differ in degree (runnering, leaf growth, etc.). Several of the newer day-neutral clones are commercial successes. Cultural systems have had to be adjusted to grow them. Floral inductive cycle number seems to be as variable for everbearers as for Junebearers. Two Dutch everbearing cultivars flowered in Norway in all combinations of temperatures and photoperiod (Heide, 1977).

Fruit development. Vestiges of the original strawberry unisexual condition are still found in modern cultivars. Primary flowers have a strong tendency toward femaleness, many of the anthers being shrunken or not present at all. This can present pollination problems in wet weather or when the opening of later flowers is delayed by cool temperatures. Later-maturing flowers usually have abundant pollen, but often are effectively male. Pistils of late flowers often do not develop (set) even though coated with pollen, especially if early fruit set is good. There is considerable seasonal variation in such phenomena, but the exact cause is not known. Perhaps temperatures might have been too warm or too cool when the anthers were being differentiated in the primary flowers. Other abnormalities that seem to have a seasonal influence are fasciation and "receptacle reversion". In fasciation several stems and receptacles appear to grow together in the bud stage and emerge contorted. Fasciation actually results from a broadening and contorting of the receptacle when fall growth conditions are favorable (Darrow, 1966). 'Receptacle reversion' occurs when portions of the floral tissue become leaf or stem-like and even differentiate plantlets at the achenes or from around the calyx. In an unusual case, the senior author observed a runner growing from the tip of a partially developed fruit. The remainder of the berry appeared to be a normal green berry, and the short runner was already forming a daughter plant. Darrow (1966) illustrates a flower cluster growing from the end of a fruit.

Spring frost is the most common environmental hazard preventing normal fruit development. Parts of the flower show varying sensitivity to cold injury. Havis (1938) listed the order of cold sensitivity from most to least as receptacle, anthers, petals, stamen filaments. The most common cold damage injury observed after a light to medium freeze is a darkened receptacle with all other floral parts appearing sound. Achenes must be the most tender part of the receptacle, for distorted fruit resulting from killed embryos may have a normal-appearing receptacle surface. Perry and Poling (1986) established for two eastern U.S. and two western U.S. cultivars a critical temperature of 26.4°F (-3.1°C) for open and popcorn flower stages for frost injury. Blossoms will be killed below that temperature, not at or above it. Boyce and Strater (1984) established the temperatures at which 50% (T_{50}) of the appropriate flower stages would be killed. Eight cultivars with open blossoms had T_{50} values of 22.8 to 23.7°F (-5.1 to -4.6°C). Injury was more severe if ice crystals were present than if tissues were supercooled. Immature berries were one of the tenderest organs, having a T_{50} value of 29.1°F (-1.6°C) with ice crystals and 24.3°F (-4.3°C) without ice crystals. Unopened buds with visible petals were the least tender, with T_{50} values of 26.4°F (-3.1°C) with ice crystals and 22.3°I (-5.4°C) without ice crystals.

A number of physical and chemical characteristics of the fruit (shape, size, flavor, etc.) vary with climate. One of the most unusual was a report from Scotland in which strawberry yields were increased by 56% over three cropping years in sheltered as opposed to unsheltered plots. Crop differences between sheltered and unsheltered plots were greatest in spring after windy fall seasons. The shelters reduced the mean wind speed an average of 31%. Plant width, number of flower trusses per plant, and number of crowns per plant were increased in sheltered plots. Berry size, plant survival, number of trusses per crown and, number of berries per truss were not influenced by the wind. The author attributed the reduced yield in exposed plots to reduced vegetative vigor because of damage to leaf tissue. Whether the damage affected photosynthetic leaf activity from damage to the leaf mesophyll or whether the stomatal apparatus had been impaired was not clear (Waister, 1972).

Biological Competitors: Weeds, Diseases, and Pests

One of the most common causes of strawberry crop failure or lowered economic returns is competition from other plants, animals, or microorganisms for the strawberry plants' water, air, and nutrients. Strawberry plant growth and fruiting is reduced by competitors in one of three general ways: crowding (out), plant part destruction or removal, or invasion and parasitism.

Weeds are the principal cause of crowding competition. Fast-spreading grasses may literally "choke out" the strawberry by stealing its water and nutrient supply. Taller or vining broadleaf weeds may "shade out" the strawberry by intercepting most of the light before it reaches the berry plant leaves, or strangle the strawberry with creeping vines, tendrils, and so on. Highly successful seed-producing annual weeds may literally carpet the soil area with thousands of rapidly developing seedlings, which can crowd out the strawberry plants. Occasionally, parasitic plants such as dodder will invade a strawberry field and kill strawberry plants before the grower notices the invasion.

Plant part destruction or removal is most often caused by animal feeding, nesting, egg laying (oviposition), burrowing or passage through the field. Species of mammals, birds, and chewing or tunneling insects or slugs may eat all or part of strawberry leaves, crowns, roots, or fruit. Bird damage is usually confined to fruit pecking or removal. Plant crowns may be flattened by nesting birds and small mammals. Tunneling ants or rodents can badly damage root systems. Sucking insects, mites, and nematodes siphon off water and plant juices needed by the invaded plant part and others that it feeds. Sucking pests may also be vectors of virus pathogens. Wounds caused by animal feeding or passage may often be entry sites for other fungal and bacterial pathogens. Some plant losses are indirect. The loss of the most valuable primary berries because the adult female bud weevil lays her eggs in buds and damages the pedicles of early-maturing flowers was noted in Chapter 2. The unrotted portion of partially rotted strawberry fruits, often used by the consumer, may not be eaten because of unpleasant flavors produced by some fungi (e.g., leather rot, caused by *Phytophthora cactorum*).

Parasitism either weakens a strawberry plant and eventually reduces its vigor, runnering, and fruit production, or it kills the plant outright. Fungi, viruses and virus-like disorders, bacteria, and nematodes are the principal disease-causing organisms in strawberries (see Fig. 3–6). Infective stages of these organisms are microscopic in size. By the time these organisms cause visible symptoms of illness in strawberry plants, the disease is serious. Visible symptoms of diseases and the severity of infections vary in strawberries. Some infections result in distinctive local lesions on leaves, stems, and runner — examples are the fungus diseases leaf blight and crown rot. Mild infestations are confined to the infected plant part and often die out with senescence of the affected part. With severe infestations and proper conditions for disease spread, lesions grow, coalesce, and kill the affected plant part, or render it unsalable, as in the case of fruit rots. With root diseases, top

FIGURE 3-6 Red stele–infected strawberry field, showing the difference in survival of resistant and susceptible cultivars.

symptoms are not visible until the disease has killed most of the root system. Then, as top growth demands sustenance from a weakened or reduced root system, plant tops typically discolor and become stunted and/or collapse (wilt).

Most virus diseases do not produce symptoms in cultivated strawberries, except for a gradual decline in plant vigor, runnering, and fruit production over a several-year period. To detect the presence of such viruses, a leaflet from the suspect strawberry is grafted into a sensitive indicator plant of a different strawberry species. If the donor plant has a virus disease that is transmitted across the graft union, new growth on the indicator plant will be dwarfed, distorted, or characteristically discolored, according to which virus(es) are present. In severe cases the indicator plant is killed.

Severe root nematode infestations will normally cause some plant top dwarfing. In very severe instances, groups of plants in drier field areas may die. Examination of the root systems of nematode-infected plants may show root galls or lesions characteristic of different plant parasitic genera. Three nematodes attack strawberry leaves and buds. Characteristic leaf distortion and plant dwarfing is visible in infected plants at certain times of the year. Bacterial diseases are very few in strawberry. The principal bacterial disease (angular leaf spot) may cause characteristic leaf lesions and occasional plant death.

Principal competitors and control measures. In strawberry culture general control strategies are used for the following purposes:

1. *Site selection* to avoid poorly drained areas, noxious weed concentrations, and areas with a history of high fungus populations.
2. *Preplanting site modification* to improve drainage by tiling, subsoiling, or raised-bed establishment; to reduce soil weed seed, nematode, and fungus populations by use of soil fumigants; to reduce competitor populations by use of nonselective herbicides on unplanted soils, by frequent tillage, and by instituting suitable crop rotations; and to reduce possible sources of infective agents by elimination of wild strawberry and related species from the vicinity of the planting.
3. *Planting* of tolerant or *resistant cultivars.* These exist for the principal fungus diseases, some mites and insects, and certain nematodes, (and for tolerance to high, unspecified virus titers) (see Maas, 1984);
4. Postplanting care.
   (a) *Sanitation:* pruning and removal from the planted area of unwanted runners, diseased leaves, and weed residues.
   Tillage: to aerate the soil, throw dirt up around crowns (rejuvenation), and destroy weeds.
   Chemical inhibitors and killers: selective compounds that eliminate or retard the growth of weeds, pests, and disease organisms.

Newer methods of biological control are becoming known to strawberry researchers, and integrated pest management (IPM) programs, so successful for other crops, are beginning to be applied to strawberry culture. An overdependence on chemical control measures in the past has led to legitimate environmental concerns by governing boards, government agencies, and the general public, and reduced effectiveness, as many weed, pest, and disease species have developed resistance to chemical pesticides.

Table 3–2 contains a sample of the weed plants that are commonly troublesome to strawberry growers in the United States. This list represents a small fraction of world strawberry weeds, since all types of plants may become pests in the culture of a crop as widely grown as the strawberry. The weeds listed can be controlled mechanically as well as chemically. Sample chemical control compounds are not listed since legal compound use approval varies from state to state and country to country.

Tables 3–3 (Pests) and 3–4 (Disease Organisms) are adapted largely from the excellent Maas reference (1984). This work could be more properly titled *Compendium of Strawberry Disorders,* inasmuch as noninfectious disorders and arthropod and mollusk pests of strawberry are included, along with infectious diseases. For more detail on control measures, disorder causes, host symptoms, areas where these disorders are important, and the history of the disorders, consult the references listed in the tables. Additionally, the Maas *Compendium* has a wealth of color and black-and-white illustrations of healthy and diseased strawberries.

TABLE 3-2 SAMPLE WEED SPECIES FREQUENTLY FOUND IN U.S. STRAWBERRY FIELDS[a]

COMMON NAME	SCIENTIFIC NAME	WEED CLASS
Quackgrass	*Agropypyron repens*	Perennial
Bermuda Grass	*Cynodon dactylon*	Perennial
Field bindweed	*Convolvulus arvensis*	Perennial
Horse nettle	*Solanum carolinense*	Perennial
Canada thistle	*Cirsium arvense*	Perennial
Hedge bindweed	*Convolvulus sepium*	Perennial
Red sorrel	*Rumex acetosella*	Perennial
Yellow nutsedge	*Cyprus esculentus*	Perennial
Crabgrasses	*Digitaria sanguinalis* and *ischaemum*	Annual grass
Barnyard grass	*Echinochola crusgalli*	Annual grass
Foxtails	*Setaria* spp.	Annual grass
Fall panicum	*Panicum dichotomiflorum*	Annual grass
Pigweeds	*Amaranthus* spp.	Broadleaf
Lamb's-quarter	*Chenopodium album*	Broadleaf, small-seeded
Spiny sida	*Sida spinosa*	Broadleaf, small-seeded
Chickweed	*Stellaria media*	Winter annual broadleaf
Peppergrass	*Lepidium* spp.	Winter annual broadleaf
Shepherd's purse	*Capsella bursa-pastoris*	Winter annual broadleaf
Prickly lettuce	*Lactuca scariola*	Winter annual broadleaf
Henbit	*Lamium amplexicaule*	Winter annual broadleaf
Cheat or chess	*Bromus* spp.	Winter annual broadleaf
Carpetweed	*Mullugo verticillata*	Small-seeded broadleaf
Horseweed	*Conyza canadensis*	Broadleaf
Purslane speedwell	*Veronica peregrina*	Broadleaf
Stinkgrass	*Eragrastis cilianensis*	Annual grass
Dandelion	*Taraxacum officinale*	Perennial
Ragweed	*Ambrosia* spp.	Broadleaf
Smartweed	*Polygonum* spp.	Broadleaf
Evening primrose	*Oenothera* spp.	Broadleaf
Morning-glory	*Ipomea purpurea*	Annual broadleaf
Cocklebur	*Xanthium* spp.	Broadleaf

Source: Hemphill (1980); Skroch and Monaco (1980); Ahrens (1982); Ag consultant (1984).

[a]Seeds sprouting from mulching materials may prove troublesome: ryes, wheats, vetch, barley, etc.

CULTURE

Fruit Production Systems

Having chosen a strawberry culture site with a particular market outlet and fruit delivery time in mind, the actual production system you use should all be geared to deliver an *optimum amount* of high-quality fruit to that market when the *price structure* is *most favorable* to you. Note that we did not say "maximum amount". Trying to produce, handle, and deliver ever-increasing amounts of fruit is a common error that strains a grower's resources and usually depresses prices. There are a number of general cultural options from which to choose.

Planting exposure: open versus protected versus forced. Planting systems are called *open* if the planting is exposed to the normal atmospheric conditions (field culture) for the entire life of the planting. Covering a planting with a winter mulch is a minor protective adjustment. Almost all North American strawberry culture is considered open. Open culture is inexpensive but subject to all of the climatic variations. *Protected* culture involves either covering a field planting to simulate greenhouse culture at weather vulnerable times, or bringing the planting "indoors" by growing them within framed areas which can be covered at appropriate times. These methods are expensive and need trained personnel to make them effective. Protected culture is usually a device for timing the harvest. Sometimes, protected culture methods are referred to as "forcing" strawberries. True *forcing* culture involves bringing specially prepared nursery stocks into a covered growing environment during the dormant season. Forcing is the most expensive option but has a great profit potential and the highest managerial input.

Planting duration: one crop versus several crops. Planting establishment costs are very high and getting higher all the time. It is less expensive to establish a multicropping planting because plant density is usually much lower in a planting that will be carried for several years, and potential profits are higher from

TABLE 3-3 MAJOR U.S. STRAWBERRY PESTS

PEST CLASS	COMMON NAME ( )[a]	SCIENTIFIC NAME
Insects		
Piercing and sucking and mites	Strawberry aphids (L)	*Chaetosiphon fragaefolii* (Cockerell), *C. thomasi* (H.R.L.), and *C. minor* Forbes, *C. jacobi* H.R.L.
	Strawberry root aphid (L, B, R)	*Aphis forbesi* Weed
	Cyclamen mite (L)	*Steneotarsonemus pallidus* (Banks)
	Spider mites, two-spotted (L)	*Tetranychus urtricae* Koch and *T. telarius* L.
	Lygus or tarnished plant bugs (S)	*Lygus lineolaris* (Palisot de Beauvois) and other *Lygus* spp.
	Strawberry bud weevil (clipper) (Fl)	*Anthonomus signatus* Say
	Potato leafhopper (L)	*Empoasca fabae* (Harris)
Chewing	Black vine weevil (L, R, C)	*Otiorhynchus sulcatus* (F.)
	Strawberry root weevil (L, R, C)	*O. ovatus* L
	Obscure root weevil (L, R, C)	*Sciopithis obscurus* (Horn)
	White grubs (R)	*Phyllophaga* spp.
	Strawberry leafroller (L)	*Ancylis comptana fragariae* (Walsh & Riley)
	Strawberry rootworm (L, R)	*Paria fragariae* Wilcox
	Strawberry sap beetle	*Stelidota geminata* (Say)
Boring	Strawberry crown borer (C)	*Tyloderma fragariae* (Riley)
	Strawberry crown miner (C)	*Aristotelia fragariae* Busck.
	Strawberry crown moth (C)	*Synanthedon bibionipennis* (Bdvl)
Slugs	Arion slug (Fr)	*Arion subfuscus*

Source: After Maas (1984).

[a]Plant part attacked: B, leaf bud; C, crown; Fl, flower parts; Fr, fruit; L, leaves; R, root; S, seed.

TABLE 3-4 COMMON U.S. STRAWBERRY DISEASES AND CAUSAL ORGANISMS

CLASS OF ORGANISM	NAME OF DISEASE	PLANT PART AFFECTED[a]	CAUSAL ORGANISM[b]
Bacterium	Angular leaf spot	L, Syst	*Xanthomonas fragariae*
Fungus	Powdery mildew	L, Fr	*Sphaerotheca macularis*
	Leaf Scorch	L, S	*Diplocarpon earliana*
	Phomopsis leaf blight	L, Fr	*Phomopsis (Dendrophoma) obscurans*
	Leaf spot	L, R, etc.	*Mycosphaerella fragariae*
	Gray mold	Fr, C, R	*Botrytis cinerea*
	Anthracnose fruit rots (black spots)	Fr	*Colletotrichum* and *Gloeosporium* spp.
	Rhizopus rot (leak)	Fr	*Rhizopus* spp.
	Leather rot (vascular collapse)	Fr, C	*Phytophthora cactorum*
	Rhizoctonia fruit rot (hard rot)	Fr, B, C, L, R	*Rhizoctonia solani* and *fragariae*
	Red stele root rot	R	*Phytophthora fragariae*
	Verticillium wilt	R	*Verticillium albo-atrum*
	Black root rot	R	*Pythium* spp. and others
	Stunt	R	*Pythium* spp.
Virus and virus-like	Strawberry mottle	Syst	Aphid-vectored strain mottle virus
	Strawberry veinbanding	Syst	Aphid-vectored strain veinbanding virus
	Strawberry mild yellow edge	Syst	Aphid-vectored strain mild yellow edge virus
	Strawberry latent C	Syst	Aphid-vectored strain latent C virus
	Strawberry crinkle	Syst	Aphid-vectored strain crinkle virus
	Strawberry leaf roll	Syst	? ? strain leaf roll virus
	Strawberry feather leaf	Syst	? ? virus-like particle
	Necrotic shock	Syst	? ? necrotic shock virus
	Strawberry pallidosis	Syst	? ? pallidosis virus
Nematodes	Root knot	R	*Meloidogyne* spp.
	Root lesion	R	*Pratylenchus* spp.
	Dagger	R	*Xiphenema* spp.
	Spring dwarf	C	*Aphelenchoides fragariae*
	Leaf and stem nematode	L	*Ditylenchus dipsaci*

Source: After Maas (1984).

[a]B, bud; C, crown; Fr, fruit; L, leaves; R, root; S, seed; Syst, systemic.

[b]Taxonomic authorities omitted in the interests of space.

several harvest seasons than from one. However, the "annual crop" system has much reduced maintenance cost, less chance of contracting disease and pest problems, and a higher per unit return because fruit is fancier in the first fruiting season and may command higher prices.

Time of planting: spring versus summer versus "winter". Normal spring plantings are usually easier to establish, and planting stocks are inexpensive then. The nursery owner has not had to put any extra storage or handling into stocks for spring planting. Summer planting depends on the availability of cold-stored dormant plant stocks. Land preparation is easier for summer planting, but the soil is drier, and supplemental irrigation is needed for establishment. "Winter" plantings are actually made in mid to late fall from fresh or recently dug nursery stocks. Like summer-planted stocks, less maintenance time is needed because the plants will fruit within a few months of planting. Summer and winter plantings are made to take advantage of nursery plant chilling history to produce higher total and early yields, respectively. Spring-planted stocks produce fruit about 13 months after planting. Summer- and winter-planted stocks yield fruit in 6 to 8 months and 3 to 4 months, respectively. Summer and winter planting fruiting can be advanced if the flower buds initiated in the nursery can be developed into fruit (usually to within 3 months after planting).

Planting and training systems: bed contour and size, bed mulching, runner plant disposition, and plant spacing.
Strawberries are planted in rows often called "beds". The rows may be prepared and the plants "set" (transplanted) into the *flat* level surface. Or the soil may be mechanically mounded into a *raised-bed* surface. Bed or row length may run the entire length of the field (*strips*), or the rows may be interrupted periodically (*blocked*) to admit cross-traffic. Plants at the edge of a row bear more berries than those in the center (better light interception). Hence there has been a tendency to narrow the row width from the traditional 24 in. (61 cm) to 12 to 18 in. (30.5 to 45.7 cm) and the planting distance between rows from 42 to 48 in. (107 to 122 cm) to 36 in. (91 cm). Both methods provide more row "edges" in the field area. The beds may be *mulched* after planting with a synthetic or organic mulch, or they may be left unmulched. Plant spacing within the row is a function of cultivar vigor and runner-making ability. Less vigorous (smaller growing) cultivars are spaced closer than more vigorous cultivars, and sparse runnering closer than free-runnering cultivars. Within row plant spacing may vary from 3 in. (7.6 cm) to 5 ft (152 cm). Transplants may be set at desired final field spacings and all runners removed so that the fruiting field consists of multiple-crowned mother plants only. Mother plants with the runners removed are said to be "hilled" and the system is called a *hill system*. More than one row of hilled plants may be planted on a bed. One, two, and four rows are common variants, called *single-hill, double-hill,* and *quadruple-hill* planting schemes.

If a predetermined small number of early daughter plants from each mother plant is anchored or "pegged down" at a suitable distance from the mother plant, the resulting plant bed is called a *spaced row*. If most of the runner plants from each mother are permitted to root in the row at random to a predetermined width, the resulting plant beds are called *matted rows*. If all runners are permitted to expand and root and no attempt is made to maintain discrete rows, the resulting entirely covered field is called *solid set* or *bed*. Hill, spaced, and matted row variants are the common training systems. The solid set system is used to maximize plant and fruit production in Michigan and Ontario for mechanical harvesting. Figure 3–7 illustrates, from several aspects, the fruiting rows of a spaced row, a matted row, and a double hill row. Figures 3–8 and 3–9 illustrate young selection fields trained to flat matted row culture and raised-bed matted row and hill culture, respectively.

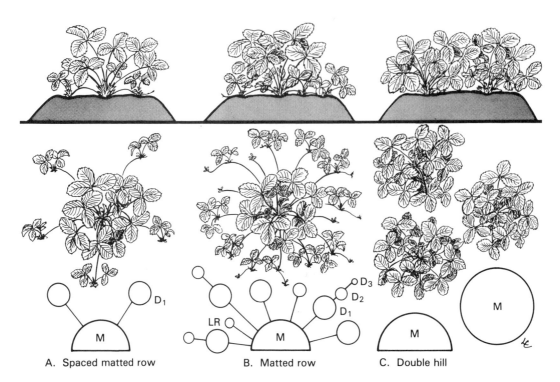

FIGURE 3-7 Comparative views of common American strawberry cultural systems. (A) Spaced matted row: mother plants and daughter plants grown to fruiting stage in a narrow row. (B) Matted row: mother plants and all but the latest runner plants form a fruiting row. (C) Double hill: close spaced mother plants only form fruiting row. Number of rows may vary from one to five. M, mother or transplanted plant; D_1, first runner or daughter plant; D_2, second daughter plant; D_3, third daughter; LR, late runner (stolon).

Planting stock: source, type, digging, and chilling history. Inexperienced growers are often tempted to secure their planting stock from a previous or neighbor's planting to save plant costs. Generally, this practice is false economy, due to increased likelihood of mislabeled cultivar and disease or insect transfer to the new area. It is wiser to purchase plants from a nursery firm specializing in strawberry plant production. These firms have experienced plant production and knowledgeable technical sales personnel. They produce plants under state agency supervision; they understand strawberry plants, cultivars, and strawberry production problems. They can give cultural and cultivar advice also. Sample types of information found in the catalog of a reputable nursery are included in Table 3-5.

Nurseries will be glad to indicate to you whether their plant production fields were set with conventional runners from isolated foundation or registered stock from a state screenhouse, or how many generations from the screenhouse it had been grown in the field. Some progressive firms have established their own tissue culture propagation facilities. Others contract with professional tissue culture firms to secure virus-free, true-to-name stocks with which to plant their plant production

FIGURE 3-8 Young strawberry selection field runnering freely. Planting was flat; training will be narrow matted rows 3.5 ft on center. Field is irrigated with trickle hoses. (From O. Mageau, U.S. Department of Agriculture.)

FIGURE 3-9 First-year everbearing strawberry selection field planted on raised beds with a straw mulch applied to the row middles. Foreground plants on beds with uncovered tops will be trained to spaced matted rows. Background plants on beds covered with black polyethylene mulch will have their runners removed (hill culture). (From O. Mageau, U.S. Department of Agriculture.)

Culture

TABLE 3-5 TYPES OF STRAWBERRY NURSERY CATALOG INFORMATION[a]

Varietal Descriptions

Earliglow (Md.-U.S. 3861): A NEW early, widely adapted, disease resistant variety that ripens 2-3 days later than Earlidawn. Berries are medium in size, firm and attractive with a glossy appearance, conical shape, and rich red flesh color. It is considered very good for freezing.

We experience Earliglow to be vigorous with good production of runners. Resistant to five strains of red stele and intermediate in resistance of verticillium wilt.

Berries withstand adverse weather and handle well because of their tough glossy skin and firm flesh. It is considered a promising pick-your-own variety.

Varietal Groupings by Characteristics

Earliest: Earlidawn, Darrow, Earliglow
Latest: Vesper, Bounty
Best flavor: Sparkle, Fletcher, Raritan, Fairfax
Freezing: Midland, Sparkle, Fletcher, Redchief, Honeoye, Bounty
Preserving: Sparkle, Catskill, Midland
Largest berries: Catskill, Robinson, Vesper, Holiday, Canoga
Verticillium wilt resistance: Catskill, Surecrop, Robinson, Guardian, Redchief, Earliglow, Darrow
Red stele resistance: Guardian, Redchief, Midway, Surecrop, Sparkle, Darrow, Earliglow
Largest yields: Raritan, Catskill, Midway, Honeoye

Cultural Information

Soil preparation: Soil preparation should be thorough and care should be taken to minimize soil compaction with equipment after plowing. Our experience has proven to us that it is best to plow and work the ground during late summer, plant an early cover crop, disc the cover crop thoroughly in the spring before it grows too rank, and then plow. Soil should be carefully levelled in order to provide a good seedbed for transplants. Where there is no natural drainage, as on a gentle slope, it is advisable to plant on raised beds. This has been standard practice with us for some time.

Source: Used by permission from 1981 Catalog, Nourse Farms, Inc., South Deerfield, Mass.

[a]Recipes, garden and club project suggestions, other uses, equipment and supplies, etc., may all be included.

fields. With tissue culture–propagated strawberries, the nursery firm realizes the benefit of enhanced and earlier runnering in the first season after tissue culture. The grower purchasing stock grown one year from tissue culture has the advantage of better survival, more vigor, and earlier growth without the extra runnering.

Summer and winter planting systems need stocky, well-rooted plants. Some nurseries bundle plants during grading for storage or subsequent sale. Machine dug and shaken plants are boxed loose for subfreezing storage in California. In Holland, plants to be stored until the summer and then late planted to secure a late yield are dug the previous September along with their regular nursery stock. Larger-crowned plants are replanted in the nursery at close spacing and runners are removed to promote multiple crown branching and flower bud initiation. Plants are redug in December and stored at slightly subfreezing temperatures [28 to 29°F (-2.2 to -1.6°C)]. They are planted the following summer at several northern European locations 60 days prior to when fruit is desired. Planting time is adjusted to secure fruit when market prices have rebounded from the early season fruit glut. These doubly dug and dormant subfreezing stored plants are called *waiting-bed* plants.

They are also an example of what the Europeans call *frigo* (frozen) plants, which are called *dormant cold stored* or just *cold-stored* plants in North America. At planting time they will show a marked vegetative response because their chilling requirement has been satisfied. They will not initiate new flowers for several months but will develop already initiated flower buds.

Fresh-dug plants with little or no chilling and intact leaves are set in Florida in October–November. The object here is high early yields. If successfully transplanted, nursery-initiated flowers will open and FBI will proceed through the winter. Similar plantings are made in southern California at the same time, but from high-elevation nurseries so that more chilling can be secured. Plants are also trimmed and sometimes stored at common refrigeration temperatures prior to planting. Optimum digging and planting dates are carefully worked out for each cultivar — see details of culture later. These California planting stocks would be called *partially chilled* or semidormant. They will make slow vegetative growth, no runners, but produce flowers in a few months following this treatment.

Cultivars: flowering habit, production region, production system and market outlet.

Strawberry cultivar choice is perhaps more crucial than in most crops, because each clone has a very definite area or climatic zone to which it is "adapted". We understand now that the range of temperature–photoperiod interactions, tolerance of extreme temperatures, and chilling requirement responses possessed by each cultivar determine the area in which they will perform consistently. The most successful cultivars are those in which FBI and FBD, fruit set, and berry ripening can proceed within the broadest microclimate variations. In Table 3-6 the major cultivars of the United States and Canada are grouped by flowering habit, production region, and production system. Other characteristics for which the cultivars are noted are coded. Good cultivars become widely planted within 5 years after their introduction and persist as leading cultivars for another 10 to 15 (25) years. A breeding cycle in strawberry (seed to introduction) takes 6 to 20 years, most frequently 10 to 15 years. There are a fair number of public and a few private strawberry breeding programs in North America. A listing as Table 3-6 should be revised about once per decade.

Input level: land, capital, personnel, and practice cost-effectiveness.

Berry producers must decide the size of enterprise with which their firm *is comfortable*. A few successful seasons often leads to overextension of strawberry acreage to the point where every part of the operation becomes a strain. Each firm must decide how much land can be incorporated into a successful strawberry rotation, whether bedding machinery is a luxury or a necessity, whether to install drip irrigation lines, and so on. Guidelines for making these decisions are given in other chapters. At this point we would caution about hasty decisions in evaluating the worth of a cultivar or a cultural practice for your farm. Low performance of a new cultivar in one season's evaluation may reflect poor planting stock, unusually poor growing conditions, or grower unfamiliarity with the growth responses of the new type, not the "long-haul" value of the clone for the area. Similarly, a new practice usually will have to be modified slightly to be effective for a particular farm.

TABLE 3-6 MAJOR NORTH AMERICAN STRAWBERRY CULTIVARS AND THEIR NOTABLE CHARACTERISTICS[a]

Single-Cropping (Junebearing or Short-Day)[b]

North	Allstar M, 2-4, 7, 8	Hood H, 3, 5, 7, 8, 11	Scott M, 2, 4, 6-8
	Badgerbelle M, 2, 3, 11	Kent M, 1, 2,	Shuksan M, 7, 8, 11, 12
	Benton H, 3, 6, 7	Linn H, 3, 4, 7, 8	Sparkle M, 1, 5-7, 11
	Bounty M, 1, 2, 11	Micmac M, 2, 8	Surecrop M, 2, 7-9
	Catskill M, 1, 3, 8	Midway M, 6, 7	Totem M, 1, 6, 7, 11, 12
	Delite M, 2, 3, 7-9, 11	Olympus H, 2, 6, 11, 12	Trumpeter M, 1, 6, 8, 12
	Earliglow M, 4-10	Ranier M, 5-8, 11, 12	Tyee M, 7, 8, 11, 12
	Fletcher M, 1, 5, 6	Raritan M, 2-4	Vesper M, 3, 11
	Guardian M, 3, 7-9	Redchief M, 2, 4-6	Veestar M, 1, 2, 6, 10
	Honeoye M, 1, 2, 6, 10	Redcoat M, 1, 2	
Central	Aiko H, 2, 12	Earlibelle M, 4, 6, 9, 10	Sunrise M, 2, 5, 7-9
	Apollo M, 2, 4, 5, 9	Heidi H, 2, 4, 12	Tenn Beauty M, 9, 11, 12
	Atlas M, 2, 4, 9	Pajaro H, 2, 12	Titan M, 3-5, 9, 10
	Cardinal M, 2-4, 6, 9	Sequoia M, H, 2, 5, 10	Tufts H, 2, 12
South	Chandler H, 2-5, 12	Douglas H, 2, 3, 10, 12	Headliner H, 10
	Dabreak H, 9, 10, 12	Dover H, 2, 10	Tangi H, 2, 3, 9

Two-Cropping (Everbearer) — usually H

Fort Laramie 1	Our Own 1	Puget Beauty 5, 9
Gem	Ozark Beauty 5, 9, 11	Quinalt 7, 9
Ogallala 1		

Multiple-Cropping (Day-Neutral) — all H

Aptos 1, 8	Fern 2	Tristar 1, 2, 4-8, 10
Brighton 3	Hecker 10	Selva 2-4
Burlington 2	Tribute 1, 2, 4, 6-9	

[a]Characteristic codes: H, usually grown as mother plants only; M, usually grown in matted rows; many cultivars can be trained to either system. 1, Very hardy; 2, productive in many environments; 3, large fruited; 4, firm fruited; 5, flavorful; 6, good for processing; 7, resistant to red stele; 8, resistant to *Verticillium;* 9, resistant to several leaf diseases; 10, early maturing; 11, late maturing; 12, virus tolerant.

[b]Clones adapted to the north have a generally high chilling requirement; those adapted to the central area need intermediate chilling levels; those adapted to the south are presumed to need little chilling. Clones such as 'Sequoia' can be grown well in either central or southern areas, as can many of the California cultivars.

Production Regions

Rather than discuss the relative merits of variations in such practices as nutrition, irrigation, and so on, we should recognize the variation in successful strawberry production methods among strawberry growing regions. Note how the successful methods are adapted to different cultivars. We can point out trends in strawberry production; the reader can then decide how best to use the information.

World production. World strawberry production for 1985 was 1949 thousand metric tons. Europe accounted for about one-half of the world production; North and Central America produced slightly over one-fourth of the total production. There was an overall increase in world production in the period 1979–1985, particularly in Africa, North and Central America, South America, and the USSR. Production for this period was stable in Asia, Europe, and Oceania (Australia and New Zealand). The 10 leading strawberry producing countries in 1985 were the United States (462 thousand metric tons), Poland (212), Japan (202) Italy (161), the USSR (120), France (92), Spain (85), Mexico (59), Korea (53), and the United Kingdom (51). The United States, Poland, the USSR, France, Spain, and Korea have shown a phenomenal increase in production. Figures are from the FAO yearbook for 1985 cited in Chapter 1. Japan, Italy, Poland, France, Spain, the United States, and Korea had experienced similar expansion in the 1970–1980 period (Childers, 1983). More recent figures indicate that the 1985 rankings in Table 1-6 are still valid, except that Korea has passed Mexico in production, and Spain's strawberry industry is continuing rapid growth.

Presumed Chinese disinterest in strawberry culture has not proved valid. Every Chinese visitor to our laboratories has requested seeds and plants. Our eastern U.S. cultivars with root disease resistance are adapted to northeastern Chinese locales with similar climates. Southeastern U.S. cultivars have been sent to similar areas for trial. New cultivars selected from seed progenies sent by the senior author several years ago have been or will be introduced. On-site consultation about disease control, virus indexing, and micropropagation was given in several Chinese provnces recently.

A remarkable set of new cultivars have been developed in Europe, often from hybridizations of New World types. Europeans have devised a number of innovative protected culture and propagation schemes. European clones have been prominent in the ancestry of recent introductions from Nova Scotia, New York, and the USDA lab in Beltsville, Maryland. Prospects for continued improvement of strawberry germplasm and expansion of strawberry production worldwide seem very favorable.

North American production. *Mexico's* modern strawberry industry began in 1948 with the establishment of a freezing plant (Emerson, 1980). The principal outlet for Mexican fruit was and is frozen berries exported to the United States. Starting with the old southern U.S. cultivar 'Klondike', the Mexicans shifted over to California cultivars, 'Tioga' becoming the principal cultivar after 1970 because of large fruit production over a longer period. Berries are grown mainly on raised beds containing one, two, or four rows of plants. Production is centered in an extensive upland valley 110 to 180 miles (200 to 300 km) northwest of Mexico City. Production is concentrated around Zamora in Michoacan state, and Irapuato in Gunanajuato state at elevations of 5000 ft (1520 m) and 5600 ft (1700 m), respectively. Berries are summer planted (July–early September) and harvested 3 to 6 months later. Peak production is in March. More of the Mexican crop is shipped fresh now. Industry expansion peaked in the 1960s and early 1970s, when Mexico was the world's third-largest strawberry-producing nation at 110 thousand metric tons. Their decline to the present level (60 to 65 thousand metric tons) resulted from rising production costs, higher sugar prices, reduced demand and profits to industry and grower. The industry, although smaller, is judged strong and durable.

Canadian strawberry production is concentrated in three major regions: the

Maritime Provinces (Nova Scotia, New Brunswick, and Prince Edward Island), Ontario and Quebec, and British Columbia (Daubeny, 1980). The Maritimes account for 15% of the production, and it is preponderantly matted row culture for fresh market and consumer harvesting [pick-your-own (PYO)]. The principal cultivar is 'Kent', with some 'Bounty', 'Micmac', 'Redcoat', and 'Veestar' grown. New red stele–resistant clones 'Annapolis' and 'Cornwallis' are available for those sites with root rot problems. Newer clones 'Blomidon' and 'Glooscap' have promise.

Ontario and Quebec account for about 60% of the Canadian production. Both provinces have overproduction problems due to earlier ripening competition from the United States. Ontario and Quebec are both actively engaged in developing strong processing outlets. Both central provinces have strong PYO and local market outlets. Although both grow berries principally on matted rows, there is some experimentation with raised-bed spaced-plant or hill culture. In Ontario there is interest in the "solid-bed" system developed in Michigan to aid in once-over mechanical harvesting. Cultivars prominent in Ontario and Quebec are 'Veestar', 'Redcoat', 'Glooscap', 'Elvira', 'Kent', and 'Gilbert'.

British Columbia produces 20 to 30% of the Canadian crop. The management system used is overwhelmingly matted row for processing fruit. 'Totem' and 'Shuksan' are leading cultivars. The newer 'Tyee' is very promising, but may be prone to June yellows (a noninfectious chlorophyll disorder).

There is considerable Canadian interest in day-neutral culture, especially in Quebec, New Brunswick, Ontario, and recently, British Columbia. The most favored cultivars to date are the U.S. cultivars 'Tribute' and, to a lesser extent, 'Tristar'. Most of these are grown for annual production on raised beds. In Saskatchewan they are experimenting with annual production systems using California day-neutral cultivars.

U.S. United States strawberry production is variously separated into six or seven producing regions. The following synopsis of U.S. regions—their production aims, practices, problems, and principal cultivars—is updated from Galletta (1984). Regional production figures for the United States are not as meaningful as for other countries because so much of the eastern U.S. production is customer-harvested and not tallied in official production figures.

California. California's cool coastal valleys are the nation's principal producers of fresh shipping, export, and also of processing strawberries (Fig. 3–10). Processing fruit is generally the small, damaged, or second-year-bed fruit. Either summer plantings of cold-stored fully dormant plants, or winter plantings of fresh-dug, partially chilled plants of specially bred varieties continue to produce flowers and fruit over a 6- to 8-month period. By judicious selection of varieties and planting dates and cultural manipulation, fruit production on the California coast is almost continuous. In the hot interior valleys or in the mountains of California, fruit production of the same varieties is over in a short time, as in comparable latitudes of the eastern or central United States.

Culture is exclusively hill culture on clear polyethylene-covered raised beds with either two or four rows of plants planted per bed. All soil is preplant fumigated for nematode and soil fungus control. Fertilizer and trickle irrigation line is set into

FIGURE 3-10 California strawberries being hand harvested.

slots as the planting beds are being formed. Most plantings are fruited for one season only. The climate is Mediterranean (mild winter, dry summer). Principal pests are viruses, verticillium wilt, leaf spot, *Botrytis* fruit rot, vascular collapse caused by the fungus *Phytophthora cactorum,* and two-spotted mite. Production has risen to a record 28 tons/acre (70 MT/ha) average in 1982, and the best growers are securing yields of 40 to 50 tons/acre (90 to 112 MT/ha). The principal cultivars in California now are the Junebearers 'Douglas', 'Chandler', 'Pajaro', 'Aiko', 'Parker', and the day-neutral 'Selva'. The day-neutral cultivars, while intended as home garden types, have sufficient quality to be used as commercial "insurance" crops if a natural disaster overtakes a Junebearing planting.

Pacific Northwest. Berries are grown in the mild, cool maritime climates of western Washington and Oregon, principally for the processing trade. Over 90% of the Oregon crop and about 75% of the Washington crop are processed. This climate, along with that of the Fraser Valley in British Columbia, is superb for fruit quality development. Eastern and midwestern strawberry processors often import berries from this region.

Cultural problems are red stele, gray mold, winter hardiness, viruses, aphids, two-spotted mites, root weevils, and adaptation for mechanical harvesting. Straw-erries are usually grown in narrow matted rows or single- or double-hill rows. The principal varieties of the area are 'Olympus', 'Benton', and 'Linn' replacing the older 'Hood' in Oregon, and 'Totem', 'Shuksan', 'Hood', and 'Olympus' in Washington. The everbearer 'Quinault' is well established in this region.

Central United States. This is an area with a continental climate marked by temperature extremes, strong winds, and lower rainfall. Cultural problems are anthracnose, red stele, leaf fungus diseases, drought tolerance, and nematodes in the south; cold hardiness, drought tolerance, weeds, leather rot, red stele, clipper, lygus bugs, and verticillium wilt in the north. The major cultural system is the matted row, with some raised bed and ribbon rows and some "solid bed" for processing berries in

Culture

Michigan. Most berries are grown for the PYO and local sales trade, with small areas of fresh fruit for shipping (principally in Arkansas) and processing fruit production (Michigan).

Principal cultivars are 'Cardinal', 'Apollo', 'Allstar', 'Delite', 'Atlas', 'Titan', 'Guardian', and 'Surecrop' in the south central area, with 'Arking', 'Sentinel', and 'Rosanne' for trial. In the north central area the cultivars are 'Honeoye', 'Earliglow', 'Redchief', 'Guardian', 'Midway', 'Kent', 'Bounty', 'Allstar', 'Redcoat', 'Veestar', 'Raritan', and 'Surecrop', with 'Lester', 'Jewel', 'Lateglow', 'Blomidon', and 'Glooscap' for trial.

Florida and Gulf Coast. This area grows berries for fresh shipment and use, with a little PYO trade becoming more common, especially at the end of the season. The Florida area uses raised-bed, black polyethylene mulch, two- or four-row double-hill culture of fresh dug, fall-set plants, usually raised north of Florida. Louisiana follows a similar system. PYO plantings in other states in the area are often matted rows.

Heat and drought tolerance, winter frost tolerance, anthracnose, nematodes, leaf diseases, mites, fruit rots, verticillium wilt, and rain damage to fruit are regional problems. The principal Florida cultivars are 'Chandler', 'Selva', 'Douglas', and 'Pajaro', with some 'Parker' and 'Dover' grown. The main cultivars in Louisiana are 'Tangi' and 'Dabreak'. 'Apollo', 'Cardinal', 'Titan', and 'Surecrop' are reasonable PYO cultivars in lower Mississippi, Alabama, and Georgia.

Mid-South (Kentucky, West Virginia, south to mid-Mississippi, Alabama, and Georgia). This is a topographically diverse region with ample rainfall, fluctuating winter temperatures, and moist, humid summers. Cultural problems are leaf and stem fungi, aphids, leafhoppers, virus reinfection of extended plantings, nematodes, mites, black root rot, red stele, weeds, and gray mold.

Commercial production is overwhelmingly from matted row culture, and the major market outlet is PYO and local sales. Important cultivars for the Coastal Plain and lower Piedmont areas of the southern portion of this region are 'Apollo', 'Atlas', 'Titan', and 'Cardinal' with 'Sunrise', 'Earlibelle', 'Sequoia', and 'Albritton' being grown in limited quantities. The newer cultivars 'Prelude', 'Summer', 'Sentinel', and 'Rosanne' are all suitable for trial in this area. For the northern and highland areas of this region, the better cultivars are 'Earliglow', 'Guardian', 'Scott', 'Delite', 'Redchief', 'Sunrise', 'Surecrop', and 'Allstar', with 'Lester', 'Lateglow', 'Honeoye', and 'Jewel' for trial. For fall-planted raised-bed, plastic mulch culture, the major cultivar is 'Chandler', with some 'Douglas', 'Pajaro', 'Atlas', and 'Selva' being tried.

Midwest, Middle Atlantic, and New England (the Northeast). This region is diverse in topography, soils, and climate, with generally ample moisture. Production is mainly for sale at the farm or locally with minor shipping and processing areas. While the narrow matted or spaced row is still the major producing system, there is a fair amount of "ribbon row" and raised-bed culture. Major problems are red stele, verticillium wilt, leather rot, gray mold, leaf fungi, aphids, viruses, clipper, lygus bugs, chewing insects, and sap beetles.

Dependable Junebearing commercial cultivars of the region are 'Earliglow',

'Redchief', 'Midway', 'Surecrop', 'Guardian', 'Raritan', 'Scott', 'Allstar', 'Honeoye', 'Kent', and 'Delite', with good results in some areas from 'Darrow', 'Bounty', 'Micmac', 'Earlidawn', 'Holiday', 'Catskill', 'Fletcher', and 'Sparkle'. Varieties for trial in this region are 'Lester', 'Lateglow', 'Jewel', 'Blomidon', and 'Glooscap'. 'Tribute' and 'Tristar' are the preferred day-neutral cultivars in this region.

Production Examples

California. United States pre–World War II acreage ranged between 150,000 and 200,000 (60,700 to 80,940 ha), dropped to about *75,000* acres (30,350 ha) in 1945, rose to about *100,000* (60,700 ha) after the war, and has now dropped to somewhat over one-third of that (42,100 = 17,040 ha in 1984). During that time yields per acre rose dramatically in California and Florida, more modestly in the rest of the United States.

Prior to World War II, Louisiana and Arkansas were the two most important commercial strawberry-producing states in the United States (both southern); Oregon (west coast) ranked third, with Tennessee (south) and Michigan (midwest) fourth and fifth, respectively. California production was relatively unimportant. The modern California strawberry industry did not develop until after the 1945 release of the first cultivars truly adapted to California growing conditions ('Shasta' and 'Lassen' by Harold E. Thomas and E. B. Goldsmith, then of the Department of Plant Pathology, University of California, Berkeley). The California south coastal industry subsequently developed around 'Lassen' and the central coastal industry around 'Shasta'. At the present time California produces over 75% of the U.S. fresh shipping and processing strawberries.

In addition to better cultivars, an industry-sponsored and partially supported university research team made many advances in disease detection and control, nursery plant production, cultural system design, postharvest fruit care, and even better cultivars. The industry was willing to accept and use their team's findings and aggressively market the increased product. This combination of people, resources, beneficial climate, and hard work has produced the strawberry preeminence of California, whose cultivars and methods have been widely used, and which we will treat therefore in more detail. Production trends in California have been recently summarized for the period 1945 to 1984 (Bringhurst, 1986).

California Commercial Cultivar Progression. Since the release of 'Shasta' and 'Lassen' in 1945, there has been a steady release of new cultivars in California, each quite popular until replaced by new and improved sorts (Table 3-7). Much of the adaptation to coastal California traces back to 'Lassen', which probably inherited it from California *F. chiloensis* ancestors. 'Lassen' was one of the parents of 'Fresno' and 'Tioga', Tioga was one parent of 'Tufts', which was one parent of 'Douglas', which was one parent of 'Chandler' and 'Parker'. All the rest also trace back to 'Lassen'. Other important ancestors were 'Howard 17', 'Nich Ohmer', 'Royal Sovereign', 'Marshall', and 'Missionary'.

Day-neutral cultivars are useful in at least two respects: (1) in obtaining fruit during off-months for winter production in places such as southern California, since

TABLE 3-7 PROGRESSION OF COMMERCIAL CALIFORNIA STRAWBERRY CULTIVARS

CULTIVAR	TYPE	YEAR INTRODUCED	COMMERCIAL PROMINENCE Years (Approx.)	Area[a]
Shasta	Short-day	1945	1947–1974	CC
Lassen	Short-day	1946	1947–1969	SC
Fresno	Short-day	1961	1965–1976	SC
Tioga	Short-day	1964	1966–1981	SC, CC
Tufts	Short-day	1972	1977–1983	CC, Fla
Aiko	Short-day	1975	1981–1986	CC
Pajaro	Short-day	1979	1981–	CC, Fla
Douglas	Short-day	1979	1981–	SC, Fla
Chandler	Short-day	1983	1984–	SC, CC, Fla, NC
Parker	Short-day	1983	1984–1985	CC
Hecker	Day-neutral	1979	1980–	Midw, W
Brighton	Day-neutral	1979	1980–	Midw, W
Fern	Day-neutral	1983	?	W, E?
Selva	Day-neutral	1983	1986–	SC, CC, Fla
Muir	Day-neutral	1987	New	
Mrak	Day-neutral	1987	New	
Yolo	Day-neutral	1987	New	
Oso Grande	Short-day	1987	New	

[a]CC, California central coast; SC, California south coast; Fla, Florida; NC, North Carolina; Midw, midwestern U.S.; W, western U.S.; E, eastern U.S.

they are easily programmed to produce a significant crop 3 to 4 months after plants are set; (2) similarly, grown as annuals, they produce fruit in a reliable pattern during the off-months for summer and fall production in the central coast of California. 'Selva' (1983) is the first major day-neutral California cultivar. 'Tristar' and 'Tribute' (1981) of similar origin are the first eastern U.S. cultivars of this type. Day-neutrals are not likely to replace short-day cultivars during the many months when the short-day types perform best, although time will prove out this point. However, they are almost certain to become more important commercially as growers become aware of their advantages and improved cultivars are released. Already they are satisfying longstanding needs of home gardeners within and outside California.

Climatic Zones of California. Strawberries perform best in the marine, Mediterranean environment of central and south coastal California, characterized by relatively warm winters and relatively cool, dry summers (data from 1941 USDA Yearbook, *Climate and Man*). For our purposes, the extraction shown in Table 3–8 is adequate, with the zonal designations as indicated.

Note the variation within a zone as well as between zones. Generally, the summer temperatures are lower near the coast and higher inland and the opposite is true in winter. Rainfall variation is associated with topographical features, particularly mountains.

Strawberry Reproduction. The apical meristem of a strawberry plant is strongly dominant. However, buds are initiated in the axils of every leaf and, depending on the conditioning imposed by prevailing environmental conditions, the axillary buds may develop as flower stocks, runners, or branch crowns. Flower production is a sexual response, while runner production is an asexual response. Sometimes the response is mixed. Crown division takes place during sexual or asexual cycles of reproduction and branch crowns are an indication of vigorous growth. The principal environmental factors that condition physiological response in strawberries are:

1. Photoperiod.
    a. Long days (= short nights) favor asexual response (plant development + runners).
    b. Short days (= long nights) favor sexual response (flower development and fruit).

All important California cultivars are "facultative" short-day (= long night) types ('Tioga', 'Tufts', 'Aiko', 'Douglas', 'Pajaro', 'Chandler'). Daylength cannot be manipulated easily; hence the only thing one can do is work around it. That is the principal reason that recommended planting dates are rather firmly fixed. (Near the equator, where day length is constant, thinking must be modified somewhat.)

TABLE 3-8 CLIMATIC ZONES OF CALIFORNIA

ZONE	MEAN TEMPERATURE [°F (°C)]		GROWING SEASON (DAYS)	RAINFALL (in.)		
	Jan.	July		Heaviest Month Winter	July	Total
South coastal						
San Diego	55 (12.8)	67 (19.4)	365	2.22	0.04	10.11
Tustin	53 (11.7)	72 (22.2)	303	2.71	0.00	12.65
Los Angeles	54 (12.2)	70 (21.1)	359	3.26	0.00	14.76
Intermediate coastal						
Santa Maria	51 (10.6)	63 (17.2)	272	2.98	0.00	14.11
Central coastal						
San Francisco	50 (10)	59 (15.0)	356	4.41	0.01	20.23
Santa Cruz	50 (10)	63 (17.2)	271	5.88	0.04	27.05
Watsonville	50 (10)	63 (17.2)	232	4.51	0.02	21.09
Salinas	50 (10)	63 (17.2)	250	3.01	0.02	13.37
San Jose	48 (8.9)	67 (19.4)	299	2.97	0.00	13.93
Central valley						
Fresno	45 (7.2)	81 (27.2)	295	1.85	0.01	9.43
Denair	43 (6.1)	77 (25.0)	254	2.08	0.00	10.80
Davis	45 (7.2)	75 (23.9)	242	3.65	0.00	16.43
Red Bluff	45 (7.2)	82 (27.8)	274	4.56	0.03	23.10
Redding	45 (7.2)	82 (27.8)	278	6.93	0.10	37.54
High elevation						
Fall River	31 (0.6)	70 (21.1)	126	2.93	0.10	17.14

2. Growing temperatures
   a. Relatively high temperatures (summer) favor asexual response.
      Relatively high temperatures (winter) favor sexual response.
   b. Relatively low temperatures (summer) favor sexual response.
      Relatively low temperatures (winter) favor asexual response.

Obviously, growing temperatures may be manipulated considerably by site selection, timing of the planting, or modification of cultural practices.

3. Chilling
   a. High amounts of chilling favor asexual response.
   b. Low amounts of chilling favor sexual response.

Here the same phenomenon that is known as "delayed foliation" in deciduous trees can be exploited in strawberries. The desirable situation is between the extremes; enough chilling to impart vigor, so that fruit quality and quantity are enhanced, but not so much that the plants produce runners. Many cultural recommendations involve controlling the amount of chilling.

Propagation. California strawberry nurseries are privately owned specialty firms of two general types:

1. *High-elevation nurseries.* These produce plants to be dug and planted fresh, under the winter planting system, and are located in northern California, near the towns of Susanville (40.4°N lat.), at about 4156 ft (1267 m) elevation; McArthur–Fall River Mills (41.2°N lat.), at about 3322 ft (1013 m) elevation; and Macdoel (41.8°N lat.), at about 4262 ft (1299 m) elevation. Macdoel has the earliest chilling temperatures [below 45°F (7.2°C)]. These nurseries are planted as early as weather permits (March–April) in order to extend the growing season as much as possible to facilitate October harvest. Normally, all plants are out of the ground by November 1.
2. *Low-elevation nurseries.* These produce plants for long-term cold storage associated with the summer planting system, and are located in the Sacramento and northern Jan Joaquin Valleys near the cities of Redding, Red Bluff, and Waterford. They are also planted in the spring but with much less urgency since they have ample growing time even when planted in mid to late May. Ideally, they should be harvested when the plants are as nearly dormant as they can get (January). In actual practice, the harvest varies from late December to as late as March, depending on the rain patterns in a given year.

All nurseries are fumigated with methyl bromide–chloropicrin before planting. Most nursery owners use modified tomato (tobacco) plant setting machines for planting. All nurseries are irrigated with sprinklers; only small heads (Rainbird 14V or equivalent) are recommended.

Plants are harvested by machine, trimmed, counted, and packed by hand.

They are sold by the thousand, with each container holding 1000 to 2000 plants, depending on the plant size.

Storage temperatures are always slightly above freezing for the high-elevation plants (short-term storage up to about 3 weeks) and below freezing for low-elevation plants [28°F (-2.2°C)]. Plants must be cooled to the desired temperature as soon as they come from the field, whether they are packed immediately or not. The storage temperature must be maintained carefully or various fungus diseases will destroy the crowns and/or roots.

Development and Propagation of Clean Nursery Stock. Ordinarily, in considering the relative merits of planting stock from a phytosanitary point of view, we are concerned with virus or virus-like infection and nematodes. However, other diseases and/or pests are frequently involved, and trueness to cultivar is critical.

Modern California cultivars are "resistant" to viruses in comparison to those formerly grown. However, this does not diminish the need for clean plants because planting stock will deteriorate rapidly if handled carelessly. This discussion will concentrate on avoidance of deterioration due to virus and virus-like infection. Soilborne nematodes are not a problem in California because of soil fumigation.

1. *Virus infection.* Infection may be simple (involving a single virus) or complex (involving two or more viruses). The effect of viruses is generally cumulative, although a given cultivar may manifest no visible symptoms from complex infection by as many as three separate entities. Single viruses are frequently referred to as virus components—meaning component of disease. The most troublesome single virus in California cultivars has been *Mild Yellow Edge* (MYE or Y), probably native to Chile. The other two most common viruses are Mottle (M) and Crinkle (C). It is more appropriate to refer to the status of a plant as "virus-negative" rather than "virus-free" since virus infection cannot be ascertained absolutely.

2. *Virus identification.* The presence and the identification of specific viruses is normally determined by graftage to selected indicator plants. The process is termed "indexing". The principle involved here is high sensitivity of the indicators to simple infection. Excised leaf graftage is the simplest procedure. The two indicators officially used in California are UC5 (an Alpine *vesca* type) and UC10 (an eastern *F. virginiana*), soon to be replaced by similar UC11. All were developed by Norman Frazier.

3. *Virus elimination.* All of the important strawberry viruses may be eliminated from cultivated clones by culturing small axillary buds, called "meristems", after the plants have been heat treated. Meristem-derived, virus-negative subclones of a given cultivar may be superior to the virus-infected old stock even in cases where there are no disease symptoms. This is mostly a vigor factor.

4. *Avoiding infection.* Virus-negative clonal stock in California is maintained through a voluntary California State Department of Agriculture Certification Program. Plants obtained from nurseries that participate in the program are as clean as it is possible to obtain. While not all nurseries participate in the

program, all benefit from it since they must obtain clean stock periodically from participants. Plants directly derived from the program are at most only several propagations removed from indexed foundation plants. The cost of the program is borne entirely by the strawberry industry and all services provided by the California State Department of Agriculture are paid for by fees levied on a cost basis.

5. *Micropropagation.* Good phytosanitary principles and practice are essential to the well-being of the industry. The advent of tissue-cultured meristem stock and rapid micropropagation techniques has removed one of the major elements of uncertainty from the business. As methodology improves, additional benefits will result, including long-term storage of plantlets or tissue.

California Planting Systems. Since performance of short-day strawberries is governed by genetic endowment, photoperiod, growing temperatures, and chilling history, it is possible to manipulate certain of the variables sufficiently to program the important cultivars for predictable annual performance, under favorable environmental conditions, with minimal risk. The planting systems of California were developed with this objective in mind. With the exception of the southeastern United States, strawberries outside California are usually planted in the spring. Only nurseries are spring-planted in California.

Only first-year production after planting is considered here, although some plantings are carried into the second year in the central coastal areas. Little manipulation is possible after the first year, and since fruit quality decreases and harvest costs increase after the first year, annual planting is recommended for all areas. This sort of decision is up to individual growers, however, and the determining factor ultimately is whether or not it pays in comparison with alternatives.

1. *Winter planting system.* So-named because success depends on how well the plants grow during the short days of winter, this system is increasing in popularity. The features of the system are as follows:

1. Winter planting in California differs from the Florida *green plant* system in that in California early plant chilling is required. Following chilling, the plants are more vigorous and have higher yield and better fruit quality, although production starts later.

2. Compared with summer planting, winter-planted fruit production starts earlier but total production is much less.

3. A high elevation nursery plant source is necessary since early chilling is required. Plants are harvested in October for optimum planting, no later than the first week of November in most cases.

4. Cultivars vary considerably in usefulness for winter planting, including tolerance to varying the date of digging and transplanting, and in their response to cold storage treatment before transplanting. 'Douglas' and 'Chandler' are the two most important winter planted cultivars in California. 'Douglas' is the earliest and most manageable, but 'Chandler' usually outyields 'Douglas', and

'Chandler' fruit quality is better. 'Selva' is also winter-planted, mostly in central coastal California. Older cultivars which have been used for winter production were 'Lassen' originally, followed by 'Sequoia', 'Aliso', 'Fresno', 'Torrey', 'Tioga' and 'Tufts'. 'Douglas' and 'Chandler' represent considerable improvement in adaptation to the winter planting system, compared to the older cultivars.

5. Plants that are dug and planted too early will lack vigor and produce small, poor quality fruit. Those planted too late will be too vigorous, tend to runner and will produce little fruit, although it may be very large. The objective is to dig early enough to achieve high yield and acceptable earliness but late enough to ensure plant vigor, fruit size and quality.

6. Obviously, this system is useful only in areas where the winter temperatures are relatively warm, particularly in south coastal California. The critical temperature for strawberry plant growth is generally assumed to be about 50°F (10°C). If the average January temperature is below this, the system won't work because the plant won't grow.

7. Planting slot placement of fertilizer and amount and type of fertilizer carrier used is important in winter plantings.

8. Clear polyethylene bed mulch applied as soon after planting as possible is necessary as a soil heating agent to enhance production in California (Fig. 3–11). (Black mulch is usually used in Florida, where low growing temperatures are not a problem.)

9. Harvesting from properly managed winter plantings is relatively easy because of accessibility and visibility of the fruit, and although production starts early, it is generally very evenly distributed.

Future possibilities for the winter planting system with some modifications are very good in central as well as south coastal California. The minimized time between planting and harvest (3 months) is a particularly attractive feature since it reduces the preharvest care and maintenance period by about 4 months and yields the earliest fruit by at least an equivalent amount. With day-neutrals such as 'Selva' the harvest season is expanded significantly into the late fall in the central coast.

2. *Summer planting system.* This system originated as an experimental tool, designed to produce consistent high yields year after year at a given location. Summer planting now dominates in the cooler central coast area of California. The features of the system are as follows:

1. Effectively, summer planting is a delayed spring planting involving cold storage of the planting stock. Nursery stock comes from low-elevation nurseries in the Sacramento–San Joaquin Valleys, harvested in the winter (preferably January, when plants are as nearly dormant as possible), and stored at 28°F (−2.2°C) until planting time. All leaves and most of the petioles are removed and the plants are packed loosely (*not bundled*) in boxes with *thin* polyethylene liners.

(a)

(b)

FIGURE 3-11 Worker burning holes in clear plastic mulch which was recently applied over strawberry planting in California (a). Plants are then pulled out through holes (b).

2. Planting time varies with the cultivar and with the planting site, starting as early as about July 20 with 'Pajaro', the dominant cultivar, at Fresno, and continuing to about September 10 in the central coast. Thus, for a given cultivar, warmer summer–colder winter sites are planted earlier than cooler summer–warmer winter sites. Stated another way, more inland areas are always planted earlier than coastal areas at a given parallel (e.g., Santa Clara Valley versus Watsonville). As with winter plantings, if plants are set too early, they lack vigor and the fruit is relatively small and of relatively low quality, although yields may be high. If planted too late, plants are very vigorous but yields are reduced greatly, although fruit quality may be very high.

3. The best cultural practices must be employed during the establishment year to maximize growth and crown development. Nitrogen must be available to the plants during this period, but placement is not as critical as with winter plantings. Sprinkler irrigation is necessary during the entire establishment period in areas where salt accumulation is a problem. It is desirable in other areas as well. Small sprinkler heads are a must (Rainbird 14V or equivalent).

4. Summer plantings always produce a "crown crop" of fruit soon after the plants are set and some growers harvest it; others remove the flower stalks before they set fruit. The economics of this practice is questionable. This crop results from buds that were initiated in the nursery during the short days preceding plant harvest. After the above-mentioned flowering ceases, runner production is normal and runners must be removed.

5. Plants become semidormant during the winter; old leaves become senescent and must be removed (pruned) about February 1, just prior to the application of the polyethylene bed mulch. White bed mulch works very well, but some use clear and others just strips over the irrigation drip line. Action to control weeds, mites, and other pests and diseases is particularly important at this time.

6. Harvest starts about 7 months after planting at the earliest (March in southern California) and may continue until fall in some areas (central coast).

7. The most desirable features of this system are dependability and high yield. Fruit quality and size is better on winter plantings. In contrast to the "winter system", summer planting is successful in all areas and is the only system to use in some.

Summer planting will continue to be used in areas where the winters are too cold for successful winter planting. In areas where winter planting is successful or potentially so, much of the present summer planted acreage will be replaced by winter planting as better varieties become available for winter planting. The economics of the business will force this issue. As better day-neutrals are developed, some spring planting may be revived to generate fruit for the late harvest season. However, improved short-day cultivars for summer planting may also be an important factor, particularly those that can be planted later (September). Some apparently will produce high-quality fruit in cycles throughout the entire summer and fall. The current principal summer planting cultivar ('Pajaro') is not suitable for winter planting because it does not yield enough in winter plantings.

3. *Day-neutral cultivar management.* Systems for the exploitation of the new day-neutral cultivars are being developed in two directions, to meet the two general needs of the industry and to provide information to guide home gardeners.

1. For winter fruiting in warmer areas such as southern California, *late* summer planting of stored strawberry plants, described previously, is one possibility. The idea is to produce fruit earlier than is possible with the short-day cultivars. This works because the 3-month rule from planting to first commercial harvest

prevails rather than the 7-month rule that prevails in this type of planting with the short-day types. The second possibility is early winter planting with fresh plants with intact leaves.

   a. The only modification may be to plant them earlier than the short-day cultivars in order to get the first fruit started by November if that is desired. This varies according to the cultivar and location (= prevailing temperatures).

   b. First flower stalks should be removed to promote more vegetative development and time the crop as desired.

   c. Day-neutral cultivars may also be summer-planted in central coastal or colder areas of California with the expectation of producing some fruit that fall; considerable if desired, depending on how early the summer planting goes in (3-month rule).

2. For late spring, summer, and fall fruiting in the central coast, modifications of the winter planting system appear necessary. These involve minimal plant handling and storage.

   a. Day-neutral plants may be planted in the nursery with, harvested at, and transplanted at about the same time as winter-planted short-day types, or dug with the short-day types but given short-term storage until it is more convenient to plant them (November, December, or even January and February). They are very flexible with regard to planting time. High-elevation nursery propagation is advantageous (earlier chilling).

   b. Day-neutral plants may also be planted in the nursery with short-day plants scheduled to be harvested about January for storage and subsequent summer planting. However, the day-neutrals so planted should be dug at the beginning of the plant harvest and then planted without storage or with holding storage of up to a few weeks and then planted (January, February, or even March or April) for cropping the same year. We have had good results at Watsonville with such plantings made about February 1.

We are only beginning to get an idea of the potentiality of day-neutral cultivars. They offer tremendous possibilities in reducing some of the costs of strawberry culture in California. As improved day-neutral cultivars are developed and the systems for growing them improve, a bright future may very well unfold.

Chronological Summary of California Cultural Systems and Important Cultural Practices. [See Voth (1986), Bringhurst (1986) and Bringhurst and Voth (1980) for summary discussions, and other of their references in the literature list that give experimental evidence underlying modern commercial practices.] California strawberries were originally planted in the spring on raised beds to permit furrow irrigation. The training system was a single- or double-hill row. Other practices, harvest duration, and yields were similar to those in other U.S. producing regions. However, it was known that yields were higher and the harvest season longer in certain cool coastal areas of the state. Production centered in the central coast

(Watsonville), and moved to include the south coast (Santa Ana) and intermediate coast (Santa Maria) areas to secure earlier fruit production.

After World War II, the new *"university varieties"* showed much increased production in the coastal areas. *Preplanting soil fumigation* with a chloropicrin-methyl bromide combination solved soil disease (verticillium wilt), nematode, and many weed problems. Soil fumigation permits annual planting on the same soil (in southern California) and in alternate years in the central coast (because the protracted harvest period ends too late to permit soil preparation and fumigation).

Planting dates were next altered to give growers as much or more yield and fruit quality as secured in spring plantings, with less growing time, and led to the development of *summer* and *winter planting* systems. Cultivar reaction to these altered planting times varied, and was found to relate to the amount of preplanting chilling that each cultivar needed to grow and fruit well. Optimum digging and planting times for each cultivar on each planting system were worked out to give maximum early or total production. Thus the need for and best length of postdigging refrigerated storage is also determined for each cultivar. Basically little or no postdigging chilling promotes early yield, slightly more chilling promotes total yield, and still more chilling suppresses yield and promotes vegetative growth.

Next came a group of nearly simultaneous improvements on the *strawberry bed and its management*. Strawberries were found to be most sensitive to soil and water salt content, particularly in the alkaline soils of the south coast, compared to the more acidic soils of the central coast. *Wider and lower beds* were cooler in the root zone and accumulated less salt than did taller, narrow beds. Hence wide beds are used in the south coast, where salt accumulation is more critical, and narrower beds in the central coast, where soil temperature is more limiting. *Clear polyethylene* soil *mulches* warmed soil temperatures and produced earlier and total yield increases. *Nitrogen* requirement differences were established for a number of California cultivars in summer plantings. All cultivars in both planting systems had improved fruit yields and fruit size at levels of 100 to 120 lb/acre (112 to 134 kg/ha) compared to no fertilizer. Intermediate rates of nitrogen [200 lb/acre (224 kg/ha)] in the south coast gave the highest total yields for all cultivars except 'Tioga'. Early-yield nitrogen rate effects varied with cultivar. High nitrogen rates of 360 to 400 lb/acre (404 to 449 kg/ha) depressed yields in the central coast only for the 'Lassen' cultivar, but on all cultivars in the south coast. Higher nitrogen levels resulted in reduced fruit appearance, size, and soluble solids; differences in appearance and size were more marked at the warmer location. Leaf nitrogen content increased as nitrogen application rates increased; the best leaf nitrogen level for optimum yield response is about 3% (Voth et al., 1967b).

Off-season (summer and winter) plantings needed sprinkler rather than surface irrigation for plant establishment. Eventually, the main water supply was applied through driplines for better water use, fewer salinity problems, and so on. With plastic mulch in winter plantings being applied shortly after planting, it became necessary to have the fertilizer in place at planting. Voth developed a wide, slotted bed that accommodates four rows of plants, with four slots for fertilizer and plants and two lines of irrigation drip tube (60-in. bed). This high density greatly increased yield potential, and the beds could be planted with the banded fertilizer and irrigation tube laid at the same time. Of course, the traditional split application ammonium salt forms of nitrogen had to be modified, as did fertilizer placement and application. For the extended winter ripening season, Voth recommends (1986) either a slot placement of 200 lb of ammonium phosphate with N-serv (slow release)/acre (224 kg/ha), or a combined planting slot–under the drip line placement of 16-20-0 + N-serv at 200 lb/acre in the slot and AN20 Drip 8 × 25 at 200 lb/acre under the drip line. Fertilizer placement in summer plantings was not critical. Of a number of newer slow-release conventional and soil-amending nitrogen carriers in slot placement, only 21-0-0 + N-serv, 18-0-0 resin, 16-20-0 + N-serv, and 13-16-0 resin, all at nitrogen rates of 300 lb/acre, produced as much yield as the standard 16-20-0 + N-serv at 200 lb/acre. Adding micronutrients or nitro-sul to 16-20-0 + N-serv at combined nitrogen rates of 300 lb/acre neither reduced nor helped the yield compared to the same rate of unamended 16-20-0 + N-serv.

Hand harvesting is used for both fresh (average 70%) and processed (average 30%) strawberries in California. Fresh fruit is harvested without stems but with the cap left on, and graded in the field by the picker (individual fruit handled once only). Fruit for processing is "plugged" (cap and stem removed) during picking. Harvested fruit is shaded and refrigerated to remove field heat as soon as possible. Additionally, pallets of refrigerated fruit containing just under one hundred 12-pint trays are covered with a polyethylene envelope into which CO_2 is injected to retard ripening and senescence and mold growth during transit. The presence of both a fresh and processing outlet, coupled with high yields per acre and an extended harvest season, strengthen the California growers' competitive position.

In south coastal California (Orange, Los Angeles, San Diego, and Ventura counties), which yields most of the fruit for processing, not much fruit is marketed fresh after May. This is because the warmer temperatures produce softer fruit that cannot compete on the fresh markets with fruit grown in the cooler central coast counties of Santa Barbara–San Luis Obispo, Monterey, Santa Cruz, and Santa Clara. The transitional change from the fresh to processing markets almost always takes place in May in southern California, when the greatest number of California strawberries are available for the fresh market.

The negative effects of warmer growing conditions (softer fruit, etc.) are just as undesirable for processing fruit as they are for fresh fruit. Furthermore, the problems are compounded by two other practices that are associated with the harvest of fruit for processing. First, the fruit is frequently left to overripen on the plants prior to harvest in order to facilitate calyx removal. Second, the calyx is removed in the field and sometimes many hours elapse before the fruit is cooled down or frozen.

These marketing problems may be alleviated by firmer-fleshed, earlier-capping cultivars. Also, extension of the harvest season earlier in the south and later in central California by new-day neutral cultivars such as 'Selva' would increase the supply of fresh market berries when prices are high.

Florida.   Production is almost entirely in the Plant City area, about 20 to 25 miles east of Tampa. Acreage is about 5500 (2225 ha), devoted to early fresh market shipping production, with limited numbers of PYO farms.

Principal cultivars: 'Chandler', 'Douglas', 'Pajaro', 'Selva;' some 'Dover', 'Parker', and 'Floridabelle' planted.

Bed configuration: raised, 7 to 9 in. (17 to 23 cm) high at crown, wide enough to accommodate two or four rows of plants, black polyethylene mulched as soon as possible after strip fumigation.

Planting date and stock: fall—after October 5 until mid-November—dates recommended for each cultivar; stocks fresh-dug, no leaves removed, well rooted, often grown in a nursery north of the anthracnose crown rot zone, with usually only the chilling received in the nursery at digging time.

Irrigation: for plant establishment right after planting in the heat of the day to prevent wilting—1 to 2 weeks on an intermittent decreasing schedule— otherwise, to keep the soil moisture within the 7 to 10% range. Overhead sprinkling mostly used with drip lines becoming more common; overhead for frost protection.

Training system: double or quadruple hill, all runners removed, plants set 12 × 12 in (31 × 31 cm) in two-row beds, and 8 to 11 × 8 to 11 in. (20 to 28 cm) in four-row beds.

Nutrition: soil tested each 2 years for P, K, Ca, Mg and pH. Adjust pH to 5.5 to 6.5 for best micronutrient availability. Apply P at soil test recommendations: K—two-row beds—broadcast 180 to 200 lb/acre (200 to 225 kg/ha) following low test, 135 to 150 lb/acre (150 to 170 kg/ha) following high test; banded between rows 1 to 2 in. (2.5 to 5 cm) deep reduce by one-third; N—175 to 200 lb/acre, (196 to 225 kg/ha) depending on soil native fertility, one-half from slow-release source such as sulfur-coated urea, IBDU, or a resin-coated material. For four-row beds apply one-third more fertilizer. Add micronutrients as needed. Minimum leaf levels for optimum yields are B 25 ppm, Ca 0.3%, Cu 5 ppm, Fe 50 ppm, Mg 0.18%, Mn 30 ppm, Mo 0.5 ppm, N 2.8%, P 0.2%, K 1.1%, S 1000 ppm, and Zn 20 ppm. Locascio (1980) summarized methods of increasing fruit yields where 50% of the N + K were applied preplant and the rest injected at intervals through the trickle system.

The Florida industry has been growing and yields have improved to over 23 MT/ha (about 10.5 tons or 21,000 lb/acre). Problems for the industry had been anthracnose disease, two-spotted mite, and securing high-quality transplants. Florida-originated cultivars have high levels of anthracnose tolerance. Anthracnose, a summer and early fall nursery disease, is avoided by growing the crop during the part of the year when anthracnose is not troublesome, and securing nursery stock grown out of the anthracnose area. Cycling (uneven production) of Florida crops due to cold or rainy winters, and late starts of fruiting, have been the biggest recent problems.

Fall-planted, annual hill system for Southeastern North Carolina.
Poling et al. (1988) report on 5 years of experimentation on this system designed to increase yield certainty in eastern North Carolina and to shift ripening forward and increase profit margins. This system is now used on 200 ares (80 ha) in the state and has been used successfully in eastern Tennessee. This modification of the Florida system uses fresh-dug plants with no additional chilling and planting as soon after digging as possible. Methyl bromide preplanting bed fumigation is recommended at 350 lb/acre (393 kg/ha). Planting is through black plastic mulch over the beds, into which either 500 lb of 10-10-10 or 100 to 150 lb/acre (560 or 112 to 168 kg/ha) of a slow-release fertilizer had been broadcast prior to bedding. The best cultivar for this culture was 'Chandler'; other less desirable alternatives were 'Douglas', 'Pajaro', 'Titan', and 'Atlas'. Optimum planting time – September 23 – had been determined for only one locale. As in California, cultivars vary in optimum planting time. Plant spacing on a two-row bed (double hill) for 'Chandler' and 'Pajaro' planted in late September to early October was 12 in. (30 cm) between rows on the bed and 10 in. (25 cm) between plants in the row when the beds were 1.52 m (5 ft) from center to center. This spacing needed 51,640 plants/hectare (20,900 plants/acre). Earlier flowering on annual hills compared to the traditional matted row required more frost and freeze protection. Research on these plots indicated that strawberry blossoms would not be injured until temperatures fell below 27°F ($-2.7°C$). This could save a good deal of water saturation. Spun-bonded polyester row covers significantly increased yield in a colder winter (1 out of 3 years in the trials). However, this suggested that the system may be expanded to cooler sites with row cover protection. A yield of 5 tons/acre (11.2 MT/ha) is considered minimum for conversion to plastic mulch culture from the matted row. Yields appeared well in excess of the minimum. Cooperating growers reported production costs of slightly less than $7400/ha ($3,000/acre) and gross revenues ranging from $12,350 to $24,700/ha ($5000 to $10,000/acre). Double-cropping vegetables with strawberries in succession was offered as an alternative for additional revenue. In practice a commercial muskmelon crop following the strawberries added $4800 gross or $1652 net revenue per acre to the operation.

The Rotthoff "ribbon row".   Walter Rotthoff of Wattsburg, Pennsylvania, near Erie, is fondly called "The Innovator" by his strawberry-growing and researcher friends in the northeastern United States. He has been growing strawberries for about 30 years on a heavy, sloping loam soil in which potatoes were formerly grown. Rotthoff started growing strawberries using the eastern U.S. traditional matted row system. He soon started using his irrigation pump and his overhead sprinkler system to apply almost all of the chemicals used on the farm, except for the high rates of Sinbar applied at renovation time (Rotthoff, 1980). After several years' experience with the matted row, Rotthoff came to the conclusion that production potential was limited and that rising production costs necessitated higher yields than the matted row would deliver. He made several visits to the South Coast Field Station (Santa Ana, California) hoping to adapt some California practices to the east, and he purchased a Marvin Land Plane. His basic theory was that having more narrow "row edges" per acre would lead to higher production.

Linear Spaced Row. Rotthoff started raised-bed culture with the row centers moved in to 3 ft (91 cm). For several years he had the land-fumigated in the fall with methyl bromide–chloropicrin. Planting was in April with mother plants set 5 ft (152 cm) apart in the row (2900 plants/acre = 7175 plants/hectare). Daughter plants were spaced by hand to an average density of 5 plants/linear foot = 30.5 cm of row. Excess runners after August 1 were pruned off by hand. This resulted in a very close-spaced narrow linear row about 12 to 15 in. (30 to 38 cm) wide at maturity. This row could be mowed and renovated by throwing up new soil, and this linear spaced row system doubled the yield. For a fuller treatment of the rationale (landlocked area, preservation of root stress prone but profitable 'Raritan' cultivar, etc.), the pinning down of runners at 2½ in. (6.35 cm) with hairpins, and the ultimate population of about 75,000 multiple crown plants/acre (185,325 plants/hectare), see the article by Wetherell (1980).

Ribbon Row. After 7 or 8 years with the linear spaced row, Rotthoff decided to plant mother plants only at the same spacing (approximately 2.5 in. in the row by 3 ft between the rows = 69,692 plants/acre) with all runners removed. He started with a summer planting in August 1979, from which he harvested the nursery-initiated fruit. His first spring-planted ribbon row was in 1980, an 8-acre block. The system has been adopted by many progressive eastern North American growers for both short-day and day-neutral clone culture.

Bed dimensions of the ribbon row (which originally may have referred to the raised-bed spaced linear row mentioned above) are 18 in. (46 cm) at the base, 10 in. (25 cm) tall, and narrowing to 10 in. at the top. Plants are set 4 in. (10 cm) apart in the rows, and the rows are 36 in. (91 cm) apart (approximately 43,560 plants/acre = 107,765 plants/hectare). The ribbon row is then a very close spaced single-hill system, designed to provide quick rooting and a relatively large rooting area per plant, which the roots fill entirely. This close spacing provides interplant competition and keeps the plants compact. Fruiting should be for 3 years only at this spacing. Beyond that the plants make too many branch crowns and fruit size is reduced.

Plants are set with the roots straight down. The plants are firmed in and the bed settles to 8 in. (20 cm) tall. After the soil is settled, 8 lb/acre (9 kg/ha) of Devrinol herbicide is applied to inhibit rooting of runners. A straw mulch is applied between the rows and up the sides of the beds within 2 weeks of planting, to conserve soil moisture and maintain more even soil temperatures. This also helps to prevent runner rooting.

Nutrition level varies according to the weather. The aim is to keep a steady supply of nutrients available, but on the low or starvation side. A preplant broadcast of lime, phosphorus, and potash is made if needed. Forty pounds per acre (45 kg/ha) of N-P-K is applied through the irrigation system shortly after growth has started. An additional 60 lb/acre (67 kg/ha) of nitrogen is added to the plants between the initial fertilization and the end of growth in November. The fertilizer is added through the irrigation system with each insecticide and miticide application, and varies in concentration from 30 lb/acre (33.7 kg/ha) of nitrogen in September prior to flower bud initiation down to 2 lb/acre (2.2 kg/ha) in November when the plants are becoming dormant.

Other concepts involved with raised-bed culture in the east include: Single rows on a bed are preferred to multiple rows because the eastern cultivars and warm spring and summer climate would result in too dense a growth on the raised beds. Also, the single row is much easier to renovate and carry for more than one season than are multiple rows. Growers and pickers alike enjoy the picking ease and display of fruit in raised-bed situations. Raised beds make water management much easier; they do have some temperature exposure problems during the dormant season.

Matted Row Culture

Matted row is the simplest form of culture and the most economical. It is recommended for inexperienced growers and those diversified growers whose specialty is not strawberries. Although attention to detail is needed, variation in timing and rates of practices is more permissible, within limits. This system also takes advantage of the strawberry's runnering tendency, and uses many of the daughter plants to make a bed and produce fruit in the next season. The system is easy to renovate (Fig. 3–12).

Recommendations for previous crop rotations, preplant soil testing, and fumigation do not vary much between northern and southern areas. Cultivars, spring planting times, and purpose of mulch protection vary from south to north. A comparison of recommended practices in the Coastal Plain of eastern North Carolina and in Ohio is given in Table 3–9. Western North Carolina practices would be much like those in a northern state.

We have not done these fine manuals justice, because they give alternative options at each step and valuable qualifying considerations for each practice. We have not included disease, pest, and specific herbicide recommendations, nor their

FIGURE 3–12 Renovation of a matted row strawberry field after spring harvest.

TABLE 3-9 COMPARISON OF MATTED ROW PRACTICES

PRACTICE	EASTERN N.C.[a]	OHIO[b]
Planting	Late fall, winter, or early spring; dormant, certified disease-free plants, $3^{1}/_{2} \times 2$ ft, proper soil line planting depth stressed	April 15–May 15, registered or certified VF plants, 36- to 40-in. rows × 12–18 in. in rows or 48-in. rows × 24–30 in. in rows, proper planting depth emphasized
Removal of nursery blooms	Yes	Yes
Cultivation	Every 10–14 days at 1–2 in. unless herbicides are used	Compaction concern — heavy soil, herbicides, and some tillage
Fertilization	30 lb N/acre 30 days after planting, 40 lb N/acre late August or early September 15–20 lb N/A January–February — sandy soils, chemigation — contamination warning	25–40 lb N/acre 10–14 days after planting, 25–40 lb N/acre mid August 5 lb 20-20-20 foliar in spring if root damage has occurred
Irrigation	When available soil moisture in upper 6–9 in. is 50% or less, apply enough to penetrate 6–8 in.	*Overhead sprinklers:* start when 50–60% of available moisture in upper 6–12 in. has evaporated, 40 × 50 ft setting with $^{1}/_{8}$-in. nozzles, varies with soil; *trickle:* essentially a daily watering system
Winter mulch	None (applied in spring to keep fruit clean)	After several freezes in low 30's and high 20's, usually between November 15 and 30, 2–3 in. deep, more on clay and raised beds; remove in early spring after danger of severe frost, usually April 1–15; rake between rows for fruit protection
Frost protection	Turn on at 34°F, turn off when ice begins and continues to melt, rate usually 0.12–0.16 in./hr; for winds above 10 mph and temperatures below 32°F, do not irrigate	Protect first-open flowers; rate depends on wind speed, difficult to protect over 20 mph; turn water on at 34°F, continue until ice melts
Training system for rows	12–18 in. wide, up to 24 in. sometimes; former should be 3–3½ ft apart, the latter 4 ft apart	Preferred width 12–18 in.
Pollination	1–2 hives bees/acre	1 colony bees/acre
Renovation	2,4-D for weeds, P and K as needed, N 25–30 lb/acre, mow tops 1 week after 2,4-D, subsoil between rows if needed; narrow beds, thin beds, throw ½ to 1 in. soil over bed, apply preemergence herbicides, set runners	2,4-D, mow 7–8 days later, subsoil, narrow row and throw 1 in. of soil over it, apply 25–40 lb N/acre, apply herbicides, irrigate

[a]From Poling et al. (1984).
[b]From Funt et al. (1985).

cultivar or harvesting option recommendations. These have been treated or refer-enced elsewhere in the book. Also, we have extracted only their matted row options.

Note that spring planting is generally as early as possible to use accumulated ground moisture and moderate temperatures for growth and that planting distances are also adjusted for cultivar vigor. This becomes even more important in day-neutral culture. Irrigation practices are now properly linked to soil moisture content. Frost-protection recommendations are necessarily conservative. Note that fertilizer recommendations for matted rows have declined (they had been 60 to 120 lb N/acre, usually 90 to 100), to control excess vegetative growth and promote fruitfulness.

The *"solid bed"* system as practiced in Ontario differs from the matted row only in the fact that runner growth is not controlled and covers the entire field (Evans et al., 1986). Pickers are carried through the field on a tractor-mounted picking aid. Yields have been 50% or more higher than in matted rows, or they can be picked by once-over machine harvesting. Fruit rot and weed control have been satisfactory with appropriate chemicals, and these plantings have been renovated a second time.

Protected Culture Systems

Protected culture systems offer a fascinating variety of practices and management schemes. Glass cloches have given way to polyethylene low tunnels 16 to 18 in. (41 to 46 cm) tall, which cover one row only, or high 'walk or drive in' tunnels, which span many rows with headroom enough for people and tractors. Protected culture has probably never become popular in the United States because consumers depend on a sequence of outdoor fresh fruit from south to north. With California supplying berries most of the year, and Mexico and Florida filling in when California is not shipping, there would appear to be small need for protected culture. Yet the quantity, quality, and price of fruit reaching eastern and central U.S. markets in the off-season is rarely in sufficient balance to promote increased consumption. So opportunities for protected culture specialists do exist.

Major problems in protected or forcing culture are lack of suitable planting stocks of suitable cultivars, inadequate flower development, poor pollination, im-proper nutrition, mite and powdery mildew infestations, and in houses using nutri-ent film or hydroponic techniques—root disease.

One example may suffice. In Japan, normal field (open) culture results in yields of 4.5 to 6.7 tons/acre (10–15 MT/ha), ripening in the period May to June (M. Minegishi, personal communication). By moving the planting date forward and providing short-day, low-temperature inductive cycles in the nursery prior to cover-ing, or by providing GA + long-day stimulation of nursery-induced flower buds under the poly cover (their "forcing" techniques), the harvest can be broken in two parts starting either December–March followed by April–June, or November–February followed by April–June. The combined yields for either forcing tech-nique are 24.5 tons/acre (55 MT/ha). Similarly, their semiforcing techniques pro-vide extended single late winter or early spring harvests of March or February through June and yields of 13.5 to 20 tons/acre (30 to 45 MT/ha. Semiforcing methods involve planting nursery stock directly into the poly tunnel following 1 month of cold storage, shading the planting prior to covering it with poly, or giving a long-day GA stimulus to preinduced buds while in the tunnel. Interestingly, the authors have seen a double- or split-harvest pattern in southern Italy, where the harvest was protected, in California cultivars such as 'Aliso' and 'Sequoia'. The Japanese strawberry cultivars contain considerable 'Donner' and 'Tahoe' germplasm (two older California cultivars of 'Shasta' and 'Lassen' age).

Home Garden Considerations

The cultural principles for home gardens are the same; although the objectives may vary. For example, a home gardener may desire a very heavy harvest at one time to have enough to eat fresh and process for use through the dormant season. Or a gardener might want modest single harvests but an extended harvest season, or both. The cultivars selected should possess high flavor and be attractive for showing to friends and neighbors; large size would be nice but is not necessary. Ability to persist with minimum care and pesticide usage might be critical. It is recommended to select the best-flavored and best-producing cultivars which are also tolerant to most root and leaf pests *and* adapted to the area. A mixture of Junebearers and one or two new day-neutrals may be desirable. Although the matted row is easier, a spaced row or a double hill can be an attractive option. Double rototill an area thoroughly and mix in a soil insecticide if possible, and lime if needed. Pick an area in full sun. Rake the rototilled area into a gently mounded bed 6 in. (15 cm) high at the crown. Plant hill system Junebearers at 12 in. (30 cm) each way and day-neutrals at 9 to 10 in. (23 to 25 cm) in rows and 12 in. (30 cm) between rows. Get a good soaker hose and slowly wet the soil after planting. Apply a good organic or polyethylene mulch after a few days. Fertilize with 7 to 11 oz per 100 ft² (200 to 315 g per 9.3 m²) 10-10-10 solid fertilizer two to three times each growing season. Use a liquid fertilizer with a polyethylene mulch. It is advisable to turn on the hose on very hot days or provide some cooling for the planting. Turning on the soaker hose several times per week for several hours in the growing season is an easy way to irrigate. You may need to spray a combination fungicide-insecticide mixture if bad spots appear on the leaves or aphids are very bad. One or two such sprays as the leaves emerge in the spring may be helpful. Dead leaves covering the crowns should be enough winter protection except in the coldest areas. The old leaves should be pruned off then and removed as growth starts in the spring. Be sure to have netting to discourage birds at fruiting time.

Trends in Production

The strawberry is increasing in popularity everywhere. There is a strong trend toward controlled growth, particularly toward maintaining compact plant size while increasing yield. Mulched raised beds, hill culture, and day-neutral cultivar culture will increase. We would expect continued interest in protected culture, possibly with better day-neutrals than we have now. There will be a trend toward reduced pesticide use, and more disease, insect, drought, and salt tolerance in our cultivars. We also expect higher fruit solids and ascorbic acid levels, longer shelf life, and firm but more succulent fruits with more delicate aromas. There is also revived interest in processing strawberries and developing new strawberry products and markets. The future looks promising for the strawberry.

REFERENCES

AG CONSULTANT. 1984. Weed control manual 1984 and herbicide guide. Meister, Willoughby, Ohio.

AHRENS, J. F. 1982. Napropamide and Terbacil for newly planted strawberries. Adv. Strawberry Prod. 1:22–26.

ALBREGTS, E. E., AND C. M. HOWARD. 1984. Strawberry production in Florida. Agric. Exp. Stn. IFAS Univ. Fla. Bull. 841.

AVIGDORI-AVIDON, H. 1986. Strawberry. p. 419–449. In S. P. Monselise (ed.). CRC Handbook of fruit set and development. CRC Press, Boca Raton, Fla.

BORTHWICK, H. A., AND M. W. PARKER. 1952. Light in relation to flowering and vegetative development. Rep. 13th Int. Hort. Congr. 2:801–810.

BOYCE, B. R., AND C. R. SMITH. 1967. Low temperature crown injury of dormant 'Catskill' strawberries. Proc. Am. Soc. Hortic. Sci. 91:261–266.

BOYCE, B. R., AND J. B. STRATER. 1984. Comparison of frost injury in strawberry buds, blossoms and immature fruit. Adv. Strawberry Prod. 3:8–10.

BRINGHURST, R. S. 1986. Trends in the California strawberry industry. p. 12–22. In E. E. Burns and E. J. Burns (eds.). Proc. 1986 Winter Conference. North American Strawberry Growers Association, Tarpon Springs, Fla.

BRINGHURST, R. S., AND D. L. GILL. 1970. Origin of *Fragaria* polyploids. II. Unreduced and double-unreduced gametes. Am. J. Bot. 57:969–976.

BRINGHURST, R. S., AND V. VOTH. 1956. Strawberry virus transmission by grafting excised leaves. Plant Dis. Rep. 40:596–600.

BRINGHURST, R. S., AND V. VOTH. 1980. Strawberry production trends in western USA. p. 13–19. In N. F. Childers (ed.). The strawberry: cultivars to marketing. Horticultural Publications, Gainesville, Fla.

BRINGHURST, R. S., V. VOTH, AND D. VAN HOOK. 1960. Relationship of root starch content and chilling history to performance of California strawberries. Proc. Am. Soc. Hortic. Sci. 75:373–381.

BROWN, H. P. (ed.). 1977. Protected strawberry cultivation. (1979 reprint.) Grower Books, London.

BYRNE, D., AND G. JELENKOVIC. 1976. Cytological diploidization in the cultivated octoploid strawberries (*F. × ananassa*.) Can. J. Genet. Cytol. 18:653–659.

CHILDERS, N. F. 1980. Foreword. p. ix. In N. F. Childers (ed.). The strawberry: cultivars to marketing. Horticultural Publications, Gainesville, Fla.

CHILDERS, N. F. 1983. Strawberry growing. p. 451–480. In N. F. Childers (ed.). Modern fruit science. 9th ed. Horticultural Publications, Gainesville, Fla.

CRAIG, D. L. 1982. Strawberry cultivars for eastern Canada. Agric. Can. Publ. 1744/E.

DANA, M. N. 1980. The strawberry plant and its environment. p. 32–44. In N. F. Childers (ed.). The strawberry: cultivars to marketing. Horticultural Publications, Gainesville, Fla.

DARROW, G. M. 1929. Inflorescence types of strawberry varieties. Am. J. Bot. 16:571–585.

DARROW, G. M. 1936. Interrelation of temperature and photoperiodism in the production of fruit buds and runners in the strawberry. Proc. Am. Soc. Hortic. Sci. 34:360–363.

DARROW, G. M. 1937. Strawberry improvement. p. 445–495. In U.S. Dep. Agric. Yearb. Wash., D.C.

DARROW, G. M. 1966. The strawberry: history, breeding, and physiology. Holt, Rinehart and Winston, New York.

DARROW, G. M., AND G. F. WALDO. 1934. Responses of strawberry varieties and species to the duration of the daily light period. U.S. Dep. Agric. Tech. Bull. 453.

DAUBENY, H. A. 1980. Strawberry production trends in Canada. p. 21–31. In N. F. Childers (ed.). The strawberry: cultivars to marketing. Horticultural Publications, Gainesville, Fla.

DURNER, E. F., J. A. BARDEN, D. G. HIMELRICK, AND E. B. POLING. 1984. Photoperiod and temperature effects on flower and runner development in day-neutral, Junebearing, and everbearing strawberries. J. Am. Soc. Hortic. Sci. 109:396–400.

EMERSON, L. P. BILL, JR. 1980. Mexico's strawberry production. p. 53–61. In N. F. Childers (ed.). The strawberry: cultivars to marketing. Horticultural Publications, Gainesville, Fla.

EVANS, W. D., A. DALE, AND C. HUNTER. 1986. The strawberry in Ontario. Minist. Agric. Food Ontario Publ. 513.

FADEEVA, T. S. 1966. Communication 1. Principles of genome analysis (with reference to the genus *Fragaria*). Genetika 2:6–16.

FORNEY, C. F., AND P. J. BREEN. 1985. Dry matter partitioning and assimilation in fruiting and deblossomed strawberry. J. Am. Soc. Hortic. Sci. 110:181–185.

FRAZER, N., et al. 1970. Virus diseases of small fruits and grapevines. Univ. Calif. Handb., Berkeley, Cal.

FUNT, R. C., B. L. GOULART, C. K. CHANDLER, J. D. UTZINGER, M. A. ELLIS, R. M. RIEDEL, R. N. WILLIAMS, AND M. A. PALMER. 1985. Ohio strawberry manual. Coop. Ext. Serv., Ohio State Univ. Bull. 436.

GALLETTA, G. J. 1984. Strawberry variety update: U.S. regional analysis and USDA synopsis. p. 35–40. In J. W. Courter (ed.). Proc. 1984 Winter Conference. North American Strawberry Growers Association, Dixon Springs, Ill.

GALLETTA, G. J., A. D. DRAPER, AND H. J. SWARTZ. 1981. New everbearing strawberries. HortScience 16:726.

GUTTRIDGE, C. G. 1985. *Fragaria* × *Ananassa*. p. 16–33. In A. H. Halvey (ed.). CRC handbook of flowering. Vol. III. CRC Press, Boca Raton, Fla.

HARTMANN, H. T. 1947a. The influence of temperature on the photoperiodic response of several strawberry varieties grown under controlled environmental conditions. Proc. Am. Soc. Hortic. Sci. 50:243–245.

HARTMANN, H. T. 1947b. Some effects of temperature and photoperiod on flower formation and runner production in the strawberry. Plant Physiol. 22:407–420.

HAVIS, L. 1938. Freezing injury to strawberry flower buds, flowers and young fruits. Bimonthly Bull. Ohio Agric. Exp. Stn. 22(194):168–171.

HEIDE, O. M. 1977. Photoperiod and temperature interactions in growth and flowering of the strawberry. Physiol. Plant. 40:21–26.

HEMPHILL, D. D. 1980. Weed control in strawberries. p. 309–317. In N. F. Childers (ed.). The strawberry: cultivars to marketing. Horticultural Publications, Gainesvlile, Fla.

References   **153**

HUGHES, H. M. 1980. Strawberries. 9th ed. Ministry of Agriculture, Fisheries and Food Ref. Book 95. London: Her Majesty's Stationery Office.

ISLAM, A. S. 1961. The haploid strawberry, *Fragaria vesca* L., and the significance of haploidy in phylogeny and plant breeding. Scientist 4:1–21.

JAHN, O. L., AND M. N. DANA. 1966. Fruiting and growth of the strawberry plant. Proc. Am. Soc. Hortic. Sci. 88:352–359.

JAHN, O. L., AND M. N. DANA. 1970. Effects of cultivar and plant age on vegetative growth of the strawberry, *Fragaria x ananassa*. Am. J. Bot. 57:993–999.

JEPSON, W. H. 1951. Manual of flowering plants of California. University of California Press, Berkeley.

LEE, D. V. 1966. Early history of the strawberry. p. 115–23. The strawberry from Chile. p. 124–39. Duchesne and his work. p. 140–72. Early breeding in Europe. p. 73–80. In G. M. Darrow (ed.). The strawberry: history, breeding and physiology. Holt, Rinehart and Winston, New York.

LOCASCIO, S. J. 1980. Nutrition application through trickle irrigation systems. p. 95–99. In N. F. Childers (ed.). The strawberry: cultivars to marketing, Horticultural Publications, Gainesville, Fla.

MAAS, J. L. (ed.). 1984. Compendium of strawberry diseases. American Phytopathological Society, St. Paul, Minn.

MARINI, R. P., AND B. R. BOYCE. 1979. Influence of low temperatures during dormancy on growth and development of 'Catskill' strawberry plants. J. Am. Soc. Hortic. Sci. 104:159–162.

MULLIN, R. H., et al. 1974. Meristem culture frees strawberries of mild yellow edge, pallidosis and mottle diseases. Phytopathology 64:1425–1429.

NICOLL, M. F. 1984. Variation in expression of the everbearing trait in cultivated strawberry, *Fragaria × ananassa* Duch. M.S. Thesis. University of Maryland, College Park.

NICOLL, M. F., AND G. J. GALLETTA. 1987. Variation in growth and flowering habits of Junebearing and everbearing strawberries. J. Am. Soc. Hortic. Sci. 112:872–880.

PERRY, K. B., AND E. B. POLING. 1986. Field observation of frost injury in strawberry buds and blossoms. Adv. Strawberry Prod. 5:31–37.

POLING, E. B., R. K. JONES, K. A. SORENSEN, R. E. SNEED, A. R. BONANNO, K. B. PERRY, AND M. J. AST. 1984. Commercial strawberry production in North Carolina. N.C. Agric. Ext. Serv. Publ. AG-05.

POLING, E. B., K. B. PERRY, W. J. LAMONT, AND J. B. EARP. 1988. Annual hill system strawberry research. Hortic. Sci. Res. Ser. 76, N.C. Agric. Res. Ser.

POPENOE, J., AND H. J. SWARTZ. 1985. Yield component comparison on strawberry plants grown in various cultural systems. Adv. Strawberry Prod. 4:10–14.

PROEBSTING, E. L., SR. 1957. The effect of soil temperature on mineral nutrition of the strawberry. Proc. Am. Soc. Hortic. Sci. 69:278–281.

REED, C. F. 1966. Wild strawberry species of the world. p. 108–121. In G. M. Darrow (ed.). The strawberry: history, breeding and physiology. Holt, Rinehart and Winston, New York.

RENQUIST, A. R., P. J. BREEN, AND L. W. MARTIN. 1982. Effects of black polyethylene mulch on strawberry leaf elongation and diurnal leaf water potential. J. Am. Soc. Hortic. Sci. 107:640–643.

ROBERTS, A. N., AND A. L. KENWORTHY. 1956. Growth and composition of the strawberry plant in relation to root temperature and intensity of nutrition. Proc. Am. Soc. Hortic. Sci. 68:157–168.

ROTTHOFF, W. 1980. Challenging practices, systems and thoughts for the '80's'. p. 77–81. In N. F. Childers (ed.). The strawberry: cultivars to marketing. Horticultural Publications, Gainesville, Fla.

SCOTT, D. H. 1951. Cytological studies on polyploids derived from tetraploid *F. vesca* and cultivated strawberries. Genetics 36:311–331.

SCOTT, D. H., AND F. J. LAWRENCE. 1975. Strawberries, p. 71–97. In J. Janick and J. N. Moore (eds.). Advances in fruit breeding. Purdue University Press, West Lafayette, Ind.

SENANAYAKE, Y. D. A., AND R. S. BRINGHURST. 1967. Origin of *Fragaria* polyploids. 1. Cytological analyses. Am. J. Bot. 54:221–228.

SHOEMAKER, J. S. 1978. Strawberries. p. 103–187. In J. S. Shoemaker (ed.). Small fruit culture. 5th ed. AVI, Westport, Conn.

SKROCH, W., AND T. J. MONACO. 1980. Weeds in strawberries. p. 318–321. In N. F. Childers (ed.). The strawberry: cultivars to marketing. Horticultural Publications, Gainesville, Fla.

STAUDT, G. 1967. The genetics and evolution of the genus *Fragaria* 2. Species hybridization of *F. vesca* × *F. orientalis* and *F. virdis* × *F. orientalis*. Z. Pflanzenzuchtg. 58:309–322.

STAUDT, G. 1968. The genetics and evolution of Heterosis in the genus *Fragaria* 3. Research with hexaploid and octaploid kinds. Z. Pflanzenzuchtg. 59:83–102.

SWARTZ, H. J., C. S. WALSH, A. F. GEYER, L. DOUGLASS, G. J. GALLETTA, AND R. H. ZIMMERMAN. 1982. Plant crown competition in strawberry matted rows. Adv. Strawberry Prod. 1:6–11.

VOTH, V. 1986. Efficient use of nitrogen fertilizers in California strawberry production. p. 31–38. In E. E. Burns and E. J. Burns (eds.). Proc. 1986 Winter Conference. North American Strawberry Growers Association, Tarpon Springs, Fla.

VOTH, V., AND R. S. BRINGHURST. 1958. Fruiting and vegetative response of Lassen strawberries in southern California as influenced by nursery source, time of planting, and plant chilling history. Proc. Am. Soc. Hortic. Sci. 72:186–197.

VOTH, V., AND R. S. BRINGHURST. 1962. Early mulched strawberries. Calif. Agric. 16(2):14–15.

VOTH, V., AND R. S. BRINGHURST. 1970. Influence of nursery harvest date, cold storage, and planting date on performance of winter planted California strawberries. J. Am. Soc. Hortic. Sci. 95:496–500.

VOTH, V., R. S. BRINGHURST, AND H. J. BOWEN, JR. 1967a. Effect of bed system, bed height, and clear polyethylene mulch on yield, salt accumulation and soil temperature in California strawberries. Proc. Am. Soc. Hortic. Sci. 91:242–248.

VOTH, V., K. URIU, AND R. S. BRINGHURST. 1967b. Effect of high nitrogen applications on yield, earliness, fruit quality, and leaf composition of California strawberries. Proc. Am. Soc. Hortic. Sci. 91:249–256.

WAISTER, P. D. 1972. Wind as a limitation on the growth and yield of strawberries. J. Hortic. Sci. 47:411–418.

WELCH, N. C., R. BRINGHURST, A. C. GREATHEAD, V. VOTH, W. S. SEYMAN, N. F. McCALLEY, AND H. F. OTTO. 1982. Strawberry production in California. Div. Agric. Sci. Univ. Calif. Coop. Ext. Leafl. 2959.

WETHERELL, R. L., JR. 1980. A spaced row planting system. p. 89–94. In N. F. Childers (ed.). The strawberry: cultivars to marketing, Horticultural Publications, Gainesville, Fla.

WHITE, P. R. 1927. Studies of the physiological anatomy of the strawberry. J. Agric. Res. 35:481–492.

WILHELM, S. 1961. Diseases of strawberry. Calif. Agric. Ext. Serv. Circ. 494.

References

WILHELM. S., AND P. E. NELSON. 1970. A concept of rootlet health of strawberries in pathogen-free field soil achieved by fumigation. p. 208–215. In T. A. Toussoun, R. V. Bega, and P. E. Nelson (eds.). Root diseases and soil-borne pathogens. University of California Press, Berkeley.

WILHELM, S., AND R. D. NELSON. 1980. Fungal diseases of the strawberry plant. p. 245–292. In N. F. Childers (ed.). The strawberry: cultivars to marketing. Horticultural Publications, Gainesville, Fla.

WILHELM, S., AND J. E. SAGEN. 1974. A history of the strawberry from ancient gardens to modern markets. Agricultural Publications, University of California, Berkeley.

SUGGESTED READING

ALBREGTS, E. E., AND C. M. HOWARD. 1984. Strawberry production in Florida. Univ. Fla. Bull. 841.

ANDERSON, W. 1963. Bibliography of world literature on the strawberry, 1920–1962. Fellowship of the Library Association, St. Louis, Mo.

CHILDERS, N. F. (ed.). 1980. The strawberry: cultivars to marketing. Horticultural Publications, Gainesville, Fla.

DARROW, G. M. (ed.). 1966. The strawberry: history, breeding, and physiology. Holt, Rinehart and Winston, New York.

DEBOR, W. H. 1976. Bibliography of international literature on strawberries. Bibliographische Relhe der technischen universitat, Berlin.

EVANS, W. D., A. DALE, AND C. HUNTER. 1986. The strawberry in Ontario. Min. of Agric. and Food, Ontario, Canada.

FUNT, R. C., et al. 1985. Ohio strawberry production, management and marketing manual. Ohio State Univ. Bull. 436.

MAAS, J. L. 1984. Compendium of strawberry diseases. American Phytopathological Society, St. Paul, Minn.

MAAS, J. L. (ed.). 1988. Advances in strawberry production. Publ. BARC-W. Fruit Laboratory, U.S. Department of Agriculture, Beltsville, Md.

PRITTS, M., AND A. DALE. 1989. Dayneutral strawberry production guide. Cornell Univ. Info. Bull. 215.

ULRICH, A., M. A. E. MOSTAFA, AND W. A. ALLEN. 1980. Strawberry deficiency symptoms: a visual and plant analysis guide to fertilization. Univ. Calif. Publ. 4098.

WELCH, N. C., et al. 1982. Strawberry production in California. Univ. Calif. Leafl. 2959.

WILHELM, S., AND J. E. SAGEN. 1974. A history of the strawberry from ancient gardens to modern markets. Univ. Calif. Publ. 4031.

Chapter 4

Raspberry Management

P. C. CRANDALL
H. A. DAUBENY

INTRODUCTION

Red raspberries require relatively cool summer and moderate winter temperatures for best production. Ideal conditions are found in only a few locations worldwide. There are intensive areas of commercial production in the western portions of Oregon, Washington, and British Columbia (the Pacific northwest region of North America) and in northern California, eastern Scotland, and southern England. Production on a more limited scale occurs in eastern Canada and the northeastern United States, as well as New Zealand, Australia, Chile, the USSR, and in various European countries. They are also grown in many home gardens and small commercial plantings as far north as Finland and Sweden and south into some of the more tropical countries where higher elevations provide low enough temperatures to satisfy the chilling requirement of the crop.

Much of the fruit grown in the Pacific northwest region of America and in Scotland is processed by freezing for retail and institutional markets and for later processing into purees, preserves, jellies, concentrates, juices, and yogurt. Because of the perishable nature of raspberries, fresh sales have frequently been restricted to local markets. However, there is increasing interest in shipping by air, truck, or rail to fresh market sale points. This interest is being stimulated by forced-air cooling, improved handling methods, and the introduction of more suitable cultivars, which produce firmer fruit with a brighter, nondarkening red color and some resistance to postharvest rots. During the winter months, fresh raspberries from the southern hemisphere are now available throughout North America and western Europe.

Primocane fruiting red raspberries are increasing in popularity. They produce fruit on the upper portions of current season canes during late summer and fall. They will also produce a second crop on the lower portion of the canes if the canes are left over winter. An increasingly common practice is to cut all canes off at ground level during the dormant season and thus to produce only the fall crop. This greatly reduces pruning labor and in colder climates, where overwintering canes are often damaged by cold, eliminates winter kill as a cultural problem. The fruit is produced during the off-season and commands a premium price on the fresh market. Recent developments in the use of growth regulators (Crandall and Garth, 1981; Brun and Garth, 1984a) and in the development of new, early, high-producing cultivars should encourage even more plantings of primocane fruiting raspberries (Lawrence, 1980b).

Black raspberries are less able to withstand cold winter temperatures than red raspberries, are more subject to diseases, produce less, and have a smaller market potential. Cold winter temperatures limit their production. They are mostly grown in home gardens and small commercial acreages for local consumption. The largest commercial production area is in the state of Oregon. There they are grown for processing to be used as flavoring for ice cream and yogurt, and for jams and jellies or pie fillings. Limited quantities are used to make edible dyes for foodstuffs.

The purple raspberry has many of the characteristics of the black raspberry except that it is more vigorous and intermediate in color. The fruit has lacked the quality necessary to compete well with either the red or the black cultivars; hence purple raspberries have largely been grown in home gardens. However, improved cultivars are being grown commercially in the northeastern United States.

CULTIVATED TYPES

Most red raspberry cultivars originated from two subspecies of diploid *Rubus idaeus* L.: *R. idaeus vulgatus* Arrhen., the native red raspberry of Europe, and *R. idaeus strigosus* (Michx.), the native red raspberry of North America and eastern Asia. The two have sometimes been given species rank but are now generally considered as subspecies. They differ in that the *R.i. vulgatus* fruits are usually a dark red color and conic or thimble-shaped with few or no glandular hairs, whereas the *R.i. strigosus* fruits are lighter red, round shaped, and have numerous glandular hairs (Ourecky, 1975). In addition, the growth habit of the *R.i. strigosus* is more open and the canes are more slender and glaucous with stiffer prickles and a darker color (Hedrick, 1922). *R.i. strigosus* is the more winter hardy of the subspecies (Darrow,

1937). The subspecies intercross with little or no sterility in the resulting seedlings (Ourecky, 1975).

Although most red raspberry cultivars are derived from both of the *R. idaeus* subspecies described, other diploid *Rubus* species have also been used or are currently being used in breeding programs. Among these, *R. occidentalis* L., the black raspberry, has figured most prominently. This species has provided a source of genes for resistance to postharvest fruit rot, mainly caused by *Botrytis cinerea* Pers. ex. Fr., and to *Amphorophora idaei* Born, the aphid vector of red raspberry mosaic virus in Europe, as well as genes for fruit firmness and late ripening (Keep, 1984). Four British cultivars, 'Malling Leo', 'Malling Joy', 'Glen Prosen', and 'Glen Moy', with *R. occidentalis* genes in their derivation have now been released (Jennings, 1982a; Keep, 1984). In North America, the primocane fruiting cultivars, 'Amity' and 'Summit', released from the Oregon State University–U. S. Department of Agriculture breeding program, also have genes from this species in their derivation.

R. arcticus L., the Arctic raspberry, has been used in red raspberry breeding programs as a source of genes for extreme winter hardiness and also for early primocane fruiting. Cultivars derived from this species are 'Merva' and 'Heija', which are winter hardy (Hiirsalmi and Sako, 1976) and 'Malling Autumn Bliss', which is early primocane fruiting (Keep, 1984).

Two Asiatic species, *R. kuntzeanus* Hemsl. and *R. parvifolius* Nutt., have been used as sources of low chilling requirement and for tolerance to fluctuating winter temperatures and high summer temperatures (Darrow, 1924; Hull, 1961; Overcash, 1972). Cultivars derived from these species include 'Van Fleet', 'Southland', and 'Dormanred'.

Most black raspberry cultivars are derived from *R. occidentalis* L. An exception is the cultivar 'Mysore', which was selected from *R. albescens* Roxb., an Asiatic subtropical species (Ourecky, 1975). Purple raspberries are usually F$_1$ hybrid selections from crosses of *R. occidentalis* × *R. idaeus*.

RELATED GERMPLASM AND UTILITY

The two *R. idaeus* subspecies still offer much potentially useful germplasm for red raspberry breeding programs. For example, in recent years new genes for resistance to *Amphorophora agathonica* Hottes, the aphid vector of the raspberry mosaic virus complex in North America, have been found in wild populations of R.i. strigosis (Daubeny and Stary, 1982). Other useful traits existing in this subspecies include winter hardiness, primocane fruiting, and resistance to cane diseases, such as spur blight *(Didymella applanata* Niessl. Sacc.) and cane *Botrytis (Botrytis cinerea* Pers. ex. Fr.) and also resistance to root rot caused by one or more *Phytophthora* species (Barritt et al., 1979; Daubeny, 1980; Daubeny and Stary, 1982; Duncan and Kennedy, 1986; Lawrence, 1980a). Among the useful traits found in recent years in wild populations of *R. i. vulgatus* are large fruit size, easy fruit abscission or removal, and resistance to fruit rots (mostly caused by *B. cinerea)* and to powdery mildew *(Sphaerotheca macularis* (Fr.) Jaczewski) (Keep et al., 1980).

Several other diploid *Rubus* species are being used in breeding programs as sources of disease and insect resistance and for desirable horticultural traits. These include the afore-mentioned *R. occidentalis* and *R. arcticus*. In addition, *R. coreanus* Mig., an Asiatic species, is a source of resistance to spur blight, cane *Botrytis*, powdery mildew, and *A. idaeii* (Keep et al., 1980; Keep, 1984). *R. crataegifolius* Bunge, also an Asiatic species, is a source of fruit rot resistance, good color, easy abscission, early ripening, and resistance to the raspberry beetle, *Byturus tomentosus* (Deg.) (Keep, 1984; Knight, 1980). *R. phoenicolasius* Maxim, the Japanese wineberry, is also being used as a source of resistance to the raspberry beetle (Knight, 1980). *R. cockburnianus,* another Asiatic species, is a source of high fruit numbers per lateral and of easy fruit abscission (Keep, 1984). *R. spectabilis,* the North American salmonberry, contains genes for early floricane and primocane fruiting, and for bright fruit color (Keep, 1984). *R. odoratus,* the purple-flowering raspberry of eastern North America, is a source of early primocane fruiting. Other diploid *Rubus* species identified in recent years as sources of useful genes for breeding programs include *R. pileatus* Focke and *R. mesogaeus* Focke, both with cane *Botrytis* resistance, and *R. lasiostylus* Focke, with easy fruit abscission and large fruit size (Jennings, 1980; Keep, 1984).

BOTANY

Red raspberries have a biennial top and a perennial root system. First-year shoots (primocanes) develop either from vegetative buds on the roots or from the basal buds of second-year canes (floricanes). In young plantings, many primocanes originate from root buds; however, as the plantings become older, more of them develop from basal buds.

Morphology and Ontogeny

Primocane development. Some of the new shoots from root buds begin growth during late summer but seldom reach more than 6 in. (15 cm) in height (Williams, 1959a). The shorter days and cool temperatures of fall cause them to remain dormant until spring, at which time they continue elongation from the terminal bud (Williams, 1959b). As growth begins in the spring, additional shoots arise from other root buds and from basal buds of floricanes (Fig. 4–1). These vegetative shoots exhibit strong apical dominance and seldom form branches in well-established plantings. Strongly growing primocanes in young plantings, where the competition from fruiting canes is minimal, often branch rather freely. Removal of the apical portion of the primocanes will also cause them to branch.

Primocanes elongate rapidly in the spring, laying down nodes spaced at varying distances apart, depending on vigor, light exposure, and cultivar. The nodes are close together at the base, farther apart on the intermediate part of the primocane, and become quite close together near the top. Each node usually produces a ternate- or quinate-compound leaf (Roberts and Colby, 1960; Engard, 1944). A cluster of buds is formed in the leaf axils, consisting of primary and secondary buds together with one or more tertiary buds (Wood and Robertson, 1957; Keep, 1969). A

FIGURE 4-1 Primocanes (new shoots) arise either from lateral buds on roots or from buds at the base of floricanes (fruiting canes). This figure shows a new shoot arising from a basal bud.

secondary cambium is formed but soon loses its ability to divide; hence the diameter of the internodes is fixed soon after development (Engard, 1944; Waldo, 1935).

The new shoots are spine-free or variously armed with many to few spines and with pubescent hairs. The color of the spines and hairiness of the newly developed shoot tip are considered to be reliable distinguishing characteristics for separating groups of cultivars (Grubb, 1922; Odyvin, 1969).

Red and black raspberry morphologies are illustrated in Figs. 4-2 and 4-3.

Flower bud initiation. The axillary buds usually remain undifferentiated until growth of the terminal bud slows or stops during early fall (Williams, 1959c). The first evidence of flower bud differentiation occurs in the terminal bud (Williams, 1959c; Vasilakakis, 1979). Soon thereafter initiation begins in the primary axillary buds near the tip of the cane. Buds between the fifth and the tenth nodes tend to advance most rapidly (Williams, 1959c; Mathers, 1952). Development proceeds generally from the tip downward. Secondary bud development closely follows that of the primary buds. Differentiation in tertiary buds seldom proceeds beyond the initial flattening of the apical meristem. Once flower buds are initiated, differentiation and development of the floral organs proceeds acropetally (Haltvick and Struckmeyer, 1965).

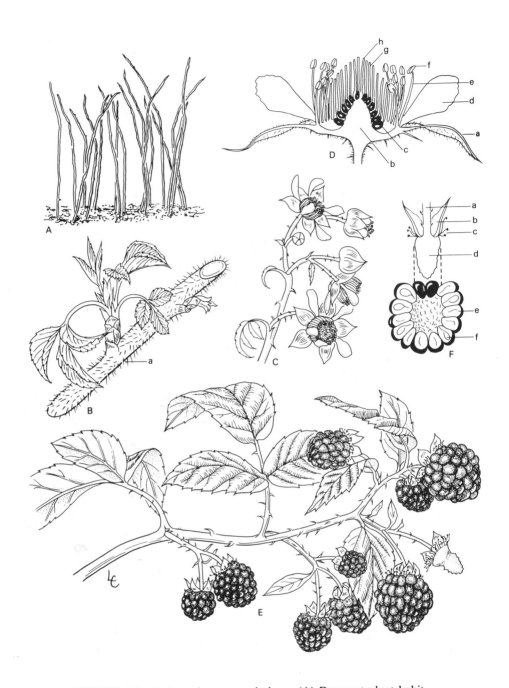

FIGURE 4-2 Red raspberry morphology. (A) Dormant plant habit. (B) Lateral spring growth from cane: a, cane and prickles. (C) Inflorescence. (D) Flower longitudinal section: a, sepal (bract); b, receptacle; c, ovary; d, petal; e, filament; f, anther; g, style; h, stigma. (E) Fruiting lateral. (F) Fruit longitudinal section: a, pedicle; b, calyx; c, dried anthers; d, receptacle (torus); e, druplet; f, pyrene (seed).

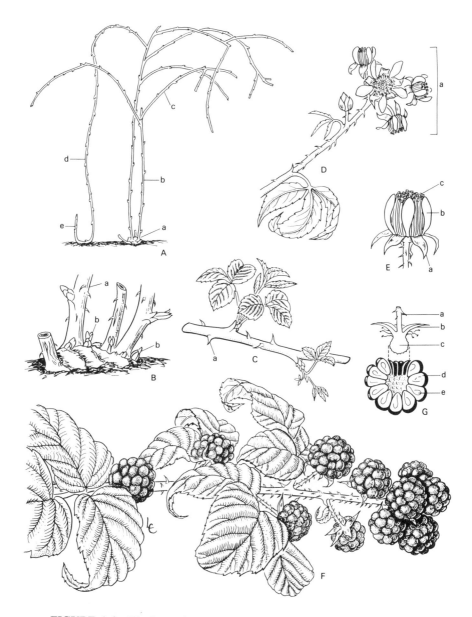

FIGURE 4-3 Black raspberry morphology. (A) Dormant plant
habit — partially pruned: a, crown base; b, overwintering cane; c, lateral
branch; d, lateral permitted to "rat-tail" and trail for layering; e, dormant shoot of tip layer. (B) Detail of crown base area: a, overwintered
floricane base; b, basal bud that will produce new primocane. (C)
Shoot emergence on lateral branch: a, prickle. (D) Flowering shoot: a,
terminal inflorescence. (E) Detail of flower: a, sepal; b, petal; c, anthers. (F) Fruiting shoot. (G) Fruit longitudinal section: a, pedicel; b,
calyx (sepals); c, receptacle (torus); d, druplets of aggregate fruit; e,
pyrene (seed).

The terminal flower of the inflorescence always develops first (Williams, 1959c). Additional flowers arise in the axils of bracts below the terminal flower to form a loose, racemose inflorescence (Reeve, 1954). In the axils of leaf primordia located below the terminal inflorescence of the fruit lateral, other inflorescences develop, which in turn consist of a terminal flower subtended by additional flower buds. These individual inflorescences are arranged along the fruit lateral, with the distal inflorescences generally having the most flower buds.

The number of microscopic flower buds (Fig. 4-4) continues to increase in number and advance in stage of development during the fall, ceasing during the cold winter months, and then continuing as weather warms in the spring. By the time growth resumes there are flower buds in all stages of development, from the initial flattening of the meristematic apex to well-advanced flower buds, depending on their location on the cane and on the individual lateral and inflorescence (Crandall et al., 1974b).

Floricane development. The primocanes overwinter as dormant canes and when growth starts in the spring produce flowers and are called floricanes. The primary axillary buds begin to elongate forming fruit laterals; the leaves unfold, and are followed by the flower buds. The general sequence is for upper laterals to begin first, followed by lower laterals. The terminal inflorescences of the lateral are usually most advanced and reach anthesis first. This sequence of growth and flowering is later reflected in the time of fruit maturity, upper and outer fruit ripening first followed by the inside and lower fruit.

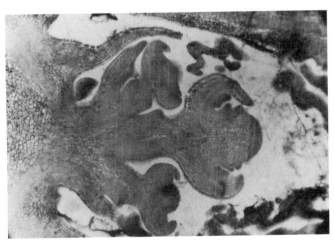

FIGURE 4-4 Flower primordia (microscopic flower buds) develop in the axillary buds of leaves of spring-flowering cultivars during the fall of the previous year. In primocane-fruiting (everbearing) cultivars, flower primordia develop in the axillary buds of the upper portions of primocanes during early summer. This flower primordium has three flowers. The terminal flower shows the initial development of sepals, stamens, pistils, and receptacle.

The calyx and corolla of the flowers are pentamerous and the stamens are numerous in two crowded whorls (Reeve, 1954). The pistils arise spirally in several ranks on an elongated receptacle. They range in number from about 80 to over 200. It requires fertilization of about 70 to 100 of the pistils to form a normal fruit.

Pollination. The peripheral pistils become receptive first and are ready to be pollinated at or just before anthesis. Therefore, plant breeders emasculate flowers at the late bud stage by cutting around the bud outside of the nectary (Topham, 1970). This removes all flower parts except the pistils and receptacle. The pollen is applied two or three times at 1- or 2-day intervals because not all the pistils are receptive at one time.

Although most commercial red raspberry cultivars are self-fruitful, they require insect transfer of pollen to provide adequate pollination (Shanks, 1969). Failure of an adequate number of ovules to set produces a fruit that crumbles when picked.

Fruit development. The fruit is classified as an aggregate fruit. Each pistil has two ovules, only one of which usually develops. This produces a single-seeded drupelet having anatomical and growth characteristics similar to those of the peach. Hill (1958) found that as the fruit enlarges it goes through a typical, double sigmoid growth curve coinciding with the following stages: (1) cell division, bloom to 10 days; (2) embryo development and hardening of the endocarp, 10 to 20 days; and (3) cell enlargement, 20 to 32 days.

The individual drupelets are held together by a network of fine, nearly microscopic, interlacing hairs (Reeve, 1954; Robbins and Sjulin, 1986). In the black raspberry and perhaps in some red raspberry fruits, there may also be some cuticular fusion at the commissural sides of the drupelets. In the center of each drupelet is a pyrene with a hard stony endocarp enclosing one or occasionally two seeds.

Raspberries separate from the receptacle (torus) at maturity. There is a weakly organized abscission zone. Reeve (1954) decided that there is no abscission tissue, but Mackenzie (1979) concluded that there is a group of specialized cells at the base of each drupelet where abscission occurs. As the fruit ripens, the mesocarp cells in this zone expand and cause the cortical and epidermal cells to rupture.

Chemical composition of the fruit. As raspberries proceed through the final cell enlargement stage of growth, ethylene production increases (Blanpied, 1972), anthocyanin pigments, pH and total soluble solids increase, and titratable acidity drops. Also, the fruit retention strength (ease of fruit removal) decreases from about 300g (underripe) to 25g (overripe) (Mason, 1974).

The root system. The root system of raspberries is extensive and consists of many fibrous and small diameter roots. Christensen (1947) found roots to a depth of 70 in. (175 cm). The upper 10 in. (25 cm) of the soil contained 70% of the root system and the next lower 10 in. (25 cm) contained 20%. This compares to the data obtained by Crandall, et al., (1969) on water extraction patterns of raspberries growing in a well drained soil. They found that 64% of the water used came from the surface 24 in. (60 cm) of the soil, 25% from the 24 to 48 in. (60 to 120 cm) zone and 11% from below 48 in. (120 cm).

Roots begin growth soon after shoots start in the spring and continue growth in the fall for a period of time after above ground growth ceases. The most active growth occurs during midsummer if adequate soil moisture is available (Atkinson, 1973).

The vegetative buds on roots undergo a dormancy cycle closely related to the cane dormancy cycle (Jennings and Carmichael, 1975). They are very unlikely to grow during May, June and July, grow somewhat better during April and August, and grow best during January, February, and March (Hudson, 1954).

Fruiting habit of primocane fruiting cultivars. The normal fruiting habit of floricane fruiting cultivars is to develop vegetative shoots one year and to fruit the next season. Some cultivars, however, when subjected to summer stress conditions, will bloom and form fruits on the distal ends of the primocanes during the fall (Keep, 1961). This tendency seems to be partly genetic but is even more closely related to early cessation of primocane elongation as a result of stress conditions. The true primocane fruiting cultivars (everbearers) initiate flowers in the buds of actively growing primocanes during the summer. This characteristic is most common in red raspberries; however, it is also present in black and purple cultivars (Keep, 1961). The first microscopic evidence of flower initiation can be observed in 'Heritage' raspberry shoots when they are about 20 in. (50 cm) tall (15 to 20 nodes) (Crandall and Garth, 1981; Vasilakakis et al., 1979). This stage of development occurs shortly after the time when Vasilakakis et al. (1980) were able to hasten flowering by cold treatment and coincides with the time when Crandall and Garth (1981) were able to increase early autumn fruitfulness with a spray application of daminozide. Only the buds on the upper one-fourth to one-third of the primocanes develop flowers and fruit during the current season. The lower two-thirds of the canes, if retained until the following spring, produce a spring crop of fruit.

Special characteristics of black and purple raspberries. The growth habit of black raspberries is similar in many ways to that of the red raspberry; however, there are some important differences. The purple raspberry, being a hybrid of the two, tends to be intermediate with the characteristics of the black raspberry parent dominant.

The primocanes of red raspberry grow upright, whereas the primocanes of purple and black raspberries bend over during late summer. Where the cane tips touch the ground, roots develop, forming a new plant. Most of the replacement canes of black raspberry arise from basal buds, very few originate as root suckers. Propagation must therefore be by tip layering (Fig. 4-5). The purple cultivars produce more root suckers but retain a strong tip-layering habit. They therefore are propagated by both root suckers and tip layers. All three types will branch when the terminal bud is removed, but the red raspberry produces weak, low-yielding branches, whereas the purple and black cultivars produce strong, very productive branches (Beach, 1934). Black and purple raspberry canes have many, stiff, sharp

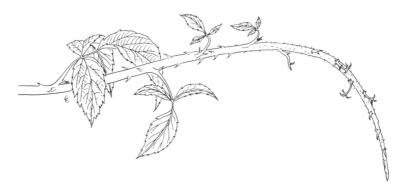

FIGURE 4-5 Primocane at "rat tail" stage of new shoot growth in black raspberry, showing proper appearance for tip layering.

spines. Spines on the red raspberry canes are finer and less stiff and in some cultivars are lacking altogether.

Red raspberry fruit is produced on slender, drooping pedicels and ripens over an extended period of time. This causes a relatively long picking season and high yield potential. The fruit of black and purple cultivars is produced on stiff, often spiny pedicels and tends to be concentrated near the distal end of the laterals. Their harvest season is therefore short and the total yield potential less.

The fruit of black and purple cultivars is nearly round, very firm, and rather "seedy". Red raspberries range from round to conical in shape and are generally considered to be less seedy.

The susceptibility to diseases varies widely among cultivars and species. Blacks and purples are generally more susceptible to viruses and soilborne diseases than are red raspberries.

Physiology

Temperature and daylength. Flower initiation in floricane fruiting red raspberries is influenced by both temperature and daylength (Williams, 1960). Plants held at 61°F (16°C) do not initiate flowers during either long or short days. At 55°F (13°C), flowers develop during short days but not in long days, and at 50°F (10°C), flowers develop during both long and short days. Young shoots that grow from root suckers during late summer remain vegetative until the following year regardless of temperature or daylength.

Primocane elongation is also related to daylength and temperature (Williams, 1959b). At 70°F (21°C) the shoots continue to grow in either long or short days. At 61°F (16°C) they stop growth during short days only and at 50°F (10°C) elongation stops regardless of daylength.

The autumn-fruiting cultivars are day-neutral (Keep, 1961). Flower primordia development can be hastened by low-temperature treatments during early flower differentiation (Vasilakakis et al., 1980), but flower induction in primocane fruiting cultivars is not considered to be temperature dependent. The date of first bloom can be advanced and the amount of early-picked fruit increased by growth regulators applied during early flower initiation (Crandall and Garth, 1981; Brun and Garth, 1984a; McGregor, 1987). There is also evidence that the total yield may be increased (Brun and Garth, 1984a).

Rest, dormancy, and cold hardiness. As the daylength shortens and temperatures decrease in the autumn, the raspberry plant goes into a state of rest (an internal, biochemically controlled condition which prevents normal growth response to favorable temperature and moisture as contrasted to dormancy, which is controlled solely by external environmental conditions). If subjected to high temperatures and/or long days during rest, the buds either fail to grow or grow poorly. The rest period of raspberries is short, usually ending by mid-December. According to Lamb (1948), it requires about 1400 hours below 45°F (7°C) to satisfy the rest requirement of the 'Latham' cultivar.

Canes are quite resistant to cold injury during the rest period. The most hardy cultivars go into a deeper rest earlier and come out more slowly (Bailey, 1948). Once rest is broken, relatively short periods of warm temperature decrease the hardiness of the canes to subsequent cold periods. The later in the winter that this occurs, the more likely canes are to be damaged. The upper portions of canes react more quickly to warm temperatures (Brierley and Landon, 1946) and thus are more likely to be damaged by cold.

Doughty et al. (1972) found that the pith in the basal part of buds is most susceptible to freeze damage, followed in order by the pith of the cane, the vascular tissue at the base of buds, and the flower primordia. Because the tissue at the base of buds is more sensitive to damage than are the buds themselves, symptoms of cold injury are variously expressed as complete failure of the lateral buds to grow, production of short, weak laterals, or as laterals that develop normally at first only to dry up and die under the stress of warm weather, or if fruit is produced, it is often small and crumbly. When the primary lateral bud is killed by late spring frosts, one or two of the secondary buds at the node frequently produce laterals (Jennings, 1979). These laterals are usually shorter and less productive than the primary laterals.

Primocanes that grow late into the fall or ones that are defoliated prematurely do not harden properly and may be damaged by unseasonal early winter cold. Doughty et al. (1972) concluded that defoliation during August, either by two-spotted spider mites or by hand, delays hardening and may result in freeze injury from early winter cold. Later defoliation has little or no effect on the hardiness of the plants.

Yield components. Total yield is determined by the number of fruits and the size of the fruits. Components that enter into the number of fruits include: (1) fruits per lateral, (2) fruitful laterals per cane, (3) canes per meter of row, and (4) row spacing. Size of fruit is determined by (1) number of drupelets, and (2) size of drupelets.

The number of fruits per lateral varies greatly among cultivars (Dale, 1979). Laterals within 30 cm of the tip of canes are usually shorter and have fewer fruits than those immediately below this portion of the cane. However, on floricanes that have this weak portion of the cane removed during the dormant season by pruning, the upper laterals may be shorter than the lower laterals, but they produce more fruits (Crandall et al., 1974b). Lower laterals have more nodes, hence probably have a higher yield potential, but because of various environmental factors, this yield potential is seldom realized (Dale, 1976). Large-diameter canes produce more fruits per lateral than do small-diameter canes (Crandall et al., 1974b). The number of fruits per lateral can be increased by more severe heading back and by reducing the number of canes left per hill when pruning. Fruitfulness of lower laterals can also be increased by removal of the competition from rapidly growing primocanes during the spring (Dale, 1977; Crandall et al., 1980).

The number of fruiting laterals per cane varies with the height of topping, the vigor of the cane, the percentage of the buds that fail to grow, and the number of nodes that produce more than one lateral (Crandall et al., 1974a). The effect of height of topping on the number of laterals is limited because as the number of nodes left per cane increases a lower percentage of the buds break to produce laterals. Also, vigorous canes have fewer nodes below the point where they are topped because the nodes on large diameter canes are usually farther apart than on small canes. Cormack and Waister (1976) found that only 71% of the buds developed fruit-producing laterals. Failure to grow is due to one or more factors, including mechanical damage, insect feeding, disease infection, lack of adequate winter chilling, and cold injury. The production of multiple laterals from a node is partially under genetic control (Jennings, 1979). Large-diameter canes tend to produce more multiple laterals. Multiple laterals generally have fewer fruits per lateral, but the total fruit number per node is often greater than for comparable single-lateral nodes.

The number of canes per length of row differs with cultivar, age and vigor of the planting, cultural practices, and pruning systems. Darrow and Waldo (1933) observed that first-year plants have few large-diameter canes with several branches and in the second year more canes with smaller diameter and fewer branches. From the third year on, there are many medium-diameter, unbranched canes. Vigorous plantings produce more and larger canes. Provided that these additional canes are retained when pruning, the increased number of canes per acre results in higher yields (Crandall et al., 1974b). Some growers, when pruning, reduce the number of canes per hill to a predetermined number of canes regardless of the original number. This pruning practice tends to offset much of the advantage of an increase in vigor. With increased numbers of canes per row, training systems that space out the canes more uniformly along the row make more efficient use of the increased cane numbers (Crandall, 1980).

Growth correlation (compensation). The raspberry plant has a remarkable ability to compensate for changes in the various yield components. Removal of some of the good floricanes when pruning causes the remaining canes to produce longer fruiting laterals with more fruits per lateral (Crandall et al., 1974a). Thus, even though total yields are reduced, the extent of loss is not nearly as great as would be indicated by the reduction of fruiting surface caused by cane removal. Waister and Barritt (1980) removed 50% of the buds on canes. The actual reduction in yield was only 30% because of the increased productivity of the nodes retained. Brun and Garth (1984b) carried out a similar trial and found that the fruitfulness of lower laterals was greatly increased. Close spacing between rows or between plants within rows increases yields per acre but not in proportion to the increase in number of canes per acre (Waister et al., 1980). Individual canes produce more fruit at wider spacing, thus partially compensating for the lower cane population. Darrow and Waldo (1933) harvested nearly as many fruits from a cane topped at 66 in. (168 cm) having 17.3 buds as from an untopped cane 125 in. (317 cm) tall with 52.4 buds.

Removal of competition due to the growth of rapidly developing primocanes during the spring causes the lower and middle fruiting laterals of floricanes to produce more fruits and sometimes larger fruits (Crandall et al., 1980). The longer the growth of the primocanes is suppressed, the greater the yield response (Dale, 1977).

A related phenomenon that is very interesting is the occasional production of basal fruiting laterals. These are very vigorous laterals that develop at or near ground level late in the season. These laterals are extensively branched and have many nodes not normally seen in upper laterals. They produce numerous flower buds (up to 250 per lateral have been counted) and the fruits are often two or three times normal size. It is not known whether all the flower buds on these laterals were present as flower primordia when growth started in the spring or whether some were initiated and developed after spring growth started. In any case, the presence of these basal fruiting laterals does give some indication of the tremendous unexpressed yield potential of the plant.

The compensation expressed by raspberries is a form of growth correlation whereby different parts and physiological processes within the plant compete for the available basic nutritional materials. Included in such materials are water, mineral nutrients, current or stored photosynthate, and hormones produced in roots or aboveground organs. The relative importance of these materials in the expression of compensation by raspberry plants is not known.

Principal Diseases

There is much variation in disease susceptibility among and within the species of raspberries. In general, black and purple raspberries are more susceptible to diseases than are red raspberries. Good descriptions of most raspberry diseases have been published (Converse, 1966; Stace-Smith, 1984).

Mosaic virus. Mosaic is a very serious disease of black and purple cultivars and of some important red raspberry cultivars. It is transmitted in North America by *Amphorophora agathonica* and causes light green or yellow mottling of the leaves. In more advanced stages, the plants develop small, often misshapen leaves with large green blisters. The plants are stunted and usually die. Some red raspberries carry the virus in a nearly symptomless condition, yet aphids feeding on such plants can readily transmit the disease to susceptible cultivars. The most effective control is to grow aphid-resistant cultivars such as 'Skeena', 'Haida', 'Chilliwack', 'Comox', 'Carnival', 'Canby', or 'Rideau'.

Leaf curl virus.   Leaf curl is spread by the aphids *Aphis rubicola* and is most often found in red raspberries; however, it sometimes affects black and purple raspberries. Some purple cultivars are very resistant. Leaves are small, with the tips and edges curled downward. The leaves may yellow but are not mottled. The canes are stunted, dry, and brittle.

Tomato ringspot virus.   This virus is spread by nematodes *(Xiphinema americanum)*. Susceptibility to the virus varies among cultivars (Freeman et al., 1975). In susceptible cultivars it causes a general weakening of the plant and is usually accompanied by crumbly fruit. The ringspot symptom appears on a few leaves of newly infected plants during early summer. Later in the season and on older infected plants this symptom disappears. The foliage on fruiting canes has a yellow cast and turns prematurely brown. Presence of the virus in the field follows the general target area pattern that is typical of nematode populations.

Raspberry bushy dwarf virus.   Bushy dwarf is pollen transmitted. Suscep-tibility varies widely among cultivars (Daubeny et al., 1978). Moreover, among susceptible cultivars, symptom expression can vary considerably. In susceptible cultivars it can cause reduced yield and fruit size and crumbly fruit. Leaves are normal in shape but may show an oak leaf pattern or interveinal chlorosis. Best control is to grow virus-free stocks and to eliminate sources of infection (Daubeny, 1980). Cultivars resistant to the common strain of the virus include 'Willamette', 'Haida', 'Chilcotin', 'Glen Clova', and 'Nootka'.

Other viruses.   Black raspberry streak, *Rubus* stunt.

Anthracnose (*Elsinoe veneta*).   Black and purple raspberries are damaged severely by the anthracnose fungus. It causes small, round to oval gray spots surrounded by reddish to purple margins on the canes and pedicels of the fruits. These often become very numerous and may girdle the canes or pedicels. Severe infections increase damage from winter injury and often cause the fruit to be misshapen or to dry up. The same type of lesions occur on the leaves, where the center of the spot often falls out, leaving a round hole. 'Skeena' and 'Glen Clova' are very susceptible to anthracnose.

Verticillium wilt (*Verticillium alba-atrum*).   Wilt is a soilborne disease that is most serious on black and purple cultivars. Primocanes stop growth during midsummer, droop, turn yellow, and lose their bottom leaves. The stems become bluish in color and gradually die. This disease is often found where raspberries have been planted following crops of potatoes, tomatoes, peppers, or eggplants.

Spur blight (*Didymella applanata*).   Spur blight affects red raspberries primarily. Dark reddish-brown discoloration develops around the buds. This browning is preceded by brown or purple spots near the buds. Severe infections cause fruit laterals to be stunted and the leaves may fall prematurely. Cultivars with some resistance include 'Haida', 'Boyne', 'Festival', and 'Newburgh'.

Crown gall (*Agrobacterium tumefaciens*). Crown gall is a bacterial disease that attacks all species of raspberries. On black and purple cultivars the crown and basal portion of canes develop wart-like galls. The galls on red raspberries occur just below ground level on the crowns and roots. Gall formation causes weakening or death of individual canes and a general reduction in growth and yield. The cultivar 'Skeena' is very susceptible, whereas 'Willamette' has some resistance.

Fruit rot (*Botrytis cinerea*). Fruit rot organisms are present nearly everywhere in the field. The disease is most serious if wet weather occurs during harvest. Blossoms are sometimes infected, but more often it is the ripe fruit that is damaged. Whereas *Botrytis* is the most common causal organism of postharvest fruit rot, *Rhizopus, Alternaria, Penicillium,* and *Cladisporium* also cause postharvest fruit rots (Converse, 1966).

Cane *Botrytis (Botrytis cinerea)* is most serious during wet growing seasons in vigorous plantings in which growth is rank and dense. Purple-brown blotches develop around the buds of new canes. Numerous elongated black pustules (sclerotia) form on the infected canes during the late fall and winter months. Infections result in bud retardation and even complete suppression. Severe infections can cause cane death. Fruit rot control sprays give some control. Removal of surplus canes in vigorous plantings also helps control the disease. Resistant cultivars include 'Chilcotin', 'Meeker', and 'Willamette' (Daubeny, 1987a).

Root rot (Various *Phytophthora* spp., including *P. erithroseptica* and *P. megasperma, Rhyzoctonia* spp., *Fusarium* spp., and *Pythium* spp.). Root rot is a general term for root diseases of raspberries. It usually occurs on plants growing in poorly drained soils. Raspberry roots are very sensitive to poor soil aeration, and under conditions of poor drainage are damaged and become susceptible to infection by *Rhyzoctonia, Pythium,* and *Fusarium*. The plants decline in vigor and may die. Floricanes may fail to leaf out in the spring, produce small, yellow leaves, or wilt and die at or near harvest. As the soil dries out, late-emerging primocanes may grow and appear nearly normal, only to decline or die the following spring. Such plantings decline in production and vegetative growth over a period of several years. The *Phytophthora* species infects roots in poorly drained soils but may also infect and cause damage in well-drained soils. The first evidence of this type of infection usually appears on the primocanes. Infection causes girdling of the basal portion of primocanes and wilting of the terminal portion of the shoot, followed by death of the entire primocane. Plants seriously infected during the summer often fail to grow the following spring. Infected plants usually die completely within a year or two after infection.

There is considerable variation in susceptibility to root rots among cultivars (Barritt et al., 1979). Resistant cultivars, cultural practices to improve drainage, and soil-applied fungicides offer hope for control (Bristow, 1980).

Other raspberry diseases. Powdery mildew *(Sphaerotheca humuli),* orange rust *(Gymnoconia peckiana),* leaf spot *(Sphaerulina rubi),* and cane blight *(Leposphaeria coniothyrium)* are diseases which can be serious.

Insects

Insects and other arthropod pests of raspberries are often more serious as contaminants of the harvested fruit than for their economic damage to the plants (Crandall et al., 1966). The seriousness of any one of them is closely related to climate and local conditions.

Crown borer (*Bembecia marginata* Harris). The crown borer is the most serious of the various species of borers that attack raspberries. The adult is a clear-winged moth (Breakey, 1963). Eggs are laid in the late summer and fall. The new larvae burrow into the crown and lower parts of the canes, weakening the plant and causing the canes to be easily broken off at ground level. Presence of damage is indicated by frass (sawdust) on the crown, by wilted or dead canes, and by the presence of a hole in the center of the stubs of canes cut off during pruning. Other types of borers burrow higher up on the canes and are usually removed when pruning. Crown borers can be controlled with a drenching spray of insecticide applied to the crown area during early or late winter. This spray kills only first-year larvae in a 2-year life cycle, so applications must be made for at least two consecutive years for full control.

Mites: two-spotted spider mites (*Tetranychus urticae*), red spider mites (*Tetranychus bimaculatus*), leaf and bud mites (*Phytopus gracilis*). Two-spotted and red spider mites are primarily leaf feeders. Heavy infestations cause speckling and browning of leaves. Spring or late summer damage can cause economic losses. Leaf and bud mites are microscopic in size. They overwinter under the bud scales and feed on the newly opened leaves and flower buds, causing stunting of laterals and crumbly fruit.

Root weevils (several species). The adults of all species of root weevil chew notches in the margins of leaves, but the principal damage is caused by larvae feeding on the roots. Adult weevils are sometimes present as contaminants on harvested fruit.

Leafrollers: orange tortrix (*Argyrotaenia citrana*), oblique-banded leafroller (*Choristonuera rosaceana*). Leafrollers do not cause serious damage to raspberry plants, but the larvae fall into the harvested fruit when disturbed. Frequent inspection of fields prior to harvest are necessary to determine whether control sprays are necessary. Pheromone traps are useful for monitoring leafroller population trends (LaLone, 1980).

Fruitworm (*Byturus* spp.). Adult beetles feed on new leaves, flower buds, and flowers. Damage to the flowers and buds causes distorted fruits. Eggs are laid on the buds and flowers and the larvae eat into the center of the fruit, where they are present at harvest. Sprays are timed to kill the adults before they lay their eggs.

Other insects. Some of the other insects that are locally or regionally important are cane maggots, thrips, tree crickets, aphids, tarnished plant bugs, and cutworms.

CLASSES OF CULTIVARS AND THEIR UTILITY

Red Raspberries

Present-day red raspberry cultivars can be divided into two main groups according to their place of origin, the Pacific northwest of North America or Britain. These places of origin coincide with two of the more important production regions in the world. Two other groups of lesser economic importance have originated from eastern Europe and the USSR and from eastern and central North America.

Important traits of some modern red raspberry cultivars are listed in Table 4–1. Cultivars from the Pacific northwest are generally a brighter or glossier red color than are those from Britain. However, in recent years some of the newer ones from the latter are more like those from the Pacific northwest. There is, also, a trend toward cultivars with firmer fruit from both places (Barritt et al., 1980). In general, cultivars bred for a particular production region do not perform as well in other regions (Dale and Daubeny, 1985).

'Willamette' has been the principal cultivar in the Pacific northwest for more than 35 years (Lawrence, 1980a). In recent years three newer cultivars, 'Meeker', 'Skeena', and 'Chilcotin' have gained wide acceptance (Daubeny, 1986). All three cultivars are higher yielding than 'Willamette' and are better for the fresh market, with 'Chilcotin' particularly well suited because of its large, bright, nondarkening red fruit and its extended harvest season. 'Willamette' has remained important for processing mainly because of suitability to machine harvesting and its dark red color. 'Meeker' and 'Skeena' are also suited to machine harvesting, but 'Chilcotin' is not. Two other newer cultivars, 'Haida' and 'Nootka', and four older ones, 'Canby', 'Fairview', 'Puyallup', and 'Sumner', are grown to a limited extent. In 1987, two new cultivars, 'Chilliwack' and 'Comox', were released for consideration in the region. Both produce large, firm fruit of good quality suited for fresh or processing markets (Daubeny, 1987b). 'Heritage' is the major primocane fruiting cultivar, but small amounts of 'Amity' and 'Summit' are now being planted. The latter two usually produce ripe fruit earlier than does 'Heritage'. However, the acceptance of 'Amity' might be limited by the difficulty in harvesting the fruit, especially under the cool

TABLE 4-1 IMPORTANT FRUIT AND PLANT TRAITS OF SOME MODERN RED RASPBERRY CULTIVARS[a]

CULTIVAR	ADAPTED REGION[b]	YIELD[c]	SIZE[c]	QUALITY[c]	HARVEST EASE[c]	HARDINESS[c,d]	OUTSTANDING RESISTANCES OR TOLERANCES[e]	COMMENT
Amity	PNW	4	3	4	1		RR	Primocane fruiting
Augustred	ENA	3	3	3	4			Very early primocane fruiting
Boyne	ENA	4	3	2	4	5	RBDV, SB, YR	Standard ENA cultivar
Canby	PNW, ENA	4	4	3	4	5	RMV, CB, YR	
Carnival	ENA	3	3	3	2	4	RMV, SB, RR	Extremely powdery mildew susceptible
Chilcotin	PNW, A	5	4	4	2	2	RBDV, CB	Fresh market standard
Chilliwack	PNW	3	4	5	5	4	RMV, SB, PrFr, PoFr, RR	New cultivar
Citadel	Mid-south ENA	3	4	4	2		RBDV	
Comet	ENA	4	3	3	4	4		
Comox	PNW	5	5	4	3	4	RMV	New cultivar
Fairview	PNW, NZ	4	4	4	3	3	RBDV, RR	
Fallred	ENA	4	3	3	3			Primocane fruiting
Festival	ENA	3	4	3	1	4	RBDV, SB	Compact growth habit
Glen Clova	UK, WE, Ch	5	3	3	3	4	RBDV	Standard UK cultivar
Glen Moy	UK	5	4	4	4	2	partial E-RMV, RBDV, CB	
Glen Prosen	UK, EE, WE	4	4	4	4	3	E-RMV	Very firm fruit
Haida	PNW, ENA	5	3	3	1	5	RMV, RBDV, SB	Compact growth habit

TABLE 4-1 IMPORTANT FRUIT AND PLANT TRAITS OF SOME MODERN RED RASPBERRY CULTIVARS[a], cont.

CULTIVAR	ADAPTED REGION[b]	YIELD[c]	SIZE[c]	QUALITY[c]	HARVEST EASE[c]	HARDINESS[c,d]	OUTSTANDING RESISTANCES OR TOLERANCES[e]	COMMENT
Heritage	PNW, ENA, E	4	3	3	4		RBDV, RR	Standard primocane fruiting
Hilton	ENA	4	4	3	2	4	RBDV	
Killarney	ENA	5	4	2	4	5	RBDV, SB	
Latham	ENA	3	2	2	3	5	RBDV, SB, RR, YR	Old standard eastern cultivar
Malling Admiral	UK	2	4	5	3	3	RBDV, SB	
Malling Autumn Bliss	UK	5	4	4	4		E-RMV	Primocane fruiting
Malling Delight	UK	5	5	2	1	4	partial E-RMV	Adapted to "pick-your-own"
Malling Jewel	UK	2	3	2	3	4	RBDV, SB	Formerly main UK cultivar
Malling Joy	UK	5	4	4	3	4	RBDV, E-RMV	Very late ripening
Malling Leo	UK	3	4	4	4	4	E-RMV, CB	Standard late fresh market
Malling Promise	UK, EE	4	2	4	3	4	RBDV	
Marcy	NZ, ENA	5	4	3	4	3	CB	Standard NZ cultivar
Meeker	PNW	4	4	4	4	1	RR, CB	
Newburgh	ENA	4	4	2	2	3	SB, RR	
Nootka	PNW, A	3	3	4	5	3	RBDV, RMV, PoFr, CB	
Nova	ENA	4	3	4	4	5	LYR	New cultivar
Puyallup	PNW	4	4	3	3	3	RBDV, CB	
Redwing	ENA	2	3	3		4		New cultivar, primocane fruiting
Reveille	ENA	5	2	3		5	RMV, SB	

Cultivar	Region						Virus/disease	Comments
Ruby	ENA	3	4	3		4		New cultivar, primocane fruiting
Scepter	ENA	3	3	3		3	RBDV	
Sentinel	ENA	3	3	3		4	RBDV	
Sentry	ENA	4	3	4		4	SB	
Skeena	PNW, ENA, NZ, A	4	4	4	4	4	RMV, PrFr	
Summit	PNW	4	3	4	3		RR	New primocane fruiting cultivar
Sumner	PNW	4	4	3		4	RBDV, RR, CB	
Taylor	ENA	5	4	4		4		
Titan	ENA	5	5	4		4		New cultivar
Willamette	PNW, A, NZ, EE	3	3	3		2	RBDV, CB, CG	Standard PNW cultivar

[a] Blank spaces usually mean trait is unknown.

[b] A, Australia; Ch, Chile; EE, eastern Europe; ENA, eastern and central North America; NZ, New Zealand; PNW, Pacific northwest; UK, United Kingdom; WE, western Europe.

[c] 1, Poor or low; 5, high or outstanding.

[d] Hardiness usually refers to the region in which the cultivar is best suited. Ratings are not given for primocane fruiting cultivars since canes are usually not overwintered.

[e] CB, cane *Botrytis*; CG, crown gall; LYR, late yellow rust; PoFr, postharvest fruit rot; PrFr, preharvest fruit rot; RBDV, raspberry bushy dwarf virus natural infection; RMV and E-RMV resistance to the aphid vector of the raspberry mosaic virus complex in North America and Europe, respectively; RR, root rot; SB, spur blight; YR, yellow rust; LYR, late yellow rust.

and wet conditions often experienced in late summer and through the fall months in the Pacific northwest.

In eastern and central portions of North America, the cultivar 'Latham', which originated in Minnesota, is still widely grown after 60 years (Lawrence, 1980a). It is exceptionally winter hardy. Among more recent cultivar releases, 'Boyne' has become a major cultivar. It is hardy to extremely low temperatures but does not tolerate fluctuating temperatures as well as 'Latham'. Other cultivars of some importance in the region include 'Festival', 'Newburgh', 'Killarney', 'Hilton', and 'Taylor'. Two cultivars, 'Nova' and 'Titan', both released since 1980, are becoming important and both are noted for improved fruit qualities compared to some of the older cultivars. Pacific northwest cultivars that have become important in the region are 'Haida', 'Skeena', and 'Canby'. 'Heritage' is the only primocane fruiting cultivar grown extensively. Cultivars with low chilling requirements adapted to the southeastern United States are 'Dormanred' and 'Southland'.

In Britain, 'Glen Clova' has replaced 'Malling Jewel' as the principal cultivar grown for the processing market. 'Glen Clova' produces higher yields and is a more vigorous grower than 'Malling Jewel'. The main fresh market cultivar is now 'Malling Leo', which is widely planted in the south of England. Other cultivars grown primarily for fresh market are 'Malling Delight', 'Malling Joy', and 'Malling Admiral'. 'Malling Delight' is an early-ripening cultivar which produces particularly large fruit desirable for the pick-your-own market. Both 'Malling Leo' and 'Malling Joy' are late ripening and thus extend the fresh market season. 'Malling Leo' is well suited to individual quick freeze (IQF). Two newly released cultivars, 'Glen Prosen' and 'Glen Moy', are rapidly gaining acceptance. 'Glen Prosen' produces firm fruit suited to either fresh or processing markets (Jennings, 1982b). 'Glen Moy' is early ripening and produces large, bright red fruit of good quality (Jennings, 1982b). Older cultivars still grown to some extent are 'Malling Promise' and 'Norfolk Giant' (Turner, 1980). 'Malling Autumn Bliss', a new high-yielding primocane fruiting cultivar, is expected to replace older cultivars such as 'Zeva Herbsternte'. The ripening season of 'Malling Autumn Bliss' overlaps that of the late-ripening summer (floricane) fruiting cultivars, 'Malling Leo' and 'Malling Joy'. With this range of cultivars, it is now possible in Britain to have a continuous supply of fresh fruit from late June to mid- or late October (Keep, 1986).

Many of the British cultivars are grown in western Europe. Other important cultivars are 'Schoenemann' in Germany and 'Veten' in Norway. 'Malling Exploit' and 'Malling Promise' are important cultivars in eastern Europe (Misic, 1980). Others grown in these countries include 'Willamette' and a series of cultivars mostly developed within the region. These include 'Valjevka', 'Jelicka', 'Bulgarian Rubin', 'Ekonomka', 'Zajecarka', 'Kapaonicka', 'Gradina', 'Krupna Dvorada', and 'Nagymarosi'. In the USSR most of the cultivars grown have been developed there. These include 'Novost Kuzmina' and 'Visluha' (Kichina, 1976). However, 'Newburgh' and 'Malling Promise' are also grown.

In raspberry production regions of the southern hemisphere (Chile, southeastern Australia, and New Zealand) important cultivars have been 'Marcy', 'Willamette', 'Fairview', 'Lloyd George', and 'Red Antwerp' (Jones and Wood,

1979). Newer cultivars gaining acceptance are 'Glen Clova', 'Skeena', 'Chilcotin', and 'Nootka'. 'Heritage' is the main primocane fruiting cultivar.

Black and Purple Raspberries

There are relatively few black and purple cultivars. Among the important blacks are 'Cumberland', 'Munger', 'Bristol', 'Morrison', and 'Blackhawk'; purple cultivars include 'Sodus', 'Brandywine', 'Marion', 'Clyde', and 'Royalty' (Table 4–2).

Hybrid Berries

Hybrid berries, which have resulted from the crossing of red raspberry and blackberry types, continue to be grown on a small scale in various parts of the world. Moreover, interest in these has increased with the release of three new cultivars, 'Tayberry', 'Tummelberry', and 'Sunberry'. These, plus three older cultivars, 'Loganberry', 'Boysenberry', and 'Youngberry', are more similar to blackberries than raspberries in that their growth habits are trailing and fruits cohere to the

TABLE 4-2 CHARACTERISTICS OF PRINCIPAL PURPLE AND BLACK RASPBERRY CULTIVARS

CULTIVAR	RIPENING SEASON[a]	PRODUCTIVITY[b]	FRUIT SIZE[b]	FRUIT FIRMNESS[b]	FRUIT QUALITY[b]	HARDINESS[b]
Purple
Amethyst	2	3	2	1	1	3
Brandywine	4	2	2	3	2	3
Clyde	3	3	2	2	1	3
Lowden	3	2	2	2	2	2
Royalty	4	3	3	2	3	3
Sodus	3	2	2	2	3	3
Success	3	2	1	2	3	3
Black
Alleghany	2	3	3	2	3	2
Allen	2	3	3	2	2	2
Blackhawk	4	2	3	3	2	2
Bristol	2	3	3	3	3	2
Cumberland	2	2	2	2	3	2
Dundee	3	3	2	2	2	2
Haut	3	2	2	2	2	2
Huron	3	2	3	3	3	2
Jewel	3	3	3	3	3	2
Mac Black	2	2	3	3	3	2
Morrison	4	2	2	2	2	2
Munger	1	2	2	2	3	2
New Logan	1	1	2	2	2	2

[a] Relative ripening season: 1, early; 4, late.

[b] Characteristics: 1, fair; 2, good; and 3, excellent.

receptacle. Culture and management of hybrid berries are similar to western trailing blackberry and have been described by Lipe and Martin (1984).

None of the hybrid berries is especially winter hardy, although the newer cultivars are more hardy than the older ones and, in particular, are more hardy than 'Boysenberry' and 'Youngberry'. The newer cultivars have been released as possible replacements for 'Loganberry'. In limited trials they have produced higher yields. Each has a distinctive flavor and, like 'Loganberry', is better suited to the processing market than to the fresh market. Unlike 'Loganberry', thornless chimeras of the newer cultivars have not been found. Thus the thorniness of their canes may limit wide-scale acceptance.

Loganberries are grown commercially in Oregon and northern California. 'Boysenberries' are also grown in the same regions and are an important crop in New Zealand.

PROPAGATION

Red Raspberries

Red raspberry plants for establishment of new fields consist of shoots (suckers) with attached roots that grow from adventitious buds on the roots of established plants. During the first two years after planting, large numbers of suckers develop around the parent plants. Excess plants are dug and transplanted to establish a new field. These are usually dug during the dormant season and either heeled in or held in cold storage until needed for planting. In some instances plants that have started growth in the spring (green plants) are used. These require extra care in handling and must be transplanted immediately. Green plants are not usually recommended because of the problems involved in handling to obtain a good stand. They are often used for small plantings or to fill in the empty spaces that may occur after planting larger fields.

Red raspberries can also be grown from root cuttings. This method of propagation is commonly used by researchers to increase plant material in the greenhouse. Torre and Barritt (1979) concluded that if 1.5 to 2.1 oz (42 to 60 g) of random-length and random-diameter root cuttings were planted per 36 in. (91 cm) of row, either in hills or as a continuous row, the field so established would be comparable with one established from dormant plants. It is a common practice for certified plant growers to sell the masses of roots removed during the processing of plants. Plantings developed from these root cuttings have been very successful. The cuttings must be kept from drying out before planting. Tissue culture is another method used for raspberry propagation (Donnelly and Daubeny, 1986).

Black Raspberries

Black raspberries are propagated by tip layering. As the primocanes develop during mid- to late summer they bow over toward the soil and the terminal growth develops a bare appearance with small curled leaves. At this stage the tips can be covered by moving soil onto them; however, it is preferable to insert the tips vertically about 2 in. (5 cm) deep in a slot made with a spade. These tips root quickly and by winter produce well-developed root systems. The parent cane is cut off to a length of about 8 in. (20 cm) at the time of digging. As with red raspberries, the plants may be heeled in or held in cold storage until planting time.

Purple Raspberries

Purple raspberries are usually propagated by tip layering. A few cultivars, however, produce some suckers, in which case it is possible to use both tip layers and root suckers for maximum number of plants.

CULTURE

Site Selection

Raspberry roots are very sensitive to poor soil aeration and deteriorate rapidly under waterlogged soil conditions. They therefore require a medium- to light-textured soil with good fertility and subsoil drainage. Sandy soils are subject to drought but are satisfactory if irrigation is available and adequate fertilization supplied.

Good sites are level or slightly rolling and not subject to spring frosts or exposed to cold winter winds. They are relatively close to markets and, if the fruit is to be hand picked, close to a source of hand labor.

Black and purple raspberries are especially susceptible to root diseases and viruses. For that reason they are not planted in soil that has been growing tomatoes, potatoes, eggplants, or peppers during the previous 4 to 5 years. Such soils often contain *verticillium* wilt, which causes serious damage to both purple and black raspberries and also to some red raspberry cultivars. It is also recommended that black raspberries not be planted close to red raspberries (Converse, 1978). Some of the common virus diseases to which red raspberries are resistant may be transmitted to the much more susceptible black raspberries.

Site Preparation

Careful site preparation is necessary for a successful planting. On low-fertility soils the organic matter is built up with green manure crops or heavy applications of manure before planting. If perennial weeds are present, they can be controlled most economically before the raspberries are planted. Clean cultivation, chemical herbicide applications, or the growing of crops on which herbicides can be used are methods that can be used to clean up a field prior to planting.

Control of nematodes. Nematodes, if present, cause varying degrees of damage, depending on the cultivar and the number and type of nematodes present (Bristow et al., 1980; McElroy, 1977). *Xiphenema americanum* is a vector for tomato ringspot virus (Teliz et al., 1966). Other species of nematodes are also known to transmit viruses to raspberries (McElroy, 1975). The presence of harmful nematodes can be determined from soil samples. The best time to collect the samples for nematode analysis is in the spring or early summer of the year prior to planting. The samples are obtained from the surface 12 in. (30 cm) of soil with a spade or soil sampling tube and include some roots of established plants (Haglund, 1974). Samples from 20 to 30 locations over the entire field are combined and mixed thoroughly in a container. A sample of 1 to 2 pints (0.5 to 1.0 liter) of the combined soil is placed in a strong plastic bag and immediately sent to the laboratory for analysis. The samples may be stored temporarily at 50°F (10°C). Either high or low temperatures or a delay of over 4 days will reduce the number of live nematodes in the sample, and since only live nematodes are counted in the laboratory procedure, proper care of the sample is important. The laboratory should be able to tell whether fumigation is needed. If the results show dangerous levels of nematodes, the best time to fumigate is during late summer of the year before planting.

Soil preparation. Fall plowing is desirable. This helps eliminate surface vegetation and usually means that the soil can be worked to prepare a plant bed earlier in the spring. An application of about 34 tons/acre (75 MT/ha) of barnyard manure applied before fall plowing is desirable for sandy soils. The following spring, as early as it is possible to work the soil properly, it is disked and harrowed into seedbed condition.

If the soil acidity is below pH 5.5, enough agricultural limestone to bring the soil up to pH 5.7 to 6.0 is broadcast and disked in during the fall before planting. Low magnesium can be corrected by using dolomitic limestone instead of calcitic agricultural lime.

Field layout. Row spacing varies depending on the expected vigor of the cultivars to be planted and the type of equipment to be used for cultivation and harvest. In the Pacific northwest region of North America, where growth is very vigorous, both black and red raspberry rows are spaced 8 to 10 ft (2.4 to 3.0 m) apart. The wider row spacing is required by the currently available machine harvesters. A spacing of 6 to 8 ft (1.8 to 2.4 m) is used for red raspberries in areas where the plants grow less vigorously. Even there, minimum row spacing for black and purple raspberries is kept at 8 ft (2.4 m) because of their more spreading growth habit. Spacing within the rows ranges from 30 to 36 in. (76 to 91 cm). Sometimes growers who expect to be able to control weeds within the row with chemical herbicides will use a hedgerow system of planting, which involves establishment of a continuous row of canes. In this system, the plants are sometimes placed as close as 24 in. (60 cm). Another method used by growers who plan to control weeds by cultivation with a garden tractor is the square system. The plants are spaced 5 to 8 ft (1.5 to 1.8 m) apart in both directions. This allows cross cultivation for easy weed and sucker control.

In hand-harvested fields, alleys 16 to 20 ft (5 to 6 m) wide are established every 330 ft (100 m) or less to permit weighing of the fruit and access for its removal from the field. Headlands of a similar width must be retained at the ends of the rows.

Wider headlands and longer distances between alleys are used when the fruits are to be machine harvested. Harvesters require a turnaround space of at least 26 ft (8 m) at the ends of rows. Alleys within the rows are needed every 330 to 1000 ft (100 to 300 m) for offloading the machine, the distance apart depending on the expected yields and the capacity of the harvester to carry flats of berries. The longer the rows, the more efficiently the machines operate.

The rows are oriented north and south where possible. This gives better overall light exposure and helps to reduce sunscald of the fruit. Rows placed across the slope of the land reduce the danger of erosion, but the soil tends to terrace as it is cultivated. This terracing effect causes problems for both hand and machine harvesting. For this reason, rows sometimes run up and down the slope. The shape of the field may also dictate the row direction. In areas where soil erosion is a major problem, rows may be laid out on the contour. This conserves moisture and greatly reduces erosion; however, the curved rows make trellis construction more difficult and often cause problems for cultural operations.

Planting

In addition to care in site preparation, the use of pathogen-free plants is essential for a successful planting. The best plants are produced by specialized growers from pathogen-free stock, are grown in pathogen-free soil, and are isolated from sources of virus infection. Such plants are labeled as certified plants.

Raspberries can be planted any time from February or March through May; however, earlier planting produces more and larger primocanes during the first year. Plants are set in a furrow opened up with a plow or disk-opener, in holes dug with a shovel, or in holes made by inserting a spade about 8 in. (20 cm) into the soil and pushing the handle back and forth to make a hole (Fig. 4–6). The latter method is quick, but the hole often is not large enough for large-rooted plants. A modified transplanting machine is sometimes used for large plantings. This requires one or more people to follow the machine to fill in skips and to make certain that all roots are well covered.

The furrow system of planting is most commonly used. Once the furrow is made, plants are dropped along the row at the proper spacing. The roots are spread out, enough soil pulled over to cover them, and then the soil is firmed around the roots, usually by foot pressure. It is especially important not to cover black raspberry crowns too deep. They are set with the growing point at or just below the soil surface. As the new shoots develop during the season, more soil can be pulled into the furrow to keep the plants from drying out and for weed control. Irrigation after planting is desirable.

Planting stocks from nurseries usually have the canes already cut back to about 8 in. (20 cm). If the canes have not already been cut back, the easiest time to do this is while they are still in bundles before planting. Cutting back prevents fruiting and helps force new sucker development. All the aboveground canes of uncertified black and purple raspberry plants are removed after planting to eliminate cane diseases that may be present.

Residual herbicides are sometimes used on new plantings to help control annual weeds (Scheer et al., 1989). These materials are applied to the moist soil

FIGURE 4-6 Raspberries are often planted by hand in the bottom of furrows opened by a plow or lister. Later cultivations pull the soil in around the plants to kill small weeds.

surface after the soil around the roots is well settled and before the seedling weeds have emerged. Water following the application moves the herbicide into the root zone of the seedling weeds and improves weed control. Sprinkler irrigation may be necessary if there is no rainfall soon after application.

Fertilization during the First Year

Fertilizer should be applied as soon as the plants show new growth. The amounts of phosphorus and potassium can be determined from a soil test. These should be combined with 30 to 35 lb/acre (35 to 45 kg/ha) of nitrogen and either broadcast on the soil surface in a 12-in. (30-cm) band over the rows or placed with a fertilizer attachment in two bands 8 in. (20 cm) apart to each side of the row and 4 in. (10 cm) deep. On sandy soils, an additional 25 lb/acre (28 kg/ha) of nitrogen is applied about 2½ months after planting. These fertilizer recommendations are high but generally applicable to most soils since it is important to obtain as much growth as possible during the first year. This ensures a good crop of fruit the season after planting.

Cultivating New Fields

The field is shallowly cultivated often enough to keep weeds under control. Deep cultivation may cause excessive root damage. Unwanted suckers that develop around and between the hills can be removed by hoeing or with special cultivators.

They are sometimes pulled by hand. Hoeing or pulling reduces the number of return suckers (Turner, 1980). In hedgerow systems, cultivation is used to maintain a row width of about 12 in. (30 cm).

Trellising

Black and purple raspberries are not usually trellised. When tipped relatively low during the summer, they do not require the additional support of a trellis. Red raspberries, however, need some type of support because of their upright growing habit. This may involve a single stake placed in the center of each hill for plants set on the square or a post and wire trellis running the length of the rows (Fig. 4–7).

Trellises are installed during the fall or winter prior to the first year of harvest. Sometimes growth of the primocanes is not enough to make it economical to harvest the first-year crop. In such a situation, all canes are mowed off during the dormant season and trellising is delayed an additional year.

Either wood or steel posts or a combination of wooden end posts with steel in-row posts are used. All posts are at least 7 ft (2.1 m) long. End posts are of a larger diameter and sometimes longer and are braced or anchored to enable them to carry the extra strain imposed when the wires are tightened. The posts are inserted into the soil about 18 in. (45 cm) and are spaced 25 to 30 ft (7.6 to 9.1 m) apart in the row. The recommended spacing for steel posts in plantings to be machine harvested is 20 ft (6.1 m).

The end of a wooden post that is inserted into the soil should be treated with a wood preservative. The most common material used for this purpose is a 4%

FIGURE 4–7 It is important that the end posts in a post-and-wire trellis system be secure. The braces in this field ensure that the end posts will stay in place when the wires are tightened prior to winter pruning and tying.

solution of pentachlorophenol. This is prepared by mixing 1 gal (4 liters) of pentachlorophenate with 10 gal (40 liters) of diesel oil. The posts are placed with the bottoms in a container filled with enough of the solution to reach 3 to 4 in. (8 to 10 cm) above the part that will be below ground. As much as 7 days of soaking, depending on the type of posts, is required to obtain adequate penetration. Only well-seasoned posts should be used.

Galvanized iron wire is used for support. Twelve-gauge wire [34 ft per pound, (23 m per kg)] is usually used for the support wires and 14 gauge [60 ft per pound, (40 m per kg)] wire for the training wires.

Many different trellis systems are used to support the canes, including the following:

1. A single stake for each hill.
2. A single support wire at a height of 5 ft (1.5 m) with no training wires. This system is used in some fields where the crop is machine harvested. It requires that the machine always travel in the same direction on the row each time it is picked to prevent serious damage to the primocanes.
3. A single support wire at a height of 4.5 to 5 ft (1.4 to 1.5 m) with two training wires, one on each side of the posts. The canes are tied to the support wire. The training wires are made adjustable in height through the use of hooks or bent nails positioned at heights of 16 and 30 in. (40 and 75 cm). The training wires are laid on the ground or placed on the lower hooks at the start of the season. As the primocanes develop, the wires are lifted to hold the canes in the row out of the way of pickers and cultivation equipment.
4. Two upper support wires and two adjustable training wires. The floricanes are held between the two support wires by clipping or tying the wires together at frequent intervals.
5. A 2 × 4 in. (5 × 10 cm) cross-arm ranging in length from 18 to 24 in. (45 to 60 cm) is fastened to the top of the posts at a height of about 46 in. (1.4 m). A support wire is stapled on top of each end of the cross-arm. When pruning, the floricanes are divided and tied to the two support wires. Two adjustable training wires are used with the shorter cross-arms. They are not needed where the longer cross-arms are used since most of the primocanes grow up through the middle between the two support wires.

In New Zealand, a specialized cross-arm trellis has been developed to be used with the Lincoln canopy machine harvester (Dunn et al., 1976; Thiele, 1980) (Fig. 4–8). The trellis consists of T-shaped supports with cross-arms 10 ft (3 m) long and several support wires. The floricanes are trained horizontally. This system requires that the raspberry rows be spaced 16 ft (4.9 m) apart.

Row Management Systems

Raspberries are most commonly maintained in hills or in hedgerows. Hills are kept in rows with plants spaced 30 to 36 in. (76 to 91 cm) (lineal system) or may be spaced

(a)

(b)

FIGURE 4-8 The Lincoln harvester was developed at Lincoln College, Canterbury, New Zealand. It handles the fruit gently and is quite efficient, but because of the expense and labor required for the special trellis system needed, it has not had a wide commercial acceptance.

at 4 to 6 ft (1.5 to 1.8 m) and cross cultivated (square system). In the hedgerow system primocanes are allowed to develop between hills to form a continuous row. Excess primocanes that develop outside the narrow row [about 12 in. (30 cm) wide] are removed by cultivation or mowing. This system is most successful when herbicides are used within the rows for weed control. The number of fruiting canes left per lineal foot (meter) of row after dormant pruning is approximately the same for the hedgerow and lineal systems. The wider plant spacing of the square system results in fewer floricanes per acre after pruning, hence it has a lower yield potential. Some growers prefer it, however, because cross-cultivation provides an easy, efficient way to control weeds and excess suckers.

Culture

Soil Management

Soil management practices are designed to control weeds and excess suckers, conserve moisture, maintain soil structure, and to obtain high yields with large berry size. The most common practice used to accomplish these objectives is clean cultivation. The area between rows is cultivated as early in the spring as soil moisture conditions permit. Rototillers (Fig. 4-9) are especially good for cultivation because they are easily adjusted for depth and they also cut up and incorporate into the soil the canes left on the surface after pruning. It is very important that cultivation be limited to a depth of 2 to 4 in. (5 to 10 cm) because much of the root system of raspberry plants is shallow. Deeper cultivation is liable to cut off many roots and reduce yields. The first cultivation is followed by additional cultivations, as needed to control weeds, up to the beginning of harvest. Cultivation is suspended during harvest and one additional cultivation is made after harvest is completed.

Weeds and excess suckers within the rows are controlled by hand, by means of mechanical cultivation equipment that can be directed around and between hills, by the use of herbicides, or by a combination of these methods. In-row weed and sucker control is made easier by maintaining the plants in hills. Hedgerow plantings are maintained by cultivation to keep the sucker plants confined to a narrow strip [about 12 in. (30 cm) wide] and with herbicides to control weeds in the row.

An over-winter cover crop of spring barley or other cereal grain is sometimes planted between the rows in the fall after harvest. This helps to slow growth and harden the canes so they are better able to withstand cold winter temperatures. It also helps maintain soil organic matter and reduces soil erosion. The cover must be turned under early in the following spring.

The advent of chemical weed killers has greatly reduced the amount of hand labor needed for weed and sucker control. It has also made possible a chemical nontillage cultural system. Under this system, weeds are controlled with residual or

FIGURE 4-9 A rototiller is commonly used for weed control in clean cultivated fields and to incorporate the canes removed during pruning.

contact herbicides applied over the entire field (Fig. 4–10). Unwanted suckers are either mowed off with rotary or flail-type mowers or killed with contact herbicides. The soil surface, under a chemical nontillage program, soon becomes stable and provides good footing for hand labor and machinery. If the weed and primocane population is kept under control, this soil management system is at least as good as clean cultivation for maintenance of soil structure and yields (Uprichard et al., 1974).

Another cultural system that has many advantages if properly managed involves chemical weed control in the rows combined with a permanent cover crop between the rows (Chamberlain and Crandall, 1979). This system is best adapted to moderately heavy soils that have a high moisture-holding capacity. Irrigation is necessary on light or sandy soils. The cover crop is usually planted during the first 1 to 2 years of the planting; if started in an older field, at least 2 years is required before the root systems of the cover crop and the raspberries establish equilibrium. Yields and growth may be reduced during this adjustment period. This system reduces erosion, provides good footing for hand laborers and equipment, helps prevent soil compaction from heavy machinery, reduces cultivation costs, decreases energy consumption, and hastens the hardening of canes during the fall, thus making them less susceptible to winter injury. Success depends on how well growth and yields are maintained. The cover crop is mowed frequently during the preharvest period to decrease competition for water and nutrients during the time when there is the greatest demand by developing primocanes and fruit. Additional nitrogen fertilizer and supplemental water may be necessary.

FIGURE 4–10 Weeds in the rows can be controlled by dormant applications of residual herbicides. This sprayer is adjusted to apply the chemical spray to an 18-in. band of soil on each of two rows.

Culture

A permanent mulch is sometimes used by home gardeners and small commercial growers. In this system of culture a thick mulch of weed-seed-free straw, sawdust, ground corncobs, or other material is applied in the plant rows, and the row middles are cultivated. Occasionally, the entire area may be mulched. The mulch is applied thick enough to smother most emerging weeds. This system is especially good for black raspberries because excess sucker growth is not a problem. Red raspberry cultivars require considerable hand labor to control suckers.

Primocane Suppression

A recent development, which involves temporarily suppressing the growth of red raspberry primocanes during the early spring, is used on vigorous plantings to increase yields and to make harvesting operations more efficient (Norton, 1973; Freeman and Daubeny, 1986; Sheets, 1973; Waister et al., 1977) (Fig. 4–11). During the spring, from the time of bud break through fruit set, new primocanes are growing rapidly and apparently compete with the developing fruiting laterals for both the storage and current products of photosynthesis. In Scotland, elimination of

FIGURE 4-11 The primocanes (new shoots) in this planting are at the maximum desirable height for chemical suppression (cane burning).

the suckers from between the hills increased yields 18 to 20% (Dale, 1977). In Washington, increases in yields of up to 70% were obtained with two cane-suppression sprays (Crandall et al., 1980). These increases resulted from the development of more fruits and sometimes larger fruits on the middle and lower fruiting laterals of the canes.

Dinoseb, a desiccant-type, contact herbicide proved to be very effective for this purpose. However, in 1987, the use of this chemical was banned. If this ban is lifted, or if a suitable substitute is found, the practice will continue to be useful for increasing yields and for increasing the efficiency of mechanical harvest. Hand cutting of primocanes has the same effect but is very labor intensive.

Fertilizers

Nitrogen. Provided that the supply of moisture is adequate, the amount of nitrogen fertilizer applied mostly determines the size and number of primocanes that develop. Vigorous primocanes usually have long internodes; thus fewer fruiting laterals remain after topping than on small-diameter canes. However, the fruiting laterals that are produced have more fruits per lateral (Crandall et al., 1974a). Thus the total number of fruits per cane is not much different for large-diameter canes than for small-diameter canes. The other effect of nitrogen fertilizer is to increase the number of trainable canes. If, during dormant pruning, the number of canes left per hill or per lineal foot (meter) of row is arbitrarily limited to a fixed number, the effect of nitrogen fertilizer applications is largely masked. However, when a dormant pruning system is used that leaves a variable number of canes per hill or per foot (meter) of row, depending on the vigor of the plants, the positive effect of nitrogen fertilization on yields is more fully realized. Therefore, within limits, growers regulate the size and number of canes produced by varying the nitrogen rate. An adequate number of moderate-sized canes is best. Where cane vigor and numbers are difficult to obtain because of less-than-optimum growing conditions, closer row spacing may be used to obtain a satisfactory cane population per acre (hectare).

Nitrogen fertilizer is applied in the spring just before growth starts. One application is usually adequate on established plantings (Crandall, 1980). Most nitrogen fertilizers are readily soluble, so they can be spread on the soil surface in a narrow band on each side of the rows. Rates of application vary from 25 to 100 lb (28 to 112 kg/ha) actual nitrogen per acre, depending on the original fertility of the soil and the growth response desired.

Phosphorus and potassium. If the soil test shows that phosphorus and/or potassium are needed, they can be combined and applied with the nitrogen.

Micronutrients. Additional nutrients, such as B, Mg, Mn, Zn, S, or Fe, are sometimes needed. Deficiencies may be indicated by a soil test, by foliar analysis, or by plant symptoms. These nutrients can be applied either to the soil or to the foliage. They are required in very small amounts. If too much is applied, they may be toxic to the plants. They should never be concentrated in a narrow band.

Culture

Manure.   Manure is a good source of nutrients, and the organic matter it contains helps to maintain good soil structure. It is usually applied during the winter at rates of about 10 tons/acre (22 MT/ha) of horse or cow manure or about half that rate for chicken or hog manure. Manure is low in phosphorus, so the application should be supplemented with about 100 lb/acre (112 kg/ha) of phosphorus. Some additional nitrogen fertilizer may be necessary, depending on the amount of raw organic matter such as straw or sawdust contained in the manure. Problems can develop if too much manure is applied. Excess nitrogen released late in the summer may cause the plants to continue growth into the late fall. This delays maturity of the canes and causes them to be more subject to cold injury.

Irrigation

More and more raspberries are being grown with irrigation since additional water will increase yields (Fig. 4–12). This results from increased numbers and size of canes and larger fruit size (Kongsrud, 1969). Also, where irrigation is not available, a year of high yield is often followed by a year of low yield because primocane growth is suppressed by lack of water during the year of the high yield. Supplemental irrigation helps to prevent this year-to-year fluctuation.

Most of the water used by raspberries growing in a well-drained soil comes from the upper portion of the soil profile (Crandall et al., 1969). Highest yields and growth are obtained when not more than two-thirds of the available water in this 4-ft (1.2-m) soil profile is used between irrigations. Crandall et al. (1969) measured

FIGURE 4–12   Irrigation increases cane growth and fruit size. This field is being irrigated with overhead sprinklers.

Raspberry Management   Chap. 4

the actual amount of water removed from the soil profile by raspberry plants and compared it to the amount of water evaporated from the free water surface of an evaporation pan during the same period. They found a ratio of approximately 1:1. During the time that the raspberry plants withdrew 1 in. (2.5 cm) of water from the soil, the evaporation pan showed a comparable loss of 1 in. (2.5 cm). This relationship can be used as a means of estimating water usage for scheduling irrigation.

Sprinkler irrigation is the most common method of application. This may be done with hand-moved sprinklers, with solid-set sprinkler installations, or with one of a number of types of large-nozzle, self-moving sprinklers that cover up to a hectare per set. Furrow irrigation has been used, but soils for which this method is suitable are often not good raspberry soils, and also, there is considerable danger of overwatering. Drip irrigation is also frequently used for raspberries. This system is expensive to install, but once installed, it requires less than half as much water as other methods and the hand labor to operate it is greatly reduced. This type of irrigation is common in regions where water is scarce.

Pruning and Training

Pruning and training red raspberries. Red raspberries differ from black and purple raspberries in the way they are pruned and trained. Whereas the primocanes of black and purple cultivars are pinched back during the summer to cause branching, red raspberries are left unpinched and normally develop upright, unbranched canes (Fig. 4–13).

Pruning of red raspberries involves three steps: (1) removal of old floricanes, (2) thinning out undesirable or excess 1-year canes, and (3) topping. These steps may

FIGURE 4–13 This field of raspberries has been pruned and trained on a cross-arm trellis. A ½-in. plastic drip irrigation line is supported by the crossarms. An emitter is placed on the line between every other plant at an interval of about 5 ft apart.

Culture

be spread out over the entire period from the end of harvest to early spring, or they can all be done during the dormant season.

The floricanes die after harvest. They are sometimes removed at that time. Often, they are left until winter and removed at the same time that unwanted 1-year canes are thinned out. Removal of the old canes immediately after harvest tends to conserve moisture but has little effect on primocane growth (Brierley, 1932). There is not much advantage of removal at this time. The effect on diseases appears to be minimal. In the past it has been recommended that the old canes be cut off close to the ground and removed at this time to eliminate some of the crown borers that are present in the basal portions of the canes (Breakey, 1963). This is only partly effective for their control since most of the borers are still below this portion of the canes. Present methods of control with insecticides are very effective and have eliminated this reason for postharvest cane removal (Scheer et al., 1989). The old canes are sometimes left to support and protect the new canes from damage by strong winds. It appears, then, that the time of cane removal largely depends on the work schedule of the individual grower.

Cane thinning and selection may be done any time during the dormant season. Weak canes and broken canes are removed at this time using either a pruning hook or long-handled pruning shears. The number of canes left per hill or foot (meter) of row is highly variable. Some growers reduce the population of canes to a predetermined number regardless of the vigor of the planting or growing conditions. The number left ranges from a low of five to a maximum of eight or nine canes per hill depending on the decision of the individual grower. Low populations of fruiting canes may have some advantages in fruit size and in the reduction of fruit rot, but yields are usually reduced below the maximum potential for the planting. Modern large-fruited cultivars greatly reduce the need to increase fruit size by pruning. In vigorous plantings, the conditions favoring fruit rot development are influenced more by the crowding and shading effect of primocanes than by the number of fruiting canes. Also, reduction in the number of floricanes tends to increase the number of new shoots that develop, thereby offsetting the advantages of having fewer fruiting canes (Waister et al., 1977).

A system of cane thinning that leaves variable numbers of canes depending on the vigor of the individual plant is now in common use (Crandall, 1980). All broken and weak canes are removed and all the strong canes are retained. The reason for this method of cane thinning is that plants which produce many large canes have the capacity to produce more and larger berries than plants which develop only a few good canes. Properly done, this method of determining cane number when pruning best utilizes the full yield potential of the planting. The greater number of canes left per acre (hectare) tends to reduce per cane yields, but this loss is more than offset by having more canes per acre (hectare). In this system, the number of canes left per foot of row varies from one up to over five (3 to 15 per meter). It has been shown that there is no advantage to leaving more than about five (Crandall, 1980). Trellising systems, such as the cross-arm trellis, where the canes are spread out along the trellis, are better adapted for high cane numbers than are upright, bundle training systems.

Both the fixed-number method of thinning and the method of thinning according to plant vigor can be improved if the more productive canes are kept and the less productive canes are removed. Optimum-quality canes are those of medium to large diameter with close internodes. Such canes produce more fruits per lateral and more berries per cane than do small-diameter canes.

Once the canes are thinned out, they are tied to the support wire and topped. Topping is delayed until after the coldest winter weather is past, to prevent cold injury to the upper buds. The height at which they are topped has some influence on yield (Crandall et al., 1974b). Higher topping increases the number of laterals but tends to reduce the number of fruits per lateral. The effect on number of fruits per lateral is determined more by the amount of cane removed than by the height of topping. The fruiting response of laterals from severe topping is seldom, if ever, great enough to make up for the number of laterals removed. Weaving the canes on the trellis, a training system that retains most of the cane length, increases total yield (Locklin, 1931). The height of topping therefore depends upon the method of harvest. Canes to be hand picked should be topped at about 5 ft (1.5 m) since higher topping of vigorous cultivars places much of the fruit out of reach of the pickers and they will either not pick it or break the fruiting laterals trying to reach it. Fields that are machine harvested can be topped at 5.5 to 6 ft (1.7 to 1.8 m). The higher topping tends to increase yields and also causes less fruit to be borne on laterals close to the ground.

All prunings are placed in the middle of the rows during the pruning operation. They can then be cut up into small pieces with a rotary mower or rototiller. They break down quite rapidly once they are incorporated in the soil and help maintain soil organic matter. They appear to cause little increase in disease or insect problems.

Training and tying. There are two general types of training, the bundle system and the spread system, with many variations of each (Figs. 4–14 and 4–15). The training systems that spread out the canes over the entire fruiting area are more productive than the bundle systems (Crandall, 1980).

The simplest method is the bundle system. All canes from a hill or section of row are gathered together into a single bundle and tied to the support wire with heavy twine. A second tie is sometimes placed around the center of the bundle for added support. Before tying, the support wire is pulled taut and the training wires are either lowered to the bottom hooks on the posts or laid on the ground along the rows. In the teepee bundle system, the canes of a hill are divided into two groups and the tops of the halves of two adjacent hills are tied together. This spreads the canes out more than the single-bundle system and also provides more self-support. When a cross-arm trellis is used, the canes are divided into either two or four bundles. All of these variations reduce the number of canes per bundle and spread them out for better light penetration. Instead of tying the canes, two lighter-weight support wires are sometimes used. The canes are spaced between the two wires and held in place by tying or clipping the wires together at frequent intervals. In Scotland, the canes are spread out along a single support wire and tied or laced individually to the wire using a continuous piece of twine (Turner, 1980).

The weaving system requires a cross-arm trellis and spreads the canes out

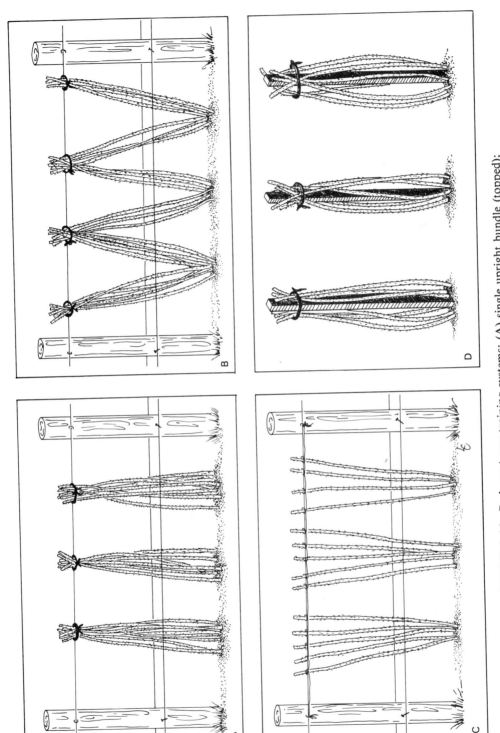

FIGURE 4-14 Red raspberry training systems: (A) single upright bundle (topped); (B) teepee (topped); (C) spread linear (topped); (D) staked hill (topped).

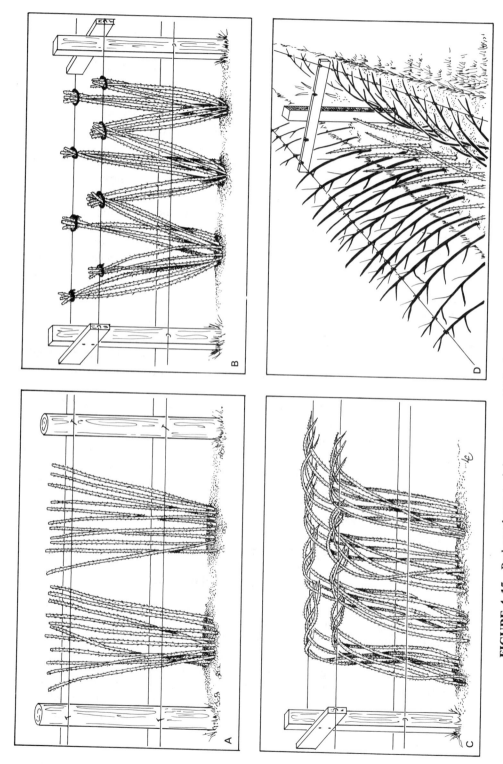

FIGURE 4-15 Red raspberry training systems: (A) hedgerow (topped); (B) cross-arm with tied spread bundle (topped); (C) cross-arm with cane weaving; (D) cross-arm with movable wires (Gjerde).

uniformly along the two support wires. No training wires are necessary because the new primocanes grow up through the center of the row and are kept in place by the woven canes. Canes are left nearly full length, thus taking advantage of the natural habit of vigorous canes to have buds closer together near the top of the canes. The canes are divided between the two wires. In weaving, one to three canes are placed inside the support wire, bent over the wire to the outside and down. The ends are locked in place by tucking them behind the next set of canes, which are brought up inside and over the wire. This forms a continuous basket weave system that requires little or no tying. The weaker tip growth of long canes is broken or cut off during the training process. This eliminates the small, crumbly fruits that are formed near the tips of canes. Weaving usually results in higher yields than those with training systems involving heading back. Fruits are concentrated along the wires and are easily harvested. The primocanes require very little summer training to keep them between the wires and they are well protected from damage by the pickers. Fruit size, however, is smaller, and especially if the weak tip growth of canes is not removed when training, there are more small, crumbly fruits produced. Also, under conditions favorable for fruit rot development, the concentrated fruiting area increases the possibility of developing fruit rot. This is especially noticeable with cultivars that produce long laterals.

The training system used varies with plant vigor, number of canes to be trained, and individual grower's needs. In general, those systems that spread out the canes produce the highest yields. Present-day machine harvesters in the United States require an upright, single-support-wire trellis and training system.

Pruning primocane fruiting cultivars. The fruiting of many commercial plantings of primocane fruiting raspberries is limited to the fall crop. This is done by cutting off all floricanes during the dormant season. These plants are often grown without a supporting trellis. Even though the fall crop is usually less than that of summer cropping cultivars, the reduced costs of pruning and trellising, the elimination of the problem of winter injury to overwintering floricanes, and the increased price for out-of-season fruit make the production of primocane fruiting cultivars economically attractive.

Pruning and training black and purple raspberries. Black and purple cultivars have a different primocane growth habit than that of red raspberries, and they require different pruning and training methods (Fig. 4–16).

Summer Pinching. Black and purple raspberry primocanes, if not pinched to induce branching, develop long, slender canes with small unfruitful branches. The total yield of unpinched canes is approximately the same as that of pinched canes (Beach, 1934). Such unpinched canes, however, require staking or trellising for support. Summer pinching causes the canes to form strong fruitful branches and keeps the plant low. Pinching at a low height tends to reduce yields over high pinching, but the cost of production is much less because the plants do not need a supporting trellis. Supports, if used, consist either of individual plant stakes or a

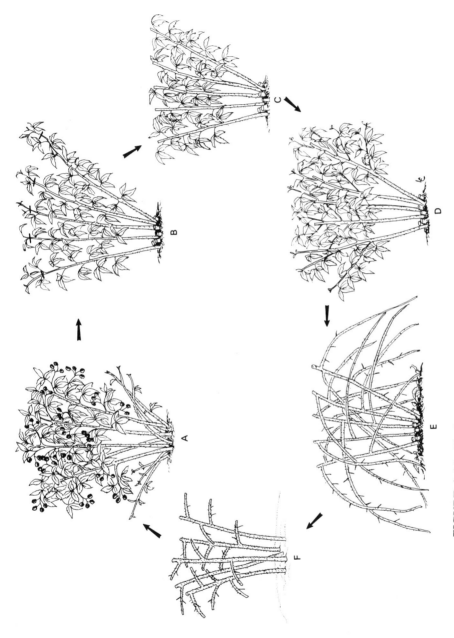

FIGURE 4-16 Black raspberry development and pruning cycle: (A) summer fruiting of floricanes and growth of primocanes; (B) primocanes prior to summer topping after fruited floricanes have been removed; (C) primocanes after topping; (D) lateral branching of primocanes in response to topping; (E) dormant canes prior to winter pruning; (F) laterals pruned back during dormant season.

simple two-wire trellis, one wire on each side of the row. Fruits for machine harvest are grown without a trellis.

Summer pinching is done during the summer before harvest. The primocanes of low-headed, unsupported black raspberries are pinched at a height of 14 to 20 in. (35 to 50 cm). High-headed, supported plants are pinched at heights ranging from 24 to 40 in. (60 to 100 cm), depending on plant vigor. Purple raspberries produce more vigorous, heavier primocanes and are therefore pinched about 8 to 12 in. (20 to 30 cm) higher than black raspberries.

Primocanes should be pinched when they reach the proper height. This involves removal of the terminal 2 to 3 in. (5 to 8 cm) of the shoot with pruning shears or by hand. Since the primocanes develop at different rates, it is necessary to go over the field two or three times at weekly intervals to tip all shoots at the same height. Pinching causes strong branches to develop from several of the axillary buds below where the cane is tipped.

Removal of Fruiting Canes. Fruiting canes of black and purple cultivars are either removed right after harvest or during the winter. Removal right after harvest is recommended where cane diseases are present. However, if canes are left, they provide support and help prevent wind damage to the primocanes during late summer and fall.

Dormant Pruning. If fruiting canes have not been removed, they are cut off close to the ground along with all weak, spindly 1-year canes. The lateral branches are cut back. Since the largest fruits are produced toward the base of the branches and on the larger-diameter branches, proper heading back effectively eliminates much inferior fruit (Beach, 1934). The length of lateral to leave depends on the vigor of the plant. Weak, small-diameter laterals are cut back to 2 to 4 in. (5 to 10 cm). Strong laterals are left up to 14 to 18 in. (30 to 45 cm) long. There is no advantage to leaving longer laterals. The laterals of purple raspberries are left longer than those of black raspberries, primarily because the purple cultivars are more vigorous.

Harvesting

Raspberries soften and loosen from the receptacle as they ripen. At the time the fruits can first be readily separated from the receptacle, they are fully colored, firm, and have a good flavor. Fruits at this stage of maturity remain in good condition for several days if handled properly. When left on the plant longer, the fruit continues to soften and the color darkens. Such fruits are more susceptible to fungal rots. Since all of the fruits do not ripen at the same time, they must be picked a number of times at frequent intervals to maintain good quality. The harvest season for red raspberries often lasts 4 to 6 weeks, whereas the black and purple cultivars have a harvest season of only 1 or 2 weeks.

Red raspberries for fresh market. Fruit for fresh market is picked and handled very carefully (Fig. 4–17). It must be firm and well colored. Pickers must be carefully supervised and instructed to harvest only high-quality, sound fruit, free of rot. Overripe fruit not suitable for fresh market must be sold through other channels. Fruit must be harvested every 1 to 3 days to maintain high quality. Fruit can be picked directly into containers holding about 1 pint or 1 quart (250 to 500 g) and transported to a holding or precooling station without further sorting or handling. Harvesting early in the day while temperatures are cool is desirable. After harvest, fruit to be shipped long distances is placed in precooling units, where it is subjected to forced-air cooling that removes the field heat rapidly and brings the core temperature down to near 32°F (0°C). The more rapid the cooling, the less the moisture loss and the longer the fruit can be held before use. Once precooled, the fruit is ready for shipment. Sometimes flats of fruit are unitized on pallets, enclosed in polyethylene film, and the initial CO_2 content of the interior atmosphere is raised to around 30% (Winter et al., 1939). This high CO_2 level dissipates during shipment but does much to keep down mold development during transportation. Fruit is shipped by refrigerated trucks or by airplane, depending on market demand and distance.

Raspberries have a short shelf life and tend to settle in the container during transport. They also tend to darken and become dull appearing. Some of the newer cultivars, such as 'Chilcotin', 'Meeker', 'Skeena', and 'Chilliwack', are better adapted to the fresh market than are older ones such as 'Willamette' (Daubeny, 1986).

Red raspberries for processing.   Fruit for processing is usually picked on a 4- to 6-day interval. The interval is kept shorter when mechanical harvesting. This causes a wide range of fruit maturity with some overripe fruit. The picking interval, and indeed, the care in handling to a degree, depend on the processing market. Fruit to be frozen in small 8-oz (250-g) retail packages or individually quick frozen (IQF) must be whole fruits in good condition. Overripe or crumbly fruits are not suitable. Fruit for freezing and reprocessing into jams, jellies, preserves, or for ice cream and yogurt flavoring can be softer and can include crumbly fruit. The softest, overripe fruit is often used for concentrates, dehydration, juices, or wine.

Fruit can be picked directly into the flats in which it will be transported to the processing plant, or picked into smaller containers and poured carefully into the processor flats. The flats are either divided into sections holding about 1 quart or contain individual containers (hallocks) of the same size (Fig.4–18). Filled flats hold about 12 to 13 lb (5.5 to 6.0 kg) of fruit. Once filled, the flats should be placed in the

FIGURE 4–17 Fruit for fresh market must be picked at the proper stage of maturity and placed directly into the special market containers in the field.

FIGURE 4-18 Stand designed to hold the empty containers enables hand pickers to harvest fruits with both hands.

shade until time for loading and transport. No more than 2 to 3 hours should elapse between picking and transfer to the processor, especially on hot days.

Hot weather or rain during harvest causes the fruit to be soft and more subject to rot. Under such conditions the fruit must be harvested more frequently. Overripe fruit, left from one picking to the next, rots and contaminates the sound fruit.

Black and purple raspberries. Black and purple raspberries have a more concentrated ripening period than red raspberries. For this reason and because the berries are more firm, it is possible to harvest most of the fruit in one to three pickings. Procedures for harvesting are similar to those for red raspberries except that they are much less likely to be damaged during harvesting and handling and are not nearly as susceptible to fruit rot.

Most black and purple raspberries are handpicked and marketed on the local market or at the farm. Very few are processed except on the west coast of the United States in Oregon. There large plantings of black raspberries are grown for processing, and nearly all of them are machine harvested.

Machine harvesting. Fruits of many raspberry cultivars loosen from the receptacle as they ripen and will fall off the plant when shaken. Operation of all commercial raspberry machine harvesters is based on this principle. The machine shakes the plants to remove the fruits and catches them as they fall (Fig. 4–19). They are then conveyed to an air cleaner for trash and insect removal, moved across a sorting belt, and finally deposited in containers. At the present stage of development, all machine-harvested fruit is sold for processing because of the advanced stage of maturity and the damage that is caused to some of the berries during handling.

First attempts to develop a machine harvester for red raspberries apparently began soon after World War II in the Puyallup Valley of western Washington. Several growers, working independently, built their own harvesters (Schwartze and Myhre, 1952). All of them operated on the "shake and catch" principle.

Currently, four commercial machine harvesters are used for raspberries in the United States. They are the Weygandt, the Blueberry Equipment Incorporated (BEI) (Fig. 4–20), the Littau (Fig. 4–21), and the Korvan machines. At present, expansion in number of harvesters is divided between BEI, Littau, and Korvan. Nearly 100% of the Oregon black raspberry crop, 85% of the red raspberries in Oregon and Washington, and 40% in British Columbia are machine harvested. More of the crop is handpicked during years when hand labor is plentiful and prices are high.

All of the harvesters mentioned above straddle the raspberry row and shake the fruit loose. Two general types of shaking mechanisms are used. One type uses

FIGURE 4–19 The Weygandt harvester uses oscillating, revolving drums with steel fingers for fruit removal. The fruit is elevated to the upper level, where it is air cleaned, hand sorted, and placed in containers.

FIGURE 4-20 The Blueberry Equipment (BEI) harvester uses long, flexible rods for fruit removal. The fruit is elevated to the rear of the machine for cleaning and handling.

FIGURE 4-21 The Littau harvester has long, flexible rods that shake the plants from side to side for fruit removal. The fruit is elevated to one side for cleaning and sorting. The Littau harvester is available as either a self-propelled model or a tractor-pulled model.

vertically mounted, many-fingered cylinders, one on each side of the row. The fingers extend into the plant canopy and shake off the fruit. The cylinders are free to rotate as the machine moves down the row.

The other type is patterned after the blackberry harvester developed by the University of Arkansas (Nelson et al., 1965). The fruit is removed by vertical banks of semiflexible rods mounted on each side of the row. These rods are hinged at the front end and impart a horizontal shaking motion.

Once the fruit is shaken loose, it falls onto spring-loaded, overlapping catching plates that work in and out of the row around the base of the plants. The fruit is carried by conveyor belts across an air cleaner and a handsorting belt and then deposited in the containers.

The shift from hand picking to machine harvesting created some new problems and placed increased emphasis on others. An important new problem was psychological. The grower must accept the fact that a field that has just been machine harvested will look different from one that has been hand picked. Many fruits that a hand picker would remove are still left on the plant. There is a strong temptation to increase the speed of the picking mechanism to remove more fruit. Such action increases fruit and plant damage, removes more green fruits and fruits with stems attached, and increases the amount of leaves and trash that must be removed from the harvested fruit. Expensive, complicated machinery requires careful maintenance, adjustment, and operation. Also, many insects that normally remain in the foliage during handpicking are shaken off and, if not removed, become contaminants of the harvested fruit. The advanced maturity of the harvested fruit makes it more susceptible to fruit rot both before and after it is removed from the plant. In general, a higher percentage of the fruit is suitable only for markets that can use overripe, softer fruit and less is therefore available for market outlets that require whole, sound berries. The proportion of better-quality fruit is greatly influenced by the cultivar and the carefulness of the grower.

Trellising for Machine Harvest. Raspberry plants for machine harvest are supported by an upright, single-support-wire trellis. Small-diameter posts can be used within the row but should be spaced closer together than for hand harvesting. Steel posts are often used in conjunction with larger, wooden end posts. Use of training wires is optional. The canes are tied in single bundles or spread out along the support wire. In the teepee system, half of the canes from two adjacent hills are tied together at the top. Cane topping height is usually 6 to 12 in. (15 to 30 cm) higher than for hand harvesting. Row ends are marked so that the machine always enters the row from the same end each time it is picked.

Insect Control for Machine Harvest. Many insects and other arthropods live in the raspberry foliage. When the plants are shaken, these fall along with the harvested fruit and unless removed, become contaminants (Crandall et al., 1966). Control requires a two-step approach. First, it is necessary to spray to obtain good control of the common insect pests. Just before first harvest, a thorough application of a broad-spectrum insecticide is applied to eliminate most of the remaining insects and other arthropods present. The foliage is very thick at this time and thorough coverage requires large amounts of spray material applied at high pressure. The second step in insect control occurs during machine harvest. The speed of the blower for the air cleaner is adjusted to slightly below the point where it blows out the ripe fruits with the trash. This speed varies depending on the condition of the foliage and the amount of moisture present. Many insects are removed with the trash. The remainder of the insects are removed on the sorting belt. It is not possible to remove many insect contaminants, but some of them can be removed.

Disease Control for Machine Harvest. Fruit rot *(Botrytis)* is a major problem during machine harvest. Once rotted fruits are in the container, it is nearly impossible to sort them out. The rot must be prevented before harvest or eliminated on the sorting belt. Spray programs for rot control prior to harvest are only partially successful, but an intensive fungicide program needs to be used. When weather conditions favor rot development during harvest, the interval between harvests is reduced. A limited amount of rotted fruit can be removed on the sorting belt. Slowing the ground speed of the machine helps. If these measures are not adequate, the machine is sometimes run through the field to shake the crop onto the ground to eliminate rotted fruits. Once the weather clears and the plants dry off, the incidence of rot decreases. Machine harvested fruit is not allowed to remain in the field for extended periods after it is picked. The fruit deteriorates rapidly, especially during hot weather.

Supervision and Adjustment. The success of a machine harvest operation depends on careful supervision. The best ground speed, beater adjustment, and air cleaner speed vary with temperature, moisture, cultivar, and crop condition. The appearance of the product when it reaches the sorting belt is a good indication of how well the machine is adjusted. Too many fruits that are green or have the stems still attached means that the beater action is too vigorous. Excess numbers of insects or trash indicates that the blower speed needs to be adjusted. One person on the machine must monitor the picking operation and make the necessary adjustments. The best location for this person is at the sorting belt.

REFERENCES

ATKINSON, D. 1973. Seasonal changes in the length of white unsuberized roots on raspberry plants under irrigated conditions. J. Hortic. Sci. 48:413–419.

BAILEY, J. S. 1948. A study of the rest period in red raspberries. Proc. Am. Soc. Hortic. Sci. 52:265–270.

BARRITT, B. H., AND L. C. TORRE. 1974. Cold storage and handling of red raspberry planting stock. HortScience 9:344–345.

BARRITT, B. H., P. C. CRANDALL, AND P. R. BRISTOW. 1979. Breeding for root rot resistance in red raspberry. J. Am. Soc. Hortic. Sci. 102:92–94.

BARRITT, B. H., L. C. TORRE, H. S. PEPIN, AND H. A. DAUBENY. 1980. Fruit firmness measurements in red raspberry. HortScience 15:38–39.

BEACH, G. A. 1934. A preliminary study of the fruiting habit of the black raspberry *(Rubus occidentalis)*. Colo. Agric. Exp. Stn. Tech. Bull. 8.

BLANPIED, G. D. 1972. A study of ethylene in apples, red raspberry, and cherry. Plant Physiol. 40:627–630.

BREAKEY, E. P. 1963. Biology and control of the raspberry crown borer, *Bembesia marginata* (Harris). Wash. Agric. Exp. Stn. Tech. Bull. 39.

BRIERLEY, W. G. 1931. Transpiration in new and old canes of the Latham raspberry. Proc. Am. Soc. Hortic. Sci. 28:188–193.

BRIERLEY, W. G. 1932. The effect of removal of fruiting canes after harvest upon the growth of new canes in the Latham raspberry. Proc. Am. Soc. Hortic. Sci. 29:300–301.

BRIERLEY, W. G., AND R. H. LANDON. 1946. Some relationships between rate of hardening, loss of cold resistance and winter injury in the Latham raspberry. Proc. Am. Soc. Hortic. Sci. 47:224–234.

BRISTOW, P. R. 1980. Raspberry root rots in the Pacific northwest. Acta Hortic. 112:39–46.

BRISTOW, P. R., B. H. BARRITT, AND F. D. McELROY. 1980. Reaction of red raspberry clones to the root lesion nematode. Acta Hortic. 112:39–43.

BRAUN, J. W. 1986. Growth and fruiting of 'Heritage' primocane fruiting red raspberry in response to paclobutrazol. HortScience 21:437–439.

BRAUN, J. W., AND J. K. L. GARTH. 1984a. Growth and fruiting of 'Heritage' primocane fruiting red raspberry in response to daminozide and ethephon. J. Am. Soc. Hortic. Sci. 109:207–209.

BRAUN, J. W., AND J. K. L. GARTH. 1984b. Intracane yield compensation in the red raspberry. J. Am. Soc. Hortic. Sci. 109:526–530.

CHAMBERLAIN, J. D., AND P. C. CRANDALL. 1979. Permanent cover crop studies in red raspberries: progress report. Proc. West. Wash. Hortic. Assoc. 69:142–144.

CHRISTENSON, J. R. 1947. Root studies. XI. Raspberry root systems. J. Hortic. Sci. 23:218–226.

CONVERSE, R. H. 1966. Diseases of raspberries and erect and trailing blackberries. U.S. Dep. Agric. Handb. 310.

CONVERSE, R. H. 1978. Controlling diseases of raspberries and blackberries. U.S. Dep. Agric. Farmers' Bull. 2208.

CORMACK, M. R., AND P. D. WAISTER. 1976. Effects of machine harvesting on yield in the following year. Hortic. Res. 16:121–129.

CRANDALL, P. C. 1980. Twenty years of red raspberry research in southwestern Washington state. Acta Hortic. 112:53–58.

CRANDALL, P. C., C. H. SHANKS, JR., AND J. E. GEORGE. 1966. Mechanically harvesting red raspberries and removal of insects from the harvested product. Proc. Am. Soc. Hortic. Sci. 89:295–302.

CRANDALL, P. C., M. C. JENSEN, M. E. MIDDLETON, AND J. D. CHAMBERLAIN. 1969. Scheduling the irrigation of red raspberries from evaporation pan data. Wash. Agric. Exp. Stn. Circ. 497.

CRANDALL, P. C., D. F. ALLMENDINGER, J. D. CHAMBERLAIN, AND K. A. BIDERBOST. 1974a. Influence of cane number and diameter, irrigation, and carbohydrate reserves on the fruit number of red raspberries. J. Am. Soc. Hortic. Sci. 99:524–526.

CRANDALL, P. C., J. D. CHAMBERLAIN, AND K. A. BIDERBOST. 1974b. Cane characteristics associated with berry number of red raspberry. J. Am. Soc. Hortic. Sci. 99:370–372.

CRANDALL, P. C., J. D. CHAMBERLAIN, AND J. K. L. GARTH. 1980. The effects of primocane suppression on growth, yield and chemical composition of red raspberries. J. Am. Soc. Hortic. Sci. 105:194–196.

CRANDALL, P. C., AND J. K. L. GARTH. 1981. Yield and growth response of 'Heritage' raspberry to daminozide and ethephon. HortScience. 16:654–655.

DALE, A. 1976. Prospects for breeding higher yielding raspberries. Acta Hortic. 60:159–167.

DALE, A. 1977. Yield response to cane vigour control. Bull. Scot. Hortic. Res. Inst. Assoc. 13:12–18.

DALE, A. 1979. Varietal differences in the relationships between some characteristics of red raspberry fruiting laterals and their position on the cane. J. Hortic. Sci. 54:257–265.

DALE, A., AND H. A. DAUBENY. 1985. Genotype-environment interactions involving British and Pacific northwest red raspberry cultivars. HortScience 20:68–69.

DARROW, G. M. 1924. The Van Fleet raspberry, a new hybrid variety. U.S. Dep. Agric. Circ. 320.

DARROW, G. M. 1929. Effect of light, temperature and transpiration on elongation of canes of red raspberry and other brambles. Proc. Am. Soc. Hortic. Sci. 26:308–311.

DARROW, G. M., AND G. G. WALDO. 1933. Raspberry and blackberry cane measurements. Proc. Am. Soc. Hortic. Sci. 30:269–274.

DARROW, G. M. 1937. Blackberry and raspberry improvement. In Yearbook of U.S. Dep. Agric. p. 496–533.

DAUBENY, H. A. 1980. Red raspberry cultivar development in British Columbia with special reference to pest response and germplasm exploitation. Acta Hortic. 112:59–67.

DAUBENY, H. A. 1986. The British Columbia raspberry breeding program since 1980. Acta Hortic. 183:47–58.

DAUBENY, H. A. 1987a. A hypothesis for inheritance of resistance to cane *Botrytis* in red raspberry. HortScience 22:116–119.

DAUBENY, H. A. 1987b. 'Chilliwack' and 'Comox' red raspberries. HortScience 22:1343–1345.

DAUBENY, H. A., AND D. STARY. 1982. Identification of resistance to *Amphorophora agathonica* in the native North American red raspberry. J. Am. Soc. Hortic. Sci. 107:593–597.

DAUBENY, H. A., R. STACE-SMITH, AND J. A. FREEMAN. 1978. The occurrence and some effects of raspberry bushy dwarf virus in red raspberry. J. Am. Soc. Hortic. Sci. 103:519–522.

DONNELLY, D. J., AND H. A. DAUBENY. 1986. Tissue culture of *Rubus* species. Acta Hortic. 183:305–314.

DOUGHTY, C. C., P. C. CRANDALL, AND C. H. SHANKS, JR. 1972. Cold injury to red raspberry and the effect of premature defoliation and mite damage. J. Am. Soc. Hortic. Sci. 97:670–673.

DUNCAN, J. M., AND D. M. KENNEDY. 1986. Root rot and die-back of raspberry. Scot. Crop Res. Inst. Ann. Rep. 1985, p. 190.

DUNN, J. S., M. STOLP, AND G. G. LINDSAY. 1976. Mechanical raspberry harvesting and the Lincoln canopy system. Am. Soc. Agric. Eng. Pap. 76-1543.

ENGARD, C. J. 1944. Organogenesis in *Rubus*. Univ. Hawaii Res. Publ. 21.

FREEMAN, J. A., AND H. A. DAUBENY. 1986. Effect of chemical removal of primocanes on several raspberry cultivars. Acta Hortic. 183:215–222.

FREEMAN, J. A., R. STACE-SMITH, AND H. A. DAUBENY. 1975. Effects of tomato ringspot virus on the growth and yield of red raspberry. Can. J. Plant Sci. 55:749–754.

GRUBB, N. H. 1922. Commercial raspberries and their classification. J. Pomol. 3:11–35.

HAGLUND, W. A. 1974. Nematode sampling. In W. P. A. Scheer and R. Garren (eds). Commercial red raspberry production. Wash. State Univ. PNW Bull. 176.

HALTVICK, E. T., AND B. E. STRUCKMEYER. 1965. Blossom bud differentiation in red raspberry. Proc. Am. Soc. Hortic. Sci. 87:234–237.

HEDRICK, V. P. 1922. Cyclopedia of hardy fruits. Macmillan, New York. p. 270–271.

HIIRSALMI, H., AND J. SAKO. 1976. The nectar raspberry, *Rubus idaeus* × *Rubus arcticus:* a new cultivated plant. Acta Hortic. 60:151–157.

HILL, R. G., JR. 1958. Fruit development of the red raspberry and its relation to nitrogen treatment. Ohio Agric. Exp. Stn. Res. Bull. 803.

HUDSON, J. P. 1954. Propagation of plants by root cuttings. I. Regeneration of raspberry root cuttings. J. Hortic. Sci. 19:27–43.

HULL, J. W. 1961. Progress in developing red raspberries for the south. Fruit Var. Hortic. Dig. 16:13–14.

JENNINGS, D. L. 1977. Somatic mutations in the raspberry. Hortic. Res. 17:61–63.

JENNINGS, D. L. 1979. The occurrence of multiple fruiting laterals at single nodes of raspberry canes. New Phytol. 82:365–374.

JENNINGS, D. L. 1980. Recent progress in breeding raspberries and other *Rubus* fruits at the Scottish Horticultural Research Institute. Acta Hortic. 112:109–116.

JENNINGS, D. L. 1981. A hundred years of loganberries. Fruit Var. J. 35:34–37.

JENNINGS, D. L. 1982a. New raspberry cultivar Glen Moy. Scot. Crop Res. Inst. Ann. Rep. 1981:71–72.

JENNINGS, D. L. 1982b. New raspberry cultivar Glen Prosen. Scot. Crop Res. Inst. Ann. Rep. 1981:72–73.

JENNINGS, D. L., AND E. CARMICHAEL. 1975. Some physiological changes occurring in overwintering raspberry plants in Scotland. Hortic. Res. 14:103–108.

JENNINGS, D. L., A. DALE, AND E. CARMICHAEL. 1976. Raspberry and blackberry breeding at the Scottish Horticultural Research Institute. Acta Hortic. 60:129–133.

JOHNSON, F., P. C. CRANDALL, AND J. R. FISHER. 1972. Soil fumigation and its effect on raspberry root rot. Plant Dis. Rep. 56:467–470.

JONES, A. T., AND G. A. WOOD. 1979. The virus status of raspberries (*Rubus idaeus* L.) in New Zealand. New Zealand J. Agric. Res. 22:173–182.

KEEP, E. 1961. Autumn-fruiting in raspberries. J. Hortic. Sci. 36:174–185.

KEEP, E. 1969. Accessory buds in the genus *Rubus* with particular reference to *R. idaeus* L. Ann. Bot. 33:191–204.

KEEP, E. 1976. Progress in *Rubus* breeding at East Malling. Acta Hortic. 60:123–128.

KEEP, E. 1984. Breeding *Rubus* and *Ribes* crops at East Malling. Sci. Hortic. 35:54–71.

KEEP, E. 1986. Bringing on varieties full of promise for the English grower. Grower 106:27–30.

KEEP, E., J. H. PARKER, AND V. H. KNIGHT. 1980. Recent progress in raspberry breeding at East Malling. Acta Hortic. 112:127–134.

KICHINA, V. V. 1976. Raspberry breeding for mechanical harvesting in northern Russia. Acta Hortic. 60:89–94.

References

KNIGHT, V. H. 1980. Screening for fruit rot resistance in red raspberries at East Malling. Acta Hortic. 112:127–134.

KONGSRUD, K. L. 1969. Irrigation experiments with raspberries. Kies (Norway) State Exp. Stn. Rep. 22.

LALONE, R. S. 1980. Pest management of leafrollers in caneberries grown in Oregon. Acta Hortic. 112:135–141.

LAMB, R. C. 1948. Effect of temperatures above and below freezing on the breaking of rest in the Latham raspberry. Proc. Am. Soc. Hortic. Sci. 51:313–315.

LAWRENCE, F. J. 1980a. The current status of red raspberry cultivars in the United States and Canada. Fruit Var. J. 34:84–89.

LAWRENCE, F. J. 1980b. Breeding primocane fruiting red raspberries at Oregon State University. Acta Hortic. 112:145–149.

LIPE, J. A., AND L. W. MARTIN. 1984. Culture and management of blackberries in the United States. HortScience 19:191–193.

LOCKLIN, H. D. 1931. Effects of different methods of pruning raspberries on earliness, weight of fruit and yield. Proc. West. Wash. Hortic. Assoc. 27:185–189.

MACKENZIE, A. D. 1979. Structure of the fruit of red raspberry (*Rubus idaeus* L.) in relation to abscission. Ann. Bot. 43:355–362.

MARTIN, L. W. 1985. Cultural modifications for improving mechanical harvesting of red raspberries and blackberries. HortScience 20:1014–1015.

MASON, D. T. 1974. Measurement of fruit ripeness and its relation to mechanical harvesting of the red raspberry (*Rubus idaeus* L.) Hortic. Res. 14:21–27.

MATHERS, B. A. 1952. A study of fruit-bud development in *Rubus idaeus*. J. Hortic. Sci. 27:266–272.

MCELROY, F. D. 1975. Nematode control in established red raspberry plantings. p. 445–446. In F. Lamberti, C. E. Taylor, and J. W. Seinhorst (eds.) *Nematode vectors* of plant viruses. Plenum Press, New York.

MCELROY, F. D. 1977. Effect of two nematode species on establishment, growth, and yield of raspberry. Plant Dis. Rep. 61:277–279.

MCGREGOR, G. R. 1987. Daminozide affects growth and yield of 'Heritage' red raspberry. HortScience 22:38–40.

MISIC, P. D. 1980. Red raspberry breeding in Yugoslavia up to 1979. Acta Hortic. 112:163–166.

MONEY, R. W., AND W. A. CHRISTIAN. 1934. Analytical data on some common fruits. J. Sci. Food Agric. 1:8–12.

NELSON, G. S., R. H. BENEDICT, A. A. KATTAN, AND G. A. ALBRITTON. 1965. Design and development of a blackberry harvester. Am. Soc. Agric. Eng. Pap. 65-619.

NORTON, R. A. 1973. Red raspberry cane control research at Mount Vernon. Proc. West. Wash. Hortic. Assoc. 63:152–155.

NORTON, R. A. 1980. Red raspberry primocane control research and practice in the Pacific northwest. Acta Hortic. 112:191–193.

OURECKY, D. K. 1975. Brambles. p. 98–129. In J. Janick and J. N. Moore (eds.). Advances in fruit breeding. Purdue University Press, West Lafayette, Ind.

OVERCASH, J. P. 1972. Dorman red raspberry: new variety for Mississippi. Miss. Univ. Agric. Exp. Stn. Bull. 793.

ODYVIN, J. P. 1969. Repeatabilities of measurements of cane production and scores of yield characters in the raspberry (*Rubus idaeus* L.). Hortic Res. 9:103–111.

REEVE, R. M. 1954. Fruit histogenesis in *Rubus strigosus*. I. Outer epidermis, parenchyma, and receptacle. Am. J. Bot. 41:152–160.

ROBBINS, J., AND T. M. SJULIN. 1986. A comparison of two methods for measurement of fruit strength in red raspberry. HortScience 21:1054–1055.

ROBERTS, O. C., AND A. S. COLBY. 1960. Red and purple raspberries: their identification from plant primocanes. Mass. Agric. Exp. Stn. Bull. 523.

SCHEER, W. P. A., C. A. BRUN, C. B. McCONNELL, AND A. L. ANTONELLI. 1989. Pest Control Guide for Commercial Small Fruits. Wash. Coop. Ext. Serv. EB 1491.

SCHEER, W. P. A., AND R. GARREN. 1981. Commercial red raspberry production. Wash.–Oreg.–Idaho. Coop. Ext. Serv. Bull. PNW 176.

SCHWARTZE, C. D., AND A. S. MYHRE. 1952. Some experiments and observations on mechanical harvesting of red raspberries. Proc. West. Wash. Hortic. Assoc. 42:21–24.

SHANKS, C. H., JR. 1969. Pollination of raspberries by honeybees. J. Apic. Res. 8:19–21.

SHEETS, W. A. 1973. Chemical pruning of caneberries with dinoseb at Aurora. Proc. West. Wash. Hortic. Assoc. 63:150–152.

SJULIN, T. M., AND J. ROBBINS. 1987. Effects of maturity, harvest date, and storage time on postharvest quality of red raspberry fruit. J. Am. Soc. Hortic. Sci. 112:481–487.

STACE-SMITH, R. 1984. Red raspberry virus diseases. Plant Disease 68: 274–279.

TELIZ, D., R. G. GROGAN, AND B. F. LOWNSBERRY. 1966. Transmission of tomato ringspot, peach yellow bud mosaic, and grape yellow vein virus by *Xiphenema americanus*. Phytopathology 56:658–663.

THIELE, G. G. 1980. Economic assessment of mechanized raspberry production under the Lincoln canopy system. Acta Hortic. 112:249–264.

TOPHAM, P. B. 1970. Some effects of gibberellin and synthetic auxins on the development of raspberry fruits and seeds. Hortic. Res. 11:18–28.

TORRE, L. C., AND B. H. BARRITT. 1979. Red raspberry establishment from root cuttings. J. Am. Soc. Hortic. Sci. 104:28–31.

TURNER, D. H. 1980. Raspberry production. Scot. Agric. Coll. Publ. 54.

UPRICHARD, S. D., D. J. ALLOT, AND D. W. ROBINSON. 1974. A comparative study of various systems of soil management in raspberries. Hortic. Res. 14:9–19.

VASILAKAKIS, M. D., B. H. McCOWN, AND M. N. DANA. 1979. Hormonal changes associated with growth and development in red raspberries. Physiol. Plant. 45:17–22.

VASILAKAKIS, M. D., B. H. McCOWN, AND M. N. DANA. 1980. Low temperature and flowering of primocane fruiting red raspberries. HortScience 15:750–751.

WAISTER, P. D., AND B. H. BARRITT. 1980. Compensation in fruit numbers following loss of lateral buds in the red raspberry. Hortic. Res. 20:25–31.

WAISTER, P. D., M. R. CORMACK, AND W. A. SHEETS. 1977. Competition between fruiting and vegetative phases in the red raspberry. J. Hortic. Sci. 52:75–85.

WAISTER, P. D., C. J. WRIGHT, AND M. R. CORMACK. 1980. Potential yield in red raspberry as influenced by interaction between genotype and cultural methods. Acta Hortic. 112:273–283.

WALDO, G. G. 1935. Fruit bud formation in small fruits and its relation to cultural practices. Oreg. Hortic. Soc. Proc. 1935:75–81.

References

WATT, B. K., AND A. L. MERRILL. 1963. Composition of foods. U. S. Dep. Agric. Handb. 8.

WHITING, G. C. 1958. The non-volatile organic acids of some berry fruits. J. Sci. Food Agric. 9:244–248.

WILLIAMS, I. H. 1959a. Effects of environment on *Rubus idaeus* L. II. Field observations on the variety Malling Promise. J. Hortic. Sci. 34:170–175.

WILLIAMS, I. H. 1959b. Effect of environment on *Rubus idaeus* L. III. Growth and dormancy of young shoots. J. Hortic. Sci. 34:210–218.

WILLIAMS, I. H. 1959c. Effects of environment on *Rubus idaeus* L. IV. Flower initiation and development of the inflorescence. J. Hortic. Sci. 34:219–228.

WILLIAMS, I. H. 1960. Effects of environment on *Rubus idaeus* L. V. Dormancy and flowering of the mature shoot. J. Hortic. Sci. 35:214–220.

WINTER, J. D., R. H. LANDON, AND W. H. ALDERMAN. 1939. Use of CO_2 to retard the development of decay in strawberries and raspberries. Proc. Am. Soc. Hortic. Sci. 37:583–588.

WOOD, C. A., AND M. ROBERTSON. 1957. Observations on the fruiting habit of the red raspberry (*Rubus idaeus* L.) and on an occurrence of cane "die-back" in Scotland. J. Hortic. Sci. 32:172–183.

SUGGESTED READING

ANON. 1970. Growing raspberries. U. S. Dep. Agric. Farmers' Bull. 2165.

ANON. 1978. Controlling diseases of raspberries and blackberries. U. S. Dep. Agric. Farmers' Bull. 2208.

ANON. 1987. Berry production guide for commercial growers, 1987. British Columbia Ministry of Agriculture and Fisheries, Victoria, British Columbia, Canada.

CHILDERS, N. F. 1976. Modern fruit science. 7th ed. Horticultural Publications. Rutgers University, New Brunswick, N. J.

CORMACK, M. R., AND P. D. WAISTER. 1976. Sources of yield loss in machine harvested raspberries. Acta Hortic. 60:21–26.

CRANDALL, P. C., AND E. B. ADAMS. 1979. Primocane pruning to increase red raspberry production. Wash. Coop. Ext. Serv. Publ. EM 4398.

DALE, A. 1989. Productivity in red raspberry. Hortic Rev. Vol. 11.

DAUBENY, H. A. (ed.) 1980. Symposium on breeding and machine harvesting of *Rubus*. Acta Hortic. 112.

FUNT, R. C., et al. 1988. Brambles: production, management, and marketing. Ohio Coop. Ext. Serv. Bull. 783.

HILL, R. G. 1960. Red raspberry growth and yield as affected by soil management, nitrogen fertilization, and training systems. Ohio Agric. Exp. Stn. Res. Bull. 857.

HILL, R. G., J. D. UTZINGER, AND R. C. FUNT. 1979. Growing bramble fruit. Ohio Coop. Ext. Serv. Bull. 411.

JENNINGS, D. L. (ed.). 1976. Symposium on breeding and machine harvesting of *Rubus* and *Ribes*. Acta Hortic. 60.

JENNINGS, D. L. 1988. Raspberries and blackberries: their breeding, diseases, and growth. Academic Press, San Diego, Calif.

PRITTS, M. P. (ed.). 1989. The bramble production guide. Northeast Region. Agric. Engineer. Serv. Publ., Cornell Univ., Ithaca, N. Y.

REDALEN, G. (ed.). 1986. Fourth international *Rubus* and *Ribes* symposium. Acta Hortic. 183.

SHOEMAKER, J. S. 1978. Small fruit culture. 5th ed. AVI, Westport, Conn.

SWARTZ, H. J. (ed.). 1988. Bramble. North American Bramble Growers Association, Department of Horticulture, University of Maryland, College Park.

TOPHAM, P. B. 1970. The histology of seed development in diploid and tetraploid raspberries (*Rubus idaeus* L.). Ann. Bot. 34:123–135.

TURNER, D. H., AND K. MUIR. 1985. The handbook of soft fruit growing. Croom Helm, Beckenham, Kent, England.

WILLIAMSON, B., H. M. LAWSON, J. A. T. WOODFORD, A. J. HARGREAVES, J. S. WISEMAN, AND S. C. GORDON. 1979. Vigour control, an integrated approach to cane, pest and disease management in red raspberry (*Rubus idaeus*). Ann. Appl. Biol. 92:359–368.

WINTER, J. D., R. H. LANDON, AND W. H. ALDERMAN. 1939. Use of CO_2 to retard the development of decay in strawberries and raspberries. Proc. Am. Soc. Hortic. Sci. 37:583–588.

WOOD, C. A. 1960. Commercial raspberry growing, the integration of cultural factors. Sci. Hortic. 14:97–103.

Chapter 5

Blackberry Management

J. N. MOORE
R. M. SKIRVIN

INTRODUCTION

Blackberries, in the genus *Rubus,* subgenus *Eubatus,* consist of a highly variable and complex group of plants, found throughout the world except in desert regions, but most numerous in the temperate parts of the northern hemisphere. Most species of blackberries produce biennial canes which vary from erect to procumbent in growth habit and are usually armed with sharp prickles.

Although blackberry species are native to many parts of the world, little domestication and commercial use has been made of them except in North America and Europe. There is evidence that they were domesticated by the seventeenth century in Europe and during the nineteenth century in North America (Jennings, 1988). Early settlers in North America considered blackberries to be a pestiferous and persistent weed, and their primary interest was in finding ways to destroy the pest. Nevertheless, there is evidence that fruit was harvested from wild stands and used as food and in the making of wine (Hedrick, 1925).

As forests were cleared in the westward migration of settlers, native species of blackberries spread into the cleared areas and a massive natural breeding program was established among the various interfertile, heteroploid, and highly heterogeneous species (Darrow, 1937). From nature's breeding program, two superior cultivars, 'Lawton' and 'Dorchester,' were selected and introduced in the 1850s. The superiority of these cultivars contributed greatly to developing interest in cultivating blackberries and led to a considerable amount of activity in selecting and breeding blackberries by private breeders in the latter half of the nineteenth century. The products of these activities were the foundation on which public breeding programs of the twentieth century developed the present cultivars of commerce.

CULTIVATED TYPES

Since present blackberry cultivars originated from the interbreeding of many genetically heterogeneous and morphologically variable species, it is not strange that present cultivars differ greatly in fruit and plant habit. For ease of grouping, American blackberry cultivars are often classified as erect thorny, western trailing, semierect thornless, dewberries, or raspberry–blackberry hybrids, based on gross morphology. However, there are often variations bridging two or more of these classes. The major blackberry cultivars of North America are characterized in Table 5-1.

Erect thorny cultivars (e.g., 'Cherokee,' 'Eldorado,' 'Shawnee,' 'Darrow') probably descended from hybridization of such erect native species as *R. alleghe-niensis, R. argutus,* and *R. frondosus,* with some introgression of other species (Darrow, 1967). Cultivars in this class are characterized by erect, sometimes arching, spiny canes, and prolific production of primocanes arising from adventitious buds on roots and crowns. They are large clustered and produce large, sweet fruits (Fig. 5-1). Cultivars in this group are among the most winter hardy.

The western trailing blackberries (also sometimes called dewberries) of the Pacific coast of North America (e.g., 'Logan,' 'Boysen,' 'Olallie') are largely derived from *R. ursinus, R. macropetalus,* and *R. loganobaccus.* Many of these cultivars also contain genes of the red raspberry, *R. idaeus.* In addition, two common cultivars of the Pacific coastal area, 'Himalaya' and 'Evergreen,' were derived from *R. procerus* and *R. laciniatus,* respectively, of European origin. Cultivars in this group produce very vigorous trailing to semierect canes, and large, roundish to elongated, wine-colored to black fruits of distinct flavor.

In the past 70 years a number of thornless blackberries have been isolated. Most of these thornless cultivars have originated as mutations ("sports") of thorny types. Most of these plants have the thornless character only in the outer epidermal layers of cells, while the internal tissue retains the thorny genes. This particular arrangement of tissues is known as a *periclinal* or "hand-in-glove" *chimera.* Because blackberry roots originate in internal tissues of the blackberry stem, adventitious shoots that develop on roots ("suckers") of chimeral plants are thorny. Also, since gametes develop from internal tissue, chimeral plants breed as if they were thorny.

TABLE 5-1 MAJOR BLACKBERRY CULTIVARS OF NORTH AMERICA, 1988

CULTIVAR	STATE OF ORIGIN	YEAR INTRODUCED	MAJOR CHARACTERISTICS	AREA OF ADAPTATION
			Erect	
Brazos	Texas	1959	Very early, very large fruit, bushy, spreading plant, small clusters, large seeds	Gulf coast, north to central Arkansas; hardy only to 0°F (−17°C)
Cherokee	Arkansas	1974	Early; fruit medium-large, firm, good flavor; plants very erect, productive, resistant to anthracnose but susceptible to rosette	Southeastern and midwestern U.S.; hardy to −10°F (−23°C)
Cheyenne	Arkansas	1976	Early; very large, firm; plants productive, erect, resistant to orange rust, susceptible to rosette	Southeastern and midwestern U.S.; hardy to −10°F (−23°C)
Comanche	Arkansas	1974	Very early; very large, firm, productive, erect, resistant to orange rust, susceptible to rosette	Gulf coastal areas, north to central Arkansas; hardy to −5°F (−20°C)
Darrow	New York	1958	Early; very erect; fruit medium size, firm, good flavor; plants vigorous, hardy	Northeastern and midwestern U.S.; hardy to −20°F (−29°C)
Humble	Texas	1942	Early; fruit small, soft; plant spreading, medium vigor, not high yielding, resistant to rosette, susceptible to orange rust	Texas and Gulf coast; hardy to −5°F (−20°C)
Shawnee	Arkansas	1985	Late; very large fruit, very productive, resistant to orange rust	Southeastern and midwestern U.S.; hardy to −10°F (−23°C)
Choctaw	Arkansas	1988	Very early; large fruit, very productive, small seeds	Southeastern and midwestern U.S.; hardy to −5°F (−20°C)
Illini Hardy	Illinois	1988	Late; fruit medium, good flavor, plants vigorous	Northeastern and midwestern U.S.; hardy to −15°F (−26°C)
Navaho	Arkansas	1988	Late; medium fruit, good flavor, plants are erect, thornless	Southeastern and midwestern U.S.
			Semierect	
Black Satin	Illinois	1974	Very late; fruit large, firm, tart; plants very vigorous, productive, thornless	Midwestern and mid-Atlantic states

216

Cultivar	Origin	Year	Description	Region/Hardiness
Chester Thornless	Illinois	1985	Very late; fruit large, very firm, sweet, productive, thornless	Midwestern and mid-Atlantic states
Dirksen Thornless	Illinois	1974	Late; fruit large, firm; plants vigorous, productive, thornless	Midwestern and mid-Atlantic states
Flint	Georgia	1957	Midseason; fruit large, firm, good flavor; plants very vigorous, productive, thorny.	Gulf coast region; not hardy in cold areas
Georgia Thornless	Georgia	1967	Midseason; fruit large, good flavor; plants productive, thornless	Gulf coast region; not hardy below 10°F (−12°C)
Hull Thornless	Maryland	1981	Very late; fruit large, firm, sweet; plants very vigorous, productive, thornless, large clusters	Mid-Atlantic and midwestern states
Smoothstem	Maryland	1966	Very late; fruit large, firm, tart; large seeds; plants very vigorous, productive, thornless, large clusters	Mid-Atlantic states
Thornfree	Maryland	1966	Very late; fruit medium-large, firm, good flavor, large seeds; plants medium vigor, productive, thornless	Lower midwest and mid-Atlantic states; not hardy in North
Trailing				
Boysen[a]	California	1935	Early; fruit very large, soft, good flavor; plant very vigorous, very productive	Pacific coast states; not hardy in cold areas
Chehalem	Oregon	1948	Late; fruit small, seeds small, flavor excellent; plants vigorous, very productive	Pacific coast states
Flordagrand	Florida	1958	Very early; fruit large, soft, good flavor; plants vigorous, productive; requires cross-pollination; short chill requirement	Florida and Gulf coast region
Gem	Georgia	1967	Early; fruit large, firm, good flavor; plant vigorous, productive, thorny	Gulf coast region
Lincoln Logan	New Zealand	1986	Identical to thornless Logan, derived from tissue culture; this plant passes the thornless character through hybridization	Pacific coastal states
Logan[b]	California	1883	Early; fruit large, maroon, soft, outstanding flavor; plant vigorous, productive	Pacific coast states

TABLE 5-1 MAJOR BLACKBERRY CULTIVARS OF NORTH AMERICA, 1988, cont.

CULTIVAR	STATE OF ORIGIN	YEAR INTRODUCED	MAJOR CHARACTERISTICS	AREA OF ADAPTATION
Marion	Oregon	1956	Late; fruit medium-large, medium firm; plants very vigorous and productive	Pacific coastal areas
Oklawaha	Florida	1964	Very early; fruit medium size, soft, good flavor; plants vigorous, semi evergreen; short chilling requirement	Florida and Gulf coast region
Olallie	Oregon	1950	Midseason; fruit large, firm, excellent for processing; plant vigorous, very productive, short chilling requirement	California, western Oregon, and Gulf coast region
Thornless Evergreen[c]	Oregon	1926	Very late; fruit large, very firm, good quality, seeds large; plants vigorous, drought resistant	Pacific coastal areas; hardy to −10°F (−23°C) with protection
Young	Louisiana	1926	Midseason; fruit very large, sweet, wine color; plants vigorous, very productive, susceptible to rosette	Gulf coast region and California

[a]Thornless clones exist which originated as mutations from the original thorny cultivar. The thornless cultivar is similar to the original thorny clone with the exception of producing thornless canes. The thornless cultivar has, in many cases, become more popular than the original thorny cultivar. Since the thornless condition of the canes is chimeral, propagation must be by tip layering to maintain the thornless condition.

[b]The original 'Logan' was selected in 1883 by J.H. Logan. The time of its actual introduction is unknown. The thornless mutant of 'Logan' was discovered in California in 1929.

[c]This cultivar resulted from the selection of a thornless mutation found on the original thorny 'Evergreen' by Philip Steffes in Oregon about 1926. The thornless clone has rapidly replaced the original thorny 'Evergreen'.

FIGURE 5-1 Fruit of 'Cheyenne' blackberry.

For these reasons, when chimeral plants are propagated from roots or when the canes freeze back, so that shoots come from below the crown, they are always thorny. These thorny shoots tend to be more vigorous than the original thornless canes and they can overgrow the thornless shoots unless they are removed.

Within recent years, a series of semierect genetically thornless cultivars, adapted to eastern United States, has been introduced by the U.S. Department of Agriculture. These cultivars ('Black Satin,' 'Chester Thornless,' 'Dirksen Thornless,' 'Hull Thornless,' 'Thornfree,' and 'Smoothstem') were derived from hybridization of a thornless cultivar from Great Britain ('Merton Thornless') with erect, thorny cultivars of the eastern United States. Cultivars in this group are characterized by vigorous, semierect, smooth canes, large fruit clusters, high productivity, and late ripening.

The term "dewberry" is commonly applied to any species or cultivar of trailing blackberry. In nature dewberries propagate from tip-layering, whereas blackberries propagate by suckering. Also, the flower clusters of dewberries are generally small, and the center flowers open first, so that the inflorescence is a cyme. In contrast, in the erect blackberries, the outer flowers open first, so that the inflorescence is corymbose or racemose (Hedrick, 1925). Since many cultivated semierect blackberries are hybrids between dewberries and blackberries, these distinctions are no longer obvious.

The most common dewberry species in the United States are *R. baileyanus* of the eastern United States, and *R. ursinus* of the western United States. We have seen that *R. ursinus* has been important in the origin of cultivars of the Pacific coast. *R. baileyanus* was involved in the development of 'Lucretia' dewberry and its derivatives, while *R. trivalis* was important in the development of 'Nessberry' and its descendants, which include the present-day cultivars 'Flordagrand' and 'Oklawaha.' Dewberry cultivars have prostrate canes that produce large, early ripening, high-flavored fruits.

Interest in hybridizing blackberries and raspberries dates from 1881. Some of the most important cultivars of commerce originated from hybridization of raspberries and blackberries (Darrow, 1955). The most famous product of such a cross is the 'Loganberry,' but 'Phenomenal,' 'Primus,' 'Paradox,' and 'Nessberry' were similarly derived. The 'Phenomenal' was later crossed with a dewberry to produce 'Young,' and 'Boysen' is believed to have a similar origin (Darrow, 1955). 'Tayberry' was produced by hybridization of blackberry and red raspberry (Jennings, 1981).

UTILITY

Blackberries have fruits that can be eaten fresh, canned, frozen; used in pies and cobblers; processed to jams or jellies; or fermented. Traditionally, blackberries have been gathered from the wild in regions of abundance. Although there are *Rubus* species to be found in the northern and southern regions of the United States and Canada, the blackberry is primarily a crop of the warmer regions of the United States. It is found in abundance along the western and eastern seaboards and in the southern two-thirds of the United States.

Most blackberry cultivars have relatively soft fruits that are susceptible to rots. It is not unusual for a quantity of blackberries to be overgrown with fungus within 24 to 48 hours following harvest. Although some growers ship berries to specialty markets, most fresh blackberry sales take place near the site of production. The majority of these berries are sold "pick-your-own" (PYO).

Much of the blackberry crop of the United States is frozen. These blackberries are a regular stock item of most grocery outlets. Until very recently a large portion of the frozen blackberry crop was sold in bulk quantities to institutions such as schools and hospitals for dessert preparation. This outlet for blackberries was very important as long as the prices of blackberries were fairly low and competitive with other frozen fruits, such as cherries and peaches. In recent times, the prices for blackberries have become so prohibitive that this market may disappear. There are some packing houses in Oklahoma and Arkansas that utilize frozen blackberries to make ready-to-bake pies and cobblers.

Another traditionally important use for blackberries has been canning. Canned berries can be eaten from the can, used in pies, or served over ice cream. At one time there were at least a dozen important blackberry canneries in the United States. Now there are only a few, located in the Pacific Northwest. The demise of this industry has been due to the high price of the canned product. Because of high cost, both homemakers and institutions have lost interest in blackberries and switched to less expensive fruits.

Making jams, jellies, syrups, bakery fillings, and ice cream toppings has always been the most important use for blackberries. It is likely that 80% or more of the commercial production is utilized in this manner. In the past few years a new and potentially large market has emerged for blackberries as a yogurt flavoring.

The use of nonfermented blackberry juice is important in Europe but minimal in the United States. Fermented blackberry products such as wines and brandies are of some importance. The increased availability of blackberry raw products should expand this market.

TAXONOMY

Blackberries are taxonomically classified in the genus *Rubus,* in the Rosaceae family. There are 12 subgenera in *Rubus* (Hedrick, 1925), but only two, *Idaeobatus* and *Eubatus,* have attained significant commercial importance as fruit crops. The subgenus *Idaeobatus* contains the raspberries of commerce, while blackberries are classed in *Eubatus.* While many morphological differences exist between these subgenera, the most commonly used criterion for classification is the method of separation of the mature fruit from the plant. In the *Idaeobatus* (raspberries), the fruit, an aggregate of small drupelets, separates from the receptacle and has the appearance of a thimble. In contrast, the drupelets of *Eubatus* (blackberries) cohere with the receptacle, which becomes a part of the edible fruit.

The subgenus *Eubatus,* comprising the blackberries and dewberries, is a highly variable, heterogeneous, and complex group of plants. Bailey (1941–45) recognized over 350 species of *Eubatus.* This subgenus primarily inhabits the temperate regions of northwestern Asia, Europe, northern Africa, North America, and the mountains of South America. There is a naturally occurring ploidy range from diploid ($2x = 2n = 14$) to dodecaploid ($12x = 2n = 84$) (Darrow, 1937). Plant types range from procumbent to rigidly erect and from evergreen to deciduous. Reproduction varies from apomictic to sexually fertile. Since homoploid blackberry species are mostly interfertile, and biological systems encouraging outcrossing are common, native populations of blackberries in much of the world are highly hybrid in nature, making exact taxonomic classification difficult or impossible (Darrow, 1967).

BOTANY

Vegetative and reproductive thorny and thornless blackberry morphology is illustrated in Figs. 5–2 and 5–3.

Vegetative Growth

The crown and root systems of blackberries are perennial, while canes are biennial. In the spring, new canes emerge from buds on crowns or roots. During their first year these canes are termed *primocanes,* and usually do not flower. In the second year, following a dormant period, the canes flower and fruit and are termed *floricanes.* Primocanes grow in length rapidly following emergence and usually produce compound leaves. In contrast, floricanes do not increase in length, but produce a number of short lateral branches with a few leaves and a terminal inflorescence. The leaves of floricanes are often partly simple, smaller, and of a different shape than those of primocanes.

The protodermal or epidermal (Fig. 5–4) outgrowths of blackberries which we call "thorns" vary in their form and size of development (Fig. 5–5) and correctly are termed *prickles.* The actual number of prickles and hairs that develop on a stem is

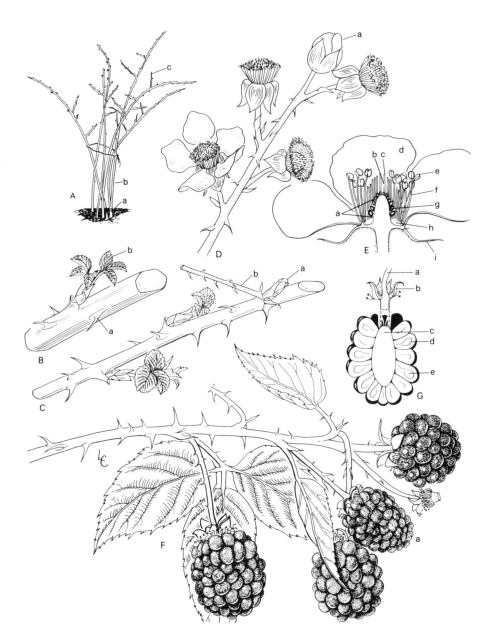

FIGURE 5-2 Thorny blackberry morphology. (A) Dormant plant
habit—pruned: a, crown area; b, overwintering cane; c, lateral shoot.
(B) Emerging cane: a, prickle; b, compound leafy shoot emerging from
bud. (C) Emerging lateral shoot: a, mixed buds; b, previous season leaf
petiole. (D) Inflorescence: a, flower bud (popcorn stage). (E) Flower: a,
pistil (carpel); b, styles; c, stigmas; d, petal; e, anther; f, filament; g,
receptacle; h, nectariferous area; i, sepal. (F) Fruiting shoot: a, aggregate fruit. (G) Longitudinal section detached—fruit: a, pedicle; b, calyx; c, receptacle (torus); d, drupelet; e, pyrene (seed).

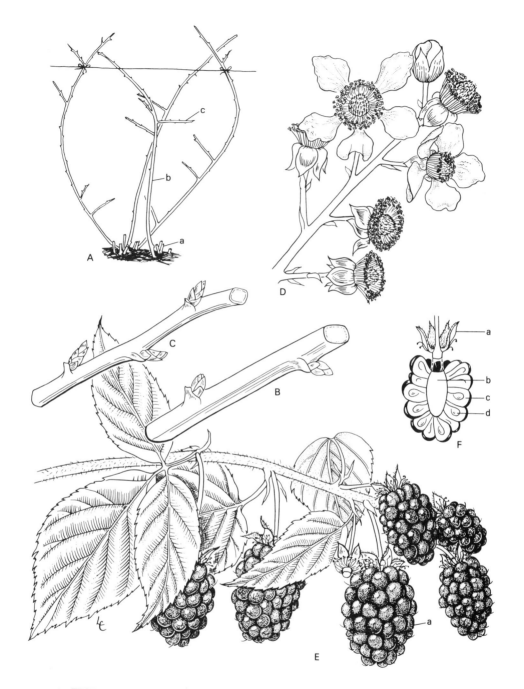

FIGURE 5-3 Thornless blackberry morphology. (A) Plant habit — dormant pruned: a, crown area; b, overwintering cane; c, lateral shoot. (B) Dormant cane. (C) Lateral shoot. (D) Inflorescence. (E) Fruiting shoot: a, aggregate fruit. (F) Fruit longitudinal section: a, calyx; b, receptacle (torus); c, drupelet; d, pyrene (seed).

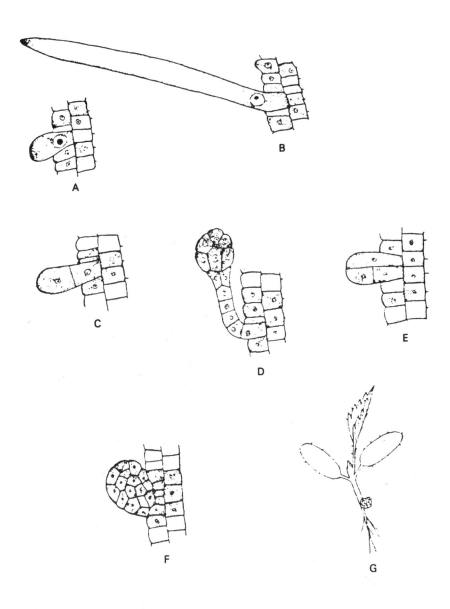

FIGURE 5-4 Prickle development from epidermal cells of blackberry: (A) section through outer portion of growing tip, showing enlarged protodermal cell, which may later develop into a single hair; (B) enlarge cell of protoderm developed into a single hair; (C) tangential division of a protodermal cell which may develop into either a prickle or a glandular hair; (D) aborted glandular hair; (E) two protodermal cells entering into the formation of a glandular hair or prickle; (F) rapid periclinal and anticlinal division of protodermal cells, which will later develop into a conspicuous glandular hair or prickle; (G) glandular hairs and prickles on a seedling. [From Peiterson (1921).]

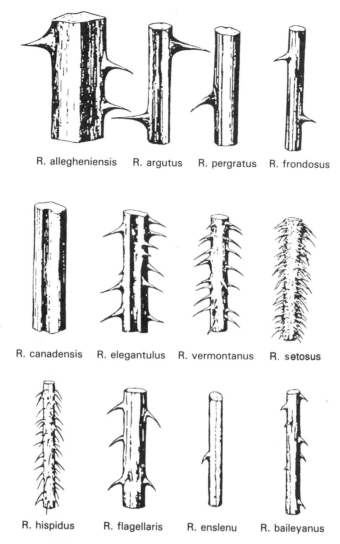

FIGURE 5-5 Prickles of various *Rubus* species.

somewhat influenced by light, and plants grown in full light have more prickles than do those grown with indirect light (Peitersen, 1921). Although thorns and prickles are anatomically distinct, the terms are used interchangeably.

Blackberries grown in the temperate climate of the northern hemisphere go through a period of dormancy which is initiated by short days and cool temperatures. There has been little study, however, of the time of onset and length of dormancy in blackberries. In contrast, the phenomenon of dormancy has been studied extensively in raspberry. In raspberry, dormancy is terminated by an accumulation of chilling temperatures below a maximum threshold. Temperatures below 41°F (5°C) (Bailey, 1948; Brierly and Landon, 1946) and 45°F (7°C) (Lamb, 1948) have been suggested as being effective. Lamb (1948) found that from 1100 to 1400 hours of accumulated temperatures below 45°F (7°C) were necessary for terminating raspberry bud dormancy in Minnesota. Different clones and species of blackberries apparently enter dormancy in the fall and emerge in the spring at different times.

Reproductive Growth

The onset, progression, and completion of the flowering process in the blackberry is controlled or influenced by a number of factors, both external and internal (Moore and Caldwell, 1983). It has been suggested that in the closely related raspberry, the primocane may have an endogenously controlled cycle in which flowering is the final stage (Lockshin and Elfving, 1981), and this seems likely in blackberry also.

Flower initiation. The time of flower bud initiation in most forms of *Rubus* is believed to be triggered by shortening day lengths and lowering temperatures (Waldo and Darrow, 1941; Williams, 1960). However, there are conflicting research finding as to when flower initiation occurs in blackberries. MacDaniels (1922) reported that flower initiation had clearly begun in New York by mid-September, while Waldo (1933), in Oregon, did not find evidence of initiation in 'Himalaya' until January, and initiation of blackberry occurred in Scotland from mid-October to late March, depending on cultivar (Robertson, 1957). It is obvious that time of flower initiation in *Eubatus* is more variable than in *Idaeobatus* (Ourecky, 1975) and is probably dependent on both plant genotype and prevailing environment.

Inflorescence development. Once initiation has occurred, the rate of inflorescence development is largely governed by prevailing temperature, periods of low temperature arresting development and retarding what would otherwise be a continuous process. Waldo (1933) observed little development of *Rubus* flower buds from December until March in Oregon, and Mathers (1952) and Robertson (1957) reported a cessation of differentiation during December and January in Scotland. In early spring, differentiation resumes and rapid development takes place prior to bud break.

Following bud break, short lateral leafy branches emerge which usually terminate in an inflorescence. The number of flowers per inflorescence varies greatly among cultivars and species of blackberries. A few species produce predominately solitary flowers, but most produce clusters which range from 3 to 75 flowers (Fernald, 1950). All species fruit predominately at the terminals of canes, with the extent of flowering at subterminal nodes varying among species and cultivars.

Inflorescences of various blackberry species vary greatly as to form and structure. Most species produce corymbose or racemose inflorescences, but some trailing types (dewberries) produce cymose inflorescences, similar to raspberry (Hedrick, 1925).

Most modern blackberry cultivars produce hermaphroditic flowers and are self-fertile (Perry and Moore, 1985), but a few are self-sterile and some wild forms are functionally dioecious (Darrow, 1937). The flowers consist of many pistils atop a succulent receptacle, surrounded by whorls of many stamens (Figs. 5–2 and 5–3).

Petals are usually pentamerous and white in color, although pink or reddish forms are occasionally seen. Each pistil will develop into a single miniature drupe fruit know as a drupelet or drupel. Each drupelet contains a single hard seed. The entire structure that we call the fruit actually consists of a large number of drupelets which cling to each other and a common receptacle (the *torus*). Collectively, the edible structure is called an *aggregate fruit*.

Blackberry flowers are not dependent on insects for pollination, although insects and wind no doubt aid in uniform dispersal of pollen, which results in more complete pollination of all pistils within a flower (Perry and Moore, 1985). Heavy rains during the bloom period may prevent complete pollination, resulting in malformed fruits. Although most modern blackberry cultivars are self-fertile, self-pollination may result in reduced fruit size and incomplete drupelet set in some cultivars (Perry and Moore, 1985; Lawrence, 1976). Therefore, plantings consisting of more than one cultivar may be advantageous.

Following pollination and ovule fertilization, the fruit of blackberries develop rapidly. The period of development from bloom to ripening usually varies from 40 to 60 days, depending on the cultivar. Individual fruits may weigh up to 10 g, but most polyploid cultivars produce fruit in the range 5 to 8 g. The largest berries are produced by the primary flower in a cluster, with secondary flowers in the inflorescence producing slightly smaller fruit. In commercial operations, a quart of blackberries is assumed to weigh 1½ lb (6 lb/gal), although weight may vary slightly depending on berry size. For a more detailed discussion of flowering in *Rubus,* see the review by Moore and Caldwell (1983).

PROPAGATION

Fruit growers are generally not encouraged to produce their own planting stock, since plants obtained from certified nurseries are usually of higher quality and may be virus free. However, blackberries are easy to propagate, and if proper vigilance is maintained, clean planting stocks can be produced. Methods of propagation differ according to type of blackberry. Many laboratories now use tissue culture to propagate and maintain virus-free cultivars.

Erect Type

Cultivars of erect blackberries can be propagated from either root suckers or root cuttings. Suckers arising from the roots of existing plants can be dug in late winter or early spring, before growth begins (Fig. 5–6). After digging, canes are shortened to 12 to 18 in. (30 to 45 cm) for planting.

The most rapid method of propagating erect cultivars is by the use of root cuttings. Root cuttings can be used to grow nursery plants or may be planted directly in fields to produce fruiting plants. Research has shown that planting root cuttings can result in the establishment of a fruiting field as quickly as the use of plants (Moore et al., 1978).

The production of plants from root cuttings is possible due to the presence of

FIGURE 5-6 Root sucker development in thorny blackberry.

adventitious buds on roots of the blackberry. When placed in warm, moist soil, these buds quickly grow to produce canes. Although almost any size root piece will produce plants, the strongest plants develop from cuttings that are ¼ to ⅜ in. (5 to 9 mm) in diameter and produce higher yields the year following planting (Moore et al., 1978). Larger cuttings may not produce canes. Root cuttings should be 3 to 4 in. (7.5 to 10 cm) in length. Root cuttings may be dug at any time during the dormant season and held by burying in well-drained soil below the freeze line, or stored in plastic bags at 32 to 36°F (0 to 2°C). They should not be dug after buds have begun to grow since handling will destroy many of the emerging shoots.

For the production of nursery plants, root cuttings may be planted in the spring in nursery rows at a spacing of 3 to 6 in. (7.5 to 15.0 cm) apart with 3 ft (90 cm) between rows. They are placed horizontally at the bottom of a 2- to 3-in. (5.0- to 7.5-cm) furrow, completely covered with soil, and firmed. A light mulch such as sawdust may be placed over the row to prevent crusting of the soil so that shoots can easily emerge. Plants may be dug after one growing season for setting or marketing.

Trailing Types

Most cultivars of trailing blackberries do not produce root suckers as freely as do erect types; therefore, propagation has primarily been by tip layering or the use of stem cuttings. In fact, some cultivars of thornless blackberries, (e.g., 'Thornless Evergreen', 'Thornless Logan') must be tip-layered, as propagation by other methods gives rise to thorny plants.

In the late summer and fall, the tip portions of primocanes of trailing blackberries rapidly elongate and turn light in color. At this time, the tips may be covered with soil to a depth of 3 to 4 in. (7.5 to 10.0 cm). During the fall (and winter in warm areas) the cane terminal initiates roots. By late fall, or the following spring, the new plants may be dug and the cane from the parent plant cut so that a "handle" of 6 to 8 in. (15 to 20 cm) of the old cane remains. Because tip-layered plants develop from a preformed axillary or terminal bud on the parent plant, chimeral integrity is preserved and this system is useful for propagating chimeral types.

Most cultivars of blackberry root readily from softwood stem cuttings placed under mist. Cuttings one to two nodes in length with two or three leaves taken from healthy growing canes are inserted into a porous rooting media, such as perlite, under mist. These cuttings root quickly and may be potted or transplanted to a nursery area.

Recently, interest has developed in rapid multiplication of blackberry cultivars by tissue culture techniques (Caldwell, 1984). Under this system shoot tips are aseptically transferred to tissue culture medium and allowed to grow. Axillary buds begin to break and soon a single shoot tip will have increased to six or more. By subculturing each of these tips onto fresh medium, more axillary shoots can be obtained; within a year one could theoretically produce millions of shoots. Individual shoots can be rooted on special rooting medium and the young plants handled as if they were seedlings and moved to soil. This system is amenable to both nonchimeral and chimeral blackberries. The use of tissue culture has facilitated the isolation of pure-thornless (nonchimeral) forms of 'Thornless Evergreen' and 'Thornless Loganberry'. These plants produce thornless root suckers and breed for the thornless gene (McPheeters and Skirvin, 1983; Hall et al., 1986a, b; Rosati et al., 1986).

CLIMATIC REQUIREMENTS

The major limiting factor to the successful culture of blackberries in much of North America is a lack of cold hardiness in current cultivars. Blackberry canes can be injured when winter temperatures fall below $-10°F$ ($-23°C$). Blackberry breeders are attempting to develop cultivars with greater resistance to cold for expansion of culture into colder areas. The western trailing blackberries, grown in the Pacific northwest and California, are especially prone to winter injury when grown in the eastern United States, and the southeastern trailing types (dewberries) also lack cold hardiness.

The physiological chilling requirement of blackberries is not well established, although observations indicate that this requirement varies among cultivars. Cultivars have been developed that grow and fruit in areas of very low winter chilling, where many northern-developed cultivars fail.

SITE AND SOIL SELECTION

Selection of a suitable site for planting is the first important step toward success in growing blackberries. In addition to economic considerations such as nearness to markets, availability of labor, and accessibility, several topographical and biological factors require consideration. The two most important factors to consider in choosing a planting site for blackberries are air drainage and water drainage. Blackberries, as most fruit crops, are subject to damage from spring frosts at bloom time.

Planting on sloping sites or level elevated areas will allow cold air to drain away from the blackberries on frosty nights. Low-lying sites or areas surrounded by trees that would impede air drainage should be avoided.

Blackberries are damaged when water stands around their roots at any time of the year, and plantings on poorly drained soils are generally unproductive and short-lived. Poorly drained soils also encourage the development of such diseases as *Phytophthora* root rot. An elevated site providing air drainage usually also has good water drainage.

Another site characteristic worthy of consideration is the previous cropping history of the site and the nature of nearby crops. Blackberries should not be planted immediately following potatoes, tomatoes, peppers, or eggplant since this increases the risk of infection with verticillium wilt. Also, any site previously planted to fruit crops with a history of crown gall should be avoided. When possible, new blackberry plantings should be separated from other cultivated or wild brambles by at least 350 ft (100 m) to restrict disease infection.

Since blackberries do best in full sunlight, any trees bordering the planting site should be removed. Trees not only shade the planting but also compete for soil moisture, impede air drainage, and provide shelter for depredatory birds during fruit ripening. However, in large open windy areas, windbreaks may be essential to prevent cane breakage.

While the direction of the site slope is not a critical factor in selection, it can affect the time of bloom and fruiting. In most areas, blackberries on a southern slope will bloom and fruit slightly earlier than will those planted on a northern slope. The availability of water for irrigation near the planting may be an important consideration in areas in which irrigation is necessary to obtain maximum production.

Blackberries grow and produce satisfactorily on a wide range of soil types, from sandy to heavy clay loams, provided that the drainage is good. Good soil characteristics for blackberry production are deep sandy loams, moderately fertile, high in organic matter, easily worked, and retentive of moisture but well drained. If the subsoil has a hardpan or the water table is high, the root system will be restricted and the plants will suffer during periods of drought. Blackberries are tolerant of a wide range of soil pH, and grow satisfactorily within a pH range of 4.5 to 7.5, but a soil pH of 6.0 to 6.5 is considered ideal.

CULTURE

Preplanting Operations

Preparing the land. Ideally, the site should be selected and preparations for planting begun the year before planting. This will allow time for proper soil preparation, elimination of perennial weeds and grasses, fertility adjustments, elimination of some soil insect problems, and installation of an irrigation system.

It is advisable to grow a clean-cultivated row crop on the site the year prior to planting. This helps to eradicate weeds and improve soil tilth. Planting directly after turning-under sod increases the risk of damage from white grubs and other soil insects. If perennial grasses exist on the site, they should be destroyed by herbicides or tillage prior to planting blackberries.

If the soil is low in organic matter, growing and turning under a well-fertilized green manure crop or 10 to 20 tons/acre (22 to 44 MT/ha) of barnyard manure in the fall prior to spring planting is desirable. Lime, if needed, may be incorporated at this time.

The site for planting should be prepared as early in the spring as possible. The soil should be plowed deep and disked and harrowed until well pulverized. If a hardpan exists, subsoiling is recommended. During land preparation, fertilizer may be incorporated into the soil. The amount of fertilizer used should be based on need as determined by a soil test.

Obtaining planting stock

Selecting Cultivars.   Following site selection, the next most important decisions a grower makes relate to the choice of cultivar and the source of planting stock. A wrong decision on these matters is irreversible and cannot be corrected without starting over.

There are many cultivars of blackberries available from which to choose; however, generally only a few are well adapted to any specific region. A person planning to grow blackberries should determine which cultivars are adapted to the region by inquiring of local agricultural extension agents, the state experiment station, or successful growers in the area. A potential grower must also determine the type of blackberry to be grown, whether erect or trailing, since planting and culture differs greatly for the two types. In many cases, the market outlet to be used dictates the type and cultivar to be grown.

Sources of Planting Stock.   After determining the cultivars to be planted, a grower must next locate a source of planting material. This is a critical decision since many serious production problems are directly associated with the planting material used, and once introduced, may be difficult or impossible to eliminate. An essential prerequisite to success in blackberry production is to start with disease-free planting stock, since the length of life of the planting and the annual productivity are directly related to the health of the plants.

To assure getting healthy, true-to-name plants, a reputable source must be used. Many nurseries offer plants bearing certificates of state certification. This indicates that the plants have been grown from special healthy stock under regulated conditions designed to eliminate, as much as possible, disease and insect pests. Every effort should be made to obtain planting stock developed under such a program. One should never use plants from an old planting unless they are carefully inspected by a person knowledgeable about blackberry disease and insect pests.

Caring for the planting stock. Planting should be done when planting stock is dormant; generally, early spring is the most desirable time. It is often necessary to store temporarily planting stock received from a nursery since weather and other factors may delay planting. Plants and root cuttings can be held successfully in storage at 34 to 36°F (1 to 2°C) for several months if drying is prevented.

When plants or root cuttings arrive, the package should be opened and the condition of the planting stock checked. If dry, they should be moistened. Unless planting is to be done within a few days, the plants should be heeled-in in a trench deep enough to cover the roots, or wrapped in plastic and placed in a refrigerator. Whichever method is used to store the plants, precautions must be taken to prevent drying.

Planting

Blackberries are generally planted in the spring of the year. Fall planting is possible, but in areas of freezing winter temperatures, fall-set plants must be protected by a mulch to prevent heaving. While early spring planting is desirable, planting should not be done until the soil is dry enough to work. The planting row should be prepared with the same care as that used for a seedbed for planting corn.

Blackberries should be planted in rows spaced 10 to 12 ft (3.0 to 3.6 m) apart. The distance between plants in the row depends on the type of blackberry being grown and the training system to be used. Generally, plants of erect, thorny cultivars are set 4 ft (1.2 m) apart in the row and allowed to fill in for establishment of a solid hedgerow (Fig. 5–7). If root cuttings are used for planting, they often are set 2 ft (0.6 m) apart for more rapid row establishment. Most trailing and semitrailing cultivars, both thorny and thornless, are set 6 to 8 ft (1.8 to 2.4 m) apart in the row, depending on vigor of the cultivar, and trained to a hill system of culture.

Under certain conditions, the direction to run the plant row deserves consideration. Where slopes are involved, cross-slope planting is better for irrigation and erosion control. In areas of occasional strong winds, it is best, where possible, to orient rows in the direction of strong winds, since a cross-wind can result in considerable breakage of primocanes. In areas of high temperatures during harvest, the fruit on the west side of north–south rows may sunburn.

During the planting operation, it is very important to prevent the plants or root cuttings from drying. Plants should be held in the field prior to planting in wet burlap bags in shade and should be set as soon as dropped. Plant roots and root cuttings can be protected from drying during planting by coating with a layer of mud. Other important points in planting are to set at the proper depth, allow proper space for spreading the roots laterally, and to firm the soil well. In many cases, irrigation will need to be applied soon after setting to ensure proper soil moisture for root survival and development.

Planting may be done in a furrow or in individual holes. Plants should be set at about the same depth as they grew in the nursery. Root cuttings should be covered 4 to 5 in. (10 to 12 cm) deep on sandy soils and 2 to 3 in. (6 to 8 cm) deep on heavier

FIGURE 5-7 Hedge row of erect blackberries, 'Cherokee' cultivar.

soil types. Generally, blackberries are planted on flat land, as raised beds tend to dry too rapidly.

Weed Control

The first consideration following planting should be to control weeds effectively. Blackberries may be shallowly cultivated during the first growing season, but care must be taken to prevent breaking the tender, newly emerging primocanes. Herbicides are also available which, when properly used, can be effective in weed control. Generally, blackberry plantings are clean-cultivated between the rows by shallow tilling or disking. As the planting ages, blackberry roots will invade the area between the rows, and cultivating too deeply will injure roots and induce unwanted suckering between the rows. If sod is allowed to develop between rows, it should be mowed several times during the growing season. Whether clean cultivation or sod is used in the middles, the row area must be kept free of weeds by either physical or chemical means.

Fertilization during the First Year

Any fertilizer needs for the initial growing season should have been identified by soil tests and corrected during preplant land preparation. However, if the plants fail to initiate vigorous growth, additional nutrients can be applied in the spring. Use of

Culture   **233** nitrogen fertilizer should be avoided later than June since this may result in subsequent winter injury.

Training and Pruning

Erect types

Training. Cultivars of erect blackberries are self-supporting and can be grown without a trellis system. However, in small, home garden plantings, some type of support will minimize cane breakage from wind, cultivation, and picking operations. In commercial operations, erect types are grown in hedgerows, wherein the sucker plants arising from roots fill in the entire row space (Fig. 5–6). The base of the row should be kept to a width of about 1½ ft (45 cm) [1 ft (30 cm) for mechanical harvest] by removing suckers that arise beyond this limit. The best plant density for the hedgerow system is four to six vigorous canes per lineal foot (30 cm) of row.

Pruning. Both summer and winter pruning is practiced with erect blackberries. During the summer, primocanes are topped, by cutting or pinching out the shoot tip, when they reach 3 to 4 ft (0.9 to 1.2 m). This removes apical dominance and allows lateral branches, which produce fruiting wood, to develop (Fig. 5–8). It also prevents long, arching cane growth, which is more likely to result in cane breakage. Since primocanes emerge at different times, summer topping must be done several times during the growing season. During the summer also, unwanted suckers should be removed.

Since blackberry canes are biennial, the second year canes (floricanes) die soon

FIGURE 5-8 Axillary bud break on blackberry primocane following summer topping.

after fruiting. Dead canes can be removed at any time from the end of harvest to the next spring. Since old dead canes may serve as a reservoir of inoculum of disease and insect pests, early removal and burning is desirable.

During the dormant season, pruning consists of shortening laterals, removing weak and red-necked cane borer–infested canes, and thinning canes in areas missed during the preceding summer. Maximum productivity and largest fruit size will be realized when lateral branches are pruned to lengths of 12 to 18 in. (30 to 45 cm).

Trailing types

Training. Trailing and semierect cultivars must be trained to some type of support system (Fig. 5–9). The support may simply be a strong post or stake, 4 to 5 ft (1.2 to 1.5 m) tall, to which the canes are tied, or one of several variations of a wire trellis system. Generally, a greater yield and ease of harvest is obtained from training to a wire trellis. The most common trellis is a two-wire, vertical system constructed by stretching wire between posts set 15 to 20 ft (4.5 to 6.0 m) apart in the row. One wire is attached 3½ ft (1 m) above the ground and the other 5 ft (1.5 m) above the ground. Canes are tied to these wires, running in both directions from the plant, during the early spring (Waldo and Hartmann, 1946).

Pruning. Trailing blackberries are not topped during the growing season as are erect types. Instead, the primocanes are allowed to grow on the ground along the row until after harvest and old canes are removed or until early spring. In areas of cold winter temperatures, canes may be protected from cold injury by covering with soil or straw. In the spring, canes are uncovered and trained to the trellis system. Spring training should be done before bud break to avoid injury to newly emerging shoots.

Following harvest, old floricanes should be cut off at ground level, removed and burned. No other summer pruning operations are required with trailing types, since they generally do not sucker as do erect types.

During the latter part of the dormant season, 8 to 10 vigorous canes should be selected, cut back to 6 to 8 ft (1.8 to 2.4 m) in length, and tied to the trellis. All other canes are removed. Lateral branches on the fruiting canes should be pruned to 12 to 18 in. (30–45 cm) in length. If training and pruning is delayed until after bud break, care must be taken to prevent damage to the tender new shoots.

Pruning and training trailing blackberries that are to be mechanically harvested requires special attention. In Oregon (Martin and Lawrence, 1976), many fields are trained to a two-wire trellis, with the top wire usually 5 to 5½ ft (1.5 to 1.6 m) above the ground. Posts must be of the proper height and diameter to allow the harvest mechanism to pass without damage. A basal herbicide spray is used to control the early-season primocanes and to remove low-growing fruiting laterals.

In Oregon, some growers use an alternate year (A-Y) system of production on trailing blackberries (Sheets et al., 1975). In this system primocanes are produced one year and allowed to fruit the following year. In the fruiting year, early emerging primocanes are removed to prevent interference with harvesting. While yields from the A-Y system are reduced about 15% in comparison with the every-year system, less labor and less pest control applications are required over a 2-year fruiting cycle.

Culture   235

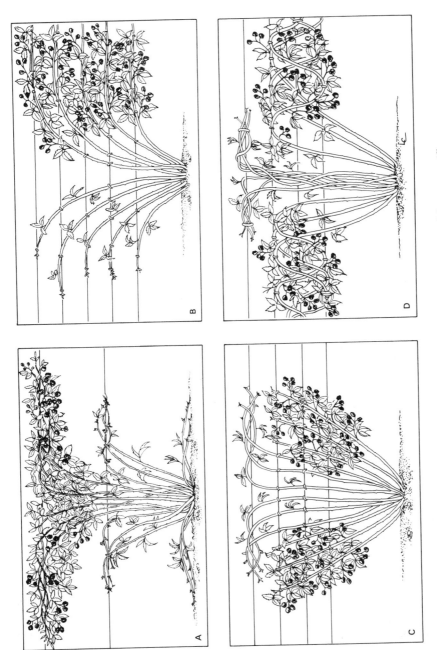

FIGURE 5-9 Trailing blackberry training systems: (A) Fruiting canes (floricanes) woven on top wire with new shoots (primocanes) allowed to run along ground; (B) fan system with fruiting canes and new shoots trained in opposite directions; (C) fan system with fruiting canes spread to each side and new shoots trained up vertically; (D) weave system with fruiting canes trained to each side and new shoots trained up vertically.

Fertilization of Established Plantings

The type and amount of nutrient elements to apply to a blackberry planting should be determined by soil or foliar analyses. In this way, a grower can apply only those elements that are actually needed. In the absence of soil or foliar tests, plant growth is a good indication of nutrient requirements. The nutrient element most likely to be needed is nitrogen. Blackberries utilize nitrogen in producing vegetative growth, which is directly related to future productivity. In most areas nitrogen will need to be applied annually.

The initial fertilizer application should be made during land preparation prior to planting. This application should be sufficient for the first growing season. In the second and following seasons, a general recommendation is to apply 50 to 100 lb/acre (56 to 112 kg/ha) of actual nitrogen. This should be applied broadcast into the row area in early spring before growth begins. If the rows are mulched, the amount of nitrogen should be increased by 50 to 100% for the first 3 years. If plants show excessive growth, the amount of nitrogen applied should be reduced accordingly.

Animal manures are very good sources of nitrogen and also add organic matter to the soil. A general rate for applying manures is 6 to 8 tons/acre (13.4 to 17.9 MT/ha) of cow or horse manure and 2 to 3 tons/acre (4.5 to 6.7 MT/ha) of poultry manure. Manures should be applied during late fall or winter when plants are dormant. Unless composted, animal manures may be a source of weed seeds.

If blackberry middles are clean cultivated, a winter cover crop is recommended. Cover crops planted in late summer between the blackberry rows will check erosion, help harden the blackberry canes for winter by competing for moisture and nutrients, and provide valuable organic matter to the soil when turned under in the spring. Also, legume cover crops are available which will add nitrogen to the soil. Some good cover crops for blackberries are cowpeas, oats, and rye. Care must be taken with aggressive crops such as vetch to prevent the seeds from getting in the blackberry row.

Irrigation

Although blackberry species survive extended periods of drought in their native habitats, a shortage of soil moisture can seriously reduce yields and fruit size of cultivated plantings. Lack of sufficient moisture in the spring will affect fruit development, and insufficient moisture at any time of the growing season may have a detrimental effect on the subsequent years crop. Irrigation may be especially important in obtaining good survival and growth of first-year plantings. Later yields are dependent on rapid establishment of well-filled hedge rows.

In general, blackberries require about 1 in. (2.54 cm) of water per week during the growing season. More may be required during fruit development in the spring and during hot, windy weather periods. When this amount is not supplied by rainfall, supplemental irrigation should be used. Any method of distributing irrigation water to the plants is satisfactory. Many growers use sprinkler irrigation, but recently trickle irrigation systems have become popular in blackberry culture.

Pest Control

Many of the pest problems on blackberries can be avoided by starting with clean planting stock and the subsequent application of good sanitary measures. By eradicating all wild *Rubus* plants in the area, and isolating new plantings from old ones, many disease and insect problems can be avoided. Plants showing symptoms of virus, crown gall, orange rust, or red-necked cane borer should be pulled from the field and burned. Timely removal and burning of dead floricanes after harvest, and the removal and burning of winter prunings, will reduce populations of destructive pests.

The most common disease and insect pests of blackberry are listed in Table 5–2. Although there are many such pests that occasionally are damaging to blackberries, only a few are so consistently destructive that a regular control program is warranted. Since insect and disease pests differ in different areas, growers should determine local recommendations for controlling pest problems.

Winter Protection

Most trailing blackberry varieties are not hardy and are suggested for southern areas only. With special protection they might be grown in northern regions, but even then winter injury may occur. The canes can be protected by covering them lightly with soil or preferably with straw after they become dormant in the fall (about mid-December). When danger of severe cold weather is past in the spring, uncover the canes, do dormant pruning, and tie the canes to a support.

One progressive grower reported that 'Thornfree' canes can be detrellised in the late fall, laid on the soil, covered with straw, and then weighted with old rubber tires. The combination of insulation from the soil and mulch has proved to be of value, and he reports a crop most years in central Illinois. Interestingly, one would expect that many of the canes would break, but the grower feels that the loss of a few canes is no problem since they should be thinned anyway.

Cultivars of erect blackberries differ greatly in winter hardiness, although none is sufficiently hardy for the coldest areas of the United States. Many cultivars developed in southern areas of the United States (e.g., 'Flordagrand', 'Oklawaha', 'Brazos') are very cold tender. Among the most hardy erect cultivars is 'Darrow', developed in New York.

Erect blackberries may be made more winter hardy by fall preconditioning. Slowing vegetative growth and hardening canes by withholding water and nutrients late in the growing season conditions the plants to survive at lower temperatures. Allowing other plants, such as natural grasses or cover crops, to compete with the blackberries for water, nutrients, and light will give similar results.

Harvesting and Marketing

Blackberries are a very perishable fruit and must be harvested, packed, stored, and marketed with utmost care if they are to remain in good condition. The best index of maturity is the ease of separation of the fruit from the pedicel. Fruit color is a poor

TABLE 5-2 IMPORTANT DISEASE AND INSECT PESTS OF BLACKBERRIES

PATHOGEN OR PEST	SYMPTOMS	CONTROL MEASURES[a]	AREA WHERE IMPORTANT
Diseases			
Virus or virus-like agents			
Mosaic	None to large greenish-yellow blisters on leaves; dwarfing of plant	Use VF stocks; control aphid vectors	All areas except Pacific northwest
Calico	Yellow leaf blotch	Use VF stock, rogue infected plants	Common everywhere untested stock of 'Loganberry' is grown
Sterility	Vigorous growth, but flowers set no or few drupelets	Use clean stocks, rogue infected plants	Many parts of U.S.; 'Darrow', 'Lawton', and 'Eldorado' notably infected
Stunt	Dwarfed, weak plants	Use VF stock, control leafhopper vector	Europe; not known in U.S.
Fungi			
Anthracnose[b]	Purple-gray lesions on canes and leaves; dry, woody drupelets	Apply fungicide; remove old canes after harvest	All areas, especially southeastern U.S.; 'Evergreen' resistant
Cane blight[c]	Light-colored fissured bark extending for several nodes; lateral shoots wilt and die	Time pruning to allow wounds to callus before rain; cut out old canes below ground level	Widespread
Cane and leaf rust[d]	Yellow spores on bark and underside of leaves of floricanes in early summer	Remove diseased canes after fruiting; apply fungicide	Pacific northwest and southeast
Orange rust[e]	Orange spores on underside of leaves in spring; new shoots spindly	Use healthy stock; rogue all infected plants in and near planting	Throughout U.S.; 'Boysenberry' immune
Rosette (double blossom)[f]	Witches-brooms of pale green leaves develop in early spring on floricanes; large, elongated flower buds; flowers on infected shoots are sterile	Destroy wild plants in area; remove infected flower clusters before bloom; treat with fungicide	Southeastern U.S., west to Texas
Leaf and cane spot[g]	Circular lesions on leaves with purple border and white center; elongate lesions on canes and petioles	Prune and burn infected canes after harvest; apply fungicide	Southeast and Pacific northwest

TABLE 5-2 IMPORTANT DISEASE AND INSECT PESTS OF BLACKBERRIES, cont.

PATHOGEN OR PEST	SYMPTOMS	CONTROL MEASURES[a]	AREA WHERE IMPORTANT
Diseases			
Verticillium wilt[h]	Young canes wilt and leaves turn yellow in summer; as fruit ripens, floricanes collapse	Use clean stock; avoid infested soil; fumigate soil; use resistant cultivars	Northern and Pacific coast states
Gray mold fruit rot[i]	Gray mycelium growth develops on harvested fruit and on overripe fruit before harvest	Apply fungicide during ripening period; avoid bruising during harvest; refrigerate	All areas
Powdery mildew[j]	Leaves covered with whitish mycelium; twisting and dwarfing of leaves	Apply powdery mildew fungicide; use wide plant spacing for quick drying of leaves after rain	All areas
Bacteria Crown gall[k]	Whitish warts on crown or develop on canes, causing canes to split	Use clean stock on uninfested soil, rogue infected plants, use proprietary competitive bacterial preparations	All areas
	Rough small to large wartlike growths on roots and crowns; plants stunted	Use clean stock on uninfested soil; rogue infected plants; dip pruning tools in formaldehyde frequently to reduce spread	
Nematodes (Various spp.) especially *Pratylenchus* spp.	General weakening of plant	Use clean stock; fumigate soil	All areas
Insects			
Aphids	None to severe leaf curling in early spring; general weakening of plants (some are virus vectors)	Apply insecticide as needed	All areas
Raspberry crown borer	Larvae feed and tunnel in crowns and roots, weakening plants	Apply insecticide in early October	All areas

Pest	Description	Control	Area
Red-necked cane borer	Larvae burrow in canes, producing swellings on cane; girdled canes may die	Apply insecticide in early spring; prune out infected canes in winter	All areas
Strawberry weevil	Flower buds cut off before opening	Apply insecticide as needed	All areas
Japanese beetle	Adults feed on leaves	Apply insecticide as needed	Eastern U.S.
Orange tortrix	Larvae web and feed on foliage and ripening fruit	Apply insecticide when blossoms appear in spring	Pacific northwest
Redberry mite	Parts or all of the berries do not ripen normally, but remain red and hard	Apply insecticide in early spring when new shoots are 1 in. long	Western U.S.
Spider mites	Reduced plant vigor; leaves turn brown and drop	Apply miticide, as needed	All areas
Raspberry fruit worm	Adults feed on leaves and flower buds; larvae feed within flower buds and developing fruit	Apply insecticide when flower buds appear	All areas

[a] Readers should consult the latest officially approved lists of pesticides for their area since chemical recommendations and approval for use vary from place to place and from time to time.

[b] Caused by *Elsinoe veneta* (Burkh.) Jenkins.

[c] Caused by *Leptosphaeria coniothyrium* (Fck1.) Sacc.

[d] Caused by *Kuehneola uredinis* (Lk.) Arth.

[e] Caused by *Gymnoconia peckiana* (Howe) Trott.

[f] Caused by *Cercosporella rubi* (Wint.) Plakidas.

[g] Caused by *Septoria rubi* West.

[h] Caused by *Verticillium albo-atrum* Reinke and Berth.

[i] Caused by *Botrytis cinerea* Pers. ex. Fr.

[j] Caused by *Sphaerotheca humuli* (DC.) Burr.

[k] Caused by *Agrobacterium tumefaciens* (E.F. Smith and Town.) Conn.

indicator since most blackberries color before they are fully ripe, and there is a tendency of most pickers to harvest fruit that is still underripe and sour.

Blackberries ripen from May in the southeastern U.S. production regions to July in the Pacific northwest. The fruiting period of individual cultivars ranges from 4 to 7 weeks at a given location.

Fruit should be picked as frequently as every second or third day. Berries left on the plants until overripe will become soft, moldy, and may fall to the ground. The best time of day to pick is in the cool of morning, but berries should never be picked when wet with dew or rain, since wet berries mold very quickly.

Berries should be picked by gently lifting with thumb and fingers. Very few berries should be held in the hand at one time. Harvested berries should be placed gently in the container in which they are to be marketed; transferring from container to container results in unnecessary bruising. Harvested fruit should be protected at all times from the sun, since exposure for even a short time will result in the fruit turning red and the flavor becoming bitter. Removing field heat by rapid cooling will greatly extend the shelf life of the fruit.

Recently, mechanical harvesters have been developed to rapidly harvest large acreages of blackberries for processing. Generally, the machines selectively harvest higher-quality fruit than hand pickers, since the machine utilizes a shaking principle that removes fully ripe fruit, while immature fruit remains on the plant for later harvest. Unfortunately, existing cultivars of blackberry do not have adequate fruit firmness to be machine harvested for fresh market use.

The pick-your-own concept of direct marketing has greatly stimulated interest in blackberry culture in many areas of the United States. Where adequate population density exists, this is an ideal method of marketing blackberries. Unless direct marketing or local marketing is to be used, potential growers should establish a marketing outlet prior to planting blackberries.

A partial crop of fruit may be expected the second summer after planting blackberries. By the third harvest season, full production is reached. A properly managed blackberry planting should yield 6000 to 8000 lb/acre (6700 to 9000 kg/ha), and even higher yields are possible. Since the crowns and roots of blackberries are perennial, a well-cared-for planting should remain productive for many years.

REFERENCES AND SUGGESTED READING

BAILEY, J. S. 1948. A study of the rest period in red raspberries. Proc. Am. Soc. Hortic. Sci. 52:265–270

BAILEY, L. H. 1941–1945. Species Batorum. The genus *Rubus* in North America. Gentes Herb. 5:1–918.

BRAINERD, E., AND A. K. PEITERSEN. 1920. Blackberries of New England: their classification. Vt. Agric. Exp. Stn. Bull. 217.

BRIERLEY, W. G., AND R. H. LANDON. 1946. Some relationships between rest period, rate of hardening, loss of cold resistance and winter injury in Latham raspberry. Proc. Am. Soc. Hortic. Sci. 47:224–234.

CALDWELL, J. D. 1984. Blackberry propagation. HortScience 19:193–195.

DARROW, G. M. 1937. Blackberry and raspberry improvement. p. 496–533. In Better plants and animals 2. U.S. Dep. Agric. Agric. Yearb.

DARROW, G. M. 1955. Blackberry: raspberry hybrids. J. Hered. 46:67–71.

DARROW, G. M. 1967. The cultivated raspberry and blackberry in North America: breeding and improvement. Am. Hortic. Mag. 46:203–218.

FERNALD, M. L. 1950. p. 818–864. In Gray's manual of botany. 8th ed. American Book Company, New York.

FUNT, R. C., ET AL. 1988. Brambles: production, management, and marketing. Ohio Coop. Ext. Serv. Bull. 783.

HALL, H. K., M. H. QUAZI, AND R. M. SKIRVIN. 1986a. Isolation of a pure thornless Loganberry by meristem tip culture. Euphytica 35:1039–1044.

HALL, H. K., R. M. SKIRVIN, AND W. F. BRAAM. 1986b. Germplasm release of 'Lincoln Logan', a tissue culture–derived genetic thornless 'Loganberry'. Fruit Var. J. 40:134–135.

HEDRICK, U. P. 1925. The small fruits of New York. J.B. Lyon, Albany, N.Y.

JENNINGS, D. L. 1981. A hundred years of Loganberries. Fruit Var. J. 35:34–37.

JENNINGS, D. L. 1988. Raspberries and blackberries: their breeding, diseases and growth. Academic Press, San Diego, Calif.

LAMB, R. C. 1948. Effect of temperatures above and below freezing on the breaking of rest in the Latham raspberry. Proc. Am. Soc. Hortic. Sci. 51:313–315.

LAWRENCE, F. J. 1976. Sterility in *Rubus*. Fruit Var. J. 30(1):22.

LOCKSHIN, L. S., AND D. C. ELFVING. 1981. Flowering response of Heritage red raspberry to temperature and nitrogen. HortScience 16:527–528.

MACDANIELS, L. H. 1922. Fruit bud formation in *Rubus* and *Ribes*. Proc. Am. Soc. Hortic. Sci. 19:194–200.

MARTIN, L. W., AND F. J. LAWRENCE. 1976. A synopsis of mechanical harvesting of *Rubus* in Oregon. Acta Hortic. 60:95–98.

MATHERS, B. A. 1952. A study of fruit-bud development in *Rubus idaeus*. J. Hortic. Sci. 27:266–272.

McPHEETERS, K. D., AND R. M. SKIRVIN. 1983. Histogenic layer manipulation in chimeral 'Thornless Evergreen' trailing blackberry. Euphytica 32:351–360.

MOORE, J. N., AND J. D. CALDWELL. 1983. *Rubus* (Tourn.) L. In A. H. Halevy (ed.). CRC handbook of flowering. CRC Press, Boca Raton, Fla.

MOORE, J. N., G. C. PAVLIS, G. R. BROWN, AND C. A. LUNDERGAN. 1978. Establishing blackberry plantings with root cuttings. Arkansas Farm Res. 27(2):4.

OURECKY, D. K. 1975. Brambles. p. 98–129. In J. Janick and J. N. Moore (eds.). Advances in fruit breeding. Purdue University Press, West Lafayette, Ind.

PEITERSEN, A. K. 1921. Blackberries of New England: genetic status of the plants. Vt. Agric. Exp. Stn. Bull. 218.

PERRY, J. L., AND J. N. MOORE. 1985. Self and cross-compatibility in tetraploid blackberry cultivars. HortScience 20(4):738–739.

PRITTS, M. P. (ED.). 1989. The bramble growers production guide. Northeast Region. Agric. Engineer, Serv. Pub. Cornell Univ., Ithaca, N.Y.

ROBERTSON, M. 1957. Further investigation of flower-bud development in the genus *Rubus*. J. Hortic. Sci. 32:265–273.

References and Suggested Reading

ROSATI, P., D. GAGGLIOLI, AND L. GIUCHI. 1986. Genetic stability of micropropagated Loganberry plants. J. Hortic. Sci. 61:33–41.

SHEETS, W. A., T. L. NELSON, AND A. G. NELSON. 1975. Alternate-year production of 'Thornless Evergreen' blackberries: technical and economic feasibility. Oreg. State Univ. Agric. Exp. Stn. Bull. 620.

SWARTZ, H. J. (ED.). 1988. Bramble. North American Bramble Growers Association Department of Horticulture, University of Maryland, College Park.

WALDO, G. F. 1933. Fruit bud formation in brambles. Proc. Am. Soc. Hortic. Sci. 30:263–267.

WALDO, G. F., AND G. M. DARROW. 1941. Breeding autumn-fruiting raspberries under Oregon conditions. Proc. Am. Soc. Hortic. Sci. 39:274–278.

WALDO, G. F., AND H. HARTMANN. 1946. Culture of trailing berries in Oregon. Oregon Agric. Exp. Stn. Bull. 441.

WILLIAMS, I. H. 1960. Effects of environment on *Rubus idaeus* L. V. Dormancy and flowering of the mature shoot. J. Hortic. Sci. 35:214–220.

Chapter 6

Currant and Gooseberry Management

L. HARMAT
A. PORPACZY
D. G. HIMELRICK
G. J. GALLETTA

CULTIVATED TYPES

Currants and gooseberries are closely related, berry-bearing shrubs, presently classified in the *Ribes* genus of the Saxifrage botanical family. Currants and gooseberries are similar enough in usage, plant and fruit habit, and climatic and cultural requirements that they can be considered together. However, minor differences in plant longevity, seasonal moisture and temperature tolerances, position of the fruiting wood (type of shoot upon which flowers and fruits are borne), and fruit market outlets make some cultural practices more economical for one species than for another (Ministry of Agriculture, Fisheries and Food, 1981).

Some *Ribes* species are grown for their edible fruit, such as *R. uva-crispa, R. hirtellum, R. nigrum, R. odoratum,* and *R. sativum;* and others for their ornamental habit and flowers, such as *R. aureum, R. odoratum, R. speciosum,* and *R. viburnifolium.* The red and white currants are generally listed as *Ribes sativum,* the black currant as *R. nigrum,* and the flowering currant as *R. odoratum.* The gooseberries of American origin are forms of *R. hirtellum* or hybrids from it; and the European gooseberries, which are much more subject to mildew, are *R. uva-crispa*.

There are approximately 140 to 160 species, which belong to the *Ribesia, Eucoreasma,* and *Grossularia* subgenera. They are native to the northern hemisphere in the cool circumpolar region. Native species can be found in Europe, Asia, and North America, and most of the cultivated species have been selected from these areas. The number of species greatly decreases in more southern regions of the northern hemisphere. In the development of cultivated types (cultivars) the species listed in Table 6-1 had important roles.

The red currant was cultivated in Germany in the fifteenth century. The *Main Herbarius* published in 1488 describes currants; however, at that time only wild species were grown for medicinal use. Reallius in France, in 1536, mentions currant as a plant suitable for garden borders. Matthiolus in 1558, and Mizaldus in 1560, write about currant as a cultivated plant. In sixteenth-century English literature, Geralde's *Herbal* mentions currant for the first time as a garden fruit. Mave in 1778, in the *Dictionary of Gardening and Botany,* described 10 currant cultivars and mentions that some of them were purchased in Holland.

The black currant was first described by the French Monk Montrand in his book *The Wonderful Characteristics of Black Currants.* He described many diseases that could be cured by black currants. Several travelers in the eighteenth century reported that black currant had been marketed in Russian cities in farmers' markets.

The currant arrived in North America probably with the first settlers. The 'Red Dutch' and 'White Dutch' cultivars were the first to arrive in the New World. The

TABLE 6-1 SPECIES THAT HAVE CONTRIBUTED TO THE DEVELOPMENT OF MODERN CULTIVARS

SUBGENUS	SPECIES
Ribesia (red currants)	*Ribes picatum* (Robbs.) (*Ribes rubrum*)
	Ribes sativum (Syme.) (*Ribes vulgare*)
	Ribes petraeum (Wolf.)
	Ribes longeracemosum (Jancz.)
Eucoreosma (black currants)	*Ribes nigrum* L. tax. conc. *europaeum* (Jancz.) tax. conc. *sibiricum* (Pavl.) tax. conc. *scandinavicum* (Vaara.)
	Ribes dikuscha (Fisch.)
	Ribes ussuriense (Jancz.)
	Ribes americanum (Mill.)
	Ribes bracteosum (Dougl.)
	Ribes petiolare (Dougl.)
	Ribes husdsonianum (Rich.)
Grossularia (gooseberries)	*Grussularia uva-crispa* (Mill.)
	Ribes grossularia L.
	Ribes aciculare (SM.)
	Ribes burejense (Fr. Schm)
	Ribes hirtellum (Michx.)
	Ribes cynosbati (L.)
	Ribes divaricatum (Dougl.)

Source: A. Terpo in Gyuro (1974).

first records in North America are from 1770. Prince's nursery catalog in 1826 recommends '7' and 'Downing;' their 1857 catalog lists 25 cultivars, all European in origin. Fuller in 1867 describes 28 cultivars and mentions 40 synonyms.

Gooseberry production started around 1700 in Europe. According to Sorge (1984), in England by 1740 about 100, and by 1810 more than 400 cultivars were named and grown. The large-fruited English cultivars spread slowly to German gardens. In 1852, L. von Pauser described 966 cultivars, not all of which were cultivated. In 1913, L. Maurer, in his book, still the most detailed description of gooseberry cultivars, lists only 133 cultivars as worthy of cultivation. Numerous gooseberry cultivars have been named and cultivated over the past several hundred years. It is noteworthy that Lucka [cited by Hriczovsky (1969)] estimates the number of gooseberry cultivars worldwide as 3004 red, 675 yellow, 925 green, and 280 white-fruited.

During the early part of this century the production of red and black currants spread in Europe to those areas where the winter cold is sufficient to break dormancy. Presently, practically the entire red and black currant production is restricted to Europe. Gooseberry production has traditionally been important in England. North American production of gooseberries and currants has been hampered by adaptation and disease problems.

RELATED GERMPLASM AND UTILITY

The Saxifrage family (Saxifragaceae) is a dicot group of herbs and shrubs differing from the Rose family (Rosaceae) mostly in having more abundant endosperm in the seeds and in usually not having stipules on the leaves. Floristically, the Saxifrage family is also similar to the succulent Orpine family (Crassulaceae) (Lawrence, 1955). The genus *Ribes* is characterized by Jepson (1951) as being in the Ribesieae tribe, which differs from the rest of the family in bearing berry-like fruit which develops from a wholly inferior floral ovary (sepals, petals, and stamens are inserted, or arise from above the ovary). The Ribesieae are shrubs having alternate leaves with stipules and flowers with two styles, more or less united into one. The nearest relatives of the *Ribes* plants are shrub genera of the tribe Hydrangeae (in which the fruit is a capsule, the leaves are opposite without stipules, and the floral styles vary from three to five), such as *Philadelphus* (mock orange), *Carpenteria, Jamesia,* and *Whipplea.*

The genus *Ribes* L. (*Grossularia* Mill.) is a member of the Rosales series of the Saxifragaceae family. The genus contains about 150 species of low shrubs in temperate regions of the northern hemisphere, and extends into the southern hemisphere in the Andes of South America. The plant may be with or without prickles. Leaves are alternate, often clustered, usually deciduous, simple, palmately veined, and lobed. Flowers are small, in few- to many-flowered racemes, or solitary. Flowers are usually bisexual, or unisexual and borne on separate plants (dioecious). They are pentamerous with a one-celled inferior ovary and having two separate or united styles. The fruit is a berry, glabrous or glandular or with prickles, crowned by calyx remnants. The genus comprises two distinct groups, the currants and the gooseberries, considered by some to be separate genera, *Ribes* and *Grossularia,* respectively. Currants mostly lack nodal spines and are usually otherwise unarmed; the flowers are mostly in racemes on pedicels jointed at the summit; the fruit disarticulating at the joints. Gooseberries have nodal spines and are usually prickly; the flowers are solitary or few, the pedicels commonly not jointed at the summit, and fruit not disarticulating. (Bailey, 1976).

Currants and gooseberries are available as fresh market fruit from mid-May to the end of July. Fresh consumption, although practiced in all of the producing countries, consumes only a small fraction of the production. Most of the fresh fruit is processed for cake fillings, puddings, pies, jams, and toppings.

Ribes fruit is utilized almost exclusively for processing. It is marketed frozen and processed as juice, jam, jelly, and compote. Black currants are prized for their distinctive flavor in juice, jam, jelly, pies, and other desserts. In France, black currants are used for brandy, with the 'Noir de Bourgogne' cultivar being most popular. Leaves and buds of the black currant are used as herbs for medicinal use. Red currants are used mainly for jelly or jam. White currants are not as popular as black and red currants. Gooseberries are eaten fresh or made into jam, pies, and other desserts. Both currants and gooseberries can be frozen easily and kept for later use.

The fruit of the *Ribes* species is rich in vitamins A, B, and C, in pectins, mineral elements, citric acid, and fructose. Their fruit or fruit products are useful and valuable for balanced nutrition.

BOTANY

Root Systems

Seed-propagated plants of both types usually have a taproot system, in comparison with vegetatively propagated plants, which have a fiberous adventitious root system. The root system is shallow, located primarily in the top 8 to 16 in. (20 to 40 cm) of soil. Occasional roots, especially from seed-propagated plants, may grow as deep as 32 to 39 in. (80 to 100 cm). The root system's diameter is rarely larger than 28 to 32 in. (70 to 80 cm). Roots occasionally extend beyond the canopy of the bush. There is a direct correlation between the height of the plant and the diameter of the root system. Roots that are close to the soil surface are especially abundant in root hairs.

Aerial Plant Habit

Currant and gooseberry morphology of aboveground organs is illustrated in Figs. 6–1 and 6–2, respectively. The canopy of the bush is 3 to 6 ft (1 to 2 m) tall. Gooseberries range in height from 2 to 5 ft (0.6 to 1.5 m), while red currants range from 3 to 5 ft (0.9 to 1.5 m), and black currants to 5 ft (1.5 m) and taller. Currants have a smooth stem, whereas gooseberries are thorny, especially at nodes. The center of new shoot production (branching point) is close to the surface of the soil, or occasionally below it. Shoots can be short spurs with short internodes, small

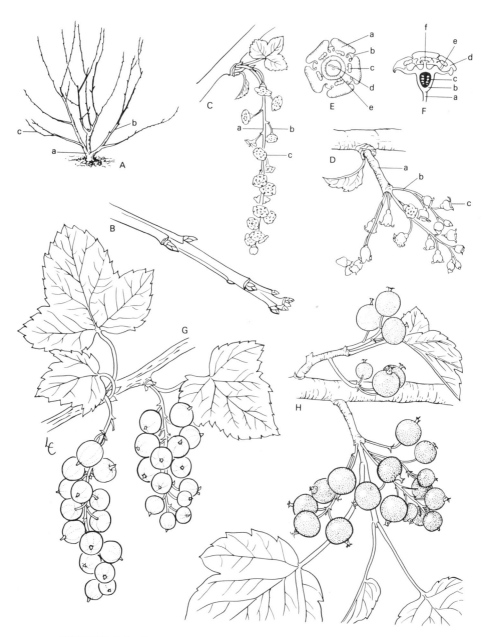

FIGURE 6-1 Currant morphology. (A) Plant habit dormant pruned: a, crown base; b, overwintering stem; c, lateral branch. (B) Dormant red currant cane. (C) Red currant raceme: a, penduncle (rachis); b, pedicel; c, flower. (D) Black currant raceme: a, peduncle; b, pedicel; c, flower. (E) Red currant flower: a, sepal; b, petal; c, stamen; d, stigmas; e, ring. (F) Red currant flower (longitudinal view): a, pedicel; b, ovary; c, ovules; d, sepal; e, anther; f, stigmas and style. (G) Red currant fruiting branch. (H) Black currant fruiting branch.

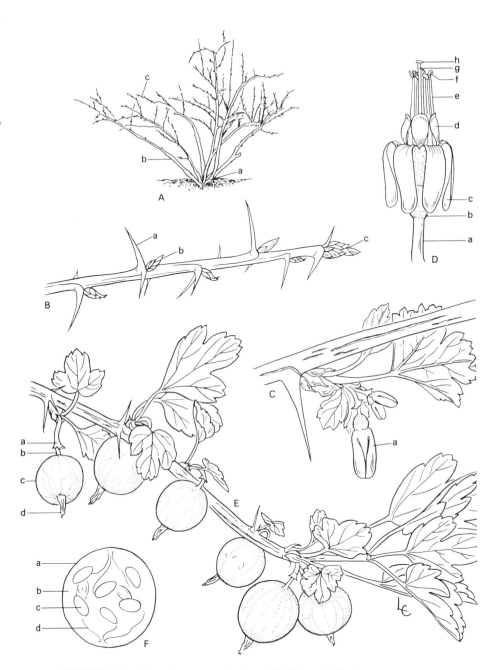

FIGURE 6-2 Gooseberry morphology. (A) Plant habit dormant: a, crown base; b, overwintering cane; c, lateral branch. (B) Dormant cane: a, nodal spine; b, axillary bud; c, terminal bud. (C) Detail of emerging axillary bud: a, flower bud. (D) Flower: a, pedicel; b, receptacle; c, sepal; d, petal; e, filament; f, anther; g, style; h, stigma. (E) Fruiting shoot: a, peduncle; b, pedicel; c, berry; d, dried stamens. (F) Berry cross section: a, epidermis; b, pulp; c, seed; d, vascular trace.

leaves and terminal flowers, or long with large leaves, as in the gooseberry. Leaves of some cultivars have hairs along the veins. Petioles are shorter than the leaf blade.

Buds are located on the 1-year-old shoots. Currant and gooseberry buds are long, pointed, light brown, and can be leaf or flower buds. On the sides of long shoots, the buds are usually leaf buds, with the terminal buds of the short shoots usually being flower buds in red currant and gooseberry. The flower buds of the black currant are usually located laterally along the 1-year-old shoots.

Flowering and Fruiting

Flower buds in all cases are terminal buds, including those developing on the sides of long shoots. These buds may develop as terminal buds of secondary shoots which often are too small to be readily visible. From the flower buds, short internode fruiting structures develop, which in gooseberries contain 1 to 3, and in currants, 8 to 30 flowers. The flower cluster branches are commonly referred to as *strigs*.

Flower buds usually differentiate from the middle of July to early August. At this time flower primordia are visible microscopically. In late September, flower bud development reaches the point where the flower is visible between the bud scales. Flower primordia continue to develop during the winter. During the spring the development of flowers is intensified. About 7 to 10 days before opening, the sexual organs of the flowers are fully developed (Fernquist, 1961).

The flowers are greenish yellow or red. They are insect pollinated. The majority of cultivars are self-fertile (the red currants and gooseberries can be planted without pollinizing cultivars). Most black currants are self-sterile.

Fruit-setting characteristics of the cultivated species vary. For example, productivity of many black currant cultivars is increased in Europe by interplanting with pollinizer cultivars (Table 6–2). In black currant flowers, stigmas are usually

TABLE 6-2 PRODUCTIVITY OF BLACK CURRANTS AND RECOMMENDED POLLINIZERS

NO.	CULTIVAR	POSSIBLE PRODUCTION (kg/bush)[a]	REALIZED PRODUCTIVITY (%)		RECOMMENDED POLLINIZERS (CULTIVAR NO.)
			Self-Pollinated	Cross-Pollinated	
1.	Altajszkaja deszertnaja	2.51	16.8	49.3	2, 3, 7, 9, 10
2.	Fertodi 1	2.66	49.7	76.1	1, 3, 5, 7, 10
3.	Hidasi botermo	2.72	34.4	70.1	2, 5–7, 10–12
4.	Neoszopajuscsajaszja	2.38	36.1	63.4	2, 5, 6, 8, 11, 12
5.	Silvergieter F. 59	2.14	37.8	59.2	2–4, 6, 8, 11, 12
6.	Wellington XXX	2.04	26.4	68.2	2–5, 7, 8, 11, 12
7.	Brodtorp	1.87	53.2	72.1	1–3, 9, 10
8.	Ben More	2.29	41.5	69.2	3–6, 11, 12
9.	Junnat	1.94	37.6	66.1	2, 3, 5, 10, 11
10.	Ben Sarek	2.96	43.2	71.6	1–3, 5, 7, 9
11.	Onix	2.19	45.2	66.3	2, 3, 5, 6, 9, 12
12.	Titania	2.98	36.5	69.2	2–8

[a] 1 kg = 2.2 lb.

Botany

receptive prior to pollen maturation, but the reciprocal situation is occasionally encountered. Pollen shedding is negligible from evening through early morning, improves between 10 A.M. and 2 P.M., and is optimal between 2 and 6 P.M. (Baldini and Pisani, 1961).

Nyeki et al. (1980) followed pollen tube growth with flourescence microscopy. They found that with black currant, the pollen tube entered only 4 to 6 out of 100 ovules. The rest of the seeds form by parthenogenesis induced by the developing pollen tubes.

Cross-pollination of cultivars depends largely on their blooming simultaneously. Time of bloom also depends on the length of the flower cluster. The time interval between the bloom of the terminal and basal flowers of the long-clustered cultivars may be as long as 20 days. This may change the requirement for pollen. For good pollination, the pollinizer cultivar must provide pollen for a long period of time. Good pollinizer cultivars not only assure good fruit set, but also affect the size of the berries. For example, the self-incompatible cultivar 'Coronet', when pollinated by the self-compatible 'Ri 270' or 'Brodtorp' cultivars, produces larger fruit than when it is pollinated by the poorly self-compatible 'Ri 1166' cultivar (Tamas and Porpaczy, 1967).

Although red currant and gooseberry cultivars are self-fertile, the degree of self-fertility depends on the year and the location. For this reason it is recommended that 1 to 2% of the planting be planted to a pollinizer cultivar. Pollination is facilitated by bees and one hive per acre (5 per 2 ha) is recommended to assure good pollination.

Climatic Requirements

Currants and gooseberries are very hardy and can be grown in areas having very cold winter temperatures which preclude the production of many temperate fruits. Summer heat is the southern limiting factor in climate adaptability, with gooseberries being slightly more tolerant of high temperatures. Species of the genus *Ribes,* as indicated by their geographic distribution, require cooler climates. In warm climates at temperatures of 86°F (30°C) or higher, leaves are frequently injured; and often the plants are defoliated. Occasionally, gooseberry fruit is also injured. The cultivated types are less sensitive to low temperatures and can withstand −22 to −31°F (−30 to −35°C) during the period of deep rest, 21 to 18°F (−6 to −8°C) after the rest is completed, 23 to 19°F (−5 to −7°C) at bud opening, 27 to 23°F (−3 to −5°C) in the closed flower stage, 31 to 28°F (−0.5 to −2.0°C) in full bloom, 28 to 27°F (−2 to −3°C) when the small fruits are developing, and 18 to 14°F (−8 to −10°C) when leaves are senescing.

The degrees days, using the average daily temperatures above 40°F (5°C), required for bud break are 20 to 60, and for bloom, about 160 to 200. The length of the vegetative period is satisfied with 120 to 140 frost-free days.

Water requirements of currants and gooseberries are not very high (an average of 0.6 in. (15 mm) per week from April to September satisfies the growth and fruiting requirement in Hungary). However, production is improved with a higher rate of water supply of about 1 in. (25 mm) per week during the growing season. If this amount of water is not supplied by precipitation, irrigation is needed. During the hot summer days, leaf injury may result from insufficient water uptake. In such cases (Dobos, 1960), morning shade is beneficial, but can be utilized practically only in home gardens.

A radiation range between 1900 and 2000 footcandles (177 to 186 lux) satisfies the requirement of *Ribes* species. Several observations indicate that *Ribes* species could be grown with much less radiation. The lower demand of these species for light intensity allows the utilization of semishade for production of gooseberries and currants. Although the plants will tolerate partial shade, a sunny site with good air movement will give higher yields.

Wind does not normally cause economic damage in currants and gooseberries, but may be a consideration during bloom, due to its limiting bee activity, or permitting plants to dry off and not be as subject to mildew, or helping to prevent spring frost damage.

Soil Requirements

For production of currants and gooseberries, the most advantageous sites are those with northern-, northeast-, or northwest-facing slopes. Sites that have good air drainage are desirable. Because summer heat may injure the plants, southern exposures are less suitable.

Currants and gooseberries require well-drained, deep loam soils with a desired organic matter content of more than 1%. The optimum soil pH is between 5.5 and 7.0. Currants and gooseberries are not very sensitive to the calcium content of the soil. They prefer slightly acidic soils, but grow well also on calcium-containing soils. When the calcium content is higher than 15%, the more sensitive cultivars, such as 'Fertodi hosszufurtu', may become chlorotic. These species do not have high soil nutrient requirements. P_2O_5 and K_2O levels of 10 and 15 mg per 100 g soil, respectively, in the upper 16 in. (40 cm) of soil suffice. The total salt content of the soil should not be more than 0.15%, nor the sodium content more than 0.05%. It is advantageous if the water table is between 3 and 6 ft (1 to 2 m), but if it is closer to the soil surface than 3 ft (1 m), it could endanger production.

Principal Diseases and Pests

In the early part of the twentieth century, both the federal and state governments in the United States took action against growing currants and gooseberries to prevent the spread of a fungal disease, white pine blister rust (*Cronartium ribicola*), which attacks *Ribes* and white pines (at that time a very important group of American timber trees). *Ribes* and white pines must live together for the blister rust fungus to complete its life cycle. Black currants and white pines are extremely susceptible, while red currants and gooseberries exhibit varying degrees of susceptibility. The federal ban was rescinded in 1966, but many state laws still prohibit the planting or cultivation of black currants (*Ribes nigrum*). Interested persons should contact their state department of agriculture to determine the legalities of growing these plants. Naturally, this quarantine sharply reduced currant and gooseberry culture in the United States. Interest in *Ribes* culture is presently increasing.

It is often said that currants and gooseberries do not have many diseases and pests, but this is inaccurate. Currants and gooseberries are often grown in isolated small plantings. As plants become older, or as *Ribes* plants are concentrated in certain areas, disease-inciting organisms and pests build up, causing severe economic losses and usually requiring pest control measures. The principal European and American *Ribes* diseases and pests are listed in Tables 6-3 and 6-4, together with the species and plant parts affected.

CULTURE

Since currants and gooseberries are slow to reach full production (black currants, 4 to 5 years; red currants, 5 years; gooseberries, 5 to 7 years), and since they persist for many years (black currants, 10 or more cropping years; red currants and gooseberries, 15 to 20 or more cropping years), it is prudent to use care in choosing sites and cultivars for commercial production and in preparing those production sites for planting.

Cultivars

Black currants. Black currants are sensitive to climatic adaptation; and a whole range of cultivars have developed in Europe. In the northern European countries (Finland, Sweden, and Norway) with their long 17- to 18-hour days, the 'Ojebyn' and 'Brodtorp' cultivars are used. These cultivars make a smaller bush and are less productive in central Europe. In central Europe, those cultivars that retain the self-fertility and the powdery mildew resistance of the northern cultivars, but which are adapted to the warmer climate, give good results. An example is the 'Fertodi 1' (Porpaczy, 1974) (Fig. 6-3). In Europe the greatest production of black currants is in England. The major cultivar is 'Baldwin', which accounts for about 80% of the production. Average yields are about 2 tons/acre (4.5 MT/ha), but its productivity is greatly influenced by the weather. The 'Blackdown' cultivar is produced in a smaller area. More productive cultivars such as 'Ben Lomond' and 'Ben More', developed in Scotland, are spreading relatively slowly. In the Scandinavian countries, Poland, and Germany, the major cultivar is 'Ojebyn', which originated in Finland. In Holland, the 'Tenah' and 'Tsema' cultivars are used. In northern areas of the USSR, where there are no fertility problems, the 'Altajszkaja deszertnaja Golubka' and 'Sztahanovak Altaja' are the major cultivars (Pavlova, 1962). In southern regions, where early bud break often results in spring frost injury, and fruit set is not assured, growers use a number of cultivars. In many regions of Europe, they still grow the old Dutch cultivar 'Silvergieter' and its pollinators, 'Boskoop Giant' and 'Wellington 30'.

Recently, the very productive early ripening 'Fertodi 1' has become popular in several European countries. In middle and southern France the 'Noir de Bourgogne'

TABLE 6-3 COMMON DISEASES OF CURRANTS AND GOOSEBERRIES

DISEASE AND CAUSAL ORGANISM	AREA OF IMPORTANCE[a]	AFFECTED PLANT PARTS[b]		
		Black Currant	Red and White Currant	Gooseberry
Fungus Diseases				
American powdery mildew *Sphaerotheca mors-uva (Schw.)*[c]	E, NA	L, Sh, Fr	—	L, Sh, Fr
European powdery mildew *Microsphaera grossulariae* (Wallr.)	E, NA	L	L	L
Leaf spot or anthracnose *Pseudopeziza ribis* Kleb.[c]	E, NA, O	L	L	L
Septoria leaf spot *Mycospharella ribis* (Fckl.) Feltg.	E, NA	L	L	L
Angular leaf spot *Cercospora angulata* Wint.	NA	L	L	L
Currant or white pine blister rust *Cronartium ribicola* Fisch.[c]	A, E, NA	L	L (minor)	L (minor)
Gooseberry or cluster cup rust *Puccinia ribesii-caricis* Kleb.	E, NA			L, Fr
Cane blight or wilt *Botryosphaeria ribis* Gross. & Dug.	NA	C	C	C
Dieback and fruit rot *Botrytis cinerea* Pers.[c]	E, NA	L, C, Fl, Fr	L, C, Fl, Fr	L, C, Fl, Fr
Coral spot or dieback *Nectria cinnabarina* Tode ex Fr.	NA, E	C	C	C
Root rots or molds *Rosellina necatrix* (Hart.) Berk.	E	R	R	R
Phellinus ribis (Schum.) Quec.	E	R	R	R
Armillaria mellea Vahl ex Fr.	E, NA	C, R	C, R	C, R
Virus Diseases (Systemic)				
Reversion virus (gall mite vector)	E	Susc	Tol	Res
Gooseberry veinbanding virus (aphid vectors)	E	Tol	Susc	Susc
Currant mosaic (American nematode vector)	NA	?	Susc	?

[a] A, Asia; E, Europe; NA, North America; O, Australia and New Zealand.
[b] C, canes; Fl, flowers; Fr, fruits; L, leaves; R, roots; Sh, shoots; Res, resistant; Susc, susceptible; Tol, tolerant.
[c] Widespread pathogen.

TABLE 6-4 COMMON PESTS OF CURRANTS AND GOOSEBERRIES

COMMON AND SCIENTIFIC NAMES	AREA OF IMPORTANCE[a]	AFFECTED PLANT PARTS[b]		
		Black Currant	Red and White Currant	Gooseberry
Insects and Mites				
San Jose scale *Aspidiotus perniciosus* Comst.	NA, E	L, Fl, Sh, C	L, Fl, Sh, C	L, Fl, Sh, C
Currant borer or Clearwing moth *Synathedon tipuliformis* Cl.	E, NA	Sh, C	Sh, C	Sh, C
Black currant gall mite *Cecidophyopsis ribis* Westw.	E	B, L	B, L	—
Black currant leaf midge (leaf curling midge) *Dasyneura tetensi* Rubs.	E	L, Sh	—	—
Currant-sowthistle aphid *Hyperomyzus lactucae*	E	L	(L)	—
Red currant blister aphid *Cryptomyzus ribis* L.	E	(L)	L	—
Permanent currant aphid *Aphis schneideri* Cl.	E	L	L	—
Red spider mite *Tetranychus telarius* L.	E	L	L	L
Currant aphid *Capitophorus ribis* L.	NA, E		L	L
Gooseberry aphid *Aphis grossularia* Kalt.	E	—	L	L
Hyperomyzus pallidus (H.R.L.)	E	—	—	L
Nansonovia ribis-nigri (Mosley)	E	(L)	(L)	L
Gooseberry sawfly[c] *Nematus ribesii* (Scop)	E	—	(L)	L
Pale-spotted gooseberry sawfly *N. leucotrochus* Hart.	E	—	(L)	L
Black currant sawfly *N. olefaciens* Benson	E	L	L	—
Currant sawfly *Pristiophora pallipes* Lep.	E	L, Fl	L, Fl	L, Fl
Currant maggot or fruit fly *Epocha canadensis* Loew	NA	Fr	Fr	Fr

Common name / Species	Region				
Currant moth					
Incurvaria capitella Cl.	E	Fr	Fr	Fr	Fr
American buffalo hopper					
Caresa bubatus Fabr.	E	Sh, C	Sh, C	Sh, C	Sh, C
Common green capsid					
Lygocaris pabulinus	E	L, Sh	L, Sh	L, Sh	L, Sh
Gooseberry inchworm or magpie moth					
Abraxus grossulariata L	E	L, Fl	L, Fl	L, Fl	L, Fl
Flat-headed borer					
Chrysobothris mali Horn	NA	R, C	R, C	R, C	R, C
Currant root louse					
Eriosoma ulmi	E	R	R	R	R
Black gooseberry borer					
Xylacrius agassizii Lee	NA	R			R
Currant borer					
Ramosia tipuliformis	NA	–	C	C	C
Fourlined plant bug					
Poecilocapsus lineatus	NA	L, Sh	L, Sh	L, Sh	L, Sh
Gooseberry fruitworm					
Zophodia convolutella	NA	Fr	Fr	Fr	Fr
Slugs and Snails					
Helix aspersa and *Cepaea* spp.	E, NA	Fr	Fr	Fr	Fr
Nematodes					
Bud and leaf nematode					
Aphelenchoides ritzemabosi (Schwartz) Steiner & Buhrer	E, O	B	B	B	–
Birds					
Bullfinch	E	B	B	B	B
Sparrow	E	Fl, Fr	Fl	Fl	Fl
Blackbird	E	Fr	Fr	Fr	Fr
Thrush	E	Fr	Fr	Fr	Fr
Starling	E	Fr		Fr	Fr

[a] E, Europe; NA, North America; O, New Zealand.
[b] B, buds; C, canes; Fl, flowers; Fr, fruit; L, leaves; R, roots; Sh, shoots; ( ), species infested to a lesser extent; –, species not usually infested.
[c] May also be known as imported currant worm of NA (*Pteronidea ribesii* Scopoli).

257

FIGURE 6-3 Black currant cultivar 'Fertodi 1'.

is the major cultivar. It is quite aromatic and is well suited for brandy production. The pollinator for this cultivar is also 'Boskoop Giant'. Among the new cultivars for central Europe, 'Ben Lomond', 'Ben Sarek', and 'Titania' are promising (Turner and Muir, 1985).

Although black currants are legally prohibited from culture (alternate host of white pine blister rust fungus) in many U.S. states, their culture is climatically feasible in the northern United States and adjoining parts of Canada. Three rust-resistant black currants have been developed in Canada and are named 'Consort', 'Crusader', and 'Coronet'. American cultivars of note are the early clones 'Topsy', 'Kerry', and 'Magnus'; the midseason 'Consort' and 'Seabrook'; and the late 'Champion' and 'Tinker'. Older European cultivars that perform well in Canada include 'Medip Cross' and 'Topsy' (early), 'Seabrook's Black' (midseason), and 'Baldwin' and 'Daniel's September' (both late). Newer European clones which may be tried in North America are the U.K. offerings 'Ben Lomond', 'Ben More', 'Ben Nevis', 'Ben Sarek', 'Blackdown', 'Black Reward', 'Malling Jet', and the Dutch clones 'Tenah' and 'Tsema'. The cultivar 'Crandall' is productive and has the added ornamental appeal of having yellow blossoms with a pleasant fragrance.

White currants. White currant cultivars, the most reliably productive [may produce 9 tons/acre (20 MT/ha)], are grown in East Germany ('Werdavia' and 'Zitavia') and Czechoslovakia ('Meridian' and 'Victoria'). The fruit of these cultivars is used mostly for baby food. In the United Kingdom, 'White Versailles' is grown to a limited extent. In the United States, 'White Imperial' is particularly well adapted to the northeast and the somewhat poorer quality 'White Grape' is reliably hardy, even in North Dakota. 'Golden Prolific' is an amber gold selection from the native *Ribes odoratum*.

Red currants. The red currant is a cosmopolitan plant. Cultivars originating from *Ribes sativum* and *R. vulgare* can be grown even in southern Europe. Cultivars with an *R. picatum* origin require longer chilling and their flowers do not develop in warmer climates.

In the northern part of Europe the main cultivar is the Dutch 'Jonkheer van Tets', which produces 4.5 to 7 tons/acre (10 to 16 MT/ha). Another popular cultivar, 'Rondom' (Fig. 6–4), is planted less extensively because of its sensitivity to mycoplasma-caused diseases. The new cultivars 'Rosetta Rotet', and 'Rovoda' from Holland are promising. In home gardens the high-quality 'Red Lake' cultivar is preferred. In more southerly areas such as southern France, 'Jonifer' is planted along with 'Fertodi hoszszufurtu', which also gives good results under these conditions.

Red currants in England are grown principally for their juice and for use in jellies. Cultivars still in use include (early)—'Earliest of Fourlands', 'Jonkheer van Tets', and 'Laxton's No. 1'; (midseason)—'Laxton's Perfection', 'Minnesota No. 71', 'Red Lake', 'Rondom', and 'Stanza'; and (late)—'Wilson's Long Bunch'.

In North America, prior to the rescinding of the blister rust quarantine (Darrow and Detwiler, 1940), the red currant cultivar recommendations listed 'Perfection', 'Wilder', and 'Red Cross' for the northeastern United States; 'London Market', 'Wilder', 'Red Cross', and 'Perfection' for the midwest; 'Perfection', 'London Market', 'Red Cross', 'Wilder', 'Fay', and 'Victoria' for the Pacific coast; and 'Red Lake' for all regions. 'Fay', 'Perfection', 'Cherry', 'Red Cross', and 'London Market' were judged 'entirely hardy in North Dakota and should be hardy anywhere in the United States'. Newer cultivars for trial in the United States include 'Cascade' (early), 'Diploma' (midseason), 'Stephens No. 9' (midseason), 'Prince Albert' (very late), and 'Viking' (blister rust resistant). Some of the recent Dutch introductions should also be tried. 'Minnesota No. 71' and 'Red Lake' have proven to be two of the best red cultivars for the northeastern United States. Several cultivars are shown in Fig. 6–5.

Gooseberries. The cultivated gooseberry has several thousand named cultivars. Obviously, only a few could be considered for commercial use. The processing industry uses only green, white, and yellow-fruited cultivars that are fully ripe, and does not use the red-fruited types.

FIGURE 6-4 Red currant cultivar 'Rondom'.

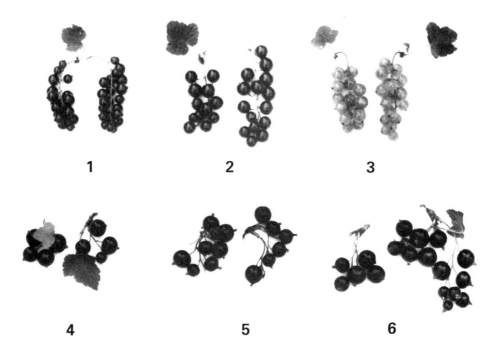

FIGURE 6-5   Red currant cultivars: 1, 'Fertodi hosszufurtu'; 2, 'Neo-szu-pajuscsajaszja'; 3, 'Wellington xxx'. Black currant cultivars: 4, 'Roodcnop'; 5, 'Silvergieter F59'; 6, 'Hidasi prolific'. (Note that 1 through 3 are taken at a different focal distance than 4 through 6.)

Most European gooseberries are grown in the USSR, the most popular cultivars being 'Ruszkij', 'Szemena', 'Kohoznig', and 'Rekord'. In England the cultivars 'Careless', 'Leveller', and 'Invicta' are common. Both countries grow their own cultivars exclusively. In other European countries the old well-established cultivars are grown, such as 'Weise Triumphbeere', 'Rote Triumphbeere', 'Weise Voltragenda', 'Lady Delamere', 'Honings Fruheste', and 'Triumphant'. In Hungary, the 'Green Giant' and its variant, the 'Pallagi Oriast', are grown.

In the United Kingdom, gooseberry cultivars are additionally categorized as for the "green berry trade" (underripe for processing or culinary use) or "ripe" (for fresh "dessert" use). The principal cultivar is 'Careless', which is pale green to milky white at its midseason maturity, and used for jam making, canning, and picking green. Two red-fruited cultivars, 'Lancashire Lad' (midseason) and 'Whinham's Industry' (midseason), are used either for the green berry or dessert trade. The early cultivars 'May Duke' and 'Keepsake' are gathered before 'Careless' for the green berry trade at favorable sites. 'Howard's Lancer' and 'Whitesmith' are high-flavored, vigorous, and productive clones which ripen later than 'Careless'. The very large, yellow-fruited dessert cultivar, 'Leveller', requires care in culture and is very sensitive to poor soil drainage (Ministry of Agriculture, Fisheries and Food, 1981). 'Crown Bob', 'Captivator', 'Invicta', and 'Golden Drop' have also become popular (Elfving et al., 1985).

Unfortunately, the larger-fruited and better-flavored European gooseberry cultivars are not as hardy and are more subject to disease than their American counterparts. Suitable American gooseberry cultivars are: reds—'Poorman', 'Ross', 'Silvia', 'Abundance', 'Welcome', 'Houghton', and 'Josselyn (Red Jacket)'; and greens, pinks, and yellows—'Oregon Champion', 'Captivator', 'Downing', and 'Pixwell'. Some of the European gooseberries that have performed well in North America are 'Clark' (red), 'Fredonia' (red), 'Glenashton' (red), 'Chautauqua' (green), and 'Industry' (red).

Site Preparation

It is advisable to use a cover crop the year before planting. Perennial weeds such as quack grass, Canada thistle, and bindweed should be destroyed the year prior to planting by the use of a nonresidual systemic herbicide. The site should be maintained so that no weeds are permitted to go to seed.

The soil should have a good supply of organic matter (more than 1%). Apply 4 to 5 bushels per 100 ft² (15 to 20 liters/m²) of well-rotted manure in late summer or fall before planting and work it thoroughly into the soil. Other organic materials (straw, hay, leaves, etc.) can be used in place of manure but should be well decomposed by planting time. If poorly decomposed material other than manure is used, additional nitrogen should be added to aid in decomposition. If manure is not available, the organic content of the soil may be increased by growing and turning under green manure crops prior to planting. The roots of all three species are sensitive to chlorine. Chlorine-containing fertilizers such as muriate of potash should be applied at least one month before planting. The plants grow best in loose soil; therefore, plowing to a depth of 18 in. (46 cm) is advisable. If possible, the soil should be tested and the pH range adjusted to 6.2 to 6.5.

Planting Systems

Planting can be done either in early spring or in the fall. Fall planting in Europe is advisable since the plants have more time for root growth. Planting holes can be small since the soil is usually well loosened before planting. Roots are usually pruned before planting. Planting depth should be the same as or slightly deeper than the plants were growing in the nursery. If planting older bushes, the lower branches should be covered up to two to three buds. This allows for the development of a large root system; and from these buds many new shoots will develop. The renewal of such bushes is thus assured. Those plants that are planted high develop into small bushes and age quickly. Plants should not be allowed to dry out during the planting procedure. Spring-planted stocks may be pruned back (headed and/or thinned just before or after planting); fall-planted stocks should not be pruned until spring.

Obtain plants as close to planting time as possible. If necessary, plants can be stored for several days by putting them in a plastic bag in a refrigerator, cold storage, or other cool place. If roots are very dry, they can be sprinkled with water before putting them in the plastic bag. Do not let roots sit in water or they may die. If plants must be kept longer than about 2 weeks prior to planting, dig a trench in well-drained soil, spread out the plants, set them in the trench, and cover the roots with soil. Water the soil if it is dry.

The actual planting system used will vary with the species and cultivar being grown, the purpose for which it is grown, and the type of planting stock used. Currants and gooseberries may be grown as bushes from either stooled plants with the point of branching at or below the ground, or plants on a short 'leg', where the canes or main stems originate from a single stem at about 6 to 12 in. (15 to 30 cm) above the soil line. The bushes may be close spaced at planting and treated as a hedge; or they may be pruned to a flat, thin fan or wing shape and trellised. These species can be grown as small trees such as tree roses, on a short trunk, either own-rooted or grafted to a suitable rootstock. Additionally, it is possible to use unrooted cuttings or 1- or 2-year-old rooted cuttings or layers as planting stocks. Plantings may be made also as single rows or multiple-row beds. Modern herbicides and mechanical harvesting make closer plant spacings more attractive and economical. Supplemental irrigation and chemical herbicides also encourage tree-form culture.

Nature of planting stock. Currants and American-type gooseberry varieties can be propagated from cuttings. Take stem cuttings in late fall from healthy wood produced that summer. Make cuttings 6 to 8 in. (15 to 20 cm) long for currants and 10 to 12 in. (25 to 30 cm) long for gooseberries with the bottom cut just below a bud, and the top cut about ½ in. (10 mm) above a bud. That fall, set cuttings 6 in. (15 cm) apart in well-drained soil in a nursery area. Remove the buds on the lower half of red currant and gooseberry cuttings to produce a bush with a leg. Plant them deep enough so that one or two buds extend out of the soil and cover them with straw. In the spring, the straw can be removed or left as mulch around the cuttings. Cuttings can also be taken in early spring before buds leaf out. Store the cuttings in a plastic bag in a refrigerator and plant them out in the nursery row as soon as possible. After one or two seasons' growth, rooted plants grown from the cuttings can be planted in their permanent location.

European-type gooseberries do not root well from hardwood stem cuttings made as described above. They can be propagated by bending down branches, still attached to the plants, and partly covering them with soil. It may be necessary to use pegs to hold down the branches. This type of propagation is called layering and is done in fall or spring. Roots form along the branches where they touch the soil. After a season's growth, the branches should be rooted well enough for digging. Often several plants can be obtained from one branch. In an even more productive method, separated rooted stem layers from stool beds are mounded up with soil around them to cover a portion of each stem during the growing season (mound or stool layering).

Planting distances. Plant gooseberries and red currants 3 to 4 ft (1.0 to 1.25 m) apart in rows. Black currants are more vigorous and should be spaced about 4 to 5 ft (1.25 to 1.5 m) apart for hand harvesting. Spacing of 2.5 to 3 ft (0.75 to 0.9 m) with 2-year-old plants intended for mechanical harvesting, and 1 ft (30 cm) for unrooted cuttings is common. Rows can be as close as 6.5 ft (2 m) apart, but 10 to 12 ft (3 to 3.5 m) is preferable for commercial plantings of black currants and 8 to 9 ft (2.4 to 2.7 m) for red currants and gooseberries.

Training Systems

Black and red currants and gooseberries can be grown in three ways: as freestanding bushes, as bushes trained to a continuous hedgerow (Fig. 6-6), or as tree-like shrubs branching from a monostem "trunk". Note that the bush form with the short monostem "leg" can be thought of as a compact variation of the small-tree type, since they are both initiated by partial disbudding of the initial propagation cutting.

All three production systems can be utilized with any of the cultivars, but the bush is the most popular in Europe and North America. The development of the bush is simple, and it requires the least investment and the least care. Its main advantage is that the bush is constantly renewed by crown sprouts. Propagation is by woody cuttings. The plants are usually planted 10 to 12 ft (3.1 to 3.7 m) between rows and 3 to 4 ft (0.9 to 1.2 m) within the row. Initial pruning consists of cutting back all canes to two to four buds. Yearly, four to five shoots are allowed to develop until 15 to 16 canes comprise the mature bush. Later the old canes are cut out as a renewal pruning.

The hedgerow is best suited for machine harvesting of currants. It differs from the bush in that the plants are planted closer within the row forcing the canes to bow out from the row. This eases the task of machine harvesting. Pruning is similar to that of a bush; however, the outer canes are often pruned by automatic hedging–pruning machines. Additional selective pruning is done with the help of pneumatic pruners.

The "winged" or "fan" bush is advantageous in home gardens. Plants trained to this system have a pleasant appearance and produce with relative abundance. Because the bush canopy is flat, light penetration into the canopy and air circulation is good; diseases are relatively limited; and the fruit colors well. With this system, rooted cuttings are planted along a trellis with three to five wires. The distance between the plants depends on whether single plants or three- to four-winged plants

FIGURE 6-6 Bush cultivation of currants.

are to be developed. The distance is 1.6 to 2.4 ft (49 to 73 cm) and 3 to 4 ft (0.9 to 1.2 m), respectively. Side branches are tied to the wires as they develop. Long branches should be removed, while the shorter strong branches should be pruned. Weak shoots should not be pruned. With this technique a narrow hedge or 'fruiting wall' can be developed.

The development of the small-tree form eases the tasks of soil cultivation, weed removal, and the use of mechanical harvesters. Tree bushes developed with a trunk must be grafted. Such a planting is started with 2.3-ft. (70-cm)-long whips. Buds usually need to be removed from the bottom half of the whip, including the below-ground portion. Usually, fall planting is advantageous and the planting can be done into black plastic mulch. The row and plant distances are 8.2 to 9.2 ft (2.5 to 2.8 m) and 2 to 3 ft (0.6 to 0.9 m), respectively. After bud break all shoots are removed with the exception of those needed for canopy development. Usually, the plants are grown between two wires, although some stronger-growing cultivars, if the trunk is not longer than 1 ½ ft (46 cm), can stand unsupported. Along the Atlantic coast of France where precipitation is sufficient, red and black currants are grown as short own-rooted trees and are harvested with grape harvesters. Grafting can be used for any of the species. A later section describes the development of a grafted gooseberry system in Hungary in warm dry climates.

Pruning

The purpose of pruning is to develop the producing surface rapidly and to distribute it evenly around the bush. This is usually accomplished by thinning, with no heading cuts being used (Fig. 6–7). One should aim for balanced growth; long vegetative and short generative shoot development should be about equal. Pruning should allow high light penetration into the canopy and should aid pest control and harvest.

Pruning can be done either in the summer or during the dormant season. Summer pruning usually weakens the bush, while winter pruning invigorates it. The degree of pruning depends on the strength of the growth. If growth was strong, pruning should be light; if growth was weak, pruning should be more severe. The size of the canopy on poor soils is smaller than on fertile soils. There is no reason to head back producing bushes.

Black currants produce the best fruit on 1-year-old wood. Strong 1-year-old shoots, and 2- or 3-year-old branches that have an abundance of strong 1-year-old wood, are the most productive. Red currants and gooseberries produce most of their fruit on spurs on 2- and 3-year-old wood. Try to keep a total of 10 to 12 canes per mature bush, with about half being 1-year-old canes. A few more canes may be kept if plant vigor is very good. Remove all canes that are more than 3 years old. Make pruning cuts close to the ground. Black currants are stronger, larger plants than red or white currants or gooseberries.

One method to achieve the previously stated pruning aims follows. After the first season of growth, remove from currants and gooseberries all but six to eight of the most vigorous branches. After the second season, retain four or five 1-year-old shoots and three or four 2-year-old branches. Following the third season, keep three or four branches each of 1-, 2-, and 3-year-old wood. When plants have finished the

FIGURE 6-7 Black currant bush before pruning (A), and after pruning (B).

fourth season, remove all 4-year-old canes; and repeat the renewal process annually as described above for the third season. After pruning, a healthy bush should have 9 to 12 branches (three to four each of 3-, 2-, and 1-year-old canes).

Irrigation and *pollination* needs of currants and gooseberries were considered in the botany section.

Nutrition, Soil Management, and Weed Control

Nutrient fertilization usually starts in the second year after planting with 4 oz (10 g) of nitrogen per plant. During the third year broadcasting of 50 lb/acre (56 kg/ha) of nitrogen on the entire area should be adequate. During the following years usually 90 lb/acre (100 kg/ha) of nitrogen is necessary. The time of application depends on the growth of the plants. If shoot growth needs to be encouraged, application time is early spring. If shoot growth is satisfactory, application of nitrogen should be done during the summer or fall, perhaps in a split application (one-third during spring,

Culture

two-thirds summer or fall). In producing plantations, good crops usually require 18 lb/acre (20 kg/ha) of phosphorus and 36 lb/acre (40 kg/ha) of potassium application during fall. In the United States, $1/4$ to $1/2$ lb (114 to 227 g) of 10-10-10 is typically applied per mature bush each spring.

Gooseberry and currant plantings may be clean cultivated and tilled during the first growing season between the rows and hoed within the rows. Alternatively, tillage may be continued during the growing seasons between rows with a cover crop sown each fall and disked in in the spring. A third alternative is the establishment of a permanent sod cover between the rows at the end of the first growing season. Placing a suitable organic mulch along the rows to control annual weeds is effective, particularly if perennial weeds that grow through the mulch are killed before planting. Some growers apply mulch over the entire planting on clean soil. Mulches are especially useful in garden sites and small plantings, where they aid in cooling soil temperatures and conserving moisture, in addition to helping control weeds. Mulches should be applied 2 to 4 in. (5 to 10 cm) deep and replenished annually. Fresh mulches bind nitrogen during degradation; and their use necessitates adding more nitrogenous fertilizer to the planting.

Large commercial plantings, particularly in Europe, have eliminated all tillage by relying on selective chemical herbicides. These bush fruits tolerate a wide range of herbicides.

Pest Control

A sample pest control program is shown in Table 6–5 to illustrate the timing and type of control measures necessary in commercial plantings.

Harvesting

Red currants and gooseberries range from 5 to 10 quarts per plant or from 2 to 5 tons/acre (4.5 to 11.2 MT/ha). Black currant yields are typically half this amount.

The harvest of currants and gooseberries is a labor-intensive process. It may take 65 to 70% of the total labor requirement of the crop. A person can harvest about 8.8 lb (4 kg) of black currants, 17.6 lb (8 kg) of red currants, and 22 lb (10 kg) of gooseberries per hour. Hand vibrators can speed up harvest. They are either pneumatic or electric vibrators with a V- or U-shaped fork or with a shaking comb.

The berries on a currant bush ripen over a 2-week period. Once a berry ripens, it can usually be left on the bush a week or more without dropping or becoming overmature. Therefore, most of the berries on a bush can be harvested in one or two pickings. With more frequent picking, there is a tendency to pick berries that are not fully ripened. Currants for jelly are picked slightly underripe, when the pectin content is highest. For juice, spiced, in jams, or for the market, they are picked fully ripe. The entire cluster is harvested carefully at the peduncle base when an occasional berry is still slightly green. Currants cannot be held moist, as they will mold easily, especially if berries are broken. Black currants are usually picked as individual berries. With red currants, whole clusters are picked and berries are stripped

TABLE 6-5 OUTLINE OF CROP PROTECTION PROGRAM FOR CURRANTS AND GOOSEBERRIES IN CENTRAL EUROPE

	TYPES OF DISEASES AND PESTS[a]				
STAGE	Miticide	Insecticide	Surface Diseases	Internal Diseases	*Botrytis* Protection[b]
At bud break	C	C	C	C	C
After bud break			C	S	S
Before bloom	C	C	S	S	S
After bloom		S	C	S	
Before harvest		C	C	C	
After harvest	C		C	C	
During July		S		C	
During August		C	C	C	

[a]C, contact material; S, systemic material.

[b]For protection against *Botrytis*, usually special fungicides are used, and for this reason this disease is handled in a separate column.

from the stems later. For making juice or jelly, the berries may be crushed without removing them from the fruit stems, since the products are strained.

Gooseberries are picked green at maximum size over a period of 4 to 6 weeks. For fresh market they are picked individually. For processing they are often raked or stripped from the bush with heavy gloves or a cranberry scoop. The leaves are later air separated from the fruit by a fan. Harvested fruit should be kept in the shade and cooled as soon as possible. Machine harvesting for processing by suction after ethephon treatment is possible if care is taken not to damage too much foliage, and if the bush is pruned so that a frame may be put under the branches to collect berries.

In large plantings continuous harvesters are used. The most popular continuous harvester is made in the United Kingdom by the Pattenden Co. (Fig. 6-8). There are several other harvesters, such as the Finish Jonas, the Hungarian RKB, the Danish Danpluk, the East German E880, and the Polish KP52-3.

Harvest is speeded by the use of ethephon sprays to enhance the development of the abscission layer. For the black and red currant, a spray of ethephon at 240 ppm active ingredient 10 to 12 days before harvest is recommended. When sprays are applied, the timing and capacity of harvesters needs to be considered. If berries are not harvested at the proper time, considerable drop may occur. Ethephon at 240 ppm usually does not affect the vegetative parts of the plant.

Gooseberry Grafted "Tree" Production

The possibility that gooseberries (*Ribes grossularia*) could be grafted onto *R. aureum* has been known since the seventeenth century. Originally, grafted trees (Figs. 6-9 and 6-10) were used only in home gardens as an ornament or curiosity. Grafts were made during the winter on hardwood stems, which was too difficult a technique to be applied on a large commercial scale. In Hungary, the commercial

Culture

FIGURE 6-8 Pattenden mechanical currant harvester.

use of gooseberry "trees" started around 1920 on sandy soils. Grafts were made with green-grafting methods, which increased planting stock considerably. Hungarian gooseberry tree production now ranges between 5000 and 8000 tons (4500 to 7300 MT), usually on small plots. The supporting nurseries produce as much as half a million grafts per year. However, many growers produce their own grafts for replacement of trees.

The major advantage of "tree gooseberries" is the height of the plant. It is difficult to protect gooseberries against powdery mildew if they are grown close to the ground. The grafted tree canopies are borne in a warmer air layer, where mildew infection is reduced. The taller canopy also protects somewhat against spring frosts. The trees produce more fruit and increase harvesting efficiency. The establishment of grafted tree plantations is more costly and requires some kind of trellis. Another disadvantage of grafted trees is that a complete renewal of the plantation is not possible; because the new shoots from the ground are those of the rootstock and not of the edible gooseberry. Consequently, a certain percentage of grafted trees need to be replanted, and aging plants replaced annually.

Ribes aureum clones 'Brecht' and 'Pallagi 2' are the most commonly used rootstocks. These were selected for strong growth and a relatively low rate of suckering. Both have good graft compatibility with most cultivars, are relatively disease and insect resistant, and long-lived. Rootstock clones are produced in stool beds planted 47 by 16 in. (120 by 40 cm). The plants are pruned to a "head"; the growing shoots are covered with wet soil and rooted. Shoots are grafted when they reach 32 to 40 in. (80 to 100 cm) in height. Green grafting (essentially a whip graft made during the growing season) is the best method for grafting gooseberry. In the past, preparation of the rootstock was done at the same time that grafting was performed. Today this is done 2 to 3 days earlier than grafting. The rootstock is cut back over a bud with a slanted cut. The top two to three leaves are removed from the

FIGURE 6-9 Own-rooted gooseberries trained to tree form.

FIGURE 6-10 Well-developed grafted "tree" gooseberry.

remaining shoot. The second bud from the top is removed (but not the top bud); and a small PVC tube $3/16$ in. in diameter and $1/2$ in. in length (4 to 6 mm by 15 to 20 mm) is pulled over the shoot. Within 2 to 3 days the wounds are dry and the top bud starts to swell and will later start to grow. This is the preferred time to graft.

Successful grafting requires that both the rootstock and the scion are un-differentiated. At the point of the graft, the woody portion of the shoots should not be visible and the shoots should not be too young. Young shoots lose water too quickly and often dry out before the grafts heal. Scions are 2 to 4 in. (5 to 10 cm) long and should come from the top portion of the mother trees. Most of the leaves of the scion are removed; and the remaining leaves are cut back to reduce water loss. On top of the rootstock parallel to the remaining top bud a vertical ½ in. (10- to 15-mm)-long cut is made with a sharp knife. The bottom of the scion is cut as a wedge about ½ in. (10 mm) long with one bud in the middle. The scion is placed into the split rootstock, pushed down to the bottom of the split, and the PVC tube is pulled up to fasten the pieces together. The rootstock and scion should be of the same thickness. If a PVC tube is not available, grafting tape can be used.

A variation of green grafting is the insertion of semiwoody (semihardwood) scions into the green rootstock. In this case the scion is a short, thick, woody, 2- to 4-in. (5- to 10-cm)-long shoot tip with a terminal bud, or a second-year-old side branch with two to three buds, and the leaves removed. Nurseries that perform a large number of grafts prefer to use this method because the percentage of 'takes' with woody scions is better.

The grafted rootstock is removed from the stool bed during the fall, and immediately planted in a nursery in double rows 8 in. (20 cm) apart and 4 ft (120 cm) between double rows. Plants require only a 4- to 6-in. (10- to 15-cm) distance within the row. Irrigation of the nursery is necessary. After bud break, during the spring, the developing shoots on the rootstock must be removed when they are about ½ to ¾ in. (1 to 2 cm) long. Shoots should be removed only partially beginning on the top; and removal should be continued when the lower buds develop. Removal of all the buds at once weakens the roots; and the root system will develop very slowly. Removing the buds with a knife is better than rubbing them out. After cutting with a knife, fewer side shoots develop and a better stem can develop. When the buds are removed, the ties from the graft can be removed in the same operation. The grafted trees are grown in the nursery until fall.

Since the gooseberry is one of the earliest plants to start growing in the spring, the time for spring planting is very short. It is more convenient to plant during the fall. Planting distance for gooseberry trees is usually 63 to 79 in. (160 to 200 cm) between rows and 32 to 39 in. (80 to 100 cm) within the row in Europe. Broken roots are usually cut back along with the longer roots, which should be shortened for easy planting. Plants with large roots are often damaged by fungi and dehydrate easier.

It is convenient to prune the canopy of the planting material before planting. Side branches should have a distance of 1.5 to 2 in. (4 to 5 cm) between them. Usually, three side branches are optimal. The side branches should be headed back as far as possible from the trunk. This assures that they branch as far as possible from the center.

Tall gooseberry trees about 3 ft (80 to 100 cm) in height usually cannot stand without support. There are several methods of supporting them. A one-wire trellis with a number 11 (2.5 to 3.5 mm) wire is the most convenient. The wire is above the plants and the trees are attached to the wire with a 3- to 6-in. (10- to 15-cm)-long string. It is convenient to make the rows not more than 300 ft long (100 m). This requires three 4 by 4 in. (10 by 10 cm) poles (one on each end and one in the middle). It also requires that after every 8 to 10 trees a smaller support be used. The wire is usually attached to the top of the poles. The poles should not be taller than the wire because they interfere with the various cultivation techniques. The trees are fastened with various types of string or fasteners which are hooked on the tree loosely and onto the wire tightly. This assures that the trees remain upright. The trunk can support the weight of the crop. The support is only needed to assure vertical tree positioning. The cultivation of the tree planting is similar to that of the bush planting. The machinery used in such plantings is an overrow straddle tractor.

Acknowledgment

The editors gratefully acknowledge the contribution of Miklos Faust, who translated much of this chapter from the original Hungarian to English.

REFERENCES

BAILEY, L. H. 1976. Hortus third. Macmillan, New York.

BALDINI, E., AND P. L. PISANI. 1961. Research on floral biology and fruit set of black currant. Riv. Ortofloro frutticoltura Ital.

DARROW, G. M., AND S. B. DETWILER. 1940. Currants and gooseberries. U.S. Dep. Agric. Farmers Bull. 1398.

DOBOS, L. 1960. Production of gooseberries in Debrecen. Mezogazdasagi Kiado, Budapest, Hungary.

ELFVING, D. C., A. DALE, K. H. FISHER, N. MILES, AND G. TEHRANI. 1985. Fruit cultivars. Ont. Minist. Agric. Food, Publ. 430.

FERNQUIST, I. B. 1961. Flower biology of red currant. Akad. Tidskr. 100. (Ref. P1 Breed Abst., 31.)

GAUCHER, G. R. 1896. Handbook of fruit production. Paul Parey, Berlin.

HARMAT, L., ET AL. 1969–1973. Production of berry crops. Mezogazdasagi Kiado, Budapest, Hungary.

HRICZOVSKY, J., ET AL. 1969. Bogyosgyumolcsuek termesztese es felhasznalasa. (Production and utilization of berry crops.) Priroda, Bratislava, Czechoslovakia.

JEPSON, W. L. 1951. Saxifragaceae. Saxifrage family. p. 454–475. In W. L. Jepson. Manual of the flowering plants of California. University of California Press, Berkeley.

LAWRENCE, G. H. M. 1955. An introduction to plant taxonomy. Macmillan, New York.

MAURER, L. 1913. Maurer's stachelbeerbuch. Stuttgart, West Germany.

MILES, N. W. 1983. Currants and gooseberries. Ont. Minist. Agric. Food Agdex 236/12.

MINISTRY OF AGRICULTURE, FISHERIES AND FOOD. 1981. Bush fruits. 2nd impression. Her Majesty's Stationery Office, London.

NYEKI, J., ET AL. 1980. The biology of flowering and fertility of fruit cultivars. Mezogazdasagi Kiado, Budapest, Hungary.

PAVLOVA, M. A. 1962. Breeding currants for winter hardiness in the USSR. Proc. 14th Int. Hortic. Congr. Brussels 1:178.

PORPACZY, A. 1974. Improvement of yield of black currants with crossbreeding. Proc. 14th Int. Hortic. Congr. Warsaw 1:336.

SORGE, P. 1984. Beerenobstsorten. (Berry cultivars.) Neumann, Leipzig, East Germany.

STANG, E. J., J. HOVELAND, D. L. MAHR, AND D. M. BOONE. 1982. Growing currants, gooseberries and elderberries in Wisconsin. Univ. Wisconsin Bull. A1960.

TAMAS, P., AND A. PORPACZY, JR. 1967. Some physiological and breeding problems in the fertilization of *Ribes*. Zuchter 37:32.

TERPO, A. 1974. Basic principles of fruit growing. In Gyuro (ed.). Mezogazdasagi Kiado, Budapest, Hungary.

TURNER, D., AND K. MUIR. 1985. The handbook of soft fruit growing. Longwood, Wolfeboro, N.H.

WRIGHT, C. J. 1985. Ribes. In A. H. Halevy (ed.). CRC handbook of flowering. CRC Press, Boca Raton, Fla.

SUGGESTED READING

ANON. 1977. Growing currants and gooseberries. Mich. Ext. Bull. E-856, SF-8.

BERGER, A. 1924. A taxonomic review of currants and gooseberries. New York State Agric. Exp. Stn. Tech. Bull. 109.

DARROW, G. M., AND S. B. DETWILER. 1940. Currants and gooseberries: their culture and relation to white pine blister rust. U.S. Dep. Agric. Farmers' Bull. 1398.

GARDNER, R., ET AL. 1981. Bush fruits. Minist. Agric. Fish. Food Ref. Book. Her Majesty's Stationery Office, London.

KEEP, E. 1975. Currants and gooseberries, p. 197–268. In J. Janick and J. N. Moore (eds.). Advances in fruit breeding. Purdue University Press, West Lafayette, Ind.

KEEP, E. 1984. Breeding *Rubus* and *Ribes* at East Malling. Sci. Hortic. 35:54–71.

KEMP, I. F., AND F. R. BROWN. 1975. Mechanical harvesting of black currants. National Institute of Agricultural Engineering, Silsoe, England. ARC Res. Rev. 1:17–32.

MARTIN, L. W., R. GARREN, AND D. L. RASMUSSEN. 1972. Gooseberry and currant culture. Oreg. Ext. Circ. 766.

MILES, N. W. 1983. Currants and gooseberries. Ont. Minist. Agric. Food Agdex 236/12.

NES, A., AND R. J. CLARK. 1980. A computer-based bibliography of the black currant literature. Hortic. Res. 20:83–85.

REDALEN, G. 1986. Fourth international *Rubus* and *Ribes* symposium. Acta Hortic. 183.

SHOEMAKER, J. S. 1978. Currants and gooseberries. p. 251–260. In J. S. Shoemaker. Small fruit culture. AVI, Westport, Conn.

STANG, E. J., J. HOVELAND, D. L. MAHR, AND D. M. BOONE. 1982. Growing currants, gooseberries and elderberries in Wisconsin. Univ. Wisconsin Bull. A1960.

WRIGHT, C. J. 1985. Ribes. In A. H. Halevy (ed.). CRC handbook of flowering. CRC Press, Boca Raton, Fla.

Chapter 7

Blueberry Management

P. ECK
R. E. GOUGH
I. V. HALL
J. M. SPIERS

CROP ORIGINS

Although considerable confusion exists over the proper taxonomic classification of the blueberry, most authorities now consider it as belonging to the Vacciniaceae, a subfamily of the Ericaceae (Robinson and Fernald, 1908; Galletta, 1975). Camp (1942) has further divided this subfamily into two tribes, the monogeneric Gaylussacieae (huckle-berries), and the Vaccinieae (whortleberries, bilberries, cranberries, and blueberries). The genus *Vaccinium* belongs to the latter tribe and is further divided into the subgenera *Batodendron, Euvaccinium, Oxycoccus,* and *Cyanococcus* (Fernald, 1970). The true blueberries belong to the ancient genus *Vaccinium,* subgenus *Cyanococcus.* According to Camp (1942), some segments of this genus had become highly differentiated prior to the Cretaceous period. The temperate forms of the genus are thought to have been derived from tropical forms, becoming firmly established predominantly in eastern North America after the Pleistocene glaciations (Camp, 1942; Eck, 1966). Plants of this genus often hybridize freely in the wild and are excellent colonizers, quickly moving into disturbed areas such as burned-over land or abandoned fields. They are widely disseminated through seeds dropped by wild animals (Eaton, 1957).

Although species ranging in height from 5 to 23 ft (1.5 to 7 m) are classified as 'highbush', the cultivated highbush blueberry has been developed primarily from two species, *V. corymbosum* L. and *V. australe* Small, although several other species have also been utilized in breeding and selection programs. Plants of these species are naturally distributed in sunny, acidic, swampy areas in the eastern coast of North America from Nova Scotia and southern Quebec west to Wisconsin and south to extreme northern Florida and southeastern Alabama (Fernald, 1970). Other localized areas of distribution include extreme northwestern Pennsylvania, northern Ohio and Indiana, and southern Michigan (Eck, 1966). Southern populations are primarily composed of *V. australe* Small, while the northern population is predominantly *V. corymbosum* L. The latter species, however, may intermingle with others, primarily *V. lamarckii* and *V. brittonii,* near its northern limits, and *V. arkansanum, simulatum, australe,* and *marianum* near its southern. Intermediate forms among these species have been noted (Eck, 1966).

The term 'lowbush blueberry' includes several species, among them *V. myrtilloides* Michaux, which ranges from Vancouver Island east to Labrador and south to New York, Indiana, and Pennsylvania. This is the most abundant species found in fields recently established from wood lots (Barker et al., 1964). *V. angustifolium Aiton,* ranging from parts of southern Canada, south through New England, eastern New York, and into eastern West Virginia, is the 'lowbush' of greatest commercial importance in the United States and is the most abundant species found in older Canadian fields (Barker et al., 1964). *V. lamarckii* Camp. and *V. brittonii* Porter have a range similar to that of *V. angustifolium* but are somewhat less important commercially. Aalders and Hall (1961) consider *V. lamarckii* within the *angustifolium* species.

The rabbiteye blueberry (*V. ashei* Reade), which can attain heights of approximately 33 ft (10 m), ranges throughout most of northern Florida, southern Alabama, and Georgia (Darrow et al., 1944). This species is often considered by plant breeders to offer the greatest possibilities for improvement because of its tolerance to a relatively wide soil pH range and high temperatures, its inherent drought resistance, and its short chilling requirement. Several other relatively minor *Vaccinium* species are found from Canada to Florida and often contribute to local trade and/or to breeding programs.

Selection and Improvement

No doubt the selection and transplanting of good wild bushes of the highbush blueberry have been occurring for hundreds of years. One of the oldest transplantings for which we have records is that on the grounds of the Smithsonian Institution. Bushes of *V. atrococcum* there date from the mid-nineteenth century (Coville, 1910). Early work on blueberry culture was begun at experiment stations in Maine,

Rhode Island, New York, and Michigan near the end of the nineteenth century. Card (1903) initiated the Rhode Island program in 1898, selecting the best wild bushes for study of transplantability and propagation techniques. The demand and wholesale price for this fruit on the Boston market, and the tremendous potential for crop improvement the species offered attracted the attention of Frederick V. Coville, a botanist with the Bureau of Plant Industry of the U.S. Department of Agriculture. In the autumn of 1906 he began cultural experiments on the genus and in 1908 embarked on a program of selecting and propagation bushes bearing large berries for use in his breeding program (Coville, 1910). His first selection of a highbush type was 'Brooks', from New Hampshire (1908). In 1909 and 1910, Coville attempted to self-pollinate 'Brooks' but met with little success. In 1911 he crossed 'Brooks' with 'Russell', a lowbush selection made in 1909. This was the first reported successful attempt at controlled crossing of the blueberry (Moore, 1966). Elizabeth White of Whitesbog, New Jersey, becoming interested in Coville's work, furnished both land for growing the trial seedlings and the aid of her blueberry picking crew, whom she instructed to mark wild bushes bearing the largest fruit. The combined efforts of White and Coville resulted in the selection of eight cultivars from the wild. Intercrosses among several of these native selections resulted in the first improved cultivars—'Pioneer', 'Katharine', and 'Cabot', introduced in 1920. These, in addition to the wild selection 'Rubel', formed the basis for the new blueberry industry.

At the time of Coville's death in 1937, nearly 70,000 hybrid seedlings had been fruited and 15 cultivars released, some of which were third-generation hybrids. During the period 1939 to 1952, an additional 15 cultivars originating from stock left by Coville were released. Many cultivars presently being planted bear fruit over five times larger than their wild progenitors and are the result of breeding efforts by Coville's successors, notably George M. Darrow, D. H. Scott, A. D. Draper, and their associates. More than 45 improved cultivars had been named as of 1975 (Galletta, 1975).

Perhaps the first commercial collection of rabbiteye blueberry was made by M. A. Sapp in Florida in 1893. He selected and transplanted wild plants, but eventually failed in his business because of competition from the highbush trade.

One of the first experimental collections of wild rabbiteye bushes selected from Florida and Georgia was established at the Georgia Coastal Plain Experiment Station in Tifton in 1925. From this collection, a joint breeding program was initiated between the University of Georgia and the U.S. Department of Agriculture in 1940. North Carolina, Florida, Mississippi, and Texas are also involved in rabbiteye breeding programs. Breeding efforts for this species have resulted in scores of newer cultivars with much improved fruit size, color, and texture compared to native selections (Scott and Moore, 1961).

This truly 'American' fruit domesticated entirely in the twentieth century has developed a world market, and programs for its improvement have been initiated in the Netherlands, Germany, Canada, Ireland, Italy, Finland, Yugoslavia, England, Denmark, and Scotland, some as early as 1923 (Galletta, 1975). From the first shipment of fruit of cultivated highbush blueberry from New Jersey in 1916, the present world highbush industry is worth in excess of $100 million.

Genetic Improvement

According to Longley (1927), the genus *Vaccinium* has a basic genome of 12. Since no fundamental sterility barriers exist between homoploid *Vaccinium* species, many polyploids have arisen naturally (Coville, 1927; Newcomer, 1941). These polyploids, particularly tetraploids ($2n = 48$), are thought to be responsible for the wide range of adaptation of the genus (Newcomer, 1941). Both parent highbush species *V. corymbosum* L. and *V. australe* Small are natural tetraploids. Species hybridization at the tetraploid level, including germplasm from the tetraploid lowbush blueberry *V. angustifolium,* has provided the richly diverse seedling highbush blueberry populations, from which new cultivars and parent clones for continued breeding have been selected.

There has been a greater breeding effort in the highbush blueberry than in any other *Vaccinium* species (Draper and Scott, 1971). The objectives proposed in initial breeding programs have, for the most part, been realized. Large, firm light blue fruit having small fruit pedical scars have been developed. Major objectives of breeding work in the northern United States involve the development of cultivars with greater winter hardiness, drought and disease resistance, and adaptation to mechanical harvesting. Objectives in the mid-south states include development of cultivars that ripen earlier and have greater resistance to fungus diseases and mites.

Kender (1966) outlined the objectives for a lowbush breeding program, which included the development of larger, better-flavored, lighter-colored fruit that ripen uniformly. Breeders should also strive to achieve higher-yielding, late-blooming, self-fruitful plants with a higher degree of disease resistance and more vigorous rhizome growth. (See the section on the culture of the lowbush blueberry for progress to date.) Several newer cultivars are particularly adapted to the north. Among them are 'Bluehaven', 'Northland', 'Northsky', and 'Northblue', all of which have both highbush and lowbush parentage.

Broadening early blueberry improvement hybridization programs, a series of low-chilling, upland-adapted tetraploid species hybrids have recently been introduced by Draper and colleagues. *Vaccinium darrowi* and *V. corymbosum* parentage is prominent in these hybrids, which possess flavors and textures superior to those of the parent species. These hybrids should extend blueberry culture into new areas, particularly since they ripen earlier than rabbiteye blueberry clones.

While rabbiteye blueberry improvement to date has been confined to intra-varietal crosses within the hexaploid *V. ashei* species, hybridizations between *V. ashei* × *V. corymbosum* are considered of value in promoting earlier ripening of larger fruit on bushes adapted to southern and/or mineral soil conditions. Unfortunately, such crosses result in self-sterile pentaploids (Darrow et al., 1954). This problem may be alleviated somewhat, however, by crossing the rabbiteye with diploids, resulting in tetraploids compatible with the highbush (Moore et al., 1964). Recent work by Vorsa (1987) has demonstrated that aneuploid individuals from *V. ashei-corymbosum* crosses are viable, possess varying levels of fertility, and can be used as parents in either direction to effect direct transfer of traits between these polyploid species.

The 'highbush' blueberry is a term applied to those North American species that range in height from 5 to 23 ft (1.5 to 7 m), while the term 'lowbush" applies to those species less than 3 ft (1 m) in height. The 'half-high' category refers to bushes intermediate in height between highbush and lowbush. The rabbiteye, attaining heights of 5 to 19 ft (1.5 to 6 m), can be considered as a highbush type (Eck, 1966).

The cultivated highbush blueberry has a root system composed of primarily fine, thread-like roots less than 0.04 in. (1 mm) in diameter (Gough, 1980), and often only 0.2 to 0.3 in (50 to 75 mm) in diameter. The roots begin growth sometime before bloom and can, under favorable conditions, grow about 0.04 in. (1 mm) per day (Coville, 1910). They are devoid of root hairs but do possess an endotrophic mycorhizza (Coville, 1910) located exterior to the epidermal cells (Doak, 1928).

Most of the roots are distributed within the dripline of the bush, but some may extend to distances of up to 6 ft (180 cm) from the crown and to depths of up to 32 in. (81 cm). Absolute distribution is dependent on plant age and climatic and edaphic conditions (Gough, 1980).

Mahlstede and Watson (1952), studying the rooting of hardwood cuttings of the highbush, reported that roots often originated immediately adjacent to a xylem ray in the cambium/phloem region. Cells that will become root initials have a large, central nucleus and a small vacuole prior to differentiation. The young rootlets contain three to five rows of epidermal cells, are devoid of hyphae, and are transparent. Anatomy of an older root is similar to that of a stem.

The major portion of the root system of the lowbush blueberry is adventitious, originating from rhizomatous activity (Mahlstede and Watson, 1952). In fact, it has been estimated that up to 85% of the stem tissue in these species is rhizomatous. The rhizomes are usually 0.12 to 0.18 in. (3 to 6 mm) in diameter, sympodial in their habit of growth, and primarily occur 1/4 to 1 in. (6 to 25 mm) below the soil surface. In moderately heavy soil, they may grow about 2 to 3 in. (5 to 7.5 cm) per year, or up to 15 in. (37 cm) per year with no competition (Hall et al., 1975). Young rhizomes are pink in color, with brown scale leaves borne near their distal end, while older ones are dark brown and suberized (Eck, 1966).

The yearly growth cycle may be thought of as beginning with shoot emergence in the spring. In the highbush blueberry, most new shoots arise from vegetative buds formed the previous season. However, dormant buds formed several seasons prior may give rise to new shoots near the base of older canes. This is particularly true if those canes have received a severe pruning. In some cases, new shoots may also arise from roots (Gough, unpublished data). Vegetative bud break usually occurs a week or two prior to bloom (Gough et al., 1978a).

Most shoots of the lowbush blueberry develop from dormant buds on the rhizomes (Hall and Aalders, 1975). Trevett (1956) reported that most new shoots appear to arise from buds near the rhizome tip, although they may originate along the entire length of the rhizome. Development of new shoots apparently occurs exclusively in those rhizomes fairly close to the surface. In some cases, a rhizome may actually emerge from the soil and directly become a shoot.

Growth of individual shoots of the blueberry is sympodial (zigzag or irregular form) and episodic, being accompanied by a varying number of apical abortions (Gough and Shutak, 1978; Bell, 1950). Each abortion terminates a 'flush' of growth. In the highbush blueberry, the number of flushes is apparently cultivar and vigor dependent, with cultivars ripening their fruit early in the season having more flushes than those ripening fruit later (Gough et al., 1976b). Bell (1950), working with *V. angustifolium* Ait. var. *laevifolium,* reported only a single apical abortion for that species. Seasonal shoot growth seems to have two distinct peaks, one in June, about 2 weeks after the first peak of root growth, and the second in August, about 2 weeks before the second peak in root growth (Abbott and Gough, 1987a).

Several authors, including Gough et al. (1976a), Bailey and French (1946), Clark (1941), and Clark and Gilbert (1942), have used leaf characteristics as aids in cultivar identification. Microscopic axillary bud primordia appear during the expansion of vegetative buds in the spring and become readily visible when young shoots are a few millimeters in length (Gough and Shutak, 1978). The buds continue to increase in size but remain vegetative until termination of the final growth flush. At this time, the uppermost bud on a highbush blueberry shoot will begin to swell noticeably and the bud scales will begin to develop an intense red coloration. Differentiation of the reproductive apex occurs at approximately this time (in Rhode Island, about the end of July). Bell (1950), working with a lowbush species, reported development of a flowering branch primordium in the axil of the penultimate leaf coincident with apical abortion and necrosis of the distal portion of the shoot axis (early June).

Flower bud differentiation occurs in the basipetal fashion, proceeding from the uppermost bud on a shoot. The number of flower buds that may develop on a highbush blueberry shoot is apparently related to shoot thickness (Gough et al., 1976b), cultivar (Darrow and Moore, 1966), and the influence of various growth regulators (Shutak, 1968). Gough et al. (1978b) reported as many as 15 to 20 flower buds on some shoots, although most had only five to seven. A similar number has been reported for the lowbush (Aalders and Hall, 1964).

Flower buds usually form singly at the upper nodes of the current year's shoots, but Shutak (1968) reported that occasionally more than one bud occurred at some nodes on highbush blueberry. Gough and Shutak (1978) concluded that the occurrence of multiple flower buds appeared independent of the cultivar ripening season but dependent on shoot vigor (i.e., thicker shoots had a greater incidence of multiple flower buds than thinner shoots). These buds differentiate and bloom at approximately the same time as single flower buds.

Flower bud differentiation proceeds basipetally along the shoot axis. By mid-autumn, all flower buds are usually clearly distinguishable, having assumed a nearly spherical shape and a size two to three times that of a vegetative bud.

In highbush blueberry, differentiation of individual florets within a bud proceeds acropetally while the peduncle apex is continuing to initiate new axillary meristems (Gough et al., 1978b). In lowbush blueberry, Bell (1950) reported simultaneous differentiation of proximal floret primordia after abortion of the peduncle apex. This was then followed by differentiation of distal primordia.

Flattening of proximal meristems and appearance of sepal primordia is followed by centripetal differentiation of additional floral parts. Nearly all flower parts were visible on highbush blueberry in Rhode Island by the beginning of October, and by November, petals completely enclosed the floret and ovular lobes were apparent. Pedicels also become apparent at this time. Cellular activity occurred into early December, then apparently ceased. No further activity was noted until the beginning of bud swell in March. Pollen grains appeared by mid-April, approximately 3 weeks prior to bloom (Gough and Shutak, 1978).

Normally, the highbush blueberry will bloom after undergoing approximately 800 hours of chilling below 45°F (7.2°C) (Darrow, 1942). It may, however, be forced to bloom under proper conditions immediately after fruiting, provided that it has not already entered rest. In fact, the author has maintained blueberry bushes in the greenhouse and observed them in flower, fruit, and full leaf all at once. The rabbiteye blueberry may require as little as 25 hours below 45°F (7.2°C) to break rest (Darrow, 1942).

The epigynous blueberry flower is born on a raceme and is generally urn-shaped and usually inverted. The five-lobed calyx is adnate to the ovary, glaucous, and glabrous. Petals usually number five and are fused into a five-lobed corolla which is generally white but may have some pink coloration along the ribs (Eck, 1966; Gough et al., 1976a). They reach lengths of ¼ to ½ in. (6 to 12 mm) and breadths of ³/₁₆ to ¼ in. (4 to 6 mm) at their widest portion. The stamens number 8 or 10, and correspond to the four or five corolla lobes. Each bears a bi-awned anther attached to a flattened, pubescent filament. Anther dehiscence is terminal via apical pores (Mathews and Knox, 1926).

In a study of blooming patterns, Shutak et al. (1956) reported that blossoms on thin wood [less than 0.1 in. (0.25 cm) in diameter] normally opened before those on thick wood [greater than 0.2 in. (0.50 cm) in diameter]. Within each flower cluster, blossoms at the base open first and those at the tip last; that is, bloom pattern within the cluster parallels the pattern of floret differentiation (Hindle et al., 1957). In addition, cluster opening along the shoot proceeds basipetally, that is, in the same order as flower bud differentiation. Later ripening cultivars often bloom later than early ripening ones, but this sequence is highly variable, depending on temperature (Gough, unpublished data).

Gough (1983a), examining the effect of pruning time on bloom, reported that plants which were not pruned generally reached full bloom before pruned plants. Plants pruned early, in September, reach full bloom last. In general, the earlier plants were pruned, the later they bloomed. This delay was as much as 5 days in some cases.

The period of bloom often occupies about a week, depending upon temperature. Stigma receptivity may last about a week (Merrill, 1936), although fruit set is not likely if pollination has not occurred within 3 days after flower opening (Chandler and Mason, 1935). This may be due to the progressive degeneration of the embryo sac after bloom. Eaton and Jamont (1966) reported that about 33% of the embryo sacs in the cultivar 'Rancocas' had degenerated within 3 days after anthesis. About a week after pollination, fertilization usually occurs, followed immediately by two cellular divisions of the endosperm.

The ovary begins enlargement soon after fertilization and will continue until ripe, a period of time ranging from approximately 1½ to 2½ months, depending on location, season, and cultivar. Shutak et al. (1980) and others have reported that blueberry fruit enlargement follows a double sigmoid growth curve. In stage I the fruit undergoes rapid pericarp development with cell division and accelerated endosperm growth. Stage II is characterized by rapid endosperm and embryo development, but little or no growth of the mesocarp. In stage III there is a final, rapid mesocarp growth due to cell enlargement. On a volume basis, the first one-third of total berry volume takes about 60% of the total ripening period, the second one-third about 30% of the time, and the last one-third about 10% of the total time.

Fruit Size

Berry size has been correlated with shoot vigor; that is, more vigorous shoots generally produce larger berries. In addition, earlier-ripening fruit of a particular cultivar are often larger than those that ripen later, and proximal berries within a cluster are often, but not always, larger than distal fruit. Finally, seed number is positively correlated with fruit size, there being about three times more seeds in large than in small fruit of a given cultivar.

Fruit Anatomy

During fruit growth, brachysclereids (stone cells) develop within the berry (Gough, unpublished data). Their presence is apparently dependent on location within the fruit and on cultivar.

As the berry enlarges, it passes through various color grades due to the increasing presence of anthocyanin pigments in the epidermal and hypodermal layers (Ballinger et al., 1970, 1972). These are often arbitrarily separated into several stages for descriptive purposes. One such separation is outlined in Table 7–1 and will be referred to in future descriptive points.

Ripening

Soluble solids. A berry is generally considered to initiate ripening at the first sign of red coloration. In the stages outlined above, this would be at about the green-pink stage of development. During ripening, which is highly temperature

TABLE 7-1 STAGES IN BERRY DEVELOPMENT

STAGE	DESCRIPTION
Immature green	Berry hard, dark green over 100% of fruit surface
Mature green	Berry softer, light green over 100% of fruit surface
Green-pink	Primarily light green, some pink showing at calyx end
Blue-pink	Primarily blue, some pink showing at stem end
Blue	Nearly completely blue, very little pink showing immediately around the scar
Ripe	100% blue coloration

dependent, the soluble solids (sugar) content increases. In general, depending on the cultivar and the cultural and environmental conditions, the soluble solids content of the blueberry will range from 7% in a green fruit to about 15% in a ripe fruit. Within cultivars, earlier ripening fruit tend to have a greater soluble solids content than those that ripen later (Shutak et al., 1980). Berries will continue to ripen after harvest, and soluble solids will increase correspondingly. For example, 'Lateblue' berries harvested at the 'Blue' stage averaged 11.7% soluble solids, but after 5 days at room temperature averaged 13.4%. However, a berry ripened off the bush will never achieve the soluble solids content of one that ripens on the bush. Where practical, allow berries to ripen fully on the bush, delaying harvest for several days after they turn blue. Respiration rate as well as transpiration rate has been positively linked with keeping quality (Shutak et al., 1980).

Abscission. Separation of the berry from the bush is effected by the formation of an abscission zone between the pedicel and the proximal end of the fruit (Gough and Litke, 1980). No specific separation layer(s) forms. Initial loss of tissue integrity occurs in the berry tissue in the area between the divergent vascular bundles entering from the pedicel. This coincides with the green-pink stage of berry ripening. Further tissue breakdown occurs in a crescent-shaped area between the vascular tissue and the berry epidermis. Separation of the fruit occurs apparently by mechanical rupture of the epidermis and the vascular bundles, since these tissues are apparently not included in the disintegration process. Another abscission zone apparently forms between the pedicel and the peduncle but has yet to be described. Characteristics of this zone would probably explain the reasons for 'stemminess' (separation of the berry with the attached pedicel) in some harvest situations.

HIGHBUSH BLUEBERRY CULTURE

The highbush blueberry industry in North America is concentrated in the six states of Michigan, New Jersey, North Carolina, Arkansas, Washington, and Oregon, and in British Columbia, Canada. Commercial plantings have also been started in Europe, and in New Zealand and Australia in the southern hemisphere. About 42,000 acres (17,000 ha) are harvested annually in North America for either the fresh market or for processing. Michigan leads in production with 50 million pounds (22,700 metric tons) per year, followed by New Jersey with 40 million pounds (18,000 metric tons), Washington and Oregon with 10.8 million pounds (4900 metric tons), North Carolina with 5.5 million pounds (2500 metric tons), and Arkansas with 1.1 million pounds (500 metric tons).

British Columbia produces 13 million pounds (5900 metric tons) annually on 3000 acres (1200 ha). In recent years, the average annual production for all the commercial cultivated blueberry areas has been approximately 120 million pounds (54,000 metric tons) for a farm gate value of $104 million (Eck, 1988).

Figure 7–1 shows the highbush blueberry morphology.

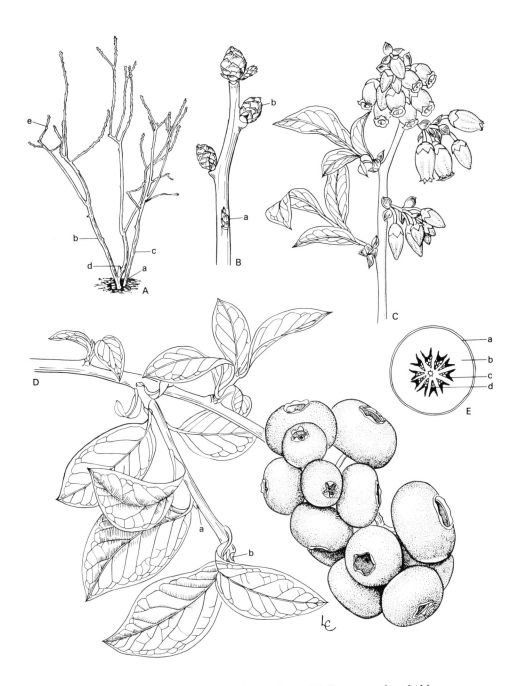

FIGURE 7-1 Highbush blueberry morphology. (A) Dormant plant habit: a, crown area; b, major cane; c, renewal canes or whips; d, pruning cut; e, lateral shoot (current season) bearing both flower and vegetative buds. (B) Dormant lateral shoot: a, vegetative bud; b, flower bud. (C) Lateral shoot in flower. (D) Fruiting branch: a, aborted apical shoot tip; b, axillary bud. (E) Berry cross section: a, epidermis; b, pulp; c, locule; d, placenta and seeds.

Cultivated Types

The original blueberry varieties used in the industry were selections from the wild propagated asexually. These included the varieties 'Rubel', 'Sooy', 'Grover', 'Chatsworth', 'Brooks', 'Harding', 'Sam', 'Russell', 'Adams', and 'Carter'. Today only 'Rubel' remains a commercially important variety in Michigan. In 1920 the first improved cultivars 'Pioneer', 'Cabot', and 'Katharine' were introduced from the USDA breeding program of F. V. Coville. These improved cultivars were larger in size, lighter in color, and had a smaller stem scar and improved flavor. During the period from 1925 until his death in 1937, Coville introduced another group of noteworthy cultivars, including 'Concord', 'June', 'Jersey', 'Rancocas', 'Scammell', 'Stanley', 'Weymouth', and 'Dixi'. These cultivars can still be found in New Jersey and Michigan fields. The 'Jersey' cultivar represents a significant segment of the industry in Michigan, as does the 'Weymouth' cultivar in New Jersey.

From 1937 until 1957, Coville's work was continued by G. M. Darrow of the USDA. Darrow introduced just prior to World War II the 'Atlantic', 'Burlington', and 'Pemberton' cultivars. 'Burlington' is still found in commercial plantings which are machine harvested because the fruit remains ripe on the bush in excellent condition, thus enabling the harvesting of the crop in one mechanical operation. Known to the highbush blueberry industry as the 'Big Seven', they are the cultivars 'Berkeley', 'Bluecrop', 'Blueray', 'Collins', 'Coville', 'Earliblue', and 'Herbert'. These large-fruited cultivars, that represent a major portion of the acreage in New Jersey, Michigan, Washington, and Oregon at present, were introduced in the period 1949 to 1960.

'Bluecrop' has been a particularly dependable cropper in all growing areas. More recent introductions from the USDA breeding program have been 'Bluetta', 'Spartan', 'Patriot', 'Darrow', 'Duke', 'Toro', 'Lateblue', and 'Elliott'. One of the main objectives of the variety improvement program has been to develop a series of cultivars that will extend the harvest season and be consistently productive. The extended harvest season for the northeastern United States is illustrated by the grouping of newer cultivars listed in Table 7-2, beginning with the earliest harvested cultivars, 'Weymouth' and 'Bluetta', and ending with 'Lateblue' and 'Elliott'. The 'Nelson', 'Bluegold', 'Sierra', and 'Sunrise' cultivars have just been introduced for the northern United States.

In North Carolina cultivars that were resistant to stem canker, caused by the fungus *Botryosphaeria corticis,* had to be developed if the industry was to survive. The mild winters of this region made this organism, as well as the bud mite, serious economic problems. The first cultivars resistant to *B. corticis* were introduced during the 1950s and named 'Angola', 'Croatan', 'Ivanhoe', 'Murphy', and 'Wolcott'. More recent introductions have been 'Morrow', 'Harrison', 'Bluechip', and 'Bounty'.

Hybrids between highbush cultivars and species native to the southern United States (particularly *V. darrowi* and *V. ashei*) have produced a series of low-chilling-requirement highbush types adapted to the south. These include the cultivars 'Flordablue', 'Sharpblue', and 'Avonblue' (Florida), 'Georgiagem' (Georgia), 'Cooper' and 'Gulfcoast' (Mississippi), and 'Cape Fear', 'Blue Ridge', and 'O'Neal' (North Carolina).

TABLE 7-2 RATINGS OF HIGHBUSH BLUEBERRY CULTIVARS FOR SOME BERRY CHARACTERISTICS[a]

CULTIVAR	SEASON	SIZE	COLOR	SCAR	FLAVOR	REMARKS
Morrow	10	8	7	6	6	Very early, canker-resistant
Angola	10	8	5	7	6	Very fine bush, canker-resistant
Harrison	9	9	8	8	8	Cane canker-resistant, very firm
Wolcott	9	8	6	9	6	Very fine bush, canker-resistant
Croatan	9	8	7	8	6	Very fine bush, canker-resistant
Weymouth	9	8	5	6	5	Poor bush, productive, poorest flavor
Bluetta	9	7	8	7	7	Short, compact, spreading, vigorous; consistent production; susceptible to red ringspot virus; recommended to replace Weymouth
Earliblue	9	9	8	7	8	Fine bush, won't drop, good flavor
Duke	9	8	8	8	6	Vigorous; consistent production; alternative to Bluetta
Collins	8	9	8	7	8	Fine bush, won't drop
Murphy	8	8	6	6	7	Spreading bush, canker-resistant
Bluechip	8	10	8	8	8	Cane canker-resistant, firm, fine texture and quality
Cabot	8	5	7	6	5	Spreading bush, berries crack
June	8	5	6	5	6	Bush usually weak
Spartan	8	10	9	8	10	Vigorous, upright plants lend themselves to mechanical harvesting
Patriot	8	8	8	9	10	Resistant to low winter temperature and phytophthora root rot
Meader	8	9	8	9	6	Good concentration of ripening
Rancocas	7	6	7	6	6	Berries crack, resistant to stunt
Ivanhoe	7	9	7	9	10	Buds not hardy, hard to propagate
Stanley	7	6	7	4	9	Easy to prune, berry size runs down
Blueray	7	10	8	7	9	Bush hardy, easy to propagate
Bluehaven	7	7	9	9	6	Vigorous; not winter hardy; productive
Bluejay	7	9	9	9	7	Resistant to mummy berry and low winter temperature; good concentration of ripening
Bluecrop	6	9	9	9	7	Drought-resistant, hardy, fine color
Concord	6	7	7	6	8	Fine cluster size
Pioneer	6	6	6	6	9	Berries crack
Scammell	6	7	6	6	7	Sets too large clusters
Northland	6	6	8	8	6	Cold tolerant; recommended for upper Michigan
Berkeley	5	10	10	8	7	Berries drop some, lightest blue
Atlantic	4	8	7	7	8	Berries drop some
Pemberton	4	8	6	4	7	Bush very vigorous, most productive

Rubel	4	6	7	7	6	Bush hardy, hard to prune
Jersey	4	7	7	7	6	Bush hardy, long picking season
Dixi	4	10	6	5	9	Berries crack, run down in size
Herbert	3	10	7	7	10	Berries tender, bush hardy
Darrow	3	10	8	8	9	Bush erect, vigorous, berries do not drop
Wareham	2	6	6	7	10	Berries tender, bad mildew
Burlington	2	7	7	10	6	Bush hardy, berries store well
Coville	2	10	7	6	9	Berries won't drop, fine processed
Lateblue	2	8	7	8	7	Erect, vigorous; good concentration of ripening; hard to pick
Elliott	1	7	9	9	8	Resistant to mummy berry; consistent production; very late

[a]For season: 1, latest; 10, earliest. For color: 1, dark; 10, light. For other characters: 1, poorest; 10, best.

Environmental Relationships

Temperature. Temperature is an overriding factor in determining whether the highbush blueberry can be produced commercially in an area. A growing season of 160 days is required to produce good crops and healthy plants that can sustain consistent production. Most cultivars require an accumulation of chilling hours below 45°F (7°C) of 650 to 850 hours. With the introduction of the 'low-chill' southern highbush cultivars, this has been reduced to 250 hours. The southern limit for highbush blueberry production had been the northern portion of South Carolina, but now the highbush blueberry can be grown as far south as central Florida.

Blueberry buds generally attain their maximum cold hardiness by mid-January, at which time they can withstand temperatures as low as −15°F (−27°C). Buds that have not fully hardened in the fall and early winter and buds that have begun to deharden during the post-rest period may be damaged by less severe winter temperatures. Fully opened buds can be killed by 30°F (−1°C). Buds that are at some stage less than fully opened can tolerate somewhat lower temperatures. Below 24°F (−5°C) considerable damage to the flower ovary can be expected in closed buds that are ready to flower.

Blueberry stem tissue is more tolerant of low temperature than bud tissue, but again the degree of hardening of the tissue is extremely important. Fully hardened wood in mid-January can withstand temperatures of −20°F (−29°C). Prolonged periods below this temperature can result in root destruction particularly if the ground is not snow covered. Most highbush cultivars are not hardy north of southern Maine and central Michigan. Several highbush cultivars, such as 'Patriot' and 'Northland', that have lowbush in their parentage can withstand colder temperatures, particularly if there is a snow cover over the root and crown areas.

Blueberries also need a considerable amount of heat input to attain maximum fruit quality during their ripening. Planting of highbush in northern portions of the United Kingdom and in southern parts of the Scandinavian countries has been disappointing because of the failure of fruit to attain the sweetness needed for good dessert quality. The cloudy and cool summers of this region reduce the energy available for sugar formation and are also favorable for the spread of *Fusicoccum* canker, a disease for which the highbush blueberry appears to have little immunity.

Light. Highbush blueberry vegetative growth is promoted under long days and it is not until the days begin to shorten in the northern growing region in late July and early August that flower buds are initiated. If growing temperatures are maintained, the initiated flower buds will develop without a rest period and flowering occurs without the plants' entering a period of dormancy. Sixteen-hour daylengths in the greenhouse can maintain blueberries in the vegetative growth state. Light intensities of about 200 footcandles are sufficient to prevent flower bud initiation, provided that temperatures remain optimum for growth.

Blueberries grow best and produce the best-quality fruit when grown in full sunlight. Experiments in which outdoor light intensity was reduced by 50% reduced blueberry growth and fruit production. Although blueberries will develop their blue color in the absence of light, bushes are pruned to open the center of the bush to light so that flower bud formation and vegetative growth are not reduced.

Moisture. Blueberry plants can suffer from either too much, or not enough soil moisture during their critical growth phase (Abbott and Gough, 1987b, c, d). During fruit development plants require about 2 in. (5 cm) of water per week, and if this cannot be provided through subirrigation or natural rainfall, some form of surface irrigation must be provided. The source of water is most often the natural rainfall that is impounded in farm ponds, although many large growers rely on large deep wells to provide a source of irrigation water. No matter what the water source, it should not exceed 0.1% total salts and 300 ppm chloride in solution.

Soil factors. The best soils for blueberries are well-drained acid sandy loams. Blueberries are members of the *Ericaceae* family, which are natural acid soil–loving plants and thrive in soils with a pH of 4.5 to 5.2. Increasing soil pH results in the development of nutritional imbalances within the plant, especially that of iron. Calcium saturation on the soil cation-exchange complex should not exceed 20%. Acid clay loams may make suitable blueberry soils provided that they have a friable structure brought about by the formation of water-stable soil aggregates. Such structure is enhanced by well-decomposed organic matter in the soil; and soils, whether of a sandy or loam texture, should contain at least 3% organic matter. Good internal drainage is absolutely essential. The most common soil type found in the commercial blueberry growing areas is a podzol with an organic matter content of the A horizon ranging from 3 to 20%. Muck soils with organic matter contents of 20 to 50% make good blueberry growing soils provided that they can be well drained and are allowed to subside following initial drainage. Peats containing more than 50% organic matter are not as ideally suited for blueberries because of the difficulty in draining them, excessive subsidence when drained, and pH ranges that may be too acid (less than pH 4.0). Other limitations of peat soils are their tendency to warm up slowly in the spring, and the possible excessive nitrogen release from decomposing organic matter during late summer, which can lead to autumn growth that is very susceptible to winter injury.

Propagation

Hardwood.   The principal method of highbush blueberry propagation is by rooting of hardwood cuttings (Fig. 7–2). Well-hardened dormant 1-year-old shoots about pencil thickness make the best propagation wood. These shoots or whips may arise from the crown of the bush or from an older cane on mature plants. A preferred method of obtaining suitable cutting wood is from mother block plants, from which the shoots are removed completely each year by cutting them to the crown. The whips are most often used immediately as cutting material or they can be stored at 36°F (2°C) for a few weeks provided that they are kept in a moist environment. Cuttings are prepared by first removing and discarding the top section of the whip, which contains the flower buds. The remaining portion of the whip is cut into 5-in. (13-cm) sections, usually with the distal cut just above a vegetative bud. Location of the cut relative to the bud position can be observed when cuttings are made by hand, but if a large volume of cuttings is being made, the whips are often cut to size on bandsaws. If the cuttings are to be stored for any length of time before being planted, they should be dipped in a suitable fungicide, placed compactly into plastic bags, and stored at 36°F (2°C).

Propagation beds are normally constructed outdoors and located in full sunlight. To ensure good drainage, they are positioned above the ground either on posts or blocks, allowing a few inches of clearance. A convenient width for propagation beds is 4 ft (1.2 m), which will enable cuttings to be struck from either side of the bed. A depth of 8 in. (20 cm) provides for adequate amounts of media to allow for good root development. The lengths of the bed may be varied as to need. The

FIGURE 7–2   Highbush blueberry cuttings showing the progressive states in rooting.

propagation frames are constructed of a suitably treated wood, for maximum life, which is usually of 2-in. (5-cm) stock size. The bottom of the frame has cross pieces for supporting heavy-gauged turkey wire, which in turn supports hardware cloth or screen that prevents loss of the propagating mix. This 'open bottom' allows for the excellent drainage necessary for good rooting of the hardwood cuttings.

The beds are filled with a 1:1 mixture by volume of acid sphagnum peat moss and coarse-washed concrete sand. The mixture should be thoroughly mixed in a cement mixer and then placed into the frame, firmed but not unduly compressed, and watered thoroughly. More media may be required if settling occurs, allowing about 1 in. (2.5 cm) between the surface of the media and the top of the bed. No fertilizers are incorporated into the media, and bottom heat is not required.

Cuttings are stuck vertically into the propagation media, allowing only the most distal vegetative bud to remain above the surface. Care must be taken to orient the cutting so that the buds on the cutting point upward before it is stuck. No rooting hormone is used since research has shown that no rooting response occurs to any of the common rooting hormones used for hardwood cuttings. After sticking the cuttings they are thoroughly watered by hand and are watered automatically thereafter to ensure a moist substrate for rooting. The cuttings are normally stuck in mid-April in New Jersey. By mid-May vegetative buds have produced young leaves, although rooting has not yet occurred. By mid-June a second flush of growth from the cutting signifies that functioning roots have formed on the cutting. At this time the first fertilizer applications are applied usually in the form of a soluble complete fertilizer in solution. Weekly applications of a suitable complete soluble fertilizer at the rate of 1 oz per 2 gal (30 g per 8 liters) until mid-August will ensure good root and top development.

The rooted cuttings are usually allowed to overwinter in the propagating frames and are removed in early spring for planting. The media is removed entirely from the beds and fresh media is prepared and placed into the beds, which are reused annually as long as they remain structurally sound.

Softwood. Softwood cuttings are taken during the active growing period of the blueberry plant. Plant material most suitable for softwood cuttings are the shoots of the first seasonal growth flush (Douglas, 1967). The first shoot flush is at the optimum physiological age for rooting when a second flush of growth first appears from axial buds in the shoot.

A 4-in. (10-cm) cutting is generally adequate and two to three leaves are allowed to remain on the cutting. The cutting is stuck at least 2 in. (5 cm) into the propagating medium, which consists of equal volumes of acid peat moss and perilite thoroughly mixed. Rooting hormones generally increase the percentage rooting of softwood cuttings. A mist system ensures an adequate moisture supply. Good air circulation is essential to reduce disease incidence. A weekly spray of a fungicide such as ferbam is a good prophylactic measure. Normally, bottom heat is not used when the cuttings are stuck in the summer. If used, however, substrate temperatures should be maintained at 72°F (22°C).

Softwood cuttings should root in 4 to 6 weeks, after which they can be potted into 3-in. (7.5-cm) pots. These plants can be forced in a greenhouse during the winter to produce additional vegetative growth provided that night temperatures are not allowed to drop below 60°F (15°C) and daylength is maintained at 16 hours. About 200 footcandles is sufficient to keep the plants from entering dormancy. Weekly applications of dilute soluble complete fertilizer will ensure good root and top growth.

Tissue culture. Blueberry shoot tips have been successfully induced to produce multiple shoots in agar media supplied with modified standard culturing solutions. After subculturing, the shoots are cut off and placed into a peat–perilite rooting mixture under mist, where they root readily.

Establishment

Site selection. Summarizing from the environmental relationships section, highbush blueberries need a growing season of at least 160 days, at least 900 to 1000 hours below 45°F in the north and at least 200 to 300 hours in Florida and along the Gulf coast, with winter minimum temperatures above −15 to −20°F for best production. Highbush blueberries should be planted in full sunlight, on acidic, well-drained soils of coarse to medium texture (Ballinger, 1966) with high organic matter content (best ranges: pH 4.5 to 5.2, organic matter more than 3%). Blueberry soils must be well drained both internally and on the surface, or special land preparation may be required. Adequate air drainage around the acid lowlands usually planted to blueberries is particularly important to reduce the spring frost hazard.

Land preparation. Newly cleared land is best allowed to remain fallow for a year and periodically disked during the year. All roots should be removed so as not to support any unwanted fungal growth. The use of a soil fumigant is recommended in some cases. If the land is marshy, it must be drained by a series of ditches and canals. Heavy soils may require the additional expense of tile drains to ensure adequate internal drainage. Final preparation of the land includes the establishment of a grade of 1 foot per 300 ft (10 cm per 30 m) in all directions from the center of the field. To further ensure good surface drainage during wet periods, plants can be planted into hills of topsoil of 6 to 8 in. (15 to 20 cm) in height. Soils that do not have the ideal acid soil reaction may require the addition of elemental sulfur to lower the pH to the desired level.

Planting. Plantings are generally made from 2- or 3-year-old nursery-grown plants, although direct planting of 1-year-old rooted cuttings is also possible. Planting rooted cuttings directly requires greater care, particularly in providing sufficient water by supplemental irrigation. Spring planting is recommended over fall planting because of the greater probability of losses of fall-planted plants to frost heaving. Spring rains are also a more reliable occurrence than a wet fall season. The traditional spacing of plants for commercial production has been a 4.5 by 9 ft (1.35 by 2.70 m) spacing. The tendency now is to increase the row spacing to 10 ft (3 m) to facilitate the movement of harvest machinery through the row. Plant spacings within the row are also being varied, the most common spacing now being 4 ft (1.2

m). A 4 by 10 ft (1.2 by 3 m) spacing would require 1089 plants per acre (2690 per hectare). Fertilizers are not placed in the planting hole but are applied as a light side dressing of 90 lb/acre (100 kg/ha) of 10-10-10 after planting. Moistened peat moss, however, is sometimes placed in the planting hole at the time of planting. During the first two growing seasons in the field, pruning consists of removing all flower buds to encourage vegetative growth. A small crop is usually harvested during the third growing season.

Mulches. Mulches (Fig. 7–3) are not generally used in commercial blueberry plantings, where the water table is controlled to provide the moisture requirements of the plant. However, on clay soils some form of mulch will greatly improve the chance of blueberry roots developing adequately. Critical root system development occurs at the interface of the mulch and soil and a few inches into the clay soil. On clay soils, the mulch must be maintained for the life of the planting. A mulch is essential where supplemental irrigation is not feasible. The mulch acts to conserve moisture in the soil and prevents weed growth, which can rob the soil of its moisture. The ideal mulching material is one that disintegrates slowly, thus placing less strain on the nitrogen supply of the soil and requiring less frequent reapplication. Sawdust makes an excellent mulch in this respect. Pine needles may also be used, but deciduous leaves are less desirable because they tend to pack and do not allow adequate water penetration. When mulches are used, a thickness of 4 to 6 in. (10 to 15 cm) is generally maintained, which often requires the annual addition of new

FIGURE 7–3 Highbush blueberries with a recent mulch application of wood chips and shavings.

material. Supplemental nitrogen fertilizer must be added with the mulch to compensate for the removal of nitrogen from the soil by the microbes that break down the organic mulch.

Nutrition

pH. Blueberries require an acid substrate for normal growth. The acidity range for satisfactory growth appears to be between pH 4.0 and 5.2 with an optimum from pH 4.5 to 4.8. The most common method used to acidify the soil is by the application of sulfur prior to planting. The ratio of sulfur application varies with the buffering capacity of the soil; for sandy soils, 0.8 lb per 100 ft^2 (0.36 kg per 9 m^2) of sulfur, and for loam soils, 2.4 lb per 100 ft^2 (1.09 kg per 9 m^2) is recommended to reduce the pH one full unit (see Table 2-11). The sulfur is thoroughly mixed into the soil 1 year prior to planting. Fertilizers that leave acid residues, such as ammonium sulfate, can then be used to maintain an acid soil reaction.

Soils with a pH below 4.0, such as may develop on some muck and peat soils, may require the addition of limestone to make them suitable. Blueberries have been observed to respond to limestone applications at these low pH levels. Again the limestone must be thoroughly worked into the soil prior to planting.

Plant composition. Although mineral element deficiencies in blueberries have been produced under controlled conditions, only nitrogen, magnesium, and iron deficiencies have been observed in field plantings. Under controlled nutrient studies, deficiency symptoms were observed at the following plant composition levels on a dry weight basis: nitrogen 1.50%, phosphorus 0.07%, potassium 0.40%, calcium 0.30%, magnesium 0.09%, iron 60 ppm, manganese 20 ppm, zinc 10 ppm, copper 10 ppm, and boron 10 ppm. Optimum levels of the essential mineral elements that have been proposed as standards for plant analysis diagnostic purposes based on the analysis of midshoot leaves from fruiting shoots in mid-July (dry weight basis) are as follows: nitrogen 1.98%, phosphorus 0.16%, potassium 0.53%, magnesium 0.28%, calcium 0.74%, iron 150 ppm, manganese 170 ppm, boron 50 ppm, copper 15 ppm, and zinc 20 ppm (Ballinger et al., 1958; Doughty et al., 1981).

Fertilizers. Highbush blueberries will respond to fertilizer applications. To maintain plant mineral composition levels at the optimum level, a complete chemical fertilizer in a 1-1-1 (N:P$_2$O5:K$_2$O) ratio is applied annually, usually at the rate of 600 lb/acre (675 kg/ha) of a 10-10-10 analysis fertilizer. The ammonium form is preferred over the nitrate form of nitrogen; therefore, ammonium sulfate is the principal nitrogen form in complete fertilizers. Blueberries are sensitive to chlorides; potassium sulfate is preferred over potassium chloride as a source of potassium. In muck and peat soils a supplemental superphosphate application of 350 lb/acre (400 kg/ha) may be beneficial. Magnesium deficiencies have been reported in field plantings in most of the blueberry growing areas; therefore, magnesium is often included in the complete fertilizer mix at 3% MgO. An alternative source of magnesium may be applied as Epsom salts (magnesium sulfate). Since most blueberry soils are of a sandy texture with relatively low cation-exchange capacities, it is generally recommended that the complete fertilizer applications be applied as a split application 1 month apart in the spring of the year. Well-composted manures have been used successfully on blueberry plantings at the rate of 10 tons/acre (9MT/ha).

Plant and Fruit Development

Bush development.   See the Botany section.

Fruiting habit.   See the Botany section.

Pollination.   Blueberries require that at least 80% of their flowers set fruit in order to achieve a profitable commercial yield. A pollinating agent is required to achieve fruit set since ripe pollen falls out of the inverted flower and not onto the receptive stigma. Pollination is effected by wild bumblebees or domesticated honeybees. Although the blueberry is self-fruitful, larger fruit and better set are obtained if cross-fertilization of cultivars occurs. Rows of one cultivar are often alternated with rows of another cultivar which bloom at about the same time in order to facilitate cross-pollination. When wild bee pollinators are insufficient in number for adequate pollination, hives of honeybees must be introduced into the field at the rate of one to two strong hives per acre (five per hectare) when about 25% of the flowers are in bloom.

Berry growth.   See the Botany section.

Pruning.   Mature blueberry plants must be pruned annually to maintain a desirable balance between vegetative and reproductive growth (Fig. 7–4). Failure to prune results in overbearing and lack of new shoot development and leads to the eventual loss of plant vigor. The best-quality fruit is attained when weak wood [less than 0.2 in. (5 mm) in thickness] is eliminated from the bush. To accomplish this objective, canes more than 4 years old are removed at the crown, and weak shoots are cut back to a strong lateral in the younger canes. This ensures the production of new vigorous canes from the crown of the plant. Occasionally, additional detailed hand pruning is necessary to eliminate weak wood in the remaining laterals. Pruning is normally carried out during the dormant period, although it is sometimes easy to recognize weak canes during the late summer and to remove them at this time.

Pest Control

Insects.   The highbush blueberry industry has developed in regions where wild blueberries were indigenous. It was a simple matter for existing insect pests to migrate to the new commercial fields. To obtain high production of good-quality fruit, growers must monitor insect populations and be ready to counteract population increases with timely insecticide sprays. Integrated pest management based on actual insect population buildup has led to reduced costs, reduced numbers of

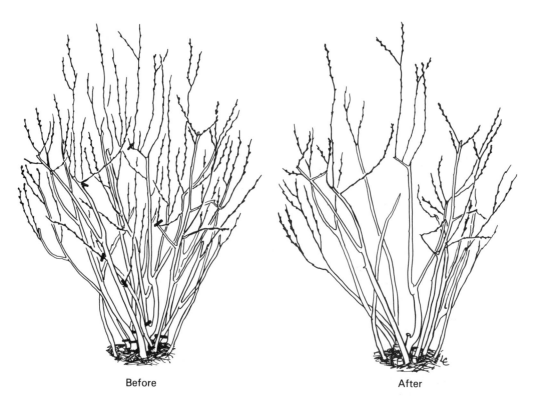

Before   After

FIGURE 7-4   Mature highbush blueberry bush before and after pruning.

insecticide applications, and superior control. Insects that must be controlled virtually every year in the highbush blueberry areas are blueberry maggot (*Rhagoletis
pomonella* Walsh), cranberry fruitworm (*Mineola vaccinii* Riley), cherry fruitworm
(*Grapholitha packardi* Dell.), plum curculio (*Conotrachelus nenuphar* Herbst.), and
in North Carolina the blueberry bud mite (*Aceria vaccinii* Keifer). The Putnam scale
(*Ospidiotus ancylus* Putnam), blueberry blossom weevil (*Anthonomus musculus*
Say), and the sharp-nosed leafhopper (*Scaphytopius magdalensis* Prov.) also require
control measures occasionally in New Jersey. Control of these insect pests can often
be enhanced by timely and thorough execution of other cultural practices, such as
clean cultivation and pruning. Insecticides such as malathion, parathion, guthion,
thiodan, and seven are used either as liquid concentrates, wettable powders, or as
dusts. Applications may be made either dry or wet by surface or by aerial application.

Diseases.   Highbush blueberries can be seriously affected by a number of
fungus and virus diseases. One of the most serious of the fungus diseases affecting
blueberries is mummy berry disease (*Monilinia vaccinii-corymbosi* Read), characterized by the formation of dried-out mummified fruit at harvest. Control is best
obtained by maintaining a clean cultivated soil below the plants, thereby preventing
the fungal fruiting bodies or apothecia from releasing their ascospores in the spring.

Sometimes granular applications of urea are made at the time of apothecia formation in order to destroy these fruiting structures. Triforine gives effective chemical control at this stage also. Control of the blight phase with ferbam or zineb is much more difficult and less effective.

A serious fungus disease in North Carolina is stem canker (*Botryosphaeria corticis* Demaree and Wilcox), which weakens and kills canes of susceptible cultivars over several growing seasons. The only practical means of controlling this serious pest is the use of canker-resistant cultivars that have been developed for the region. Another stem canker is *Fusicoccum putrefaciens,* which is troublesome in the more northern regions of highbush blueberry production. The organism is difficult to control by fungicides and immune cultivars are not known. Stem blight (*Botryosphaeria dothideae*) has become a more serious pest in recent years, seemingly mild infections causing a plant to wilt and die within a single season.

Blueberry *Botrytis* or gray mold (*B. cinerea*) develops under conditions of cool temperatures and high humidity. This organism can cause serious damage to both twigs and blossoms. Ferbam and zineb dusts have been used successfully to control both twig and blossom blight. Powdery mildew (*Microsphaera pencillata* var. *vaccinii* Schu.) develops on leaves late in the growing season and is usually treated with sulfur applications. Blueberry *anthracnose* (*Glomerella cingulata* Spaulding and von Schrenk) has become an increasingly important economic disease because of its deleterious effect on blueberry fruit. The fungus develops as an unsightly orange-colored mold on the fruit, which makes it unsalable. Ferbam and ziram are the principal fungicides used for control.

The principal viruses affecting the highbush blueberry are blueberry stunt disease (now classified as a mycoplasma), red ringspot, necrotic ringspot, mosaic, and shoestring. Control of virus diseases is implemented by the control of the vector, if known, as for example the control of the sharp-nosed leafhopper for stunt control, and by the persistent roguing and destruction of virus-infected plants.

Weeds. In the commercial production of highbush blueberry, weeds must be eliminated since they effectively compete with the blueberry for the limited available moisture and nutrients in the soil. The principal methods of weed control are mulching, tillage, and herbicides. For mulching to be effective, the mulch must be at least 6 in. (15 cm) deep, thus requiring annual amendments of mulch to replace the portion that decomposes. Clean cultivation is the most common method of weed control but is also very labor intensive, requiring frequent hoeing within the row and disking between the rows. Chemical weed control is becoming increasingly popular as new herbicides are developed for control of the wide spectrum of weeds that are found in blueberry plantings. Materials that have been used as successful pre-emergent herbicides are diuron (Karmex), terbacil (Sinbar), and simazine (Princep). Chlorpropham (Chloro IPC) has been used against chickweed and dodder, and dichlobenil (Casoron) has been used against certain perennial weeds and winter annuals. Paraquat applied in early spring before bud break is also used to control perennial weeds. Herbicides are generally directed under and between the bushes for weed control. The areas between the rows are either disked or mowed if maintained in permanent sod.

Birds.   Commercial blueberry plantings that are located near areas where general farming is carried out may be troubled by birds during the harvest season. Blackbirds, starlings, and members of the thrush family are common fruit-eating species that have been known to present problems. Where losses can be expected to be substantial, it is necessary to cage the plants securely enough to prevent access by the birds (Fig. 7–5). This usually requires the construction of some permanent frame over which netting can be stretched. Other methods of bird control have not proven effective, although recent experiments with the bird repellant 'Mesurol' have shown promise for blueberries.

Harvesting, Processing, and Storage

Blueberries are hand harvested for the fresh market and machine harvested for processing. Casual workers are most often used for hand harvest and are paid approximately 20% of the gate value for a pint of blueberries. Most of the North Carolina crop is hand harvested for the fresh market. About 50% of the New Jersey crop is hand harvested and most of the Michigan crop is machine harvested for processing.

When hand picked, the fruit is placed directly into pint containers in field trays. The trays are either moved directly to packing lines or held in cold storage at 55°F (13°C) until ready for packing. Individual pints are capped (overwrapped) without undergoing further inspection and placed into transport trays containing 12 pints each. The trays are palletized and transported to market in refrigerated trucks.

FIGURE 7–5   Blueberry bushes enclosed in a netted cage to exclude birds. Note sod middles and chemical weed control in rows.

Machine packaging of hand-harvested fruit is becoming more common as the temporary labor force continues to diminish.

Machine-harvested fruit is removed from the bushes using a vibration method which produces a force that will cause the fruit to abscise (Fig. 7–6). The vibration can be produced with either hand-held vibrators or with large over-the-row harvesting machines that are designed to detach the fruit, collect it, and to give it an initial winnowing in order to remove debris that accompanies the abscised fruit. The fruit must be further treated to remove trash, usually by aerodynamic separation, and is then washed, drained, and inspected before the fruit is packaged for freezing, usually into 20- or 30-lb (9- to 14-kg) containers.

Economics and Marketing

The highbush blueberry industry in the United States is valued at approximately $104 million per year at the farm gate. Only minor increases in acreage and production have occurred in recent years. The most significant change in blueberry production within the last decade has been in crop utilization. Whereas the fresh fruit market was the major form of crop utilization 10 years ago, today over 70% of the fruit is processed. Significant increases in export of processed fruit to Europe and Asia have contributed to the demand for processed fruit. Paradoxically, the per capita consumption of blueberries in the United States has changed little in the last decade. Of increasing importance in recent years has been the pick-your-own operation as a method of marketing blueberries. These operations are particularly successful in localities situated close to urban centers.

Blueberry production remains a profitable horticultural venture, in part due to the successful attempts to mechanize the operations and the development of a process market. Fruit harvested for the fresh market has returned about $1 a pound in recent years, and fruit for the process market about 50 cents per pound. For more detailed information on the costs of highbush blueberry production, see *Blueberry Science* (Eck, 1988).

FIGURE 7–6 Highbush blueberries being harvested using a hand-held vibrator with catch frames under the bush.

REFERENCES

AALDERS, L. E., AND I. V. HALL. 1961. Pollen incompatibility and fruit set in lowbush blueberry. Can. J. Genet. Cytol. 3:300–307.

AALDERS, L. E., AND I. V. HALL. 1964. A comparison of flower-bud development in the lowbush blueberry *Vaccinium Angustifolium* Art. under greenhouse and field conditions. Proc. Am. Soc. Hortic. Sci. 84:281–284.

ABBOTT, J. D., AND R. E. GOUGH. 1987a. Seasonal development of highbush blueberry roots under sawdust mulch. J. Am. Soc. Hortic. Sci. 112:60–62.

ABBOTT, J. D., AND R. E. GOUGH. 1987b. Reproductive response of the highbush blueberry to root-zone flooding. HortScience 22:40–42.

ABBOTT, J. D., AND R. E. GOUGH. 1987c. Growth and survival of the highbush blueberry in response to root-zone flooding. J. Am. Soc. Hortic. Sci. 112:603–608.

ABBOTT, J. D., AND R. E. GOUGH. 1987d. Prolonged flooding effects on anatomy of highbush blueberry. HortScience 22:622–625.

BAILEY, J. S., AND A. P. FRENCH. 1946. Identification of blueberry varieties by plant characters. Mass. Agric. Exp. Stn. Bull. 431.

BALLINGER, W. E., ET AL. 1958. Relation between nutrient element content of blueberry foliage and fruit. Mich. Agric. Exp. Stn. Quart. Bull. 40:906–911.

BALLINGER, W. E. 1966. Soil management practices. In P. Eck and N. F. Childers (eds.). Blueberry culture. Rutgers University Press, New Brunswick, N.J.

BALLINGER, W. E., E. P. MANESS, G. J. GALLETTA, AND L. J. KUSHMAN. 1972. Anthocyanins of ripe fruit of a "pink-fruited" hybrid of highbush blueberries. J. Am. Soc. Hortic. Sci. 97:381–384.

BALLINGER, W. E., E. P. MANESS, AND L. J. KUSHMAN. 1970. Anthocyanins in ripe fruit of the highbush blueberry, *Vaccinium corymbosum* L. J. Am. Soc. Hortic. Sci. 95:283–286.

BALLINGTON, J. R. 1984. The history of blueberry improvement in North America. In T. E. Crocker and P. Lyrene (eds.). Proc. 5th North American Blueberry Research Workers Conf., Feb. 1–3, 1984, University of Florida, Gainesville, Fla.

BARKER, W. G., I. V. HALL, L. E. AALDERS, AND G. W. WOOD. 1964. The lowbush blueberry industry in eastern Canada. Econ. Bot. 18:357–365.

BELL, H. P. 1950. Determinate growth in the blueberry. Can. J. Res. 28:637–644.

BERGMANN, H. F. 1929. Changes in the rate of respiration of fruits of the cultivated blueberry during ripening. Science 70:15.

CAMP, W. H. 1942. A survey of the American species of *Vaccinium*, Subgenus *Euvaccinium*. Brittonia 4:205–247.

CAMP, W. H. 1945. The North American blueberries with notes on the other groups of Vacciniaceae. Brittonia 5:203–275.

CARD, F. W. 1903. Bush-fruits. R.I. Coll. Agric. Mech. Arts Bull. 91.

CHANDLER, F. B., AND I. C. MASON. 1935. Blueberry pollination. Maine Agric. Exp. Stn. Bull. 380:215–216.

CLARK, J. H. 1941. Leaf characters as a basis for the classification of blueberry varieties. Proc. Am. Soc. Hortic. Sci. 38:441–446.

CLARK, J. H., AND S. G. GILBERT. 1942. Selection of criterion leaves for the identification of blueberry varieties. Proc. Am. Soc. Hortic. Sci. 40:347–351.

CONSTANTE, J. F., AND B. R. BOYCE. 1968. Low temperature injury of highbush blueberry shoots at various times of the year. Proc. Am. Soc. Hortic. Sci. 93:267–272.

COVILLE, F. V. 1910. Experiments in blueberry culture. U.S. Dep. Agric. Bull. 193.

COVILLE, F. V. 1927. Blueberry chromosomes. Science 66:565–566.

DARROW, G. M. 1942. Rest period requirements of blueberries. Proc. Am. Soc. Hortic. Sci. 41:189–194.

DARROW, G. M. 1960. Blueberry breeding: past, present, and future. Am. Hortic. Mag. 39:14–33.

DARROW, G. M., AND W. H. CAMP. 1945. *Vaccinium* hybrids and the development of new horticultural material. Torrey Bot. Club Bull. 72:1–21.

DARROW, G. M., J. H. CLARK, AND E. B. MORROW. 1939. The inheritance of certain characters in the cultivated blueberry. Proc. Am. Soc. Hortic. Sci. 37:611–616.

DARROW, G. M., AND J. N. MOORE. 1966. Blueberry growing. U.S. Dep. Agric. Farmers Bull. 1951.

DARROW, G. M., E. B. MORROW, AND D. H. SCOTT. 1952. An evaluation of interspecific blueberry crosses. Proc. Am. Soc. Hortic. Sci. 59:277–282.

DARROW, G. M., D. H. SCOTT, AND H. DERMAN. 1954. Tetraploid blueberries from hexaploid × diploid species crosses. Proc. Am. Soc. Hortic. Sci. 62:266–270.

DARROW, G. M., R. B. WILCOX, AND C. S. BECKWITH. 1944. Blueberry growing. U.S. Dep. Agric. Farmers' Bull. 1951.

DOAK, K. D. 1928. The mycorrhizal fungus of *Vaccinium*. Phytopathology 18:148.

DOUGHTY, C. C., E. B. ADAMS, AND L. W. MARTIN. 1981. Highbush blueberry production in Washington and Oregon. Washington State Univ. Bull. PNW 215.

DOUGLAS, J. 1967. The propagation of highbush blueberries by softwood cuttings. International Society of Horticultural Science Working Group Symposium on Blueberry Culture in Europe, July 27–28, Venlo, The Netherlands, p. 95–104.

DRAPER, A. D., AND D. H. SCOTT. 1971. Inheritance of albino seedling in tetraploid highbush blueberry. J. Am. Soc. Hortic. Sci. 96:791–92.

DRAPER, A. D., AND D. H. SCOTT. 1973. Recent developments in blueberry breeding work of the U.S. Department of Agriculture. Jugosl. Vocarstro 7:203–208.

DRAPER, A. D., AND D. H. SCOTT. 1974. Current blueberry breeding work. Proc. 9th Annual Meeting of the North American Blueberry Council.

DRAPER, A. D., A. W. STRETCH, AND D. H. SCOTT. 1972. Two tetraploid sources of resistance to *Phytophthora cinnamomi* Rands. HortScience 7:266–268.

EATON, E. L. 1957. Spread of blueberry seed through manure and by migrating robins. Proc. Am. Soc. Hortic. Sci. 69:293–295.

EATON, G. W., AND A. M. JAMONT. 1966. Megagametogenesis in *V. corymbosum*. Can. J. Bot. 44:712–714.

ECK, P. 1966. Botany. In N. F. Childers and P. Eck (eds.). Blueberry culture. Rutgers University Press, New Brunswick, N.J.

ECK, P. 1988. Blueberry science. Rutgers University Press, New Brunswick, N.J.

ECK, P. AND N. F. CHILDERS. 1966. Blueberry culture. Rutgers University Press, New Brunswick, N.J.

FERNALD, M. L. 1970. Gray's manual of botany. 8th ed. Van Nostrand Reinhold, New York.

GALLETTA, G. J. 1975. Blueberries and cranberries. In J. Janick and J. N. Moore (eds.). Advances in fruit breeding. Purdue University Press, West Lafayette, Ind.

GOUGH, R. E. 1980. Root distribution of 'Coville' and 'Lateblue' highbush blueberry under sawdust mulch. J. Am. Soc. Hortic. Sci. 105:576–578.

GOUGH, R. E. 1983a. Time of pruning and bloom date in cultivated highbush blueberry. HortScience 18:934–935.

GOUGH, R. E. 1983b. The occurrence of mesocarpic stone cells in the fruit of cultivated highbush blueberry. J. Am. Soc. Hortic. Sci. 108:1064–1067.

GOUGH, R. E., R. J. HINDLE, AND V. G. SHUTAK. 1976a. Identification of ten highbush blueberry cultivars using morphological characteristics. HortScience 11:512–514.

GOUGH, R. E., AND W. LITKE. 1980. An anatomical and morphological study of abscission in highbush blueberry fruit. J. Am. Soc. Hortic. Sci. 105:335–341.

GOUGH, R. E., AND V. G. SHUTAK. 1976. Effect of SADH on leaves of cultivated highbush blueberry. HortScience 11:514–515.

GOUGH, R. E., AND V. G. SHUTAK. 1978c. Anatomy and morphology of cultivated highbush blueberry. R.I. Agric. Exp. Stn. Bull. 423.

GOUGH, R. E., V. G. SHUTAK, AND R. L. HAUKE. 1978a. Growth and development of highbush blueberry. I. Vegetative growth. J. Am. Soc. Hortic. Sci. 103:94–97.

GOUGH, R. E., V. G. SHUTAK, AND R. L. HAUKE. 1978b. Growth and development of highbush blueberry. II. Reproductive growth, histological studies. J. Am. Soc. Hortic. Sci. 103:476–479.

GOUGH, R. E., V. G. SHUTAK, AND N. D. WINDUS. 1976b. Observations on the vegetative and reproductive growth of the cultivated highbush blueberry. HortScience 11:260–261.

HALL, I. V., AND L. E. AALDERS. 1975. Lowbush blueberry production and management. Can. Dep. Agric. Publ. 1477 (rev. 1975).

HALL, I. V., AND F. R. FORSYTH. 1967. Respiration rates of developing fruits of the lowbush blueberry. Can. J. Plant Sci. 47:157–159.

HALL, I. V. ET AL. 1975. Lowbush blueberry production. Can. Dep. Agric. Publ. 1477.

HINDLE, R. J., V. G. SHUTAK, AND E. P. CHRISTOPHER. 1957. Growth studies of the highbush blueberry fruit. Proc. Am. Soc. Hortic. Sci. 69:282–287.

ISMAIL, A. A., AND W. J. KENDER. 1969. Evidence of a respiratory climacteric in highbush and lowbush blueberry fruit. HortScience 4:342–344.

JANICK, J., AND J. N. MOORE (EDS.). 1975. Advances in fruit breeding. Purdue University Press, West Lafayette, Ind.

JOHNSTON, S. 1942. Observations on the inheritance of horticulturally important characteristics in the highbush blueberry. Proc. Am. Soc. Hortic. Sci. 40:352–356.

JOHNSTON, S. 1946. Observations on hybridizing lowbush and highbush blueberries. Proc. Am. Soc. Hortic. Sci. 47:199–200.

KENDER, W. J. 1966. Domesticating the lowbush blueberry. In Proceedings of the North American Blueberry Workers' Conference. Maine Agric. Exp. Stn. Misc. Rep. 118.

LILLY, J. P., V. S. JENKINS, AND C. M. MAINLAND. 1975. Investigations of soil and other factors influencing plant failure of North Carolina highbush blueberry. N.C. Agric. Exp. Stn. Tech. Bull. 230.

LONGLEY, A. E. 1927. Chromosomes in *Vaccinium*. Science 66:566–568.

MAHLSTEDE, J. P. AND D. P. WATSON. 1952. An anatomical study of adventitious root development in stems of *Vaccinium corymbosom*. Bot. Gaz. 113:279–285.

MAINLAND, C. M. 1966. Propagation. In P. Eck and N. F. Childers (eds.). Blueberry culture. Rutgers University Press, New Brunswick, N.J.

References

MARUCCI, P. E. 1966. Insects. In P. Eck and N. F. Childers (eds.). Blueberry culture. Rutgers University Press, New Brunswick, N.J.

MATHEWS, J. R., AND E. M. KNOX. 1926. The comparative morphology of the stamen in the Ericaceae. Trans. Proc. Bot. Soc. Edinb. 29:243–281.

MEADER, E. M., W. W. SMITH, AND A. F. YEAGER. 1954. Bush types and fruit colors in hybrids of highbush and lowbush blueberries. Proc. Am. Soc. Hortic. Sci. 63:272–278.

MERRILL, T. A. 1936. Pollination of the highbush blueberry. Mich. Agric. Exp. Stn. Bull. 151.

MILHOLLAND, R. D., AND G. J. GALLETTA. 1967. Relative susceptibility of blueberry cultivars to *Phytophthora cinnamomi*. Plant Dis. Rep. 51:998–1001.

MOORE, J. N. 1965. Improving highbush blueberries by breeding and selection. Euphytica 14:39–48.

MOORE, J. N. 1966. Breeding. In N. F. Childers and P. Eck (eds.). Blueberry culture. Rutgers University Press, New Brunswick, N.J.

MOORE, J. N., H. H. BOWEN, AND D. H. SCOTT. 1962. Response of highbush blueberry varieties, selections, and hybrid progenies to powdery mildew. Proc. Am. Soc. Hortic. Sci. 81:274–280.

MOORE, J. N., D. H. SCOTT, AND H. DERMAN. 1964. Development of a decaploid blueberry by colchicine treatment. Proc. Am. Soc. Hortic. Sci. 84:274–279.

NELSON, J. W. AND H. C. BITTENBENDER. 1971. Mummy berry disease occurrence in a blueberry selection test planting. Plant Dis. Rep. 55:651–653.

NEWCOMER, E. H. 1941. Chromosome numbers of some species and varieties of *Vaccinium* and related genera. Proc. Am. Soc. Hortic. Sci. 38:468–470.

ROBINSON, B. L., AND M. L. FERNALD. 1908. Gray's new manual of botany. 7th ed. American Book Company, New York.

SCOTT, D. H., AND J. N. MOORE. 1961. Status of blueberry breeding program, United States Department of Agriculture and cooperating agencies. U.S. Dep. of Agric. Crops Res. Div. Mimeo.

SHUTAK, V. G. 1968. Effect of succinic acid 2, 2-dimethylhydrozide on flower bud formation in the 'Coville' highbush blueberry. HortScience 3:225.

SHUTAK, V. G., R. E. GOUGH, AND N. D. WINDUS. 1980. The cultivated highbush blueberry: twenty years of research. R.I. Agric. Exp. Stn. Bull. 428.

SHUTAK, V. G., R. HINDLE, AND E. P. CHRISTOPHER. 1956. Factors associated with ripening of highbush blueberry fruits. Proc. Am. Soc. Hortic. Sci. 68:178–183.

SHUTAK, V. G., R. J. HINDLE, AND E. P. CHRISTOPHER. 1957. Growth studies of the cultivated blueberry. R.I. Agric. Exp. Stn. Bull. 339.

STRETCH, A. W., AND E. VARNEY. 1966. Diseases. In P. Eck and N. F. Childers (eds.). Blueberry culture. Rutgers University Press, New Brunswick, N.J.

TREVETT, M. F. 1956. Observations on the decline and rehabilitation of lowbush blueberry fields. Maine Agric. Exp. Stn. Misc. Publ. 626.

VORSA, N. 1987. Meiotic chromosome pairing and irregularities in blueberry interspecific backcross hybrids. J. Hered. 78:395–399.

WINDUS, N. D., V. G. SHUTAK, AND R. E. GOUGH. 1976. CO_2 and C_2H_4 evolution by highbush blueberry fruit. HortScience 11:515–517.

YARBOROUGH, J. A., AND E. B. MORROW. 1947. Stone cells in *Vaccinium*. Proc. Am. Soc. Hortic. Sci. 50:224–228.

Zimmerman, R. H., and O. Broome. 1980. Blueberry micropropagation. Proc. Conf. on Nursery Production of Fruit Plants Through Tissue Culture: Applications and Feasibility. U.S. Dep. Agric. Agric. Res. Results, AGR-NE-11:44–47.

SUGGESTED READING

Doughty, C. C., E. B. Adams, and L. W. Martin. 1981. Highbush blueberry production. Wash.–Oreg.–Idaho Coop. Ext. Serv. Bull. PNW 215.

Eck, P. 1988. Blueberry science. Rutgers University Press, New Brunswick, N.J.

Eck, P., and N. F. Childers (eds.). 1966. Blueberry culture. Rutgers University Press, New Brunswick, N.J.

Gough, R. E., and V. G. Shutak. 1978. Anatomy and morphology of cultivated highbush blueberry. R.I. Agric. Exp. Stn. Bull. 423.

Gough, R. E., V. G. Shutak, and D. Wallace. 1985. Highbush blueberry culture. R.I. Coop. Ext. Bull. 143.

Hindle, R. J., V. G. Shutak, and E. P. Christopher. 1957. Growth studies of the highbush blueberry fruit. Proc. Am. Soc. Hortic. Sci. 69:282–287.

Johnston, S., J. Mouten, and J. Hull, Jr. 1969. Essentials of blueberry culture. Mich. State Univ. Ext. Bull. E-590.

Liebster, G., H. W. Debor, and O. Palm. 1976. Bibliography of international literature on the blueberry (*Vaccinium* sp.). Bibliographische Reihe der Technischen Universität Berlin. Herausgegeben von der Universitätsbibliothek, Berlin.

Mainland, C. M., and J. F. Brooks. 1982. Commercial blueberry production guide for North Carolina. N.C. Agric. Ext. Publ. AG-115.

Moore, J. N. 1976. Adaptation and production of blueberries in Arkansas. Arkansas Agric. Exp. Stn. Bull. 804.

Scott, D. H., A. D. Draper, and G. M. Darrow. 1978. Commercial blueberry growing. U.S. Dep. Agric. Farmers' Bull. 2254.

*LOWBUSH BLUEBERRY CULTURE**

Up to the present, harvesting of the lowbush blueberry has been from native stands of *Vaccinium* species in the northeastern United States and eastern Canada (Hall, 1955). The principal species is *V. angustifolium,* commonly known as the sweet lowbush blueberry, the biology of which has recently been described in detail (Hall et al., 1979). It is a highly variable species consisting of a multitude of clones whose flowering, fruiting, and vegetative characteristics vary greatly (Hall et al., 1972). Most authors agree that it is tetraploid species (Newcomer, 1941; Hall and Aalders, 1961; Whitton, 1964; Hersey and Vander Kloet, 1976) and separate from a low-growing, diminutive species, *V. boreale,* which is found locally on the peaks of the Adirondack Mountains and in Newfoundland–Labrador. The latter species is a diploid (Aalders and Hall, 1962). The only diploid species of commercial importance is *V. myrtilloides,* sour-top blueberry, which is found in stands recently developed from cutover woodlands (Hall, 1959). The ploidy of a species is impor-

*This discussion was prepared by Ivan V. Hall.

tant since Coville (1927) and Longley (1927) reported that *Vaccinium* species of the same chromosome number intercross and produce normal fruit, whereas those differing, seldom, if ever, produce berries. The lowbush blueberry morphology is shown in Fig. 7–7.

Growth and Development

Most lowbush blueberry fields are under a 2-year cycle of management (Barker et al., 1964). The results of a 9-year rotational burning study on blueberry fields on Prince Edward Island indicated that fruit production was greater from burning every second year than from every third year (Black, 1963).

The year following burning, vigorous shoots arise from dormant buds on the rhizomes (Barker and Collins, 1963b) and/or lower portions of the stems that survived burning. Shoot growth begins in early to mid-May in southern Maine (Eggert, 1957) and as late as mid-June in parts of Newfoundland. Shoot growth continues until a black tip forms at the end of the shoot about the first week of July in new burn and approximately a month earlier on year-old shoots (Barker and Collins, 1963a). This formation of a black tip is the death of the apical meristem (Bell, 1950) and sets the stage for a change from a vegetative state to one of flower bud formation. By late August it is possible to note that the buds developing at the tip of the shoot are larger and more plump than those at the base, which are spear-shaped. The latter are the vegetative buds from which side branches are produced the following year, whereas the terminal flower buds will break into a raceme or cluster of flowers (Bell and Burchill, 1955a). Flower buds continue to develop through late summer and early fall provided that temperatures remain above 46°F (8°C) (Hall and Ludwig, 1961). Bell and Burchill (1955b) have shown that the anther is fully formed and the female gametophyte is represented by a mature archesporium during the winter resting stage.

The second year following burning sees first the flowers and later the fruit. Flowering may be in advance of vegetative growth, concomitant with it, or in some clones may follow. In southern Maine bloom occurs in mid- to late May, while in the large producing area of Washington County, Maine, it is usually 1 week to 10 days later. The commercial fields of New Brunswick and Nova Scotia are in bloom the last week of May and the first 2 weeks of June, depending on site location (Bell, 1953).

Lowbush blueberries are insect pollinated (Boulanger et al., 1967). Many growers supplement the native pollinating force with at least one hive of honeybees per acre (two per hectare) (Karmo, 1958; Ismail, 1980). The hives of bees are brought into the fields on a trailer or similar vehicle and left in a sheltered place facing south. If the hives are placed on the ground, special care should be taken to prevent destruction by bears. As lowbush blueberries are highly self-sterile (Aalders and Hall, 1961), it is essential that pollen (Fig. 7–8) from one plant be available to pollinate flowers of a different genotype (Aalders and Hall, 1975a). Blueberry flowers are ready for pollination shortly after they open and remain highly receptive up to 4 days and to a lesser degree to 6 days (Wood, 1962a). Under field conditions it takes from 4 to 6 days of warm temperatures for fertilization to occur. Following

FIGURE 7-7 Lowbush blueberry morphology. (A) Plant habit: a, underground rhizome; b, upright stems. (B) Dormant shoots: a, vegetative buds; b, flower buds. (C) Shoot in flower. (D) Fruiting branch.

Lowbush Blueberry Culture

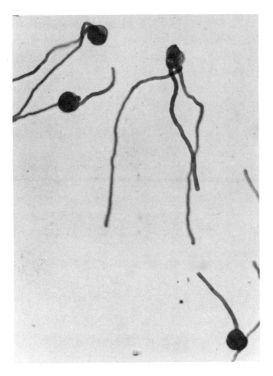

FIGURE 7-8 Germinating pollen of the lowbush blueberry. Each pollen grain may produce up to four germ tubes. These grow down through the pistil into the ovary, where fertilization occurs.

fertilization the flowers first turn pink, wither, and finally drop off. The calyx of nonpollinated flowers assumes a purplish tinge and eventually dehisces. Bell (1957) has detailed the stages of blueberry seed development and Bell and Giffin (1957) have shown the morphological development of the ovary.

Blueberry seeds play an important role in the development of the berries. Bell (1957) found that each berry contained 13.3 perfect seeds and 49.9 imperfect seeds. Hall et al. (1979) found considerably higher values in crosses involving six selected clones. Berries harvested from areas suspected of receiving below-freezing temperatures during bloom had lower seed counts than did areas free from frost (Jackson et al., 1972).

Under field conditions it takes 70 to 90 days for berry development. Following fertilization the fruit is in an active state of metabolic activity, with rapid increase in size, rate of respiration (Forsyth and Hall, 1969), and ethylene production (Hall and Forsyth, 1967). Following the initial increase in berry size there is a period in which metabolic activity decreases markedly, during the month of July (Forsyth and Hall, 1969). The final increase in size is due to enlargement of individual cells. The fruits ripen during mid- to late summer. In Cumberland County, Nova Scotia, where 80% of the Nova Scotian crop is harvested, harvesting begins approximately August 20. A field study at Nappan, Cumberland County, conducted over a 3-year period showed that from 70 to 80% of the fruits were ripe by August 10, and by August 30 more than 90% were ripe (Aalders et al., 1972b). Harvesting may continue as late as the first week of October in Newfoundland on the Avalon Peninsula provided that frost does not occur. Berries subjected to frost become soft and of poor quality in 2 to 3 days (Hall and Leefe, 1966).

Pruning

Pruning is usually done by burning with oil, propane, or straw (Hall et al., 1975). The object is to apply enough heat to kill the stems to about ½ in. (1 cm) from the soil surface. Many of the charred stems remain during the first year following burning, but generally they become flattened by pressure from snow and ice in the winter and thus do not interfere with raking in the crop year. Many growers find it a sound practice to mow the vegetation on their fields before burning. On reasonably smooth terrain growers have found pruning with oil the most economical. With these burners (Fig. 7-9) they use from 400 to 500 gal/acre (375 to 475 liters/ha) of furnace oil. Propane is used only on small fields where access to fields is difficult, especially in the spring. Burners should be adjusted so that 200 to 275 lb/acre (225 to 300 kg/ha) of propane gas is needed. Straw or marsh hay is an excellent burn material because it can be spread in late fall at a time when other farm duties are not as pressing as in spring. It can also be burned in the spring as soon as the last patch of snow has melted from the field. At this time there is generally snow in the woods, which gives an added amount of fire protection. The scattering rate is 1300 to 2200 lb/acre (1500 to 2500 kg/ha) of straw. Results of burning trials indicate that fall burning is as good as early spring burning. No burning should be done on stands of plants where vegetative growth has started (Eaton and White, 1960).

FIGURE 7-9   Oil burner being used to renovate a lowbush blueberry field.

Weed Control

Most weeds of lowbush blueberry fields are woody shrubs or woodland species which thrive under the present cultural practices (Chandler and Mason, 1946). Pruning stimulates the rhizomes of weeds such as bunchberry (Hall and Sibley, 1976) or sweet fern (Hall et al., 1976) to produce new shoots. The purpose of weed control is to eliminate the weeds while they are still small patches. Several chemicals have been tested and the susceptibility of various species is given in various extension bulletins (Trevett, 1952) and weed control guides. Those herbicides registered for use on blueberries in Canada are 2,4-D, dicamba, terbacil, asulam, and hexazinone (Jensen, 1985). Dicamba and 2,4-D are used primarily as spot sprays against species not controlled by hexazinone.

The introduction in the early 1980s of the herbicide hexazinone drastically changed weed control practices in lowbush blueberry stands. Applied at 1.7 to 2.2 lb/acre (2.0 to 2.5 kg/ha) in the spring after pruning and before new growth begins it controls many herbaceous and woody weeds, including lambkill, meadow sweet, Labrador tea, and trailing blackberry. Jensen and Kimball (1985) demonstrated that blueberry stand and fruit yield were increased by 33 to 55% on plots receiving 1.7 and 3.4 lb/acre (2.0 and 3.5 kg/ha) of hexazinone, respectively. Increased yields were related to increases in number of flower buds per shoot and to the density of fruiting shoots. Studies in Maine (Yarborough and Ismail, 1985) showed a highly significant decline in meadow sweet and goldenrod with an increase in hexazinone rate. Weeds resistant to hexazinone, such as alder, choke pear, honeysuckle, bracken, and hay-scented fern, are generally treated by spot spraying with a specific herbicide, for example, 2,4-D and dicamba. For hay-scented fern, terbacil is the most effective herbicide.

Fertilization

Although lowbush blueberries are often found growing on very light sandy soils, the proof of the need for applications of fertilizer is difficult to show (Trevett, 1962, 1965b). After many years of extensive research in Maine, Trevett (1969b) stated that nitrogen was the one element that had given a consistent response. The amounts to be added were quite small, 35 lb/acre (39 kg/ha). Growers should assess their need for fertilizer by setting out small test plots in their fields and comparing the flower bud count and yield of fertilized with nonfertilized areas.

The nutrient deficiency symptoms for the lowbush blueberry have been described and resemble those found in other species (Lockhart, 1959; Kender and Anastasia, 1964). The percent dry weight of minerals in leaves has been reported by several authors, including Trevett (1962) and Lockhart and Langille (1962) and from rhizomes and associated leaves by Townsend et al. (1968). On the basis of their own work, as well as that of others, Townsend and Hall (1970) suggested that the levels of the various nutrients in the leaves at the time of flower bud initiation should be as listed in Table 7-3.

Several problems have been encountered in the use of fertilizer. Nitrogen

TABLE 7-3 NUTRIENT LEVELS FOR BUD INITIATION

NUTRIENT	RANGE OF CONCENTRATION (%)
N	1.50–2.00
P	0.08–0.12
K	0.40–0.55
Ca	0.40–0.65
Mg	0.15–0.20

applied too late in the year following burning has promoted new growth that is subject to winter killing (Trevett, 1969a). Areas receiving regular applications of fertilizer have shown a marked increase in populations of black chokeberry (Hall et al., 1978). Fertilizer applications with quantities of phosphorus and potassium have sometimes stimulated grass growth, which interferes with raking.

Fertilizer applications have been most successful when adequate moisture was available. Some growers are now setting up irrigation systems which will ensure movement of nutrients in dry weather and provide good frost protection, especially during the bloom period (Anon., 1979).

Diseases

Several pathogenic fungi have been recognized on lowbush blueberries (Conners, 1967), but only three diseases are considered serious. Twig and blossom blight caused by *Monilinia vaccinii-corymbosi* (Hilborn, 1955) infects the buds, twigs, leaves, flowers, and the fruit of the blueberry plant. Infected fruit becomes hard or mummified and is capable of surviving the winter months. In the spring, a stalked cup-shaped structure called an apothecium is formed from the mummies about the same time that buds begin to swell and open (Lockhart, 1961). Spores are discharged at this time, infecting leaf and flower buds. Two to three weeks after infection leaf shoots and flower clusters wilt and turn brown. Conidia formed on infected tissue infect flower ovaries. The resulting fruit shrivels and falls to the ground prior to harvest. The mummified fruit overwinters to complete the cycle. *Monilinia* blight can be controlled by two spring applications of triforine.

Botrytis blight, caused by *Botrytis cinerea,* occurs during bloom and shortly thereafter and may be a consistent problem in some fields or in seasons when extended wet periods occur during bloom or shortly after petal fall. The fungus attacks the blossoms and young fruit, causing them to turn brown. During damp weather typical gray mold can be seen on the infected tissue. Control is achieved by applying suitable fungicides during the bloom period.

A systemic disease that is considered serious in coastal areas of eastern Canada is red leaf disease, caused by *Exobasidium vaccinii* (Lockhart and Delbridge, 1979). It is recognized in fruiting fields in June and July by the bright red foliage of infected plants. The lower surface of infected leaves becomes covered with a white felt-like spore-bearing layer of the fungus. By midsummer infected leaves drop and the disease is inconspicuous the rest of the season. The symptoms reappear on the same plants in subsequent years because the fungus overwinters in stems and rhizomes. Since infected plants fruit poorly, eradication of diseased clones is recommended.

Insects

The approach to insect control in stands of the lowbush blueberry has been to avoid a general insecticide program. Selective insecticides have been applied only to areas where a problem insect has been identified (Wood and Small, 1978). Some insects that have been troublesome during the last 30 years have been the blueberry maggot (Wood, 1962b), black army cutworm (Wood and Neilson, 1956), case beetle (Wood, 1966), flea beetles (Maxwell et al., 1954), red-striped fireworm (Wood, 1972), and tussock moth (Wood, 1959).

The adult fly of the blueberry maggot emerges just as the first berries turn blue and they lay their eggs in the pulp of the fruit (Lathrop and Nickels, 1932). Two aerial applications 7 days apart of axinophos-methyl at 1.5 gal/acre (14.4 liters/ha) will control this pest. Where maggot is a problem, growers are advised to burn refuse from winnowing machines and to burn-prune all areas of their fields every second year. The black army cutworm begins to feed as soon as growth begins in the spring. The larvae eat out the interior of the flower buds and later under epidemic proportions will feed on the foliage. Feeding is generally at night. Carbaryl 5% dust applied at 20 lb/acre (22.4 kg/ha) or carbaryl 25% dust at 4 lb/acre (4.5 kg/ha) will control spring caterpillars on bearing fields.

Blueberry case beetle has been found throughout the greater part of the producing areas but has assumed epidemic proportions in only one localized area. Larvae feed on leaves immediately following bloom, whereas the adults emerge in late summer and feed on the bark of shoots until early winter. Trichlorfon 80% S.P. at 1.2 lb/acre (1.3 kg/ha) or carbaryl (same rate as for cutworm) following bloom will control case beetle.

Flea beetle infections are generally quite localized and feeding begins shortly after growth of the lowbush blueberry begins. The feeding stage of this insect is a black grub about 0.4 in. (1 cm) long. Trichlorfon 80% S.P. at 1.2 lb/acre (1.3 kg/ha) is recommended for control.

Red-striped fireworm has recently developed into a pest causing serious damage. The larvae tie two or more leaves together and skeletonize them. In a bearing field the activity of this insect can result in severe dessication of the plant and in reduction of fruit quality by squashing of fruit due to fused stems. For control use carbaryl at the rate recommended for cutworms.

Tussock moths attack a whole host of woody plants, including lowbush blueberries. Populations tend to decline rapidly, as the species is susceptible to disease and climatic conditions. The yellow and black larvae are easily recognized. Trichlorfon at the same rate as used on flea beetle or case beetle is the control measure. In wet weather more than one application may be necessary.

Insect problems are changing as cultural methods change. In areas where little burning has been employed, leaftiers and leafrollers have assumed epidemic proportions. With increasing oil prices growers are considering longer periods between burning or are pruning by mowing. These practices may create further problems.

Harvesting

The purpose in harvesting is to remove the berries as efficiently as possible and to retain an attractive pack of fresh fruit (Abdalla, 1963). Growers have found it beneficial to line off the field in strips about 3 ft (1 m) wide and to assign one picker to each lane. The berries are collected by passing a rake (Fig. 7–10), a specially designed aide for harvesting this crop, upward and forward through the stems of the plant. After two or three passes the raker tips the rake sideways and allows the berries to fall into a pail or suitable container (Fig. 7–11). When this is full the raker carries it to a foreman, who inspects the product and records the weight. Rakers may be paid on the basis of number of containers filled, but the more general practice is to pay according to total weight harvested per day. Berries are quickly moved from the field to a receiving station or delivered directly to a cold storage plant, where they are frozen by an individual quick freeze (IQF) process. As more blueberry land is developed the need for labor increases, and several growers as well as research teams are vigorously trying to develop mechanical harvesters. Machines are available that will work reasonably well on land that was originally cultivated and is relatively free of weeds (Hall et al., 1975).

New Plantings

The idea of setting out fields to superior clones of the lowbush blueberries goes back many years (Brierley and Kenety, 1920; and Duis, 1941). At Kentville, Nova Scotia, a program of selecting clones from native stands began in 1961, and by 1966 nearly 1000 clones had been selected from fields in the Atlantic Provinces and the province

FIGURE 7–10 Rake for harvesting lowbush blueberries.

Lowbush Blueberry Culture

FIGURE 7-11 Lowbush blueberries after hand-rake harvest being separated from leaves and stems in a cleaning machine. (Courtesy of North American Blueberry Council.)

of Quebec and from the Blueberry Station at Jonesboro, Maine. Since then, selections have been made from original clones and crosses made using the selected clones as parent material. Several projects have been initiated to plant out rooted cuttings of superior clones or progenies of seedlings. Data from experimental plots have shown that plantings of our best clones have outyielded related seedling progenies (Aalders et al., 1979). There is, however, much interest in using seedlings, as the growth habit is more conducive to early rhizome growth (Aalders et al., 1972a) and the price per plant is lower. Seed can be stored in the fruit or dry at temperatures just below freezing (Aalders and Hall, 1975b). Seeds germinate well if sown on the surface of media consisting of equal parts of peat and sand. Pelleting of seeds improves germination (Aalders and Hall, 1979). Anderson and Teeter (1976) have outlined the economic advantages of select clone plantings. Recently, tissue culture techniques have been developed for rapid propagation of lowbush blueberries from seedling tissues (Nickerson, 1978) and from shoot tips of mature plants (Nickerson, unpublished; Smagula and Lyrene, 1984).

REFERENCES

AALDERS, L. E., AND I. V. HALL. 1961. Pollen incompatability and fruit set in lowbush blueberries. Can. J. Genet. Cytol. 3:300–307.

AALDERS, L. E., AND I. V. HALL. 1962. New evidence on the cytotaxonomy of *Vaccinium* species as revealed by stomatal measurements from herbarium specimens. Nature 196:694.

AALDERS, L. E., AND I. V. HALL. 1975a. A study of variation in fruit yield and related characters in two diallels of the lowbush blueberry, *Vaccinium angustifolium* Ait. Can. J. Genet. Cytol. 17:401–404.

AALDERS, L. E., AND I. V. HALL. 1975b. Germination of lowbush blueberry seeds stored dry and in fruit at different temperatures. HortScience 10:525–526.

AALDERS, L. E., AND I. V. HALL. 1979. Germination of lowbush blueberry seeds as affected by sizing, planting cover, storage, and pelleting. Can. J. Plant Sci. 59:527–530.

AALDERS, L. E., AND I. V. HALL, AND A. C. BRYDON. 1979. A comparison of fruit yields of lowbush blueberry clonal lines and related seedling progenies. Can. J. Plant Sci. 59:875–877.

AALDERS, L. E., I. V. HALL, AND L. P. JACKSON. 1972a. Growth of lowbush blueberry seedlings as compared with clonal cuttings. Can. J. Plant Sci. 52:655–656.

AALDERS, L. E., L. P. JACKSON, B. G. PENNY, A. F. RAYMENT, R. STAR, AND I. V. HALL. 1972b. Selection of an 'optimum' time to harvest lowbush blueberry fruit. Can. J. Plant Sci. 52:701–705.

ABDALLA, D. A. 1963. Raking and handling lowbush blueberries. Univ. Maine Coop. Ext. Serv. Bull. 497.

ANDERSON, R. W., AND J. J. TEETER. 1976. Atlantic lowbush blueberries. Can. Farm Econ. 11:1–37.

ANON. 1979. Cultivated lowbush blueberries. Production guidelines. New Brunswick Department of Agriculture, Plant Industry Branch.

BARKER, W. G., AND W. B. COLLINS. 1963a. Growth and development of the lowbush blueberry: apical abortion. Can. J. Bot. 41:1319–1324.

BARKER, W. G., AND W. B. COLLINS. 1963b. The blueberry rhizome: *in vitro* culture. Can. J. Bot. 41:1325–1329.

BARKER, W. G., I. V. HALL, L. E. AALDERS, AND G. W. WOOD. 1964. The lowbush blueberry industry in eastern Canada. Econ. Bot. 18:357–365.

BELL, H. P. 1950. Determinate growth in the blueberry. Can. J. Res. C28:637–644.

BELL, H. P. 1953. The growth cycle of the blueberry and some factors of the environment. Can. J. Bot. 31:1–6.

BELL, H. P. 1957. The development of the blueberry seed. Can. J. Bot. 35:139–153.

BELL, H. P., AND J. BURCHILL. 1955a. Flower development in the lowbush blueberry. Can. J. Bot. 33:251–258.

BELL, H. P., AND J. BURCHILL. 1955b. Winter resting stages of certain Ericaceae. Can. J. Bot. 33:547–561.

BELL, H. P., AND E. C. GIFFIN. 1957. The lowbush blueberry: the vascular anatomy of the ovary. Can. J. Bot. 35:667–673.

BLACK, W. N. 1963. The effect of frequency of rotational burning on blueberry production. Can. J. Plant Sci. 43:161–165.

BOULANGER, L. W., G. W. WOOD, E. A. OSGOOD, AND C. O. DIRKS. 1967. Native bees associated with the lowbush blueberry in Maine and eastern Canada. Maine Agric. Exp. Stn., Can. Agric. Res. Stn. Bull. T26.

BRIERLEY, W. G., AND W. H. KENETY. 1920. Blueberry culture in Minnesota: a report of progress. Proc. Am. Soc. Hortic. Sci. 17:243–249.

CHANDLER, F. B., AND I. C. MASON. 1946. Blueberry weeds in Maine and their control. Maine Agric. Exp. Stn. Bull. 443.

CONNERS, I. L. 1967. An annotated index of plant diseases in Canada and fungi recorded on plants in Alaska, Canada and Greenland. Can. Dep. Agric. Res. Branch, Publ. 1251, p. 310–312.

COVILLE, F. V. 1927. Blueberry chromosomes. Science 66:565–566.

DUIS, W. H. 1941. Selection of the lowbush blueberry in West Virginia. Proc. Am. Soc. Hortic. Sci. 38:434–437.

EATON, E. L. 1954. Horticulture p. 7–12. In Progress report 1949–1953. Dominion Blueberry

Substation, Tower Hill, N.B. Canada Department of Agriculture Experimental Farms and Science Services.

EATON, E. L., AND R. G. WHITE. 1960. The relation between burning dates and the development of sprouts and flower buds in the lowbush blueberry. Proc. Am. Soc. Hortic. Sci. 76:338–342.

EGGERT, F. P. 1957. Shoot emergence and flowering habit in the lowbush blueberry (*Vaccinium angustifolium*). Proc. Am. Soc. Hortic. Sci. 69:288–292.

FORSYTH, F. R., AND I. V. HALL. 1969. Ethylene production with accompanying respiration rates from the time of blossoming to fruit maturity in three *Vaccinium* species. Nat. Can. 96:257–259.

HALL, I. V. 1955. Floristic changes following the cutting and burning of a woodlot for blueberry production. Can. J. Agric. Sci. 35:143–152.

HALL, I. V. 1959. Plant populations in blueberry stands developed from abandoned hayfields and woodlots. Ecology 40:742–743.

HALL, I. V. 1975. The biology of Canadian weeds. 7. *Myrica pennsylvanica* Loisel. Can. J. Plant Sci. 55:163–169.

HALL, I. V., AND L. E. AALDERS. 1961. Cytotaxonomy of lowbush blueberries in eastern Canada. Am. J. Bot. 48:199–201.

HALL, I. V., AND F. R. FORSYTH. 1967. Production of ethylene by flowers following pollination and treatment with water and auxin. Can. J. Bot. 45:1163–1166.

HALL, I. V., AND J. S. LEEFE. 1966. The effects of frost injury before harvest on yield of marketable lowbush blueberries. Can. J. Plant Sci. 46:205.

HALL, I. V., AND R. A. LUDWIG. 1961. The effects of photoperiod, temperature, and light intensity on the growth of the lowbush blueberry (*Vaccinium angustifolium* Ait.). Can. J. Bot. 39:1733–1739.

HALL, I. V., AND J. D. SIBLEY. 1976. The biology of Canadian weeds. 20. *Cornus canadensis* L. Can. J. Plant Sci. 56:885–892.

HALL, I. V., F. R. FORSYTH, L. E. AALDERS, AND L. P. JACKSON. 1972. Physiology of the lowbush blueberry. Econ. Bot. 26:68–73.

HALL, I. V., L. P. JACKSON, AND C. F. EVERETT. 1973. The biology of Canadian weeds. 1. *Kalmia angustifolia* L. Can. J. Plant Sci. 53:865–873.

HALL, I. V., L. E. AALDERS, L. P. JACKSON, G. W. WOOD, AND C. L. LOCKHART. 1975. Lowbush blueberry production. Can. Dep. Agric. Publ. 1477.

HALL, I. V., L. E. AALDERS, AND C. F. EVERETT. 1976. The biology of Canadian weeds. 16. *Comptonia peregrina* (L.) Coult. Can. J. Plant Sci. 56:147–156.

HALL, I. V., G. W. WOOD, AND L. P. JACKSON. 1978. The biology of Canadian weeds. 30. *Pyrus melanocarpa* (Michx.) Willd. Can. J. Plant Sci. 57:499–504.

HALL, I. V., L. E. AALDERS, N. L. NICKERSON, AND S. P. VANDER KLOET. 1979. The biological flora of Canada. 1. *Vaccinium angustifolium* Ait., sweet lowbush blueberry. Can. Field-Nat. 93(4):415–430.

HERSEY, R., AND S. P. VANDER KLOET. 1976. IOPB chromosome number reports L11. Taxon 25:241–346.

HILBORN, M. T. 1955. Blueberry diseases and their control. *In* Producing blueberries in Maine. Maine Agric. Exp. Stn. Bull. 479:27–32.

ISMAIL, A. A. 1974. Terbacil and fertility effects on yield of lowbush blueberry. HortScience 9:457.

ISMAIL, A. A. 1980. Honey bees and blueberry pollination. Coop. Ext. Serv. Univ. Maine Bull. 629.

JACKSON, L. P., L. E. AALDERS, AND I. V. HALL. 1972. Berry size and seed number in commercial lowbush blueberry fields of Nova Scotia. Nat. Can. 99: 615-619.

JENSEN, K. I. N., AND E. R. KIMBALL. 1985. Tolerance and residues of Hexazinone in lowbush blueberries. Can. J. Plant Sci. 65:223-227.

KARMO, E. A. 1958. Honeybees as an aid in orchard and blueberry pollination in Nova Scotia. Proc. International Congress on Entomology 10th Meeting, Montreal, Quebec, 1956, 4:955-959.

KENDER, W. J., AND F. ANASTASIA. 1964. Nutrient deficiency symptoms of the lowbush blueberry. Proc. Am. Soc. Hortic. Sci. 85:275-280.

LATHROP, F. H., AND C. B. NICKELS. 1932. The biology and control of the blueberry maggot in Washington County, Maine. U.S. Dep. Agric. Tech. Bull. 275.

LOCKHART, C. L. 1959. Symptoms of mineral deficiency in the lowbush blueberry. Plant Dis. Rep. 43:102-105.

LOCKHART, C. L. 1961. *Monilina* twig and blossom blight of lowbush blueberry and its control. Can. J. Plant Sci. 41:336-341.

LOCKHART, C. L., AND R. W. DELBRIDGE. 1979. Diseases. p. 29-37. *In* Lowbush blueberry production. Agric. Can. Publ. 1477.

LOCKHART, C. L., AND W. M. LANGILLE. 1962. The mineral content of the lowbush blueberry. Can. Plant. Dis. Surv. 42:124-128.

LONGLEY, A. E. 1927. Chromosomes in *Vaccinium*. Science 66:566-568.

MAXWELL, C. W. B., G. W. WOOD, AND W. NEILSON. 1954. Insects in relation to blueberry culture. p. 13-16. In Progress report 1949-1953. Dominion Blueberry Substation, Tower Hill, N.B. Canada Department of Agriculture Experimental Farms and Science Services.

NEWCOMER, E. H. 1941. Chromosome numbers of some species and varieties of *Vaccinium* and related genera. Proc. Am. Soc. Hortic. Sci. 38:468-470.

NICKERSON, N. L. 1978. In vitro shoot formation in lowbush blueberry seedling explants. HortScience 13:698.

PLAFREY, G. D. 1957. Weed control in wild blueberries. Pamphlet 5. N.S. Dep. Agric. Market.

SMAGULA, J. M., AND P. M. LYRENE. 1984. Blueberry. p. 383-401. In P. V. Ammirato, D. A. Evans, W. R. Sharp, and Y. Yamada (eds.). Handbook of plant cell culture. Vol. 3. Macmillan, New York.

TAYLOR, E. M. 1954. Fertilizer and mulching experiments. p. 12-13. In Progress report 1949-1953. Dominion Blueberry Substation, Tower Hill, N.B. Canada Department of Agriculture Experimental Farms and Science Services.

TOWNSEND, L. R., AND I. V. HALL. 1970. Trends in nutrient levels of lowbush blueberry leaves during four consecutive years of sampling. Nat. Can. 97:461-466.

TOWNSEND, L. R., I. V. HALL, AND L. E. AALDERS. 1968. Chemical composition of rhizomes and associated leaves of the lowbush blueberry. Proc. Am. Soc. Hortic. Sci. 93:248-253.

TREVETT, M. F. 1952. Control of woody weeds in lowbush blueberry fields. Maine Agric. Exp. Stn. Bull. 499.

TREVETT, M. F. 1956. Observations on the decline and rehabilitation of lowbush blueberry fields. Maine Agric. Exp. Stn. Misc. Publ. 626.

References   **313**

TREVETT, M. F. 1961. Controlling lambkill in lowbush blueberries. Maine Agric. Exp. Stn. Bull. 600.

TREVETT, M. F. 1962. Nutrition and growth of the lowbush blueberry. Maine Agric. Exp. Stn. Bull. 605.

TREVETT, M. F. 1965a. Spring or fall fertilization for lowbush blueberries. Maine Farm Res. 12:11.

TREVETT, M. F. 1965b. Fertilizing lowbush blueberries is tricky. Maine Farm Res. 12:35–42.

TREVETT, M. F. 1966. A small weed roller for lowbush blueberries. Maine Farm Res. 14:48–54.

TREVETT, M. F. 1968. Side effects of fertilizers in lowbush blueberries. Res. Life Sci. 16:3–8.

TREVETT, M. F. 1969a. Winter injury and fertilizers in lowbush blueberries. Res. Life Sci. 16:4–15.

TREVETT, M. F. 1969b. Nitrogen fertilizers increase the stand of lowbush blueberry stems. Res. Life Sci. 16:48–50.

TREVETT, M. F., AND R. E. DURGIN. 1971. Regulating soil acidity in lowbush blueberry fields. Res. Life Sci. 19:1–11.

TREVETT, M. F., P. N. CARPENTER, AND R. E. DURGIN. 1968. A discussion of the effects of mineral nutrient interactions on foliar diagnosis in lowbush blueberries. Maine Agric. Exp. Stn. Bull. 664.

WEBSTER, D. H. 1962. Entry of 2,4-dichlorophenoxyacetic acid into lambkill leaves at varied 2,4-D/Tween 20 ratios. Weeds 10:250–251.

WHITTON, L. 1964. The cytotaxonomic status of *Vaccinium angustifolium* Aiton in commercial blueberry fields of Maine. Ph.D. thesis. Cornell University, Ithaca, N.Y.

WOOD, G. W. 1959. Insects. p. 10–12. In Progress report 1954–1959. Blueberry Station, Tower Hill, N.B. Canada Department of Agriculture Experimental Farms and Science Services.

WOOD, G. W. 1962a. The period of receptivity in flowers of the lowbush blueberry. Can. J. Bot. 40:685–686.

WOOD, G. W. 1962b. The blueberry maggot in the Maritime Provinces. Can. Dep. Agric. Publ. 1161.

WOOD, G. W. 1966. Life history and control of casebearer, *Chlamesus cribripennis* (Coleoptera:Chrysomelidae) on blueberry. J. Econ. Entomol. 59:823–825.

WOOD, G. W. 1972. Effects of feeding by the red-striped fireworm on lowbush blueberry production. Can. J. Plant Sci. 52:397–398.

WOOD, G. W., AND W. T. A. NEILSON. 1956. Notes on the black army cutworm, *Actebia fennica* (Tausch.) (Lepidoptera:Phalaenidae), a pest of lowbush blueberry in New Brunswick. Can. Entomol. 88:93–96.

WOOD, G. W., AND D. M. SMALL. 1978. Trichlorfon: a selective insecticide for lowbush blueberry. J. Econ. Entomol. 71:219–220.

YARBOROUGH, D. E., AND A. A. ISMAIL. 1985. Hexazinone on weeds and on lowbush blueberry yield. HortScience 20:406–407.

Of the species of blueberries (*Vaccinium* spp.) native to the southeastern United States, the most important commercially is the rabbiteye (*V. ashei* Reade). The first known commercial planting of rabbiteye blueberries was made in western Florida in 1893, using bushes transplanted from the wild or propagated from early plantings (Darrow and Moore, 1966). Similar plantings were later made in Alabama, Georgia, Louisiana, Mississippi, North Carolina, and South Carolina, often using plants obtained from Florida. At one time, more than 3500 acres (1400 ha) were planted in the southeast, consisting mainly of unselected bushes, many of which produced small, black, gritty-fleshed berries that were lacking flavor. These characteristics gave the rabbiteye a poor reputation in markets and most of the commercial plantings were finally abandoned.

In 1940 a cooperative breeding program between the Georgia Coastal Plain Experiment Station, North Carolina Agricultural Experiment Station, and the U.S. Department of Agriculture was initiated to improve the horticultural quality of rabbiteye blueberries (Darrow et al., 1944). Subsequently, the University of Florida began rabbiteye blueberry breeding studies, and presently most southern states conduct research on rabbiteye blueberries. Considerable progress has been made in improving the color, size, and quality of the rabbiteye blueberry, and the acreage of commercial blueberry plantings in the south is expanding using varieties developed mainly by the Universities of Georgia and Florida, North Carolina State University, and the U.S. Department of Agriculture.

Successful commercial plantings of rabbiteye blueberries are presently found in all southern states and acreage is expanding. Georgia has the most acreage (3000 acres, 1200 ha by 1987) followed by Florida (1400 acres, 560 ha), Mississippi (900 acres, 360 ha), Texas (650 acres, 260 ha), South Carolina (500 acres, 200 ha), Louisiana (200 acres, 80 ha), and Alabama (200 acres, 80 ha). North Carolina, a large producer of highbush blueberries, has about 200 acres (80 ha) of rabbiteye blueberries grown in small commercial plantings and 'pick-your-own' operations (Brooks, 1970). Arkansas, another state with highbush plantings, has less than 100 acres (40 ha), grown primarily in the southern half of the state.

Figure 7–12 shows the rabbiteye blueberry morphology.

Cultivated Types

'Tifblue': leading rabbiteye cultivar. Very vigorous and widely adapted. Mid- to late-season. Fruit large, round, light blue, sweet, very firm with a small dry scar. Berries appear to be ripe several days before full flavor develops. Berries remain on plant several days after fully ripe. Georgia, 1955.

'Woodard': early, 7 to 10 days before 'Tifblue'. Bush size is the shortest and most spreading of Georgia varieties. Produces many suckers. Berries are light

*This discussion was prepared by J. M. Spiers.

FIGURE 7–12 Rabbiteye blueberry morphology. (A) Plant habit dormant: a, crown area; b, major cane; c, renewal cane or whip; d, lateral shoot (current season) bearing both flower and vegetative buds. (B) Dormant lateral shoot: a, vegetative bud: b, flower bud. (C) Lateral shoot in flower. (D) Inverted blueberry flower: a, ovary; b, ovule; c, sepal; d, filament; e, anther; f, pore; g, style; h, stigma; i, corolla. (E) Fruiting branch: a, peduncle; b, pedicle; c, calyx; d, aborted apical shoot tip.

blue, firm, large, with excellent quality when full ripe, but very tart until ripe. Georgia, 1960.

'Climax': upright, open plants. Berries are medium in size, medium dark blue in color, have a small scar and good flavor. Early season, ripening 3 to 5 days before 'Woodard'. Concentrated ripening, excellent for machine harvest. Georgia 1976.

'Briteblue': Moderately vigorous, grows upright and open. Midseason, generally before 'Tifblue'. Berry firmness, heavy bloom, and small dry scar combine to make this a good shipper. Fruit with good flavor when fully ripe. Georgia, 1969.

'Bluebelle': good 'pick-your-own' (PYO) cultivar. Berries large, round, light blue with excellent flavor, maintain size well throughout the season. Midseason. Plants moderately vigorous with upright growth. Scar tends to tear, not recommended for shipping. Georgia, 1976.

'Delite': upright bush, moderately vigorous. Season slightly later than 'Tifblue'. Berries are light blue, often with reddish undercoat; large, firm with excellent flavor. Berries are not tart before reaching maturity. Georgia, 1969.

'Southland': moderately vigorous, dense upright plant. Berries are light blue, medium large with good flavor. Tend to lose size as season progresses. Same season as 'Tifblue'. Scar is small and dry. Georgia, 1969.

'Brightwell:' early, same season as 'Woodard'. Berries are medium in size and blue in color, with small dry scars and good flavor. Plant growth is vigorous, upright, and produces enough new canes to renew the plant. Georgia, 1981.

'Premier': earlier (2 to 3 weeks) than 'Tifblue'. Large fruit with good flavor. Vigorous, disease resistant, productive. North Carolina, 1978.

'Powderblue': vigorous, disease resistant, productive. Same season as 'Tifblue', with better fruit color and more foliage disease resistance. North Carolina, 1978.

'Centurion': later than 'Tifblue'. Adds one or more weeks to the rabbiteye ripening season in North Carolina. Good flavor, not as firm as, and darker than 'Tifblue'. North Carolina, 1978.

'Beckyblue': early ripening. Low chilling requirement (less than 400 hours). Extends the cultural range of rabbiteye blueberries into south central Florida. Should be interplanted with 'Aliceblue'. Not recommended north of northern Florida. Florida, 1978.

'Aliceblue': early ripening with low chilling requirement. Similar to and should be interplanted with 'Beckyblue'. Florida, 1978.

'Baldwin': productive, late-ripening cultivar with good flavor and firm, dark-blue fruit. Has lengthy ripening period; adapted to PYO and backyard plantings. Georgia, 1985.

The following cultivars are low-chilling tetraploid (southern highbush) plants and are included since their climatic adaptability is within the range of rabbiteye blueberries:

'Avonblue': adapted to north central Florida. Ripens after 'Sharpblue' but before any rabbiteye cultivars. Fruit quality high. Florida, 1977.

'Flordablue' and 'Sharpblue': adapted to central and south central Florida, considerably south of the best range for present rabbiteye cultivars. Suitable for PYO and local markets. Interplant both cultivars for cross-pollination. Florida, 1976.

'Blue Ridge': early–midseason cultivar with medium-large, firm, high-acid-flavored fruit. Recommended for local sales and PYO in Piedmont and lower mountains of southeastern United States. Chilling requirement of 500 to 600 hours. North Carolina, 1987.

'Cape Fear': mid-early cultivar similar in season to 'Croatan' in North Carolina. Productive, with very large fruit of good color, scar, and firmness and average quality. Recommended for hand harvest and commercial shipment or PYO plantings. Chilling requirement of 500 to 600 hours. North Carolina, 1987.

'O'Neal': very early ripening cultivar with large, very high-quality fruit. Adapted for PYO or hand harvest for commercial shipment. Chilling requirement of 400 hours. North Carolina, 1987.

'Cooper' and 'Gulfcoast': moderately vigorous, upright, productive cultivars with high-quality medium-size fruit. Fruit size of 'Cooper' is larger and 'Gulfcoast' is more productive. Flower later than 'Climax' and ripen 2 to 3 weeks earlier than 'Climax' or 'Premier'. Mississippi, 1987.

'Georgiagem': moderately vigorous, upright, productive with medium-size fruit that has good color, small scar, and is firm. Blooms later than 'Climax' but earlier than 'Sharpblue' and 'Avonblue' and ripens 2 weeks before 'Climax'. Georgia, 1987.

Environmental Relationships

Rabbiteye blueberries are grown from North Carolina and the mountainous areas of north Georgia south to Gainesville, Florida, and westward to east Texas. Native to the Gulf South, this crop inherently has a low-chilling requirement. Since plants tend to bloom before danger of frost is past, they are subject to frost damage in colder areas (Kender and Brightwell, 1966; Darrow, 1942). Severe temperatures can damage even dormant rabbiteye plants. A temperature of $-17°F$ ($-27°C$) in January killed fruit buds and injured some shoots on rabbiteye seedlings grown in Beltsville, Maryland (Darrow et al., 1944). In Tennessee a drop to $-8°F$ ($-22°C$) before mid-December damaged 'Tifblue' plants and killed 'Homebell' plants (Kender and Brightwell, 1966). 'Woodard' plants were not damaged. In controlled cold damage studies, severe damage was prevalent in rabbiteye blueberry plants that had broken dormancy and were subjected to $-4°F$ ($-20°C$) and $10°F$ ($-12°C$) killed all new growth and some small stems but did not damage larger canes.

A freeze ($16°F, -9°C$) on March 1, 1980 was estimated to reduce the fruit in southern Mississippi from 30 to 90%, depending on cultivar, with 'Briteblue',

'Tifblue', and 'Climax' the most cold tolerant and 'Delite' and 'Woodard' the most susceptible (Spiers, 1981).

Rabbiteye blueberries require a shorter rest period [chilling hours less than 45°F (7°C)] than do highbush cultivars. Darrow (1942) reported that 200 hours below 45°F (7°C) were not sufficient to break dormancy in the rabbiteye blueberry 'Pecan' but that after 250 chilling hours the plants appeared to have completed their rest period. Other studies have shown that 'Woodard' required more than 200 hours chilling, while 'Tifblue' needed more than 400 hours to break dormancy (Spiers and Draper, 1974). Leaf removal reduced the rest requirement period of vegetative buds. Additional chilling above the required number of hours to break dormancy increases the amount and rate of floral bud break (Gilreath and Buchanan, 1981; Spiers and Draper, 1974). Field studies in Florida (Sharpe and Sherman, 1971) and growth chamber data in Mississippi (Spiers, 1976) indicate that 'Tifblue' requires 500 hours of chilling for plants to grow and flower normally. 'Tifblue' is not recommended for central Florida for this reason.

Propagation

Rabbiteye blueberries are usually propagated by rooting softwood or hardwood cuttings, but other methods, such as transferring suckers or offshoots and budding on native rootstock, can be used. Rabbiteye blueberries are considered more difficult to root than highbush blueberries. There appear to be little or no differences in ease of rooting among rabbiteye varieties (Brightwell, 1971; Spiers, 1978c; Austin and Mason, 1978).

Softwood cuttings are taken from young shoots just nearing the end of their spring period of growth (Ware, 1930), which is normally the last of April through May, depending on latitude and growing season. Hardwood cuttings are made from shoots or whips which are commonly 12 to 36 in. (31 to 91 cm) long. These shoots must be well hardened and can be collected in late January through February (Spiers et al., 1974) (Fig. 7–13). Shoots collected earlier should be stored at cool temperatures between 35 and 40°F (1.7 to 4.4°C) with adequate moisture and air ventilation until they are placed in the propagation bed. Cuttings should not be taken from diseased plants, and flower buds should be removed from the terminals of hardwood whips before sticking.

Establishment

Rabbiteye blueberries will grow well on various soil types but do best on light, well-drained soils with a soil pH between 4.2 and 5.5. If soil pH values are higher than 5.5, elemental sulfur can be applied the year before planting to increase soil acidity (lower the pH). These plants possess a fibrous root system that penetrates more deeply into a well-drained soil than does the root system of the highbush, but penetration is still relatively shallow (Ballinger, 1966). The roots develop best in a moist, well-drained soil with good fertility. Soil drainage is necessary to prevent root injury from excessive moisture. The water table should be a minimum of 20 in. (50

FIGURE 7-13 Rabbiteye blueberry plant from the nursery prior to planting.

cm) below the soil surface (Ferree and Austin, 1979). This can be accomplished by the use of drainage ditches or by setting the plants on wide raised beds.

The growth and yield of highbush blueberries generally are considered proportional to the amount of organic matter in the soil (Cain and Eck, 1966). This also appears to be true for rabbiteye blueberries. Since most soils used for blueberry production in the South are extremely low in organic matter, general planting instructions often include incorporating peat moss into the backfill soil at planting (Arnold and Sherman, 1974; Brightwell, 1971; Moore, 1970; Spiers et al., 1985). Peat moss is important for improving the soil structure and increasing retention of moisture. Also, the cation-exchange capacity of many upland soils of the Southeast is usually low, and peat moss with a high exchange capacity reduces the leaching of plant nutrients. Nitrogen may be held on the exchange complex of peat moss in the ammonium form, which is readily absorbed by blueberry plants (Cain, 1952). One study showed that 30% more plants survived and plant growth doubled over a 2-year period when peat was incorporated into the planting hole of an upland soil (Spiers, 1980).

Noxious weeds should be eliminated completely prior to planting. This usually requires extensive cultivation and/or the use of a systemic herbicide for weeds with rhizomes.

Rabbiteye blueberries can be planted any time during the dormant season. Plants should be set approximately ½ to 1 in. (1.3 to 2.5 cm) deeper than they grew in the nursery. Plant spacing usually ranges from 5 to 8 ft (1.5 to 2.4 m) between plants in a row and from 12 to 14 ft (3.7 to 4.3 m) between rows. The closer spacings might be more efficient for mechanical harvesting, and the wider spacings are often used in pick-your-own operations (Ferree and Austin, 1979).

Young rabbiteye blueberry plants are extremely sensitive to fertilizer (Spiers, 1982a). When planted under irrigation with incorporated peat moss, little fertilization should be needed the first growing season.

Nutrition

Available information on the effects of fertilizer on rabbiteye blueberries is limited, but the number of reports are increasing as this crop gains importance. Darrow (1957) reported that rabbiteye blueberries responded to applications of complete fertilizers containing 4% nitrogen. An 8-4-8 analysis with ammonium sulfate as the nitrogen source was used on rabbiteye types in Florida at the rate of 800 lb/acre (897 kg/ha) (Mowry and Camp, 1928). Later studies from Georgia indicated that two rabbiteye cultivars had little or no response to fertilizer over a 6-year period (Austin and Brightwell, 1977). Another study indicated similar results, in which 'Tifblue' did not respond to fertilizer levels during the first 5 years after planting. Increasing fertilizer levels increased unmarketable fruit, the amount of pruned wood, and time required to grade fruit (Austin and Mullinix, 1980). Austin and Gaines (1984) reported that old (36 years) rabbiteye blueberry plants on a typical low-fertility Coastal Plain soil grew and fruited well after receiving no fertilizer for 14 years.

In a study of blueberries grown in nutrient solutions rabbiteye plants were considered to be iron inefficient since they did not respond to iron stress by inducing biochemical reactions that make iron more available for use (Brown and Draper, 1980). Compared to highbush types, rabbiteye blueberries were reported to be more susceptible to iron-deficiency symptoms, and also had less iron in their leaves. The addition of $CaCO_3$ to nutrient solutions decreased iron transport from roots to leaves, indicating calcium competition with iron resulting in iron chlorosis (Brown and Draper, 1980). Another greenhouse nutrient study using $CaCl_2$ as the calcium source showed no differences in leaf content of iron at three levels of calcium fertilization (Spiers, 1979b). Variable fertilization treatments (20, 40, and 80 ppm of calcium) did not affect plant growth, fruit yield, and the elemental uptake of nutrients, with the exception of calcium.

Rabbiteye blueberries grow best in acid soils with the pH between 4.2 and 5.5 (Ferree and Austin, 1979; Shoemaker, 1978). Brightwell (1971) reported that rabbiteye blueberry plants on soils with pH values above 5.5 became chlorotic and grew poorly. Cummings et al. (1981) found that the growth and yield of rabbiteye blueberries decreased as soil pH of a fine sand was raised from 4.5 to 7.0. Plant survival decreased at pH 6.0 and 6.5, and all bushes died at pH 7. With a fine sandy loam soil, Spiers (1984) found better rabbiteye blueberry plant survival at pH 6.5 to 7.0 than at pH 3.0 to 3.5. Both studies indicate possible plant damage due to excess sulfur additions to the soil (Cummings et al., 1981; Spiers, 1984). The reported poor growth of blueberries in soils with high pH values is probably due to the unavailability of essential elements at high pH levels. Another possible cause of poor growth at high pH levels is an increase of nitrates present in soils with high pH values (Oertli, 1963). Available nitrogen in acid soils is mainly in the NH_4+ form, which is considered by some workers to be the most suitable nitrogen source for blueberries (Cain, 1952; Spiers, 1978a, 1979c). Studies comparing nutrient uptake in rabbiteye blueberry plants fertilized with either $(NH_4)_2SO_4$ (reduced nitrogen) or $NaNO_3$ (oxidized nitrogen) indicated much greater uptake of nutrients and plant vigor in plants receiving reduced nitrogen. This reduction in mineral indicated that NO_3- is less available than NH_4+ (Spiers, 1978a, 1979c). Studies have shown that rabbiteye blueberry plants receiving NO_3- had a higher pH within the leaves than plants fertilized with NH_4+ (Spiers, 1979c). This higher leaf pH could cause some nutrient precipitation and be detrimental to blueberry growth (Cain, 1954). Optimum time for the collection of leaf samples from rabbiteye blueberries for mineral analysis appears to be during the latter part of the harvest season through a 1- to 2-week period immediately following harvest.

Most fertilizer recommendations include a complete fertilizer, with $(NH_4)_2SO_4$ as the preferred nitrogen source (Spiers et al., 1985; Brightwell, 1971; Scott et al., 1978; Ferree and Austin, 1979; Puls, 1978). This form of nitrogen supplies available nitrogen to the plants and tends to reduce the pH of soil also. Nutrient element balances appear to be important in the nutrition of blueberries. Rabbiteye blueberries may lack a mechanism to regulate sodium uptake and have a low tolerance to salinity (Spiers, 1983b). Studies in Texas found plant growth in rabbiteye blueberries was negatively correlated with the sodium content of irrigation water (Haby et al., 1986). Creech et al. (1986) stated growers should avoid using irrigation water containing over 50 ppm sodium.

Fruit and Plant Development

The rabbiteye blueberry has a fruiting habit similar to that of the highbush blueberry, which produces fruit from buds on 1-year-old wood (Darrow, 1962). Flower buds are initiated during the late summer and bud development continues throughout the fall and winter. Due to this long development period and the vigor of rabbiteye blueberries, plants pruned immediately after fruit harvest (mid-July) can produce new fruiting wood and initiate flower buds during summer through late fall, thus producing fruit the following year (Spiers, 1979a) (Fig. 7–14).

Since rabbiteye plants are sufficiently vigorous to produce a heavy crop and still produce enough new fruiting shoots at the same time, little yearly pruning is required (Brightwell, 1962). However, it is desirable to prune in order to keep the bushes from becoming too dense and tall, and selective summer pruning can be effective in maintaining both plant size and satisfactory fruit yields the following year.

In early spring, after receiving sufficient chilling, fully formed flower buds with no visible swelling progress from the visible swelling stage to the fully expanded and open corolla stage in about 25 to 40 days, depending on environmental conditions (Fig. 1 of Spiers, 1978b). After pollination, fruit development in rabbiteye blueberries is characterized by three divisions of growth: an early period of acceler-

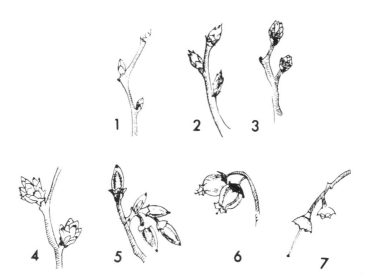

FIGURE 7-14 Stages of flower-bud development in rabbiteye blue-berry: 1, no visible swelling, bud scales completely enclose inflores-cence; 2, visible swelling of bud, scales separating, flowers still completely enclosed; 3, bud scales separated, apices of flower visible; 4, individual flowers distinguishable, bud scales abscised; 5, individual flowers distinctly separated, corollas unexpanded and closed; 6, corollas completely expanded and open; 7, corollas dropped.

ated growth, a second period with a slower rate of increase in size, and a third period with another spurt of rapid growth which continues until fruit is mature (Spiers, 1981b). Fruit size is usually largest at the first harvest and smallest at the last harvest, with some cultivars showing a greater decrease in fruit size than that shown by others. In general, the fruit is mature about 90 days after corolla drop (petal fall).

Titratable acidity levels in ripening fruit decrease as the fruit becomes mature, and these levels remain relatively stable throughout the harvest period. Soluble solids (an indication of sugar content) increase in developing rabbiteye blueberry fruit until fruit is mature and stay relatively constant through harvest. Cultivar differences are present in rate of fruit development, titratable acidity, and percent soluble solids.

Water Relations

Rabbiteye blueberry plants are shallow-rooted, yet capable of surviving periods of drought. They are tolerant to high summer temperatures and productive in habitats too dry for highbush blueberries (Eck and Childers, 1966). Andersen et al. (1979a) found that *V. ashei* has some characteristic adaptations to drought conditions, such as wax rodlets observed in and adjacent to stomatal pores. Also, relatively higher stomatal resistances in rabbiteye blueberries result in efficient water use, enabling them to withstand drought (Teramura et al., 1979). In greenhouse studies the rabbiteye cultivar 'Woodard' recovered from flooding stress more quickly than did the highbush 'Bluecrop', indicating more tolerance to excess soil moisture (Davies and Flore, 1986).

Many areas of the southeastern United States have sufficient annual precipitation, but seasonal distribution is not always uniform enough for highest yields. Irrigation is usually considered necessary for maximum production. In Florida, drip irrigation increased berry yields by 2000 lb/acre (2245 kg/ha) in a dry year but was marginally profitable in a wet year (Buchanan et al., 1978). Both yield and berry weight were increased 20 to 25% by irrigation in Florida (Andersen et al., 1979b). In studies in southern Mississippi, irrigation increased plant survival 25 to 35% (Spiers, 1980). Plant dry weight and fruit yield were doubled in plants grown with irrigation for 2 years. Fruit yield from 'Tifblue' grown for 3 years in a sandy loam soil averaged 4.4 lb per plant (2000 g) with irrigation compared to 0.8 lb per plant (360 g) without irrigation (Spiers, 1983a). Differences exist between cultivars in response to irrigation. Drip irrigation has significantly increased yields of 'Tifblue' and 'Bluegem' but had little influence on 'Woodard' even during extremely dry periods (Andersen et al., 1979b). The use of an absorbent gel at planting increased mortality of bare-rooted plants (Gupton, 1985).

Pruning

Rabbiteye blueberries are vigorous and can support and develop heavy crops of large-sized fruit (Scott et al., 1978). Therefore, rabbiteye blueberries generally require less pruning than do highbush blueberries (Fig. 7–15).

Before planting, blueberry plants should be cut back to a height of 4 to 6 in. (10 to 15 cm). Remove all weak shoots and fruit buds. Generally, no additional pruning is needed during the year of establishment. In the next 2 to 5 years, pruning consists of removing the lower twiggy growth, dead or damaged shoots, and weaker growth. Pruning can be done in the dormant season with young plants and immediately after harvest with older plants. Tall shoots can be cut back by one-third to one-half. Plants can be shaped for mechanical harvesting by removing all shoots growing outside a 12-in. (31-cm) band within the row (Ferree and Austin, 1979). In Florida, Lyrene (1984) found that removal of shoot tips as late as October induced flower bud formation below the cut even though no new vegetative growth occurred.

When plants become too tall to harvest easily, selectively remove about one-third of the older canes (Spiers, 1979a). These selective cuts should be made to open up the center of the plant for better light penetration. Compared to selective pruning, plants pruned to a hedge 4 ft (12 m) high had a greatly reduced yield the following year and hand harvesting was more difficult. Application of naphthaleneacetic acid has delayed shoot growth of pruned, rapidly growing plants (Austin, 1983). This and other growth regulators may prove useful in controlling growth.

(a)   (b)

FIGURE 7-15   (a) Before and (b) after pruning rabbiteye blueberry bush.

Pollination

Rabbiteye blueberries, in general, have some degree of self-incompatability. Meader and Darrow (1944) found that most varieties were either partially or completely self-unfruitful, with larger berries being produced when cross-pollinated than when self-pollinated. Also, a study from North Carolina reported that the rabbiteye cultivar 'Tifblue' can naturally self-pollinate or have parthenocarpic fruit development (Ambrose and Mainland, 1978). Cross-pollination in rabbiteye blueberries resulted in an increase in berry size and seed content and an earlier ripening of berries. Studies from Japan confirmed that cross-pollination usually increases the percentage of fruit set, size of berries, and number of large seeds per berry and results in earlier ripening than does self- or open-pollination (Tamada et al., 1977). Hence planting of two or more varieties for cross-pollination is included in instructions for rabbiteye blueberry culture in most southern states (Moore, 1970; Scott et al., 1978; Brightwell, 1971; Spiers et al., 1985).

Diseases

Diseases are seldom a serious problem in rabbiteye blueberry plantings. Stem canker has been found on wild plants throughout the southern blueberry sections and is probably indigenous to this area. Canker is at present no problem in rabbiteye blueberry plants because all leading varieties are either immune or highly resistant to stem canker. It appears that researchers who made the original rabbiteye selections from the wild took only canker-free plants even though they were unaware at the time that abnormally rough bark was the symptom of a serious disease (Varney and Stretch, 1966).

In general, rabbiteye cultivars are more resistant than the highbush to the predominant fungal pathogens. Root rot (*Phytophthora cinnamomi*) is widespread in Arkansas and North Carolina blueberry plantings, but workers found rabbiteye cultivars more tolerant to P. *cinnamomi* than highbush cultivars (Milholland and Galletta, 1967; Erb et al., 1986).

Cercospora stem blotch disease of rabbiteye blueberries was isolated in 1977 from plantings in Georgia and North Carolina (Milholland, 1977). Symptoms of the disease appear as red blotches on the previous season's growth.

'Tifblue' and 'Woodard', two of the leading rabbiteye cultivars, are susceptible to blueberry anthracnose caused by *Gloeosporium fructigenum* (Milholland, 1975). Infection of succulent stems results in either the development of red flecks on more resistant plants or severe stem dieback on the more susceptible cultivars. This disease and other reported diseases are found only in isolated incidents and are not considered a serious problem at present (Ferree and Austin, 1979). Presently, there is no disease spray program for rabbiteye blueberries.

Insects

The number of insect species that attack the rabbiteye blueberry is relatively small (Brightwell, 1971) and damage occurs only occasionally in isolated cases. Generally, rabbiteye varieties are more resistant than highbush varieties to insect damage. Neunzig and Galletta (1977) found a much greater infestation of blueberry bud mite (*Acarina eriophyidae*) in highbush than in rabbiteye blueberries on plants grown in the same location. As more plantings of rabbiteye blueberries are made, the need for insect control will probably increase.

Insects that are known to attack rabbiteye blueberries include stem borers, cranberry fruit worm, leafrollers, mites, bagworm, orange-striped oak worm, yellownecked caterpillars, and wax scale (Neunzig and Sorensen, 1976; Ferree and Austin, 1979). Since insect infestations are infrequent, an insecticide spray program is not necessary. Growers, however, should inspect their plantings often for insects and spray with approved insecticides if infestation occurs.

Weed Control

No chemical herbicide has been found yet that is completely effective in controlling weeds and that will not damage young blueberry plants, especially during the first growing year (Ballinger, 1966). Therefore, the eradication of persistent weeds such as Johnsongrass, Bahiagrass, Bermudagrass, honeysuckle, and so on, the year before planting is very important to the success of establishing and growing weed-free rabbiteye blueberries. If the more noxious weeds are eradicated before planting, weed control during the first year of growth should be minimal and in subsequent years, recommended herbicides can be safely applied.

Depending on the soil type, topography, and probability of erosion, one of two or more systems of managing the planting site can be used once the planting is established. Where erosion is likely, a sod strip system between rows while maintaining a weed-free row is recommended. The sod middle permits the movement of equipment during wet periods, in addition to reducing soil erosion. Another real advantage is for convenience to workers, pickers, or customers in pick-your-own operations. The sod strip can be either seeded grasses or natural vegetation but should be a type that provides very little competition with the blueberry plants and is easily controlled.

Clean cultivation can be used in areas where erosion is not a problem. The row is kept free of weeds usually with the use of herbicides and the row middles are disked periodically to keep weeds from seeding. Often a winter-annual crop is planted in the middles and then disked under in early spring (Ferree and Austin, 1979). Regardless of the system used, herbicides are used to maintain a weed-free row in which the rabbiteye blueberry plants grow.

Harvesting

Harvesting of commercial rabbiteye blueberries begins in late May in Florida and continues into August in North Carolina (Lyrene and Sherman, 1976; Brooks, 1970). A 6-year study in south Mississippi comparing the harvest interval of six major rabbiteye blueberry cultivars showed that the harvest period was usually 6 to 8 weeks long, starting in the first week of June (Spiers, 1981c). Highbush types ripen early in May in Florida (Lyrene and Sherman, 1976) and in mid- to late May in south Georgia and Mississippi.

In 1982, most rabbiteye plantings consisted of 10 or fewer acres and the crop was usually hand harvested for fresh market or by pick-your-own customers. Berries should be hand-picked at approximately weekly intervals, depending on rate of ripening. With most cultivars, picking should begin 1 to 2 weeks after the first blue color appears (Shoemaker, 1978). Too-early harvesting results in reduced berry size and poorer quality of fruit with less sugar content. Mature rabbiteye plants should produce 20 pints or more per bush. From four to six pickers are required per acre (10 to 15 per hectare) to hand harvest rabbiteye blueberries. To reduce fruit damage, it is preferable to pick directly into the containers in which the fruit will be sold on the fresh market (Ferree and Austin, 1979).

Rabbiteye blueberry acreages are increasing in the south. This, plus the relatively high cost of hand harvesting and uncertain labor supply, has resulted in more blueberries being machine harvested. Two types of mechanical harvesting aids are available for larger acreages: a hand-held battery-powered vibrator and an over-row harvester. Both types remove some twigs, leaves, and undesirable fruit, and therefore grading (cleaning) is necessary. Grading usually consists of a blower unit that removes most leaves, small twigs, and small immature berries and a conveyer belt for hand removal of the remaining undesirable fruit and foreign matter.

Mechanical-harvesting increased loss of marketable fruit and resulted in softer berries than with hand harvesting (Austin and Williamson, 1977). Ground losses can be reduced by training rabbiteye blueberry plants to accommodate over-row harvesters. Hand-harvested fruit has a better shelf life than that of machine-harvested fruit, so growers using mechanical harvesters should have a ready market or plan not to move machine-harvested fruit into the fresh market (Austin and Williamson, 1977).

Economics

Growing rabbiteye blueberries is a small, relatively new horticultural industry that is expanding rapidly in most southeastern states. In 1973, Sheridan and Seelig (1973) stated that rabbiteye blueberry production in Georgia and Florida approached 1 million pounds (454,000 kg). Expanded acreage in the south continues to make the rabbiteye a significant factor in the blueberry market.

Studies of pick-your-own operators in Florida indicated net revenues of about $250 per acre ($600 per hectare) for a hobbyist grower to over $2000 per acre ($5000 per hectare) for larger-acreage growers (Degner et al., 1981; Crocker et al., 1979). Customers rated the freshness and overall quality plus price as the major reason for shopping at the pick-your-own operations. Fowler et al. (1981) found that the internal rate of return for a 10-acre (4-ha) blueberry planting was 24.6% and appears to be economically feasible for small-acreage landowners.

With the present rabbiteye varieties, production would compete with highbush plants grown in North Carolina primarily, and to a lesser extent, to those grown in New Jersey (Sheridan and Seelig, 1973). Since 90 to 95% of all the blueberries marketed are distributed in the northeastern quarter of the United States, a primary market area for rabbiteye blueberries could be in the southeast and western states, where blueberries are not marketed on a large scale (Walkup and Glover, 1970).

Rabbiteye blueberries have proven suitable for storage, with storage in pint containers at 35°F (1.7°C) and 95 + % humidity resulting in 88% marketable fruit after 5 weeks (Dekazos and Smith, 1976). A textural (woodiness or grittiness) problem in blueberries frozen for more than 6 months, caused by the random development of schlereids, was controlled in rabbiteye blueberries by coating the berries with a hydrocolloid mixture prior to storage at −30°F (−34°C) (Dekazos, 1977).

Reports on consumer acceptance of fresh and processed rabbiteye blueberries indicate considerable potential for the product itself but point to a need for promotion to introduce rabbiteye blueberries to natives of the southern United States who are not familiar with cultivated blueberries (Knapp and Sherman, 1974; Walkup and Glover, 1970; Flora, 1979; Flora and Nakayama, 1980).

REFERENCES

AMBROSE, J. T., AND C. M. MAINLAND. 1978. Rabbiteye blueberry (*Vaccinium ashei*) pollination tests. Proc. 4th International Symposium on Pollination. Md. Agric. Exp. Stn. Misc. Publ. 1:149–155.

ANDERSEN, P. D., D. W. BUCHANAN, AND L. G. ALBRIGO. 1979a. Antitranspirant effects on the water relations and fruit of rabbiteye blueberry. J. Am. Soc. Hortic. Sci. 104(3):378–383.

ANDERSEN, P. D., D. W. BUCHANAN, AND L. B. ALBRIGO. 1979b. Water relations and yields of three rabbiteye blueberry cultivars with and without drip irrigation. J. Am. Soc. Hortic. Sci. 104(6):731–736.

ARNOLD, C. E. 1975. Grass *Agnostis perennans, Paspalum nonatum* control in rabbiteye blueberries. Proc. South. Weed Sci. Soc. 28:161–165.

ARNOLD, C. E., AND W. B. SHERMAN. 1974. Growing blueberries in Florida. Univ. Fla. Ext. Circ. 397:P-3.

AUSTIN, M. E. 1983. Naphthaleneacetic acid and fruiting of rabbiteye blueberry 'Tifblue.' J. Am. Soc. Hortic. Sci. 108(2):314–317.

AUSTIN, M. E., AND W. T. BRIGHTWELL. 1977. Effect of fertilizer applications on yield of rabbiteye blueberries. J. Am. Soc. Hortic. Sci. 102(1):36–39.

AUSTIN, M. E., AND T. P. GAINES. 1984. An observation of nutrient levels in old, unfertilized rabbiteye blueberry plants. HortScience 19(3):417–418.

AUSTIN, M. E., AND J. S. MASTON. 1978. Comparison of regular and concentrated sphagnum peat moss for rooting cuttings of rabbiteye blueberries. Ga. Agric. Res. 19(3):15–17.

AUSTIN, M. E., AND B. G. MULLINIX. 1980. Plant populations and fertility studies on rabbiteye blueberries. J. Am. Soc. Hortic. Sci. 105(1):111–114.

AUSTIN, M. E., AND R. E. WILLIAMSON. 1977. Comparison of harvest methods of rabbiteye blueberries. J. Am. Soc. Hortic. Sci. 102(4):454–456.

BALLINGER, E. 1966. Soil management, nutrition, and fertilizer practices. In P. Eck and N. F. Childers (eds.). Blueberry culture. Rutgers University Press, New Brunswick, N.J.

BRIGHTWELL, W. T. 1962. Rabbiteye blueberries. Ga. Agric. Ext. Stn. Mimeo N.S. 131.

BRIGHTWELL, W. T. 1971. Rabbiteye blueberries. Univ. of Ga. Agric. Exp. Stn. Res. Bull. 100.

BROOKS, J. G. 1970. Blueberries: production guide for North Carolina. N.C. State Univ. Ext. Circ. 474.

BROWN, J. C., AND A. D. DRAPER. 1980. Differential response of blueberry (*Vaccinium*) progenies to pH and subsequent use of iron. J. Am. Soc. Hortic. Sci. 105(1):20–24.

BUCHANAN, W. D., F. S. DAVIES, AND A. H. TERAMURA. 1978. Yield responses of three rabbiteye cultivars to drip irrigation and vapor guard. Proc. Fla. State Hortic. Soc. 91:162–163.

CAIN, J. C. 1952. A comparison of ammonium and nitrate nitrogen for blueberries. Proc. Am. Soc. Hortic. Sci. 59:161–166.

CAIN, J. C. 1954. Blueberry leaf chlorosis in relation to leaf pH and mineral composition. Proc. Am. Soc. Hortic. Sci. 64:61–70.

CAIN, J. C., AND P. ECK. 1966. Blueberry and cranberry. p. 101–129. In N. F. Childers (ed.). Fruit nutrition: temperate to tropical. Horticultural Publications, New Brunswick, N.J.

CREECH, D. L., R. SMITH, AND T. BELL. 1986. Rabbiteye blueberry field study. Proc. 1983 Texas Blueberry Growers Conference. p. 42–55.

CROCKER, T. E., P. M. LYRENE, AND C. P. ANDREWS. 1979. The blueberry. Fruit crop fact sheet. Fla. Coop. Ext. Serv. Univ. Fla. Circ. 4-10M-79.

References

CUMMINGS, G. A., C. M. MAINLAND, AND J. P. LILLY. 1981. Influence of soil pH, sulfur, and sawdust on rabbiteye blueberry survival, growth, and yield. J. Am. Soc. HortScience 106(6):783–785.

DARROW, G. M. 1942. Rest period requirement of blueberries. Proc. Am. Soc. Hortic. Sci. 41:189–194.

DARROW, G. M. 1957. Blueberry growing. U.S. Dep. Agric. Farmers' Bull. 1951 (revised).

DARROW, G. M. 1962. The blueberry goes modern. Am. Fruit Grow. 82:13, 50–52.

DARROW, G. M., AND J. N. MOORE. 1966. Blueberry growing. U.S. Dep. Agric. Farmers' Bull. 1951.

DARROW, M., O. WOODARD, AND E. B. MORROW. 1944. Improvement of the rabbiteye blueberry. Proc. Am. Soc. Hortic. Sci. 45:275–279.

DAVIES, F. S., AND J. A. FLORE. 1986. Gas exchange and flooding stress of highbush and rabbiteye blueberries. J. Am. Soc. Hortic. Sci. 111(4):565–571.

DAVIES, F. S., A. H. TERAMURA, AND D. W. BUCHANAN. 1979. Yield, stomatal resistance, xylem pressure potential, and feeder root density in three rabbiteye blueberry cultivars. HortScience 14 (6):725–726.

DEGNER, R. L., L. W. RODAN, AND K. MATHIS. 1981. Farmer to consumer direct marketing of blueberries in Florida: producer and consumer benefits. Fla. Agric. Mark. Res. Cent. Ind. Rep. 81-2.

DEKAZOS, D. 1977. Sclerid development and prevention of woodiness and/or grittiness in rabbiteye blueberries. Proc. Fla. State Hortic. Soc. 90:218–224.

DEKAZOS, E. D., AND C. J. B. SMITH. 1976. Effect of variety, packaging and storage conditions on the shelf life and quality of rabbiteye blueberries. Ga. Agric. Res. 18(2):19–23.

ECK, P., AND N. F. CHILDERS. 1966. Blueberry culture. Horticultural Publications, New Brunswick, N.J.

ERB, W. A., J. N. MOORE, AND R. E. STERNE. Attraction of *Phytophthora cinnamomi* to blueberry roots. HortScience 21:1361–1363.

FERREE, M. E., AND M. E. AUSTIN. 1979. Commercial rabbiteye blueberry culture. Ga. Coop. Ext. Serv. Circ. 713.

FLORA, L. F. 1979. Processing rabbiteye blueberries: acceptability of beverages. Proc. North American Blueberry Workers Conference. p. 259–270.

FLORA, L. F., AND T. O. M. NAKAYAMA. 1980. Consumer acceptance of rabbiteye blueberry beverages. Fruit South 5(1):4–6.

FOWLER, S. R., W. L. BATEMAN, AND J. M. SPIERS. 1981. Costs and returns for small-acreage blueberry production in the mid-Gulf region. Miss. Agric. Forest. Exp. Stn. Res. Rept. Vol. 6, No. 2.

GILREATH, P. R., AND D. W. BUCHANAN. 1981. Temperature and cultivar influences on the chilling period of rabbiteye blueberries. J. Am. Soc. Hortic. Sci. 106(5):625–628.

GLAZE, N. C., AND S. C. PHATAK. 1977. Abstract. Weed control in rabbiteye blueberries. South. Weed Sci. Soc. 30:166.

GUPTON, C. L. 1985. Establishment of native *Vaccinium* species on a mineral soil. HortScience 20(4):673–674.

HABY, V. A., K. D. PATTEN, D. L. CAWTHON, B. B. KREJSA, E. W. NEUENDORFF, J. V. DAVIS, AND S. C. PETERS. 1986. Response of container-grown rabbiteye blueberry plants to irrigation water quality and soil type. J. Am. Soc. Hortic. Sci. 111(3):332–337.

KENDER, W. J., AND W. T. BRIGHTWELL. 1966. Environmental relationships. In P. Eck and N. F. Childers (eds.). Blueberry culture. Rutgers University Press, New Brunswick, N.J.

KENWORTHY, A. L., AND L. MARTIN. 1966. Mineral content of fruit plants. In N. F. Childers (ed.). Temperate to tropical fruit nutrition. Horticultural Publications, New Brunswick, N.J.

KNAPP, F. W., AND W. B. SHERMAN. 1974. Consumer acceptance testing of processed Florida blueberries. Proc. Fla. State Hortic. Soc. 87:260–264.

KRAMER, A., AND A. L. SCHRADER. 1942. Effects of nutrients, media, and growth substances on the growth of the Cabot variety of *Vaccinium corymbosum* L. J. Agric. Res. 65:313–328.

KREWER, G. 1986. Used carefully, fertilizer can yield dramatic results for rabbiteye blueberries. Fruit South 7(3):7–11.

KUSHIMA, T., AND M. E. AUSTIN. 1979. Seed number and size in rabbiteye blueberry fruit. HortScience 14(6):721–723.

LYRENE, P. M. 1984. Late pruning, twig orientation, and flower bud formation in rabbiteye blueberry. HortScience 19(1):98–99.

LYRENE, P. M., AND W. B. SHERMAN. 1976. Blueberry cultivars for Florida. Fruit Var. J. 32(1):9–12.

MEADER, E. M., AND G. M. DARROW. 1944. Pollination of the rabbiteye blueberry and related species. Proc. Am. Soc. Hortic. Sci. 45:267–274.

MILHOLLAND, R. D. 1975. Pathogenicity and histopathology of *Phytophthora cinnamomi* on highbush and rabbiteye blueberry. Phytopathology 65:789–793.

MILHOLLAND, R. D. 1977. Cercospora stem blotch disease of rabbiteye blueberry. Etiology 67:816–819.

MILHOLLAND, R. D., AND G. J. GALLETTA. 1967. Relative susceptibility of blueberry cultivars of *Phytophthora cinnamomi*. Plant Dis. Rep. 51:998–1001.

MINTON, N. A., T. B. HAGLER, AND W. T. BRIGHTWELL. 1951. Nutrient-element deficiency symptoms of the rabbiteye blueberry. Proc. Am. Soc. Hortic. Sci. 58:115–119.

MOORE, J. N. 1970. Blueberry variety performances in Arkansas. Univ. Arkansas Agric. Exp. Stn. Rep. Ser. 186:P-16.

MOWRY, H., AND A. F. CAMP. 1928. Blueberry culture in Florida. Univ. of Fla., Gainesville, Fla.

NEUNZIG, H. H., AND G. J. GALLETTA. 1977. Abundance of the blueberry bud mite (*Acarina eriophyidae*) on various species of blueberry. J. Ga. Entomol. Soc. 12(2):182–184.

NEUNZIG, H. H., AND K. A. SORENSEN. 1976. Insect and mite pests of blueberry in North Carolina. N.C. Agric. Exp. Stn. Bull. 427.

OERTLI, J. J. 1963. Effect of form of nitrogen and pH on growth of blueberry plants. Agron. J. 55:305–307.

PULS, E., JR. 1978. Growing rabbiteye blueberries in Louisiana. La. State Univ. Coop. Ext. Serv.

SCOTT, D. H., A. D. DRAPER, AND G. M. DARROW. 1978. Commercial blueberry growing. U.S. Dep. Agric. Farmers' Bull. 2254.

SHARPE, R. H., AND W. B. SHERMAN. 1971. Breeding blueberries for low-chilling requirements. HortScience 6:146–147.

SHERIDAN, P., AND R. A. SEELIG. 1973. Blueberries. *In* Fruit and vegetable facts and pointers. United Fresh Fruit and Vegetable Association, Alexandria, Va.

References

SHOEMAKER, J. S. 1978. Small fruit culture. 5th ed. AVI, Westport, Conn.

SPIERS, J. M. 1976. Chilling regimes affect bud break in 'Tifblue' rabbiteye blueberry. J. Am. Soc. Hortic. Sci. 101(1):88–90.

SPIERS, J. M. 1977. Growing the rabbiteye blueberry. U.S. Dep. Agric. Publ. SR ca-S-2.

SPIERS, J. M. 1978a. Effects of pH level and nitrogen source on elemental leaf content of 'Tifblue' rabbiteye blueberry. J. Am. Soc. Hortic. Sci. 103(6):705–708.

SPIERS, J. M. 1978b. Effect of stage of bud development on cold injury in rabbiteye blueberry. J. Am. Soc. Hortic. Sci. 103(4):452–455.

SPIERS, J. M. 1978c. Rabbiteye blueberry propagation in south Mississippi. Miss. Agric. For. Exp. Stn. Res. Rep. 4(6).

SPIERS, J. M. 1979a. Blueberry variety studies in south Mississippi. Miss. Agric. For. Exp. Stn. Res. Rep. 4(10).

SPIERS, J. M. 1979b. Calcium and nitrogen nutrition of 'Tifblue' rabbiteye blueberry in sand culture. HortScience 14(4):523–525.

SPIERS, J. M. 1979c. Influence of oxidized and reduced N on 'Tifblue' rabbiteye blueberry growth. p. 64. In Proc. 4th North American Blueberry Research Workers Conference, Fayetteville, Ark., Oct. 16–18, 1979.

SPIERS, J. M. 1980. Influence of peat moss and irrigation on establishment of 'Tifblue' blueberry. Miss. Agric. For. Exp. Stn. Res. Rep. 4(18).

SPIERS, J. M. 1981a. Freeze damage in six rabbiteye blueberry cultivars. Fruit Var. J. 35(2):68–70.

SPIERS, J. M. 1981b. Fruit development in rabbiteye blueberry cultivars. HortScience 16(2):175–176.

SPIERS, J. M. 1981c. Harvest intervals of six rabbiteye blueberry varieties. Miss. Agric. For. Exp. Stn. Res. Rep. 5(14).

SPIERS, J. M. 1982a. Influence of fertilization and incorporated organic matter on establishment and early growth of rabbiteye blueberry. J. Am. Soc. Hortic. 107(6):1054–1058.

SPIERS, J. M. 1982b. Seasonal variation of leaf nutrient composition in 'Tifblue' rabbiteye blueberry. J. Am. Soc. Hortic. Sci. 107(2).

SPIERS, J. M. 1983a. Irrigation and peat moss for the establishment of rabbiteye blueberries. HortScience 18(6):936–937.

SPIERS, J. M. 1983b. Influence of N, K, and Na concentrations on growth and leaf element content of 'Tifblue' rabbiteye blueberry. HortScience 18(2):223–224.

SPIERS, J. M. 1984. Influence of lime and sulphur soil additions on growth, yield, and leaf nutrient content of rabbiteye blueberry. J. Am. Soc. Hortic. Sci. 109(4):559–562.

SPIERS, J. M., AND A. D. DRAPER. 1974. Effect of chilling on bud break in rabbiteye blueberry. J. Am. Soc. Hortic. Sci. 99:398–390.

SPIERS, J. M., J. H. BRASWELL, AND C. P. HEGWOOD, JR. 1985. Establishment and maintenance of rabbiteye blueberries. Miss. Agric. For. Exp. Stn. Bull. 941.

SPIERS, J. M., W. A. LEWIS, AND A. D. DRAPER. 1974. Hardwood propagation of rabbiteye blueberry. HortScience 9(1):24–25.

TAMADA, T., H. IWAGAKI, AND S. ISHIAWA. 1977. The pollination of rabbiteye blueberries in Tokyo. Acta Hortic. 61:335–341.

TERAMURA, A. H., F. S. DAVIES, AND D. W. BUCHANAN. 1979. Comparative photosynthesis and transpiration in excised shoots of rabbiteye blueberry Vaccinium ashei. HortScience 14:723–724.

VARNEY, E. H., AND A. W. STRETCH. 1966. Diseases and their control. In P. Eck and N. F. Childers (eds.). Blueberry culture. Rutgers University Press, New Brunswick, N.J.

VORSA, N. 1987. Meiotic chromosome pairing and irregularities in blueberry interspecific backcross hybrids. J. Hered. 78:395–399.

WALKUP, T. B., AND R. S. GLOVER. 1970. The feasibility of blueberry production and marketing in Georgia and the southeast. Ga. Blueberry Assoc. Publ. SR 101.

WARE, L. M. 1930. Propagation studies with the southern blueberry. Miss. Agric. Exp. Stn. Bull. 280.

WHATLEY, B. T., AND J. J. LACKETT. 1979. Effects of honey bee pollination on fruit set, yield, and quality of rabbiteye blueberries, *Vaccinium ashei* Reade. 4th International Pollination Symposium.

Chapter 8

Cranberry Management

M. N. DANA

INTRODUCTION

The cranberry industry has developed through the manipulation of the native ecosystem in which the cranberry species evolved. The cranberry of commerce, *Vaccinium macrocarpon* Ait., native to the acid bogs of the northeastern United States and southern Canada, was harvested by the indigenous people of the area before the European settlers started the conquest of this land and instituted different agricultural methods. The initiation of improvements for the development of an industry based on culture and management dates from the early nineteenth century when enterprising individuals in the Cape Cod area of Massachusetts started building ditches and dikes to facilitate water control in the cranberry fields. The removal of excess water during seasons of heavy precipitation was coupled with the resupply of water for cold protection in winter and during frosts in the growing season. From this meager beginning has grown the sophisticated practices now used that provide a carefully managed production environment.

The Massachusetts industry grew slowly for a century or more and reached a peak of 15,000 acres (6000 ha) in 1950. A gradual decline in acreage has occurred since that time due to failure of poorly located bogs and the pressure for land development for other uses. The industry located in the Pine Barrens region of southern New Jersey began in the nineteenth century and grew to a peak of 11,000 acres (4500 ha) in 1920. Since 1920 the acreage has slowly declined to about 3000 acres (1200 ha) by 1987. Low production and poor economic returns, coupled with the conversion of land to blueberry culture, were responsible for this decline in acreage.

The Wisconsin industry began in the 1860's with the improvement of native stands and grew in size and sophistication to reach 8000 acres (3200 ha) in 1987. The industry in Washington started with the first planted bog in 1882. Acreage has increased slowly to about 1100 acres (450 ha) in 1987. The Oregon industry has developed to about 800 acres (325 ha) since its initial plantings in the early twentieth century. A small area, 100 acres (40 ha), is harvested in the Maritime Provinces of Canada, and there are a few small developments in Quebec and eastern Ontario. About 1500 acres (600 ha) of cranberries are grown in the Vancouver area of British Columbia, Canada. The total U.S. acreage remained between 24,000 and 25,000 acres (9700 to 10,000 ha) from 1905 to 1953 and now stands at 22,000 acres (9000 ha) (see Table 8-1).

Production of cranberries showed a steady growth from 318,000 barrels (15,900 tons) in 1900 to 982,700 barrels (49,135 tons) in 1950 (100 lb in a barrel). From 1950 to 1986 a rapid increase in production occurred, reaching 3,400,000 barrels (171,400 tons) in 1985. A dramatic increase in production per acre (from approximately 15 barrels in 1900 to over 100 barrels in 1985) accounts for the increase in production in spite of stable or declining acreage (Table 8-1).

SPECIES

Cranberry cultivars are from native plant selections or controlled hybridization in the species *Vaccinium macrocarpon* Ait., the large or American cranberry. This is a perennial, woody, evergreen species in the Vacciniaceae family, native to bogs from Newfoundland south to North Carolina and west to Minnesota. The plants root in the surface layers of peat bogs and the stems creep over the sphagnum moss and

TABLE 8-1 CRANBERRY PRODUCTION IN MAJOR STATES: 1985

STATE	PRODUCTION (1000 TONS)
Massachusetts	84.0
New Jersey	16.0
Oregon	4.9
Washington	8.3
Wisconsin	58.2
Total in United States	171.4

other low-stature species found in the ecological association. The American cranberry has the following morphological description: *V. macrocarpon* Ait. — creeping, evergreen shrub, leaves alternate, oblong, 1/3 to 1/2 in. (0.8 to 1.3 cm) long, obtuse, margins entire, one to seven solitary flowers at successive axils on the flowering shoot, four sepals, four reflexed pink petals, eight stamens with anthers opening in a terminal pore, a single inferior ovary with four cells, few to many ovules; fruit red at maturity, oblong, globose, or nearly pyriform berry 1/3 to 3/4 in. (0.8 to 1.9 cm) in diameter.

Related species of some interest are *V. oxycoccus* L., mossberry or small cranberry, and *V. vitis idaea* L., lingonberry, mountain cranberry, or cowberry. The mossberry differs from the large cranberry in having smaller, pointed leaves, more thread-like stems, smaller and more highly colored flowers, and smaller, round, often speckled fruit. This is a tetraploid species and does not hybridize with *V. macrocarpon,* although it grows in the same ecological association. No development of this species as a horticultural crop has occurred. The lingonberry or mountain cranberry is an upland species growing far north in circumpolar distribution. It is a creeping, evergreen species with terminal inflorescences and small, very acid red berries. Lingonberries are harvested for local use in Alaska and Scandinavia. A small quantity are harvested and processed for export from the Scandinavian countries; but no commercial production has been developed in North America.

MORPHOLOGY

Figure 8–1 shows the cranberry morphology.

Roots

The cranberry has a very fine, fibrous root system that develops in the top 1 to 3 in. (2.5 to 7.5 cm) of soil. The roots have no root hairs. Roots live in close association with mycorrhizal organisms, but no proof of interdependence of fungus and cranberry has yet been shown. Due to the cultural practice of sanding, one may find functional roots at depths of several inches. These roots did not penetrate to that depth; rather, they remained functional after new layers of sand were added to the bog surface.

Stem

The initial growth of a new cranberry plant is normally a creeping (procumbent) stem (runner) that may grow several feet horizontally in one season. In the second season some of the axillary buds break to produce vertical shoots called uprights. Eventually, the surface area of the field becomes covered with runners, which give rise to many uprights, up to 550 per square foot (5000 per square meter). The upright produces 2 to 4 in. (5 to 10 cm) of new growth annually. This structure becomes a decumbent stem (i.e., the terminal 5 to 8 in. (12 to 20 cm) remain upright, while the base of the stem sags down against the floor of the bog). Thus, after many

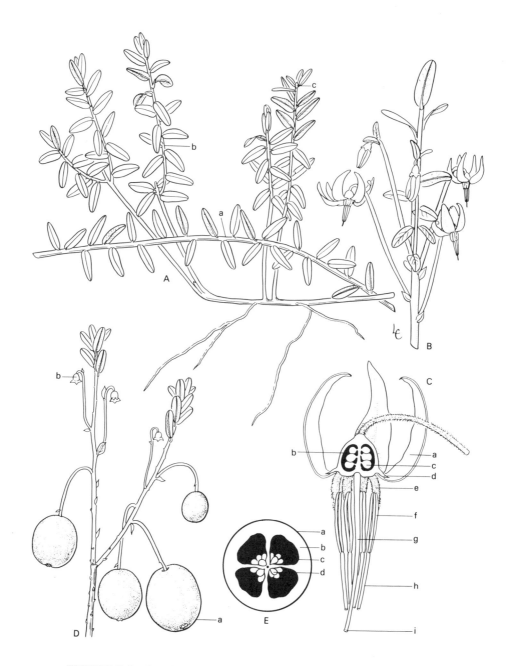

FIGURE 8-1 Cranberry morphology. (A) Plant habit: a, runner (procumbent stem); b, upright (vertical shoot): c, terminal bud. (B) Flowering shoot. (C) Flower longitudinal section; a, petal; b, ovary; c, ovule; d, sepal; e, filament; f, anther; g, style; h, pollen delivery tube; i, stigma. (D) Fruiting uprights: a, mature berry; b, unfertilized ovary and calyx. (E) Berry cross section: a, epidermis; b, flesh; c, locule; d, seeds.

Morphology

years, an upright may be several yards (meters) long, but only the terminal portion remains upright. At this point the old, woody portion of an upright is indistinguishable from that of a runner. These decumbent stems do not initiate roots unless they are covered with a moist medium.

The apical region of the upright is the point of flower bud development. The terminal mixed bud is induced about July 1 and continues differentiation of flower parts during the remainder of the summer and in the spring of the following year. The terminal apex remains vegetative; and with the return of warm spring temperatures, the embryonic, overwintering bud (Fig. 8-1) elongates with leaves and new stem growth at the terminal, and the solitary, axillary flowers appearing at the base of the shoot growth. Each flower is subtended by a bract (a very much reduced leaf). The pedicel has two bracteoles about midway between the upright and the flower. The buds of individual flowers become evident about 2 weeks after emergence of the terminal bud, with the start of flowering (June 20 in Wisconsin) about 30 days after initiation of growth. The flowers point downward on the stiff pedicels. Flowers open by separation of the petal tips, which in a matter of hours reflex against the pedicel and expose the stamens in a tube arrangement (Fig. 8-1). Twenty-four to thirty-six hours later the style elongates and protrudes through the center of the staminal tube, eventually exceeding the length of the stamens by $1/16$ to $1/8$ in. (2 to 4 mm). The open flower has the appearance of a crane's head, and thus the name 'craneberry' was applied, which later, due to someone's error in spelling, became accepted as the cranberry. The stigma is pollen receptive before its emergence through the stamen tube, and, if not pollinated, will remain receptive for several days. The pollen is shed in tetrads through the terminal pores of the anthers. Agitation of the flower (usually by air currents or insects) is necessary for pollen shedding. Following pollination, the pollen tubes penetrate the stylar tissue and deliver the generative nuclei to the ovary, where fertilization takes place. A period of 24 hours or more elapses between pollination and fertilization. The temperature has a major impact on this period, with warm conditions favoring development and cooler temperatures delaying development. Each ovary is divided into four locules in which as many as 50 ovules are distributed. Occasionally, seedless fruit may develop; but usually, fruit set and fruit enlargement follow fertilization of a portion of the ovules (seeds). Shortly after fertilization, the petals and stamens fall, leaving the calyx lobes and the dried, thread-like style on the rapidly enlarging berry. The fruit matures 60 to 120 days or more after fertilization. The actual time of maturity depends on cultivar characteristics, seasonal heat, and sunlight accumulation. Maturing berries change from grass green to a lighter green and sometimes white, with slow development of red pigment in the surface tissue layers. The mature berry is bright red, often with a waxy bloom, which on highly colored cultivars, makes the berry appear almost black. At maturity the fruit does not separate from the pedicel by the formation of an abscission layer; it may remain attached to the plant through the winter and into the next growing season. Harvest of the fruit demands either breaking the pedicel or tearing the pedicel from the fruit. A portion of the pedicel may remain attached to the harvested fruit and may be evident when the fresh fruit reaches the market.

Leaves formed on the uprights are light green as they enlarge to maturity, and assume a glossy, dark green, leathery condition at maturity. With the onset of short days and cool temperatures in the autumn, the leaves take on a deep red color, due to a decline in chlorophyll concentration and an increase in red pigment. During the dormant season, the overall appearance of the marsh from a distance is distinctly brown. With the return of warm weather in the spring, the red color disappears and the green color returns (Fig. 8-2). A leaf formed the previous summer usually is shed in late summer of the second season; but some may persist to the third growing season. Premature leaf drop is a clear indication of cultural problems such as oxygen deficiency, inadequate nutrition, or pesticide injury.

CULTIVARS

Cultivars grown commercially are named selections from native populations of vines. Fruit size, yield, and maturity season have been the major factors attracting the attention of those interested in discovering improved selections. Over 150 cultivars have been introduced to the industry by this selection method. Six cultivars have been released from controlled breeding programs conducted by the U.S. Department of Agriculture and cooperating state experiment stations. One cultivar has arisen from the breeding program at Washington State University.

The cultivar situation changes very slowly. There has been little or no effort to market berries on the basis of cultivar characteristics and little commercial incentive to plant particular cultivars for purposes other than maximum tonnage. Furthermore, the removal of an established planting and replacement with a new planting are costly in labor and planting material, and require the sacrifice of cropping on that acreage for a period of 4 to 8 years.

Approximately 90% of U.S. production is 'Early Black', 'Howes', 'Searles', and 'McFarlin', all native selections (Table 8-2). Small acreages are planted with 'Bergman', 'Stevens', 'Wilcox', and 'Crowley', developed from breeding programs and several cultivars selected from the wild.

Howes: selected from the wild by Eli Howes, East Dennis, Massachusetts, around 1843. This is the standard late cultivar in the eastern United States.

FIGURE 8-2 Fruiting cranberry plant in mid-August.

TABLE 8-2 LEADING CRANBERRY CULTIVARS IN UNITED STATES

NAME	ORIGIN	RIPENING SEASON	ESTIMATED ACREAGE
Early Black	Native selection	September	10000 (4000 ha)
Howes	Native selection	October	5000 (2000 ha)
McFarlin	Native selection	October	3000 (1200 ha)
Searles	Native selection	Early October	5000 (2000 ha)
Stevens	McFarlin × Potter	Early October	200 (75 ha)
Bergman	Early Black × Searles	September	200 (75 ha)
Ben Lear	Native selection	September	200 (75 ha)

Fruit ripens late, being a glossy, oblong, uniform berry with good storage quality and very good processing quality.

Early Black: selected from the wild on the property of Nathaniel Robbins in Harwich, Massachusetts, about 1852. This is the standard early cultivar in the eastern United States. Fruit ripens in September, being very dark red, fairly glossy, uniform in size, slightly smaller than 'Howes', with excellent processing quality but only fair keeping quality in common storage.

McFarlin: selected by T. H. McFarlin at South Carver, Massachusetts, in 1874. This is the leading cultivar in Washington and Oregon, and is planted on about 20% of the acreage in Wisconsin. Fruit ripens in October with high color, waxy bloom, large size, good processing quality, and good storage quality.

Searles: selected by Andrew Searles at Walker, Wisconsin, in 1893. The leading cultivar in Wisconsin, it is highly productive in that state. Fruit ripens in early October, being bright red when fully colored, oblong in shape, of good size, with fair processing and storage quality.

CULTURE

Selection of a Planting Site

The production of cranberries has evolved by modification of sites on which cranberries were native, or on sites with topography and structure similar to these sites. Such sites are normally wetlands with a high water table and a low soil reaction, pH 4.0 to 5.0. Many have a substantial quantity of peat deposition, although some are sand or may have a very thin layer of peat.

A cranberry field is a long-term investment and once properly established, becomes a permanent agricultural enterprise. The selection of a site with all possible favorable characteristics is mandatory to minimize the possibility of economic loss.

The characteristics of a desirable site are:

1. A soil reaction in the acidity range pH 4.0 to 5.0.
2. A peat or sand soil.

3. A large supply of fresh water for frost protection, irrigation, harvesting, and winter protection.

4. A convenient supply of coarse sand for surfacing the prepared planting bed and for regular applications as a cultural practice over the life of the planting.

5. An area with sufficient grade to permit drainage of excess water from the area.

6. An elevated site that will encourage air drainage to lower undeveloped areas.

7. A large enough area for development of an economic unit. Small plantings do not lend themselves to the utilization of mechanical equipment for pest control. harvesting, fertilization, and other cultural needs. The total acreage may include water supply, sand supply, roadways, dikes, and ditches as well as the area planted to cranberry vines.

8. An area that is uniform in soil condition and topography. Working around or removing islands and rock outcroppings adds substantially to the cost of establishing drainage patterns and leveling surfaces for planting.

The native vegetation on suitable sites will be leatherleaf, *Chaemadaphne calyculata* Moench.; sphagnum moss, *Sphagnum* sp.; wiregrass sedge, *Carex oligosperma* Michx.; labrador tea, *Ledum groenlandicum* Oeder; bog laurel, *Kalmia* sp.; larch, *Larix laricina,* Koch; rush species, *Juncus* sp.; and other genera and species characteristic of northern wetlands. A heavy population of *Larix laricina* tends to lower the desirability because of the cost of tree removal during site preparation.

Establishment of the Field

The area to be planted is carefully surveyed to determine the natural drainage, which will be enhanced by the construction of canals and ditches for the removal of excess water. The water supply should be located to take advantage of gravity flow for putting water on the field at critical periods. Many operators, however, pump water onto the field and then allow gravity to drain the water from the field after use. After designing the water control system, the field is divided into beds or planting sections. These may be from 2.5 to 12.5 acres (1 to 5 ha) in Wisconsin to as little as ²/₃ acre (¼ ha) in Oregon, Washington, and Massachusetts, with much larger plantings in British Columbia. The size may be controlled by the extent of field available for development. The beds of 2.5 to 5 acres (1 to 2 ha) in Wisconsin were established to provide flexibility in water management (flooding). The advent of sprinkler irrigation for frost protection has removed the need for frost control by flooding, and allows for the development of larger areas under a single water control structure.

Heavy equipment is used to dig the main drainage canals to drain the area for further development. Planting areas are prepared by scalping (removal of the surface vegetation) and leveling the surface of the bed. Scalpings are pushed to the side to provide a dike, and ultimately are the base for the road surrounding the bed. Scalping should remove the roots of woody species such as leatherleaf, Labrador tea, and willows. These species regenerate shoots and become weed problems in the cranberry bed. Scalping to a depth of 6 in. (15 cm) is usually adequate when care is used to remove remnants of potentially bothersome woody species.

It is standard practice to apply 2 to 4 in. (5 to 10 cm) of clean sand over the entire surface of the section before planting. A layer of sand stabilizes the underlying peat, provides a well-aerated planting medium, establishes a firm surface for equipment maneuverability, and is convenient for leveling the surface of the bog. If the native soil is sand, obviously the supplemental sand application at planting time is not required.

Major emphasis is placed on the need for level beds. In all growing areas these fields are flooded for harvesting and, in most areas, for winter protection. It is imperative to have a uniform depth of water over the flooding section if equipment is to harvest efficiently and if winter protection for all parts of the section is to be uniform.

Sources of Planting Stock

Planting material is obtained by mowing vines of the desired cultivar from an established planting (Fig. 8-3). Mowed vines are handled loosely with forks or power equipment or may be bailed for long-distance shipment. These 'cuttings' must be kept moist to maintain viability. Cuttings are sold by weight, usually by the ton. An acre of vines will yield 2 to 6 tons (5 to 15 MT/ha) of cuttings.

Planting

Planting is normally completed during the month of May except in western growing areas, where fall planting has been successful. Cutting material may be mechanically chopped into lengths of 3 to 24 in. (8 to 60 cm) for convenience in planting. No attempt is made to select, grade, or otherwise arrange the mass of material before planting.

Planting is accomplished by hand if stock material is in short supply, or mechanically if stock material is plentiful. Hand planting may use as little as 450 lb/acre (500 kg/ha), while mechanical planting may use up to 3 tons/acre (7 MT/ha). A

FIGURE 8-3 Vines in field after mowing.

Cranberry Management   Chap. 8

hand dibbler pushes the ends of three or four cuttings into the planting surface to a depth of 2.5 to 4 in. (6 to 10 cm). Clumps of cuttings may be spaced at 9-in. (23-cm) intervals over the entire bed, or if maximum space is to be covered with minimum material, the spacing may be at 16- to 24-in. (40- to 60-cm) intervals. Mechanical planting is done by spreading the unsorted vines loosely over the surface of the bed (Fig. 8–4), followed by any of a number of pieces of power equipment that push the vines into the wet sand or peat (Fig. 8–5). Various disk devices have been used, and a crawler tractor with dull cleats run both ways over the field will do an acceptable job of planting. A shallow flood after planting helps settle the soil around the vines and encourage a good stand. This crude planting method leaves vines in all orientations with relation to top and bottom and finds many not covered at all. However, the economy of planting with minimum labor outweighs any benefits to be gained from higher-quality hand planting.

Maximum rooting and survival are gained from keeping the soil surface damp but not waterlogged. Very light applications of sprinkler irrigation for an hour per day during hot weather and at thrice-weekly intervals during cool weather maintain a high relative humidity and good soil aeration, both of which minimize stress on the cuttings.

Two to four weeks after planting, roots are initiated on the stems underground and axillary buds start shoot elongation above ground. Under favorable circumstances and good management, the surface of the bed will be covered with new runners by the end of the first season.

FIGURE 8–4 Scattering vines over prepared surface with planting machine in background.

FIGURE 8-5 Appearance of newly planted field, showing slots into which the vines have been pressed.

Newly planted fields may be treated with a suitable preemergence herbicide to minimize weed seedling invasion in the first year. If weed-free sand is used to cover the surface before planting, there should be a minimum weed problem in the first year.

Fertilizer application to the newly set vines is commonly delayed until the cuttings have initiated growth. Soluble fertilizers may be applied through the irrigation system starting about June 15. A rate of 15 to 20 lb (16 to 22 kg/ha) of nitrogen in the ammonium form may be repeated at 2- to 3-week intervals until September 1. The goal of the relatively high nitrogen level is to stimulate as much vegetative growth as possible in order to cover the soil surface with cranberry vines at the earliest possible time, both to compete against weed invasion and to provide plants for fruit bearing at an early age.

See Table 8-3 for a summary of cultural operations.

BOG MANAGEMENT

Water Management

The cranberry grower makes more extensive use of water as a management tool than any other producer of agricultural crops. Only fish and seafood farmers and kelp harvesters rely more heavily on water for success with their operation. An extensive

TABLE 8-3 SEASONAL DEVELOPMENT AND CULTURAL OPERATIONS
FOR COMMERCIAL CRANBERRY PRODUCTION

MONTH	CRANBERRY PLANT STAGE	CULTURAL PRACTICES
January–March	Dormant	1. Apply sand. 2. Maintain winter flood. 3. Service equipment.
April	Dormant; bud swelling	1. Remove winter flood. 2. Restore sprinkler irrigation to operable condition. 3. Repair water control structures. 4. Apply granular herbicides and fertilizers. 5. Maintain frost protection. 6. Prepare new land for planting. 7. Rake trash from beds.
May	Dormant; hook stage	1. Maintain frost protection. 2. Apply herbicides and fertilizers. 3. Apply insecticides as needed. 4. Plant new fields. 5. Maintain water control structures. 6. Hand-weed woody species.
June	Bud development to blossom	1. Maintain frost protection. 2. Apply herbicides and fertilizers. 3. Look for early season insects and treat as needed. 4. Finish planting early in the season. 5. Hand-weed willows, hardhack, etc. 6. Place bees in field for pollination. 7. Clean ditches and maintain dikes.
July	Blossom, fruit set, flower bud initiation for next year	1. Maintain frost protection. 2. Irrigate for soil moisture maintenance. 3. Make insecticide applications. 4. Make fungicide applications for foliar diseases. 5. Remove bees from the field. 6. Apply supplemental nitrogen.
August	Developing fruit	1. Maintain frost protection. 2. Maintain insecticide and fungicide treatments. 3. Prepare new land for planting.
September	Maturing fruit	1. Maintain frost protection. 2. Harvest early cultivars.
October	Mature fruit, dormant vines	1. Maintain frost protection. 2. Harvest. 3. Clean up trash. 4. Prepare irrigation lines for winter storage.
November–December	Dormant	1. Pack and market berries. 2. Apply winter flood. 3. Apply sand.

and reliable supply of good-quality fresh water is mandatory for efficient management of a cranberry bog. The water is used for (1) winter mulching in the colder production areas, (2) growing season frost protection in all areas, (3) summer cooling in the continental climate areas, and (4) soil moisture maintenance in all areas. Historically, water was used for insect and weed control; but this has been superseded by more reliable methods.

Cranberry plants are evergreen; thus transpiration from leaf surfaces is a year-round concern. It was long ago discovered that in regions with severe winter climates, the vines would suffer lethal desiccation during those cold periods of winter when there was no snow cover over the vines. With temperatures in the range -4 to $-40°F$ (-29 to $-40°C$) there may also be a direct kill of buds and foliage from cold even without desiccation. Early in the history of the development of commercial culture, it was also discovered that this plant could be submerged under water for considerable periods without suffering damage to the fruit buds or leaves. These two bits of knowledge were soon brought together with the development of the now standard practice of winter flooding in those climatic areas where the hazards of desiccation and/or freezing injury are prevalent.

Winter flooding is not without hazard. The cranberry plant continues metabolic activity (respiration), albeit at a very low rate, during the low temperatures of winter. For this activity oxygen is necessary. With water temperatures near freezing the cranberry plant can extract sufficient oxygen from water with a dissolved oxygen content of 2.00 ppm. As temperatures increase, the demand for oxygen by the cranberry plants and by other organisms also increases; for the respiration rate rises with increasing temperatures. It is significant that oxygen solubility in water increases with decreasing temperature. Therefore, a plant may be submerged in cold water for a longer period than in warm water.

The replenishment of the oxygen may be by dissolution from the atmosphere at the air–water interface or from the oxygen released by photosynthesis in submerged leaves. The amount dissolved from the air is directly related to temperature and to the surface exposure gained from agitation of the water supply. Photosynthetic release of oxygen is a direct function of the amount of light reaching the leaves. Dirty water, deep flooding, cloudy conditions, and ice and snow cover minimize photosynthesis and sunshine, while clean water and a shallow flood favor light penetration.

The common practice in Wisconsin is to apply the winter flood in late November or early December, or as soon as the temperature is low enough to freeze the water within a day or two. Growers commonly build up the flood by applying a 2- to 3-in. (5- to 8-cm) layer of water, which is allowed to freeze solid before adding another layer of water for freezing. Successive layers are added over a period of a week or more until all vines are totally encased in an ice blanket. Any free water in ditches and under the ice is drained away to leave the planting in ice storage until late March or early April. Oxygen deficiency is never a problem when a good, quick freeze-down occurs. Problems may develop in the spring when thawing is erratic and the water cannot be removed promptly with the return of warm temperatures, and when free water develops under the ice due to the insulation of a heavy snow cover.

Eastern growers cannot be assured of sufficiently low temperatures to freeze down the flood. Under these circumstances, the flood should be applied in December or even January, but not before the root zone is completely frozen and the weather forecasts call for low temperatures and desiccating conditions (moderate winds and low relative humidity). The flood should be removed as soon as practicable, usually March 15 in Massachusetts. Cranberries grown in the relatively mild-winter-temperature areas of Oregon, Washington, and British Columbia do not need the protection of a winter flood.

Cranberries are grown in the most frost-prone areas of the local topography (i.e., the lowest elevations). Until the development of economic means for sprinkler irrigation, cranberries were protected against frost by the application of water over the surface of the bed by gravity flow. Protection of the plants was afforded by the conduction and convection of heat from the water to the air in the microenvironment of the sensitive shoot tips. The amount of water applied was determined by the intensity of the frost conditions—the lower the temperature, the greater the depth of the frost flood. Under severe conditions, total plant submergence might be necessary, but this was avoided if possible. A frost flood was removed as soon as temperature conditions warranted, for metabolically active vines cannot tolerate submergence for more than a few hours without suffering damage to developing flower buds. Again, the temperature of the water is the determinant of the safe period.

Sprinkler irrigation for frost protection has been standard practice in western growing areas for over 50 years; but it was not widely adopted in Wisconsin until the 1960s and has moved into the eastern areas since that time. Protection depends on an adequate water supply and solid set irrigation so that all portions of the field may be protected at once. Water is applied at 0.1 to 0.2 in. (0.25 to 0.50 cm) per hour to maintain a constant wetting of all surfaces during the frost period. As the water on the plant surface freezes, it releases heat at the rate of 80 cal/g. Some of this heat is conducted to the plant buds and maintains them at temperatures at or just below freezing and above lethal conditions. Protection to air temperatures of 14°F ($-10°C$) has been recorded, but few growers wish to hazard that much. A forecast of temperatures that low would normally call for flood protection. Sprinkler irrigation is a precise, quickly responsive, and often automated method of frost protection. It uses much less water than the flooding system because the quantity applied may be less than 0.25 in. (1 cm) for a frost as opposed to 2 to 6 in. (5 to 15 cm) for a flood. The slowness of flooding often required anticipatory water application when, in fact, a frost did not occur, and sprinklers may be delayed until the precise moment before damage occurs.

Sprinkler irrigation is a useful means of lowering temperatures on exceedingly warm days in summer. The enclosed nature of cranberry beds with surrounding dikes and roadways creates pockets with low convection heat loss. Temperatures may be several degrees warmer than at exposed locations in the same vicinity. The application of sprinklers for a few minutes during the heat of the day reduces temperatures by evaporative cooling. This treatment is especially beneficial during the blossoming season to encourage the activity of pollinating insects. Whether the cooling and moisture benefit nectar flow or merely make temperatures more appealing to the pollinators is not known. Certainly, the moisture stress on the plants is reduced due to lower temperatures and a higher relative humidity in the leaf zone.

The root system of cranberries is not an efficient mechanism for extracting soil moisture. The roots are concentrated near the surface, do not have any root hairs, and commonly are in a sand soil. Frequent irrigations to maintain adequate moisture in the surface 3 to 6 in. (8 to 15 cm) are mandatory. One inch (2.5 cm) of water every 4 days during hot weather in the absence of rainfall is recommended. Unfortunately, symptoms of summer desiccation do not become evident for several days after the damage occurs. Thus a preventive program is necessary rather than attempting a cure after the fact.

Sanding

Maintenance of cranberry plants in a vigorous and productive condition is an important part of the management program. With most fruit crops, this is accomplished in part by a pruning program designed to remove old unproductive wood and replace it with vigorous new shoots that produce revitalized fruit spurs. The low-growing, slender myriads of cranberry uprights do not lend themselves to a controlled pruning program. Many years ago an enterprising grower concluded that a step in the right direction could be the application of a thin layer of sand over the entire surface of the bed. This sand would cover the old stems (runners and bases of uprights) and stimulate new rooting of stems closer to the fruiting zone of the plant. This new rooting could revitalize the plant and stimulate new upright formation. The response would be the same as pruning. It worked. Applying ½ to 1 in. (1.25 to 2.5 cm) of sand on a 3- to 4-year rotation is now standard practice in most cranberry fields.

The side benefits of a good sanding program are:

1. The fresh sand reflects light upward into the vine canopy, and presumably enhances photosynthetic activity during the first summer after sanding.
2. It slowly builds a hard surface on peat soils for better machinery operation.
3. Soil drainage improves with a long-term sanding program.
4. Newly sanded bogs have a slightly lowered frost hazard because the sand takes up and releases heat more readily than peat or the accumulated duff on the bog surface.
5. The weight of the sand tends to hold down the underlying peat and reduce the hazard of portions of the bog floating away on the winter flood.
6. Sanding re-anchors the vines at intervals and facilitates mechanical harvest.

In Wisconsin the sand is applied with trucks and spreaders driving on top of the ice during the winter. When the ice melts, the sand settles on the bog surface. Growers in other areas apply the sand from various machines adapted to move onto the field without doing excessive damage to the vines. Usually, the sanding is done in early spring or late fall when there is not a crop of fruit on the vines. The sand should be free of pebbles and stones, for these may be picked up by picking machines and do mechanical damage.

Fertilization

The cranberry plant evolved under highly acid bog conditions with low natural supplies of the mineral elements. Mineral elements needed were supplied in surface runoff water and from the recycling of nutrients in very slowly decaying organic matter. The survival of the species under these circumstances could indicate a relatively low requirement for the major elements. This appears to be the case. There are few reports of favorable response to fertilization with elements other than nitrogen.

A soil test level of 60 lb/acre (65 kg/ha) of available phosphorus indicates a sufficiency of this element for cranberry growth. Soil should be raised to this level by the use of phosphate fertilizer before planting. A maintenance program may be applied as needed when soil test results indicate. This fertilizer is normally applied in early spring as a dry, granular material either by air or with ground equipment.

Potassium is normally supplied in adequate quantities from the sand applied as a cultural practice and from the decaying organic material. There is no experimental evidence to show that cranberry soils are ever deficient in potash. As an insurance against possible deficiencies, a soil test level of 100 lb/acre (110 kg/ha) available potassium should be maintained.

Cranberry plants are known to show a response to supplemental nitrogen fertilization. Vegetative growth can be overstimulated by mismanagement of nitrogen fertilization. Given suitable conditions, a high nitrogen level may stimulate previously fruitful uprights into becoming vigorous, unproductive runners. A loss of fruit production ensues.

In 1929, Addoms and Mounce in New Jersey first showed the preference of cranberries for the ammonium form of nitrogen rather than the nitrate form. This characteristic was further elaborated by Greidanus et al. (1972), who showed that the cranberry plant had a strong preference for NH_4^+ in nutrient culture experiments and in field plots. There was evidence that NO_3^- was utilized poorly by the cranberry plant. Other workers have not substantiated the near essentiality of NH_4^+, but all studies show a quick response to ammonium applications. The amount of nitrogen needed is determined by the growth status of the producing vines. New upright growth should be in the range of 2.5 to 4 in. (6 to 10 cm) annually. With new growth on the uprights of less than 2 in. (5 cm), a grower should apply 30 lb/acre (34 kg/ha) of nitrogen; with 2.5 in. (6 cm) of growth, 25 lb/acre (28 kg/ha) of nitrogen, and with 4 in. (10 cm) of growth, about 25 lb/acre (17 kg/ha) of nitrogen. Growth in excess of 4 in. (10 cm) indicates an adequacy of nitrogen supply from environmental sources, and no supplementation is needed. The material may be applied as a single application in mid-May as a dry fertilizer by air or ground equipment, or it may be applied through the irrigation system. Many growers have started using split applications, with half of the nitrogen applied in May and the other half applied just before blossom in mid-June. A third application of 5 to 10 lb/acre (5 to 9 kg/ha) of nitrogen in late July may be used to sustain leaf efficiency and increase berry size.

Nitrogen must be used carefully and in moderate applications. Excessive vine growth from overfertilization decreases production, interferes with harvest, delays fruit color development, and increases the potential for rot development in the fruit crop. Excessive nitrogen also stimulates weed growth in those fields that have a weed population present.

Pollination and Fruit Set

The cranberry is self-fruitful (i.e., pollen of a cultivar will fertilize the ovules of the same cultivar). A limited amount of work has been reported showing that fertilization by a different cultivar may increase fruit set and the number of seeds per fruit. Both are important for maximum production; for more berries mean more yield, and there is a good correlation between seed number and berry size. On a practical basis all cranberries are planted in solid stands of only one cultivar.

Cranberry flowers are pollinated by insects, air currents, and possibly by gravity. A small amount of fruit set occurs in experimental areas that are screened to exclude insects and minimize wind. Numerous studies in recent years have clearly shown the benefits of insect pollination for the setting of commercial crops. Although wild bees and other insects provide adequate pollination in some years, most growers provide insurance pollination by transferring honeybees to the field at blossom time. Recommendations call for one strong colony of honeybees per acre to be located in protected areas adjacent to the field. Two colonies per acre is helpful, especially in those years when poor pollination conditions prevail during the flowering period. A field with heavy flowering will have 40,000,000 flowers per acre (100,000,000 per hectare), each of which is potentially capable of becoming a fruit if properly pollinated, fertilized, and developed.

Fruit set follows pollination, germination of the pollen tube, fertilization of the ovules, and the initiation of seed and fruit development. The stigma of an unfertilized flower may remain receptive to pollen for several days if weather conditions are moderate. The germinating pollen tube requires at least 24 hours to reach the ovary and effect fertilization. Apparently, a developing fruit exercises some control over the fertilization and development of later-opening flowers on the same upright. Growers have long recognized that when the first flowers on the bottom of the new shoot set fruit, there is a tendency for later-produced flowers higher on the upright to fail to produce fruit. It is unknown whether this condition is due to an intraplant competition for energy resources or the production and export of inhibitory substances by developing ovules. The fertilized fruit develops rapidly with favorable weather conditions. Once 'set' there is no natural drop or loss of fruit from the vines.

Pruning

The amount of light reaching an individual upright determines the long-term fruit-fulness of that upright. Excessive runner growth over the top of the vines, too many uprights per unit area, and tall weed growth restrict the amount of light reaching an upright. Roberts and Struckmeyer (1942) concluded that 200 to 300 uprights per square foot and a terminal growth of 2.5 to 3.5 in. (6.4 to 8.9 cm) per upright was optimal for 'Searles'. The heavier vined 'McFarlin' reached optimum conditions at 2.5 to 3 in. (6.4 to 7.6 cm) of growth. Optimum growth for other cultivars is in the same range as that for 'Searles' and 'McFarlin'.

Control of upright populations is in part a function of fertilizer levels and water management. A direct control is imposed by nonselective pruning of vines after harvest or in the early spring. Cranberry pruning machines are usually a series of vertical knives set at a slight angle to the direction of movement and spaced at 1-ft intervals along a rotation frame. The vertically mounted knives move through the vines and cut off excess runners and some uprights. The severity of pruning is controlled by knife spacing and the speed of operation of the machine. Stems that are cut off are raked and removed from the bed. This material may be used for planting stock if it is properly handled to prevent desiccation.

The adoption of mechanical rakes for harvesting has resulted in substantial pruning and thinning of vines, especially in overly vegetative beds. The planned pruning with special devices has been less common as mechanical harvesters have become widely adopted.

Weed Control

Removal and suppression of weed competition is a major management concern of the cranberry grower. The cranberry plant is a weak competitor in the ecological niche created by the drainage, leveling, sanding, fertilization, and irrigation of the field. Wetland species in the sedge and grass families are particularly serious invaders. In addition, ferns of several species, willows, several ericaceous shrubs, and annual and perennial broadleaved wetland species may become serious problems. There is no opportunity for cultivation because the vines totally cover the surface of the bed.

Mowing of the dikes surrounding the beds and clipping of weed flower stalks over the top of the vines may be helpful in slowing the spread of annual species. Hand weeding of willows (*Salix* spp.), hardhack (*Spirea* spp.), and isolated plants of other species is a common practice.

Herbicides have been used in cranberry bogs for many years. Iron sulfate, sulfuric acid, sodium nitrate, and copper sulfate were used in the early twentieth century for treatment of particularly difficult species. In the mid-1920s, it was discovered that mineral spirits (petroleum derivatives) could provide top-kill of many species without damage to the cranberry vines. Kerosene, gasoline, stove oil, and Stoddard solvent with various additives, when applied at 300 to 500 gal/acre

(2800 to 4700 liters,ha) before cranberry growth was initiated in the spring would suppress perennial sedges and grasses without damage to the cranberry plants. The high cost of these materials since the early 1970s has discouraged continued reliance on this type of herbicide.

With the development of the herbicide 2,4-dichlorophenoxy-acetic acid (2,4-D) in the 1950s, a new approach to weed control was available. The cranberry is susceptible to 2,4-D injury, but the selective and carefully controlled application of 2,4-D to individual weeds provided a useful adjunct to hand weeding and petroleum solvent sprays. The labeling of dichlobenil in 1964, chlorpropham and naptalam combination in 1968, norflurazon in 1971, and glyphosate in 1981 has permitted the gradual development of weed control applications on an annual basis to establish and maintain nearly weed-free plantings. With the exception of glyphosate, these herbicides are applied as granular formulations in the spring before much new growth is evident on the cranberry vines. The development and availability of glyphosate applied by over-the-top wiping techniques for summer treatment of established herbacious perennials has changed weed control practices substantially. Over 400 species of plants may occur as weeds in cranberry fields.

Fruit Development, Harvesting, and Handling

The cranberry fruit matures between 60 and 120 days after blossom. Cultivars with early-ripening characteristics, such as 'Early Black', 'Ben Lear', and 'Bergman', will be harvested in September; while 'McFarlin', 'Stevens', and 'Howes' will be harvested in October and as late as early November in the coastal growing areas. The trend is to leave the berries on the vines as long as possible in order to gain maximum red color development, because the marketability of berries for both fresh and processed uses is related to the extent of color development.

The demand for a highly colored fruit to be used in the preparation of juice products with no artificial color added has encouraged interest in finding means to hasten and intensify development of red pigment. Application of the insecticide malathion as early as 3 weeks before anticipated harvest has been shown to increase color in cranberries (Eaton et al., 1969). The use of malathion for this purpose was recommended for several years. In the early 1970s the ethylene stimulator ethephon, (2-chloroethyl)phosphonic acid, was shown to stimulate color formation in cranberries. This material is useful only when temperatures are above 60°F (15°C). Unfortunately, there is often a shortage of hours and days during late September and October when temperatures in cranberry growing areas reach that level. Furthermore, frost protection with sprinklers or flooding is a frequent need at that season and surface-applied chemicals are diluted and removed before they can be absorbed and become metabolically active. As a result of the erratic responses to ethephon under field conditions, there has not been widespread acceptance for this method of color enhancement.

Berries are machine harvested either dry or 'on the flood'. Dry raked fruit is stripped from the vines by mechanical rakes that pass through the plants, hold the berries on the teeth (tines) of the machine, and allow the slender uprights to pass through the teeth. The effect is similar to combing one's hair. The vines are trained in a given orientation and must be harvested in the same direction each year to minimize disruption of the plants. Berries collected by the machine are deposited in bags or boxes and carried from the field for transfer to the warehouse or receiving station for storage, packing, or processing.

Harvesting 'on the flood' takes advantage of the buoyant nature of the fruit. It lifts the unharvested berries from the bog floor for easy and complete removal by the machines and facilitates movement of berries from the field to the dikes, where waiting trucks transfer them to the handling facilities (Figs. 8-6 and 8-7). The field is flooded to a depth of 4 to 8 in. (10 to 20 cm). The actual depth needed depends on

FIGURE 8-6 Cranberries harvested with a machine-mounted rake and moved in boats to a collection point.

FIGURE 8-7 Boats lifted from the section and emptied into a truck for transport to handling and storage facilities.

Bog Management

vine growth, evenness of the field, and method of harvest. Historically, water raking was done with hand rakes that were a set of closely spaced teeth on the front of a box that was used to capture the harvested fruit. This process was mechanized in the 1940s and 1950s, and self-propelled machines with a set of teeth in front and a conveyor belt in back were used to strip the berries from the vines and carry them to metal or fiberglass boats trailing beside or behind the machines. The boats, holding up to 10 barrels of berries, were hoisted from the beds and emptied into trucks for movement to the warehouse.

In the 1970s, the water reel or 'eggbeater' became widely adopted in all growing areas (Figs. 8-8 and 8-9). This machine is a series of horizontal bars that rotate on a shaft as the machine moves forward. The horizontal bars are carried in the water about 1 to 2 in. (2.5 to 5 cm) off the ground, and as they rotate, the pedicel of the fruit is broken and the buoyant berry pops up to the surface of the flood. All berries in a flooding section are knocked off and float on the water. It is simple to construct a wooden boom that traps the floating mass of berries and moves them to the chosen loading area. Often, wind will do a nice job of floating the berries to one corner of the section, where they may be elevated to trucks.

Fruit harvested by the water reel is removed from the flooding section by conveyor belt elevators constructed with horizontal bars to hold the berries as they move up the incline from the bog to the truck (Fig. 8-10). The loaders float the berries to the base of the conveyor, which picks them up and carries them to the truck.

Water raking harvests some weeds, vines, and leaves (i.e., trash) with the berries. The trash is removed by passing the harvested mass over a coarse grating

FIGURE 8-8 Self-propelled but manually directed water reel moving through a field. Once broken free of the plants, the berries float to the surface and are not injured by machinery driving through the field.

FIGURE 8-9 Large water reel completing a trip across the field. Each reel unit is 8 ft long.

FIGURE 8-10 Elevator for lifting berries to the truck.

that allows the fruit to pass through, and screens out the coarse weeds and vines. Commonly, the wet berries and small trash fall to a wide rubberized belt inclined at 45° and moving at a modest speed. The berries roll down the belt while the small trash sticks to the belt and is carried up and away from the fruit.

Wet harvested berries must have the surface moisture removed before transfer to storage facilities. This is accomplished by moving the berries over a fine screen through which a current of warm air passes. The berries may be moved horizontally on a conveyor belt, or may travel slowly by gravity down an inclined screen. The rate of flow by gravity is controlled by baffle boards that maintain a constant depth of fruit over the screen, with the movement of the entire mass controlled by a rotating, horizontal reel at the bottom of the incline. The surface-dried berries are cooled to ambient temperature by fresh-air fans installed down the line from the dryers.

In comparison with dry harvested fruit, wet harvested fruit generally has poorer storage quality. The wet harvesting procedures encourage the transfer and invasion of decay organisms and cause greater bruising and mechanical damage to the fruit. The water reel is particularly damaging to the fruit. For this reason, berries harvested with the water reel are sorted immediately after harvest, and sent to freezer storage to be used for processing later in the marketing season. Dry raked fruit and some wet raked fruit are held for fresh market packaging. Refrigerated storage at temperatures between 32 and 40°F (0° −5°C) will hold fresh berries for several months, and common storage holds berries for 2 to 3 months if autumn temperatures are not excessively warm.

Mature Fruit

The mature fruit has a firm, crisp flesh surrounding the open locules in the center. The outer tissues contain all of the red pigment in the fruit at maturity. In storage at temperatures above 50°F (10°C) many cultivars continue to develop color which may diffuse into the flesh as the fruit becomes overripe.

Cranberries are sold fresh for home processing and are processed commercially into whole-fruit sauce, strained sauce, juice cocktail, juice blends with other fruits (apple, raspberry, blueberry, grape, apricot), cranberry–orange relish, candied and spiced cranberries, and liqueurs. Over 80% of the crop was commercially processed in the late 1970s.

Marketing

Cranberries are marketed through a national grower cooperative that handles approximately 80% of the crop. The remainder are packaged or processed by private concerns in Massachusetts, New Jersey, and Wisconsin. A very small portion of the crop is packaged and enters trade channels directly from the producer.

Berries in Massachusetts, New Jersey, Washington, Oregon, British Columbia, and a large portion of the Wisconsin crop are transported directly from the growers' fields to large, centrally located receiving stations operated by the handlers.

At the receiving station, the grower is credited with the quantity of berries delivered; and from that point on the berries belong to the national pool of berries. Berries received are cleaned, surface dried, sorted to remove decayed and damaged fruit, and placed in containers for storage. Fruit destined for processing is dumped into large bulk bins and shipped to freezer storage, where it may be held for many months without deterioration. Fruit for the early fresh market is placed in shallow, ventilated crates and stored in common storage (warehouse) until needed for marketing. A small amount of fresh fruit is held in refrigerated storage at 40°F (5°C) for the post-Christmas fresh fruit market. Fruit for the fresh fruit market is graded, sorted, and packed in polyethylene film packages for entrance into marketing channels.

Cranberries are graded for size by passing the fruit over sizing screens. The small berries ('pie berries') are sent directly to the processor for freezer storage; the larger fruit may be held for fresh market sales.

Two methods are used to separate good and bad cranberries. The traditional cranberry mill consists of a series of seven bounce boards arranged so that the berries fall against the board slanted at 45° to the angle of flow. Parallel to and facing the slope of the bounce board is a vertically placed barrier board whose height may be adjusted up or down. The cranberries fall against the bounce board; and if of good quality and thus resilient, they bounce up and off at an angle and hopefully over the barrier board. The soft, decayed, and nonresilient berries do not bounce. They merely slide or fall off the bounce board rather than hurdling the barrier board. There are normally seven bounce boards arranged in a vertical series with 10 in. (25 cm) between them, so a berry has seven chances to be a good berry before it finally falls into the 'slush pile'.

The flotation sorter operates on the principle that sound berries have different specific gravity and surface tension properties than those of unsound berries. By passing the fruit through a carefully monitored flotation tank, it is possible to separate unsound from sound fruit.

Berries coming from either of the sorting machines are passed over sorting belts, where sharp-eyed workers pick out unripe fruit and any unsound fruit that may have escaped the sorting machine.

Diseases

The false blossom disease was endemic in Wisconsin and became a problem as the industry developed in that state. The introduction of contaminated vines to other growing areas spread the disease to all growing areas, where its prevalence threatened the industry. The discovery that this systemic disease was caused by a virus entity (later classified as a mycoplasma), and that the vector was the blunt-nosed leafhopper, *Scleroracus vaccinii,* has led to near eradication of this disease. Insecticides for control of the leafhopper have become available and widely used. Infected plants produce a "witch's broom" growth, with several shoots arising from axillary buds at the terminal region of the upright. These shoots produce flowers with an excessive amount of red pigment. The flowers remain erect instead of becoming pendulous as a normal flower does. Usually, the flowers do not set fruit.

Fungi may attack leaves and stems of the cranberry plant as well as the fruit. Rose bloom and red leaf spot, caused by *Exobasidium oxycoccus* Rostr. and *E. vaccinii* Fekl. Wor., respectively, attack the stems and leaves.

Other leaf diseases of cranberry are caused by black spot. *Mycosphaerella nigro-maculans* Shear, and gibbera spot, *Gibbera compacta* (Pk) Shear. These fungi induce minute, dark lesions on the leaves. The 'berry speckle disease' on 'Searles' in Wisconsin is caused by *Gibbera* fruit infections.

Two serious diseases cause twig blight or shoot dieback in cranberries. *Lophodermium oxycocci* (Fr) Karst. causes severe upright kill in certain bogs in Washington and Oregon but is no problem in other areas. *Phomopsis* causes shoot dieback in other cranberry growing areas.

The most serious disease problems of cranberries are caused by the fruit-rotting fungi. Early rot caused by *Guignardia vaccinii* Shear is the most common field rot in the eastern growing areas. A closely related *Guignardia* species is of minor significance in Wisconsin and the West coast. This is the most common organism causing 'scald' or rot in the field in New Jersey and Massachusetts.

End rot caused by *Godronia cassandrae* Peck is the most common storage rot in Wisconsin. Losses may reach 30% of berries held in common storage for fresh market sales during the holiday season. Infection occurs in the field, with rot development being delayed until after harvest. The practice of freezing fruit immediately after harvest has reduced the impact of this disease to a relatively minor problem.

Black rot, *Ceuthospora lunata* Shear, is recognized by the jet black rotted berries in the field and in storage. Affected berries are firm at first, but later shrivel and dry out like miniature prunes, and later still, mummify and harden. This disease is usually of minor significance, but in some marshes in some years may destroy 10% of the crop.

Numerous other organisms—*Sclerotinia oxycocci* Wor., *Acanthorynchus vaccinii* Shear, *Glomerella cingulata vaccinii* Shear, and *Sporonema oxycocci* Shear—may cause rotting of cranberries in the field and in storage. These are of minor significance commercially.

Insects

Cranberry plants are attacked by many different types and species of insects. Fortunately, only about a dozen are of enough significance to demand control programs. The roots are attacked by several species of soil-inhabiting insects. The larvae of the common white grub, *Phyllophaga anxia* Lec., the cranberry root grub, *Lichnauthe vulpina* (Hentz), grape *Anomala, Anomala lucicola* Fab., and cranberry rootworm, *Rhabdopterus picipes* (Oliv.) have all been found attacking roots of cranberries in eastern areas. The black root weevil *Brachyrynus sulcatus* Fabr. is the most serious root pest in Washington and Oregon. The damage from each of these pests is localized in nature but destroys plants totally in affected areas. Many species of insects attack cranberry leaves and stems. Only a few are a general problem in all areas and warrant control measures as standard practice.

Cranberry tipworm, *Dasyneura vaccinii* Smith, adults are minute flies. The first brood adults emerge from the pupal cases in late spring (late May in Wisconsin). The females lay tiny eggs at the leaf margins near the shoot tips. These eggs hatch and the maggots move to the developing meristem, where they feed on the embryonic leaves and destroy the shoot tips. Terminals destroyed by first brood maggots produce no fruit. Axillary buds below the injured tips develop new shoots, which may produce fruit buds for the next year's crop. Terminals destroyed by second brood maggots do not recover to produce fruit buds in that season. Control of the first brood is particularly important to restrict the second brood population.

The black-headed fireworm, *Rhopobota vacciniana* Pock., is a lepidopterous insect whose larvae feed first on old leaves, then migrate to the new shoots, where they consume the upper surface of the leaves. Characteristically, several leaves are webbed together, and on occasion more than one upright may be involved. The injured leaves turn brown. A heavy population of larvae may destroy all the uprights in an area, leaving the appearance that a fire swept through the area (hence the name).

The black-headed fireworm overwinters as an egg on the underside of a leaf near the base of an upright. The eggs hatch in late May. The larval stage lasts about 3 weeks. The pupa rests in the injured vines or on the trash on the field floor. Two weeks after the beginning of pupation the adults emerge. Females may lay eggs within a day after emergence. The cycle is repeated, with the second-brood adults laying the overwintering eggs in August.

The black-headed fireworm is the most destructive of all the insects attacking cranberries. Of less importance, but present in some years, are the red-striped fireworm *Aroga trialbamaculella* (Cham.), Hill's fireworm *Ilascala finitella* (Wlk.), spotted fireworm *Archips parallela* (Rob.), and yellow-headed fireworm *Peronea minuta* (Rob.).

Scale insects may on occasion be serious pests. The oyster shell *Lepidosaphes ulmi* (L.) and *Lecanium* sp. scales are reportedly problems in Washington; oyster shell scale, cranberry scale [*Aspidaspis oxycoccus* (Woglum)], and Dearness scale [*Rhizaspidiotus dearnessi* (Ckll.)] in Massachusetts; and the Dearness scale in Wisconsin.

Cranberry girdler, *Crambus hortuellus* Huebner, is a lepidopterous insect whose larvae attack the bark tissues of runners and uprights near the soil surface.

The cranberry fruitworm. *Acrobasis vaccinii* Riley, is the most common and serious pest attacking the fruit. The insect overwinters as a cocoon under the surface of the soil. In April and May the larva in the cocoon changes to a pupa. In July the adult moth emerges, and the females soon lay small, whitish eggs under the calyx lobes of the young fruit. The newly hatched larvae migrate from the blossom end to the stem end of the berry, where they eat a small hole and penetrate to the seed cavity. The developing seeds and most of the internal tissues of the fruit are consumed before the larva eats its way out of the berry and goes on to another fruit, where the process is repeated. A larva may consume the interior of up to six berries on its way to maturity.

The sparganothis fruitworm or false yellow-headed fireworm, *Sparganothis sulfureana* (F.), has become a problem in eastern growing areas following the widespread use of organic phosphate insecticides beginning in the 1950s. This insect overwinters as a larva. In the spring these larvae feed on new shoot growth and may feed on developing flower buds. The larvae mature, pupate on the vines, and the adult moths emerge in August. The female moths lay eggs on leaves, fruit, and weeds; and in about 10 days the new crop of larvae appear. These larvae feed preferentially on developing fruit, causing external damage to the fruit.

Green spanworms *Itame sulphurea* (Pack), brown spanworms *Ematurga amitaria* (Gn.), cutworms, gypsy moth *Porthetria dispar* (L.), larvae, and cranberry sawfly *Pristiphora idiota* Norton larvae have all been found as occasional serious pests feeding on cranberry foliage. The blunt-nosed leafhopper is a common inhabitant of cranberry fields and was a problem because of its relationship to transfer of false blossom disease. Cranberry weevil, *Anthonomus musculus* (Say.), and leaf miner may be locally abundant. Southern red mites, *Paratetranychus ilicis* (McG.), may build up, damaging populations in an occasional poorly managed bog that has no provision for winter flooding.

Miscellaneous Damage

At least four species of mammals may be problems in cranberry culture. Muskrats, *Ondatra zibethicus,* may tunnel through dikes and around water control structures, thus contributing to washouts and dike breakage during high-water periods. These creatures also feed under the ice in winter and may cause substantial damage to small areas within cranberry beds. On occasion a colony of beavers, *Castor canadensis,* may choose to construct a dam in a critical drainage area, an activity that interferes with necessary water-level control. Meadow voles (meadow mice), *Microtus* sp., may establish nests in the cranberry field. They chew the stems of the cranberry and leave the tips to die. Such damage is localized and not prevalent. In Wisconsin there is considerable concern about damage from the white-tailed deer, *Odocoileus virginianus.* These game animals make paths across beds as they travel the shortest distance between their chosen habitats. Occasionally, they bed down in the vines. They eat cranberry fruit as they travel across the beds. Perhaps most damaging of all, economically, is the habit of leaving droppings in the bed. The droppings are about the same size as a cranberry, and a certain number of these 'deer berries' are picked up by harvesting machines. These 'deer berries' go through the mills and bounce like a cranberry and must be hand sorted from the fruit going to market. Deer problems are generally of minor concern.

The cranberry plant demands specialized soil and water conditions for successful commercial production. The plant evolved under acid wetland conditions in north temperate regions. Commercial producers have discovered that growth and fruit production of the cranberry may be benefited by modification and control of factors in the growth environment. These modifications comprise the science and art of cranberry culture.

The industry has grown rapidly in production per acre in recent years, while acreage devoted to cranberries remained static. A slow acreage increase is under way in the 1980s as market acceptance of products has absorbed the expanded production. The cranberry industry, though small, promises to continue as a successful small fruit enterprise.

REFERENCES AND SUGGESTED READING

ADDOMS, R. M., AND F. C. MOUNCE. 1931. Notes on the nutrient requirements and the histology of the cranberry (*Vaccinium macrocarpon* Ait.) with special reference to mycorrhiza. Plant Physiol. 6:653–668.

BRICK, A. R., JR. 1981. Energy inputs in cranberry production. In CRC handbook of energy utilization in agriculture. CRC Press, Boca Raton, Fla.

CHANDLER, F. B., AND I. E. DEMORANVILLE. 1959. Cranberry varieties of North America. Mass. Agric. Exp. Stn. Bull. 513.

CROSS, C. E., ET AL. 1976. The modern art of cranberry cultivation. Coop. Ext. Serv. Univ. Mass. Publ. 112.

CROSS, C. E., ET AL. 1982. Modern cranberry cultivation. Coop. Ext. Serv. Univ. Mass. Publ. SP-126.

DANA, M. N., AND G. C. KLINGBEIL. 1966. Cranberry growing in Wisconsin. Univ. Wisc. Coop. Ext. Serv. Circ. 654.

DOUGHTY, C. C., AND J. C. DODGE. 1966. Cranberry production in Washington. Wash. State Univ. Coop. Ext. Serv. Publ. EM2619.

EATON, G. W., ET AL. 1969. Effect of preharvest sprays on cranberry fruit color. J. Am. Soc. Hortic. Sci. 94:590–595.

EATON, G. W., AND T. R. KYTE. 1978. Yield component analysis in the cranberry. J. Am. Soc. Hortic. Sci. 103:578–583.

ECK, P. 1986. Cranberry. In S. P. Monselise (ed.). CRC handbook of fruit set and development. CRC Press, Boca Raton, Fla.

ECK, P. 1990. The American cranberry. Rutgers University Press. New Brunswick, N.J.

FELLERS, C. R., AND W. B. ESSELEN. 1955. Cranberries and cranberry products. Mass. Agric. Exp. Stn. Bull. 481.

FRANKLIN, H. J. 1948. Cranberry insects in Massachusetts. Mass. Agric. Exp. Stn. Bull. 445. 1950. Ibid. Parts II–VII. 1952. Ibid. Supplement.

GREIDANUS, T., L. A. PETERSON, L. E. SCHRADER, AND M. N. DANA. 1972. Essentiality of ammonium for cranberry nutrition. J. Am. Soc. Hortic. Sci. 79:272–277.

HALL, I. V. 1966. Growing cranberries. Can. Dep. Agric. Publ. 1282.

LIEBSTER, G., AND H. W. DEBOR. 1974. Bibliography of international literature on the cranberry, *Vaccinium macrocarpon* Ait. Bibliographische Reihe der Technischen Universität, Berlin. Herausgegeben von der Universitätsbibliothek, Berlin.

PETERSON, B. S., C. E. CROSS, AND N. TILDEN. 1968. The cranberry industry in Massachusetts. Common. Mass. Dep. Agric. Bull. 201.

ROBERTS, R. H., AND B. E. STRUCKMEYER. 1942. Growth and fruiting of the cranberry. Proc. Am. Soc. Hortic. Sci. 40:373–379.

SHAWA, A., G. W. EATON, AND P. A. BOWEN. 1981. Cranberry yield components in Washington and British Columbia. J. Am. Soc. Hortic. Sci. 106:474–477.

SHAWA, A. Y., ET AL. 1984. Cranberry production in the Pacific northwest. Wash.-Oreg.-Idaho Coop. Ext. Serv. Publ. PNW 247.

SHEAR, C. L. 1907. Cranberry diseases. U.S. Dep. Agric Bull. 110.

SHEAR, C. L., N. E. STEVENS, AND H. F. BAIN. 1931. Fungus diseases of the cultivated cranberry. U.S. Dep. Agric. Tech. Bull. 258.

TOMLINSON, W. E., JR. 1982. Cranberry insects. Coop. Ext. Serv. Univ. Mass. Publ. SP–137.

Chapter 9

Elderberry, Highbush Cranberry, and Juneberry Management

E. J. STANG

INTRODUCTION

Native Americans and early settlers made extensive use of the abundant fruit from wild species stands of these three widely distributed woody shrub genera, usually in preserved, beverage, dyestuff, or extract forms. Improved clonal selections have been made from the wild and from breeding efforts, largely in the twentieth century. Improved selections of elderberry have come largely from the American elder, *Sambucus canadensis* L.; of highbush cranberry from the American cranberrybush, *Viburnum trilobum* Marsh.; and of Juneberry, from *Amelanchier alnifolia* Nutt., the western serviceberry.

Cultivars of these berry plants are easily propagated by softwood stem cuttings, but they can also be propagated from hardwood cuttings, by layering, or from root sprouts. These large shrubs take 3 to 5 years to attain full fruit production. Planting site selection should stress good soil and air drainage and fertile loam soils. Frequent shallow cultivations and watering during the first few years aid establishment by promoting root growth and suppressing weed competition. The fertilizer needs of these plants are modest. Fruiting in these species is often heaviest on 2- to 3-year-old canes. Older canes are thinned out annually, after the plant is mature, leaving five to nine younger, vigorous canes per plant. This light-to-moderate pruning stimulates new growth as canes and branches, removes weak and diseased wood, and promotes regular annual bearing.

Figure 9-1 shows the Juneberry, cranberry, and elderberry morphologies.

ELDERBERRIES

Origin of Cultivated Forms

Elderberries, members of the *Caprifoliaceae* (honeysuckle) family, are deciduous shrubs or small trees distributed through temperate and subtropical regions worldwide. The elderberry genus *Sambucus* includes at least 20 species, with at least eight species native to North America (Ritter and McKee, 1964). Prior to the early twentieth century, fruit was obtained mostly from the wild, with little recorded effort in the selection of improved cultivars. Selection and breeding for improved fruiting have been confined largely to the American elder, *S. canadensis* L. At least 12 cultivars of American elder are recorded within this species. Many ornamental selections have been made, included mostly within *S. canadensis, S. racemosa,* and *S. cerulea.*

Related Germplasm and Utility

Genus *Sambucus.* Elderberries found in North America include both native and introduced species. Common names and general characteristics of some elderberry species are described in Table 9-1.

Cultivars. Of the many cultivars of American elderberry (*S. canadensis*), only a limited number have become economically important, with small-scale production in the United States reported in New York, Ohio, and Oregon (Way, 1981). General characteristics of the more common cultivars are outlined in Table 9-2. The Scotia elderberry is shown in Fig. 9-2.

Utility. The genus name *Sambucus* is derived from *sambuce,* Latin for an ancient musical instrument. The pith of the stem is bored out easily, leaving a hollow tube. Stems have long been used for musical flutes and pipes for conducting liquids. North American Indians and early pioneers adapted the hollow stems as a tap in drawing sap from sugar maple trees.

Tannin in the bark and roots of elderberry was used in tanning leather. Leaves, flowers, and fruit provided dyes for leather, clothing baskets, and artifacts made by North American Indians.

In Europe, berries and oil pressed from elderberry seeds have been used to flavor wine. All parts of the elderberry have at some time been used in medicine.

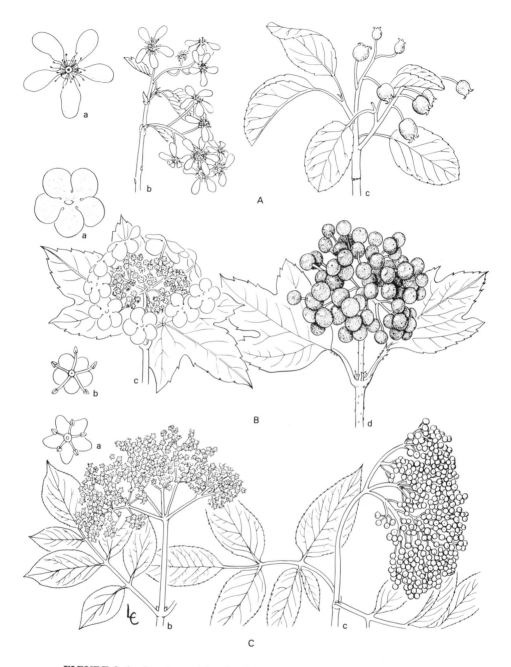

FIGURE 9-1 Juneberry (*Amelanchier alnifolia*), highbush cranberry (*Viburnum trilobum*), and elderberry (*Sambucus canadensis*) morphology. (A) Juneberry: a, flower; b, inflorescence; c, shoot with fruit and leaves. (B) Highbush cranberry: a, sterile marginal flower; b, perfect flower; c, inflorescence; d, shoot with fruit and leaves. (C) Elderberry: a, flower; b, inflorescence; c, shoot with fruit and leaves.

TABLE 9-1 COMMON NAMES AND CHARACTERISTICS OF ELDERBERRY (*SAMBUCUS*) SPECIES FOUND IN THE UNITED STATES

SPECIES	COMMON NAME	CHARACTERISTICS
S. callicarpa	Pacific red elder	Clump forming, large shrub, prolific annual growth, principal use as browse for sheep, cattle, and wildlife, found from west coast of California to Washington
S. ebulus L.	Dwarf elder or danewort	Herbaceous perennial up to 5 ft (1.5 m) high, native to eastern Europe, common in western U.S.; fruit small, black; leaflets narrow, sharply serrate
S. leiosperma	None	Possibly a clone of *S. pubens*; range extends to Alaska
S. melanocarpa Gray	Blackhead elder	Moderately vigorous growth, found along Pacific coast from British Columbia to California, shorter internodes than other species, primarily a forage for wildlife
S. mexicana Presl.	Mexican elder	Large shrub or small tree, evergreen, requires long growing season, bears fruit continually in native habitat, ranges from Mexico to southwestern U.S.
S. microbotys Rydb.	Bunchberry elder	Medium or small shrub, up to 6.5 ft (2 m); found in western states, California to Colorado, north to North Dakota, mostly in moist, fertile sites
S. nigra L.	European elderberry	Small tree, 13 to 26 ft (4 to 8 m); rough bark; wood yellow, hard and fine grained; used by cabinetmakers; similar to *S. canadensis*; berries black or dark green
S. pubens Michx.	Stinking elder	Large shrub, up to 16 ft (5 m); sometimes confused with *S. racemosa*; new stems glaucous; bark darker gray than other species with large corky lenticels
S. racemosa	European or red elder	Medium shrub, up to 13 ft (4 m); reddish-scarlet fruit, new shoots distinctly reddish; native to Europe and Western Asia, found as escapes from cultivation in U.S.
S. sieboldiana Graebn.	Siebold elder	Native to China and Japan, found wild in U.S.; leaflets oblong and distinct from other species; black fruit on small cymes
S. simponii Rehd.	Southern elder	Large shrub or small tree, to 20 ft (6 m); evergreen; fruit ripens throughout the year; widely adapted; forms dense thickets; common throughout the southeastern U.S.
S. cerulea or *S. glauca*	Blueberry elder	Vigorous growing tall shrub, to 20 ft (6 m); found from Pacific coast in western U.S. to New Mexico and Montana; fruit blue skinned with waxy bloom; large fruited, sweet and juicy; cultivated for fruit since 1850
S. canadensis L.	American or common elder	Moderately tall shrub, 6.5 to 16 ft (2 to 5 m); found from Nova Scotia to Minnesota south to Florida and Texas; bark grayish brown with tan lenticels; frequently used as an ornamental for its pleasantly scented flowers; fruit important food for wildlife and commonly harvested from the wild or cultivated for human consumption; first reported under cultivation in U.S. in 1761

Source: Ritter and McKee (1964).

TABLE 9-2 CHARACTERISTICS OF SELECTED ELDERBERRY (*SAMBUCUS*) CULTIVARS

CULTIVARS	CHARACTERISTICS
Adams 1, Adams 2	Introduced in 1926 by the New York Agricultural Experiment Station; vigorous [to 6 ft (2 m)] and productive plants, large fruited; late season ripening in northern regions; Adams 2 is more productive and ripens a few days later than Adams 1; distinguished by more reddish bark on Adams 2 in late fall
Johns	Selected more than a century ago; named in 1954 at Kentville, Nova Scotia Research Station; very vigorous growth to 10 ft (3 m); productive with larger fruit clusters than Adams cultivars; maturing 10 days earlier than either of the Adams cultivars
Scotia	Open pollinated seedling of Adams 2, named in 1960 at Kentville Research Station; medium-sized, productive plant noted for high soluble solids content of fruit
York	Seedling from cross of Adams 2 × Ezyoff, named in 1964 at New York Experiment Station; fruit matures 3 days later than Adams cultivars; very large berries, generally more productive than most other cultivars
Nova	Open pollinated seedling of Adams 2, named in 1959 at Kentville Experiment Station; fruit large, maturing early and uniformly; similar to Kent and Victoria but sweeter
Kent	Open pollinated seedling of Adams 2, introduced in 1957 at Kentville Experiment Station; fruit large, maturing early and uniformly
Victoria	Open pollinated seedling of Adams 2, introduced in 1957 by Kentville Experiment Station; fruit similar to Adams; ripens 3 to 6 days earlier; plant moderately vigorous and productive
Ezyoff	Originated in Ithaca, New York, by S.H. Graham; introduced in 1938; berries larger than native types, cluster size medium; fruit easily removed from clusters when ripe; plant medium in vigor and productivity

Source: Way (1981).

At present, elderberry fruit is used for various culinary purposes: in sauces, alone or combined with other fruit in pies and tarts, as fruit juice and red wine.

Botany

Systematic plant description of *Sambucus canadensis* L.: family Caprifoliaceae—stoloniferous shrub to 12 ft (3.6 m) in height with white pith and pale yellowish-gray, slightly lenticillate branches; leaves bright green, leaflets usually seven, elliptic to lanceolate 5 to 6 in. (15 cm) long, acuminate, sharply toothed on short petiolules, the lower surface smooth or slightly downy; flowers white, produced in June to July in five-rayed cymes to 10 in. (25 cm) across; fruit purplish black, usually four-celled, about ¼ in. (0.6 cm) in diameter in September (Bailey, 1949).

Climate and soil requirements. Elderberries are widely adapted from the temperate northern to mid-southern regions of the United States. Winter injury to roots and 1-year-old canes of the *canadensis* species has not been reported (Ritter and McKee, 1964). Plants will grow under a wide range of soil conditions, from very moist to fairly dry. Generally, vigorous growth will result on moist but well-drained

FIGURE 9-2 Prolific flowering and early fruit development in 'Scotia' elderberry.

fertile silt loam soils. Where extended drought may occur, plants will benefit from timely irrigation since elderberry roots are fibrous and relatively shallow.

Principal diseases and pests. Of the diseases affecting elderberries, several viruses appear to be among the most devastating. Tomato ringspot virus, spread by nematodes and through pollen transfer, is particularly serious, resulting in weakened plants, reduced productivity, and eventually plant death. Control involves preplant soil fumigation to kill nematodes, and eradication of wild elderberry plants within an area of 100 ft (31 m) surrounding cultivated plants, prior to planting (Way, 1981).

Fungus diseases include the stem and twig cankers (*Cytospora, Nectria,* and *Sphaeropsis*), which are controlled by pruning and removal or burning of infected canes (Pirone, 1970). At least four species of powdery mildew can infect leaves and berries in late summer and early fall. Less common diseases include leaf spotting fungi, thread blight, root rots, and verticillium wilt.

The larval stage of the elder shoot borer (*Desmocerus dalliatus*) may cause substantial dieback and loss of canes. Left uncontrolled, this pest may cause plant death. Infested canes should be pruned out and either burned or buried promptly.

Larvae of the cecropia moth can cause substantial loss of foliage during feeding. Control involves hand removal and destruction of the large caterpillar. Additional pests may include aphids, eriophyid mites, potato flea beetles, grape mealybugs, thrips, and San Jose scale. No insecticides or fungicides have label clearance for use in elderberry plantings in the United States.

Birds feeding on ripe fruit are among the most serious pests in elderberries. A variety of control means may be required, such as plant netting, noise cannons, distress calls, and prompt harvesting of ripe fruit to reduce fruit loss.

Culture

Elderberries are adapted to a wide variety of soils, ranging from sandy to clay loams. Wet, poorly drained soils are not suitable, and their use often results in plant loss. Open fields receiving full sunlight and located away from woods or other obstructions allow free air movement, thus reducing disease problems and potential insect and pest bird depredation.

All cultivars of elderberries are considered partially self-fruitful. Fruit production is significantly increased with cross-pollination; thus plantings should include two or more cultivars in close proximity (Way, 1981).

Preplant soil tillage and use of nonresidual herbicides before planting to eliminate troublesome perennial weed infestations are vital to optimum plant establishment and subsequent growth.

Elderberry planting stock should be purchased from a virus-free source. Plants are readily propagated from hardwood or softwood cuttings, root cuttings, or suckers at home if a known virus-free source of plant material is available. Dormant hardwood cuttings with one or more nodes can be cut from 1-year-old canes in early spring, and set directly in nursery rows or into the field in their permanent location. Plants in the nursery row can be left in the field over winter or dug in fall and stored in moist sand under refrigeration until spring planting.

Dormant rooted plants should be set in early spring at the same depth as grown in the nursery. Plant spacing, depending on tillage and harvesting equipment size, may range from 5 to 6.5 ft (1.5 to 2 m) apart in the row and 10 to 13 ft (3 to 4 m) between rows. Watering at or immediately following planting improves initial root establishment and subsequent plant growth and survival.

Fertilizer application is not suggested in the year of planting. Where phosphorus and potash levels were determined by a preplant soil test to be below optimum levels, these nutrients can be broadcast and tilled in prior to planting. Alternatively, the annual banded row application of a complete fertilizer beginning in the second growing season is suggested, applying 1 oz (28 g) actual nitrogen per year of plant age up to a maximum of 0.5 lb. (225 g) of nitrogen per plant.

No herbicides are approved for use in elderberry plantings. Weed populations in newly established plantings will result in severe competition and suppressed growth of the elderberry plants. Frequent shallow, careful cultivation in the row and between plants is suggested. Hand hoeing probably will be needed close to plants, although caution is necessary to avoid damaging elderberry roots near the surface. Weed-free straw, waste hay, or sawdust mulch around plants can help to suppress weeds.

The American elder fruits principally on branched 2-year-old canes. Fruiting clusters are borne terminally on current season's growth also. Thus new canes will bear only a single cluster of fruit, which usually ripens later than that on 2- and 3-year-old canes. To maintain consistent, productive plantings, pruning should consist of removing weak, diseased, or broken canes, and leaving equal numbers of 1-, 2-, and 3-year-old canes. Canes older than 3 years should be removed, leaving a total of seven to nine canes per plant, or one to two canes per square foot of row in narrow hedgerow plantings.

Elderberry plants will bear a limited crop the first year after planting. Full production of up to 12 to 15 lb (5.5 to 6.8 kg) of fruit per plant may be expected in 3 to 4 years. In mature, vigorous, disease-free hedgerow plantings, yields of up to 12,000 lb/acre (13,500 kg/ha) or more are possible.

Depending on the cultivar and location, elderberry fruit will mature from mid-August to mid-September. Depending on the age of the bearing cane and the air temperature at the time of harvest, clusters will ripen over a period of 5 to 15 days. Entire fruit clusters are harvested for later stripping of individual berries and immediate processing or freezing. Fruit in containers should not be held at room temperature for periods of more than 2 to 4 hours, as internal heating from respiration will reduce quality and cause rapid spoilage.

HIGHBUSH CRANBERRIES (AMERICAN CRANBERRYBUSH)

Origin of Cultivated Forms

Of the more than 200 species of *Viburnum*, family *Caprifoliaceae*, most are grown as ornamentals for their attractive foliage and colorful fruit (Egolf, 1962a) (Fig. 9-3).

The cranberrybush *Viburnums* include several very similar species, formerly classed as varieties of the species *V. opulus*. More recently, taxonomists have identified distinct species, based on leaf form and fruit characteristics. Fruits of these species are a bright translucent red or yellowish orange at maturity. Unlike the

FIGURE 9-3 Highbush cranberry (*Viburnum trilobum*) in flower.

oval-shaped leaves of most other members of the genus, leaves are three- or five-lobed, with three to five major veins branching palmately from the base. Cranberrybush *Viburnums,* with the exception of several dwarf clones, are medium-sized shrubs ranging from 8 to 12 ft (2.5 to 3 m) in height, spreading or arching to a similar width (Wood, ca. 1976). The cranberrybush *Viburnums* are among the showiest and most attractive in bloom. Flowers are small, borne in a large cyme, with the outer flowers enlarged and sterile, providing an attractive unusual lacy display at full bloom.

The native viburnum, *Viburnum trilobum* Marsh., alternately called the highbush cranberry or pembina, ranges in Canada from New Brunswick to British Columbia, in Alaska and in the northern United States from New York to Michigan, South Dakota, and Oregon (Dirr, 1983).

Viburnum trilobum sometimes is treated as a subpopulation of *V. opulus,* the European cranberrybush. Characteristics of fruiting species are noted in Table 9-3. Characteristics that distinguish *V. trilobum* from *V. opulus* include somewhat greater cold hardiness, more attractive red leaf coloration in fall, and the production of edible fruits (Flint, 1983).

Viburnum trilobum fruits are similar to those of the true cranberry, *Vaccinium macrocarpon,* only in size and color, but they can be used in making preserves and jellies. Fruits of *V. opulus* are considered very bitter and inedible.

Related Germplasm and Utility

Genus Viburnum. General characteristics of some species of cranberrybush *Viburnums* are outlined in Table 9-3.

Cultivars. Plants of *V. trilobum* often are sold as a species, with only a few cultivars named and described. Named cultivars of *V. trilobum* include 'Andrews', 'Hahs', and 'Wentworth', tall shrubs to 9 ft (3 m), originating as selections from a

TABLE 9-3 CHARACTERISTICS OF SELECTED HIGHBUSH CRANBERRY (*VIBURNUM*) SPECIES

SPECIES	COMMON NAME	CHARACTERISTICS
V. opulus	European cranberrybush	Shrub, 3 to 13 ft (1 to 4 m) includes some dwarf cultivars; tolerant of dry soils; fall leaf colors not as attractive as *V. trilobum*; fruits bitter and classed as inedible; leaves susceptible to aphid injury; native to Europe
V. sargentii	Sargent viburnum	Tall shrub, 13 to 16 ft (4 to 5 m); similar in form to other species; purple anthers; darker, corkier bark than other species; fruit often smaller than *V. trilobum* or *V. opulus*; native to Japan
V. trilobum	American cranberrybush	Open, spreading shrub, 6.5 to 13 ft (2 to 4 m) includes one compact cultivar; may be slightly more hardy than *V. opulus* or *sargentii*; excellent red or orange fall leaf color; leaves not damaged by aphids; fruit tart; edible in preserves or jelly

Source: Wood (1976).

population of native seed and cuttings collected by A. E. Morgan, East Lee, Massachusetts, in northern New England and eastern Canada about 1914 (Wilson, 1977). These cultivars were selected about 1922 on the basis of fruit quality, plant habit, and season of fruit ripening [i.e., 'Wentworth' (early), 'Hahs' (midseason), and 'Andrews' (late)].

'Compactum', a shrub to 6 ft (2 m) in height with a strong upright branching habit, is available more readily than the older cultivars. At least two distinct 'Compactum' clones have been reported (Snyder, 1976). One of these, 'Compactum Alfredo', reputed to be a denser, broader form with improved fall foliage coloration, was introduced by Bailey Nurseries, Inc., St. Paul, Minnesota, in about 1976.

'Manitou Pembina', syn. 'Manitou', a standard-sized Canadian selection noted for large fruit size, was introduced at the Morden Research Station, Manitoba, Canada, in 1947 (Darrow, 1975). More recent *V. trilobum* introductions include 'Garry Pink', with slightly pink-tinged flowers, and 'Phillips', selected in 1965 at the University of New Hampshire for its superior fruit quality. Fruit of 'Phillips', is described as being free of the musky flavor and odor common in cooking fruit of the species, making its jelly equal in flavor and color to that of red currant (Flint, 1982).

Utility. Fruit of the highbush cranberry, *V. trilobum,* is used most often in making jelly, in pies, or as a substitute for cranberry sauce with seeds removed. The large seeds of these fruits preclude their use in whole-fruit products. The fruit is particularly high in pectin when harvested either before the fully ripe stage or before fall frost occurs.

Botany

Systematic plant description of *Viburnum trilobum* Marsh.: family *Caprifoliaceae* — deciduous shrub to 12 ft (3.6 m) with gray glabrous branches, winter buds scaly; leaves broad-ovate 2 to 5 in. (5 to 13 cm) long, lobes coarsely toothed or nearly entire, pubescent on the veins beneath or nearly glabrous; petioles with shallow groove and small, usually stalked glands; cymes 3 to 4 in. (7.6 to 10 cm) across, short peduncled, with marginal showy sterile flowers produced in early summer; stamens exserted, fruit bright scarlet beginning to color by the end of July and keeping their color until the following spring; fruit 1/3 in. (0.8 cm) long (Bailey, 1949).

Climate and soil requirements. *Viburnum trilobum* is native and widely adapted to soils of the northern United States and southern Canada (Darrow and Yerkes, 1937). Although adapted best to cool, moist, and fertile soils the species will grow in soils of moderate fertility but is subject to severe injury or death under extended drought conditions. Although tolerant of partial shade, exposure to full sunlight encourages flowering, fruiting, and fall foliage coloration (Hasselkus, 1982).

Principal diseases and pests. Bacterial diseases affecting *Viburnum* include bacterial leaf spot (*Pseudomonas viburni*) and occasionally crown gall (*Erwinia tumefaciens*) (Pirone, 1970). The fungus diseases, powdery mildew and shoot blight (*Botrytis cinerea*), may cause severe leaf, shoot, and fruit injury, but can be controlled with fungicides.

Viburnum trilobum and other *Viburnum* spp. are susceptible to feeding injury by the tarnished plant bug (*Lygus lineolaris*) on blossoms and young shoots, particularly on the developing inflorescence. Two species of thrips may infest the plant. Thrips and tarnished plant bugs are controlled by conventional home insecticide sprays.

V. trilobum may be attached by aphids, but generally is not subject to the severe injury reported on *V. opulus,* the European cranberrybush.

Other insect pests may include the potato flea beetle, dogwood twig borer, and various scale insects. Where soil populations of the southern root-knot nematode (*Meloidogyne*) are high, infestation and plant injury are likely to occur. No insecticides, fungicides, or herbicides are labeled for use on commercial plantings in the United States.

Culture

As for most other small fruit crop species, proper preplant site and soil preparation involves selecting a well-drained loam or silt loam soil with good moisture-holding capacity and a pH of 6.0 to 7.5. Preplant fertilization generally is considered unnecessary in soils with normal phosphorus and potassium content (Hasselkus, 1982). Tilling or use of nonresidual preplant herbicides to eliminate competing perennial weed species before planting is suggested.

Although *V. trilobum* can be propagated by hardwood cuttings, softwood cuttings taken in midsummer, rooted in sand or perlite under glass or mist, are considered the most successful propagation method (Hartman and Kester, 1975). For best survival, cuttings should be allowed to develop a secondary root system before being transplanted to nursery rows or directly to the field. Simple layering is also an effective propagation method for *V. trilobum* plants. The base of either current season's growth layered in midsummer or previous season's growth layered in early spring will develop strong root systems in 12 to 18 months.

Young dormant plants from either cuttings or layerage may be transplanted by hand or machine to the field in early spring. Plants of standard-sized cultivars should be spaced 6.5 to 8 ft (2 to 2.5 m) in the row with 13 to 20 ft (4 to 6 m) spacing between rows to permit traffic of sprayers and other tillage or harvesting equipment. Plants should be set at a depth they were growing in the nursery row and watered immediately after planting. Frequent watering and the addition of nitrogen fertilizer either through nutrient solution application or banding beside plants is recommended to maintain continued growth.

Pruning is needed only for removal of broken, diseased, or crowding stems as plants develop. As plants mature, productivity may be improved by limited annual renewal pruning to encourage new growth. Remove one-third of the mature shoots and leave five or more mature fruiting stems per plant.

Limited fruit development occurs during the third season after planting, with full production anticipated in the fifth season. Expected yields have not been reported or documented.

Fruit can be hand harvested when fully mature in mid-September through early October. Maximum fruit pectin content develops prior to frost.

JUNEBERRIES (SERVICEBERRY, SASKATOON)

Origin of Cultivated Forms

The genus *Amelanchier,* family Rosaceae (Rose), is among the most diverse of native North American species. The many common names attributed to members of this genus reflect the extensive distribution, the relative ease of hybridization, and the rich history of utility as a desirable fruiting and ornamental shrub or small tree. Common names include Juneberry, serviceberry, saskatoon, sarvis or sarvistree, shadblow, shadbush, swamp sugar pear, currant tree, snowy mespilus, or Indian pear, among others (Jones, 1946). The widely used common name serviceberry may include such diverse types as the Allegheny serviceberry (*A. laevis*), running serviceberry (*A. stolonifera*), and the Chinese serviceberry (*A. asiatica*), although the latter may be more often termed a shadblow. Depending on the regional location, *A. canadensis* may be called by either name.

The term sarvistree, used to include both *A. arborea* or *A. laevis,* is among the oldest common names. Apparently, early English colonists confused *Amelanchier* with the European *Sorbus domestica,* whose common name at that time was sarvis or service tree. The genus *Amelanchier,* as usually estimated, includes some 24 species (Miller and Stushnoff, 1971), although over 40 scientific names have been used in describing them. With the exception of *A. asiatica* (native to China) and *A. ovalis* (from Europe), the genus is nearly exclusive to North America. One or more species have been found in almost every state in the United States and in every province in Canada. *Amelanchier alnifolia* Nutt. is the dominant species among the named cultivars; although a few cultivars of other eastern species are reported (Hilton, 1982).

Related Germplasm and Utility

Genus *Amelanchier*. General characteristics of native North American *Amelanchier* species are described in Table 9-4.

Cultivars. Many of the cultivars of *Amelanchier* are dual-purpose plants used both for their improved fruit size, quality, or yield, and as ornamentals for their flowering and fall foliage coloration. A recent compilation of recognized cultivar names and some of their characteristics is outlined in Table 9-5 (Hilton, 1982).

As noted by Hilton, some cultivars of *Amelanchier* are apparently compatible with and readily propagated on rootstocks of *Sorbus aucuparia* L. and *Cotoneaster acutifolia.* Interspecific hybrids of *A. alnifolia* with male parents of crabapple, pear, and mountain ash (*Sorbus* × *alnifolia*) are reported to be under test by G. Grainger at the Tree Nursery and Horticulture Centre in Edmonton, Alberta, Canada.

Utility. *Amelanchier* species are widely used as ornamentals for their masses of showy flowers in early spring and for their edible fruit. The fruit was used by North American Indians in making pemmican, a semidry mixture of fruit and meat. Early pioneers used the Juneberry or serviceberry as a major source of fruit. *Amelanchier* fruit may be eaten fresh, in pies or other baked desserts, canned, frozen, or made into wine, jellies, jams, preserves, and syrup.

Botany

Systematic plant description of *Amelanchier alnifolia* Nutt.: family Rosaceae—slender shrub 6 to 15 ft (1.8 to 4.6 m) high, leaves oblong to elliptic oblong, about 1 ½ in. (3.8 cm) long, mostly obtuse at ends, coarsely toothed toward the apex to subentire; usually subglabrous above, somewhat tomentose beneath; flowers white in more or less tomentose racemes to 1½ in. (3.8 cm) long, petals spatulate to ⅓ in. (0.8 cm) long, ovary wooly at summit; fruit dark purple, bloomy (Bailey, 1949).

Climate and soil requirements. The extensive distribution of the *Amelanchier* species indicates wide adaptability to varying climate and soil types. *A. alnifolia,* the dominant species among the named cultivars, is adapted throughout Canada and the northern and north central prairie states. *Amelanchier* will grow well in all soil types, with the exception of poorly drained soils or poorly aerated clay soils lacking humus (Harris, 1972).

Principal diseases and pests. Several rusts (*Gymnosporangium* spp.) attack the leaves and fruit of *Amelanchier,* sometimes causing defoliation and loss of fruit. Alternate hosts of these disease organisms are the red cedar, common juniper, and southern white cedar. Primary control, if possible, is the eradication of the alternate hosts within a 1-mile radius of the planting (Pirone, 1970).

As with most other Rosaceae, serviceberries are susceptible to fire blight (*Erwinia amylovora*) bacterial infection. Severe fruit loss and plant injury may occur. Principal control consists of pruning infected shoots below the point of visible injury, and removing and burning or burying infected plant material. Pruning shears should be disinfected in a 1:10 sodium hypochlorite (household bleach) or alcohol-water solution between cuts to avoid spreading the bacteria to uninfected tissue. Streptomycin or agromycin sprays may be helpful also.

Less common diseases include several species of powdery mildew, leaf spot (*Fabraea* spp.), and *Monolinia* fruit rots, occurring most often in humid rainy seasons. There are no fungicides cleared for use on *Amelanchier* in the United States.

Various borer insects, including the lesser peach tree, apple bark, roundheaded apple tree, and shot hole borer, are known to occasionally infest *Amelanchier.* As with other plant species, most borers will preferentially infest weakened, diseased,

TABLE 9-4 NORTH AMERICAN *AMELANCHIER* SPECIES

SPECIES	PLANT CHARACTERISTICS AND HABITAT
A. alnifolia	Stoloniferous shrub, 3 to 10 ft (1 to 3 m); erect dense raceme; sweet, juicy, purple fruit; habitat: plains, thickets, river banks; distribution: Ontario to British Columbia, South Dakota, Nebraska, New Mexico, and California
A. arborea	Fastigiate shrub or small tree, 16 to 65 ft (5 to 20 m); spreading, pendulous raceme; reddish-purple dry fruit; habitat: woods, slopes, open areas; distribution: New England to Minnesota and Iowa, Georgia, and Louisiana
A. bartramiana	Fastigiate shrub, 1.5 to 8 ft (0.5 to 2.5 m); corymbose raceme; fruit insipid, purplish black; habitat: bog borders, mountain slopes; distribution: Labrador to Ontario, Pennsylvania, and Michigan
A. basalticola	Shrub, 3 to 10 ft (1 to 3 m); terminal raceme habit; fruit dark purple, glabrous, juicy; habitat: basaltic cliffs and ledges; distribution: southeastern Washington
A. canadensis	Fastigiate shrub or tree, 16 to 33 ft (5 to 10 m); dense, nodding racemes; fruit insipid, dark purple, glabrous; habitat: swamps, dry hillsides in Minnesota to Nova Scotia to South Carolina, west to Iowa, Missouri
A. cusickii	Shrub with slender branches, 3 to 10 ft (1 to 3 m); juicy bluish-black fruit; habitat: basaltic ledges and river banks; distribution: Oregon and Washington to Idaho
A fernaldi	Stoloniferous, short shrub, 1 to 3 ft (0.3 to 1 m); spreading racemes; juicy glabrous purplish-black fruit; habitat: wet woods; distribution: Newfoundland and Quebec
A. florida	Tree with erect branches, 3 to 16 ft (1 to 5 m); erect racemes; juicy, purplish-black fruit; habitat: open woods, hillsides; distribution: Alaska to California, east to Idaho
A. gaspensis	Dense suckering shrub, 1 to 3 ft (0.3 to 0.9 m); erect racemes; glabrous, purplish-black juicy fruit; habitat: cliffs, ledges, lake shores; distribution: Quebec, New Brunswick to Ontario, northern Michigan to Minnesota
A. humilis	Stiff, stoloniferous shrub, 1 to 26 ft (0.3 to 8 m); erect terminal and lateral racemes, juicy black, glabrous, sweet fruit; habitat: rocky lake shores; distribution: Vermont to Ontario and Alberta, south to New York and Iowa
A. huronensis	Fastigiate shrub or tree, 10 to 23 ft (3 to 7 m); loose racemes; very sweet, juicy, dark purple fruit; habitat: calcareous cliffs, woods, lake shores; distribution: Ontario and Manitoba, Michigan, Wisconsin, and Minnesota
A. interior	Straggly, nonstoloniferous shrub or tree, to 33 ft (10 m); loose racemes; juicy, purplish-black fruit; habitat: hillsides and stream banks; distribution: Wisconsin, Minnesota, Iowa, and South Dakota
A. intermedia	Tall, fastigiate shrub, to 26 ft (8 m); erect compact racemes; juicy, dark purple fruit; habitat: bogs and marsh edges; distribution: New England to Ontario, Florida, and Louisiana
A. laevis	Fastigiate, irregular branching shrub or tree, to 43 ft (13 m); drooping racemes, sweet, dark purplish-black, glaucous fruit; habitat: dry thickets or swamp borders; distribution: Newfoundland to Michigan, Kansas, Georgia, and Alaska
A. mucronata	Slender stemmed shrub, 3 to 10 ft (1 to 3 m); erect racemes; juicy, purplish-black fruit; habitat: burned woods, open wet thickets; distribution: Minnesota and Manitoba
A. neglecta	Slender stemmed shrub, 3 to 10 ft (1 to 3 m); erect racemes; juicy, purplish-black fruit; habitat: burned woods, open wet thickets; distribution: New England

A. obovalis	Stoloniferous shrub with slender stems, 0.7 to 5 ft (0.2 to 1.5 m); dense racemes; glabrous, purplish-black, juicy fruit; habitat: sandy pine barrens, lowland; distribution: Maine to South Carolina, Georgia, and Alabama
A. pallida	Erect, branching shrub, 3 to 10 ft (1 to 3 m); racemes somewhat corymbose; purplish-black, juicy fruit; habitat: gravelly ridges or rocky woods; distribution: California
A. pumila	Shrub, 3 to 10 ft (1 to 3 m); short, somewhat erect racemes; glaucous, dark purplish fruit; habitat: mountain ridges and plains; distribution: Michigan to Oregon and Washington
A. sanguinea	Straggly shrub with few stems; racemes loose, pendulous; very sweet, juicy, dark purplish-black fruit; habitat: dry ridges and stream banks; distribution: New Brunswick to Minnesota, Alaska, North Carolina, and Michigan
A. spicata	Suckering shrub, 1 to 6.5 ft (0.3 to 2 m); racemes erect, dense; fruit juicy, purplish black; habitat: gravelly shores and calcareous cliffs; distribution: Ontario to Michigan, Iowa, Pennsylvania, and North Carolina
A. stolonifera	Stiff, upright, stoloniferous shrub, 1 to 5 ft (0.3 to 1.5 m); erect, dense racemes; fruit blackish, juicy, sweet; habitat: dry, acid rocky areas; distribution: Newfoundland to Minnesota and Virginia
A. utahensis	Clumped, highly branched shrub, 1.5 to 16 ft (0.5 to 5 m); racemes not characterized; fruit purplish black, drying on plant; habitat: rocky banks and slopes, desert; distribution: Utah and Arizona
A. wiegandii	Arching shrub, 10 to 16 ft (3 to 5 m); racemes loose, pendulous; juicy sweet, purplish-black fruit; habitat: rocky slopes and banks; distribution: Newfoundland to Ontario, New York, Michigan, Wisconsin, and Minnesota

Source: Miller and Stushnoff (1971); Krussman, (1984).

or winter-injured specimens. Judicious fertilization and watering can help to maintain *Amelanchier* in good vigor, reducing possibilities for borer injury.

Minor insect problems may include infestation and leaf injury by leaf miners, pear slug, sawfly, and pear leaf blister mite. Scale insects are only rarely a problem on *Amelanchier*. No insecticides are registered for use on *Amelanchier* in the United States.

Birds may feed heavily on *Amelanchier,* causing substantial yield losses. Control is difficult and may require a variety of methods, including noise cannons, bird distress calls, and in severe cases, netting on plants. Prompt harvesting of mature fruit may be of some help.

Culture

Serviceberries bloom relatively early in the season, in May in northern states (Fig. 9-4). Late spring frosts may injure bloom; thus planting sites with a moderate slope should be selected to provide for cold air drainage during frosts and freezes. Preplant soil preparation should include tillage and use of nonresidual herbicides prior to planting to eliminate perennial weed infestations. Where irrigation is available, grass sod between planting rows may be maintained by mowing. Soil pH is not critical, and plants will grow and produce adequately in a wide pH range (6.0 to 7.8).

Juneberries (Serviceberry, Saskatoon)

TABLE 9-5 CHARACTERISTICS AND ORIGIN OF *AMELANCHIER* CULTIVARS

CULTIVAR AND SPECIES	CHARACTERISTICS
Altaglow *A. alnifolia* Nutt.	Shrub to 16 ft (5 m), pyramidal; white-fruited; introduced by the Horticultural Research Centre, Brooks, Alberta, Canada, ca. 1935
Ballerina *A.* × *grandiflora* Rehd.	Shrub to small tree; large flowered; named and described by H. J. van de Laar, Holland, 1980
Forestburg *A. alnifolia* Nutt.	Shrub to 10 ft (3 m); few root suckers; large berries with fair quality; selected by A. Nixon, Alberta, Canada, ca. 1975
Hollandia *A. spicata hollandia*	Shrub to 6.5 ft (2 m); profuse suckering; from Hillier and Sons, Winchester, England, ca. 1971.
Honeywood *A. alnifolia* Nutt.	Plant size unknown; produces large fruit clusters; introduced by A. J. Porter, Saskatchewan, Canada, in 1973
Indian Species unknown	Reported to be dual purpose for fruit and foliage; selected by D. Maclison, River Rouge, Michigan, ca. 1960
Moonlake *A. alnifolia* Nutt.	Large-fruited, erratic bearing, introduced by G. Krahn, Saskatoon, Saskatchewan, Canada, in 1974
Northline *A. alnifolia* Nutt.	Small shrub to 5 ft (1.5 m); suckers freely; large fruited; selected and described at Beaverlodge Research Station, Alberta, Canada, in 1960
Paleface *A. alnifolia* Nutt.	Shrub to 6.5 ft (2 m); few suckers; productive; large, white fruit, mild flavored; introduced by W. Oaks, Manitoba, Canada, date unknown
Parkhill Species uncertain	Originated in Michigan; listed by Parkhill Nursery, Bismarck, North Dakota, in 1974
Pembina *A. alnifolia* Nutt.	Shrub to 8 ft (2.5 m); few suckers; productive; highly flavored fruit; selected by J. A. Wallace in 1932, introduced by Beaverlodge Research Station, Alberta, Canada, in 1956
Regent Probably *A. alnifolia* Nutt.	Small shrub 5 to 6.5 ft (1.5 to 2 m); dual purpose for fruit and foliage; selected by J. Caudrian, Regent, North Dakota, date unknown
Rubescens *A.* × *grandiflora* Rehd.	Small tree with purplish buds; flower white tinged with pink
Robin Hill *A.* × *grandiflora* Rehd.	Large flowers in slender racemes; pink fading rapidly to white
Shannon Species unknown	Reported to be dual purpose for fruit and foliage; collected in Michigan by D. Maclison, River Rouge, Michigan, ca. 1960
Shanty Rapids Possibly *A. bartramiana*	Shrub with unusually broad flowers, petals; collected in Michigan by D. Maclison, River Rouge, Michigan, ca. 1962
Smoky *A. alnifolia* Nutt.	Shrub, to 6.5 to 10 ft (2 to 3 m); suckers freely; very productive with large, sweet berries; selected by W. D. Albright, Beaverlodge, Alberta, Canada; introduced in 1952
Sturgeon *A. alnifolia* Nutt.	Shrub to 10 ft (3 m); large fruit in large clusters; selected by J. A. Wallace, Beaverlodge Nursery, Beaverlodge, Alberta, Canada, in 1971
Success Possibly *A. sanguinea* Pursh.	Shrub to 6.5 ft (2 m); suckers freely; originated early nineteenth century, possibly in Michigan; introduced by H. D. Van Deman, Kansas, ca. 1878
Thiessen *A. alnifolia* Nutt.	Selected for fruit quality; introduced by G. Krahn, Saskatoon, Saskatchewan, Canada, in 1976

Source: Hilton (1982).

FIGURE 9-4 Flowering habit of low shrub form of *Amelanchier anifolia* (Juneberry).

Amelanchier are propagated readily from seed, root sprouts, root cuttings, or softwood cuttings. Seed propagation for fruit production is not suggested since plants will not come true from seed, and progeny may vary widely from the parent in plant size and productivity.

One of the principal limiting factors to the advancement of this crop is the inability to propagate the large-fruited, more productive cultivars in quantities to meet the demand for plants at an economical cost.

Depending on the tendency of the cultivar to produce root suckers, sprouts with roots may be removed during the dormant season, shortened to a uniform length of 2 to 4 in. (5 to 10 cm), and transplanted to nursery rows. After growth in the nursery row for a season, plants may be transplanted in the following spring to their permanent location.

Similarly, root cuttings may be taken in early spring. Cuttings ³⁄₈ to ⁵⁄₈ in. (1 to 1.5 cm) in diameter and 4 to 6 in. (10 to 15 cm) long are preferred (Harris, 1972). Plant in the nursery row with the stem end up and near ¼ in. (0.5 cm) of the surface. Frequent, light watering and shading will encourage vigorous shoot growth.

Softwood cuttings root readily when taken from actively growing shoots in late spring or early summer. Cuttings 3 to 6 in. (7.5 to 15 cm) long are preferred. More extensive rooting is promoted by dipping shoot bases in 0.3 to 0.8% indolebutyric acid in talc and the application of bottom heat of 68 to 70°F (20 to 21°C) in an intermittent mist propagation bed. Cuttings can be left in the propagation bed through winter and transplanted to nursery rows in early spring.

For commercial plantings, space *Amelanchier* at least 8 ft (2.4 m) apart in each direction if cross-cultivation is desired. For hedgerow plantings, set plants 5 to 6 ft (1.5 to 1.8 m) apart in the row with 13 to 16.5 ft (4 to 5 m) between rows, depending on the type of equipment to be used in tillage and harvesting.

Dormant, well-branched young plants 6 to 12 in. (15 to 30 cm) tall are preferred for transplanting to the field. At transplanting, prune off one-third of the plant top growth, and water plants at or immediately following planting to encourage rapid establishment and growth.

No herbicides are approved for use on *Amelanchier* in the United States. Periodic, shallow cultivation and some hand hoeing will be necessary to control weeds. Straw, sawdust, or waste hay mulch around plants can be beneficial in soil moisture retention and weed suppression. Most *Amelanchier* species are shallow rooted hence irrigation can be particularly beneficial in early years of establishment to maintain consistent vigorous growth.

Fertilizer requirements for *Amelanchier* have not been established. Moderate to highly fertile loam soils generally will not require supplemental fertilization. On less fertile or sandy soils, the annual banding of nitrogen fertilizer at a rate of 1.0 oz (28 g) of nitrogen per plant per year of plant age up to a maximum of 0.5 lb (227 g) may be beneficial if growth is inadequate. Where fire blight (*Erwinia amylovora*) is common on other Rosaceae, avoid inducing excessively vigorous growth through the application of large amounts of nitrogen-containing fertilizers.

Amelanchier fruit is borne on previous years' growth and older wood. Pruning young plants consists of removing weak, diseased, and broken shoots, retaining five to seven primary, vigorous shoots. On mature plantings, prune to remove low branches and cut tops to 5 to 6.5 ft (1.5 to 2.0 m) for ease of harvesting. Occasional renewal pruning to remove older, less productive wood and encourage regrowth of new shoots will be necessary to maintain productivity.

Juneberries begin to bear fruit 2 to 4 years after planting. Maximum productivity is attained after 7 to 11 years. Yields of up to 6 tons/acre (13 MT/ha) are reported for small plantings (Harris, 1972). Fruit ripens evenly in midsummer (late June to early July), and the crop can be harvested all at once. As with other Rosaceae species, fruit harvested at the early stage of maturity is high in pectin, thus best for jelly, freezing, and processing. Fully mature fruit is higher in sugar content and preferred for wine making. Mature fruit can be harvested rapidly without damage, using a small power vibrator and catching frame, as for highbush blueberries.

REFERENCES AND SUGGESTED READING

BAILEY, L. H. 1949. Manual of cultivated plants. Macmillan, New York.

DARROW, G. M. 1975. Minor temperate fruits. p. 269–284. In J. Janick and J. N. Moore (eds.), Advances in fruit breeding. Purdue University Press, West Lafayette, Ind.

DARROW, G. M., AND G. E. YERKES. 1937. Some unusual opportunities in plant breeding. U.S. Dep. Agric. Agric. Yearb. p. 545–558.

DIRR, M. A. 1983. Manual of woody landscape plants. 3rd ed. Stripes, Champaign, Ill.

EGOLF, D. R. 1962a. Ornamental deciduous flowering viburnums. Am. Hortic. Mag. 41(3):139.

EGOLF, D. R. 1962b. Ornamental fruiting and autumnal foliage viburnums. Am. Hortic. Mag. 41(4):209.

FLINT, H. 1983. Landscape plants for eastern North America. Wiley, New York.

HARRIS, R. E. 1972. The saskatoon. Can. Dep. Agric. Bull. 1246.

HARTMAN, H. T., AND D. E. KESTER. 1983. Plant propagation principles and practices. Prentice-Hall, Englewood Cliffs, N.J.

HASSELKUS, E. R. 1982. University of Wisconsin–Madison. Personal communication.

HILTON, R. J. 1982. Registration of *Amelanchier* cultivar names. Fruit Var. J. 36(4):108–110.

JONES, G. N. 1946. American species of *Amelanchier*. University of Illinois Press, Urbana, Ill.

KRUSSMAN, G. 1984. Manual of cultivated broad-leaved trees and shrubs. Vol. 1, A–D. Timber Press, Portland, Oreg.

MILLER, W. S., AND C. STUSHNOFF. 1971. A description of *Amelanchier* species in regard to cultivar development. Fruit Var. Hortic. Dig. 25(1):3–10.

OURECKY, D.K. 1972. Minor fruits in New York State. Cornell University Bull. 11, Plant Sciences, Pomology 2.

PIRONE, P. P. 1970. Diseases and pests of ornamental plants. New York Botanical Garden, Ronald Press, New York.

RITTER, C. M., AND G. W. MCKEE. 1964. The elderberry: history, classification, and culture. Pa. Agric. Exp. Stn. Bull. 709.

SNYDER, L. C. 1976. Viburnums. Univ. Minn. Agric. Ext. Serv. Arboretum Rev. 30.

WAY, R. D. 1981. Elderberry culture in New York State. N.Y. State Agric. Exp. Stn. Geneva, N.Y. Food Life Sci. Bull. 91.

WILSON, K. A. 1977. Lowdown on highbush 'cranberry' . . . and other native viburnums. Flower Garden Mag.:34, 43.

WOOD, K. W. ca. 1976. Viburnum collection. Section *Opulus:* Cranberrybush Viburnums. University of Wisonsin–Madison arboretum field book. Madison, Wisc.

SUPPLEMENTARY READING

BROOKS, R. M., AND H. P. OLMO. 1972. Register of new fruit and nut varieties. University of California Press, Berkeley.

DARROW, G. M. 1923. Viburnum americanum as a garden fruit. Proc. Am. Soc. Hortic. Sci. 21:44–54.

KVAALEN, R. 1979. What are the best viburnums for Indiana? In Plants and the Landscape 2(3):3–12.

NIELSEN, E. L. 1939. A taxonomic study of the genus *Amelanchier* in Minnesota. Am. Midl. Nat. 22:160–208.

Slate, G. L. 1955. Minor fruits. Nat. Hort. Mag. 34:139–149.

Stimart, D. P. 1985. Viburnum. In A. H. Halevy (ed.). CRC handbook of flowering. CRC Press, Boca Raton, Fla.

Swink, F. 1967. Confusing viburnums. Morton Arboretum Q. 3:33–39.

Wiegand, K. M. 1912. The genus *Amelanchier* in eastern North America. Rhodora 14:116–164.

Chapter 10

Grape Management

M. AHMEDULLAH
D. G. HIMELRICK

INTRODUCTION

Grapes have been an integral part of human society for thousands of years and are the single most important fruit crop grown in the world today in terms of both total acreage and dollar value (Harlan, 1976). They are produced in every country of the world where environmental conditions permit successful growth and maturation. The value of grapes for wine, juice, raisins, table fruit, jam and jellies, and other products far surpasses that of any other fruit crop. Their processed value in the United States alone exceeds $1 billion dollars each year.

The United States is the fifth-largest grape-producing country in the world, following Italy, France, the USSR, and Spain. The primary use of grapes worldwide is for wine production. The United States typically ranks sixth in wine production behind Italy, France, Spain, the USSR, and Argentina (Table 10-1).

The most important grape-producing state in the United States is California, which accounts for approximately 93% of the total production each year. Other significant grape-producing states are New York, Washington, Pennsylvania, and Michigan (see Table 10-2).

TABLE 10-1 WORLD GRAPE AND WINE PRODUCTION, AND GRAPE ACREAGE, 1986

COUNTRY	GRAPES (thousands of tons)	WINE (thousands of gallons)	ACREAGE (thousands of acres)
Italy	12812	2,028,850	2711
France	10287	1,934,352	2592
USSR	8972	898,872	3304
Spain	6381	907,458	3936
USA	5226	500,542	823
Turkey	4124	9,246	1962
Argentina	2825	528,360	702
Greece	1820	66,045	415
Yugoslavia	1674	148,496	566
Romania	1569	229,837	744
Portugal	1333	213,008	964
South Africa	1192	219,639	272
West Germany	1109	265,818	250
Australia	1100	106,359	158
Iran	990	none	460
Chile	961	87,179	269
Bulgaria	860	92,463	348
Hungary	761	81,896	363
Mexico	717	6,605	146

Source: Wine Institute Economic Research Report, 1988. Data based on reports from Office International de la Vigne et du Vin, Paris.

TABLE 10-2 GRAPE PRODUCTION IN MAJOR STATES, 1987

STATE	TONS
California	
Wine	1,900,000
Table	530,000
Raisin	2,100,000
Total	4,530,000
Washington	230,100
New York	174,000
Pennsylvania	60,000
Michigan	58,000
Arizona	21,500
Ohio	9,500
Arkansas	5,000
Missouri	2,600
North Carolina	2,500
Georgia	2,100
South Carolina	700
United States total	5,096,000

Source: USDA Fruit Situation. Other important grape producing states include Oregon, Texas, Virginia, Florida, and New Mexico.

Genus *Vitis* The genus *Vitis* belongs to the botanical family Vitaceae (vine family), which is composed of 11 genera and 600 species (Einset and Pratt, 1975). *Vitis* is the only food-bearing genus in the family. The grapevine plant habit is a woody liana (climbing vine) which bears nonshowy flowers and true berry fruits. Related American plants include the kangaroo vine (*Cissus*), Virginia creeper (*Parthenocissus*), and pepper vine (*Ampelopsis*).

Vitis plants are perennial, woody deciduous vines that have tendrils opposite many leaves which aid the plant in attachment to supports in cultivation and to surrounding vegetation in nature. Grape flower parts are in fives or multiples thereof, and the leaves are simple and palmately lobed. Grape plants are confined primarily to the temperate zones of the world, although they are also grown in subtropical and tropical climates. The genus is divided into two subgenera, *Euvitis* and *Muscadinia*, based on various morphological criteria and somatic chromosome number, with the former having 38 and the latter having 40 (Dearing, 1947; Winkler et al., 1974; Einset and Pratt, 1975; Weaver, 1976). The American bunch grape cultivars, such as 'Concord' or 'Niagara', are often thought to be derived mostly from the native *V. labrusca* species commonly known as the "fox grape". However, Snyder (1937), Munson (1909), Einset and Pratt (1975), and McGrew (1981) point out that most American cultivars are hybrids among a number of native species. Many of these also contain some of the European type *V. vinifera* germplasm. The term *bunch grape* refers to the fact that these cultivars have berries that are borne in a cluster and have a concentrated harvest period during which the entire cluster, or bunch, is harvested as a uniformly ripe intact unit. In contrast, muscadine cultivars are harvested as individual berries that ripen over an extended harvest period.

Although there has been sporadic success in crossing the *V. rotundifolia* (muscadine) and the *V. labrusca* (bunch grape) cultivars in the United States since Munson's nineteenth-century experiments (Munson, 1909), most muscadine grape cultivars are hybrids derived from the principal muscadine species *V. rotundifolia*. Much of the difficulty with such interspecific crosses is due to the difference in somatic chromosome numbers, with *V. labrusca* having 38, while *V. rotundifolia* has 40.

Native American Species

There are about 30 species of grapes native to extensive areas of the United States, and a number of these have played important roles in the grape industry of the United States, as well as in that of Europe (Einset and Pratt, 1975; Rogers and Rogers, 1978). Representatives of some of these have been grown extensively as standard cultivars, while cross-breeding between native species, hybridizing with different representatives of *Vitis vinifera* L., and interbreeding with grapes thus derived have given rise to many of the grape cultivars grown in America. The wild species have also been important in grape culture, either as pure species or as hybrids developed for rootstock purposes. They have often been found invaluable where own-rooted vines have failed because of their inherent resistance to certain insect pests and their adaptation to specific regions.

Among those natives species that have proved most valuable, at least seven species of bunch grapes should be noted.

Vitis labrusca L. (fox grape). This species also has the accepted classification name *Vitis labruscana* Bailey. Derived cultivar examples: 'Concord', 'Niagara', 'Isabella'.

Vitis riparia Michaux (riverbank grape). Derived cultivar examples: 'Beta', 'Clinton', 'Baco noir', 'Marechal Foch', 'C 3309', '5BB', 'SO 4'.

Vitis aestivalis Michaux (summer, pigeon, or winter grape). Derived cultivar examples: 'Norton', 'Cynthiana'.

Vitis rupestris Scheele (rock, July, or mountain grape). Derived cultivar examples: 'St. George', '99 R', '140 Ru', 'AXR 1'.

Vitis lincecumii Buck1. (post oak grape, sometimes included under *V. aestivalis*). Derived cultivar examples: 'Bailey', 'Beacon', 'Ellen Scott', 'Marguerite'.

Vitis champini Planch. Derived cultivar examples: 'Champanel', 'Lomanto', 'Nitodal'.

Vitis candicans Engelm. Derived cultivar examples: '1616 C', 'Salt Creek', 'Dogridge', 'Harmony', 'Freedom'.

Several other species of American grapes have been used, particularly in the development of valuable rootstocks. These include *Vitis berlandieri* Planch., *V. cordifolia* Lam., *V. doaniana* Munson, *V. longii* Prince, *V. cinerea* Engelm., and *V. monticola* Buckl.

Two other species of American grapes call for special mention: *Vitis rotundifolia* Michx. and *V. munsoniana* Simpson. These belong to an entirely distinct botanical group, differing widely from the bunch-grape types in the character of vine and fruit. They do not hybridize readily with the bunch-grape species and do not form satisfactory graft unions with them. Although not immune to some of the diseases to which the bunch grapes are subject (e.g., Pierce's disease, downy mildew, etc.), they do show considerable resistance to them; this makes them particularly valuable in sections of the South, where these diseases are prevalent.

Vitis rotundifolia Michx. (muscadine, bullace, or southern fox grape). Derived cultivar examples: 'Scuppernong', 'Magnolia', 'Carlos', 'Noble'.

Vitis munsoniana Simpson (bird or everbearing grape). There are no named cultivars of *V. munsoniana*.

The Vinifera

The various forms of the *vinifera,* European, or Old World, grape, which have been grouped under the species *Vitis vinifera* L., are of somewhat uncertain lineage. This species is believed to have originated in the region south of the Caspian Sea in Asia

Minor, from where it has been widely disseminated (Winkler et al., 1974). Cultivars derived from it are grown commercially between 20 and 51°N. latitude and between 20 and 40°S. latitude. *V. vinifera* grapes not only furnish the major world production, but have also played a vital part in the improvement of native American types. There are an estimated 5000 named cultivars, such as 'Cabernet Sauvignon', 'Pinot noir', 'Thompson Seedless', and the '41 B' rootstock. The cultural range of *V. vinifera* grapes is limited mainly by climatic factors. In general, they require a long growing season, relatively high summer temperatures, low atmospheric humidity, a ripening season free from rain, and mild winter temperatures. The numerous cultivars furnish fruit types ranging from the small-berried currant grapes (e.g., 'Black Corinth'), and the medium-sized fruit of the wine cultivars (e.g., 'Zinfandel'), to the large-berried table cultivars (e.g., 'Tokay'). Detailed varietal descriptions can be found in the ampelographic references cited elsewhere in this chapter.

V. vinifera grape cultivars can be divided into basically six usage categories: wine, juice, table, raisin, canning, or rootstock. Some cultivars, such as 'Thompson Seedless', have several uses, including table, wine, and raisin.

French-American Hybrids

Hybridization of native American species assumed importance in France when the devastations by the grape phylloxera insect made necessary the grafting of *V. vinifera* on resistant roots in the last quarter of the nineteenth century (Snyder, 1937). The phylloxera is an insect (*Daktylosphaira vitifoliae* Fitch), indigenous to eastern and central United States, that feeds on roots of vines and also forms galls on the leaves of some *Vitis* species. This insect was carried to France from the United States before 1860, probably on rooted vines imported because they were resistant to powdery mildew (*Uncinula necator* Burr.). To combine the most desirable characteristics of different species, interspecific crosses were made between various native American species and between *V. vinifera* and the American species (Cattell and Stauffer, 1978). Some work was done by official institutions but much by private breeders and nurserymen such as M. Contassot, G. Couderc, and A. Seibel (Einset and Pratt, 1975).

An extension of the early work resulted in the production through breeding of the so-called 'direct producers' or 'French hybrids', which would combine the resistance of the American species with the fruit qualities of *V. vinifera*. As a result of these crosses, many of the French hybrids combine the excellent wine quality of the European *V. vinifera* with the hardiness and insect/disease resistance of the wild American species, making them a versatile choice in many geographical areas (Barrett, 1956).

In regions where early spring frosts are common, French hybrids exhibit an important advantage over American cultivars. They have the ability to produce a commercial crop from secondary and even tertiary buds if the primary bud, or its developing shoot, is destroyed by adverse weather. However, the high degree of fruitfulness of primary shoots, along with the growth of fruitful adventitious shoots, typically poses a problem of overbearing. McGrew (1981) traces the development of modern grape hybrids through three stages (F1, F2–8, and backcross generations) and notes the variable contributions made by different American species at the different stages.

Muscadine Grapes

There are three species of muscadine-type grapes found in the southern United States: *V. rotundifolia* Michx., *V. munsoniana,* and *V. popenoei.* All of the commercially grown cultivars are of the *V. rotundifolia* species. These grapes have commonly been called many names, including Bullace, Bullis, and Muscadine. Modern cultivated grapes of this species are commonly called muscadines, with the bronze-colored types occasionally referred to as "scuppernongs". The 'Scuppernong' is the oldest and the first bronze cultivar to be planted commercially. Although there are several newer bronze cultivars which are larger and more productive, 'Scuppernong' is still popular because of its excellent flavor.

Areas of adaptation. Muscadines are generally limited in their production to the cotton belt areas of the southern United States which have a moderate climate. Vines should not be planted where temperatures drop below 10°F (−12°C). Some damage or death of vines may occur as temperatures drop below 0°F (−18°C), depending on the rapidity of temperature drop, preconditioning, age, cultivar, and condition of the vine.

Fruit Characteristics. In addition to wine production, muscadine grapes are also used in unfermented juice, pies, jellies, and sauces. The distinctive fruity flavor and aroma of most muscadine cultivars is retained in fermented and unfermented products. Muscadine clusters are small, usually containing 6 to 24 berries. Mature berries of most cultivars do not adhere to the stems as do those of bunch grapes, and berry fall (shattering) of early ripening berries results in loss of some of the crop. Berries ripen unevenly because of the long flowering period (early May until mid-June), and the main crop (primary fruit set) is set over a 3- to 4-week period. Consequently, each cluster may contain flower buds, flowers, and small berries at the same time. Also, each shoot has from one to three or more clusters. The order of blooming of clusters is the one nearest the base of the shoot first, the one next to it second, and the one farthest from the base of the shoot last. Another important harvesting characteristic is berry tear (wet stem scars). Berries often tear at the point of attachment to the cluster, with berry maturity affecting the amount of tear. Berries that are fully mature when harvested usually fall with a dry stem scar, and many of those harvested before they are fully ripe have wet stem scars. The percentage of berries with dry stem scars is higher for some cultivars (e.g., 'Carlos' and 'Southland') than for others. If a vineyard is being established for fresh market sales other than pick-your-own (PYO) or roadside stands, planting cultivars with the highest percentage of dry stem scars should be considered (Hegwood et al., 1983).

Muscadine grapes are normally harvested when the pH reaches 3.2 and total acidity values range from 0.3 to 0.5. Soluble solids (sugars) typically range from 15 to 19° Brix. Varietal white wines are made from 'Magnolia', 'Carlos', and 'Scuppernong', while 'Noble' gives a deep red wine. If properly fermented, excellent sweet, semidry, and dry wines can be produced. In addition to these, many white wine cultivars are combined in the production of wines that are labeled as muscadine or scuppernong. The largest portion of the white muscadine production is used in wines that combine other grape species, and the label does not indicate cultivar or species. Champagne and brandy are also produced from muscadine grapes. Those cultivars showing the most promise for wine production include 'Carlos', 'Magnolia', 'Summit', 'Sterling', 'Doreen', 'Roanoke', 'Regale', and 'Nevermiss'. Fruit marketed fresh is primarily sold locally, with limited numbers of commercial shipments to cities in the southeastern states. Muscadine grapes have a shorter storage and shipping life than those of *V. vinifera* grapes. Rapid cooling following harvest and a cultivar with a dry stem scar such as 'Carlos' is required for shipment if quality is to remain acceptable for more than a few days. Grapes for fresh market should be refrigerated at 35 to 40 °F (1.7 to 4.4°C) immediately after harvesting. Proper refrigeration can maintain berry quality up to 14 days. The best cultivars for storage or shipping to distant markets are 'Carlos' and 'Southland'. Large-fruited cultivars such as 'Jumbo', 'Fry', and 'Higgins' and 'Big Red' are good choices for fresh market and PYO vineyards. 'Watergate' and 'Sugargate' have potential for fresh market sales because their berries are very large, skins are thinner, and flavors are different from 'Jumbo'. Disadvantages are that they both have pistillate flowers, and 'Sugargate' has low yields. Yields range from 3.5 to 8 tons/acre (8 to 18 MT/ha) for cultivars trained on a modified Geneva double curtain (GDC) type of trellis. Yields of double-cordon trained vines on a GDC trellis are about 50% greater than on a single-cordon trellis.

Juice production is about a third less per ton than for bunch grapes, with muscadines yielding about 130 gal/ton, while other grapes average 180 gal/ton (Hegwood et al., 1983; Brooks, 1978).

Space limitations do not allow for a complete treatment of specific cultural practices used in muscadine grape production. Readers should refer to the citations listed in the suggested reading section for further information.

Rootstocks

The use of rootstocks is a standard practice for grape propagation in most areas of the world where *V. vinifera* grapes are grown. The resistance of grape rootstocks to pests or environmental stresses is relative. Injury is simply less with resistant or tolerant rootstocks than would typically be experienced by *V. vinifera* roots. With several factors influencing the performance of rootstocks, they need to be examined in many different situations before a final judgment is made on their ability to perform. It should be recognized that there is no universal rootstock that is good for all conditions (Morton, 1979). There are several reasons for using rootstocks for *V. vinifera* cultivars. Primary among them are the extreme susceptibility of the roots to the attack of phylloxera and nematodes.

Grape phylloxera has been a destructive pest in many *V. vinifera* growing regions of the world for more than 100 years. The use of resistant rootstocks appears to be the best means of combating this problem. Sandy soils are not as conducive to the spread of this pest as are heavier clay and loam soils (Bioletti et al., 1921;

Husman et al., 1939; Jacob, 1942a; Snyder and Harmon, 1948; and Lider, 1957).

Tolerant and resistant rootstocks have also been used to overcome nematode problems. The nematodes most seriously affecting grapes are the root knot (*Meloidogyne incognita* var. *acrita*), root lesion (*Pratylenchus vulnus*), and dagger (*Xiphinema index*) nematodes. The dagger nematode is a vector of fan leaf and other grape viruses.

Snyder (1937) showed that all *V. vinifera* species are susceptible to injury by nematodes. The species *V. solonis, V. champini,* and *V. doaniana* show moderate to high resistance to this pest. Harmon and Snyder (1956) and Lider (1960) have described nematode-resistant rootstocks for California. The grape rootstock situation has been described in Israel (Spiegel-Roy et al., 1971) and for Washington and Oregon (Ahmedullah, 1980). Other important characteristics for rootstocks may include drought, salt, limestone, and soil flooding (wet feet) tolerance, iron chlorosis resistance, resistance to diseases such as oak root fungus and cotton root rot and to viruses such as fanleaf, stem pitting, corky bark, and tomato ringspot. Rootstocks are also used to impart or decrease vigor in scion cultivars, along with hastening or delaying fruit and vine maturity. Vigor control is a very important vineyard management concept and may affect such wide-ranging elements as yield, fruit quality, winter hardiness and vine survival. Other factors, such as cold tolerance, soil type performance, ease of rooting of the cuttings, and budding and grafting compatibility, are also important. Table 10-3 lists some of the most popular rootstocks currently in use around the world.

There are many other rootstocks not listed here which have limited use. Rootstocks may be chosen for their specific adaptation or tolerance to particular biotic or abiotic stresses. For example, the following rootstocks might be good choices for the indicated situations. Good lime tolerance on high pH soils where iron chlorosis is a problem: '99 R', '41 B', '161–49 C', '140 Ru', or 'Dogridge'. Those that perform best on acid soils where the opposite conditions prevail might include '140 Ru', '110 R', '99 R', and '196–17 Cl'. Rootstocks with good drought tolerance include '110 R', '140 Ru', and '44–53 M', while '101–14 Mgt', '3306 C', 'Ramsey', '143–B Mgt', and 'Dogridge', among others, comprise those that are most tolerant of high soil moisture. Those showing the greatest salt tolerance are '1616 C', '216–3 Cl', 'Salt Creek', and '1103 P'.

Rootstocks are used in specific geographical areas for localized problems. For example, the presence of cotton root rot fungus in Texas requires the use of resistant rootstocks such as 'Champanel', 'Dog Ridge', or 'La Pryor'. Sites with a *Phytophthora* problem may benefit from the use of resistant rootstocks such as '143–B Mgt or 'Jacquez. In other geographical areas in the South, such as Florida, a rootstock like 'Tampa' or 'Dogridge' may be best suited to local conditions.

The University of California has recently released two patented rootstocks, '039–16' and '043–43', which are resistant to the fanleaf virus. They are immune to feeding by the nematode vector for grape fanleaf virus (*Xiphenema index*) and have good nematode and phylloxera resistance. Other investigations have shown the rootstock cultivars 'SO 4', '039–16', and '044–4' to have the highest levels of resistance to biotype A and B grape phylloxera in California (Granett et al., 1987). In the

TABLE 10-3 CHARACTERISTICS OF IMPORTANT GRAPE ROOTSTOCKS

ROOTSTOCK	VIGOR[a]	ADAPTABILITY TO:[b]				RESISTANCE TO:[c]			TOLERANCE FOR:	
		Wet Soil	Dry Shallow Clay	Deep Silt or Dense Loam	Deep Dry, Sandy Soil	Phylloxera	Nematode	Drought	Lime (%)	Salt (g/liter)
Riparia Gloire	2	3	1	2	2	5	2	1	6	0.7
Rupestris St. George	4	1	2	3	1	4	2	2	15	—
196-17	3	2	1	2	3	3	1	3	6	—
125 AA	4	—	3	1	1	4	3	2	—	—
420 A	2	2	3	2	2	4	2	2	20	—
5 BB	2	3	2	2	1	4	2	1	20	—
SO 4	2	3	1	2	1	4	3	3	17	—
5 C	3	—	3	3	1	4	4	1	17	—
161-49 C	3	3	1	2	2	4	4	2	25	—
110 R	3	1	4	3	3	4	—	4	17	—
99 R	4	2	2	4	2	4	2	3	20	—
140 Ru	4	3	3	3	4	4	3	4	17	0.6
1103 P	3	3	3	3	3	4	3	3	11	0.4
3309 C	2	3	2	2	2	4	2	2	11	0.4
3306 C	3	3	1	2	2	4	1	1	9	—
101-14	2	3	2	2	1	4	1	1	10	—
44-53 M	3	3	2	3	2	4	2	4	11	—
1616 C	3	2	1	2	2	4	4	1	13	—
1202 C	3	—	3	3	2	3	1	2	13	0.8
A×R #1	3	1	3	3	2	2	1	2	13	0.8
41 B	2	1	1	1	1	2	1	2	13	0.8
333 EM	1	2	1	1	1	4	1	3	40	Very sensitive
1613 C	3	2	2	2	3	2	1	2	40	Very sensitive
Dogridge	4	2	2	2	4	2	4	2	Low	—
Salt Creek	4	2	1	3	4	2	4	2	High	—
Harmony	3	2	1	2	3	2	4	2	—	—
Freedom	3	—	1	1	3	2	4	2	—	—

Source: Adapted from Howell (1987); Pongracz (1983); Galet (1979); Winkler et al. (1974); Kasimatis and Lider (1980); Strauss and Archer (1986); Carbonneau (1985).

[a] 4, High; 1, low.   [b] 4, Good; 1, poor.   [c] 5, Very resistant; 1, very susceptible.

eastern United States the best adapted and most popular rootstocks are 'SO 4', '5 BB', '3309 C', and '1616 C'.

Cultivars

There are more than 5000 cultivars of grapes that have been named and described. The majority of the cultivars described belong to *V. vinifera*. Of these, about 80 to 90 are considered important in the *V. vinifera* grape growing countries of the world (Winkler et al., 1974).

It is a difficult task to assess the relative importance of particular grape cultivars to overall grape industry in the United States. Table 10-4 lists the most important grape cultivars in several U.S. states and a Canadian province. Certain cultivars are of notable importance to particular categories of the industry such as 'Concord' and 'Niagara' to the juice market, or 'Thompson Seedless', 'Black Corinth', and 'Muscat of Alexandria' to the raisin market. The 'Thompson Seedless' and 'Flame Seedless' cultivars currently dominate the table grape industry. The relative importance of various cultivars to the wine grape market, if viewed from a tonnage crushed basis, shows 'French Colombard', 'Thompson Seedless', and 'Chenin blanc' to lead the field.

An informative survey of the varietal wine market in the United States in 1988 by *Wines and Vines* magazine showed 'Chardonnay' to be the *V. vinifera* varietal which is produced by the largest number of wineries. It was followed by 'Cabernet Sauvignon', 'White Riesling', 'Pinot noir', 'Sauvignon blanc', 'Zinfandel', 'Merlot', 'Gewurztraminer', and 'Chenin blanc'. Among American varietals 'Catawba' ranked first, just ahead of 'Niagara' and 'Concord'. 'Seyval' was the leading French-American cultivar wine, followed by 'Vidal blanc' and 'Marechal Foch'.

Proper cultivar selection for any given location must be collectively based on many cultural, environmental, marketing, and economic factors which are covered in detail in other sections.

Detailed descriptions of cultivars are given by Viala and Vermorel (1909) and Galet (1979) in French; Constantinescu et al. (1960) in Romanian, and Frolov-Bagreev (1946-1958) in Russian. In addition, the work of Hedrick (1907) and the translation of Galet's book by Morton (1979) are important references for cultivar descriptions. Orffer (1979) has described the important cultivars grown in South Africa. Grape cultivars must be compatible with the conditions within a general climatic region as well as being specifically adapted for a given site. In addition to the major grape producing areas, specialized growing locations may require cultivars adapted to climate extremes. For example, the following are the few choices for extremely cold northern climates such as might be found in Minnesota: 'Valiant', 'Beta', 'Worden', 'Bluebell', 'St. Croix', 'Kay Gray', 'Swenson Red', and 'Edelweiss'.

On the other extreme, in addition to the muscadine cultivars, the following bunch grapes can be grown in the hot and humid conditions found in the deep South. For dessert fruit: 'Orlando Seedless', 'Conquistador', 'Lake Emerald', 'Suwanee', 'Blue Lake', and 'Stover'. For white wine: 'Blanc Du Bois'.

A very brief description of some of the important cultivars is given in Tables 10-5 to 10-9.

TABLE 10-4 IMPORTANT GRAPE CULTIVARS GROWN IN SELECTED U.S. STATES AND A CANADIAN PROVINCE[a]

CALIFORNIA	NEW YORK	WASHINGTON	MICHIGAN	OREGON	MISSOURI	ONTARIO
Thompson Seedless	Concord	Concord	Concord	Pinot noir	Concord	Concord
French Colombard	Catawba	White Riesling	Niagara	Chardonnay	Catawba	Elvira
Chenin blanc	Niagara	Chardonnay	Vidal blanc	White Riesling	Seyval	De Chaunac
Chardonnay	Aurore	Chenin blanc	Delaware	Gewurztraminer	Vidal blanc	Niagara
Zinfandel	Delaware	Cabernet Sauvignon	Seyval	Cabernet Sauvignon	Vignoles	Seyval
Cabernet Sauvignon	Chardonnay	Sauvignon blanc	Vignoles	Muller-Thurgau	Cynthiana	Vidal blanc
Flame Seedless	Seyval	Chardonnay	White Riesling	Sauvignon blanc	Niagara	Fredonia
Flame Tokay	De Chaunac	Merlot	De Chaunac	Pinot gris	Chancellor	Catawba
Emperor	Elvira	Semillon	Baco noir	Merlot	Chambourcin	Marechal Foch
Sauvignon blanc	Baco noir	Niagara	Marechal Foch	Semillon	De Chaunac	S.V. 23–512
Grenache	White Riesling	Gewurztraminer	Chardonnay	Chenin blanc	Baco noir	Agawam
Carignane	Cayuga White	Grenache	Aurore	Gamay	Marechal Foch	Ventura
Barbera	Dutchess	Pinot noir	Chelois	Sylvaner	Cayuga White	New York Muscat
Perlette	Fredonia	Muscat Canelli	Cayuga White	Zinfandel	Chelois	Dutchess
Pinot noir	Marechal Foch	Limberger		Muscat Ottonel	Rougeon	Baco noir
Muscat of Alexandria	Rougeon	Campbell Early		Early Muscat	Villard noir	Le Commandant
Ruby Cabernet	Vidal blanc	Muller-Thurgau		Marechal Foch	New York Muscat	Villard noir
White Riesling	Ives	Black Monukka		Pinot blanc	Leon Millot	Veeblanc
Rubired	Cabernet Sauvignon	Muscat of Alexandria		Pinot Meunier	Couderc noir	Chelois
Ruby Seedless	Vignoles	Thompson Seedless				
		Gamay Beaujolais				

[a]Cultivars are listed in approximate order by acreage.

393

TABLE 10-5 IMPORTANT CALIFORNIA TABLE GRAPE CULTIVARS, 1988

CULTIVAR[a]	COLOR[b]	SEEDLESS	PRODUCTION (% OF TOTAL)
Thompson Seedless	W	Yes	39
Flame Seedless	R	Yes	21
Emperor	R	No	9
Perlette	W	Yes	6
Ruby Seedless	R	Yes	6
Ribier	B	No	3
Calmeria	W	No	3
Exotic	B	No	2
Redglobe	R	No	2

Source: California Table Grape Commission.

[a]Other important black cultivars include "Beauty Seedless," "Black Corinth," "Niabell"; red cultivars include "Queen," "Flame Tokay," "Christmas Rose," "Cardinal"; white cultivars include "Superior Seedless," "Italia," and "Almeria."

[b]B, black, blue; R, red, pink; W, white, green, yellow.

TABLE 10-6 IMPORTANT CALIFORNIA WINE GRAPE CULTIVARS, 1987

CULTIVAR	COLOR[a]	APPROXIMATE TONNAGE (CRUSHED)	HARVEST PERIOD	PRODUCTIVITY (TONS/ACRE)
French Colombard	W	620,000	Midseason	8–13
Thompson Seedless	W	398,000	Early	8–11
Chenin blanc	W	290,000	Early-mid	8–11
Zinfandel	B	143,000	Mid	5–9
Grenache	B	108,000	Mid	9–15
Chardonnay	W	101,000	Early	3–5
Tokay	B	99,000	Early	8–10
Barbera	B	74,000	Late-mid	6–9
Carignane	B	72,000	Late	8–12
Cabernet Sauvignon	B	65,000	Late-mid	5–7
Sauvignon blanc	W	59,000	Early	5–7
Rubired	B	51,000	Mid	8–10
Ruby Cabernet	B	43,000	Late	6–9
Muscats	W	39,000	Early	2–8
Pinot noir	B	30,000	Early	4–5
Burger	W	26,000	Late-mid	8–11
White Riesling	W	25,000	Mid	3–5
Emerald Riesling	W	16,000	Early	9–13
Semillon	W	14,000	Early	6–10
Gewurztraminer	W	12,000	Early	2–4
Petite Sirah	B	11,000	Late-mid	5–8
Napa Gamay	B	11,000	Late	7–9
Palomino	W	11,000	Early	9–13
Malvasia Bianca	W	11,000	Mid	7–10

Source: California Crop and Livestock Reporting Service.

[a] B, black, blue, red, pink; W, white, green, yellow.

TABLE 10-7 CHARACTERISTICS OF EASTERN GRAPE CULTIVARS

CULTIVAR	RIPENING SEASON[a]	COLOR[b]	PRINCIPAL USE[c]	WINTER HARDINESS
American Hybrids				
Alden	M	B	D	Fair
Alwood	VE	B	D	Fair
Beta	E	B	D, J	Very good
Bluebell	E	B	D	Very good
Buffalo	E	B	D	Fair
Caco	L	R	D	Good
Catawba	L	R	W	Good
Cayuga White	M	W	W	Fair
Concord	LM	B	D, J	Good
Delaware	M	R	W	Good
Diamond	M	W	W	Good
Dutchess	LM	W	W	Poor
Edelweiss	VE	W	D	Very good
Elvira	M	W	W	Good
Festivee	LM	B	D	Poor
Fredonia	VE	B	D, J	Good
Horizon	M	W	W	Good
Isabella	EM	B	W	Fair
Ives	L	B	W	Good
Kay Gray	VE	W	D	Very good
Melody	M	W	W	Good
Monticello	E	B	D	Fair
Moored	L	R	D	Fair
New York Muscat	E	B	D, W	Fair
Niagara	LM	W	W, J	Good
Ontario	VE	W	D	Good
Price	VE	B	D	Good
St. Croix	VE	B	D, W	Very good
Schulyer	VE	B	D	Fair
Seneca	VE	W	D	Poor
Sheridan	L	B	D	Good
Steuben	L	B	D	Good
Swenson Red	VE	R	D	Very good
Urbana	L	R	D	Good
Valiant	VE	B	D	Very good
Van Buren	VE	B	D, J	Good
Veeblanc	M	W	W	Good
Ventura	LM	W	W	Good
Vinered	L	R	D	Good
Worden	VE	B	D	Very good
Yates	L	R	D	Good
French-American Hybrids				
Aurore (Seibel 5279)	VE	W	W	Good
Baco Noir (Baco 1)	M	B	W	Fair
Cascade (Seibel 13053)	VE	B	W	Good

TABLE 10-7 CHARACTERISTICS OF EASTERN GRAPE CULTIVARS CONT.

CULTIVAR	RIPENING SEASON[a]	COLOR[b]	PRINCIPAL USE[c]	WINTER HARDINESS
French-American Hybrids				
Chambourcin (J. Seyve 26–205)	L	B	W	Poor
Chancellor (Seibel 7053)	LM	B	W	Good
Chelois (Seibel 10878)	M	B	W	Fair
Colobel (Seibel 8357)	LM	B	W	Poor
De Chaunac (Seibel 9549)	M	B	W	Good
Leon Millot (Kuhlmann 194-2)	E	B	W	Good
Marechal Foch (Kuhlmann 188-2)	VE	B	W	Very good
Rosette (Seibel 1000)	LM	B	W	Very good
Rougeon (Seibel 5898)	M	B	W	Good
Seibel 10868	M	W	W	Fair
Seyve-Villard 23-512	M	W	W	Fair
Seyval (Seyve-Villard 5-276)	M	W	W	Fair
Verdelet (Seibel 9110)	M	W	W	Poor
Vidal blanc (Vidal 256)	L	W	W	Fair
Vignoles (Ravat 51)	M	W	W	Fair
Villard blanc (Seyve-Villard 12-375)	L	W	W	Fair
Villard noir (Seyve-Villard 18-315)	LM	B	W	Fair
V. vinifera for the northeast				
Cabernet Sauvignon	L	B	W	Poor
Chardonnay	LM	W	W	Fair
Gamay	M	R	W	Poor
Gewurztraminer	LM	W	W	Poor
Pinot noir	M	B	W	Poor
White Riesling	L	W	W	Fair

[a] VE, very early; E, early; M, midseason; LM, late midseason; L, late.

[b] B, black, blue; R, red, pink; W, white, green, yellow.

[c] W, wine; D, dessert; J, juice.

TABLE 10-8 CHARACTERISTICS OF EASTERN SEEDLESS TABLE GRAPE CULTIVARS

CULTIVAR	RIPENING SEASON	COLOR	FLAVOR	BERRY SIZE	CLUSTER SIZE	CLUSTER COMPACTNESS	VINE VIGOR	YIELD/ VINE	WINTER HARDINESS
Canadice	Early	Red	Good	Medium	Medium	Tight	Medium	High	High
Challenger	Mid	Red	Good	Large	Medium	Loose	Medium	Medium	Medium
Concord Seedless	Late–mid	Blue	Fair	Small	Small	Loose	Medium	Low	High
Glenora	Mid	Blue	Good	Medium	Medium	Compact	Medium	Low	Low
Himrod	Early	White	Excellent	Medium	Medium	Loose	Medium	Low	Medium
Interlaken	Very early	White	Good	Medium	Medium	Compact	Medium	Medium	Low
Lakemont	Mid	White	Good	Medium	Large	Compact	High	High	Low
Mars	Early	Blue	Good	Medium	Small	Compact	Medium	Medium	Medium
Einset	Mid	Red	Excellent	Medium	Medium	Compact	Medium	High	Medium
Reliance	Early	Red	Good	Medium	Medium	Loose	High	Medium	High
Remaily	Late–mid	White	Fair	Large	Large	Compact	Medium	High	Low
Romulus	Late	White	Fair	Small	Large	Compact	Medium	Medium	Medium
Saturn	Mid	Red	Excellent	Large	Medium	Compact	Medium	Medium	Medium
Suffolk Red	Mid	Red	Excellent	Large	Medium	Loose	High	Low	Low
Vanessa	Mid	Red	Good	Medium	Medium	Compact	Medium	Medium	High
Venus	Very early	Blue	Good	Large	Large	Tight	High	High	Medium

TABLE 10-9 CHARACTERISTICS OF SELECTED MUSCADINE GRAPE CULTIVARS

CULTIVAR	FLOWER TYPE[a]	FRUIT COLOR[b]	BERRY SIZE[c]	VINE VIGOR[d]
Albemarle	SF	Bl	M	M
Bountiful	SF	Bl	S	M
Carlos	SF	Br	M	H
Chief	SF	Bl	S	M
Chowan	SF	Br	M	M
Cowart	SF	Bl	L	M
Creek	P	Bl	S	M
Dearing	SF	Br	S	L
Dixieland	SF	Br	L	M
Dixie Red	SF	BR	L	M
Doreen	SF	Br	M	H
Dulcet	P	Bl	S	L
Fry	P	Br	VL	H
Golden Isles	SF	Br	M	M
Higgins	P	Br	VL	M
Hunt	P	Bl	L	M
Jumbo	P	Bl	VL	M
Magnolia	SF	Br	M	H
Magoon	SF	Bl	S	L
Nesbitt	SF	Bl	VL	M
Nevermiss	SF	Br	M	H
Noble	SF	Bl	S	M
Pamlico	SF	Br	M	H
Pride	P	Bl	L	VL
Redgate	SF	BR	S	H
Regale	SF	Bl	M	H
Roanoke	SF	Br	M	M
Scuppernong	P	Br	M	M
Southland	SF	Bl	M	M
Sterling	SF	Br	L	M
Surgargate	P	Bl	VL	M
Summit	SF	Br	L	H
Tarheel	SF	Bl	S	H
Thomas	P	Bl	S	M
Topsail	P	Br	S	M
Watergate	P	Br	VL	M
Welder	SF	Br	M	H
Yuga	P	Br	S	H

Source: Adapted from Hegwood et al. (1983); Poling et al. (1984).

[a]P, pistillate (female); SF, self-fertile.

[b]Bl, black; Br, bronze; BR, bronze-red.

[c]S, small, 2.1–4.0 g/berry; M, medium, 4.1–6.0 g/berry; L, large, 6.1–8.0 g/berry; VL, very large, 8.1–10.0 g/berry.

[d]L, low; M, medium; H, high.

Propagation

Grapevines are propagated by seeds, cuttings, layering, budding, or grafting. New plants have been produced by several in vitro techniques, including embryoid formation and fragmented shoot tip cultures (Krul and Mowbray, 1985). Seeds are used only in breeding programs to produce new cultivars. Grape propagation methods have been modernized by the use of virus-indexed, 'clean' planting stock, mist-propagation techniques for leafy cuttings, and rapid machine-grafting procedures. Most commercial propagation is by dormant hardwood cuttings. For types difficult to root, such as muscadines (*V. rotundifolia*), layering or the use of leafy softwood cuttings under mist is necessary (Sharpe, 1954). Budding or grafting on rootstocks may be used to increase vine life, regulate vigor, and yield. Where noxious soil organisms such as phylloxera (*Daktulosphaira vitifoliae*) or root-knot nematodes (*Meloidogyne* spp.) are present, and cultivars of susceptible species such as *V. vinifera* are to be grown, it is necessary to graft or bud onto a resistant rootstock.

Dormant cuttings. Most grape cultivars are traditionally propagated by dormant hardwood cuttings, which root readily. Cutting material should be collected during the winter from healthy, virus-free, vigorous, mature vines. Well-developed current season's canes should be used; they should be of medium size and have moderately short internodes. Cuttings ⅓ to ½ in. (8 to 13 mm) in diameter and 14 to 18 in. (36 to 46 cm) long are generally used, planted in the spring deep enough to cover all but one bud. One season's growth in the nursery should produce plants large enough to transplant in the vineyard. Auxin-type growth regulators have not been particularly helpful in rooting difficult-to-root hardwood grape cuttings (Harmon, 1943).

Layers. In layering, adventitious roots are caused to form on a cane while it is still attached to the parent plant. The rooted plant is detached to become a new plant. The main use of layering is to propagate grape cultivars which are difficult to root by cuttings, or to replace a missing vine in an established vineyard. Layers can be simple, trench, or mound.

Grafting. The most common method of grafting is bench grafting (Harmon, 1943). Scions are grafted on either rooted or unrooted disbudded rootstock cuttings by the whip graft, or by various techniques using machines which more accurately match the two pieces. The grafts are made in late winter or early spring from dormant scion and stock material. The stocks are cut to 12 to 14 in. (30.5 to 35.5 cm), with the lower cut just below a node and the top cut an inch or more above a node. All buds are removed from the stock to prevent subsequent suckering. Scion wood should have the same diameter as the stock.

After grafting, using a one-bud scion, the union is stapled together or wrapped with a budding rubber. The grafts should be held for 3 to 4 weeks in well-aerated, moist wood shavings or peat moss at about 80°F (26.5°C) for callusing.

The callused grafts are removed from the callusing boxes or plastic bags and any roots and the scion shoot are carefully trimmed back to a ½ -in. (18-mm) stub. The scion is dipped quickly into a temperature-controlled container of melted (low-melting-point) paraffin to a depth of 1 in. (2.5 cm) below the graft union and then quickly into cool water. The paraffined bench graft is then planted into a 2 by 2 by 10 in. (5.0 by 5.0 by 25 cm) milk carton or planting tube, which contains a mixture of perlite and pumice, or perlite and peat moss. The cartons or tubes are placed upright in flats. The flats are set on pallets and moved into a heated greenhouse for 6 to 8 weeks. The growing bench grafts are then transferred to a 50% shade screen house for about 2 weeks for hardening off prior to planting in the nursery or vineyard.

The bench grafts are planted deeply so that the top of the carton or planting tube is at least 2 to 3 in. (5 to 7.5 cm) below the soil level to ensure that water will get inside the carton or tube. At no time, however, should bench grafts be planted in the vineyard with the graft union at or below ground level or the scion may become rooted. If disbudding is not properly done, this will encourage growth of suckers from the rootstock (Weaver, 1976; Winkler et al., 1974).

Greenwood grafting.   Greenwood grafting is a simple and rapid procedure for propagating *V. vinifera* grapes on resistant rootstocks (Harmon, 1954). A one-budded greenwood scion is splice-grafted during the active growing season on new growth arising either from a 1-year-old rooted cutting or from a cutting during midseason of the second year's growth.

Budding.   A satisfactory method of establishing grape cultivars is by field budding on rapidly growing, well-rooted resistant rootstock cuttings that were planted in their permanent vineyard location the previous winter or spring. T-budding in late spring can be done using dormant budwood held under refrigeration. Shortly after budding, the trunks should be cut with diagonal slashes at the base to allow the 'bleeding' to take place there rather than where the bud was inserted (Alley and Koyama, 1978). In another method chip budding is performed in late summer or early fall just as soon as fresh mature buds from wood with light brown bark can be obtained and before the stock begins to go dormant. In areas where mature buds cannot be obtained early in the fall, growers may store budsticks collected in the winter under refrigeration and bud them in late spring or early summer.

The bud is inserted in the stock 2 to 4 in. (5 to 10 cm) above the soil level, preferably on the side adjacent to the supporting stake. It is tied in place with budding rubber but is not waxed. The bud is covered during the winter with 5 to 10 in. (13 to 25 cm) of well-pulverized, moist soil to prevent drying. In areas of extremely hot summers, or in soils of low moisture, variable results are likely to be obtained, and bench- or nursery-grafted vines should be used. If the buds are tied with white ½ -in. (13-mm) plastic tape, it is unnecessary to mound them over with soil.

Top-grafting grapevines. Two methods can be used for changing cultivars of mature grapevines:

1. The tops of the vines are cut off in early spring 12 to 21 in. (30 to 53 cm) below the lower wire and vines are side whip-grafted, using a two-bud scion of the desired cultivar. The scions are wrapped with 1-in. white plastic tape and the cut surfaces are covered with grafting wax.

2. After the bark 'slips' in late spring, the vines may be T-budded with the inverted T and wrapped with white plastic tape. No grafting compound is needed. Both methods give highly successful takes (Hartmann and Kester, 1983; Zabadal, 1985a).

STRUCTURE AND ANATOMY OF THE VINE

The effective management of grapevines requires a fundamental understanding of the structure and physiology of the plant. Proper application of such cultural practices as pruning, shoot tipping, shoot and leaf thinning, cultivation, propagation, crop control, crop estimation, winter damage evaluation, girdling, and growth regulator application demands a basic knowledge of grape plant anatomy. The morphological and anatomical details of vegetative anatomy of the vine at microscopic levels have been reviewed by Pratt (1974). The following account of the anatomy of stem, shoots, and root system of *V. vinifera* is based on Pratt's detailed review (1974). Grapevine morphology is illustrated in Fig. 10–1, while Fig. 10–2 shows the general structure of a stylized grapevine.

Stem

The *stem,* also called the *trunk,* supports the aboveground parts of the vine (arms, shoots, and leaves). The stem originally develops from a bud. It starts as new and succulent growth (*shoot*) from the bud of a rooted cutting after planting. The mature shoot after it has dropped its leaves in the autumn is called a *cane.* The stem (shoot or cane) has nodes, internodes, buds, tendrils, and lateral shoots. The apical part of the shoot, the growing tip, is 4 to 8 in. (10 to 20 cm) long. It consists of the grouping of tiny young leaves, unopened, pressed and closed together. The hairiness, color, and form of its growing tip and the color of the stipules are important taxonomic traits in the identification of cultivars (Morton, 1979). Growth in the shoot tip takes place by cell elongation and cell division. Slightly bulged areas exist on the shoot at regular intervals on which buds develop and the leaves arise. These are the *nodes.* The area between two nodes is called an *internode.* The internodes do not increase in length. Increase in the diameter of the trunk takes place by radial growth.

In *Vitis* species other than *V. rotundifolia* and *V. munsoniana,* the pith of the

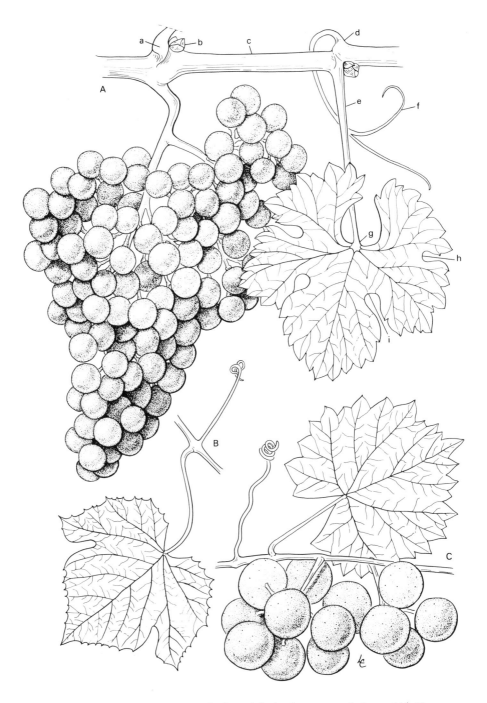

FIGURE 10-1 Grape cane, leaf, and fruit cluster morphology. (A) *V. vinifera:* a, petiole; b, bud; c, internode; d, node; e, petiole; f, tendril; g, petiolar sinus; h, inferior sinus; i, superior sinus. (B) *V. labrusca* leaf and tendril. (C) *V. rotundifolia* leaf, tendril, and fruit cluster.

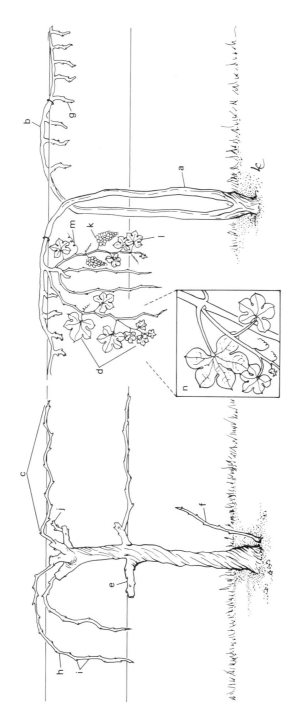

FIGURE 10-2 General structure of a grapevine: a, trunk; b, cordon; c, cane; d, shoot; e, arm; f, sucker; g, spur; h, cane; i, internode; j, renewal spur; k, cluster; l, leaf; m, tendril; n, summer lateral shoot.

shoot at each node is interrupted by a woody layer. This interruption in the pith, called a *diaphragm,* can be seen by cutting the internodal area longitudinally.

Leaf

The leaf, an expanded lateral outgrowth of the shoot, consists of the *blade* (lamina), *petiole,* and a pair of *stipules.* The petiole at the point of attachment to the leaf divides into five large veins, one of these going to each of five lobes of the leaf. Leaf shape, surface, color, contour, and margin (dentation or teeth) are important characteristics in the identification of certain cultivars (Morton, 1979). The leaves of 'Chardonnay', for example, are entire (unlobed), whereas the leaves of 'Cabernet Sauvignon' are orbicular with overlapping edges hiding the sinus, giving the impression of holes punched in the leaf.

The space between the lobes is referred to as the *sinus.* The petiolar sinus, an important ampelographic character, is the attachment of the petiole to the leaf blade and lies between the lobes of the two petiolar veins (Morton, 1979).

Bud

Buds begin development from the meristem axillary to a leaf or bract. The buds are compound, consisting of three growing points: primary, secondary, and tertiary (Fig. 10–3). European literature refers to compound buds as *eyes.* The primary bud is located in the middle and consists of a compressed partially developed shoot. Normally, only the primary bud grows in spring and gives rise to the shoot. If the primary bud is damaged or killed, the secondary bud will grow. The secondary is fruitful and will bear flower clusters. In *V. labrusca* cultivars, shoots that develop from secondary buds will produce approximately 50% of a normal crop. Sometimes two or all the three growing points may give rise to shoots. This happens when the vine is damaged, severely pruned, or is deficient in boron (Pratt, 1974).

In addition to the three buds in the eye, there is another growing point, sometimes referred to as an *axillary bud, lateral bud,* or *summer lateral,* in the axil of leaves which develops into a lateral shoot on the current season's growth. This sometimes grows into a lateral shoot in the same season, or grows very little (Pratt, 1974; Fournioux, 1972). The underground suckers or water sprouts on the trunk are developed from lateral buds.

Tendrils

Tendrils and flower clusters have a common origin. In *V. vinifera* the first two to three basal leaves lack tendrils.

Flower Cluster and Fruit

Grape flowers are borne in an inflorescence which is always opposite a leaf. In *V. vinifera* and *V. labrusca* there are two or three inflorescences per shoot, while

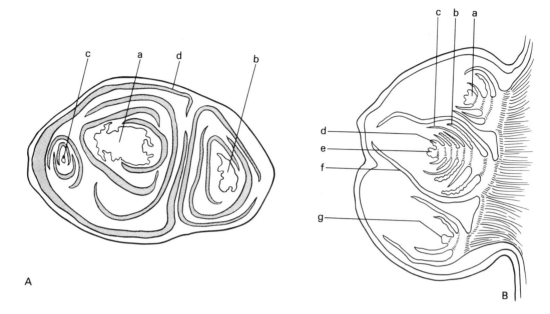

FIGURE 10-3 Dormant grape bud. (A) Cross section: a, primary bud; b, secondary bud; c, tertiary bud; d, leaf primordia. (B) Longitudinal section: a, lateral growing point (secondary bud); b, tendril primordia; c, leaf primordia; d, flower cluster primordia; e, main growing point; f, leaf primordia; g, lateral growing point (tertiary bud).

French-American hybrids may produce five clusters per shoot (Morton, 1979). The main axis of the inflorescence is the branched *rachis,* whose length varies with the cultivar.

The grape flower has the following parts. Five sepals, forming the outer part, are the *calyx.* The *corolla,* also called *cap* or *calyptra,* is made up of five petals (Fig. 10-4). Unlike the flowers of other fruit trees, it is joined at the top and as it opens it detaches from the base and falls off at bloom. The male part consists of five stamens opposite the petals. The *stamens* consist of the *filament* and the *anther,* which produces pollen. There are five *nectaries* at the base alternating with the stamens. The female part, the *pistil,* consists of a *stigma,* a *style,* and an *ovary,* which has two *carpels* having two *locules.* In each locule there are two *ovules.* Each ovule has an *embryo sac,* containing an egg. The fertilized egg becomes the *embryo* within the *seed,* with a possible maximum of four seeds per berry. The majority of the *V. vinifera* cultivars have perfect or hermaphroditic flowers with functional stamens and pistils.

The grape cluster consists of *peduncle, cap stems* (pedicels), *rachis,* and *berries.* The berry consists of skin, pulp, and seeds. The thin waxy layer on the skin of several cultivars, called *bloom,* prevents water loss. The anthocyanins, flavoring and aromatic compounds in the berry, are located in the skin (Fig. 10-5).

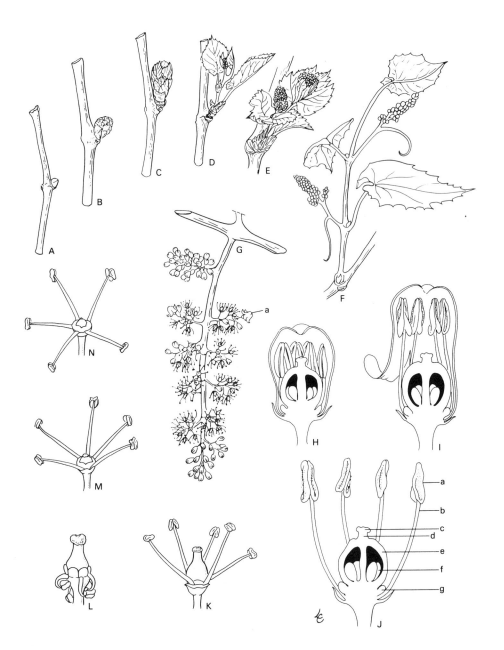

FIGURE 10-4 Development of a new shoot and flowering. (A) Dormant bud. (B) Bud swell. (C) Bud burst. (D) Leaf separation. (E) Clusters visible. (F) Extended shoot with clusters. (G) Flower cluster during bloom: a, calyptra. (H) Flower with attached calyptra. (I) Flower with calyptra separating. (J) Open flower: a, anther; b, filament: c, stigma; d, style; e, ovary; f, ovule; g, nectary. (K) Perfect flower. (L) Female flower. (M) Physiologically male with partially aborted ovary. (N) Male flower.

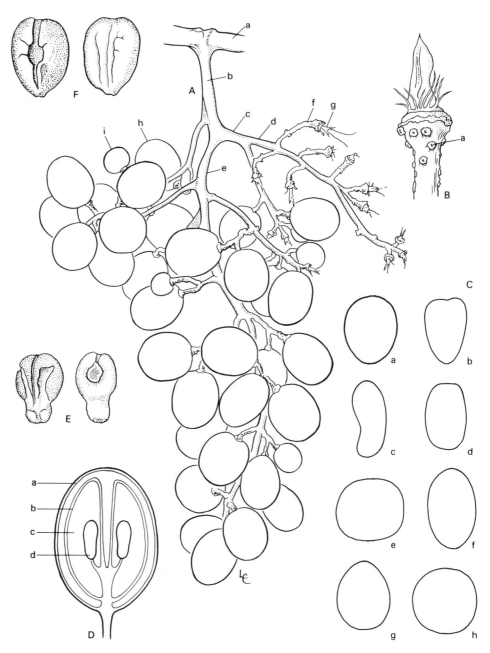

FIGURE 10-5 Grape fruit cluster and berry morphology. (A) Fruit cluster: a, shoot; b, peduncle; c, primary branch; d, secondary branch; e, rachis; f, pedicle; g, brush; h, berry; i, shot berry. (B) Brush on pedicle: a, lenticle. (C) Berry shapes: a, ovoid; b, truncate; c, falcoid; d, cylindrical; e, oblate; f, ellipsoidal; g, obovoid; h, spherical. (D) Longitudinal section of a berry: a, epidermis; b, vascular strand; c, pulp; d, seed. (E) *V. vinifera* seed. (F) *V. rotundifolia* seed.

Structure and Anatomy of the Vine

Root

The root system consists of the main roots, branch roots, and rootlets or feeder roots. The bulk of the roots of mature grapevines are in the upper 2 to 5 ft (0.6 to 1.5 m) of soil; however, vine roots have been found up to 40 ft (12 m) in depth (Winkler et al., 1974). The rootlets at their growing end have a cream-colored region about 1 in. (2.5 cm) or shorter. They consists of root tip (root cap), zone of elongation, and zone of absorption (Winkler et al., 1974). The most favorable soil temperatures for root growth is 86°F (30°C). An excellent review of the grape root system has been compiled by Richards (1983).

CULTURE

Crop Yield Components

Yield depends on several factors. There are many interactions and interrelationships between various anatomical, physiological, developmental, and environmental factors, which annually combine to determine the quantity and quality of grapes that a vine will produce. The relationship between crop yields and the components of yield is shown in Fig. 10-6.

Growth and Berry Development

The annual growth cycle of a typical grape vine is expressed in Fig. 10-7. In this cycle several different events occur simultaneously. The exact timing of specific events may shift by several weeks at a given location from one year to the next, depending on weather conditions. The relative timing of events may also be notably

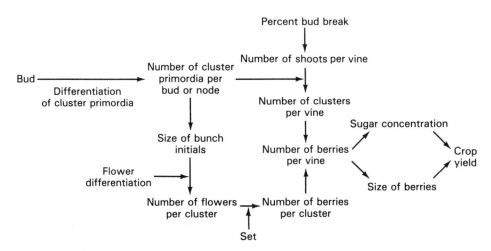

FIGURE 10-6 Interrelationships between crop yield and components of yield. (Courtesy of Mark Kliewer, University of California, 1980.)

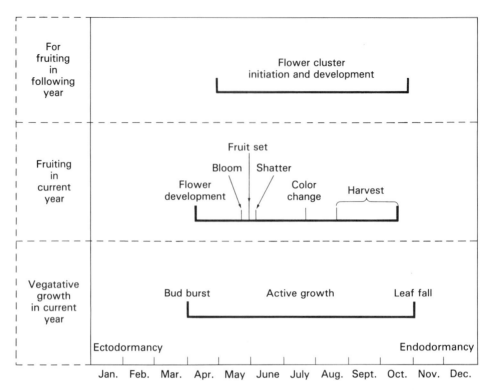

FIGURE 10-7 Calendar showing when the stages in the growth and fruiting of a *vinifera* grapevine occur. (Adapted from Pratt 1971; used by permission)

different, depending on geographical location. For example, bloom may occur in mid-May in many California locations, while it may not normally occur until mid-June in the Great Lakes area.

Flower clusters begin their differentiation the summer prior to the year the grapes are actually harvested. This differentiation is complete by the time the vines lose their leaves during the fall months. Following pruning and bud burst the shoots begin to grow rapidly. When the shoots reach 4 to 6 in. (10 to 15 cm) in length, the flower clusters are easily distinguishable, and by 12 in. (31 cm) the flower clusters are well separated on the growing shoot. Because of the size and shape of the flower clusters, some people confuse them with developing berries. The average bloom period for grape begins in May or June, whereas the flower clusters can be seen developing within the closed compound bud from mid-March up to the beginning of bloom. The grape flowers have a protective cap called a *calyptra,* which covers the stamens, ovary, pollen, and other flower parts. As the bloom period approaches, the calyptra or cap begins to crack along the seams and begins to curl up from the bottom, exposing the flower parts.

Following pollination the flower parts fall off and the berries begin to grow and develop. Berries that begin to develop from flowers which were not pollinated are aborted and fall to the ground in what is referred to as the "shatter" stage. In

addition to physiological responses to adverse environmental conditions, poor pollination can also result from nutrient deficiencies such as zinc or boron, or from certain virus infections. Shatter typically occurs 7 to 10 days after full bloom. For example, only 20 to 40% of the florets in 'Concord' clusters normally develop into berries. The pollinated flowers begin to form berries which continue to grow in size and develop sugar until the harvest period. Useful reviews of the physiology of flowering in the grapevine can be found in Lavee (1985), Lavee and Nir (1986), and Srinivasan and Mullins (1981).

Factors Affecting Cultivar Adaptation

The major viticultural areas of the world are contained primarily within two belts between the parameters of 30 to 50°N. latitude, and 30 to 40°S. latitude. Virtually all of the good-quality wines of the world are produced between isotherm regions in temperate zones that have average yearly temperatures between 50 and 68°F (10 and 20°C).

The genetic composition of grape cultivars has an important bearing on their adaptation to various sections of the country. This largely determines the character of growth of the vine, its hardiness, time of flowering and fruit maturity, resistance to fungus diseases and insect pests, tolerance to drought, and other inherent properties. There are a number of other factors, concerned primarily with environmental conditions, that affect cultivar adaptation. Among these are (1) the severity of winter temperatures; (2) the length of the period from the last killing frost in the spring to the first killing frost in the fall; (3) the amount, seasonal distribution, and availability of moisture; (4) the average temperature level of the growing season; (5) the physical and chemical character of the soil; (6) the relative humidity of the air during the growing season; (7) the amount and quality of sunshine; and (8) the latitude, which determines the day length and season as well as the period of winter dormancy. In some areas the severity of winter cold precludes the growing of any grapes at all, and even in more favored locations it sharply restricts the types and cultivars that can be grown successfully. This applies particularly to the northern parts of the country and to the higher elevations, but winter killing of vines is by no means confined to these areas.

One of the most critical factors determining cultivar adaptation in the northern parts of the country, is the length of the frost-free period. Cultivar selection is normally limited in regions having a short growing season of less than 150 days by the fact that only the most hardy cultivars will thrive. With the exception of those cultivars derived largely from southern species, most of the standard cultivars succeed best where the frost-free period is 150 to 180 days. They may grow and produce crops in regions having longer growing seasons, but there is an increasing tendency, as they are grown farther south, for the berries to mature unevenly in the cluster and for the vine to become gradually weaker and to die while it is still relatively young.

Factors other than the length of the frost-free period are operative here also, and it is often difficult, if not impossible, to judge which are most important. The northern limit for the growing of the southern muscadine cultivars coincides rather

closely with the line marking the upper boundary of the region with a 200-day frost-free period. The zone extending from the Gulf of Mexico to this northern boundary also has been found best suited to the growing of those standard cultivars that have been developed in the deep South.

Heat units during the growing season. While low winter temperatures and the length of the growing season are two of the major factors limiting the survival of grapes, another factor is the temperature during the growing season. Grapes will not grow if the temperature is below 45°F (7°C) and will not produce adequate shoot growth or acceptably ripen a crop if the mean temperature during the growing season is too cool. In order for most cultivars to grow vigorously and mature large crops with a high sugar content, relatively warm temperatures are needed.

Heat during the season is particularly important in wine grapes. During cool seasons, grapes tend to be lower in sugar and higher in acid. Warmer weather results in increased sugar with somewhat less acid and higher juice pH. This relationship is expressed in accumulated heat units, calculated from monthly mean temperatures over 50°F (10°C) multiplied by the number of days in the month. The total for a season (April through October) depends not only on high temperatures during the summer, but also on the length of the growing season.

The level of heat units needed for best production depends on the cultivar of grape and its use. In general, most American-type grape cultivars are grown under conditions of over 1800 but less than 2500 heat units. With over 3000 heat units per season, vine vigor is more difficult to maintain, while grape production and quality is lower. The sugar content can be high, but the acid is low and the color is less desirable.

Some European-type grape cultivars and a number of hybrids grow well with less than 2500 heat units, but a range of 2500 to 3000 heat units favors higher production, higher sugar, and better quality. With 3500 heat units and above, European and hybrid grape cultivars develop more sugar and the acid content is lower. Growing degree days are discussed in detail in Chapter 2.

Because of its influence on the development of fungus diseases that attack the grape, relative humidity is perhaps the next most important single factor in varietal adaptation. The *V. vinifera,* or European cultivars, which are very susceptible to fungus diseases, are favored in the hot, dry central valleys of California and the hot irrigated sections of Arizona and Texas, where these diseases cannot thrive, whereas the same cultivars in the humid regions of the south and east are quickly destroyed unless given special care. On the other hand, some cultivars, including the muscadines, appear to thrive best in regions where the humidity is relatively high. The presence of fungus diseases and the degree of susceptibility of American cultivars to them often determine what cultivars may be grown successfully in various regions.

In some parts of the country, temperature, length of growing season, and character of the soil may be satisfactory for the successful growing of grapes, yet many cultivars fail because of the character of their root systems and in their inability to penetrate deeply into the soil. Where rainfall is light and water for irrigation is not available, only those cultivars that are able to send their roots deep into the soil will be adapted to the region. This is particularly true in the semiarid and arid sections of the southwest (Magoon and Snyder, 1943; Richard, 1983; Mielke et al., 1980).

Factors in Site Selection

Length of growing season. The length of the growing season within a given latitude is influenced by elevation, climate moderation by relatively large bodies of water, and slope, which can export cold, dense air to adjacent lower areas. As a conservative general rule, a minimum frost-free period of 165 days is essential for most early to midseason cultivars, with 180 days or more being preferable. This frost-free period must begin early enough in the spring to protect shoots as growth begins, and extend long enough in the fall to ensure maturity not only of the crop, but of the vegetative parts of the vine as well. Although a cultivar may mature its fruit early, it may still require a substantial frost-free postharvest period with functional leaves to mature the vine itself adequately.

The length of time between bud break and harvest of a particular cultivar in relation to the length of the growing season of a given site is a major factor in the selection of grape cultivars. Involved is not only the maturing of the crop but also the recovery and maturation of the vines after harvest. This site characteristic is most important in cool regions with limited growing seasons. The production recommendations based on this relationship may be expressed as follows:

Areas with less than 150 frost-free days. Consider only American-type grapes and the earliest-maturing French hybrids.

Areas with 150 to 160 frost-free days. Most American-type grape cultivars and several early-maturing hybrids can be grown. A season of only 160 frost-free days is marginal for all but the earliest-maturing European-type (*V. vinifera*) grapes.

Areas with 160 to 170 frost-free days. Some early-maturing European-type and hybrid-type cultivars can be grown under cultural practices and soil conditions that favor early maturity.

Areas with 170 to 180 frost-free days. Many European-type and hybrid-type grape cultivars can be grown.

Areas with over 180 frost-free days and higher. This is the most desirable length of the growing season for many European-type and French hybrid grape cultivars.

Areas with over 200 frost-free days and higher. This long growing season is required for many late-maturing European-type cultivars and muscadines.

Minimum winter temperatures. Data concerning the magnitude and frequency of winter minimum temperatures at a potential site should be interpreted in the light of the proposed cultivar selection and vineyard management guidelines. A general guide to the selection of sites for the avoidance of winter damage to vines can be estimated as follows:

Excellent. Winter temperatures reach −5°F (−20.5° C) three times or less in 10 years; winter temperatures reach −10°F (−23°C) no more than once in 10 years, with the long-term minimum temperature not lower than −10°F. Suitable for all current commercial American, French hybrid, and selected winter-hardy *V. vinifera* cultivars.

Good. Winter temperatures reach −5°F (−20.5°C) five times or less in 10 years; winter temperatures reach −10°F (−23°C) no more than once in 10 years, with the long-term minimum temperature not lower than −15°F (−26°C). Suitable for most current cold-hardy commercial cultivars, but cold-tender cultivars can be expected to sustain severe damage at least once in 10 years and lesser damage more often.

Acceptable. Winter temperatures reach −5°F (−20.5°C) almost every year; winter temperatures reach −10°F (−23°C) four times or less in 10 years, with the long-term minimum temperature of −15°F (−26°C) or less occurring no more than once in 10 years. In general, these sites are suitable only for cultivars of medium or greater hardiness.

Poor. Winter temperatures reach −10°F (−23°C) five or more times in 10 years; winter temperatures reach −15°F (−26°C) 3 or more times in 10 years. Not suitable for commercial grape production (Jordan et al., 1981; Tukey and Clore, 1972).

It is important to note that the preconditioning of the vine, its state of acclimation, and the rate and amount of temperature change can dramatically affect the amount of injury sustained.

Anticipated responses to low temperatures. The types of response or injury that can be anticipated from low temperatures are as follows. Temperatures of 0°F (−18°C) occurring during midwinter, following a period of cool weather, may cause some loss of primary buds or even canes of all grapes that have grown late into the fall. Little, if any, injury and no loss would be anticipated with well-matured vines. If these low temperatures followed a period above 30 to 40°F (−1.1 to 4.4°C), they might result in some damage to European-type grapes as well as to some hybrids.

Temperatures down to −10°F (−23°C) during midwinter are likely to cause injury to both buds and trunks of European-type grapes and, probably, crop loss. Killing of some primary buds on American-type grapes with injury to trunk and arms may occur with weaker vines. Hybrids should be intermediate between these two, with significant bud damage occurring.

Temperatures down to −20°F (−29°C) during midwinter would be expected to severely damage or kill most unprotected European grapes and seriously injure hybrid grape trunks and canes. Injury to American-type grapes would be less, but would probably result in significant crop reduction. Some of the lesser known European cultivars developed for colder regions of Europe and Asia have shown good survival and production following exposure to these low temperatures but are not readily available from commercial nurseries.

An early freeze in mid-November with temperatures down to $-10°F$ ($-23°C$) may cause serious injury to European grapes with crop loss, except on the more hardy cultivars and well-hardened-off vines. Such temperatures may cause some loss of buds on American-type grapes, with greater injury on hybrids.

Soil. Although grapevines will survive and produce a crop under a wide range of soil conditions, the establishment of economically feasible vineyards is increasingly dependent on selecting soils that have good internal drainage and sufficient rooting depth. The minimum depth should be at least 30 in. (76 cm); 40 in. (102 cm) is preferable, with additional benefits likely as rooting depth increases up to 5 or 6 ft (1.5 to 1.8 m).

Good yields of some cultivars are common on imperfectly drained soils that have been improved through tiling. However, within the major grape-producing areas, the better the soil drainage, the better the site will be for grape production. Where the option exists, it will usually be false economy to purchase a less expensive site with heavy, imperfectly, or poorly drained soil, because the cost of artificial drainage, which at best is only a partial remedy, may exceed any savings on the original purchase price of the land.

Vineyard Preparation and Planting

Preparation of the vineyard site is very important and should begin at least the year before planting. Among the major items for consideration in such preparation should be land leveling, installation of drainage tile (if needed) and sod waterways, fertility and lime adjustment, and removal of persistent weeds. Since a vineyard, once planted, will usually be maintained for many years, correction of as many site imperfections as possible before planting will add materially to its longevity and productivity.

The land should be plowed at least 8 to 10 in. (20 to 25 cm) deep, and cleared of the existing vegetation. The land should be leveled if furrow irrigation is planned. Test pits 4 ft deep (1.2 m) and 2 ft (61 cm) in diameter should be dug in different parts of the vineyard to detect the presence of hardpan or other root-obstructing layers. If such a layer is found within a depth of 2 to 3 ft (61 to 92 cm), deep-plow to break it up before planting. A hardpan layer may eventually cause root growth and water infiltration problems even when deep plowing is performed during vineyard preparation.

A plan of the vineyard showing location of rows, roads, and storage or work shed should be drawn up. Large fields should be divided into blocks of suitable size using surveying instruments. Main avenues in the vineyard should be 20 ft (6.1 m) or wider to give farm machinery room to turn around. Space equal to the row spacing is usually allowed on all sides of the vineyard for normal farm operations. In very large vineyards, large blocks are separated by wide avenues to allow for air movement.

The position of the rows, and plants in the row, should be marked using temporary wooden stakes and surveyor's chain. Straight rows can be set in by preparing a deep furrow for planting. Individual planting holes may also be dug by hand or by the use of a tractor-powered posthole auger. A planting machine can also be used for planting a large vineyard. The holes should be deep enough to accommodate the roots fully.

The size of the field, topography, the irrigation system chosen, and soil type determine the length of the rows. With furrow irrigation, row length should not be more than 360 ft (110 m) on sandy soils. On heavy soils row length can be up to 700 ft (214 m). With drip irrigation the length of the rows ranges from 300 to 600 ft (92 to 183 m). With sprinkler irrigation, rows can be up to 1000 ft (305 m) long, depending on the volume and output of the irrigation lines.

Direction of rows.   Factors important in deciding the direction of rows are wind velocity, slope of the land, and the need for maximum light exposure. North–south rows intercept more light than do east–west rows. Also, light interception is greater for tall, closely spaced north–south rows (Smart, 1973). This is important in regions where the growing season is short. In areas where winds are a problem, the rows should be parallel to the wind. In rill-irrigated vineyards, the direction of the rows is the same as the direction of the slope.

In California the rows run east to west in raisin grape vineyards, so that grapes placed on the ground to dry between the rows will receive the maximum amount of sun. In table grape vineyards, rows run northeast to southwest to minimize sunburning of the clusters.

Row and vine spacing.   There have been numerous arbitrary formulas recommended in the past for the spacing of vines and rows in commercial vineyards. The most efficient and practical spacing depends on many factors and may change dramatically with climate, site, cultivar, and equipment. The row spacing is determined by equipment size, particularly tractor widths. As a general rule, row spacing has been governed by machinery width, while vine spacing has been governed by cultivar vigor.

The relative spacing of vines in the row has traditionally been determined by the expected vine size and vegetative vigor of a particular cultivar. For example, very weak *V. vinifera* cultivars such as 'Muscat Ottonel' may successfully support only about 20 buds, and such vines may be planted about 3 ft (1 m) apart. Moderately weak vines such as 'Gewurztraminer' will support 25 buds and could be planted 4 ft (1.2 m) apart. Cultivars of medium vigor such as 'Muller-Thurgau' could be allowed 35 buds and planted 5 ft (1.5 m) apart, while the vigorous 'Cabernet Sauvignon' may support 50 buds and might be planted 6 ft (2 m) apart in many areas (Jackson and Schuster, 1981). The number of buds per unit length of row for each of the examples above is about the same at 6 to 8 buds per ft (20 to 25 buds per meter). In the case of American and French hybrid vines the number of buds retained per foot of row typically ranges from 3 to 8 (10 to 25 buds per meter) depending on vine size and cultivar fruitfulness. For example, a moderate-sized 'Concord' or 'Catawba' vine might optimally support 6 buds per foot (20 buds per meter), while a similar-size 'Aurore' or 'Seyval' vine may only adequately sustain 5 buds per foot (16 buds per meter).

The close spacing of vines increases the number of nodes (buds) per unit area of land. This trend will produce a yield increase up to a point where shoot crowding and shading begin to reduce the fruitfulness of the vines. Early work by Partridge (1925) in Michigan showed that 'Concord' vines with a vigor greater than 2.5 to 3.5 lb (1.1 to 1.6 kg) of pruning weight per vine became overly vegetative and unfruitful using the spacing and training systems of that era. Even though this extra wood production has the potential for increasing the yield, the poor-quality buds being produced in the shaded canopy had fewer and smaller clusters.

Row spacing depends in part on the proposed training and trellising system, and in part on the equipment to be used in the vineyard, including the possible use of a mechanical harvester. An 8-ft (2.4-m) row spacing is satisfactory for small plantings, but is considered too restrictive for most commercial operations. In the eastern United States a 9-foot (2.8-m) spacing between rows is common and generally ample, but 10 to 11 ft (3.1 to 3.4 m) between rows may be needed to accommodate large equipment on steep slopes.

Wide spacing between rows has had the advantage of reducing harvesting labor because grapes could be hauled out from between the rows. The use of specialized over-the-row mechanical harvesters now limits the width of rows in most areas. Wide rows also cut the cost of pruning and brush disposal, facilitate the use of power spraying equipment, and make irrigation easier. Wide spacing has a direct impact on costs. Establishment costs are much less because there are fewer vines, posts, and wire per acre. Cultivation, mowing, and spraying costs are reduced on a per acre basis due to the reduced number of passes required to cover the same area.

Spacing vines in the row at 8-ft (2.4-m) intervals has proven satisfactory for most American and French hybrid cultivars under average conditions. However, closer spacings have produced somewhat higher yields under certain specific conditions. Cultivars that produce less vigorous growth, such as 'Delaware' or 'Catawba' and some French hybrids, may be set closer together than 'Concord' or other cultivars of similar vigor. Highest yields on an acre basis have generally been obtained from vineyards containing 600 or more vines per acre (1482 vines per hectare) in the eastern United States.

The best spacing is always a compromise and is normally the widest feasible that is compatible with mechanized vineyard operations without reducing the crop yield of a mature vineyard. Spacing is also influenced by climatic conditions, as evidenced by the variety of recommendations. In the interior valley in California nearly all table grapes and vigorous wine cultivars are managed well at 8 ft (2.4 m) between the vines and 12 ft (3.7 m) between rows. Moderate-growing cultivars are planted at 6 or 7 ft between vines and 12 ft (1.8 or 2.1 by 3.7 m) between rows. These wider row spacings are used because of the greater vine vigor response to the very warm growing conditions.

The overall pattern in the majority of vine spacing experiments seems to indicate an increasing yield and pruning weight per vine, with an increase in vine spacing or row spacing. However, frequently when the data are calculated per unit area, the yield decreases slightly with an increase in the vine spacing and decreases significantly with an increase in row spacing. Yield per square foot of vineyard tends to decrease much faster than do pruning weights with increases in vine or row spacings.

In summary, the efficiency of vineyards as measured by yield per unit of pruning weight decreases with increases in row and vine spacing. However, practical considerations of economic and operating efficiency dictate vine and row spacing based on costs and ease of operation (Fisher, 1987).

Planting stock.   Planting stock (1-year-old No. 1 rooted cuttings) from a reliable nursery should be ordered well ahead of planting time. State quarantine regulations designed to prevent the spread of grape viruses prohibit shipment of plants into Washington, Oregon, and California. Where phylloxera and nematodes are a problem, grafted vines on resistant rootstocks should be considered.

Land preparation.   Preparation for planting grapes is quite similar in practice to the traditional site modifications listed in other chapters of this book. Development of a site should take into account the following procedures:

1. Adjust soil pH and nutrient levels if needed.
2. Add organic matter when practical (cover crops, manure).
3. Control weed populations (cover crops, herbicides).
4. Fumigate where serious soil pathogen, nematode, or weed populations exist.
5. Develop good soil tilth and avoid erosion-causing cultural practices.
6. Correct internal or surface water drainage problems.

Weed control and cultivation.   Effective weed control after planting is critical to the success of any new vineyard planting. Weeds may be controlled by the use of polyethylene mulch, cultivation and hand weeding, and chemical herbicides.

Vine preparation and planting.   Handle young vines carefully to prevent drying out or other damage after they have been dug or received from the nursery. If vines are not planted immediately, place them in cold storage [36°F (2°C) with high relative humidity] until planting time. If proper facilities are not available, carefully heel in vines in a sheltered location. Dig a shallow trench and place individual vines in the trench so that the tops are exposed. Cover roots with moist soil and firm around plants. Transplant them to their permanent location as soon as possible. Soaking vine roots in water 2 to 3 hours before planting will also increase their chance of survival.

Before setting vines, prune off broken or dead portions of the roots. Long roots may be shortened for convenience in planting. Additional root pruning is not necessary or desirable. At the same time, reduce top growth generally to a single cane.

Vines are most conveniently set using a mechanical transplanter; otherwise, simply plow a straight furrow 10 to 12 in. (10 to 15 cm) deep for the row. It will accommodate a rather large root system without packing a mass of roots into a small hole. Spread roots well, cover with a few inches of topsoil, and tamp firmly. A plow or disk may be used to finish filling the furrow. In a small planting, the entire operation is often done by hand. When planting is completed, a node from which the lowest cane will arise should be at or just above the soil level. If vines grafted on special rootstocks are used, make sure that the union is well above the soil level. Prune the single cane remaining after planting so that only two or three live buds remain. As these shoots begin to develop, all but two of the most vigorous are pruned when about 1 in. (2.5 cm) long. This provides two shoots to develop into vigorous new canes (Cahoon and Hill, 1981).

Managing Young American and French Hybrid Vines

First year. Putting fertilizer in the furrow during planting is not advisable because of the danger of injuring roots. It is unnecessary if the soil was properly prepared. If needed, approximately 4 oz (13 g) of 10–10–10 fertilizer, or an equivalent, can be applied to the soil surface around each vine immediately after planting. However, the hazard of overfertilization and stimulation of later summer growth with increased susceptibility to winter cold damage is greater than the hazard of inadequate growth during the first year.

As soon as bud break occurs, the newly set vines, if not pruned before planting, should be pruned to the best single cane. If a trellis is to be constructed early in the first growing season, as recommended, this best single cane should be tied to the lower wire of the trellis. When the new shoots are an inch or less in length, all but two to four strong shoots near the top of the cane should be rubbed off to promote growth in height and to avoid the growth of unwanted shoots along the trunk.

As the season progresses, the retained shoots should be tied loosely to the trellis for better light exposure, to avoid damage by equipment, and to facilitate pest control. Flower clusters that develop should be removed as early as possible through midsummer. Timely flower-cluster removal, tying, and shoot removal will require two or more trips through the vineyard during early and midsummer, depending on cultivar.

If no trellis is to be constructed for several months or excess shoot and flower-cluster removal cannot be accomplished in a timely manner, the best cane should be pruned to two buds immediately before or after planting. Preventing weed competition close to the vines during the first two growing seasons is critical for early profitable vineyard production.

The primary objectives in training a young vine in the first year are the development of a large, healthy root system and a straight, semipermanent trunk. The shaping of the aboveground parts of the vine, according to a particular training system, is of secondary importance. During the first and second growing seasons, these objectives can be accomplished by eliminating or reducing the crop and increasing the leaf area. The same treatment rejuvenates very weak vines of any age (Fig. 10–8).

Second year. During the dormant period following the first growing season, the best cane should be retained to form one trunk and to take it to the top wire if possible. At the time of bud burst, 6 to 10 shoots should be retained on the upper portion of this single trunk if training systems such as umbrella Kniffin, single-

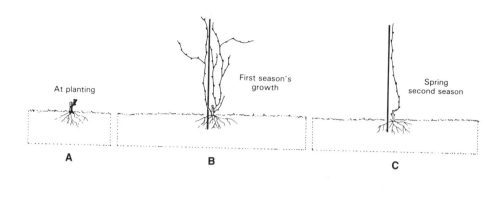

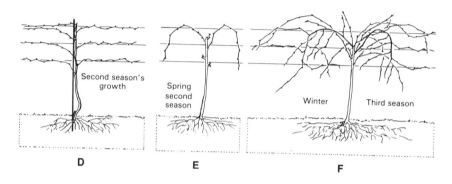

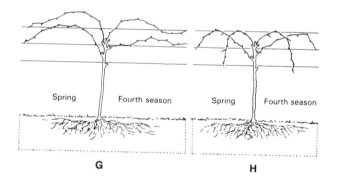

FIGURE 10-8 Growth and training of an American or hybrid type grapevine: (A) at planting time; (B) potential growth during first growing season; (C) establishing the trunk, spring of second year; (D) typical growth during second year; (E) pruned vine with selected fruiting canes, spring of third year; (F) typical growth during third year; (G) pruned vine with fruiting canes selected for fourth year's growth; (H) fruiting canes tied to trellis prior to start of fourth year's growth (umbrella Kniffen system).

Culture

curtain cordon, or Geneva double curtain are being considered, or at the proper position for arms of other training systems. All other shoots should be removed so that the growth will be concentrated in shoots located in positions most useful for future training. During the second growing season, all the flower clusters should be removed from the growing shoots as soon as they develop. This, of course, eliminates the crop for the year, but ensures greater development of the vine's roots and top.

Third year.   Vines that have grown enough to produce ¾ lb (350 g) or more of prunings during their second year should be balance pruned and fruited in the third year. However, it is important that these immature vines have the flower clusters thinned to prevent overcropping.

In areas where trunk injury is a problem, a second cane, preferably a sucker, should be pruned to the bottom wire. All but two or three shoots near the top of this cane should be removed shortly after shoot growth commences; it will become the second trunk. The double-trunk training system can also be established earlier by allowing two main shoots to develop from the crown (near ground level) after the first year of growth.

When vines produce less than ¾ lb (350 g) of prunings in their second or subsequent growing seasons, the second-year treatment should be repeated: and flower clusters should be removed to promote greater vine growth (Jordan et al., 1981).

Training Vinifera from Planting to Third Year

The training methods and cultural practices discussed in this section pertain to environmental conditions and management techniques that are commonly found in the western United States. The training of *V. vinifera* in the eastern United States commonly follows those guidelines given for American and French hybrid vines.

First year.   In the first year the main objective is to develop a good root system. No stakes are needed. Toward the end of the growing season (mid-August) irrigation frequency should be reduced to permit hardening of the canes. This is very important in areas subject to winter injury. By the end of the first year the vines should have a well-established root system with several shoots 8 to 15 in. (20 to 38 cm) in length.

After the vines have become dormant, all growth except the strongest cane is removed and that cane is pruned back to two or three buds. In regions with severe winters the vine should be completely covered with soil to protect it from the cold. This is usually accomplished by throwing soil on the plants from both sides of each row using a colter disk or grape hoe. Normally, no fertilizers are applied. Weeds should be controlled and irrigation provided. The amount and frequency of irrigation will depend on weather conditions.

Second year.   The objective of training during the second year is to develop a strong, straight cane that will become the trunk. In early spring, covered vines should be carefully uncovered before bud break. If this is delayed until after bud break, the new growth will be etiolated and subject to frost injury. The covering material (soil) can be removed by hand or by machine. In Washington a tractor-driven potato digging machine has been used successfully to remove soil. If the first year's growth was weak, nitrogen at 20 lb/acre (22 kg/ha) should be applied. Disease and pest control measures should be adopted if needed. Unless the vines are to be head-trained, the trellis should be installed early in the second year. When the vines have made sufficient growth, a cord is tied from the trellis wire to a peg inserted in the soil beside each plant and a strong shoot is tied loosely to it at 9-in. (23-cm) intervals. Care should be taken that the shoot is not girdled. Lateral shoots are allowed to grow to obtain a maximum photosynthetic leaf surface, but are left untied. If the trellis has not been installed, tie each plant to a stake temporarily. Vines that will be head-trained should be provided with sturdy stakes that will last 3 to 5 years. By late summer when the main shoot has grown approximately 12 in. (31 cm) beyond the point at which the arms of the cordon are desired, 6 to 8 in. (15 to 20 cm) below the wire, the shoot should be cut through the node immediately above the node where branching is desired. This will stop further elongation of the shoot and will usually cause two branches to develop. Tie them loosely to the wire, one on each side. These will become the arms of the cordon-trained vine. Up to this point, the training of head- and cordon-trained vines is the same.

Third year. During the third growing season, the vine will bear a crop. The size of the crop will depend on the number of buds allowed and the fruitfulness of the cultivar. It is better to keep the crop small, as the objective of training at this stage of vine development is to develop a strong head or cordon, depending on the system used. As the lateral shoot of the cordon increases in length, it should be tied again. The shoot should be cut at a point past the halfway point of the next vine at the time of pruning.

During the third winter, after the leaves have dropped, the branches of the cordon should be cut at a point where the cane is at least 3/8 in. (9.5 mm) thick. The canes are trained or wrapped one and half times around the support wire. The ends of the canes should be tied tightly to the wire. The spurs on the cordon should be spaced 8 to 12 in. (20 to 31 cm) apart. These should be pruned to one to two bud spurs to complete the cordon.

Trellis Systems

Eastern United States. Most vertical trellises for commercial vineyards in the eastern United States are of the same general type: two or three wires, one above the other, stretched tightly on firmly set posts. Two wires are adequate for single-curtain cordon, umbrella Kniffin, and four-arm Kniffin, the most common systems; but three wires are necessary for some other training systems. For average-sized vines the top wire of the trellis should be 5 1/2 to 6 ft (1.7 to 1.8 m) above the ground. This permits cane distribution that encourages good exposure to sunlight and facilitates insect and disease control. The bottom wire should be approximately 3 ft (0.9 m) above the ground to facilitate mechanical harvest.

Culture

Geneva double-curtain (GDC) training requires one trunk support wire plus two horizontal and parallel cordon-support wires, positioned 4 ft (1.2 m) apart [for 9 ft (2.8 m) rows] and 6 ft (1.8 m) above the vineyard floor on metal or wood arms attached to line posts. The arms are usually bolted to the line posts, inclined upward at about a 35° angle, and are free to move vertically up at their outer ends for mechanical harvesting. Row spacings of less than 9 ft (2.8 m) will necessitate reduced space between cordons to permit harvester and other equipment use without excessive damage.

West coast. A great diversity of trellis system designs are currently being used in vineyards on the west coast of the United States. The type of trellis used at a particular location will depend on such factors as the commercial class of grapes grown (wine, table, raisin), whether the grapes will be mechanically harvested or mechanically pruned, the climatic and geographical location, and ultimately, the grower's own preference. The following systems represent the most common trellis designs.

Wine Grape Trellis Designs. *System 1.* Consists of a 7-ft (2.1-m) two-wire and three-wire vertical system. The most common trellis currently used for wine cultivars is the two-wire vertical trellis on a 7-ft (2.1-m) stake. The head or cordon wire is located 40 to 46 in. (102 to 117 cm) above the ground surface. A catch (foliage support) wire is usually attached 12 to 14 in. (31 to 36 cm) above the cordon wire, but only 10 to 12 in. (25 to 31 cm) under windy conditions. To prevent cordon twisting, this wire should be attached the year the vine is trained. The top wire can be moved upward for better foliage support as the spur positions rise with age. Another option is the addition of a third wire at the top of the stake for additional support.

System 2. Consists of a 7-ft (2.1-m) stake with crossarm. A crossarm may be added to the two-wire vertical trellis described. Opinions vary as to the necessity or desirability of this crossarm. However, most agree that the crossarm should be installed for vigorous cultivars.

Crossarms are used principally for additional foliage support in high- to exceptional-vigor vines. They also serve to guide and support most of the shoots upright. This helps minimize spur breakage and foliage interference during harvest. Much of the foliage can be retained beyond harvest because of its position within and above the crossarm, thus escaping harvester contact.

The width of the crossarm is determined by vine vigor and the choice of mechanical harvester. For vigorous vines, use of up to a 36-in. (91-cm) crossarm width is recommended, whereas a 24- to 30-in. (61- to 76-cm) crossarm will suffice for most others. The harvester to be used must accommodate the crossarm width and design. The distance between the fruiting wire and the crossarm is a compromise between maximum foliage support, accessibility of harvester rods, and the anticipated increase in spur height.

Crossarm brace interference should be avoided when attaching crossarms. Braces should be attached from the stake top where excessive stake length is available above the crossarm. Several types of steel straps or brackets are commercially available for nailing on wooden crossarms. There are also prefabricated steel or plastic crossarms that do not require traditional bracing and wiring.

System 3. Consists of a 6-ft (1.8-m) stake, two-wire vertical system. This system can be used for low- to moderate-vigor vineyards, spur-pruned wine cultivars, or cane-pruned raisin cultivars. The lower cordon or cane wire should be at 40 to 46 in. (103 to 117 cm). The second or overhead foliage support wire is attached to the top of the stake. The distance between the two wires should be 12 to 14 in. (31 to 36 cm) under average conditions and 10 to 12 in. (25 to 31 cm) in windy areas. The top wire is especially important in catching and supporting upright shoots to prevent cordon twisting in young vines. For this reason it should be installed before training the vines.

System 4. Consists of a 6-ft (1.8-m) stake, one-wire vertical system. This trellis is used primarily for the cane-pruned 'Thompson Seedless' cultivar for raisin production. A single wire is attached to the top of the stake, usually 52 to 54 in. (132 to 137 cm) from the ground.

Table grape trellis designs. Trellis systems for table grapes generally require a crossarm attachment to a 6- or 7-ft (1.8- to 2.1-m) stake. This system is very common on cordon-trained spur-pruned table grape cultivars. For cane-pruned table cultivars, some growers use a 36- to 42-in. (91- to 107-cm) crossarm and tie fruiting canes directly onto the attached wires. Others go to a more elaborate system employing two crossarms and a cordon wire. The cordon wire is attached to the 7-ft (2.1-m) stake 42 in. (107 cm) above ground. An 18- to 24-in. (46- to 61-cm) crossarm is placed 12 to 14 in. (31 to 36 cm) above the wire with another 36- to 42-in. (91- to 107-cm) crossarm being placed about 12 in. (31 cm) above the first crossarm. For those cultivars requiring a great deal of handwork, such as girdling, thinning, leaf pulling, and so on, this system works well. It also facilitates hand harvesting by causing fruit clusters to hang separately (Christensen et al., 1973).

Posts. Posts serve two functions. The intermediate or line posts provide vertical support for the trellis wires. Although the end posts support the wire too, their main purpose is to provide anchor points for tightening and maintaining wire tension.

Cost per year of service is the basis on which posts should be selected; therefore, they should be strong and either naturally durable or treated with chemical preservatives. Steel or reinforced concrete posts may be satisfactory but are not as commonly used as wooden posts. Wooden posts that have been correctly commercially pressure treated with preservatives should last well over 20 years.

Farm-cut posts from some native tree species can also be used successfully in vineyards, but most species require preservative treatment to be economically competitive with good commercially treated posts. Nondurable species such as ash, maple, elm, larch, and pine may give a post life of 5 years or less without treatment. The use of these is uneconomical, because of frequent installation costs, even if the posts are considered free. Even normally rot-resistant tree species such as red or white cedar and black locust may fail in 7 to 10 years if fast-growing trees with little heartwood are used.

Line Posts. Line posts should be 8 ft (2.4 m) long with a minimum top diameter of approximately 3 in. (7.6 cm). They should be driven or set 24 to 30 in.

(61 to 76 cm) in the ground, depending on the trellis height desired. Tractor-powered posthole augers and post drivers are used for installing posts. Line posts are usually spaced so that there are three or four vines between posts; the exact distance between posts varies, depending on vine spacing, but should not exceed 24 ft (7.3 m) if excessive sagging of the crop-supporting or cordon wire is to be avoided.

End Structures.   End structures should not move when the trellis is subjected to the stress of large crops, wind, and wire contraction in cold weather. If movement occurs, the result will be crooked trunks, sagging cordons, less-efficient mechanical harvest, and the need for retensioning trellis wires. Therefore, end posts should be larger than line posts and preferably longer, so that they can be set 3 to 4 ft (0.9 to 1.2 m) in the ground, and should be anchored or braced. Eight-foot, round, pressure-treated posts with a top diameter of 4 in. (10 cm) have been satisfactory for single-curtain-trained vines when secured to an external anchor. However, if Geneva double-curtain training is a possibility, larger posts are advised.

The stability of an end post is increased by driving or setting the post so that the aboveground part is angled away from the vineyard at about 30° from the vertical, reducing the height of the top wire at the end post, and bracing or, preferably, anchoring it. A common method of bracing uses an extra line post to extend obliquely from a point midway up the end post to the base of the first line post. The outside angle formed by the end post and the brace should be at least 135° to avoid a lever effect, which may lift the end post from the ground when the top trellis wire is tightened. The brace should be spiked or otherwise secured in place, or mechanical harvesting is likely to dislodge it. Braces are advantageous if headland is limited, but will sometimes interfere with mechanical-harvester collector plates.

Anchors are generally superior to bracing, even though they are susceptible to damage by equipment. There are many types of anchors: screw-in anchors, a metal plate welded to a steel shank, and a concrete dead-man attached to a steel shank or heavy wire are all common. Buried railroad ties and old gas or oil line pipe have also been used successfully. Screw anchors 4 to 6 in. (10 to 15 cm) in diameter are the most popular and, with a simple adapter, can be screwed in with tractor-mounted posthole augering equipment in most soils. Anchors that require augering holes or ditching should be installed before the ground freezes in the fall. The soil is permitted to settle and pack before the connecting guy wire, cable, or rod is attached to the post, and the trellis wire is tensioned the following spring.

The anchor should be installed 4 ft (1.2 m) away from the base of the post. With straight vertical end posts it should be placed at about a 45° angle toward the end post and aligned with the row, to minimize interference with equipment entering and leaving. The holding resistance of the anchors will vary by type, size, depth, soil type, and other factors. A minimum depth of 4 ft (1.2 m) should be the goal and has generally been adequate.

Wire.   The most generally used crop-support wire has been No. 9 (steel wire gauge) black annealed wire. However, the increased use of Geneva double-curtain training and other cordon training systems, as well as the need to reduce labor, require a more-durable wire. The wire must retain its tension without annual tightening, provided that the end structures do not move. A No. 11, crimped, high-tensile (210,000 psi) steel wire, with class III galvanizing, meets this need most economically. The larger No. 10 wire of the same type is also available and widely used, but No. 11 is adequate.

The lower wire on the trellis is an aid in maintaining straight trunks, tying up trunk renewal canes and shoots, and securing (tying) the ends of canes to enhance cane distribution on the trellis. The stress on this wire is much less than on the crop-supporting wires; so it can be of lower tensile strength and cost. No. 9 black annealed wire is satisfactory for the lower wire; however, uncrimped (straight) No. 11 or 12 galvanized fence wire is more durable and is recommended because it reduces wire chafing on 1- to 3-year-old trunks.

The weight of wire needed for an acre depends on wire size, row number, row spacing, and the amount of waste. For a 9-ft (2.8-m) row spacing approximately 4900 ft (1495 m) of wire is needed per acre for each trellis wire. Thus a two-wire trellis will require about 9800 ft (2990 m) of wire.

The weight of wire of various sizes required for one strand per acre is given in Table 10–10.

Wire Installation. The high-tensile No. 11 or 10 crimped crop-support wire should be installed 5 ½ to 6 ft (1.7 to 1.8 m) above the vineyard floor. For nondivided training systems on well-drained soils where heaving of posts is unlikely, this wire can be stapled loosely to the top of the line posts with 1 ¼ to 1 ½-in. (32- to 38-mm) fence staples. On poorly drained soils, alternate freezing and thawing usually causes heaving, which necessitates periodic repounding of the posts. Here wire can be stapled in a groove in the top of the post or should be stapled loosely to the windward side and 2 to 3 in. (51 to 76 mm) below the top of each line post with 1 ½ to 1 ¾-in. (38- to 45-mm) fence staples. Staples should be driven into the posts far enough to hold the wire close but not so tight as to prevent drawing the wire through the staples for tensioning or retensioning, in the event that end structures move or the wire stretches. The lowest wire of a nondivided trellis is similarly stapled to the line posts at a height of 30 to 36 in. (76 to 91 cm) from the vineyard floor. If there is a third wire, it is typically located midway between these two.

For Geneva double-curtain (GDC) training, the two cordon and crop-support

TABLE 10-10 DESCRIPTION OF GAUGES OF WIRE TYPICALLY USED IN TRELLIS CONSTRUCTION

WIRE GAUGE NO.	APPROX. FT/100 LB	APPROX. LB/ACRE FOR ONE WIRE WITH 9-FT ROWS
12 straight	3436	143
11 straight	2632	186
11 crimped	2584	190
10 straight	2079	236
10 crimped	2000	245
9 straight	1730	283
8 straight	1443	340

Source: Jordan et al. (1981).

Culture

wires are attached at the ends of the supporting arms by metal clips, hooks, or chain links, depending on arm design. First, however, the arms should be secured to the line posts at a height that will position the taut wires 6 ft (1.8 m) above the vineyard floor. A lower wire height will reduce training and pruning options and result in machinery damage to cordons and vertical arms. A higher wire will reduce the harvesting efficiency of current mechanical harvesters. The trunk-support wire should be loosely stapled to the line posts, either just above or just below the point of arm attachment. Vine trunk training for efficient pruning mechanization and vertical movement of the arms during mechanical harvesting requires this high trunk-support wire (Jordan et al., 1981).

Pruning

Pruning refers to removal of canes, shoots, and other vegetative parts with the object of (1) establishing and maintaining the vine in desired shape and form, (2) distributing the bearing units over the vine for economic production, (3) controlling the crop, and (4) concentrating the growth of the vine into its permanent arms and bearing units. A vine can properly nourish and ripen only a certain number of clusters and canes. Pruning is done according to the capacity of the vine (potential for bearing a crop) and its vigor (rate of growth).

Terminology of pruning. The following terminology of parts of a vine in relation to training and pruning should be familiarized (Winkler et al., 1974; Weaver, 1976; Jordan et al., 1981).

Arms: the main branches of the trunk.

Base bud: a bud in the axil of a bract at the base of a cane that is not borne at a clearly defined node on the cane. Shoots that arise from these buds are often unfruitful.

Base shoot (also referred to as a *watersprout*): a shoot from a bud at the base of a cane or previously removed shoot or cane. It may be found on trunks, cordons, arms, and at the base of canes. It is often extraneous and, unless needed for renewal or fruiting, should be removed during the process commonly referred to as 'suckering'.

Bud: a compressed shoot. In the axil of each leaf is the compound bud or eye containing the primary, secondary, and tertiary buds.

Cane: the lignified, brown mature shoot that has become woody.

Canopy: the entire shoot-leaf complex of the vine; it can be defined in terms of its height, width, and division.

Capacity: the quantity of total growth and total crop of which the vine or part of the vine is capable of producing.

Cordon: extension(s) of a trunk, usually horizontally oriented and trained along a wire. Fully developed cordons can bear arms, spurs, base shoots, and canes. The cordon can be unilateral or bilateral (i.e., it can extend from the trunk in either one or two directions, respectively).

Curtain: a length of canopy that may be shoot positioned. The curtain can constitute a portion of the canopy as for Geneva double-curtain training, or can be synonymous with the canopy as for nondivided cordon-training systems (single curtain).

Fruiting spur: the basal portion of a cane normally pruned to one to two buds.

Head: the top of the trunk and short upper arms.

Internode: the portion of a cane or shoot between nodes.

Laterals: the side branches of a shoot or cane.

Node: the thickened part of the shoot or cane where the leaf and its compound bud are attached.

Renewal spur: a cane cut back to one to two buds at a place on the arm close to the spur which will be replaced, or where the growth of shoots for a fruiting cane for the subsequent year is desired.

Shoot: the leafy growth (leaves and stem) developing from the bud in spring.

Spur: a cane pruned to one to four nodes.

Sucker: a shoot from a bud below ground.

Trunk: the main unbranched stem of the grapevine.

Vigor: rate of growth, quality, or condition that is expressed by parts of the vine.

Vine size: often expressed as the weight of cane prunings on a vine.

Watersprouts: shoots arising from buds on the trunk.

Aspects of pruning. Pruning is simply the act of removing unwanted parts of the vine. The objective of pruning is to produce the maximum yield of good-quality mature grapes while maintaining adequate vine size, vigor, and fruiting wood quality for the following year. In many cases, this involves removing 70 to 90% of last year's vine growth during the winter pruning operation. Proper pruning of the vine in the dormant season is essential in matching cropping level to vine vigor (size). Careful selection of high-quality canes and the retention of proper bud numbers directly influences yield, fruit quality, vine vigor, and bud and trunk hardiness. There are two basic aspects of pruning. The first of these is vine shaping. This involves pruning so that the vine can be arranged on the trellis to facilitate maximum exposure of the leaves to light, and to aid in other operations, such as insect and disease control, cultivation, and harvesting. The second aspect of pruning is used in crop regulation, which controls not only size, but to a large extent the quality of the crop.

Bud quality, number, and distribution. When selecting the best possible canes and buds to be retained after pruning, one should consider bud quality, bud number, and bud distribution. Bud quality of the dormant canes is determined by the sunlight exposure of the leaves that subtended those buds the previous summer. Leaves originating from shoots on the outer layer of the canopy intercept most of the light striking the vine. Those buds that occupied the best light-exposure position are the most fruitful, so the best fruiting canes should be selected from the outside of the canopy (the top and sides of the trellis). Unless the vine was shoot positioned, interior canes are inferior because they were partially or completely shaded by the leaves of shoots growing outside or above them. In addition to having the highest fruiting potential, these 'sun canes' also mature earlier and more completely than canes in the interior of the canopy, making their buds somewhat more winter hardy.

The best-quality canes also have darker cane color and thicker diameter. In general, normal canes with the largest diameters have the greatest fruitfulness. Very large 'bull canes', which made excessive growth the previous summer, are usually not fruitful. However, if they have well-developed lateral branches, fruitful buds can be retained on these laterals.

In regard to cold hardiness, observations suggest that the largest canes of cold tender cultivars are more susceptible to winter injury than medium-sized canes. As a general rule, wood that is pencil sized in diameter is a good choice for selecting buds with maximum winter hardiness. When comparing canes of the same cultivar, diameter, and color, the shorter or medium-sized internode lengths have higher-quality buds. The internode length is a direct reflection of good or poor sunlight exposure during the previous growing season. This same effect is seen in the long spindly growth of house plants that are kept in low-light conditions. Howell et al. (1978) found that certain cultural practices (including balanced pruning to 30 + 10) which favored vine size maintenance and consistent production of ripe fruit also favored cold hardiness of the primary bud of 'Concord'.

The number of buds retained at pruning will be determined by vine size and vigor as evidenced by the weight of 1-year-old canes on the vine and by the cultivar. In balanced pruning, the grower is striving for maximum yields of acceptable quality fruit without a reduction in cane maturity, vine vigor, or winter hardiness in succeeding years. In pruning, it is important to be looking ahead at least 2 years.

The final consideration in effective pruning is bud distribution. It is important to provide a systematic and uniform distribution of the fruiting wood which we retain. This is of primary importance in maximizing light exposure on the developing shoots as well as affecting fruit and vine maturity, insect and disease control, and harvesting. The goal is to distribute the buds uniformly so as to occupy as much of the trellis space allotted for each vine as possible. Various training systems contribute to the distribution of buds, with each having its own advantages and disadvantages.

Balanced pruning. A system called *balanced pruning* relates the capacity of the vine to bear fruit with the number of count nodes (buds) to be retained on canes and spurs on the vine. Vines pruned in this manner are called balanced because the process of economic importance to the grower (fruit yield and quality) is in balance with the process of biological importance to the vine (shoot and root growth and carbohydrate storage in the plant). Balanced pruning involves removing a portion of a vine and leaving a calculated number of buds for fruit based on the amount of 1-year-old wood produced during the previous growing season.

Under vineyard conditions this is accomplished by leaving buds slightly in excess of the estimated final number on the vine while all other 1-year-old wood is cut into manageable lengths and bundled for weighing. It is important to note that no 2-year or older wood is included in the calculation, so 1-year-old canes must be weighed separate from all other prunings. The bundle of canes is weighed with a small hand scale to determine how many pounds of wood were produced by the vine during the previous growing season. For example, using the 30 + 10 system, a bundle weighing 3 lb (1.4 kg) would indicate the need to leave a total of 50 buds for fruit production the next season. Thirty buds are retained for the first pound of prunings plus 10 additional buds for the second and third pounds, for a total of 50 buds. For example, if a vine were estimated to have 2 lb (0.9 kg) of prunings, it would require 40 buds. Seventy-five buds might be left on the vine and the rest pruned off. If in this instance the canes actually weighed 2 lb (0.9 kg), the pruner would remove 35 of 75 buds remaining on the vine, leaving a total of 40. If, however, the canes weighed 3 ½ lb (1.6 kg), 55 buds would be retained. Table 10–11 shows the recommended pruning formulas for mature vines at standard spacings. In Washington, where high light intensities prevail, a pruning formula of 50 plus 10 with a maximum of 90 buds is typically used.

The average grapevine may have 200 to 300 buds on mature canes capable of producing fruit. Typically, only 40 or 50 buds may be left for fruiting, as dictated by the balanced pruning formula. Pruning too lightly (leaving too many buds) will lead to excessive shoot numbers, shading and poor shoot development, excessive crop levels, and reduced fruit quality, soluble solids, winter hardiness, and vine vigor. On the other hand, excessively severe pruning which leaves too few buds is undesirable because it leads to unnecessarily low yields, limited leaf area, excessive shoot vigor, and potential wood maturity and winter hardiness problems along with decreasing vine size.

Overcropping leads to delayed or inadequate fruit maturation, reduced vine size (hence reduced yield potential), and reduced wood maturity. The latter consequence is especially significant in regions where low winter temperatures occur. Although the wood may appear well matured, the starch reserves in crop-stressed vines can be so low that vegetative growth the following season may be severely depressed. Extreme cases of overcropping may produce symptoms such as tendril abortion, lack of continued shoot growth, and possibly poor foliage condition and premature leaf fall. Undercropping has an obvious direct economic disadvantage, but more subtle vine responses are also encountered. As the crop is reduced below vine capacity, vegetative development is enhanced. Excessive vegetative development leads to intracanopy shading, which further reduces vine productivity. The combination of shade and prolonged shoot elongation precludes adequate wood maturation (Pool et al., 1978).

Pruning French-American hybrids. In the production of American bunch grapes (*V. labrusca*), the use of dormant-season balanced pruning has proven to be a good method of controlling crop level and maintaining an acceptable fruit quality (°Brix, acidity, etc.). However, for many French-American hybrid grapes, balanced pruning has not resulted in adequate crop control. These hybrids characteristically have high cluster numbers per shoot (three to five), and fruitful secondary shoots, along with additional fruitful shoots which are produced from many base buds that are not counted in the balanced pruning procedure. For these

TABLE 10–11 BALANCED PRUNING FORMULAS FOR MATURE VINES AT STANDARD SPACINGS

GRAPE CULTIVAR	NUMBER OF BUDS RETAINED FOR FIRST POUND OF PRUNINGS		NUMBER OF BUDS RETAINED FOR EACH ADDITIONAL POUND OF PRUNINGS	MAXIMUM NUMBER OF BUDS FOR PLANTS AT 8-FT SPACING
Concord	30	plus	10	60
Fredonia	40	plus	10	70
Niagara, Delaware, Catawba	25	plus	10	60
Ives, Elvira, Dutchess	20	plus	10	50
French hybrids: All of these require severe "sprouting and suckering" during spring and early summer for satisfactory growth, crop, and vine maturity with the formulas suggested below.				
Small-clustered varieties such as Foch and Leon Millot, Baco noir	20	plus	10	50
Medium-clustered varieties such as Vidal blanc, Aurore, Cascade, Chelois	20	plus	10	40
In years of above-average fruit set, these may need cluster thinning; weak vines will need flower-cluster thinning and careful suckering.				
Large-clustered Varieties such as Seyval, Verdelet, Chancellor, Chambourcin, Villard blanc, DeChaunac	20	plus	10	40
These must be supplemented with prebloom thinning to one cluster per shoot and careful suckering.				
Viniferas	20	plus	20	40

Source: Adapted from Jordan et al. (1981).

reasons, overproduction can occur, which results in delayed fruit maturity and reduced °Brix, weight of cane prunings (vine size and vigor), and winter hardiness. Greater pruning severity does not overcome this problem in French-American hybrids, due to the productivity of the base buds. Consequently fruit thinning as discussed below may be required.

Cluster thinning. The need for additional crop reduction to achieve a balance between growth and fruiting is best achieved by cluster thinning. Grower acceptance of this practice has been hindered by the additional labor expense involved. The time required to cluster-thin 1 acre of grapes by hand ranges from 20 to 40 hours (50 to 100 hours per hectare) depending on cultivar, planting scheme, trellising, and timing of the thinning operation. Experimental work using growth regulators such as ethephon and gibberellic acid has been promising, but is not currently recommended (Considine, 1982; Szyjewicz et al., 1984).

The French hybrids will set fruit even in their first and second years in the vineyard. Young vines are severely stunted by a fruit load, making it important to remove all fruit in the first 2 years after planting. In the third year, one bunch may be left on each of the stronger shoots if the vine has made good growth and has reached the top wire.

Several researchers have reported that reducing leaf area may adversely affect fruit quality. Conversely, increasing the leaf area-to-cluster ratio by cluster thinning may improve quality. The maximum effects of cluster thinning are achieved by thinning before bloom (flower-cluster thinning) as opposed to thinning after fruit set. If thinning is done before set, carbohydrates are conserved and made available to the remaining clusters to form a greater number of fully developed flowers, and therefore set more berries.

Cluster thinning of French hybrids does not generally significantly reduce yield. Looney and Wood (1977) reported that thinning 'de Chaunac' to one cluster per shoot reduced yield, whereas thinning to two clusters did not. Looney (1981) observed that thinned 'de Chaunac' vines actually produced more fruit than non-thinned vines during the first 2 years of a 3-year study. Cahoon (1979) found that 'Villard noir' vines thinned to one cluster per shoot did not show increases in yield until the third year of the study.

It has been demonstrated that cluster thinning results in increased cluster weight and berry weight. In a 3-year study, Looney (1981) observed that cluster weight and berry weight increased the first 2 years, but cluster weight was reduced and berry weight was not affected the third year. Looney and Wood (1977) noted that cluster thinning increased berry weight the first year, but not the second year of a 2-year study.

Most researchers report an increase in soluble solids at harvest due to cluster thinning. Over a 3-year period, Looney (1981) observed an increase in soluble solids during the first and third years, but not the second year. Wolpert et al. (1983) found that cluster thinning 'Vidal blanc' resulted in higher weight and soluble solids/acid ratio for clusters from thinned vines.

Experiments in Canada have shown the benefit of cluster thinning mature French hybrid grape vines. Cluster thinning of 'de Chaunac' vines to one cluster per

Culture

shoot over a 15-year period produced no significant differences in the mean annual yield of thinned and unthinned vines. The mean yield was 20.9 lb (8.6 kg) per vine for thinned vines and 19.4 lb (8.8 kg) for unthinned vines. The total number of clusters produced on these balanced pruned vines was 183 and 116 clusters per vine, and 7.5 and 5.0 clusters per count bud for thinned and unthinned vines, respectively. Additional compensation by the vine is evidenced by the mean cluster weight of 251 g for thinned and 184 g for unthinned vines. This increase in cluster weight was due almost entirely to an increase in the number of berries per cluster from 112 for unthinned, to 153 for thinned vines. Desirably higher sugar levels were also achieved with thinned fruit averaging 17.3° Brix, while unthinned averaged only 15.6° Brix. Additionally, cluster thinning increased the vegetative vigor of the vines, as evidenced by a mean increase in pruning weight per vine from 1.7 lb (0.78 kg) for unthinned to 2.9 lb (1.3 kg) for thinned vines (Fisher et al., 1977).

In general, most grape cultivars respond to cluster thinning. The goal of cluster thinning is to achieve a proper balance between leaf area and fruit yield. The removal of excessive clusters generally results in a better berry set on the remaining clusters. These remaining clusters will frequently be larger in size and, therefore, may compensate for the reduced number of clusters, causing total yield to remain stable. The increased berry size and/or number accounts for the increased weight of thinned clusters.

Timing can be critical in cluster thinning. If thinning occurs too early prior to fruit set, there may be an increase in the number of berries per cluster. In loose-clustered cultivars this increase may not be a problem, but in tight-clustered cultivars bunch rot could be aggravated. If thinning occurs too late, the only net effect may be to reduce the crop with little or no effect on fruit quality or winter hardiness.

Pruning severity. With the French-American hybrid 'Baco noir', as pruning severities increased and the number of buds on the vine decreased, vine size, petiole nitrogen, fruitfulness per node, and the number of clusters per node increased. However, yield, number of clusters per vine, and total sugar were reduced. Although increased pruning severity advanced maturity and produced more favorable extract, pH, and color, taste panel preference was lowered (Byrne and Howell, 1978). They tentatively concluded that 'Baco noir' should be balance pruned to 50 + 10 nodes per vine in Michigan, which would increase yield, maintain constant vine size, not delay fruit maturity or decrease wine quality, and accelerate acclimation while only slightly reducing the maximum hardiness level. In another Michigan study, 'Vidal blanc' vines were pruned to 10, 15, and 20 nodes per pound of prunings. All vines were thinned to the basal cluster and all noncount clusters were removed. In the last year of the study a thinned and nonthinned set of treatments were superimposed on the other variables. Decreasing the pruning severity decreased soluble solids by up to 1.4%. Basal clusters from thinned vines were heavier than basal clusters from nonthinned vines. Soluble solids did not differ between the thinning treatments. Grapes from thinned vines were lower in acidity and higher in pH (which was considered advantageous in Michigan) than grapes from nonthinned vines (Wolpert et al., 1983).

In Arkansas, Morris et al. (1984b) examined the effects of balance pruning to

10 + 10 and 20 + 10 nodes per vine on six French-American hybrid cultivars: 'Chelois', 'Seyval', 'Villard noir', 'Chancellor', 'Verdelet', and 'Aurore'. There were no differences between the two pruning severities in yield, pruning weight, or grape quality. The authors concluded that the lack of difference was probably due to the productivity of noncount nodes. No differences occurred between two-node or four-node spurs in yield, pruning weight, or quality parameters (Spayd, 1985).

Work in Canada by Bradt (1965) indicated that the French hybrid cultivar 'Chelois' produced the best yields at 30 + 8 nodes per vine when compared to 15 + 4 nodes per vine. 'Verdelet' was also shown to have the same yield increase at the lower pruning level. Bradt (1964) reported that for 'Chelois' and 'Verdelet', thinning increased yields over unthinned vines. The French hybrid cultivar 'de Chaunac' was shown to produce the highest yields under a 30 + 8 pruning level compared to a 15 + 4 level.

General management guidelines for hybrids. It is difficult to give specific recommendations for pruning all French-American hybrid cultivars, but the following are good general principles. Use a 20 plus 10 balanced pruning formula with a maximum of 40 or 50 buds, depending on cultivar. Make several trips through the vineyard in the spring and early summer to remove all shoots that develop from adventitious noncount buds. In addition to the suckering operation, prebloom flower cluster thinning may also be required to prevent overbearing and to obtain high-quality fruit. The use of long-cane pruning and training systems (e.g., umbrella Kniffin), as opposed to spur-pruned cordon systems, may also help to reduce the number of noncount shoots that develop from adventitious and base buds.

Pruning *vinifera* cultivars. Pruning techniques and recommendations can vary dramatically from one climatic and geographical region to another. The pruning methods used in Germany, France, or South Africa will show a great range of variation, as will the differences in management found within a single state, such as California or New York. The reader is directed to the suggested reading section at the end of this chapter for additional sources of information on this topic.

Systems of pruning *vinifera* cultivars. There are several systems of pruning, each suited to a certain situation or cultivar (Table 10–12).

Spur Pruning (Short Pruning). In spur pruning *V. vinifera* cultivars, short spurs, usually with two to four buds, are retained as fruiting units. The number of buds left on the spur depends on the thickness of the spur and the vigor of the vine. On spurs with the diameter of a pencil (1/4 in., 64 mm), one bud is retained. On larger spurs, two, three, or four buds may be retained, depending on the vine vigor. Buds within 1/4 to 1/2 in. (64 to 130 mm) of the base of the cane usually are not counted. Spur pruning is suited to head and cordon systems of training. Spurs are spaced 9 to 12 in. (23 to 31 cm) apart on the cordon. The total number of buds allowed per vine depends on the cultivar, vigor of the vine, and cropping level, and varies between 35 and 75 buds.

Culture

CULTIVAR	TRAINING		PRUNING		
	Cordon	Head	Buds/Spur	Cane	Buds/Vine
White Cultivars					
Burger	×	×	2		20–24
Carnelian	×		2–3		24–48
Chardonnay	×	×	2	×	40–50
Chenin blanc	×		2		24–28
Emerald Riesling	×		2–3		24–42
Flora	×	×	2		10–28
French Columbard	×		2–3		20–42
Gamay	×	×	2		16–24
Gewurztraminer		×			40–50
Gray Riesling	×		2–3		24–48
Muscat Canelli	×		1–3		50–60
Muscat of Alexandria	×		2		20–32
Palomino	×		2		28–48
Saint Emilion	×		2–3		28–48
Sauvignon blanc		×		×	50–60
Semillon	×		2		16–28
Sylvaner	×		2		28–48
White Riesling	×	×	2	×	40–50
Red and Black Cultivars					
Alicante Bouschet	×		2–3		24–42
Barbera	×		2–3	×	24–48
Cabernet Sauvignon	×	×	2–3	×	40–72
Carignane	×		2–3		24–48
Grenache	×	×	2–4		28–54
Merlot		×		×	40–50
Mission	×	×	2–3		36–60
Petite Sirah	×		2		14–36
Pinot noir		×			40–50
Royalty	×		2		24–48
Rubired	×		2–3		28–48
Ruby Cabernet	×		2		20–42
Salvador	×	×	1–3	×	18–72
Tinta Madeira	×		2–3		24–42
Zinfandel	×		2		14–20

Cane Pruning (Long Pruning).   In cane pruning of *V. vinifera* cultivars,
canes having 8 to 20 buds are retained as fruiting units. The number of canes ranges
from two to six, depending on the cultivar and the purpose for which grapes are
grown (e.g., wine, table, raisin). This method is suitable for cultivars that have
unfruitful buds at the base of the cane or have small clusters. For every fruiting cane
retained, a one- or two-bud renewal spur should also be left. The fruiting canes are
pruned after the crop is harvested. Next year's canes develop from the renewal spurs.
The canes retained for fruiting should be of medium vigor and bear plump, vigorous
buds.

Summer pruning.　Pruning vegetative parts of the vine during the growing season is referred to as summer pruning. Removal of water sprouts and suckers from the trunk (suckering), arms, and main branches (crown suckering) is practiced to a limited extent. Removal of leaves around the cluster for color enhancement is practiced for table grape cultivars (e.g., 'Tokay' and 'Emperor'). Pinching and topping refers to the removal of the growing tip [3 to 6 in. (7 to 15 cm)]. Removal of several feet of the shoot is sometimes practiced to reduce damage from strong winds. In table grape cultivars such as 'Cardinal' and 'Ribier', which normally bear three clusters to a shoot, the basal cluster is removed (cluster thinning) to allow better development of the remaining clusters.

Means of improving grape quality.　In addition to training and trellising manipulation, fruit quality (color, berry size, cluster compactness, incidence of disease, chemical composition, etc.) can be improved in various situations by specific cultural manipulations. Grape quality is discussed in more detail in Chapter 12. Some of the most common practices include the following:

1. Flower cluster thinning (by hand)
2. Cluster thinning (by hand)
3. Berry thinning (by hand)
4. Chemical thinning [gibberellic acid (GA), ethephon]
5. Girdling (trunk and cane)
6. Growth regulators (ethephon, Alar, GA)
7. Leaf removal
8. Shoot positioning
9. Pruning (summer and dormant)
10. Suckering (hand, mechanical, chemical)

Seedless table grape production practices.　The use of special cultural practices is necessary for the production of quality table grapes. These practices include flower cluster and berry thinning, cluster rachis trimming, deleafing, girdling, and growth regulator application.

Girdling.　This process is the removal of a strip of bark using a double-bladed girdling knife 1/8, 3/16, or 1/4 in. (3, 5, 6 mm) in width for trunks or 3/16 in. (5 mm) for canes. Grapes are girdled at fruit set to increase berry size or at the beginning of the ripening phase to advance maturity. Fruit weights of vines girdled at fruit set, without gibberellin (GA), will increase from 40 to 60% compared to those not girdled, depending on how well the vines were thinned. With GA treatment, berry weight will increase about 20% due to girdling treatment.

Gibberellic Acid.　GA is used in some cultivars either for thinning out the number of flowers which set (a bloom thinning spray), or for increasing the size of the berries (a sizing spray applied about one week after bloom). In some cultivars both a bloom spray and one or two sizing sprays are applied. Not all cultivars

Culture

respond to bloom sprays for thinning and may respond only to GA for increasing berry size. In the case of 'Thompson Seedless' a 10 to 15 ppm GA spray is applied when 50% of the clusters on the vine are showing 50 to 70% of the flowers in bloom. When the developing berries reach a diameter of ³/₁₆ in. (5 mm) a 40 ppm GA sizing spray is applied. This may be followed by a similar sizing spray 5 to 7 days later. Modifications of these timings and concentrations have been developed for other *V. vinifera* cultivars. Guidelines for eastern seedless cultivars suggest a 20 ppm bloom spray and a 50 ppm shatter spray two weeks after bloom.

Ethephon. This chemical is sprayed on some red cultivars to enhance the ripening process and aid in the development of richer, more uniform berry color. For most clutivars this synthetic hormone (Ethrel) is applied at the rate of one pint per acre (2.3 1/ha) when the berries first begin to show a slight change in color.

Canopy microclimate model. Smart et al. (1985) have produced a conceptual model of factors that affect wine quality and yield (Fig. 10–9). Vine and fruit characteristics are basically determined by the genetic makeup of the plant, but fruit composition and wine quality are equally affected by environmental and physiological factors. These factors can be directly influenced by soil, climate, and cultural decisions.

Training Systems

Vinifera **training systems for California**

Head Training. This system has greatly declined in popularity in recent years. A mature well-trained vine under the head system will have four or five equally distributed, short branches or arms supported by a strong trunk. The point at which the trunk divides to form short branches is referred to as the *head*. The height of the trunk varies from 3 to 5 ft (0.9 to 1.5 m). Viewed from above, the head-trained vine will look like the spokes of a wheel. The fruiting units (spurs or canes) are left at the end of each arm. Except for the first 3 to 5 years, when a support stake is needed, head-trained vines do not need support. This method requires the least capital outlay and is economical in cost of pruning. Cross-cultivation is possible. Its main drawbacks are: (1) fruit clusters crowd around the head, often causing more bunch rot than other systems; (2) it requires severe pruning, which has a depressing effect on the vine; (3) it is difficult to establish and maintain; (4) it takes longer to come to production; and (5) it is not suited to mechanical harvesting. This system is suitable for cultivars that produce small to medium-sized clusters from shoots arising from the buds at the base of the cane and where the appearance of the fruit is not of foremost importance. Head-trained vines can be spur- or cane-pruned.

1. *Head-trained spur-pruned.* Spurs should be one to two buds long. More buds should be allowed on vigorous canes from the previous year's growth. On weaker vines producing canes of pencil size or smaller, only one bud per spur should be allowed. Basal buds closer than ¹/₄ in. (6 mm) to the base are not normally counted (Fig. 10–12).

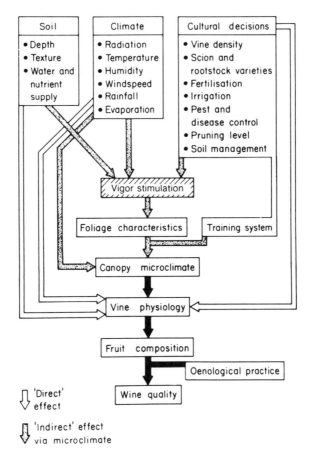

FIGURE 10-9 General model proposing how soil and climate and cultural decisions can affect wine quality via effects on canopy microclimate. (After Smart, 1985 from American Journal of Enology and Viticulture 36:3.)

2. *Head-trained cane-pruned.* Two to three short arms are allowed to develop on each side. Two to four canes (fruiting units) with 8 to 20 buds each are left at pruning time. For each cane a one-bud renewal spur is allowed, which gives rise to a fruiting cane for the next year. Cane pruning allows the vine to set a full crop on small-clustered wine grape cultivars. This system is also used for cultivars that have unfruitful basal buds (e.g., 'Thompson Seedless'). This system is easy to prune, but the cost of tying the canes makes it expensive. There is also a danger of overcropping if too many canes are left at the time of pruning.

Bilateral-Cordon Training: A vertical trunk 4 to 6 ft (1.2 to 1.8 m) in height is allowed to develop into two equal branches (arms) 8 to 12 in. (20 to 31 cm) below the lower trellis wire. These extend in opposite directions along the lower wire

Culture

(bilateral cordon) to within 10 in. (25 cm) of adjacent vines. Cordon-trained vines are spur-pruned.

Cordon-Trained Spur-Pruned. With spur pruning each cordon has equally spaced bearing units (spurs) on its upper side, each bearing one to three buds. No shoots are allowed to develop at the bend (Y) or below it. With cordon training, fruit is distributed evenly on the cordon and therefore develops good color. This system is used for many table and wine grape cultivars. It lends itself to mechanical harvesting. It is difficult to establish during the first 2 to 3 years, but once established is easy to maintain and prune (Winkler et al., 1974).

Vinifera management systems for cold climates. The most common training systems used for *V. vinifera* in cold climates include Keuka high renewal, modified Keuka high renewal, umbrella Kniffin, fan, and Mosel (low umbrella). Typical vine spacing is 9 ft (2.7 m) between rows and 6 to 7 ft (1.8 to 2.1 m) between vines, with ideal vine size being about 2.5 to 3.5 lb (1.1 to 1.6 kg), and desirable yields in the range 2.5 to 4.0 tons/acre (5.6 to 8.1 MT/ha). Vine management is designed to anticipate and compensate for cold injury. The use of multiple trunks and the periodic renewal of trunks which are 4 to 6 years old is essential to vine maintenance. Graft unions are protected by plowing a mound of earth over the base of vines in late fall to insulate the graft union and to protect the renewal zone. Under extreme conditions, canes and even entire vines can be buried to protect them from winter injury. Vines are pruned in the spring after sampling buds for percent mortality and adjusting the bud number accordingly. A 20 + 20 balanced pruning scale is typical for many cultivars (Wolf, 1987).

Training systems for American and French hybrid grapes. Conventional training of eastern grapevines has been to the Kniffin system. Three modifications of this system are in use: the four-arm Kniffin, six-arm Kniffin, and umbrella Kniffin. With the development of new knowledge about the fruiting habit of the grape and the use of the mechanical harvester, other systems have been developed and widely adopted. These include the Geneva double-curtain and single-curtain cordon systems. The selection of the best system depends on the cultivar being grown, type of harvester to be used, condition of the trellis, fertility of the soil, and personal preferences (Figs. 10–10 to 10–13).

Four-Arm Kniffin. This system is characterized by the four short arms from which the fruiting shoots arise. The arms, two on each side of the trunk, are developed from the trunk extensions and renewal spurs, and provide fruiting wood for the following year. All surplus wood is pruned away each year. If the vine can support more than four canes, the canes should be left on the top wires because they will be more productive than those arising lower on the trunk.

Six-Arm Kniffin. This system differs only slightly from the preceding one. It permits more canes to remain on the vine by tying them to each of the three trellis wires. In general, both of these systems tend to standardize the training procedure for routine pruning and handling of the vines.

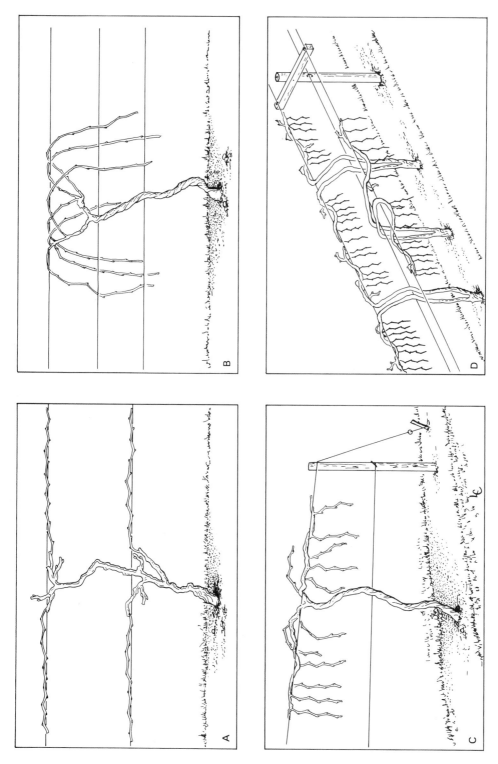

FIGURE 10-10 Common grapevine training systems: (A) four-arm Kniffen; (B) umbrella Kniffen; (C) single-curtain cordon; (D) Geneva double curtain.

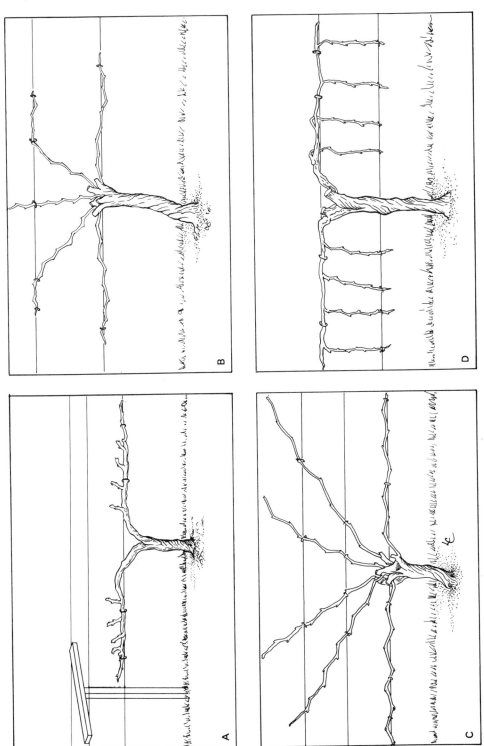

FIGURE 10-11 Common grapevine training systems: (A) low cordon, spur-prune, with crossarms and support wires; (B) modified Keuka high renewal; (C) fan; (D) Hudson River umbrella.

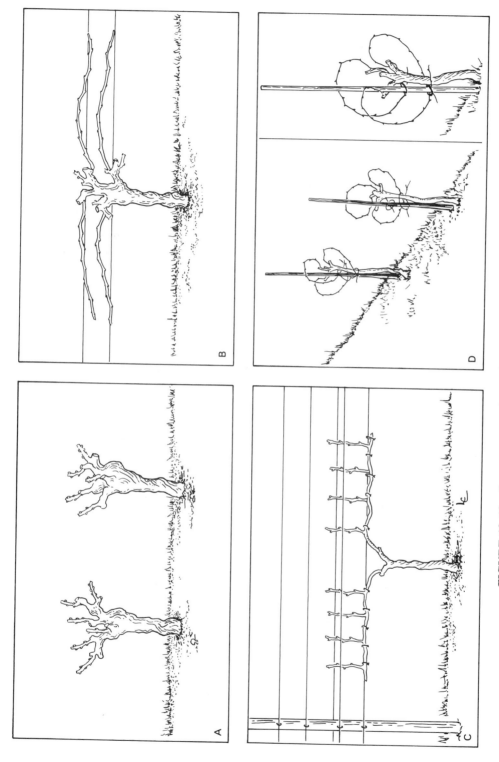

FIGURE 10-12 Common grapevine training systems: (A) head, spur-pruned; (B) head, cane-pruned; (C) low cordon, spur-pruned; (D) pole.

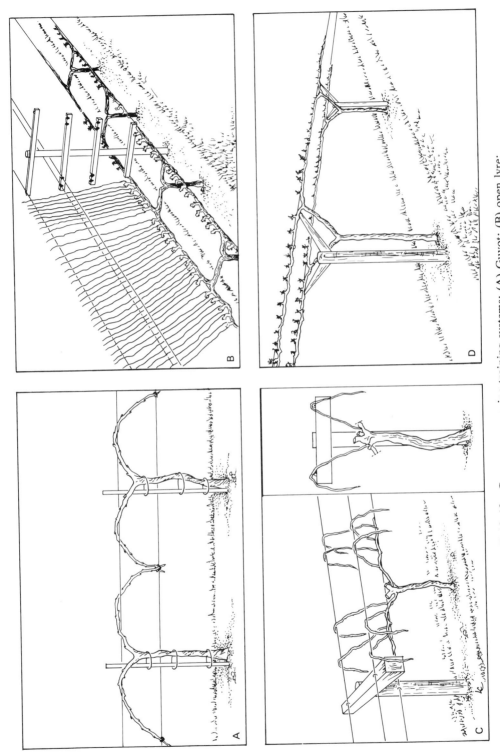

FIGURE 10-13 Common grapevine training systems: (A) Guyot; (B) open lyre; (C) Munson T-bar; (D) double curtain (muscadines).

Umbrella Kniffin. The mature vine trained according to this system consists of a single trunk trained to the top trellis wire, then headed out at this point or from 4 to 5 in. (18 to 23 cm) below the wire. All canes utilized in training originate near the head of the vine near the top wire are allowed to droop down and are tied to the lower wire or wires. With care, the canes are bent rather sharply, just enough so that the outer bark cracks. The purpose of cracking the bark is to induce more vigorous growth from the buds behind the bend rather than allowing growth to develop at the cane tip. Overall fruitfulness is presumably increased. The number of canes will vary from four to six, depending on the size of the vine.

Fan System. In the colder climates where trunk injury is more likely to occur, a multiple-trunk system is still found in some vineyards. In the fan system, three or four trunks are tied to the lower wire, which makes it possible to detach the trunks easily from the trellis for burying in winter for cold protection. Greater labor requirements for tying, untying, burying, and suckering on multiple trunks are the disadvantages of this system.

Geneva Double Curtain (GDC). This system, developed at the New York Agricultural Experiment Station at Geneva represents one of the best methods of training 'Concord' and other cultivars. It is especially adapted to mechanical harvesting and the utilization of high vine vigor. This system can increase vine productive capacity and at the same time maintain or even improve fruit and vine maturation. Better maturation and increased yields are made possible by shoot and leaf positioning, which exposes a greater proportion of the leaf area to sunlight. Vine vigor and the principles involved in balanced pruning are also fundamental concepts of this system (Cahoon and Hill, 1981).

Single-Curtain Cordon. The single-curtain cordon training system is also known by other names, such as Hudson River umbrella, top-wire cordon, bilateral cordon, and the no-tie system. In this system the trunk is extended up to the top wire and horizontal arms are established on the top wire. There may be some variation in the number and lengths of canes, renewal spurs, and the amount of tying required. This system incorporates many of the same pruning and training features as the Geneva double-curtain system, except that it is developed on a standard two- or three-wire trellis and, as the name indicates, has only a single curtain of foliage. The trunk of the single-curtain-cordon-trained vine is attached to the top trellis wire and is approximately 6 ft (1.8 m) in height. Two horizontal cordons are then developed along the top wires and extend 4 ft (1.2 m) in each direction. If the vineyard is converted from one of the Kniffin training systems, 1-year-old canes are positioned along the top wire to develop into cordons in future years. Extra canes should be retained during this transition year to maintain the balanced pruning concept.

Cordons are secured to the top wire by plastic ties or other similar material. Care must be taken to see that the cordon is not girdled by the ties as it increases in size. One advantage of the single-curtain system compared to the Kniffin systems is a reduction in tying time.

Like the Geneva double-curtain system, five-bud canes are selected from the cordon, plus adequate single-bud renewal spurs. Shoots are later positioned downward for maximum exposure to sunlight during the growing season and also to facilitate the pruning operations.

This system is suitable for low- to moderate-vigor vineyards. For high-vigor vineyards, the Geneva double-curtain system is recommended because it allows essentially twice the amount of surface area per vine as the single-curtain system, 8 ft (2.4 m) per cordon as compared to 4 ft (1.2 m). Modifications of this system are known by other names. The Hudson River umbrella system, for example, utilizes long canes (8 to 12 buds instead of 5 buds) which are tied to the bottom wire.

Training French-American hybrids. There is a wide variety of systems currently in use for training French-American hybrid cultivars, most of which are similar to those used for American types. Once again, the personal preference of the grower, cultivar, soil and climate conditions, and desired quality characteristics will influence the choice of system. Wolpert et al. (1983) found that training 'Vidal blanc' to a top-wire bilateral cordon, bottom-wire bilateral cordon, high-head umbrella Kniffin, or low-head Keuka high renewal produced no differences on measured parameters. In this case, no significant differences were noted in cluster weight, soluble solids, acidity, or juice pH in response to training system.

In a study of six French-American cultivars, Morris et al. (1984b) reported that all cultivars had higher yields on the Geneva double-curtain training system [9.7 tons/acre (21.7 MT/ha)] than on the single-wire, bilateral cordon system [8.3 tons/acre (18.5 MT/ha)]. The training system had no effect on pH or acidity, but the GDC training system produced a lower percentage of soluble solids (16.8 versus 17.4) compared to single-wire cordon.

Reynolds et al. (1985) examined the effect of seven different training systems on growth, yield, fruit composition, and wine quality of 'Seyval'. They suggested that some sacrifice in quality must be made to obtain high yields consistently. Maintaining high trunks and/or large amounts of perennial wood, as in the case of six-arm Kniffin, umbrella Kniffin, Hudson River umbrella, and midwire cordon, led to the greatest growth and yield. Increasing trunk height also led consistently to better fruit exposure, lower acidity, and higher pH. Unfortunately, the large yields of the high-trained systems led to lower sugar levels. They found that the highest sugar levels (°Brix) could be obtained on low-trunk systems such as Pendelbogen, modified Keuka high renewal, and Moselle. However, these systems produce lower yields, and their poor fruit exposure leads to higher acidity.

Shoot Positioning. Shoot positioning is a practice for increasing the light exposure of leaves on the basal portion of shoots originating from the cordons of top-wire cordon-trained vines. This enhanced light exposure of the renewal area increases bud fruitfulness, improves fruit set, and promotes crop and shoot maturation.

Shoot positioning is particularly useful with large vines of cultivars that have large leaves and a drooping-shoot growth habit, such as 'Concord' and 'Niagara'. Shoot positioning has also been used successfully with vigorous 'Catawba', 'Delaware', 'De Chaunac', 'Marechal Foch', 'Seyval', and other top-wire cordon-trained cultivars. It is considered essential for Geneva double-curtain training.

The shoot-positioning procedure is as follows. (1) During the 4-week period beginning with grape bloom, all vigorous horizontally growing shoots are placed in a vertically downward position so that the light exposure of leaves at the basal four to six nodes of fruiting and renewal shoots will be improved. (2) For Geneva double curtain, all vigorous shoots growing into the center area between the cordons must also be pulled down to maintain two separate curtains of foliage and permit light penetration to their inner sides. Although shoots can be positioned so that more than four to six nodes have an enhanced light environment, this excessive positioning should be avoided since it will result in a loss of vine size and hence capacity for high production.

The earlier shoot positioning is accomplished after the bloom to early post-bloom period, the greater its effect on fruit-bud initiation and development. Shoot positioning during bloom is not harmful; however, shoot positioning significantly earlier than the start of bloom usually results in excessive shoot breakage, and the effect on shoot direction may be negligible. Maximum benefit from shoot positioning with minimum cost is most likely with an early start and more than one trip through the vineyard. Depending on vine size and vigor, plus timing, shoot positioning may require from 20 to 30 hours per acre (50 to 75 hours per hectare). However, substantial mechanization of this procedure has been commercially accomplished (Jordan et al., 1981).

Harvest Parameters

Berry size normally increases across the growing season until the fruit reaches the optimum maturity for its intended use. Changes in berry size during ripening will influence yield. If the fruit is allowed to remain on the vine beyond optimum maturity, berry splitting or decreases in berry size due to shriveling may occur. The changes in 'Concord' fruit composition across the growing season are illustrated in Fig. 10–14. The sugar content of grapes increases with advancing harvest date or maturity, with glucose and fructose being the predominant sugars present at maturity.

The primary acids found in grapes are tartaric and malic. The percent acidity of grapes decreases during maturation. However, if the individual acids are considered on a per berry basis, it is evident that the malic acid content decreases during ripening, while the tartaric acid content remains more stable. The pH of grapes increases during maturation.

In wine, pH plays an important role in the occurrence of malo-lactic fermentation, prevention of microbial spoilage, sourness of taste, stability of soluble grape proteins, solubility of potassium bitartrate and calcium tartrate, color of red wines, and the addition of SO_2. For these reasons, Amerine and Ough (1974) have established an upper limit for pH in wines. Wines with a pH above 3.60 are potentially unstable. Furthermore, adjustments in pH are more difficult to make than the amelioration of sugar content. Adjustments in the other important grape quality parameters are easier than adjusting for high pH. Some adjustment of the sugar or acid content, or the pH of the crushed berries and juice (must) in the winery, is a

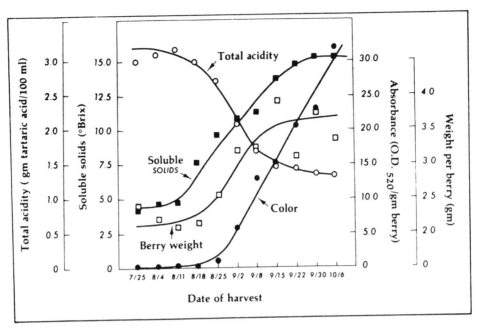

FIGURE 10-14 Changes in Concord fruit composition and berry weight during a growing season. (From R. Kluba in Jordan et al © 1981.)

common practice. Figure 10-15 shows grapes being run through a stemmer-crusher at a small winery.

Amerine et al. (1980) established ranges in degrees Brix, percent acidity, and pH in musts for making the various types of wine in California. They recommend that musts used for the production of white table wines should have a degree Brix reading between 19.5 and 23.0, the percent acidity should be greater than 0.70, and the pH should be less than 3.3. For the production of red table wines in California, it is recommended that the degree Brix reading be between 20.5 and 23.5, the percent acidity be greater than 0.65, and the pH be less than 3.4.

The yield and quality of 82 cultivars were studied from 1964 to 1973 in Washington (Clore et al., 1976). The French-American hybrids included in the study had percent soluble solids that ranged from 19.4 to 24.8, percent acidity ranging from 0.42 to 1.28, and pH ranging from 3.0 to 4.0. The *V. vinifera* cultivars had percent soluble solids ranging from 15.6 to 27.5, percent acidity ranging from 0.42 to 1.51, and pH ranging from 3.0 to 3.9.

Seventy-eight cultivars were evaluated in Ohio during the 1971 to 1975 seasons for must and wine quality (Gallander and Stetson, 1977). The French hybrid cultivars tested ranged in percent soluble solids from 14.8 to 19.9, their percent acidity ranged from 0.56 to 1.42, and the pH ranged from 2.99 to 3.48. The *V. vinifera* cultivars tested in this study ranged from 16.8 to 18.6 in percent soluble

FIGURE 10-15 Grapes being dumped into a stemmer-crusher at a small winery. This is one of the first steps in the wine-making process.

solids, their percent acidity ranged from 0.78 to 1.17, and the pH ranged from 3.10 to 3.60.

In general, the must analysis for cultivars grown in the central and eastern United States indicates that these cultivars are relatively low in pH and high in acidity. The American cultivars tend to be lowest in acidity, while the French-American hybrids are more acidic and have lower pH. Apparently, these grape types are more inherently acidic than *V. vinifera* and are even more acid when grown in a cool climate.

Carroll et al. (1971) examined the chemical composition of 12 muscadine grape cultivars in North Carolina. They found the percent soluble solids to range from 10.2 to 17.9. Total titratable acidity ranged from 0.39 to 1.6%, while pH ranged from 2.9 to 3.5.

Veraison is the stage of development of the fruit when the berries begin to change color, and in some cases, to soften. At this point in the development of the grape berry in white cultivars, the green berry begins losing chlorophyll. Other pigments that were previously masked become evident, with white grapes taking on a translucent straw color at maturity. Veraison in red, blue, or black grapes is marked by the initiation of anthocyanin development; thus the color of red, blue, or black grapes increases as they mature.

Culture

Harvesting

Unlike many other fruits, grapes do not continue to ripen after they are harvested. The proper time to harvest grapes varies depending on the intended use (table, wine, raisin, etc.). Practically all cultivars of grapes reach full size and have good color several days before they reach true maturity. There are several indices that must be considered together in determining the level of grape berry maturity. The size, color, and taste of the berry, as well as its soluble solids content, titratable acidity, pH, and sugar/acid ratio, are the major considerations for determining when to harvest. Most grape cultivars change color long before they are mature enough for harvesting. Thus grapes picked by their color alone may be harvested prior to their peak by flavor, size, and soluble solids content. Picking grapes just 2 weeks prior to full maturity can result in up to 10% decrease in yield.

For fresh market and home use, the clusters are harvested selectively according to the degree of maturity. For commercial processing, the entire crop of a vine or cultivar is picked in one harvest. Grapes that are picked by hand should be harvested by placing the hand under the cluster; then, using a small pair of shears, the cluster is clipped from the vine. The clusters after picking are carefully placed in a container. In the eastern United States, grapes for fresh market are most commonly sold in 1-, 2-, or 4-quart baskets. Those going to the processor are placed in lugs or boxes of various sizes. The most common ones hold approximately 40 lb (18 kg). Specially made, lightweight nesting plastic lugs are now widely used in commercial vineyards. A small lightweight portable picking stand is a convenient way to hold the picking containers and for moving along the row. An experienced picker can pick between 40 and 50 lugs per day. Most wine, juice, and raisin grapes are now machine harvested (Fig. 10–16). Mechanical harvesters have been developed for use in commercial vineyards for harvesting processing grapes. Most of the harvesters operate on the principle of high-frequency vibration arms moving along the vines that shake the grapes from the clusters. A single mechanical harvester can do the work of about 100 hand pickers. These speed the harvest operation as one machine can harvest 6 tons/hr (5 MT/hr). In the case of mechanical harvesting, grapes are harvested into large bins that hold approximately 2200 lb (1000 kg), or into gondolas (Petrucci et al., 1983).

Grapevine Nutrition

High yields and high fruit quality can only be obtained when vine nutrition is not limiting. The evaluation of vineyard nutrition is commonly accomplished by using soil tests and leaf petiole analysis. Tissue analysis is useful for establishing sufficiency and deficiency levels.

Petiole samples for nutrient analysis are normally collected at bloom time in warmer *V. vinifera* growing areas such as California. American and French hybrid cultivars growing in cooler regions are typically sampled 70 to 100 days after bloom in New York, and 30 to 70 days after bloom in Ohio. Table 10–13 gives the acceptable working range of some nutrients in leaf petioles. Concentrations falling

Grape Management   Chap. 10

FIGURE 10-16 A large percentage of the annual grape harvest is accomplished by the use of mechanical harvesters.

TABLE 10-13 WORKING RANGE OF LEAF PETIOLE NUTRIENT CONCENTRATIONS IN GRAPES IN CALIFORNIA, WASHINGTON, AND NEW YORK VINEYARDS COLLECTED AT BLOOM

ELEMENT	CALIFORNIA[a]	WASHINGTON[b]	NEW YORK[c]
No_3-N	0.15–0.75%	0.19–0.33%	1.8–2.2% (N)
P	0.3–0.6%	0.11–0.17%	0.08–0.3%[d]
K	1.0–2.5%	1.5–3.2%	1.1–2.0%[d]
Ca	–[e]	0.9–1.7%	0.75–1.7%[d]
Mg	0.3–1.0%	0.4–0.7%	0.25–0.5%[d]
Zn	15–20 ppm	29–77 ppm	25–50 ppm
Mn	–	18–35 ppm	50–1000 ppm[d]
B	25–60 ppm	26–37 ppm	100–1500 ppm
Fe	–	34–71 ppm	30–100 ppm[d]
Cu	–	7–14 ppm	5–15 ppm
Cl	0.05–0.5%	–	–
Mo	0.1–0.50%	–	–

[a]From Winkler et al. (1974).

[b]From Dow and Ahmedullah (1981).

[c]From Himelrick (1983).

[d]Sample collection 70 to 100 days after bloom.

[e]Data not available.

below this range may indicate potential deficiencies, while those above this range may be more than adequate, and in some instances toxic (e.g., B, Cl, N).

Under California conditions, N, K, Zn, and B are the most commonly deficient nutrients, while Fe, Mg, and Mn are less common deficiencies. Na, Cl, and B can produce toxicity problems in the vineyards. Under New York conditions, N, K, and Mg are the most commonly deficient nutrients. The range of elements differs a great deal from one grape growing state to another and even within a state, from one cultivar to another, depending on the soil, climatic conditions, rootstock used, and the vigor of the vines (Cook, 1966; Christensen et al., 1978).

Diseases

Grapes are attacked by a wide range of pathogens in every area of the world where they are cultivated. The scope of this book does not allow a detailed description of the symptoms, causal organism, disease cycle and epidemiology, and control measures for each disease. In general, disease control strategies involve careful selection of planting site and planting material, along with cultural practices and sanitation that lower disease pressure, and chemical control with a carefully managed spray program (Fig. 10–17).

The reader is highly encouraged to examine the following publications for in-depth coverage and discussion of grape pests: Pearson and Goheen (1988) and Flaherty et al (1981).

Bibliographic reports on virus and virus-like diseases of *Vitis* species have been compiled by Hewitt and Bovey (1979) and Bovey and Martelli (1986).

Common Grape Diseases

Powdery mildew (Uncinula necator). The PM fungus can infect all green tissues of the grapevine. It appears as a white or grayish white powdery covering on the upper and lower surfaces of leaves and fruit. Expanding leaves that are infected become distorted and stunted. When green shoots are infected, the fungus appears dark brown to black and remains as brown patches on the surface of dormant canes. Cluster infection before or shortly after bloom may result in poor set and considerable crop loss. Berries are susceptible to infection until their sugar content reaches about 8%. If infected when they are pea-size or larger, the epidermis stops growing but the pulp continues to expand and the berry splits. When berries of purple or red cultivars are infected as they begin to ripen, they fail to color properly and have a blotchy appearance at harvest. Such fruit is unmarketable as fresh fruit and wines made from it will have off-flavors. In late summer the PM fungus produces black spherical bodies (cleistothecia) on the surface of infected leaves, shoots, and berries.

Downy mildew (Plasmopara viticola). The fungus causes direct yield losses by rotting inflorescences, clusters, and shoots, and indirect losses by prematurely defoliating vines which increases their susceptibility to winter injury and delays ripening of the fruit. *Plasmopara viticola* can infect all green, actively growing parts of the vine that have mature, functional stomata (tiny pores or openings) which are

FIGURE 10-17 Following a regular spray schedule is essential for the successful management of grapes.

used for air exchange on plant tissues. Leaves develop yellowish-green lesions on their upper surfaces. As lesions expand, the affected areas turn brown, necrotic or mottled. White, "downy" sporulation of the fungus forms on the lower leaf surface within the borders of the lesion. When young shoots, petioles, tendrils, or cluster stems are infected, they frequently become distorted, thickened or curled. White, downy sporulation is abundant on berries during humid weather. The fruits remain susceptible as long as stomata on their surfaces are functional. After that, new infections and sporulation do not develop, but the fungus continues to grow into healthy berry tissue from previously infected areas.

Black rot (Guignardia bidwellii). All green tissues of the vine are susceptible to infection. Leaves are susceptible for about 1 week after they unfold. Brown circular lesions develop on infected leaves, and within a few days black spherical fruiting bodies (pycnidia) form within the lesions. Petiole infection may cause the leaves to wilt. Shoot infection results in large black elliptical lesions. These lesions may contribute to breakage of shoots by wind. The fruit infection phase may result in substantial economic loss. Berries are susceptible to infection from bloom until

Culture

they begin to ripen. An infected berry first appears light brown, soon the entire berry turns dark brown, and black pycnidia develop on its surface. Infected berries shrivel, turn hard and black and are called mummies.

Phomopsis cane and leaf spot (Phomopsis viticola). Phomopsis cane and leaf spot, was formerly combined with Eutypa dieback and called "dead arm". Only under conditions of very high disease pressure does crop loss occur due to this disease. Heavily infected shoots are more prone to wind damage than are healthy shoots. Severely infected leaves become yellow and drop from the vine. Infected ripe fruit drop from the cluster, resulting in crop loss.

The shoot infection phase is the most common symptom of this disease. Infections on shoots give rise to elliptical lesions that are most numerous on the first 4–6 basal internodes. Lesions may coalesce, resulting in irregular, black, crusty areas. Lesions on cluster stems are similar in appearance to those on shoots and where they coalesce, the fruit may shrivel. Infected ripe fruits develop a light brown color. Infected berries are easily detached from their pedicels. Ripe fruit is susceptible to infection during prolonged rain periods close to harvest.

Eutypa dieback (Eutypa lata). Eutypa dieback of grapevines, formerly called "dead arm," was for many years thought to be caused by the fungus *Phomopsis viticola*. Recently, however, another fungus, *Eutypa lata* (imperfect stage: *Cytosporina*), was shown to cause the cankers and dieback symptoms previously associated with "dead arm." *Eutypa lata* causes cankers on trunks and cordons (arms) of infected vines. Cankers are frequently found surrounding old pruning cuts. They may appear as flattened areas on trunk and are usually concealed by dead bark. When the bark is removed the cankered area is revealed as brown discolored wood bordered by white healthy wood. The canker tends to expand longitudinally much more rapidly than laterally. A cross section through the canker area usually shows a wedge-shaped area of darkened wood.

Characteristic leaf symptoms develop on shoots arising from infected portions of the vine. As these new shoots begin to grow in the spring they appear stunted and have short internodes. The first leaves that unfold are small, cupped, and pale green to yellow. The leaf symptoms are most obvious early in the growing season when healthy shoots are 12 to 24 inches (30–60 cm) long. Leaf symptoms become more pronounced each year until the affected portion of the vine dies.

Crown gall (Agrobacterium tumefaciens). Crown gall is characterized by galls or overgrowth that forms on the roots, trunk, and arms of grapevines. Crown gall bacteria survive in soil for several years. They enter grape roots or stems through fairly recent wounds caused by freezing injury, pruning, machinery, or anything else that injures the plant. Bacteria from soil or infected plant parts can be carried by splashing water, which then infects new plants. There may be some transfer of the pathogen through soil, either within an established vineyard or in an immediate replant situation. Swelling or galls are most common on the roots and stem near the soil line. As galls age, they become dark brown, woody, rough, and may be bigger than a baseball. Secondary galls can develop higher up on the trunk and arms. Gall formation can disrupt the food- and water-conducting tissues of the vine. Infected young vines may become stunted and grow poorly.

Foliage on affected vines show yellow discoloration that resembles the coloration associated with the onset of fall season. In uninfected vines, there must be a wound for the bacteria to enter plant cells and cause a gall to form. This commonly occurs where trunks or other vine parts are split by extreme winter temperatures. However, mechanical injury as from a grape hoe or disk can also give the pathogen entry.

Botrytis bunch rot and blight (Botrytis cinerea).

Botrytis bunch rot and blight (Botrytis cinerea). *Botrytis* bunch rot and blight of leaves, shoots and blossom clusters, is also called gray mold. *Botrytis* bunch rot is especially severe in grape cultivars with tight, closely packed clusters of fruit. *Botrytis* is also responsible for storage losses of grapes picked for fresh market. *Botrytis* infection of leaves begins as a dull, green spot, commonly surrounding a vein, which rapidly becomes a brown necrotic lesion. The fungus may also cause a blossom blight or a shoot blight, which can result in significant crop losses. The most common phase of this disease is the infection and rot of ripening berries. This will spread rapidly throughout the cluster. The berries of white cultivars become brown and shriveled and those of purple cultivars develope a reddish color. Under proper weather conditions, the fungus produces a fluffy, gray-brown growth containing spores (Pearson et al., 1984).

Pierce's Disease (Xylella fastidiosa).

Pierce's Disease (Xylella fastidiosa). Pierce's disease (PD), a killer of grapevines, is caused by bacteria and spread by certain kinds of leafhoppers known as sharpshooters. Pierce's disease seems to be restricted to portions of North America with mild winters. In the southeastern states PD is the single most formidable obstacle to the growing of *V. vinifera* grapes. Affected vines show symptoms of water stress beginning in midsummer and increasing through fall. The first evidence of PD infection usually is a drying or "scorching" of leaves. The leaf or leaves closest to the point of infection become slightly yellow chlorotic) along the margins before drying up, or the outer edge of a leaf may dry suddenly while still green. Typically, the leaf dries progressively over a period of days to weeks, leaving a series of concentric zones of discolored and dead tissue. About the time foliar scorching begins, or slightly later, some or all of the fruit clusters may wilt and dry up or portions of clusters may dry up any time following fruit set. Colored grape cultivars may develop color early before wilting and drying. The only way to reduce or prevent PD spread through vector control is to prevent sharpshooters from entering vineyards.

Armillaria Root Rot (Armillaria mellea).

Armillaria Root Rot (Armillaria mellea). Long known to occur near old creek beds and water courses where oaks once grew, *Armillaria* root rot (oak root fungus), is found on a wide range of woody plants. Affected vines decline in vigor, the leaves take on a yellow color in early summer, and cane growth becomes weaker before the vine eventually collapses. Patches of diseased vines may gradually increase in size each year if left untreated. Oak root fungus causes a moist rot of the crown and root tissue, beginning just below ground level.

Black Measles. The cause of measles is not fully known, although appearance of symptoms is invariably correlated with an internal wood rot, beginning at large pruning wounds. Species of fungi is the genera *Fomes, Cephalosporium* and *Stereum (Phellinus)* are most frequently mentioned in the literature as being associated with the disease. The most important symptom is the peculiar berry spotting, most noticeable on white varieties. The skin is peppered with small, round dark spots, each bordered by a brown-purple ring; these spots may appear any time between fruit set and ripening and affect either entire or parts of clusters. In severely affected vines the berries often crack and dry on the vine or are subject to spoilage. Leaf symptoms usually develop on canes with measled fruit, but also on canes with normal fruit. Typically, affected leaves display small, chlorotic interveinal areas which enlarge and dry out; in dark colored varieties, dark red margins surround the dead interveinal areas.

Verticillium Wilt (Verticillium dahliae). Verticillium wilt causes significant losses in several small fruit crops, but it is a minor disease of grapes. Leaves begin to wilt and collapse in early summer heat, followed by death of some shoots, vascular discoloration and streaking of wood. Frequently vines are only partially affected, and strong new growth often appears in unaffected portions. Wilted leaves normally remain attached, and fruit clusters at the base of affected canes dry up. Vines that are not killed may show complete recovery by the following year.

Anthracnose (Elsinoe ampelina). This disease is also called bird's eye rot and is most commonly found in rainy, humid regions. Young, green, succulent parts of the shoot are most susceptible, but the fungus can attack mature leaves and fruit.

Bitter Rot (Greeneria uvicola). This is a disease of ripe fruit primarily found in muscadines. The fungus attacks damaged of near senescent tissues under warm and humid conditions and produces a bitter flavor in infected fruit.

Ripe Rot (Colletotrichum gloeosporiodes). This fungus occurs on grapes as they mature and ripen and is particularly serious on muscadines. The primary symptom is rotting of ripe fruit in the vineyard at harvest.

Macrophoma Rot (Botryosphaeria dothidea). This fungus causes circular lesions on berries as they reach maturity and is most destructive on muscadines. Affected berries drop from the vine.

Viruses. Major viruses of economic importance that attack grapevines include the following: grapevine fanleaf, tomato ringspot, tobacco ringspot, peach rosette mosaic, leafroll, corky bark, and stem pitting.

Insects

Over 250 species of insects and mites attack grapes in the United States. However, fewer than 15 species are of sufficient pest status to be of concern in commercial vineyards in the eastern United States. Vineyardists must accurately identify and assess the injury caused by insects and mites to make meaningful decisions on the need for control measures. Making these decisions can be easier when the appearance of the pest injury, the time of its occurrence, and the description of the pest are known.

Summarized is information on selected insect and mite pests in vineyards. The outline divides the insect–mite complex initially on the specific part of the vine attacked, then on the appearance of the injury, and finally, when necessary for similar pests, on the time of occurrence or on the description of the pest.

The reader is encouraged to consult the following publications for a more detailed discussion of grape insects: Flaherty et al. (1981), Pfeiffer and Schultz (1986), William et al. (1986), and Pearson and Goheen (1988).

Eastern grape insects*

Subterranean Insects Injuring Roots

Grape phylloxera. Causes swelling or galls on smaller roots and rootlets; larger roots may have open lesions with root rotting at the lesion site. The root form of this insect is present on a year-round basis. It is most injurious to *V. vinifera.*

Grape rootworm. Rootlets are consumed and furrows eaten into larger roots and crown of the vine. Grubs are present underground all year but are most active during warm months.

Grape root borer. Tunnels in larger roots and crown of the vine.

Insects Boring into and Feeding in Grape Canes, Cordons, or Trunks

Grape trunk borer. A brown beetle with yellow stripes dorsally on wing covers, has long rear legs that resemble those of a grasshopper. Larvae feed in dead or dying grape wood which is usually 2 or more years old.

Grape cane borer. Beetles bore into cane at the base of a bud and feed on the pith forming a tunnel. Sap may ooze from the tunnel opening in early autumn. Small white larvae may be found in tunnels in dying canes.

Ambrosia beetle. Bores tunnels that penetrate straight into trunk for about 1 cm, then divide into three or more arms. Tunnels may allow for invasion of disease-causing organisms.

Insects Injuring Developing Primary Grape Buds in the Spring   Note: Insects in this group inflict similar injury. The insects should be located for accurate pest identification.

Grape Flea Beetle [Steely Beetle.] Small, shiny, steely-blue beetle about 3/16 inch long. Each can destroy several buds along a cane. Beetles most active on

---

*This discussion is adapted from C. W. Haeseler, G. L. Jubb, Jr., and J. W. Travis, 1983. Illustrated guideline to viticulture in Pennsylvania (mimeo).

warm, sunny days. Presence in a particular vineyard is cyclic. Usually found along woodlines and other sheltered areas.

Climbing Cutworms. Dull gray or brown caterpillars which feed on grape buds at night. They are inactive during the day and hide in debris or vegetation near the vine.

Insects Injuring Shoots and Canes.   *Note:* Many insects in this group attack shoots; however, their injury may not be noticed until the leaves have fallen or when the canes are pruned.

Swelling or galls of various shapes and colors on shoots:

> *Grape tomato gall* (*tumid gall*). Irregular shaped, fleshy, succulent galls on leaf petioles, tendrils, and young leaves. Galls vary in color from green through reddish yellow to deep red. Small orange-colored maggots are contained inside the galls. This insect is common on wild grapes and can be injurious to certain wine cultivars.
>
> *Grape cane gallmaker.* Reddish or green swellings (red on red- or blue-fruited cultivars, green on white cultivars) above nodes about twice the diameter of the cane, also a vertical row of small holes chewed into the cane at the site of the gall.

Small, sluggish insects sucking plant juices from shoots:

> *Grapevine aphid.* Small, black insects clustered in colonies, usually feeding at the shoot tips and tender young leaves.
>
> *Grape mealybug.* Whitish, oval, soft-bodied wingless insect. May be found under old bark on trunk or arms in the spring.

Shoots girdled by ring of feeding punctures; sections of damaged shoots break off, causing a tip pruning effect in the spring:

> *Grape cane girdler.* Shoots girdled by a ring of feeding punctures. Sections of damaged shoots break off, causing a tip pruning effect early in the growing season. White, legless larvae found in the center of shoots that have this ring-like girdle.
>
> *Grape plume moth.* Webs together young leaves at shoot tip: small greenish, white-haired, wooly larva feeds on young leaves and flower clusters enclosed by the webbing.
>
> *Apple twig borer.* Adults make a small hole and burrow into main stem. New growth will be killed as a result of feeding in burrow.

Insects Injuring Flower Clusters

> *Grape tomato gall* (*tumid gall*). Galls can also be formed on the stems of developing flower clusters, causing them to curl up and even envelop florets.

This form of infestation is particularly significant on French hybrid cultivars.

Rose chafer. Light brown to reddish-brown, long-legged, 1/2- to 5/8-in. (13- to 16-mm)-long beetles that feed in groups. They feed on flower buds and stems and may eventually consume the entire cluster except for the main stem. Particularly common in sandy soil areas.

Grape blossom midge. Flower buds noticeably enlarged, with the lower portion of the bud developing a reddish color. The inner parts of the flower are consumed by small yellowish-orange maggots, and the infested buds will drop off.

Banded grape bug. Nymph feeds on flower clusters, sucking sap from developing flower buds and clusters stem. Florets then dry up.

Silver webs of various sizes and shapes in flower clusters; chewing damage to flower buds and flowers:

Grape berry moth. Silver webs in flower clusters with greenish to purplish larvae feeding on flower buds and flowers.

Redbanded leafroller. Silver webs in flower clusters with yellowish-green larvae. Larvae feed on flowers, berries, and stems, causing them to shrivel and drop.

Grape plume moth. May damage flower clusters while they are enclosed in growing shoot tip.

Insects Injuring Berries and Berry Clusters

Grape curculio. Shallow cavities chewed into berries with whitish larvae feeding on pulp and seeds. Infested berries may drop.

Grape mealybug. Sluggish, whitish, wingless insect that sucks juices from the berries and excretes a sticky honeydew liquid which collects on the berries and promotes the growth of a black sooty mold. Berries may shrivel and fall if injury occurs on grape stems.

Banded grape bug. Adult sucks sap from newly set berries. White, then dark spot on berry indicates feeding injury. Adult also a predator on flies; small larvae present in vines.

Berries misshapened and shriveled; contents consumed, holes chewed through skin; silken webs in clusters:

Grape berry moth. Several berries webbed tightly together with holes chewed from one berry to another. Greenish-purple larvae feeding within the berry. Berries may be misshapened, shriveled, and their contents consumed.

Redbanded leafroller. White webbing usually along the cluster stem. Berry contents partially consumed by very active yellowish-green larvae.

Insect attracted to ripe or nearly ripe berries; berry skins cracked by birds, diseases, insects, or other causes:

Fruit fly. Pulp of the berries infested with white, translucent maggots. Small active flies on and flying around cluster. Clusters typically have a sour odor.
Polistes wasp, yellow jacket, baldfaced hornet.

Insects and Mites Injuring Leaves *Leaves with swellings or galls of varying shapes and sizes*:

Grape phylloxera. Small, wart-like greenish galls on the underside of leaves about the size of a small garden pea. Gall opening is visible on upper surface of leaf. Galls contain small yellowish nymphs. Infected leaves may eventually curl up, turn brown, and fall from the vine.
Grape tomato gall (tumid gall). Masses of irregular, succulent galls on leaves and leaf petioles. Leaves may be misshapen as a result of the galls. Galls are greenish to reddish yellow to red in color and contain small orange maggots.

Grape erineum mite. Swellings or outpocketings on the upper surface of the leaf with dense, white, hair-like growth in corresponding cavities on lower leaf surface. Dense hair-like growth on lower leaf surface which turns brown in color. Very small wedge-shaped mites are found among the hairs of the galls.
Grape blister gall. Green or purplish smooth gall on surface of leaf. Severe infestation can cause leaf to become misshapen and extend to canes. Usually present near ground on suckers or low-growing canes.

Leaves discolored by insects and mites sucking plant juices:

Grape leafhopper. Leaves at first speckled with small whitish spots; continued feeding may eventually result in entire leaf becoming a yellowish-bronze color. Small lemon-colored adults and nymphs on the underside of leaves.
European red mite. Leaves turn chlorotic and a bronze coloration begins at the base of the leaf, which eventually envelopes the entire leaf. Minute red-colored mites crawling on underside of leaf and sucking the leaf juices.
Two-spotted spider mite. Adults are yellow-white with two dark markings. Damage is similar to European red mite. (*Note:* Several other spider mites cause leaf bronzing. However, initial bronzing is confined along the main veins. A fine webbing may be associated with infestations of spider mites.)

Leaves webbed together; chewing insect injury present:

Grape plume moth. Webs together young leaves at shoot tip. Small greenish, white-haired, wooly larvae that feed on young leaves.
Grape leaf folder. Individual leaves folded over and held in place by silken

threads. Light green larvae with brown heads feeding on the upper leaf surface within the leaf fold.

Grape vine epimenis. Larva makes shelter by spinning together leaf or leaves to the shape of roundish ball. Feeds on nearby leaves.

Chewing injury to leaves; no webbing present; parts of or entire leaf can be consumed:

Eight-spotted forester. Brightly colored caterpillar with distinct orange, yellow, black, and white markings. About 1 in. (2.5 cm) long. Can completely destroy the leaves except for petiole and larger veins.

Hornworm. Large, thick-bodied caterpillars with striking color patterns on the bodies. Could be up to 3 ½ in. (9 cm) long. Adults are sphinx moths.

Grape sawfly. Many small ½ -in. (13-mm)-long larvae, light green in color. Commonly found feeding side by side on the undersurface of the leaf.

Grape vine looper. Green or reddish inchworm-like larvae mimic grape tendril. Larvae rest on shoot or under leaf, chew round holes in leaves.

Grape leaf skeletonizer. Larvae feed on upper surface of leaves and may skeletonize them.

Chewing injury on leaves; no webbing present; interveinal tissue may be either partially or completely consumed; many small veins remain untouched, to give a lace-like, skeletonized appearance to varying degrees.

Japanese beetle. Metallic green and coppery brown and white beetle about ½ in. (13 mm) long. Chewing on leaves causes lace-like appearance.

Spotted pelidnota. Large, reddish-brown beetle. It can be up to 1 in. long with eight black dots on its upper body surface. Resembles ladybug beetle, only much larger.

Grape rootworm. Small, hairy, chestnut brown snout-nosed beetle. Chain-like feeding marks apparent on upper side of leaf.

Grape flea beetle (steely beetle). Small, brownish caterpillar-like larvae with black spots. Chain-like feeding on upper leaf surface.

Line-like, zigzag, or curved holes chewed into leaf:

Grape curculio. Small, brown, snout-nosed beetles feeding early in the growing season.

Western grape insects

Grape leafhopper. Both adults and nymphs feed on leaves by puncturing the leaf cells and sucking out the contents.

Variegated grape leafhopper. Nymphs cause the principal damage, black spotting of table grapes, which detracts from their market value.

Pacific and Willamette spider mites. Feeding by small colonies of both species produces small yellow spots on upper leaf surfaces.

Omnivorous leafroller. OLR larvae cause damage to grape clusters by feeding injuries that create avenues for infection by rot organisms.

Western grape leaf skeletonizer. Leaf damage is caused by larval feeding.

Grape leaffolder. The extent of the vine damage through reduction of leaf surface by rolling and larval feeding depends on population size and the time of year or brood involved.

Orange tortrix. The prime concern in an orange tortrix infestation is the development of grape cluster rot caused by fungi, molds, and bacteria gaining entry into the fruit through larval feeding injury.

Grape phylloxera. In California the principal damage to vinifera grapevines is caused by phylloxera inhabiting and feeding on roots. It is believed that during feeding, phylloxera inject poisonous saliva that causes swelling of roots, which stops rootlet growth and ultimately causes root death. Aerial galls on leaves are not found in the western United States.

Thrips. Western flower thrips damage on grapevines consists of (1) halo spotting which can make the fruit of certain white varieties unsightly and unmarketable; (2) berry scarring on table grapes, which can also render them unsalable; and (3) shoot stunting and foliage damage.

Grape mealybug. The grape mealybug does no known harm to the plant, but it contaminates fruit with one or more of the following: the cottony ovisac, eggs, immature larvae, adults, honeydew, or black sooty mold growing on honeydew.

Cutworms. Damage to grapevines occurs between the time that buds begin to swell to when shoots are several inches long. Injury results from nocturnal feeding in spring during a 2-week bud-break period, negating or deforming growth of fruit-yielding canes.

Grape bud beetle. Like cutworms, grape bud beetles feed on opening buds at night during spring.

Branch and twig borer. The adults burrow into the canes at the crotch or bud axil and cause severe pruning.

Click beetle. Damage to buds in early spring by the click beetle is difficult to distinguish from that by bud beetles.

Hoplia beetle. About the time new grape shoots are 12 to 14 in. (30 to 36 cm) long, the beetles fly into the vineyard from adjacent areas and feed on developing flower clusters and the younger leaves. Partial destruction of developing clusters results in small, misshapen bunches at harvest.

False chinch bug. Apparently, the nymphs produce a toxin, and heavy nymphal infestations can completely kill back new growth (Flaherty et al., 1981).

REFERENCES

ADELSHEIM, D. 1983. Spacing, training, and trellising *vinifera* grapes in western Oregon. p. 25–68. In Oregon winegrape grower's guide. Oregon Wine Growers Association, Salem, Oreg.

AHMEDULLAH, M. 1980. Grape varieties, clones, and rootstocks for Washington and Oregon. Oreg. Hortic. Soc. Proc.: 215–222.

ALLEWELDT, G. 1959. Untersuchung über die Gescheinzahl der Reben. Wein-Wiss. 14:61–69.

ALLEY, C. J., AND A. T. KOYAMA. 1978. Vine bleeding delays growth of T-budded grape-vines. Calif. Agric. 32:6.

ALLEY, C. J., C. S. OUGH, AND M. A. AMERINE. 1971. Grapes for table wines in California's regions IV and V. Wines and Vines 32:20–22.

AMERINE, M. A., AND C. S. OUGH. 1974. Wine and must analysis. Wiley, New York.

AMERINE, M. A., AND E. B. ROESSLER. 1958. Methods of determining field maturity of grapes. Am. J. Enol. 9:37–40.

AMERINE, M. A., AND A. J. WINKLER. 1944. Composition and quality of musts and wines of California grapes. Hilgardia 15:493–673.

AMERINE, M. A., H. W. BERG, R. E. KUNKEE, C. S. OUGH, V. L. SINGLETON, AND A. D. WEBB. 1980. The technology of wine making. AVI, Westport, Conn.

ATANASOV, J. A. 1964. Investigations on pruning the variety 'Cabernet Sauvignon' growth without soil covering in the winter. Gradinar. Lozar. Nauka. 1:95–100. Hortic. Abstr. 1965:35, 5341.

BAILEY, L. H. 1934. The species of grapes peculiar to North America. Gentes Herb. 3:150–244.

BARANEK, P., M. W. MILLER, A. N. KASIMATIS, AND C. D. LYNN. 1970. Influence of soluble solids in Thompson Seedless grapes on airstream grading for raisin quality. J. Am. Soc. Enol. Vitic. 21:19–25.

BARCLAY, L. W. AND C. S. KOEHLER. 1981. Managing insects and diseases in the home vineyard. Univ. Calif. Leafl. 21196.

BARRETT, H. C. 1956. The French hybrid grapes. Natl. Hortic. Mag. 35:132–144.

BEATTIE, J. M. 1959. Severe pruning reduced yield and quality of Concord grapes. Ohio Agric. Exp. Farm Home Res. Bull. 44:4–5.

BERG, H. W. 1960. Grade classification by total soluble solids and total acidity (revised). Wine Institute, San Francisco.

BIOLETTI, F., AND A. J. WINKLER. 1934. Density and arrangement of vines. Hilgardia 8:179–195.

BIOLETTI, F. T., F. C. H. FLOSSFEDER, AND A. E. WAY. 1921. Phylloxera resistant stocks. Calif. Agric. Exp. Stn. Bull. 331:1–139.

BOVEY, R., AND G. P. MARTELLI. 1986. The viroses and virus-like diseases of the grapevine. Vitis 25:227–275.

BRADT, O. A. 1962. Effect of pruning severity and bunch thinning on yield and vigour of Seibel 10878 and Seibel 9110 grapes. Rep. Hortic. Exp. Stn. Prod. Lab., Vineland, Ont., 1962, p. 19–22.

BRADT, O. A. 1964. Effect of bunch thinning and pruning severity on yield and vigour of Seibel 9549 grape. Rep. Hortic. Exp. Stn. Prod. Lab., Vineland, Ont., 1964, p. 44–49.

BRADT, O. A. 1965. Training, pruning and thinning French hybrids. N.Y. State Hortic. Soc. 110:222–224.

BRANAS, J., G. BERNON, AND L. LEVANDOUS. 1948. Eléments de viticulture générale. Ecole Natl. Agric. Montpellier.

BROOKS, J. F. 1978. Muscadine grapes production guide for North Carolina. N.C. Agric. Ext. Serv. Circ. 535.

BUTTROSE, M. S. 1969. Fruitfulness in grapevines: effects of light intensity and temperature. Bot. Gaz. 130:166–173.

BYRNE, M. E. AND G. S. HOWELL. 1978. Initial response of Baco noir grapevines to pruning severity, sucker removal, and weed control. Am. J. Enol. Vitic. 29:192–198.

CAHOON, G. A. 1976a. An 8-year comparison of umbrella Kniffin and single curtain training systems on Concord grapes. Fruit crops: 1976. A summary of research. Ohio State Res. Circ. 220.

CAHOON, G. A. 1976b. Vineyard preparation and planting. Virginia Grape Short Course.

CAHOON, G. A. 1979. Crop control in grapes. Proc. Ohio Grape-Wine Short Course, p. 32–38.

CAHOON, G. A., AND R. G. HILL, JR. 1981. Grape growing. Ohio State Univ. Bull. 509.

CARBONNEAU, A. 1985. The early selection of grapevine rootstocks for resistance to drought conditions. Am. J. Enol. Vitic. 36:195–198.

CARROLL, D. W., M. W. HOOVER, AND W. B. NESBITT. 1971. Sugar and organic acid concentrations in cultivars of muscadine grapes. J. Am. Soc. Hortic. Sci. 96:737–740.

CATTELL, H., AND H. L. STAUFFER. 1978. The wines of the east: the hybrids. L & H Photojournalism, Lancaster, Pa.

CAWTHON, D. L., AND J. R. MORRIS. 1977. Yield and quality of Concord grapes as affected by pruning severity, nodes per bearing unit, training system, shoot positioning and sampling date in Arkansas. J. Am. Soc. Hortic. Sci. 102:760–767.

CHRISTENSEN, L. P., A. N. KASAMATIS, J. J. KISSLER, F. JENSEN, AND D. A. LUVISI. 1973. Mechanical harvesting of grapes for the winery. Agric. Ext. Univ. Calif.

CHRISTENSEN, L. P., A. N. KASAMATIS, AND F. L. JENSEN. 1978. Grapevine nutrition and fertilization in the San Joaquin valley. Univ. Calif. Publ. 4087.

CLORE, W. J., C. W. NAGEL, AND G. W. CARTER. 1976. Ten years of grape variety responses and wine-making trials in central Washington. Wash. State Univ. Bull. 823.

COLBY, A. S., AND L. R. TUCKER. 1933. Some effects of severity of pruning on growth and production in the 'Concord' grape. Ill. Agric. Exp. Stn. Bull. 393:179–206.

COLBY, A. S., AND A. C. VOGELE. 1924. Notes on pruning and training 'Concord' grapes in Illinois. Proc. Am. Soc. Hortic. Sci. 21:384–387.

CONSIDINE, J. A. 1982. Concepts and practice of use of plant growth regulating chemicals in viticulture. In L. G. Nickell (ed.). Plant growth regulating chemicals. Vol. I. CRC Press, Boca Raton, Fla.

CONSTANTINESCU, G., E. NEGREANU, V. LAZARESCU, I. POENARU, O. ALEXEI, AND C. BOURNEAU. 1960. Ampelografia. Academiei Republicii Populare, Bucharest, Romania.

COOK, J. A. 1966. p. 777–812. In N. F. Childers (ed.). Fruit nutrition, 2nd ed. Horticultural Publications, New Brunswick, N.J.

DEARING, C. 1947. Muscadine grape breeding. J. Hered. 8:409–424.

DETHIER, B. E., AND N. SHAULIS. 1974. Minimizing the hazard of cold in New York vineyards. Ext. Bull. 1127. Cornell University, Ithaca, N.Y.

Dow, A. I., and M. Ahmedullah. 1981. Soil fertility and nutrition management of Washington vineyards. Wash. State Univ. Ext. Bull. 0874.

Einset, J., and C. Pratt. 1975. Grapes. p. 130–153. In J. Janick and J. N. Moore (eds.). Advances in fruit breeding. Purdue University Press, West Lafayette, Ind.

Esau, K. 1948. Phloem structure in the grapevine, and its seasonal changes. Hilgardia 18:217–296.

Fisher, K. H. 1987. An investigation into the fruiting and vine size response of five grape vine cultivars (*Vitis* sp.) to four vineyard spacing patterns. Ph.D. dissertation. Cornell University, Ithaca, N.Y.

Fisher, H. K., O. A. Bradt, J. Wiebe, and V. A. Dirks. 1977. Cluster-thinning 'de Chaunac' French hybrid grapes improves vine vigor and fruit quality in Ontario. J. Am. Soc. Hortic. Sci. 102:162–165.

Flaherty, D. L., F. L. Jensen, A. N. Kasamatis, H. Kido, and W. J. Moller. 1981. Grape pest management. Univ. Calif. Publ. 4105.

Fournioux, J. C. 1972. Distribution et differérenciation des tissus conducteurs primaires dans les organes aériens de *Vitis vinifera* L. Ph.D. dissertation. University of Dijon, Dijon, France.

Frolov-Bagreev, A. M. 1946–1958. Russian ampelography. G. Pishcheromizdat, Moscow, 6 vols.

Galet, P. 1979. A practical ampelography. Translated and adapted by Lucie T. Morton. Cornell University Press, Ithaca, N.Y.

Gallander, J. F., and J. F. Stetson. 1977. Grape varieties and selections for Ohio wines. Proc. Ohio Grape-Wine Short Course. p. 16–26.

Geisler, G. 1963. Art und sortenspezifische CO^{2-} Assimiationstraten von Reben unter berücksichtigung wechselnder Beleuchtungsstarken. Mitt. Klosterneu. 13:301–305.

Granett, J., A. C. Goheen, L. A. Lider, and J. J. White. 1987. Evaluation of grape rootstocks for resistance to type a and type b grape phylloxera. Am. J. Enol. Vitic. 38:298–300.

Guillou, R. 1960. Coolers for fruits and vegetables. Calif. Agric. Exp. Stn. Bull. 773:1–65.

Hale, C. R., and R. J. Weaver. 1962. The effect of developmental stage on direction of translocation of photosynthate in *Vitis vinifera*. Hilgardia 33:89–131.

Haeseler, C. W., G. L. Jubb, and J. W. Travis. 1983. Illustrated guideline to viticulture in Pennsylvania (Mimeo).

Hamilton, J. 1953. The effect of cluster thinning on maturity and yield of grapes on the Yuma Mesa. Proc. Am. Soc. Hortic. Sci. 62:231–234.

Harlan, J. 1976. Plants and animals that nourish man. Sci. Am. 235:89–97.

Harmon, F. N. 1943. Influence of indolebutyric acid on the rooting of grape cuttings. Proc. Am. Soc. Hortic. Sci. 42:383–388.

Harmon, F. N. 1954. A modified procedure for greenwood grafting of vinifera grapes. Proc. Am. Soc. Hortic. Sci. 64:255–258.

Harmon, F. N., and E. Snyder. 1956. Comparative value of three rootstocks for Sultana grape in rootknot nematode-infected soil. Proc. Am. Soc. Hortic. Sci. 67:308–311.

Hartmann, H. T., and D. E. Kester. 1983. Plant propagation. Prentice-Hall, Englewood Cliffs, N.J.

Harvey, J. M. 1955. A method for forecasting decay in California storage grapes. Phytopathology 45:229–232.

References

HARVEY, J. M. 1960. Instructions for forecasting decay in table grapes for storage. U.S. Dep. Agric., Market Res. Rep. 393:3–12.

HEDBERG, P. R., AND J. RAISON. 1982. The effect of vine spacing and trellising on yield and fruit quality of 'Shiraz' grapevines. Am. J. Enol. Vitic. 33:20–30.

HEDRICK, H. P. 1907. The grapes of New York. N.Y. State Agric. Exp. Stn. Rep. 1907.

HEGWOOD, C. P., R. H. MULLENAX, R. A. HAYGOOD, T. S. BROOKS, AND J. L. PEOPLES. 1983. Establishment and maintenance of muscadine vineyards. Miss. Coop. Ext. Bull. 913.

HEWITT, W. B., AND R. BOVEY. 1979. The viruses and virus-like diseases of the grapevine. A bibliographic report 1971–1978. Vitis 18:316–376.

HIMELRICK, D. G. 1983. Vineyard nutrition. Vineyard Notes Newsl., Cornell Coop. Ext., Fredonia, N.Y.

HOWELL, G. S. 1987. *Vitis* rootstocks. In R. C. Rom and R. F. Carlson (eds.). Rootstocks for fruit crops. Wiley, New York.

HOWELL, G. S., AND N. J. SHAULIS. 1980. Factors influencing within-vine variation in the cold resistance of cane and primary bud tissues. Am. J. Enol. Vitic. 31:158–161.

HOWELL, G. S., AND J. WOLPERT. 1978. Nodes per cane, primary bud phenology, and spring freeze damage to Concord grapevines. A preliminary note. Am. J. Enol. Vitic. 29:229.

HOWELL, G. S., B. G. STERGIOS, AND S. S. STACKHOUSE. 1978. Interrelation of productivity and cold hardiness of Concord grapevines. Am. J. Enol. Vitic. 29:187–191.

HUGLIN, P. 1958. Recherches sur les bourgeons de la vigne: initiation florale et developpement végétatif. Ann. Amelior Plant 12:151–156.

HUGLIN, P., AND B. JULLIARD. 1959. Le contrôle de la maturation du raisin par le prélèvement base. Prog. Agric. Vitic. 152:11–16, 37–41.

HUNTER, D. M., J. WIEBE, AND O. A. BRADT. 1985. Influence of spacing on fruit yields and quality of grape cultivars differing in vine vigor. J. Am. Soc. Hortic. Sci. 110:590–596.

HUSMAN, G. C., ET AL. 1939. Vinifera grape varieties grafted on phylloxera-resistant rootstocks in California. U.S. Dep. Agric. Tech. Bull. 697.

JACKSON, D., AND D. SCHUSTER. 1981. Grape growing and wine making: a handbook for cool climates. Alister Taylor, Martinborough, New Zealand.

JACKSON, D., AND R. SMART. 1985. Yield, quality, and light use by grapes. Pacific Northwest Grape Shortcouse: Canopy Management. p. 9–23.

JACOB, H. E. 1929. The utilization of sulfur dioxide in shipping grapes. Calif. Agric. Exp. Stn. Bull. 471:1–24.

JACOB, H. E. 1942a. Examples of incompatibility between grape varieties and rootstocks. Proc. Am. Soc. Hortic. Sci., 41:201–203.

JACOB, H. E. 1942b. The relation of maturity of the grapes to the yield, composition, and quality of raisins. Hilgardia 15:321–345.

JACOB, H. E. 1944. Factors influencing the yield, composition, and quality of raisins. Calif. Agric. Exp. Stn. Bull. 683:3–44.

JORDAN, T. D., R. M. POOL, T. J. ZABADAL, AND J. P. TOMKINS. 1981. Cultural practices for New York vineyards. Cornell Univ. Misc. Bull. 111.

KAPS, M. L. 1985. The influence of leaf, cluster, and berry thinning, and leaf position and shading on yield, juice composition and vine vigor of hybrid grapes. Ph.D. dissertation, Ohio State University, Columbus.

KASIMATIS, A. N., AND L. LIDER. 1980. Grape rootstock varieties. Univ. Calif. Ext. Leafl. 2780.

KASIMATIS, A. N., AND C. LYNN. 1967. Raisin maturity. Univ. Calif. Agric. Ext. Serv. AXT-235:1-20.

KASIMATIS, A. N., L. P. CHRISTENSEN, D. A. LUVISI, AND J. J. KISSLER. 1980. Wine grape varieties in the San Joaquin Valley. Univ. Calif. Publ. 4009.

KASIMATIS, A. N., B. E. BEARDEN, AND K. BOWERS. 1981. Wine grape varieties in the north coast counties of California. Univ. Calif. Publ. 4069.

KLIEWER, W. M. 1970. Effect of time and severity of defoliation on growth and composition of Thompson Seedless grapes. Am. J. Enol. Vitic. 21:37-47.

KLIEWER, W. M. 1980. Vineyard canopy management: a review. Symposium Proceedings Grape and Wine Centennial, Davis, Calif., p. 342-352.

KLIEWER, W. M. 1981. Grapevine physiology: how does a grapevine make sugar? Univ. Calif. Leafl. 21231.

KLIEWER, W. M., AND R. J. WEAVER. 1971. Effect of crop level and leaf area on growth, composition, and coloration of 'Tokay' grapes. Am. J. Enol. Vitic. 22:172-177.

KLIEWER, W. M., L. A. LIDER, AND N. FERRIERI. 1972. Effects of controlled temperature and light intensity on growth and carbohydrate levels of Thompson Seedless grapevines. J. Am. Soc. Hortic. Sci. 97:185-188.

KOBLET, W. 1969. Wandering von Assimilaten in Rebtrieben und Einfluss der Blattfläche auf Ertrag und Qualität der Trauben. Wein-wiss. 24:277-319.

KRIEDEMANN, P. E. 1968. Photosynthesis in vine leaves as a function of light intensity, temperature, and leaf age. Vitis 7:213-220.

KRIEDEMANN, P. E., AND R. E. SMART. 1971. Effects of irradiance, temperature, and leaf water potential on photosynthesis of vine leaves. Photosynthetica 5:6-15.

KRUL, W. R., AND G. H. MOWBRAY. 1985. Grapes. p. 396-434. In W. R. Sharp et al. (eds.). Handbook of plant cell culture. Vol. 2. Macmillan, New York.

LAVEE, S. 1985. *Vitis vinifera.* p. 456-471. In A. H. Halevy (ed.). CRC handbook of flowering. Vol. IV. CRC Press, Boca Raton, Fla.

LAVEE, S., AND G. NIR. 1986. Grape. p. 167-191. In S. P. Monselise (ed.). CRC handbook of fruit set and development. CRC Press, Boca Raton, Fla.

LIDER, L. A. 1957. Phylloxera-resistant rootstock trials in the coastal valleys of California. Am. J. Enol. 8:58-67.

LIDER, L. A. 1960. Vineyard trials in California with nematode-resistant grape rootstocks. Hilgardia 30:123-152.

LIDER, L. A., A. N. KASIMATIS, AND W. M. KLIEWER. 1975. Effect of pruning severity on growth and fruit production of 'Thompson Seedless' grapevines. Am. J. Enol. Vitic. 26:175-178.

LIUNI, C. S. 1965. A preliminary study on the possibility of spur pruning in 15 varieties of *Vitis vinifera.* Agric. Venez. 19:541-554. Hortic. Abstr. 1967 37:4592.

LOONEY, N. E. 1981. Grape cluster thinning stabilizes production, improves juice quality. Goodfruit Grower, Jan. 15.

LOONEY, N. E., AND D. F. WOOD. 1977. Cluster thinning and gibberellic acid effects on fruit set, berry size, vine growth, and yield of 'de Chanunac' grapes. Can. J. Plant Sci. 57:653-659.

MAGOON, C. A., AND E. SNYDER. 1943. Grapes for different regions. U.S. Dep. Agric. Farmers' Bull. 1936.

MANEY, T. J., AND H. H. PLAGGE. 1934. A study of production and physiology of 'Concord' grape vines as affected by variations in the severity of pruning. Proc. Am. Soc. Hortic. Sci. 32:392–396.

MARKIN, A. R., AND G. B. WHITE. 1982. Economics of conversion to the Geneva double curtain training system of 'Concord' grapes. J. Am. Soc. Hortic. Sci. 107:1117–1123.

McGREW, J. R. 1981. A review of the origin of interspecific hybrid grape cultivars. Am. Wine Soc. Manual 10.

MEYER, C. L., AND A. W. MARSH. 1972. A permanent sprinkler system for deciduous orchards and vineyards. Calif. Agric. Ext. AXT-70.

MIELKE, E. A., ET AL. 1980. Grape and wine production in the four corners region. Univ. Ariz. Agric. Exp. Stn. Tech. Bull. 239.

MILLER, M. W. 1964. Study of the influence of grape maturity on the quality and yield of raisins. Twenty Yrs. Raisin Res. Calif. Raisin Adv. Fresno, p. 12–18.

MORRIS, J. R., AND D. L. CAWTHON. 1980a. Mechanical trimming and node adjustment of cordon-trained Concord grapevines. J. Am. Soc. Hortic. Sci. 105:310–313.

MORRIS, J. R., AND D. L. CAWTHON. 1980b. Yield and quality response of 'Concord' grapes to training systems and pruning severity in Arkansas. J. Am. Soc. Hortic. Sci. 105:307–310.

MORRIS, J. R., AND D. L. CAWTHON. 1981. Effect of soil depth and in-row vine spacing on yield and juice quality in a mature 'Concord' vineyard. J. Am. Soc. Hortic. Sci. 106:318–320.

MORRIS, J. R., D. L. CAWTHON, AND C. A. SIMS. 1984a. Long-term effects of pruning severity, nodes per bearing unit, training system, and shoot positioning on yield and quality of 'Concord' grapes. J. Am. Soc. Hortic. Sci. 109:676–683.

MORRIS, J. R., C. A. SIMS, J. E. BOURQUE, AND J. L. OAKES. 1984b. Influence of training system, pruning severity and spur length on yield and quality of six French-American hybrid grape cultivars. Am. J. Enol. Vitic. 35:23–27.

MORTON, L. T. 1979. A practical ampelography: grapevine identification. Comstock Publishing Associates, Cornell University Press, Ithaca, N.Y.

MUNSON, T. V. 1909. Foundations of American grape culture. 2nd ed. T. V. Munson & Son. Denison, Tex.

NELSON, K. E., AND M. AHMEDULLAH. 1970. Effect on Cardinal grapes of position of sulfur dioxide generators and retention of gas and water vapor in unvented containers. Am. J. Enol. Vitic. 21:70–77.

NELSON, K. E., AND M. AHMEDULLAH. 1972. Effect of type of in-package sulfur dioxide generator and packaging materials on quality of stored table grapes. Am. J. Enol. Vitic. 23:78–85.

NELSON, K. E., AND J. P. GENTRY. 1966. Two-stage generation of SO_2 within closed containers to control decay of table grapes. Am. J. Enol. Vitic. 17:290–301.

NENOV, S. 1964. A contribution to the study of the pruning of the wine variety 'Pinot noir'. Hortic. Abstr. 1964. 34:536.

NESTEROV, A. I., V. P. BONDAREV, AND T. N. SKORIKOVA. 1969. Special forming features on the wine variety 'Pinot noir'. Vinodelie Vinogradarstro 29:34–41. Hortic. Abstr. 1970 34:536.

ORFFER, C. J. (ED.). 1979. Wine grape cultivars in South Africa. Human & Rousseau, Cape Town, South Africa.

PARTRIDGE, N. L. 1921. A note on the fruiting habit of the 'Concord' grape. Proc. Am. Soc. Hortic. Sci. 18:193–196.

PARTRIDGE, N. L. 1922. Further observations on the fruiting habit of the 'Concord' grape. Proc. Am. Soc. Hortic. Sci. 19:180–183.

PARTRIDGE, N. L. 1925. The fruiting habits and pruning of the Concord grape. Mich. Agric. Exp Stn. Tech. Bull. 69.

PEARSON, R. C., AND A. C. GOHEEN. 1988. Compendium of grape diseases. American Phytopathological Society, St. Paul, Minn.

PEARSON, R. C., T. J. BURR, AND M. R. SCHWARZ. 1984. Grape IPM disease identification sheets 1–6. Cornell University, Ithaca, N.Y.

PETRUCCI, V. E., C. D. CLARY, AND M. O'BRIEN. 1983. In M. O'Brien et al. (eds.). Principles and practices for harvesting and handling fruits and nuts. AVI, Westport, Conn.

PFEIFFER, D. G., AND P. B. SCHULTZ. 1986. Major insect and mite pests of grapes in Virginia. Va. Tech. State Coop. Ext. Serv. Publ. 444–567.

POLING, E. B., C. M. MAINLAND, AND J. B. EARP. 1984. Muscadine grape production guide for North Carolina. N.C. Agric. Ext. Serv. Bull. AG-94.

PONGRACZ, D. P. 1983. Rootstocks for grapevines. David Philip, Cape Town, South Africa.

POOL, R. M., C. PRATT, AND H. D. HUBBARD. 1978. Structure of base buds in relation to yield of grapes. Am. J. Enol. Vitic. 29:36–41.

PRATT, C. 1971. Reproductive anatomy in cultivated grapes: a review. Am. J. Enol. Vitic. 22:92–109.

PRATT, C. 1974. Vegetative anatomy of cultivated grapes: a review. Am. J. Enol. Vitic. 25:131–150.

RANGELOV, B. 1964. Studies on the pruning of the variety 'Pinot noir'. Grad. Lozar Nauka. 1:101–107. Hortic. Abstr. 1965 35:3036.

REYNEKE, J., AND S. J. DU PLESSIS. 1943. The treatment of table grapes for local markets. Farm. South Africa, 18:443–445.

REYNOLDS, A. G., R. M. POOL, AND L. R. MATTICK. 1985. Effect of training system on growth yield, fruit composition, and wine quality of Seyval blanc. Am. J. Enol. Vitic. 36:156–164.

RICHARDS, D. 1983. The grape root system. p. 127–168. In J. Janick (ed.). Horticultural reviews. Vol. 5. AVI, Westport, Conn.

RIEDL, H., AND E. F. TASCHENBERG. 1984. Grape IPM insect identification sheets 1–7. Cornell University, Ithaca, N.Y.

ROESSLER, E. B., AND M. A. AMERINE. 1958. Studies on grape sampling. Am. J. Enol., 9:139–145.

ROGERS, D. J., AND C. F. ROGERS. 1978. Systematics of north American grape species. Am. J. Enol. Vitic. 29:73–78.

SHARPE, R. H. 1954. Rooting of muscadine grapes under mist. Proc. Am. Soc. Hortic. Sci. 63:88–90.

SHAULIS, N. J. 1980. Responses of grapevines and grapes to spacing of and within canopies. Symp. Proc. Grape and Wine Centennial, University of California, Davis.

SHAULIS, N., AND K. KIMBALL. 1955. Effect of plant spacing on growth and yield of Concord grapes. Proc. Am. Soc. Hortic. Sci. 66:192–200.

SHAULIS, N. J., AND P. MAY. 1971. Response of Sultana vines to training on a divided canopy and to shoot crowding. Am. J. Enol. Vitic. 22:215–222.

SHAULIS, N. J., AND G. D. OBERLE. 1948. Some effects of pruning severity and training on Fredonia and Concord grape. Proc. Am. Soc. Hortic. Sci. 51:263–270.

SHAULIS, N. J., AND W. B. ROBINSON. 1953. The effect of season, pruning severity and trellising on some chemical characteristics of Concord and Fredonia grape juice. Proc. Am. Soc. Hortic. Sci. 62:214–220.

SHAULIS, N. J., AND R. SMART. 1974. Grapevine canopies: management, microclimate and yield responses. 19th International Horticultural Congress, Warsaw. p. 255–265.

SHAULIS, N. J., AND R. G. D. STEEL. 1969. The interaction of resistant rootstock to nitrogen, weed control, pruning and thinning effects on the productivity of Concord grapevines. J. Am. Soc. Hortic. Sci. 94:422–429.

SHAULIS, N. J., H. AMBERG, AND D. CROWE. 1966. Response of Concord grapes to light exposure and Geneva double curtain training. Proc. Am. Soc. Hortic. Sci. 89:268–280.

SMART, R. E. 1973. Sunlight interception by vineyards. Am. J. Enol. Vitic. 24:141–147.

SMART, R. E. 1980. Vine manipulation to improve wine grape quality. Symp. Proc. Grape and Wine Centennial, University of California, Davis.

SMART, R. E. 1984. Climate, canopy microclimate, vine physiology and wine quality. Proc. internationed cool climate viticulture and enology symposium, Eugene, Oreg.

SMART, R. E. 1985. Principles of grapevine canopy microclimate manipulation with implications for yield and quality: a review. Am. J. Enol. Vitic. 36:230–239.

SMART, R. E., N. J. SHAULIS, AND E. R. LEMON. 1982a. The effect of Concord vineyard microclimate on yield. II. The interrelationships between microclimate and yield expression. Am. J. Enol. Vitic. 33:109–116.

SMART, R. E., N. J. SHAULIS, AND E. R. LEMON. 1982b. The effect of Concord vineyard microclimate on yield. I. The effects of pruning, training, and shoot positioning on radiation microclimate. Am. J. Enol. Vitic. 33:99–108.

SMART, R. E., J. B. ROBINSON, G. R. DUE, AND C. J. BRIEN. 1985. Canopy microclimate modification for the cultivar Shiraz. I. Definition of canopy microclimate. Vitis 24:17–31.

SNYDER, E. 1937. Grape development and improvement. p. 631–664. In U.S. Dep. Agric. yearbook agric.

SNYDER, E., AND F. N. HARMON. 1948. Comparative value of nine rootstocks for ten *vinifera* grape varieties. Proc. Am. Soc. Hortic, Sci. 51:287–294.

SPAYD, S. 1985. Review of research on crop load effects on vine, grape, and wine quality of *Vitis* sp. Pacific Northwest Grape Shortcourse: Canopy Management. p. 66–79.

SPIEGEL-ROY, P., J. KOCHBA, AND S. LAVEE. 1971. Performance of table grape cultivars on different rootstocks in an arid climate. Vitis 10:191–200.

SRINIVASAN, C., AND M. G. MULLINS. 1978. Control of flowering in the grapevine (*Vitis vinifera* L.): formation of inflorescences *in vitro* by isolated tendrils. Plant Physiol. 61:127–30.

SRINIVASAN, C., AND M. G. MULLINS. 1981. Physiology of flowering in the grapevine: a review. Am. J. Enol. Vitic. 32:47–63.

STRAUSS, H. C., AND E. ARCHER. 1986. Choice of rootstocks. Vitic. Enol. Publ. B3.10. Directorate Agricultural Information, Pretoria, South Africa.

SZYJEWICZ, E., N. ROSNER, AND W. M. KLIEWER. 1984. Ethephon, (2-chloroethyl) phosphonic acid, Ethrel (CEPA) in viticulture: a review. Am. J. Enol. Vitic. 35:117–123.

TUKEY, R. B., AND W. J. CLORE. 1972. Grapes: their characteristics and suitability for production in Washington. Wash. State Univ. Bull. EB635.

VIALA, P. AND V. VERMOREL. 1909. Ampelographie. 7 vols. Masson et Cie, Paris.

WAGNER, P. M. 1985. A wine-grower's guide. Alfred A. Knopf, New York.

WEAVER, R. J. 1952. Thinning and girdling of 'Red Malaga' grapes in relation to size of berry, color, and percentage of soluble solids of fruit. Proc. Am. Soc. Hortic. Sci. 60:132–140.

WEAVER, R. J. 1976. Grape growing. Wiley, New York.

WEAVER, R. J., AND S. B. McCUNE. 1959. Test of activity of plant growth-regulators on grapes. Bot. Gaz. 120:116–170.

WEAVER, R. J., AND R. M. POOL. 1968. Effect of various levels of cropping *Vitis vinifera* grapevines. Am. J. Enol. Vitic. 19:185–193.

WIEBE, J., AND O. A. BRADT. 1973. Fruit yields and quality in the early years of a grape-spacing trial. Can. J. Plant Sci. 53:153–156.

WILLIAMS, R. N., D. M. PAVUK, AND R. W. RINGS. 1986. Insect and mite pests of grapes in Ohio. Ohio Coop. Ext. Serv. Bull. 807.

WINES AND VINES. 1988. Exclusive '88 Wines & Vines U.S. varietal chart. Sept., p. 30.

WINKLER, A. J. 1969. Effect of vine spacing in an unirrigated vineyard on vine physiology, production and wine quality. Am. J. Enol. Vitic. 10:39–43.

WINKLER, A. J., AND H. E. JACOB. 1925. The utilization of sulfur dioxide in the marketing of grapes. Hilgardia 1:107–131.

WINKLER, A. J., J. A. COOK, W. M. KLIEWER, AND L. A. LIDER. 1974. General viticulture. 2nd ed. University of California Press, Berkeley.

WOLF, T. K. 1987. Dormant pruning and training of grapevines in Virginia. Virginia Coop. Ext. Serv. Publ. 423–011.

WOLPERT, J. A., G. S. HOWELL, AND T. K. MANSFIELD. 1983. Sampling Vidal blanc grapes. I. Effect of training system, pruning severity, shoot exposure, shoot origin, and cluster thinning on cluster weight and fruit quality. Am. J. Enol. Vitic. 34:72–76.

ZABADAL, T. 1983. Tightening vineyard cash flow. East. Grape Grower Winery News. Dec. 1983, p. 21–22.

ZABADAL, T. 1985a. Field grafting. Parts I and II. East. Grape Grower Winery News. Aug./Sept., p. 19–21; Oct./Nov., p. 19–26.

ZABADAL, T. 1985b. Fruitfulness of spurs versus long canes. Vineyard Notes Newsl., Cornell Coop. Ext., Penn Yan, N.Y.

ZOTKIN, I. I., AND A. M. SAFARJAN. 1966. The quality of vine crops in relation to the soil and climatic conditions and to cultural practices. Hortic. Abstr. 1966 36:554.

SUGGESTED READING

Books

AMERINE, M. A., H. W. BERG, R. E. KUNKEE, C. S. OUGH, V. L. SINGLETON, AND A. D. WEBB. 1980. Technology of wine making, AVI, Westport, Conn.

FLAHERTY, D. L., ET AL. 1981. Grape pest management. Div. Agric. Sci., Univ. Calif. Publ. 4105.

Jackson, D., and D. Schuster. 1986. The production of grapes and wine in cool climates. Butterworth, Stoneham, Mass.

Morton, L. T. 1985. Winegrowing in eastern America. Cornell University Press, Ithaca, N.Y.

Pearson, R. C., and A. C. Goheen. 1988. Compendium of grape diseases. American Phytopathological Society, St. Paul, Minn.

Pongracz, D. P. 1978. Practical viticulture. David Philip, Cape Town, South Africa.

Robinson, J. 1986. Vines, grapes and wines. Alfred A. Knopf, New York.

Vine, R. P. 1981. Commercial winemaking. AVI, Westport, Conn.

Wagner, P. M. 1985. A wine-growers guide. Alfred A. Knopf Press, New York.

Ward, J. 1984. The complete book of vine growing in the British Isles. Faber & Faber, London.

Weaver, R. J. 1976. Grape growing. Wiley, New York.

Webb, M. 1983. Oregon winegrape grower's guide. Oregon Winegrowers Association, Portland, Oreg.

Winkler, A. J., J. A. Cook, W. M. Kliewer, and L. A. Lider. 1974. General viticulture. 2nd ed. University of California Press, Berkeley.

Bulletins

Cahoon, G. A., and R. G. Hill, Jr. 1981. Grape growing. Ohio State Univ. Coop. Ext. Serv. Bull. 509.

Ferree, M. E. 1979. Muscadine grape culture. Univ. Ga. Bull. 739.

Fisher, K. H., O. A. Bradt, and R. A. Cline. The grape in Ontario. Publ. 487, Horticultural Research Institute of Ontario, Vineland Station, Ontario.

Hegwood, C. P., R. H. Mullenax, R. A. Haygood, T. S. Brooks, and J. L. Peoples. 1983. Establishment and maintenance of muscadine vineyards. Miss. Coop. Ext. Bull. 913.

Jordan, T. D., R. M. Pool, T. J. Zabadal, and J. P. Tomkins. 1981. Cultural practices for commercial vineyards. Misc. Bull 111. New York State College of Agriculture and Life Sciences at Cornell University, Ithaca, N.Y.

Macgregor, D. 1981. Growing grapes in Minnesota. Minnesota Grape Growers Association, Minneapolis, Minn.

McEachern, G. R., et al. 1982. Texas vineyard guide. Tex. Agric. Ext. Serv. Bull. B-1424.

McEachern, G. R., et al. 1988. Texas vineyard management handbook. Tex. Agric. Ext. Serv. Bull.

McGrew, J. R. 1977. Growing American bunch grapes. U.S. Dep. Agric. Farmers' Bull. 2123.

McGrew, J. R. 1980. Guide to winegrape growing. Manual 8. The American Wine Society, Royal Oak, Mich.

McGrew, J. R. 1983. Basic guide to pruning. American Wine Society, Rochester, N.Y.

McGrew, J. R., and G. W. Still. Control of grape diseases and insects in the eastern United States. U.S. Dep. Agric. Farmers' Bull. 1893.

Mielke, E. A., et al. 1980. Grape and wine production in the four corners region. Univ. Ariz. Agric. Exp. Stn. Tech. Bull. 239.

NELSON, K. E. 1985. Harvesting and handling California table grapes for market. Univ. Calif. Bull. 1913.

POLING, E. B., C. M. MAINLAND, AND J. B. EARP. 1984. Muscadine grape production guide for North Carolina. N. C. Agr. Ext. Serv. Publ. AG–94.

PULS, E., JR. 1984. Muscadine culture in Louisiana. La. State Univ. Coop. Ext. Serv. Publ. 1920.

SULLIVAN, D. T., R. E. GOMEZ, AND M. D. BRYANT. 1978. Growing grapes in New Mexico. N.M. State Univ. Coop. Ext. Serv. Circ. 483.

TUKEY, R. B., AND W. J. CLORE. 1972. Grapes: their characteristics and suitability for production in Washington. Wash. State Univ. Coop. Ext. Serv. Publ. EB 635.

ZABADAL, T., ET AL. 1988. Concord table grapes: a manual for growers. Communications Services, New York State Agric. Exp. Stn., Geneva, N.Y.

Suggested Reading

Chapter 11

Kiwifruit Management

A. R. FERGUSON

INTRODUCTION

Most of the other fruit plants described in this book have been known for thousands of years and cultivated for centuries. The kiwifruit is an exception: although it has long been known to the Chinese and was described in texts dating back to the Tang Dynasty, it has been domesticated for less than a century. The Chinese did not attempt cultivation, but instead, simply collected fruit from wild-growing plants, a practice that is still common in many parts of China.

At the beginning of this century, the kiwifruit was no more than a wild plant of the mountainous regions of south and central China. During the period from 1900 to 1910, plants or seed were introduced almost simultaneously to the United Kingdom, Europe, the United States, and New Zealand. Commercial cultivation started in New Zealand around 1930, but it was not until the development of export markets for the fresh fruit, some 20 to 30 years ago, that plantings became widespread. Commercial cultivation in California, France, Italy, and Japan started about 1970.

The common name 'kiwifruit' is very recent, dating from 1960 with the first exports of the fruit from New Zealand to the United States. Kiwifruit has now replaced the older English name of 'Chinese gooseberry'. The tendency to shorten the name to 'kiwi' should be resisted. In Italy, the common name is 'actinidia' (from the generic name). The Chinese use the name 'mihoutao' for the whole of the genus *Actinidia,* but in common usage 'mihoutao' normally refers to the kiwifruit and the closely related *Actinidia chinensis.*

The kiwifruit is now New Zealand's most important export horticultural crop. In most other parts of the world it cannot yet be really considered an established crop. The cultivars grown and the cultural practices used have all been adopted from New Zealand. This account of kiwifruit management is, therefore, largely an account of how kiwifruit are grown in New Zealand. The management practices used there are not necessarily the most suitable for the various countries in which kiwifruit are now being grown.

ORIGINS OF CULTIVATED KIWIFRUIT

The kiwifruit is dioecious; that is, pistillate (female) and staminate (male) flowers occur on different plants. Commercial orchards must therefore contain both types of plant. Only one pistillate cultivar, 'Hayward', is grown to any extent (Figs. 11–1 and 11–2), but a number of different staminate clones are used as pollenizers.

Commercial kiwifruit cultivars in New Zealand trace back to one staminate and two pistillate plants and a single introduction of seed from China in 1904. 'Hayward' (later named for its discoverer, Hayward Wright) was first sold in the late 1930s, leading to the establishment of commercial orchards of this cultivar. Cultivars such as 'Abbott', 'Bruno', and 'Monty' were initially more widely grown, but

FIGURE 11-1 Fruiting habit of 'Hayward' kiwifruit growing on a T-bar. Fruit are carried in the leaf axils on lateral shoots of the current season coming from canes of the previous season. (Courtesy of the New Zealand Kiwifruit Authority.)

FIGURE 11-2 'Hayward' kiwifruit. Note the remains of the sepals, styles, and stamens attached to the fruit. (Courtesy of the New Zealand Kiwifruit Authority.)

'Hayward' eventually predominated because of its large fruit, fine flavor, and excellent keeping qualities. The New Zealand kiwifruit industry is now a monoculture based on one pistillate cultivar. This has its drawbacks and dangers—the whole crop must be harvested and handled over about 6 weeks and there is a risk of disease epidemics. Various strains of 'Hayward' are now emerging and the best of these are being propagated and distributed.

'Hayward' is also the most important pistillate cultivar in other countries with kiwifruit industries. Hayward Wright sent a plant of a large-fruited kiwifruit strain to Chico, California, in 1935, which became the source of much propagating material for California commercial kiwifruit plantings. The cultivar 'Chico' or 'Chico Hayward', derived from this plant, is considered indistinguishable from 'Hayward'. The cultivars from New Zealand are also grown in France, Italy, and Japan. Growers in California and in other countries have found it easier to achieve good yields with cultivars such as 'Abbott' and 'Monty'. However, the clear superiority of 'Hayward' fruit has generally outweighed advantages of the other cultivars. 'Hayward', selected about 50 years ago from a very small number of seedling plants, is not perfect. But its excellent size, fine flavor, and exceptionally long storage life (up to 6 months) have permitted the remarkable development of the New Zealand kiwifruit export industry.

Staminate clones that coincide in flowering with the pistillate cultivars are required. Choice of the appropriate staminate plants for an orchard therefore depends on the particular pistillate plants grown. 'Matua' or some other long-flowering type is generally used, even though their main flowering period is usually in advance of that of 'Hayward'. A mixture of staminate clones is often planted to ensure that some will coincide with 'Hayward' each season. Most staminate plants have their flowers in small inflorescences consisting of two or three flowers. The terminal flower of an individual inflorescence usually opens at least a week before the lateral flowers and this effectively extends the flowering season. The amount and 'quality' of the pollen produced is just as important as the coincidence of flowering, and a number of promising staminate clones (the M series) are currently being evaluated. The 'Chico male' or 'California male' was selected in California to coincide with 'Chico' (i.e., 'Hayward').

BOTANICAL CLASSIFICATION

Kiwifruit clones in cultivation are large-fruited selections of *Actinidia deliciosa* (A. Chev.) C. F. Liang et A. R. Ferguson var. *deliciosa*. There are more than 50 species in the genus *Actinidia* (family Actinidiaceae) mostly from the mountains and hills of southwestern China. All are perennial climbing or creeping plants. The most obvious characteristic feature in common is the structure of the pistillate flower, which has a circle of styles radiating out from the top of the ovary (Fig. 11–4A).

Until recently, the kiwifruit was known by the botanical name *Actinidia chinensis* Planch. This species was polymorphic, however, and several variants could be identified in different parts of the wide geographic range over which the species occurs in China. The most obvious visible differences were in the size and hairiness of the fruit. One variant had small, almost spherical, smooth-skinned fruit, whereas the other variant had larger, oblong, hairy fruit. Only the hairy-fruited variant was grown outside China and this is the kiwifruit of today—it became known as *A. chinensis* Planch. var. *hispida* C. F. Liang (from 'hispid', meaning 'stiff-haired'). The smooth-skinned and hairy variants of *A. chinensis* are now treated as two separate species. The kiwifruit of cultivation therefore takes the new name *Actinidia deliciosa* var. *deliciosa*, whereas the smooth-skinned variant retains the name *Actinidia chinensis* (Fig. 11–3). This species is little known outside China, and only recently has it been cultivated in other countries.

USES OF KIWIFRUIT AND OTHER ACTINIDIA SPECIES

Large quantities of the fruit of *A. chinensis* and *A. deliciosa* are collected from the wild in China each year—possibly as much as is produced in commercial kiwifruit orchards elsewhere in the world. Much of the fruit is sold locally for fresh consumption, but some is processed into a variety of products such as fruit juices, jam, preserved fruit, wine, and spirits. Traditionally, other parts of the plants have also been used: the stems for making good-quality paper or for preparation of adhesives, the leaves as fodder, and the flowers and seed for the extraction of fragrant oils. Chinese pharmacopoeia also list a number of medicinal uses.

Fresh Kiwifruit Production

Commercial cultivation of kiwifruit elsewhere in the world (Table 11–1) is primarily to provide fruit for fresh consumption, especially for when there is a lack of other soft fruit. The fruit has a bright green color and unique flavor, and a very high vitamin C content.

Processed Kiwifruit Production

Processing of kiwifruit has often been looked upon simply as the best use for culled fruit. Only 75 to 80% of the fruit produced meet the export standards for the fresh fruit. As production has increased, so has the quantity of fruit available for

FIGURE 11-3 Kiwifruit — *Actinidia deliciosa* 'Hayward' — flanking *A. chinensis* fruit, which are smaller and much less hairy. (Courtesy of Mt. Albert Research Centre, New Zealand.)

processing. Kiwifruit, however, are not easy to process: the skin (and the hairs) must be removed; the chlorophyll, responsible for the beautiful green color of the flesh, is readily degraded to compounds of a sludgy olive-green color; and the unique flavor is lost with processing or heating. Most processed products therefore retain few of the characteristics of the fresh fruit. A variety of processed kiwifruit products are exported from New Zealand, including canned, sliced fruit, frozen fruit, slices or pulp, and wine, jam, juice concentrate, glacéed fruit, and other products.

TABLE 11-1 ESTIMATED PLANTINGS AND PRODUCTION OF KIWIFRUIT, 1987

COUNTRY	PLANTINGS (ACRES)	PRODUCTION (TONS)
New Zealand	39,200	210,000
Italy	31,700	91,000
Japan	10,800	38,000
California, USA	8,700	27,000
France	10,400	22,000
Australia	2,500	9.000
Greece	4,200	4,000
Chile	12,400	3,000
Other countries	6,100	8,000
World total	126,000	412,000

Source: International Kiwifruit Organization (Frutticoltura 50(11):79, 80 (1988). There is a lag between planting and production and in many countries most plantings are still young and have not yet reached full production.

Other Actinidia Species

Some other *Actinidia* species have potential as fruit-producing plants, although none is yet grown on a commercial scale:

A. chinensis Planch. Many groups in China are selecting high-quality individual plants from wild populations of *A. chinensis* and *A. deliciosa*. Most of the attributes being selected for, such as hairlessness, fragrance, flavor, and red or yellow flesh, are attributes of *A. chinensis,* not *A. deliciosa.* Within a few years, it is likely that *A. chinensis* will become important as a newly domesticated fruiting plant.

A. arguta (Sieb. et Zucc.) Planch. ex Miq. is more cold hardy than the kiwifruit. The fruit is small (about the size and shape of the European gooseberry, *Ribes grossularia*). The skin is smooth, the flesh is very juicy, and the fruit has a very appealing flavor which many consider much superior to that of the kiwifruit. However, it ripens on the vine and it will probably prove difficult to handle or store.

A. kolomikta (Maxim. et Rupr.) Maxim. is even more cold hardy, being able to withstand temperatures down to $-30°F$ ($-35°C$). The fruit is also small but is very sweet and has a fine aroma and flavor. It is particularly valued for its remarkably high content of vitamin C—about 1% fresh weight. Selected staminate plants of *A. kolomikta* are often grown as ornamentals because of the striking pink and white variegation of the younger leaves.

Attempts in Europe and North America to establish commercial plantings of *A. arguta* and *A. kolomikta* have largely been unsuccessful despite the selection of large-fruited strains and hybrids. These species could, however, be useful fruiting plants for amateur horticulturists, and they may have a place in countries that are too cold for kiwifruit cultivation. Fruit of other *Actinidia* species is also collected from the wild in China.

BOTANY

Vegetative Structure

The kiwifruit is a very vigorous long-lived, perennial deciduous vine requiring a strong framework on which to grow (Figs. 11–8 and 11–9). Under most systems of orchard management, the vine has a single trunk of about 6 ft (1.8 m) in height. As plants can live for 50 years or more, the trunk eventually becomes massive, sometimes more than 8 in. (20 cm) in diameter.

The mature orchard vine has a permanent framework of branches from which fruiting 'arms' or canes are developed at right angles (Fig. 11–9). Lateral shoots of the current season's growth emerge in spring from buds in leaf axils of canes produced the previous season (Fig. 11–1). Second-order lateral flowering shoots can, in turn, be produced the following year. Some lateral shoots (nonterminating shoots) are very vigorous and continue to grow throughout the season, reaching 10 to 15 ft (3 to 5 m) in length; others (terminating shoots) are less vigorous and the growing tip withers and dies, leaving shoots with three to six fully sized leaves. There are no terminal buds. Shoots coming from weaker wood, such as from the interior of the vine, and second-order lateral shoots are generally terminating shoots. Fruiting arms with their lateral and second-order lateral shoots are the typical productive units of kiwifruit vines.

The canopy of a typical 'Hayward' vine has a leaf surface area of between 300 and 450 ft² (30 to 40 m²) from some 4000 to 5000 leaves. Young leaves are thin and soft, but the older leaves, up to 8 in. (20 cm) wide, become thick and leathery during the season. The lower leaf surface is grayish white from the dense felting of stellate hairs. Leaf size and shape vary along a shoot and on different types of shoots.

Kiwifruit can have extensive root systems: the fresh weight of the root system can approach that of the total vine above ground. On deep porous soils, the roots can descend in large numbers to depths of at least 12 ft (4 m); and measurements have shown significant water extraction at depths greater than 7 ft 8 in. (2.4 m) in coarse, sandy soils. On heavier clay soils most of the roots are at a depth of up to 3 ft (1 m). Roots usually extend 6 to 10 ft (2 to 3 m) from the trunk, and in established orchards the root systems of adjacent vines would overlap.

Flower Structure

Dioecism.   Flowers of pistillate kiwifruit appear perfect (Fig. 11–4A), but their stamens produce nonviable pollen: flowers of staminate plants (Fig. 11–4B) have a greatly reduced ovary and only poorly developed styles. Occasional staminate plants do produce fruit. Bagging experiments indicate that such plants have flowers that are self-pollinating and self-setting. Fruit from partially fertile staminate plants have small ovaries with few ovules, limited stylar development, and small fruit. Some staminate plants, however, can produce larger fruit, indicating that development of a truly hermaphroditic cultivar should be possible.

FIGURE 11–4   (A) Pistillate ('Hayward') and (B) staminate kiwifruit flowers. (Courtesy of Mt. Albert Research Centre, New Zealand.)

Flowering shoots. Some shoots are purely vegetative: others develop into flowering shoots. Small inflorescences are borne at the base of flowering shoots in the leaf axils several nodes distal to those containing basal buds (Figs. 11–2 and 11–5). The following season, flowering shoots are in turn formed from buds in axils of leaves distal to the last flowering axil. Flowers are never formed at the shoot apex, which remains vegetative. Vines do not flower until they are 3 or 4 years old.

The inflorescence potentially consists of a terminal flower and successive orders of lateral flowers, but lateral flowers often do not develop. Staminate cultivar inflorescences usually contain three or more flowers. Some pistillate cultivar inflorescences have three flowers; other cultivars bear only a single flower owing to lateral flower bud abortion. 'Hayward' produces fewer flowers than do other pistillate cultivars because it bears fewer flowers per flowering shoot and fewer flowering shoots per cane.

Flowers. Pistillate flowers are generally larger than staminate flowers and often contain more perianth parts. In 'Hayward', flowers at the base of the shoot are usually larger than those more distal and they also have more perianth parts. There are usually five sepals. The flower is cup-shaped with five or more petals which are white at opening but become golden yellow. A large number of stamens encircles the ovary. In pistillate flowers stamen filaments are generally shorter than in staminate flowers. In a pistillate flower (Fig. 11–4A), the lower parts of the carpels (usually more than 30) fuse to form the ovary. Each carpel has two rows of 10 to 20 ovules attached to the central axis. In staminate flowers (Fig. 11–4B), the ovary is much smaller and the ovules and styles are only rudimentary. Flowers do not produce any nectar. Both staminate and pistillate flowers have a distinctive fragrance.

Fruit Structure and Composition

Fruit shape and hairiness varies with cultivar. Most have fruit that are oval in cross section, but some (e.g., 'Bruno') have fruit that are nearly cylindrical. 'Hayward' fruits have a characteristic shape, being broader and less elongated than fruit of other cultivars.

Botanically, the fruit is a nondehiscent berry bearing many seeds in a fleshy pericarp (Fig. 11–5C). The bulk of the pericarp tissue consists of thin-walled parenchyma cells. The central core of the fruit is formed of homogeneous, large parenchyma cells, although the stalk end is often hard and woody even when the fruit is ripe. The seeds occur in two radial rows in the locules of the inner pericarp. A fruit can contain up to 1400 seeds.

The composition of kiwifruit is unusual in several respects:

1. The bright green flesh color is due to the presence of chlorophyll, which is not lost on storage or ripening but is degraded during processing.
2. Freshly harvested 'Hayward' fruit contains 80 to 100 mg of ascorbic acid per 100 g of fresh weight. A single fruit can thus provide enough ascorbic acid to satisfy the minimum daily human requirement.

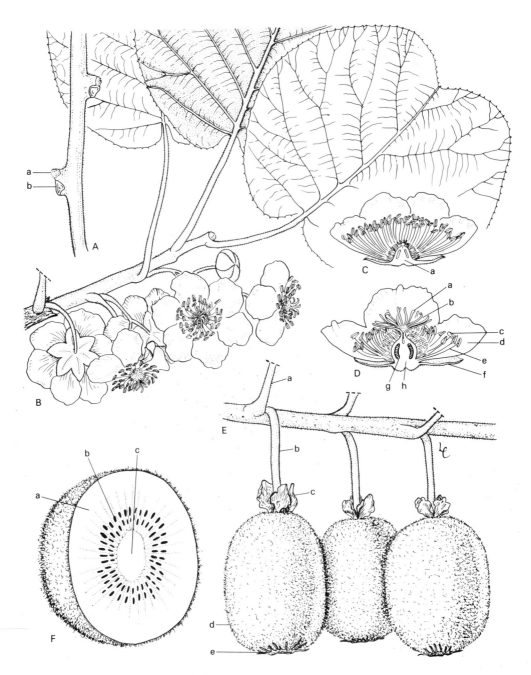

FIGURE 11-5 Kiwifruit morphology. (A) Cane: a, dormant bud; b, leaf scar. (B) Flowering shoot. (C) Staminate flower: a, rudimentary ovary. (D) Pistillate flower: a, stigma; b, style; c, anther; d, petal; e, filament; f, sepal; g, ovules; h, ovary. (E) Fruiting shoot: a, leaf petiole; b, peduncle; c, sepals; d, fruit; e, remains of styles and anthers. (F) Fruit cross section: a, outer pericarp; b, seed; c, core.

3. In mature kiwifruit there can be as much quinic acid as there is citric acid.

4. The fruit contains considerable amounts of actinidin, similar to the proteolytic enzymes from papaya, figs, and pineapples. Slices of raw kiwifruit will therefore tenderize meat or prevent gelatin-based jellies from setting.

Annual Growth Cycle

Bud formation and shoot growth. The new season's shoots emerge about a month after bud swell. These shoots had differentiated as buds the previous spring. As the shoots extend, new buds start to differentiate in the axils of leaves beyond the last developing flower. The vine is in full flower, about 2 months after bud break.

Shoot growth continues throughout spring and early summer, slowing down as water and nutrients become limiting or as competition from the developing fruit increases. By midsummer the buds have largely completed differentiation. The bud enters winter dormancy buried in the cork of the swollen leaf base, which remains after the leaf has fallen.

Flower development. In most woody plants, flower bud differentiation is largely completed before the plant enters winter dormancy. In kiwifruit, the potential flowering shoot overwinters as a bud containing differentiated vegetative structures but with few or no traces of differentiated floral structures. Evocation (flower initiation or floral induction) occurs in summer, but visible differentiation starts only in spring, about 10 days before the new shoot emerges (about 6 months between evocation and flower differentiation). Full bloom occurs relatively late in the season because flowers are borne only on current season's growth, and flower differentiation and development both take place during spring. Cultivars differ by up to a week in their time of flowering, and 'Hayward' is consistently the last pistillate cultivar to flower.

Fruit set. There is no fruit drop in kiwifruit; every flower that is set produces a fruit. The cropping capacity of the vine is thus limited by the number of flowers produced. In districts with colder winters, however, the crop has to be regulated by reducing the number of flowers or the number of set fruit allowed to remain on the vine.

Flower quality is also important. Every kiwifruit of acceptable commercial size contains hundreds of seeds (there is a strong correlation between seed number and fruit size). A high proportion of undersized, unmarketable fruit is usually ascribed to inadequate pollination. However, a small or poorly developed flower (containing a reduced number of carpels or ovules) cannot develop into a large, many-seeded fruit, no matter how effective the pollination.

Pistillate flowers can be pollinated and set fruit for up to 7 to 9 days after opening. They require multiple visits from bees to produce fruit of commercial size. Once the flower has been pollinated, the stigmata turn brown and wither. Staminate flowers can release pollen for the first 2 or 3 days after opening.

Botany

Fruit growth. Fruit growth is a continued development of the pistillate flower ovary. Developing ovary dimensions increase about 6- to 10-fold, but the relative proportions of the mature fruit do not differ greatly from those of the ovary. The fresh weight or volume increases several hundredfold. Fruit growth occurs in several stages: a very rapid growth phase in the first couple of months after pollination; followed by about 3 weeks of much slower growth; and a second period of rapid growth.

Growth Interactions

Vegetative and reproductive growth interact. They may take place simultaneously, they may compete, or one may be dependent on another. Fruit development clearly depends on the preceding flower formation and development; conversely, crop load in one season can influence flower production and vegetative growth the following season. (Older vines frequently fall into biennial bearing. The reduced flower production in the off-years is usually ascribed to depletion of nutrients by a previous heavy crop and/or to specific inhibition by growth substances, such as gibberellic acid, produced by the developing seeds.) A light fruit load may allow excessive vegetative growth.

Environmental effects on growth may not be expressed immediately. Adverse conditions during spring can affect flower and fruit development and even the vegetative buds which grow into shoots the following spring. Adverse conditions in summer might limit flower evocation, and this would not be seen until the following spring. Temperatures during winter can influence the proportion of buds that break dormancy in spring and the proportion of shoots that are reproductive.

Growth Requirements

The natural habitat of kiwifruit indicates that they should be considered as temperate, not subtropical plants. They grow well under temperate conditions, they are deciduous, and they require a period of winter chilling for adequate bud break. Kiwifruit are, however, susceptible to damage from spring and fall frosts.

Te Puke in the Bay of Plenty district of New Zealand has proved to be particularly well suited to the growth and cropping of kiwifruit, and its soils and climate should give an indication of the growth requirements of kiwifruit. At Te Puke, the mean annual temperature is 57.2°F (14.0°C); the February (summer) mean maximum and minimum 74.6°F (23.7°C) and 56.7°F (13.7°C), respectively; and the winter (July) mean maximum and minimum 56.7°F (13.7°C) and 40.6°F (4.8°C). The mean daily range in temperature is 17.1°F (9.5°C). The rainfall of about 68 in. (1725 mm) is distributed evenly throughout the year, the relative humidity stays close to 80% and there are some 2225 hours of sunshine annually. There are only a small number of frosts during winter. The significance of these values should not be overemphasized: kiwifruit in the Bay of Plenty probably receive inadequate winter chilling, and their growth in summer is excessively vigorous. Furthermore, kiwifruit can be grown satisfactorily in areas with very different climates if the management techniques originally devised for the Bay of Plenty are modified. If the comparatively exacting requirements of kiwifruit are not met, however, growth will be poor and the yields insufficient to justify the high costs of orchard establishment.

In China, kiwifruit are normally found in relatively wet and shady areas on the edge of the forest or in clearings in mixed evergreen–deciduous forests. They seldom occur on hilltops where there is exposure to strong winds. When the vines climb up into the canopy, many fruit are set. It appears that shade is required for seedling growth and subsequent establishment; more direct light is needed for growth of the mature vine and for fruiting.

Dormant kiwifruit vines can tolerate winter temperatures well below 32°F (0°C). Growing vines perform best in a relatively temperate climate having a long frost-free period, with maximum summer temperatures seldom exceeding 100°F (40°C) and abundant and well-distributed rainfall.

Climatic Effects

Wind and shelter.   The importance of shelter from wind is often underestimated. The vigorous young shoots that will be tied down to form fruiting arms the following year can be broken or are readily blown out during spring and early summer storms. Developing fruit can be scarred by rubbing against branches or adjacent fruit. More insidiously, there can also be a marked reduction in growth, particularly of younger vines.

Water.   The amount of water required by a vine will depend on the canopy area and factors such as temperature, relative humidity, the amount of sunlight, and air movement. The total daily transpiration of vines can approach 25 gal (100 liters) of water a day in summer, owing to the large leaf area and very high rates of transpiration and water conductivity.

In areas with shallower soils or where there is restricted root growth or more limited rainfall, irrigation may be essential. In California, for example, where there is little or no rain during the summer months, kiwifruit have the reputation of requiring more water more often than any other crop. A regular and constant supply of good-quality water must be provided by an irrigation system able to supplement the natural rainfall to between 30 and 45 in. (800 and 1200 mm) of water throughout the growing season. A shortage of water, even for only a brief period, can result in loss of turgor, leaf dessication, and a check to fruit growth. If water is limiting during early fruit development, fruit size never recovers.

Frost.   Kiwifruit flower about 60 days after vegetative bud break, and the fruit are mature and ready for harvesting some 150 to 160 days after flowering. Successful cropping of kiwifruit therefore requires a particularly long frost-free growing season of about 220 days (7 to 8 months).

Susceptibility to frost varies with time of year and age of the plant. Newly produced vegetative shoots, developing flower buds, and flowers are all very frost tender and can be damaged by even short exposures to temperatures of 30°F (-1°C) or lower. Frost tolerance develops throughout the season and plants may be able to withstand temperatures down to 14°F (-10°C) by midwinter. Early fall frosts can cause damage to the fruit. Severely frosted fruit rapidly become very soft, and even fruit that are less damaged do not store well and develop off-flavors.

Hail. Hail can cause severe damage to fruit as well as less important damage to shoots and leaves. It is a serious problem in parts of Italy, where antihail nets are commonly used. Nets can also help prevent fruit sunburn as well as providing some protection against spring frosts and wind.

Sunburn and high temperatures. Excessive summer heat can cause sunburn or scald on fruit and can cause scorching of leaves. Damage to fruit is particularly common on younger vines with incomplete canopy cover or where hard summer pruning has exposed fruit previously shaded.

Winter chilling. In tropical or subtropical regions with mild winters, kiwifruit vines show poor bud break over a long period, leading to low flower numbers and a much extended flowering. Winter chilling increases both the percentage and uniformity of bud break and the number of flowers that develop. It has been suggested that 'Hayward' requires 750 to 800 Richardson chilling units for satisfactory flower production, but this has not yet been tested experimentally with whole plants. Some orchardists in warmer climates have grown cultivars such as 'Abbott', 'Monty', or 'Bruno', as they seem to require less winter chilling and are more floriferous than 'Hayward'. However, they break bud slightly earlier in the season and are therefore more susceptible to spring frosts, and the quality of their fruit is inferior.

Light. Shading by natural or artificial shelter belts or by overhead shelter can decrease productivity simply by reducing the amount of light received and hence reducing photosynthetic assimilation. For vines growing under New Zealand conditions, fruit exposed to the sun are of better quality and can be stored for longer than those that are in the shade under the canopy. If fruit are susceptible to sunburn from the intense sunlight (e.g., as in California), it may be an advantage for them to be shaded. Shading can also affect flower evocation. If whole vines are shaded throughout the period of evocation in late summer, there is a reduction in the number of flowers produced the following season. Shading of individual shoots throughout the summer produces replacement canes that are weaker and that carry large numbers of shoots which remain dormant the following spring: the shoots produced from the buds that do break carry fewer flowers. For good flower production, pruning should maintain an open canopy, and the replacement canes that become fruiting arms the following year should be kept exposed to the sun. Vine management is therefore a compromise between aiming at maximum light interception and ensuring that buds or fruit within the canopy are not excessively shaded.

Soil and Nutrient Requirements

Soil. Kiwifruit prefer light, well-drained soils with adequate humus. They do not grow well on heavy clay soils that are susceptible to waterlogging, as this can result in vine decline or even rapid death. On the other hand, excessively sandy soils are also not suitable, as they dry out too quickly. The soil should be slightly acid, as kiwifruit suffer from lime chlorosis on calcareous soils.

Vine composition and turnover. The trunk and the main branches of a kiwifruit vine are permanent, but the fruiting arms are replaced every 2 or 3 years and the leaves and the fruit are lost every year. Much of the new vegetative growth is taken off in summer pruning. About 60% of the aboveground mass of the plant is thus removed during the season in the prunings, leaves, and fruit. If only the fruit is removed and the prunings are left, as is usually the case, to decompose on the orchard floor, the nutrient loss will still be significant. Kiwifruit yields in New Zealand average about 11 tons/acre (25 MT/ha), and the approximate quantities of the major nutrients removed in such a crop are 34 lb/acre (38 kg/ha) of nitrogen, 5 lb/acre (5.5 kg/ha) of phosphorus, 6.5 lb/acre (7 kg/ha) of calcium, 3 lb/acre (3.5 kg/ha) of magnesium, and 67 lb/acre (75 kg/ha) of potassium. Such estimates indicate the minimum quantities of nutrients required each year for sustained cropping.

Pests and Diseases

The present major pests and diseases of kiwifruit in New Zealand are listed in Table 11-2. Many other insect pests can also be a problem, but they are normally controlled by the spray programs used for scale and leaf roller. Young plants in the nursery or the field can be damaged by slugs and snails and rabbits. Undoubtedly, the most unexpected pests are domestic cats that are attracted to the roots and will chew young plants or seedlings.

In other countries, as in New Zealand, control programs have become necessary as plantings increase. However, the pests and diseases that are important may be different, partly because the climatic and growing conditions are different and partly because different species are present. In California, for example, the main problems at present are various types of scale, leaf rollers such as *Platynota* and *Argyrotaenia* spp., and *Botrytis*. Nematodes *(Meloidogyne* and *Pratylenchus),* *Phytophthora,* and *Armillaria mellea* (oak root fungus) can also cause problems.

TABLE 11-2 MAJOR PESTS AND DISEASES OF KIWIFRUIT IN NEW ZEALAND

SCIENTIFIC NAME	COMMON NAME	PART AFFECTED	CONTROL
		Insects	
Ctenopseustis obliquana and other tortricids	Leafroller caterpillars	Shoots, leaves, young fruit	Regular spraying to kill successive generations
Hemiberlesia rapax	Greedy scale	Stems, leaves, fruit	Best by spraying dormant vines; also postblossom to kill crawlers
Meloidogyne hapla	Root-knot nematode	Roots	Use of clean planting material or nematicide dipping before planting
Scolypopa australis	Passionvine hopper	Shoots	Removal of alternative hosts and spraying of shelter, if necessary
		Bacterial Diseases	
Pseudomonas viridiflava	Bacterial blossom blight (bud rot)	Flower buds	No commercial program
		Fungal Diseases	
Armillaria spp.	*Armillaria* root rot, honey fungus	Roots and trunk	Removal of dead tree stumps or soil fumigation partially successful
Botryosphaeria dothidea	Ripe rot	Fruit in store	Reduced by spraying shelter belts and removing prunings from orchard
Botrytis cinerea	Storage rot	Dead flowers, leaves, fruit in store	Fungicides applied postblossom and just before harvest
Phytophthora spp.	Root rot, collar rot, crown rot	Roots and base of stem	Best overcome by providing better drainage
Sclerotinia sclerotiorum	*Sclerotinia* rot, field rot	Flower buds, leaves, fruit on vine	Removal of dead flower parts, prompt pruning of male vines, postblossom fungicides

CULTURE

Although this account is based on the cultural methods used in New Zealand, the differences in season between the southern and northern hemispheres have been taken into account: the months cited are those appropriate to California.

Cultivars

'Hayward' is markedly superior to the other pistillate cultivars currently available commercially. 'Matua', selections from the 'M-series', and 'Chico male' are the best pollenizers.

Site Selection and Preparation

As kiwifruit orchards are costly to establish, it is essential that sites be carefully chosen. The amount of wind, the availability of good-quality irrigation water, winter temperatures, the topography and aspect, soil depth, and drainage must be considered. Dry windy hilltops, cold frosty hollows, heavy and poorly drained soils, and steep hillsides: all these are not worth planting.

The pH of the soil should be about 6.0. Kiwifruit do not grow well on alkaline or calcareous soils, and nitrate fertilizers should be avoided on soils that tend toward alkalinity. The land should be graded to ensure good runoff of irrigation and rainwater; waterlogging, which causes rapid death in kiwifruit, is sometimes minimized by planting the vines on ridges running along the rows. If the subsoil is heavy or there is a hardpan, drainage must be provided.

Young kiwifruit vines compete poorly with weeds and pasture plants such as clover: before planting, a strip 3 to 6 ft (1 to 2 m) wide should be cleared along the rows and the ground worked.

Shelter

Shelter is essential but not without disadvantages. The losses due to wind damage or to the deleterious effects of shelter belts are among the major limitations to kiwifruit production.

Growers in New Zealand and most other growing areas have adopted a system of closely spaced shelter belts which are established at least several years before the kiwifruit are planted. (Fig. 11-6). An effective shelter should filter the wind, not present a solid barrier to it. The shelter belts are ideally at right angles to the direction of the prevailing winds, and the blocks are usually wide enough for about six rows of kiwifruit. Species widely used in New Zealand to provide shelter include

FIGURE 11-6 Regular patterns of shelter belts and kiwifruit orchards, Bay of Plenty, New Zealand. (Courtesy of the New Zealand Kiwifruit Authority.)

Salix matsudana (Matsudana willow), *Cryptomeria japonica* (Japanese cedar), *Casuarina* sp., and *Sinocalamus oldhami* (giant bamboo).

Shelter belts occupy valuable land, they compete with the vines for water and nutrients, they can increase the risk of frost by hindering air drainage, and the shading they cause can reduce vegetative growth and flowering. They must be trimmed and maintained and they can harbor pests and diseases. Bee behavior, and hence pollination, can also be affected. There are often marked yield gradients across kiwifruit blocks, with yields being reduced alongside the shelter belt. Many existing shelter belts are now being replaced by artificial shelter, and remaining shelter belts are controlled more rigorously to ensure a porosity of between 45 and 50% and thus prevent wind turbulence. The roots of shelter trees are also pruned.

Artificial shelter provides instant shelter and allows better land utilization but at a much higher initial capital cost. Overhead artificial shelter covering the entire orchard provides good protection against wind, but the advantages may be outweighed by shading.

Propagation

Only clonal material should be planted in orchards, and this is raised by grafting seedlings, from rooted cuttings, or by tissue culture. Under good growing conditions, there are no consistent differences in vigor and fruiting between plants that are rooted cuttings and grafted seedlings. Mature plants can also be reworked using rind (bark) grafts.

Grafted seedlings. Seed is extracted by briefly blending ripe kiwifruit at low speed and washing the fruit pulp away. Seed is stored moist in a refrigerator for 3 weeks and then held at fluctuating temperatures between 50°F (10°C) at night and 70°F (20°C) in the day during germination.

Young seedlings are transplanted into seedling trays or small [3-in. (7.5-cm)] pots. They are planted outside in rows in a nursery block in spring when they are about 4 to 5 in. (10 to 13 cm) high. After a year in the nursery, the seedlings can be either grafted and left for another year in the nursery before being planted out in the orchard or transferred to the orchard and allowed to grow for a year and then grafted.

Budwood should be taken in winter only from vines known to produce good-quality fruit true to type. It is held in a cool, damp place or sealed in plastic bags in the refrigerator until grafting in January (California), before the vines bleed, or from April onward. Kiwifruit are easily grafted: cleft grafts or whip-and-tongue grafts with two or three buds are normally used.

Rooted cuttings. Softwood cuttings are taken from young growth during June to August. The top two leaves of the cutting are cut in half and the others are removed. The cuttings are dipped in rooting hormone such as IBA and then rooted while being held in a mist propagation unit. The young plants can be shifted outside to a nursery the following spring. Semihardwood cuttings and root cuttings can also be propagated successfully. It takes about 2 months for shoots taken from 'Hayward' micropropagation proliferation cultures to develop into rooted plants about 8 in. (20 cm) high and with 6 to 10 leaves.

Planting

Young vines are planted out in late winter or early spring, although planting can be delayed if there is a risk of frost. Only good, robust plants with a well-developed root system should be used (Fig. 11–7): if the plants are too small, many may be lost on transplanting or during establishment. In T-bar blocks, there is normally 15 to 16 ft (4.8 to 5 m) between the rows and 18 to 20 ft (5.5 to 6 m) between plants in each row, but with more intensive planting there may be only 8 to 10 ft or less (2.5 m) between plants in the row. On pergolas there is usually about 20 ft (6 m) between rows and 18 to 20 ft (5.5 to 6 m) between the plants in each row. Where possible, the vines should be planted midway between the posts.

Soil Management and Weed Control

Most kiwifruit orchards have a permanent ground cover of grass and clover (which can make a significant contribution to the nitrogen status but competes for potassium). Regular mowing of the sod is required — particularly during flowering when competing flowers that are attractive to bees, such as clover, should be removed. Chemical weed control is normally limited to strips running along the row, leaving the area between the rows in grass. Herbicides registered for use in vineyards or orchards are normally safe as long as they are not sprayed onto the leaves or green stems.

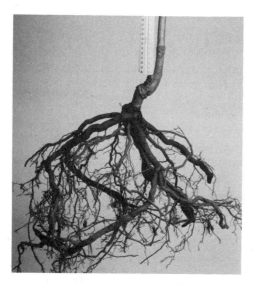

FIGURE 11-7 Root system of a 2-year-old 'Hayward' kiwifruit plant produced from a rooted cutting and ready for planting out in the orchard. (Courtesy of Mt. Albert Research Centre, New Zealand.)

Fertilizers

Young vines are very susceptible to damage from excessive fertilizer concentrations. A slow-release or organic fertilizer should be mixed with the soil in the planting hole. Young vines should then be given small amounts of a balanced fertilizer, containing nitrogen, phosphorus, potassium, and magnesium, regularly throughout the season.

Guideline maintenance dressings (on a planted area basis) for mature cropping vines are:

Nitrogen: 150 lb/acre (170 kg/ha) applied in two dressings, two-thirds in March (California), the remaining third in May after flowering.

Phosphorus: 55 lb/acre (60 kg/ha), supplied in February–March.

Potassium: 225 to 325 lb/acre (100 to 150 kg/ha). Large amounts of potassium should be added as split applications during spring (e.g., equal amounts in February–March, April, and May).

Magnesium: 55 lb/acre (50 kg/ha) should be provided at the same time as potassium.

This program should be modified according to the local soil conditions and the crop load. Other nutrients can also be applied according to a knowledge of the soil if vines show symptoms of deficiency or as indicated by leaf analysis monitoring.

Large amounts of potassium are removed in the fruit, and vines frequently show signs of potassium deficiency, often confused with drought stress. Heavy applications of potassium, however, can induce deficiencies of calcium or magnesium if these are not also supplied. Manganese deficiency can occur if the pH of the soil is too high, manganese toxicity if the pH is too low. Fertilizers should be spread evenly and the pH of the soil should be maintained at about 6.0 by the application (preferably annually) of lime or of dolomite when there is a likelihood of magnesium deficiency.

Leaf samples for monitoring nutrient status should consist of a standard type of leaf together with its stalk (petiole) taken at the same stage of growth each year, usually in late summer (August). Provisional optimal nutrient concentrations for the second leaf beyond the final fruit on a fruiting shoot collected at this time are as follows:

	PERCENT DRY WEIGHT		PPM
Calcium	3.0–3.5	Boron	40–50
Magnesium	0.35–0.45	Copper	10–15
Nitrogen	2.2–2.8	Iron	60–200
Phosphorus	0.18–0.22	Manganese	50–100
Potassium	2.0–2.5	Zinc	15–30
Sulfur	0.30–0.45		

The trends in leaf composition, and not just the absolute values, are important.

Irrigation

The method of water application depends partly on the size of the vine's rooting system. On lighter soils, drippers often supply water to only a narrow cone of soil, and frequent irrigation is necessary, particularly to young plants with their small root systems. For larger vines, up to 10 drippers per vine may be required to provide enough water. Undervine minisprinkler systems, which produce a wetted area of much greater radius, are often preferred. Overhead sprinklers, which can also be used for frost protection, are not suitable. They may leach large quantities of nutrients from the leaves, or 'water stain' the fruit.

Support Structures

Kiwifruit vines are not self-supporting; their size, vigor, and longevity, and the heavy crop loads carried means that they require strong and permanent structures on which to grow.

A support structure should allow the development of a canopy of leaves efficient at intercepting the light and capable, therefore, of high rates of photosynthetic assimilation. Fruiting arms are the productive units of kiwifruit vines — fruit are carried on shoots of the current season which come from wood of the previous season. These fruiting arms need to be fastened so that the fruit are held in a stable position to avoid windrub and are kept clear of contamination from the soil or damage by tractors. The ideal structure will also be easy to manage efficiently and be comfortable to work on. Two main types of support structures are currently used: the pergola and the T-bar. A pergola provides a single plane of canopy about 6 ft (1.8 m) above the ground (Fig. 11–8). The T-bar can be thought of as a single-wire fence in which the extra wires at both ends of the cross-bar simply hold the fruiting arms in fixed position as they hang down toward the ground (Fig. 11–9). For a T-bar system to make efficient use of the land, the fruiting arms should meet in the middle when they are lifted horizontally. T-bars are cheaper and easier to construct than pergolas and they are less labor intensive, with many growers finding them easier to manage. They are certainly more comfortable to work on, they are better suited to pollination by bees, and there is less risk of severe *Botrytis* infection. On the other hand, yields are frequently considerably higher with pergolas and the fruit is less susceptible to wind damage, as it is much easier to fasten canes down. When the full pergola canopy is established, the shade reduces weed growth and there is less mowing. In California, it has been found that the greater shade also produces not a brown-skinned fruit but a green-skinned fruit which is preferred by the market. Mature kiwifruit on a T-bar system produce a load of about 30 lb/ft (40 kg/m) spread over all the wires. It is therefore false economy to skimp on support structures, and it is particularly important that the end assemblies be sufficiently strong. Failure of support structures can lead to major crop losses and be difficult to repair.

A typical T-bar system will have posts every 16 to 20 ft (5 to 6 m) of 3½- to 4-in. (90-mm)-diameter round treated timber driven 2 to 3 ft (0.6 to 0.9 m) into the ground, leaving 6 ft (1.8 m) above ground. The cross-bar is 5 ft (1.5 m) wide of 4 ×

FIGURE 11-8 Kiwifruit trained on a pergola. Photograph taken from above just before bud break. (Courtesy of Mt. Albert Research Centre, New Zealand.)

FIGURE 11-9 Kiwifruit trained on a winged T-bar. Photograph taken from ground level just before bud break. (Courtesy of Mt. Albert Research Centre, New Zealand.)

2 in. (100 × 50 mm) timber rebated into the top of the post and braced back to the post with wire or timber. The end strainer assembly is either a horizontal stay ('box end') or a tie-back strainer ('dead man'). Three high-tensile galvanized wires, 12 or 13 gauge (2.5 or 3.15 mm), are placed on top of the cross-arm and pulled tight. A common modification of the standard T-bar is the winged T-bar (Fig. 11–10), in which there is an outrigger wire at the end of a downward wing on each side of the cross-arm. Tying down a cane onto two wires has the effect of pulling it into a more natural curve, the cane is supported farther out, its movement in the wind is reduced, and there is less tractor damage.

A pergola system has posts similar to those used for the T-bar. Two laminations of 4 × 1 in. (100 × 25 mm) timber are required for the cross members and the wires are run on top of the beams down the rows of posts and 18 to 25 in. (450 to 650 mm) apart between the rows.

Training and Pruning

If the vigorous growth of the vine is not controlled, the result is a dense and tangled mass of vegetation that carries only light loads of small fruit. Proper pruning establishes and maintains:

An organized and well-formed permanent framework of branches

A balance between vegetative growth and fruit production

A canopy that intercepts light efficiently and yet is open enough to allow sufficient penetration of the light required for fruit quality and flower evocation

An open canopy that allows access of the bees during flowering, reduces outbreaks of fungal diseases such as *Botrytis,* and makes spraying and harvesting easier.

When the vine is young it may be important to establish a good canopy cover to prevent the fruit being sunburned; in older vines it may be more important to reduce shading by removing excessive vegetative growth.

Pruning methods must take into account that:

1. Flowers are produced only on shoots of the current season and usually only on shoots growing from 1-year-old wood.

2. Shoots that grow from older wood when it is pruned back seldom produce flowers in their first season.

3. Canes that bear fruiting shoots should originate as close as possible to the center wire.

4. Shoots from buds that were heavily shaded during the preceding season will be less productive than those from buds that were exposed to the sun.

5. Ideal 1-year-old canes have short internodes with well-formed buds and are self-terminating. Such canes develop early in the season. In general, the

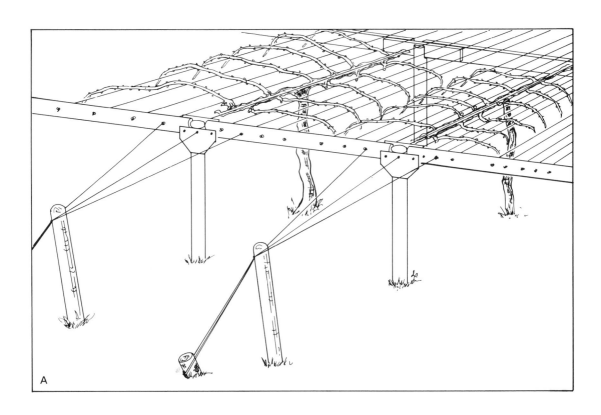

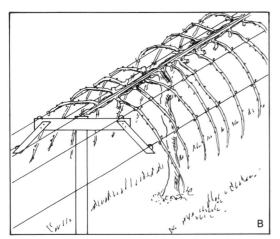

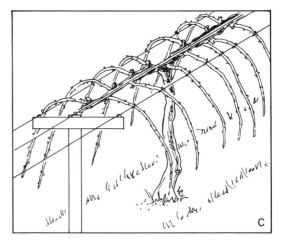

FIGURE 11-10 Kiwifruit training systems: (A) pergola; (B) winged T-bar; (C) standard T-bar.

Kiwi Fruit Management   Chap. 11

stronger canes are more fruitful, but the very vigorous 'water shoots' (strong, upright young shoots) seldom produce fruit until they are 2 years old and they can shade the rest of the vine.

6. Buds distal to the fruit on a fruiting shoot have the potential the following year to produce shoots that will flower and fruit.

7. Different pistillate cultivars respond differently to management. 'Hayward' carries lighter crops than the other cultivars and the selection of new fruiting wood is more important.

8. Pistillate and staminate plants are pruned differently.

Training young plants.   A light stake is placed next to the vine and a strong shoot is trained up the stake to the center wire to form a single straight trunk. All growths below the graft are removed. When the shoot reaches the wire it is trained in one direction as a permanent leader, and the following year a shoot is trained as leader in the opposite direction. Alternatively, the stem is cut just below the wire to produce shoots, two of which are selected as leaders. These are tied along the center wire and eventually form the main branches. If the main stem or one of the leaders becomes spindly or tangled, it is headed back to a strong bud to encourage more vigorous growth. The stem should not be allowed to twist tightly around its stake or the leaders around the center wire because the constrictions that develop can weaken the vine. Lateral canes are tied at right angles along both sides of the leaders: these canes will become fruiting arms the following year.

Winter pruning of pistillate plants.   The main branches or leaders along the center wire are permanent, although they can be renewed, if necessary, by tying down a fresh shoot. All other wood is replaced on a regular cycle. At winter pruning, the vine is tidied up by removing much of the wood that has fruited, any twisted, tangled, or broken canes and other unwanted wood. The aim is to retain the optimum number of buds on 1-year-old wood which is evenly spaced on the vine and forms a single canopy layer. This 1-year-old wood is a mixture of:

1. *Replacement canes arising close to the leader.* On a T-bar system these canes are tied down over the outer wires and cut off about knee height or tied back to keep their ends clear of the ground. On pergolas, the canes stretch over to the adjacent plants.

2. *Fruiting laterals on 2-year-old fruiting arms.* Each lateral is cut back to about six to eight buds past the last fruit.

3. *Spurs.* These are short, self-terminating laterals, usually produced by the stubbing back of strong shoots close to the central leader.

Replacement canes are generally more fruitful and produce bigger fruit than the laterals on arms that fruited the previous year. Fruiting arms are often replaced after their first year of fruiting, but are retained if reduced vegetative vigor means that sufficient replacement canes are not available. After three seasons at most, fruiting arms have to be removed, as the vine would otherwise become overcrowded. Only a small proportion of the fruit should be carried on spurs. Winter pruning can start once the leaves have fallen and should be completed well before bud break in spring, as the vines will otherwise bleed.

Summer pruning of pistillate plants. In New Zealand, summer pruning begins in midspring before flowering; unfruitful shoots that originate outside the wires are removed, flowering laterals are cut back to four or six leaves beyond the last flower, 'water shoots' are stubbed back, and any tangles are removed. During the summer months, vegetative growth can be very vigorous. Shoots not wanted the following year as replacement canes are removed, replacement canes are tipped to prevent tangling, and regrowths are pruned. It is essential that the canopy not become too dense. The amount of summer pruning required will depend on the climatic conditions and the need to protect fruit from sunburn.

Pruning staminate plants. Staminate plants are often particularly vigorous because their vegetative growth is not restricted by competition from fruit for resources. They may therefore require rigorous pruning to keep them down to size. They are usually pruned immediately after flowering when the flowering arms are cut back to new growth close to the main leader. The flowering season can be extended by heading back the developing canes several times during the year. In California it is recommended that staminate vines be pruned immediately after flowering, as the summer sun may otherwise burn the newly exposed branches and trunk.

Crop Loading and Thinning

The overcropping of young vines reduces vegetative vigor and delays the formation of full canopy cover. If a mature vine is overcropped, the fruit do not size up, and at harvest there is a greater proportion of the smaller grades of fruit, which are usually less profitable. The vine may also be thrown into biennial bearing.

Crop load can be regulated by pruning. The amount of 1-year-old wood (or more precisely, the number of large, fat buds on 1-year-old wood) left on the vine determines the potential number of fruit. However, not all buds break dormancy in spring, and some of the new shoots are purely vegetative, while the others carry variable numbers of flowers. Furthermore, the flowers that are produced may be malformed or they may be destroyed by disease or frost. By monitoring the behavior of vines from year to year it is possible to predict the likely numbers of fruit produced per winter bud laid down. In the Bay of Plenty (New Zealand), for example, it can be expected that about one-third of the winter buds will produce flowering shoots, and each of these shoots will, on average, carry a little over three flowers. This results in about 1.2 flowers per winter bud. In districts with colder winters, the ratio of flowers produced to winter buds laid down may be considerably higher.

It is no longer considered sufficient at winter pruning simply to tie down a replacement cane every 10 to 15 in. (25 to 40 mm) each side of the leaders. Rather, the strategy ('target pruning') should be to retain sufficient 1-year-old wood to provide enough flowers for a realistic target crop load. Ideally, the fruit should be spaced evenly on the vine. The number of winter buds required per square yard of canopy can be estimated, and then, by taking the average number of buds per foot of cane and the vine canopy area into account, this is converted to more useful figures, such as length of replacement cane required per vine (in typical mature vines between 200 and 225 ft or 60 to 70 m), or numbers of canes on each side of the leaders. An allowance is made for the number of spurs. Since bud break varies from season to season and since flowers can be lost during the spring, it is usually best to winter prune comparatively lightly and then thin to the required crop load. Thinning should be completed within 2 weeks of fruit set. Fasciated and flat fruit and any damaged fruit are removed first, followed by lateral fruit and then the smallest single fruit. Growers usually aim at about 40 to 45 fruit per square yard (50 to 55 fruit per square meter) of canopy. To size such a crop load successfully requires good vine management and effective pollination.

Pollination

Although wind can play a small part in pollination, honeybees are the most important agent of pollen transfer. Fruit size increases with seed number and the large number of seed in commercial-sized fruit means the transfer of at least several thousand pollen grains from the staminate flowers to the stigmata of each pistillate flower.

Kiwifruit flowers are not particularly attractive to bees—they produce no nectar and the pollen is shed in dry clumps, which the bees find difficult to pack into their pollen baskets. High densities of bees (usually, 3 hives per acre or 8 hives per hectare) are therefore required in kiwifruit orchards, particularly if cold wet weather during flowering limits foraging. Hives are moved into the orchard at about 10 to 15% 'Hayward' flowering.

Competition for pollen sources affects bee behavior. Bees visit both staminate and pistillate flowers. They can, however, distinguish between flowers, and do not visit them at random but show a preference for one or other type. Only when there is pressure on the supply of pollen (i.e., from the number of bees in the orchard) do a high proportion of bees visit both staminate and pistillate flowers. It is important that enough bees be brought into the orchard to ensure visits to both staminate and pistillate flowers, and that each pistillate flower is visited often enough to ensure good pollination.

Generally, about 10% of the canopy is reserved for staminate vines. These should be evenly distributed throughout the orchard as the fruit produced closest to the staminate vines are larger and contain more seed, probably because bees forage repeatedly in fairly restricted areas. There is also a tendency for bees to move along rows; this is very marked within T-bars blocks, less so in pergola blocks.

Orchards have commonly been planted in a 1:8 staminate/pistillate ratio, with every third plant in every third row a staminate plant. Higher ratios of 1:6 (every third plant in every second row) and 1:5 (every second plant in every second row) are accommodated by reducing the canopy area occupied by each staminate vine. Ideally, staminate plants should be grown in each row. This can be achieved, in effect, in T-bar blocks by running the staminate plants as a hard-pruned, narrow row at right angles across the top of the pistillate rows. The pistillate plants are planted between the posts and the staminate plants alongside every second post in every second row and trained along a wire 1 ft (30 cm) above the fruiting canopy. In pergola blocks, every second row can be a very thin row or band of staminate plants, and the canopy is kept open for bee access.

Pest and Disease Control

The program of sprays used in New Zealand throughout the season is designed for the growing conditions in that country to control the pests and diseases that are important there (Table 11-2), while allowing the fruit to meet the quarantine regulations and the spray residue standards insisted upon by importing countries. There is the added restriction that sprays applied during the flowering period must not harm bees. Insecticides are used mainly to control leafrollers and scale. As an example, the current program (1987/1988) recommended by the New Zealand Ministry of Agriculture and Fisheries consists of:

1. During winter, sprays of lime sulfur and chlorpyrifos to clean up greedy scale. Bordeaux or other copper fungicides can also be applied to the dormant vines.
2. Preblossom, the insecticide azinphos-methyl at least 7 days prior to bees being brought into the orchard.
3. Insecticides such as phosmet applied as soon as the bees have been taken out of the orchard and neighboring orchards, 2 weeks later, and then every month until the withholding period of 21 days prior to harvest.
4. Iprodione or vinclozolin to control *Botrytis,* applied as close as possible (but not closer than 3 days) to harvest.
5. Sprays of *Bacillus thuringiensis* can be used to control leaf roller. This spray has the great advantage of no residue limits and does not affect bees; however, it does not control greedy scale.
6. From petal fall onward, fungicides to control *Sclerotinia* if monitoring reveals infection of rotting flowers (especially staminate flowers) or the development of apothecia on litter on the orchard floor.

Harvesting

Growers normally want to pick their kiwifruit as early as possible in the season. Fruit on the vine are always at risk from frost or other bad weather; the returns for the first fruit on the market are usually high. If kiwifruit are picked when they are still immature, they have a poor color and an inadequate flavor when ripened, and a short shelf life when taken out of storage. If fruit are not picked until late in the season, occasional fruit may have ripened prematurely, and these can trigger the ripening of the remaining fruit.

The conversion of starch to sugars as kiwifruit mature can be followed by measuring the soluble solids concentration (percent soluble solids or degrees Brix) in the fruit. Under New Zealand conditions, this provides a simple but reliable measure of maturity: a block may not be picked for export until it has reached a minimum maturity index of 6.2% soluble solids, as estimated by a strictly standardized procedure; in California, the minimum maturity standard has been set at 6.5% soluble solids. For good fruit quality after 4 or more months' storage, it is generally recommended that fruit be picked at a maturity index between 7 and 10% soluble solids.

Fruit are usually harvested about the beginning of November (California). The fruit are snapped off their stalks, which remain on the vine (Fig. 11–11). Although the fruit are still hard, they must be handled gently; for example, pickers should wear gloves to avoid damaging the skin, and the fruit should not be dropped or knocked together.

Inspection, Grading, and Packing

Grading criteria and standards vary from country to country, and the standards that must be met by fruit for local markets are frequently much less rigorous than those for fruit that are to be exported. U.S. standards for grades of kiwifruit require that the fruit be intact, sound, clean, well formed, and typical of the cultivar; they must be of a certain size; they must be free of any defects that impair the appearance and keeping quality of the fruit or which are likely to make the fruit unattractive to the consumer; and they must be free from pests, diseases, and contamination with toxic materials.

A high rate of inspected fruit rejection indicates poor management or unfavorable climatic conditions, poor orchard hygiene, poor pollination, or careless fruit

FIGURE 11-11 Kiwifruit harvest. Note that the picker is wearing gloves to protect the fruit from damage by fingernails. (Courtesy of New Zealand Kiwifruit Authority.)

handling. In New Zealand about 20% of the crop is usually rejected as being unsuitable for export.

Packaging materials are designed to protect the fruit during storage and transport, as well as allowing them to be displayed attractively to consumers. Most fruit are packed into wooden or fiberboard trays (flats). The fruit are sorted by weight (sometimes by size) and are then placed into pocket packs so that each tray (California) contains about 7 lb (3.2 kg) net of fruit. In New Zealand, the trays contain about 3.5 kg of fruit, and the number of fruit per tray (the tray count) varies with fruit weight from 25 to 46. The packed fruit should not protrude above the level of the tray. A polyliner (of low-density polyethylene) is placed under the pocket pack in each tray and then folded over the fruit. Sheets of corrugated strawboard, smooth side toward the fruit, are usually placed at the top and the bottom of the tray.

Storage

Kiwifruit can be harvested while still firm, stored for long periods of 6 months or more, and then ripened to an edible, highly acceptable state. This is possible only if fruit are of good quality when they enter the store and the correct storage conditions are used. The fruit should be held as close as possible ($32 \pm 1°F$ or $0 \pm 0.5°C$) to the temperature at which they freeze (about $29°F$ or $-1.5°C$), and they should be reduced rapidly to this temperature after harvest and packing. There is a very small margin of error between the temperature at which kiwifruit should be stored and the temperature at which they freeze.

Large amounts of water can be lost by kiwifruit when they are stored at the low relative humidities found in most cold storage rooms: unprotected fruit lose weight and shrivel within a few weeks. This loss of water is reduced by wrapping the packed fruit within a polyliner inside the tray.

Kiwifruit produce little ethylene when they are harvested. They are, however, very sensitive to ethylene and even small traces of the gas will cause them to soften and ripen rapidly. Freshly harvested fruit should not be exposed to ethylene, which can be produced by damaged fruit, fruits such as apples or pears, or is present in exhaust fumes. Even fruit stored at $0°C$ will respond to as little as 0.03 ppm ethylene. Hence all forklifts used in cold storage facilities are battery driven. Kiwifruit produce ethylene as they ripen, as do fungal rots, and a few prematurely ripe or rotten fruit can thus trigger ripening in stored fruit.

Production Costs

Kiwifruit are among the most costly of all fruit plants to establish, and there is a long delay from the beginning of development until profitable cropping is achieved. In the first year there is the cost of the land and its preparation, orchard machinery such as tractors and sprayers, and the provision of irrigation for the shelter. It may take 2 years before the shelter has grown enough to allow planting of the vines. Then come the major costs: purchase of the young vines, construction of the support structures, and completion of the irrigation system. Some fruit will be produced in the fifth and sixth years, but this means further expenditure to build a packhouse or buying into existing facilities. The vines will not reach mature cropping levels until they are 8 or 9 years old (i.e., 10 or 11 years after development began). In New Zealand, it has been calculated that when interest rates are taken into account, it can take some 16 years for a standard T-bar orchard with natural shelter to break even.

Returns will be improved if vines start bearing sooner and maximum yields are achieved earlier. More rapid canopy development, or more intensive planting with two or three times as many vines as normal, should bring full production 2 to 4 years earlier. Artificial shelter probably quadruples the cost of vine establishment, but does allow the vines to be planted the first year, increasing income during the early years. The use of artificial shelter allows a greater proportion of the orchard land to be planted, thereby reducing the unit costs of land, buildings, and machinery. Pergolas, at $2000 to $3000 per acre, cost about 50 to 70% more than T-bars, but this increased capital cost may be justified by the higher yields and the reduced fruit damage.

Once an orchard has reached maturity, the costs of production (pruning, fertilizers, irrigation, weed control and mowing, spraying against pests and diseases, pollination, harvesting) are only about half the cost of grading, packing, and cold storage of the fruit.

Marketing

Large-scale production of a new crop is possible only when promotion has created market demand. The successful promotion and marketing of kiwifruit encouraged growers in New Zealand to plant more vines, confident that the fruit they produced could be stored, shipped overseas, and then marketed in good condition. The successful export of kiwifruit from New Zealand to California, Europe, and Japan subsequently encouraged growers in those countries to plant kiwifruit; they could plant with the knowledge that a profitable market had already been created for their fruit.

The promotion of a previously unknown crop is not easy and it took many years for the kiwifruit to become anything but a novelty fruit. The inherent qualities of the fruit itself made the primary appeal, but other factors were also important: the sustained and imaginative promotion, the name change from 'Chinese gooseberry' to 'kiwifruit', good and standardized packaging, and attractive presentation. Perhaps most important was the emphasis on quality and quality control.

World kiwifruit marketing patterns are changing rapidly. Initially, most countries followed the New Zealand pattern, relying on export markets. Now there is increasing competition, as world production doubles every two or three years. California has exported half of its kiwifruit crop to Japan, but as production increases in Japan and in other northern hemisphere countries such as Italy and France, Californian growers will become more dependent on their local market, sending perhaps only their larger fruit to Japan. New Zealand is still the largest producer in the world, but it is facing more competition from other southern hemisphere countries, such as Chile, which now produce appreciable amounts of fruit. There is no direct competition for much of the year between fresh kiwifruit from the northern and southern hemispheres, but the long storage life of the fruit results in some overlap at the beginning and end of the marketing seasons.

Kiwifruit are available on the market for many months, and supplies can be adjusted to demand. The long storage life of the fruit allows the maximizing of returns by the orderly progression of fruit from cold storage to the market and to the consumer.

ACKNOWLEDGMENTS

I am grateful to my colleagues for many helpful suggestions, and in particular to N. A. Turner for his assistance in preparing the section on fertilizer requirements and H.M.N. Lees, orchardist of Te Puke.

SUGGESTED READING

ALEXANDER, G. P. 1986. Kiwifruit-male vines: selection, distribution, and husbandry techniques. In Proc. Kiwifruit Pollination Seminar, Oct. 1986, Tauranga, New Zealand. Advisory Services Division, Ministry of Agriculture and Fisheries.

BEUTEL, J. A. 1986. Kiwifruit training. p. 33–39. In 1986 Kiwifruit Production Meeting Proc., Saanichton, British Columbia. Queen's Printer, Victoria, British Columbia.

BEUTEL, J. A. AND G. COSTA. 1983. The kiwifruit situation in California. p. 67–77. In Atti del II Incóntro Frutticolo SOI sull'Actinidia, Udine, 1983. Centro Regionale per la Sperimentazione Agraria per il Friuli-Venezia Giulia e Sezione Frutticoltura della SOI, Udine, Italy.

DALGETY, N. (compiler). 1986. Establishing a kiwifruit orchard: costs and returns. 2nd ed. Ministry of Agriculture and Fisheries, Hastings, New Zealand.

EYNARD, I. 1986. Ambiente colturale dell'actinidia ed aspetti biologici. p. 11–41. In G. Bargioni, F. Lalatta, and A. Febi (eds.). Incontro Frutticolo la Coltura dell'Actinidia, Verona. Cassa di Risparmio di Verona Vicenza e Belluno per l'Agricoltura, Verona, Italy.

FERGUSON, A. R. 1984. Kiwifruit: a botanical review. Hortic. Rev. 6:1–64.

FERGUSON, A. R. AND R. M. DAVISON. 1986. *Actinidia deliciosa*. p. 1–14. In A. H. Halevy (ed.). CRC handbook of flowering. Vol. 5. CRC Press, Boca Raton, Fla.

FERGUSON, A. R. AND M. LAY YEE. 1983. Kiwifruit *(Actinidia chinensis* var. *hispida)*. p. 111–116. In G. S. Wratt and H. C. Smith (eds.). Plant breeding in New Zealand. Butterworth, Wellington, New Zealand.

FISCHER, W. B. 1987. Vegetation management in kiwifruit vineyard. Calif. Fruit Grower 64(1): 33–36.

FLETCHER, W. A. 1976. Growing Chinese gooseberries. Government Printer, Wellington, New Zealand. Bull. 349 N. Z. Dept. Agric.

GOODWIN, R. M. 1986. Honey bee pollination of kiwifruit. In Proc. Kiwifruit Pollination Seminar, Oct. 1986, Tauranga, New Zealand. Advisory Services Division, Ministry of Agriculture and Fisheries.

HOPPING, M. E. 1986. Kiwifruit. p. 217–232. In S. P. Monselise (ed.). CRC handbook of fruit set and development. CRC Press, Boca Raton, Fla.

HORTICULTURAL ADVISORY OFFICERS. 1985. Kiwifruit target yield pruning: one day planning guide, Winter 1985. Advisory Services Division, Ministry of Agriculture and Fisheries, Bay of Plenty and Hamilton, New Zealand.

JAY, D., AND C. JAY. 1984. Observations of honeybees on Chinese gooseberries ('kiwifruit') in New Zealand. Bee World 65(4):155–166.

LIANG, C. F., AND A. R. FERGUSON. 1986. The botanical nomenclature of the kiwifruit and related taxa. N. Z. J. Bot. 24: 183–184.

LÖTTER, J. DE V. 1984. An evaluation of the climatic suitability of various areas in southern Africa for commercial production of Hayward kiwifruit *(Actinidia chinensis)*. Deciduous Fruit Grower 34:122–130.

LUH, B. S. AND ZHANG WANG. 1984. Kiwifruit. Adv. Food Res. 29:279–309.

PENNYCOOK, S. R. 1985. Fungal fruit rots of *Actinidia deliciosa* (kiwifruit). N. Z. J. Exp. Agric. 13:289–299.

PILARSKI, M. 1985. Actinidia enthusiasts newsletter. Friends of Trees Society, Chelan, Wash.

SALE, P. R. 1985. Kiwifruit culture. 2nd ed. D. A. Williams (ed.). Government Printer, Wellington, New Zealand.

SMITH, G. S., C. J. ASHER, AND C. J. CLARK. 1987. Kiwifruit nutrition: diagnosis of nutrition disorders. 2nd rev. ed. Agpress Communications, Wellington, New Zealand.

UNITED STATES DEPARTMENT OF AGRICULTURE, AGRICULTURAL MARKETING SERVICE. 1986. Subpart: United States for grades of kiwifruit. p. 349–354. Code of federal regulations, Title 7, Agriculture.

WARRINGTON, I. J., AND G. C. WESTON. (eds.). 1989. Kiwifruit: science and management. Ray Richards, Auckland, New Zealand, in association with the New Zealand Society for Horticultural Science (in press).

YOUSSEF, J., AND A. BERGAMINI. 1979. L'Actinidia (kiwi-yang tao) e la sua coltivazione. Frutticoltura 41(7, 8):13–67.

Chapter 12

Maturity Standards, Harvesting, Postharvest Handling, and Storage

S. E. SPAYD
J. R. MORRIS
W. E. BALLINGER
D. G. HIMELRICK

FRUIT MATURITY

Small fruits should be harvested at the time of optimum maturity. Fruit maturation can occur whether or not a fruit is attached to the plant. The postgrowth period of fruit maturation and eventual death is divided into three stages:

1. *Maturation:* a series of changes that occur between the cessation of growth and physiological maturity;
2. *Ripening:* the changes that occur from the end of the maturation period to the beginning of senescence;
3. *Senescence:* the irreversible changes that follow ripening and lead to death.

'Optimum quality' (horticultural harvesting maturity or maximum usefulness for a particular purpose) is attained just prior to or during senescence. Since small fruits are used in a wide variety of forms and products, specific criteria are used to define quality. These criteria will vary from species to species and from product to product.

Components of small fruit quality and/or maturity indices can be grouped into four general categories: (1) appearance, (2) flavor, (3) texture, and (4) nutritional value.

Appearance. Color, size, shape, and defects influence the appearance of small fruits. Insect, disease, bird, and frost injury may cause scarring or malformation of fruit which make the fruit unsuitable for fresh market or pick-your-own (PYO) sales. Fruit size and uniformity are important for fresh market, for PYO operations, and for processing into whole or sliced, frozen, or canned products. A product may have excellent nutrient content, flavor, and texture, but if it is not attractive, it will not be acceptable.

Small fruits for use in preserves, jams, jellies, purees, and juices should be free of insect damage and contamination, but certain percentages of microorganisms (such as mold) may be permitted within federal and state regulations. Fruit destined for use in wine should be free of diseases since they can cause off-flavors in the final product.

Small fruit color (a widely used maturity index) is essentially dependent on three types/classes of pigments: (1) phenolic compounds (e.g., anthocyanins), (2) chlorophyll, and (3) carotenoids. Changes in fruit color during development are due to pigment synthesis, pigment degradation, and/or chemical changes within the fruit that result in an alteration in the color expression of existing pigments.

Anthocyanins play the most important role in small fruit color. Anthocyanins give ripe strawberries their characteristic redness and blueberries their blueness. Anthocyanins absorb light in the visible wavelength range between 475 and 560 nm. Their composite colors range from red to purple. Color expression depends on type of anthocyanin, pH, presence of metallic ions, and so on. Anthocyanin concentrations increase with ripening and decrease during advanced fruit senescence.

Each type of fruit has a genetically determined complement of anthocyanin(s). For example, red *Vitis vinifera* cultivars contain anthocyanins that have one glucose unit attached to the aglycone (monoglucosides). Most red American grape species contain both monoglucoside and diglucoside forms. Therefore, it is possible to differentiate wines from American red grapes from wine from *V. vinifera*. Other types of phenolic compounds contribute to the color of ripe, white-fruited grapes.

Chlorophylls and their derivatives are the predominant pigments in green fruits such as kiwifruit and immature forms of other small fruits. In fruits that do not have chlorophyll as the predominant pigment, chlorophyll concentration decreases during fruit development. In strawberries, chlorophyll concentration decreases essentially to zero prior to initiation of red color development (the inception stage). Chlorophylls are usually yellow to bluish green in color and have absorbance maxima in the infrared region (630 to 710 nm).

Carotenoids have been found in strawberries and blueberries, but their role in small-fruit color is minor. Carotenoids are colorless, red, orange, or yellow, depending on the type present. Carotenoids absorb in the range 400 to 500 nm and are fat-soluble pigments. In addition to its contribution to color, beta-carotene is a precursor of vitamin A.

Flavor.   A consumer's initial purchase is normally based on the product's appearance or reputation, but repeat purchases of a product depend on flavor and other characteristics affecting fruit quality. Flavor is a complex sensation and is affected by the aroma of the product as well as the taste. Many attempts have been made to classify taste as well as odor or aroma. The four basic taste sensations of sweet, sour, salty, and bitter are a critical base for understanding flavor.

Numerous classes of chemical compounds make up the flavor volatiles. Volatiles vary between fruits, between cultivars within a given species of fruit, and between fruit maturities. Flavor profiles can be developed by the use of gas chromatography in conjunction with a mass spectrometer. To characterize the aroma of specific volatile compounds, the partitioned gas is split into two streams as it exits the chromatography column. One gas stream enters the mass spectrometer, while the other stream exits to a sniffing device. The individual volatiles are then characterized as to their smell (fruity, floral, citral, etc.). The 'typical' aroma of a small fruit may be due to one or more of these compounds. The contribution of a volatile to flavor is not necessarily proportional to the concentration of the volatile in the fruit. Often the combination of two or more volatiles imparts the characteristic aroma.

The sugar-to-acid ratio is an important factor in determining the flavor and quality of a small fruit. In general, as fruit ripens, sugars increase and acidity decreases. Sugar increases may be due to starch hydrolysis, translocation of sugars into the fruit, and/or sugar synthesis in the fruit. Desiccation may also contribute to increased concentration of sugars in fruit. Acidity is decreased by respiratory metabolism, primarily by the tricarboxylic acid (TCA) cycle, and by dilution as the fruit rapidly absorbs water during ripening. The most common method for determining sugar content is by use of a refractometer. It is expressed as percent soluble solids, degrees Brix, or the refractive index.

Organic acids are the major contributors to the acidity of small fruits. Many of these are intermediates of the TCA cycle. The two major TCA cycle acids are malic and citric. Tartaric acid in grapes and quinic acid in blueberries are two of the non-TCA-cycle organic acids found in appreciable amounts in small fruits.

Texture.   Cell turgor, integrity of cell membranes and walls, and intracellular integrity contribute to the texture and firmness of small fruits. Many small fruits exhibit a double sigmoid pattern of fruit growth (Fig. 12–1). During phase I, fruit growth is due to a rapid increase in cell number. Individual cells are relatively small in size and volume, and the fruit has high cell density per unit area. The immature fruit is very firm at this stage due to the high proportion of dry matter packed in a small volume with rigid cell walls. In phase II cell division slows or stops. Phase III is marked by a rapid increase in cell size due to increases in intracellular water. As long as the cell membranes and walls remain intact, the fruits retain their firmness due to turgor pressure. As the fruit ripens and advances toward senescence, proteases, pectinases, and cellulases act on cell membranes, cell walls, and intracellular materials. Hydrolysis of components of these structures results in loss of intracellular binding, increased membrane permeability, and ultimately, softer fruit.

Many methods are used to measure firmness. Most instruments determine

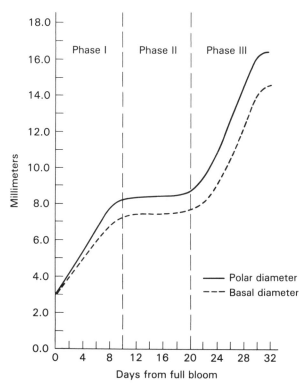

FIGURE 12-1 Changes in polar and basal diameter recorded at 2-day intervals from full bloom, June 9, to maturity, July 11, of 'Lathan' red raspberry fruits. [From Hill (1958).]

firmness as force required (1) to reach a predetermined degree of deformation, (2) to puncture or penetrate the fruit to a given depth, or (3) to shear a given weight of sample. Carbohydrate levels in cell walls and enzyme activity changes are useful indicators of fruit firmness.

Nutrients. When consumed fresh, small fruits are a good source of ascorbic acid (vitamin C), fiber, and potassium. During maturation of strawberries, ascorbic acid concentration increases during ripening and then levels off or declines as the fruit approaches senescence. Potassium concentration in grapes tends to increase steadily during fruit maturation.

Changes in Fruit during Maturation

Many physical and biochemical changes occur during fruit maturation and ripening. Figure 12–2 shows changes in strawberry composition and berry weight with maturity. One of the most striking changes during maturation is the change in fruit color. Anthocyanin-pigmented fruits (e.g., strawberries) begin to decrease in chlorophyll concentration, increase in anthocyanin concentration, and become redder and/or

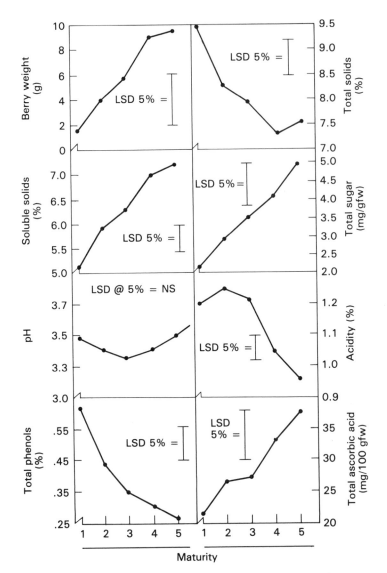

FIGURE 12-2 Changes in berry weight, total solids (%), soluble solids, total sugar, pH, acidity, total phenols (expressed as percent quercitannic acid), and total ascorbic acid with increasing maturity of strawberries: 1, small green fruit; 2, large light green fruit; 3, red color inception (less than 50% red color); 4, fresh market ripe (more than 50% red color to 100% bright red color); 5, processing ripe (dark red color). [From Spayd and Morris (1981).]

bluer in color as they mature. In kiwifruit, chlorophyll concentration does not change when fruits ripen (induced by ethephon) on the vine while carotenoid concentration decreases (Ben-Aire et al., 1982).

Sugar concentration tends to increase during maturation, and the concentration of sugars varies considerably between the different fruits. Of the small fruits, the greatest change in sugars, as measured by percent soluble solids, occurs in grape berries. At veraison (the point at which grapes begin to ripen, soften, and change color) soluble solids of 'Concord' grapes are about 8 to 10% and of wine grapes are about 12 to 15%. Depending on the intended use of the grapes, soluble solids will be allowed to increase at least twofold on the vine prior to harvest. Soluble solids in highbush blueberries increase from 6 to 7% (small deep green berries) to 10 to 12% (entirely blue berries) (Ballinger and Kushman, 1970). Percent soluble solids in strawberries (Fig. 12–2; Spayd and Morris, 1981) and kiwifruit do not change drastically during development (Ben-Aire, 1981).

Acidity decreases and pH increases during the ripening phase of development for most small fruits. Acidity loss in small fruits during ripening is due primarily to respiratory metabolism of TCA-cycle acids (malic and citric), and also results from dilution of the acid concentration as the water concentration increases rapidly during phase III of development. Increased pH in grapes during vine ripening is due at least partially to the increase in potassium concentration that occurs during maturation.

Concentrations of volatile compounds that are associated with the typical flavor of a ripe fruit also increase during ripening. Ascorbic acid concentration decreases in kiwifruit (Ben-Aire, 1981) and increases in strawberries (Spayd and Morris, 1981) as the fruit ripens.

Quality Characteristics and Utilization

The optimum quality for harvesting a fruit depends on how the fruit will be utilized after harvest. Each fruit and each type of market or product has its own set of quality requirements or standards. The goal of these standards is to deliver a finished product (whether fresh or processed) with predictable quality and shelf life.

Most small fruits for the fresh and processing markets are harvested on the basis of fruit color. Cultivars have been and are being developed with fruit that have synchronized development of optimum color, flavor, firmness, and other desirable fruit characteristics. Uniformity of fruit size and color is desirable in fresh and processed products.

Blueberries. Fruit of a deep-blue color with a dusting of light-blue waxy bloom is required for the fresh market. Removal of the waxy bloom is an indication of overripe fruit or mishandling of the fruit during or after harvest. For highbush and rabbiteye blueberries, larger fruit may command a higher price.

Most blueberries for processing are harvested with mechanical harvesters or with mechanical aids. Such fruit has a wide range of maturities in addition to stems, leaves, and other foreign matter to be removed in the packhouse or processing plant. The presence of insects, shriveled berries, pathogens, split fruit, and extraneous plant material can result in the rejection of fruit by processing plant buyers.

Brambles. When marketed fresh, red raspberries should have a glossy-bright red fruit color, no mold, and whole fruits. Since the torus is removed during harvest, raspberries have a hollow core and are easily crushed.

For processing, the mold count is a critical factor that affects the quality of bramble fruit. The Food and Drug Administration's upper permissible level for mold content is 50% by the Howard Mold Count Technique. For frozen whole fruit, color and size uniformity are important.

Strawberries.   Fruit firmness, size, color, and skin glossiness are extremely critical for strawberries sold on the fresh market. Firmness is also important to the processing industry in whole and sliced berry products. It is a prerequisite for successful machine harvest. Other quality parameters important for long shelf life of fresh strawberries are maintenance of a green calyx and freedom from mold. Uniformity of color and size is important in the production of frozen whole and sliced berry products. Internal fruit color should be stable during frozen storage. Berries for pureed products such as jellies, jams, and juice are often harvested at a later stage of ripeness than that for fresh market fruit. This ensures adequate anthocyanin concentrations for good color in the finished product. Fruit from different cultivars and regions may be blended to achieve the desired color in the final product.

Grapes.   Grape quality standards are probably the best developed and utilized among the small fruits. Appearance is the most important quality parameter for table grapes (Winkler et al., 1974). Critical components of grape appearance are (1) large berries shaped typically for the cultivar with a bright attractive color (whether green, red, or dark blue); (2) uniformity of berry size, shape, and color; (3) large ½ to 2 lb (125 to 1000 g), well-shaped, compact clusters; (4) bright green rachis; and (5) freedom from injury and disease. There are other important quality factors. Seedless table grapes are usually preferred. Flavor is affected by the sugar-to-acid ratio, aroma, and characteristic taste of the cultivars. Texture also affects the 'mouthfeel' and the perception of flavor.

Raisins should be firm but not crisp. USDA standards (Anon., 1974) for processed raisins specify that 'processed raisins are dried grapes of the vinifera varieties, such as Thompson Seedless (Sultania), Muscat of Alexandria, Muscatel Gordo Blanco, and Sultana. The processed raisins are prepared from clean, sound, dried grapes; are properly stemmed and capstemmed except for cluster or uncapstemmed raisins; and are sorted or cleaned, or both, and except for cluster or uncapstemmed raisins are washed in water to assure a wholesome product'.

Most raisins are prepared from seedless cultivars, although some seeded grape cultivars are used. Sugar and moisture content are the two most important factors that affect raisin quality. A maximum of 18 to 23% moisture is allowed in the finished product to meet the minimum USDA standard grade. Raisin quality could be increased by maximizing the sugar-to-water ratio of the raw product. Fruit size affects the rate of drying. The smaller the fruit, the greater the surface-to-volume ratio and the faster the rate of water loss.

Grape Juice and Wine.   In the United States, 'Concord' *(V. labrusca* L.) grapes are the most widely used grape in the production of unfermented juice, due to its characteristic 'foxy' flavor. Methyl anthralinate is the major flavor volatile that contributes to this flavor. Sugar content, expressed as percent soluble solids, is used as the criterion for determining the optimum maturity for harvest (between 15 and 19% soluble solids). Acidity, pH, and color are other important quality criteria. Fruit that is low in acid in relation to percent soluble solids has a flat, insipid taste. High pH values (3.5 and higher) can cause off-colors (from purple-red to purple-blue) due to a shift in the chemical structure of anthocyanins. Since 'Concord' fruit quality is greatly affected by the climate in which the grapes are grown, juices manufactured from grapes produced in various regions of the country may be blended to produce a uniform product.

Timing of harvest for wine grapes *(Vitis vinifera* and French-American hybrids) is also usually based on percent soluble solids. White wine cultivars are usually harvested when the fruits have between 19 and 21% soluble solids, while red wine cultivars are harvested when they have between 20 and 24% soluble solids. A minimum level of soluble solids is required to achieve a minimum concentration of 7% alcohol for the product to be considered wine. In some regions, in the event that the minimum level of soluble solids is not reached, sugar is added to the crushed fruit (must). With some cultivars and in regions with warm night temperatures, fruit acidity, and/or pH may be the limiting quality parameter. Therefore, depending on the cultivar and the intended style of wine, fruit may be harvested on the basis of acid content and/or pH. High acidity can be offset by leaving residual sugar in the wine. Although acidity and pH can be adjusted in the winery, a minimum acid content of 0.5 to 0.6% and a pH within the range 3.00 to 3.50 are realistic commercially. A combination of high acidity and high pH can also make adjustment in the winery more difficult.

American *Vitis* species are also used for wine production. Harvest criteria are similar to those for *V. vinifera* and its hybrids. Muscadine grapes are harvested around 16 to 17% soluble solids with low acidity (0.2 to 0.3) and pH (3.1 to 3.3).

Other small fruits. Color intensity, glossiness, and uniformity and freedom from defects are the major quality parameters for fresh and frozen cranberries. For cranberry juice, cocktail, and sauce, color uniformity is not critical as long as there is enough pigment present to produce an acceptably colored product. Gooseberries are harvested when the color changes from a bright green to dull, translucent green. Red currants are usually harvested before the color changes from a bright red to a dull dark red color. Soluble solids are usually about 12% and acidity is around 2%.

HARVESTING SMALL FRUITS AND GRAPES

The availability of an adequate and dependable supply of hand pickers at harvest time is a continuous problem for small-fruit and grape growers. In some sections of the country, growers have relied on labor of local origin, while others depend on an influx of migrant labor to harvest the crop. Mechanical harvesting has been employed mainly with crops that are destined for the processing market. Hand pickers continue to harvest most fruit for the fresh market, since fruits are bruised less when picked by hand.

Hand Harvesting

Berries for local sales and for processing should be harvested when they are fully mature and at the peak of their flavor. If they are to be shipped, they should be harvested slightly before they attain full maturity so that the berries will have a sufficiently long shelf life. All berries must be harvested and handled with the greatest of care if they are to reach the market in good condition.

It is important to instruct hand pickers carefully concerning the desired stage of maturity for a given market (fresh market or processing) and the best technique for picking. Pickers must be shown how to pick the berries with the most speed and least damage to the fruit and plant, as well as what should be done with rejects and rotten berries. Pickers should always use both hands. Their picking speed is reduced very little when the pickers are properly trained. Most growers provide their pickers with small carts designed to hold the fresh market or processing lug that can be pulled or pushed between the rows.

Cane or bramble berries are hand picked by gently lifting the berries with the thumb and fingers. Raspberries separate, leaving the torus (the center part of the fruit) on the bush. Blackberries, when harvested, separate so that the torus remains within the fruit. One of the best indices of proper harvest maturity is color; full color will usually develop before the berries separate easily from the plant. These berries are usually hand harvested directly into the containers in which they are sold. Harvesting can be facilitated by using waist carriers, which leave both hands free for picking.

These delicate berries should be removed from the sun and placed in a cool location as soon as possible after harvest. Temporary sheds are often built near the fields or a truck is covered so that the fruit can be placed in the shade immediately after each carrier is filled. The market life of berries can be extended by precooling them immediately, keeping them cool thereafter and using nondamaging post-harvest handling procedures.

Hand harvest of table grapes. The California table grape crop is hand packed either in the vineyard or in packing houses (Fig. 12–3). Some growers pack their grapes under the vine by placing the shipping containers on a small stand or by propping the container against the trunk of a vine. This method is used by small growers or for grapes that require special, gentle handling. Most of the grapes that are field packed use an avenue field-packing system. With this method one packer with a portable stand will pack the grapes that are harvested by four to six pickers. The development of a 'snap-on' lid has eliminated the need for hand nailing and has increased the practice of vineyard packing. Additional advantages of vineyard packing include low overhead, elimination of field lugs, less handling, and longer shelf life.

Today, specially designed packing houses permit mechanization of many of the packing operations and facilitate the packing of more than one grade of a given cultivar. In this system the empty field lugs are distributed in the vineyard, and the pickers place the suitable clusters stem-up, one layer deep into the lugs (Fig. 12–4). The pickers trim the clusters only minimally to remove damaged fruit. At the

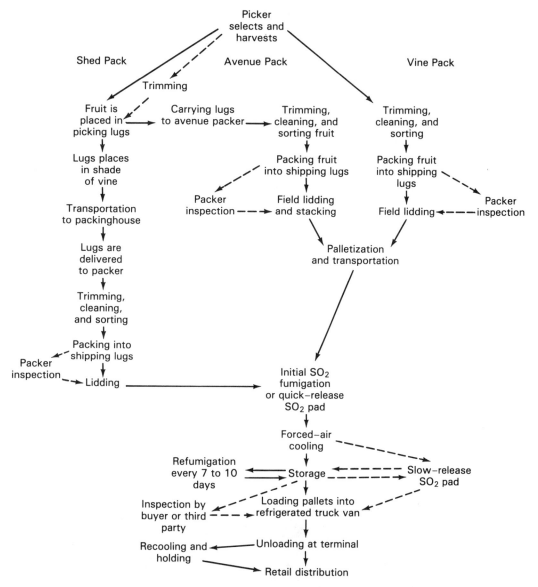

FIGURE 12-3 Handling system for table grapes in California. [Courtesy of F.G. Mitchell, *Postharvest Technology of Horticultural Crops,* Univ. Cal. Spec. Publ. 3311.]

packing house the palletized lugs are transferred by a forklift. The lugs are then placed onto conveyors that pass by the packers, who trim the clusters further to remove defective berries and then pack the clusters stem-up in the shipping containers. The packed containers move through a lidding machine, are stacked on pallets, and are then strapped securely to the pallet and are moved to a forced-air cooling, fumigation room. This system requires field lugs and the management of both a picking and a packing crew. However, packers who employ this system like the final inspection and control at the packing house.

The standard lug for shipment of California table grapes is 16 in. (41 cm) long and 14 in. (36 cm) wide with a depth of about 5 in. (13 cm). The net weight of the grapes packed in it is approximately 22 lb (10.5 kg) for the Coachella Valley district and 23 lb (11 kg) for San Joaquin Valley district.

As with any fresh fruit, the grape is alive and continually undergoes respiration during postharvest handling and marketing. Thus the most important step in prolonging the storage and shelf life of grapes is to immediately cool the packed grapes by forced air to 40°F (4°C), which slows the rate of respiration, and then to fumigate the room with sulfur dioxide. This fumigation should be completed during the day of harvest. The sulfur dioxide destroys fungi and fungal spores on the surface of the grapes. If the grapes are in good condition, fumigating with a sulfur dioxide concentration of 0.5% by volume for a 20 minute period is sufficient. After the gas is exhausted, the grapes can be moved to a common cold storage room that does not contain forced air facilities, and held at 40°F (4°C). Grapes should be refumigated with sulfur dioxide each week that they are held in storage.

Hand harvest of wine grapes. A large percentage of the wine grapes in California are still harvested by hand. Pickers drop the cut bunches of grapes into pans or plastic lugs which, when full, are dumped into gondolas with a capacity of 2 to 7 tons (2.2 to 7.7 MT) of grapes. The gondolas are designed so that they can either be dumped directly at the winery or several transferred to a truck that is equipped for dumping. If a large volume of grapes is to be moved for a long distance, the grapes from the field gondolas are usually dumped into larger gondolas on tractor/trailers which haul them to the winery. There the gondolas are hydraulically dumped by a winch crane into the winery receiving hoppers (Fig. 12-5).

FIGURE 12-4 In this California grape vineyard, empty lugs are distributed on top of the trellis and pickers cull the grapes, placing the bunches stem-up in the lugs. These grapes will be repacked at a central packing shed.

FIGURE 12-5 This California winery has the capacity of dumping two trucks at the same time. One truck is delivering a white cultivar and the other truck is delivering a red cultivar.

Mechanical Harvesting

Mechanical harvesting of cane fruits. Most mechanical harvesters utilize a shaking or beating mechanism to remove fruits from the canes. Fruits are normally caught in catching plates and air-cleaned, sorted, and loaded into containers (Fig. 12-6).

Cane fruit harvesters exploit fruit abscission as the basis of harvesting, allowing for repeated selective harvesting as the fruit matures. Ease of fruit abscission increases with maturity and can result in a machine-harvested product superior to that which is hand picked. Machine-harvested berries are larger and have a higher percentage of total soluble solids, lower acidity, and superior color than do hand-harvested berries.

One of the most important influences on quality of machine-harvested berries

FIGURE 12-6 Many of the mechanical grape harvesters operating in the United States use the horizontal shake-catch concept. The horizontal vibration is applied to the vine canopy by fiberglass rods.

Harvesting Small Fruits and Grapes

515

is temperature. Berries mechanically harvested at cool field temperatures have raw and processed quality comparable to that of hand-picked fruits regardless of berry temperature at harvest. However, berries machine-harvested at high temperature, 97°F (36°C), deteriorate more rapidly during storage than do berries hand-picked at the same temperature. Machine harvesting at the lowest possible temperature is advantageous for maintaining fruit quality during handling and storage.

Most insects can be eliminated from cane fruits prior to machine harvest by following recommended spray programs for the specific insect problem. However, insects in machine-harvested cane fruits can be removed by a washing technique in which infested berries pass through water containing a 0.1% nonalkaline anionic wetting agent. A water spray is then used to remove insects, debris, and wetting agent. Ninety-five percent of the insects can be removed by this method with no loss of quality.

Modifications to cultural systems for growing machine-harvested cane fruits are important for successful mechanical harvesting of cane fruits. It is necessary that a continuous hedgerow of plants enter the machine to obtain maximum harvest efficiency. A mechanized pruner has been developed that not only results in improved harvesting efficiency but also reduces the labor required for pruning. Mechanical pruning and leaving old canes in the hedgerow of erect blackberries has not resulted in lower yields or quality.

Mechanical harvesting of strawberries. Strawberries have been considered among the least adaptable crops to mechanical harvesting. There are two major obstacles to overcome: (1) lack of firm-fruited, uniformly ripening cultivars, and (2) increases in fruit weight of high-yielding cultivars, causing the fruit's supporting truss to sag to the ground. Mechanized harvesting and handling systems have been developed with varying degrees of success (Figs. 12–7 and 12–8).

One harvester utilizes a pneumatic stripping system in which air lifts the fruit into position and a comb-brush picking belt strips the fruit from the plant. The strawberries are given a once-over harvest when a majority of the crop has developed acceptable color. Another approach involves cutting or clipping the fruit from the plant, but many of the large fruit cannot be harvested since they remain on the ground. Most cultivars suited for machine harvesting have a 5- to 6-day optimal period for a once-over harvest.

Prior hand picking improves the quality of machine-harvested fruit from certain strawberry cultivars. Fruit remaining on the plants after one or two hand harvests had a higher percentage of ripe fruit in the once-over harvest than did machine-harvested fruit not preceded by a hand harvest.

One of the most objectionable aspects of machine-harvesting strawberries is the presence of green fruit from once-over harvests. In-plant equipment has been developed with the capability of cleaning and separating the strawberries into distinct maturity classes. Many immature fruits can be sorted from mature fruits based on differences in berry size on the in-plant cleaning line with a tapered-finger, continuous sizer. Strawberry products containing as much as 50% immature fruit can be utilized in the production of commercially acceptable jam from cultivars

FIGURE 12-7 The commercial over-the-row machine developed from the University of Arkansas prototype is self-propelled, hydraulically driven, and with a crew of five will replace 85 hand pickers. Also, this machine is equipped with lights that permit for 24-hour operation.

having high anthocyanin levels. Immature fruit does reduce the color quality of the jam but does not influence color loss and discoloration during storage.

Mechanical harvesting of blueberries. Commercial blueberry harvesters have been used since 1966. These large, over-the-row harvesters shake and dislodge berries from the bush. The fruit is caught in pans and conveyed to the rear of the machine, where trash and leaves are removed by high-velocity air blasts (similar to the diagram in Fig. 12-6 for the cane fruit harvester).

New techniques for sorting machine-harvested blueberries have been developed with varying degrees of success. These techniques include sizing, fiber optic light measurement, and vibration for sorting the berries. Sizing has not been an effective means of sorting by quality since this method does not discriminate well between ripe and overripe fruit. The fiber optic light method uses the anthocyanin content of the berries as a basis of separation. Mature berries have higher anthocyanin levels than those of immature berries; thus this method sorts berries into maturity classes (green, ripe, and overripe). The low-frequency vibration method

FIGURE 12–8 The commercial model of the University of Arkansas BEI mechanical strawberry harvester picks two rows and requires two lug tenders.

separates blueberries on the basis of firmness. This method separates green (very firm), ripe (firm to soft), and overripe (very soft) berries according to their 'bounce'. A newly developed USDA hydrohandling system for blueberries is superior to the standard grading line, due to removal of a higher percentage of undesirable fruit (green, soft, bruised, etc.).

The growth regulator Ethephon can be used to accelerate color development, abscission, and maturity of blueberries. Ethephon reduces the amount of force necessary to dislodge the berries from the bush; thus berries are damaged less during machine harvest, shelf life is increased, and there is less damage to the bush.

Mechanical harvesting of grapes. Major developments in grape harvest mechanization occurred in the early and mid-1960s, and mechanization was commercially practiced by the late 1960s. Today, many of the commercial harvesters employ the use of 'pivotal strikers', which consist of a double bank of flexible horizontal rods that strike and shake the vine to remove fruit (Fig. 12–6). In California, the 'trunk shaker' or pulsator harvesting concept is another commonly used method, which incorporates two parallel rails to impart horizontal vibration to the upper trunk and/or cordon. The trunk shaker is effective in removing fruit only in contact with a rigid trunk or cordon, and much less material other than fruit (MOG) is harvested. Some of the newer machines have combined the principles and reduced the number of horizontal rods. One commercial company refers to their unit as a 'pivotal pulsator'. Since it operates at a lower speed, this unit results in less leaf removal and vine damage. It has been reported that shorter stroke lengths result in more damage to the grapes, but the frequency of the beater does not affect the amount of damage. Fruit are removed with all harvesting methods as cluster parts and individual, torn berries. Perhaps the major quality problem with mechanically harvested grapes is the fruit damage from the beater rods or slappers and handling after harvest. The percentage of intact mechanically harvested berries may be as low as 40%.

With cultivars suited for mechanical harvesting ('Concord', 'Niagara', 'Flora', 'Thompson Seedless', 'Gewurztraminer', and 'Cabernet Sauvignon'), a mechanical harvester will deliver about the same amount of fruit to the processing unit as do hand-harvesting crews. The structure of the cluster framework and its adherence to the vine and to the berries are the main factors determining how easily, and in what condition, the fruit is removed. Fruit of most cultivars are removed primarily as single berries, this being particularly true of those with a fairly loose attachment. Cultivars with a firm berry attachment and a tough or wiry cluster are the most difficult to harvest mechanically.

Muscadine grapes present a problem for once-over harvesting as compared to the other commercial *Vitis* species. Many muscadine cultivars do not ripen uniformly. A system for sorting machine-harvested muscadine grapes into maturity classes has been developed which utilizes brine solutions of different strengths to separate grapes inexpensively according to specific gravity and/or maturity. Muscadine grapes are unique also in that an abscission layer forms as the berries mature. Abscission zone formation is so complete in some cultivars that ripe fruit will drop in advance of the mechanical harvester's collecting mechanism. New equipment designed to adapt to the front of any conventional commercial harvester can prevent the loss of these fruit.

Temperatures at time of harvest, during handling, and between harvest and processing probably influence the quality of machine-harvested grapes more than any other factor. High temperatures at harvest and a delay in processing lead to rapid deterioration of grape juice quality. Grapes harvested when fruit temperature is high [about 95°F (35°C)] produce high levels of alcohol and acetic acid, both signs of microbial spoilage, and have poor color. The alcohol and acetic acid content of mechanically harvested grapes begins to increase after 18 hours of holding at 84°F (29°C) or 24 hours at 75°F (24°C). Decreases in soluble solids and flavor parallel the increases in alcohol and acetic acid. The addition of sulfur dioxide to machine-harvested grapes has been shown to decrease quality loss during holding by delaying alcohol accumulation and loss of soluble solids for 24 hours when held at 95°F (35°C). Sulfur dioxide will discourage bacterial spoilage that might be expected to develop at high fruit temperatures over a long period; it also serves as an antioxidant to prevent juice browning.

The type of containers used for hauling the grapes to the processing unit can have an influence on product quality. Traditionally, 1-ton (0.91-MT)-capacity wooden bins with food-grade plastic liners have been used to accommodate the fruit. However, many operations on the west coast have shifted to a 4- to 5-ton (3.6- to 4.5-MT)-capacity hydraulic, self-dumping vineyard gondola that dumps the harvested grapes from the vineyard into bulk tank trucks which are hydraulically dumped at the processing plant. These bulk collection units have not reduced, and in some cases have helped, to maintain the quality of the processed product.

Harvesting Small Fruits and Grapes

Another approach to handling machine harvested grapes is to crush the grapes in the field as the fruit are discharged from the harvester, and transporting the juice to the processing unit. A closed gondola tank for collecting crushed grapes and juice from the harvester with a stemmer-crusher is effective in controlling microbial growth and oxidation since it permits injection of carbon dioxide, and sulfur dioxide into the tank.

PREPARING FOR MARKET

Grading (sorting) is the removal of objectionable fruit and separation of the remainder into one or more grades. Grades, in turn, are the enforcement arm of standards. In general, few small fruits intended for the fresh market are sorted or graded by machine because of their small size, tenderness, and high perishability. Handling during mechanical sorting can physically damage the fruit. The operation consumes precious time in the short postharvest life of many of these fruits. Exceptions are cranberries, kiwifruit, and mechanically harvested blueberries.

Strawberries and bramble fruits.   Strawberries and bramble (cane) fruits intended for fresh market are sorted for ripeness (as indicated by color) and grade as they are hand harvested into consumer packages (Fig. 12–9). They are then sent directly to precoolers and into marketing channels. This abbreviated handling reduces the physical damage to these delicate fruits.

Blueberries.   Cultivated highbush blueberry fruit intended for the fresh market are often hand harvested into shallow trays and buckets or are harvested directly into pint containers. In the packing house the ones harvested into trays or buckets are poured directly into trays lined with pint containers, or passed through a sorting line consisting of a dumper, cleaner (air blower for leaves and debris), and an inspection belt whereon defective fruits are removed by hand. The remaining berries drop from the end of the inspection belt into pint containers lined in shallow trays. Each filled pint is then covered (capped) by hand with a sheet of cellulose acetate held in place with a rubber band. Alternatively, the berries from the end of the inspection table can be fed into a mechanical filler/packaging unit.

Many highbush and some rabbiteye blueberries are harvested by over-the-row mechanical harvesters. The harvested fruits on some machines are collected in plastic lugs and later taken to the packing house, where they are sorted and packed as above. Currently, an attempt is being made to equip the harvesters with a brand of vibrating fingers that more gently detach only the ripe fruit from the bushes. Extra-strong air blasts separate leaves and debris from the collected and conveyed berries before the berries drop into shallow trays lined with 1-pint consumer containers. The filled pints are then taken to the packing house, where they are capped without further handling. This is an attempt to reduce unnecessary handling and bruising that can occur with some of the harvesting machines that detach green as well as blue fruit from the bushes. Lowbush blueberries are generally harvested with hand-held rakes or scoops.

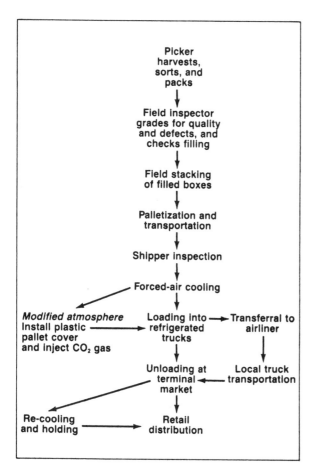

Picker
harvests,
sorts, and
packs

↓

Field inspector
grades for quality
and defects, and
checks filling

↓

Field stacking
of filled boxes

↓

Palletization and
transportation

↓

Shipper inspection

↓

Forced-air cooling

↓

Modified atmosphere
Install plastic ——→ Loading into ——→ Transferral to
pallet cover   refrigerated   airliner
and inject CO_2 gas   trucks

↓   ↓

Unloading at   Local truck
terminal   ←——— transportation
market

Re-cooling ←   ↓
and holding ——→ Retail
distribution

FIGURE 12-9 Postharvest handling system for strawberries. (Courtesy of F.G. Mitchell, *Postharvest Technology of Horticultural Crops,* Univ. Cal. Spec. Publ. 3311.)

Grapes. Bunch grapes are sorted in the vineyard during harvest and are placed directly into containers of various sizes, shapes, and materials. Muscadine grapes are harvested as single berries and end up with 50 to 80% of their stem scars torn open and oozing sugar-rich juice. Some growers of muscadine grapes sort them by hand on sorting belts and then pack them either in pint or in 18 to 24 lb containers of various kinds.

V. vinifera (European) grapes of acceptable sugar and acid contents are harvested in clusters and are either packed in the field or placed in shallow lugs and packed in the packing house (Weaver, 1976). At either location, each cluster is lifted carefully by its stem and defective berries are snipped from the cluster, as pulling them off the stem leaves a wet brush which invites decay. Care is taken to avoid crushing or tearing of the berries, since any opening in the skin invites easy entrance of decay microorganisms. These table grapes are usually packed with their stems up to allow easy removal of the clusters from the containers later in the marketing system. The box is tilted and one or more clusters are placed stem-up across the bottom width of the container. Other clusters are sequentially placed, stem-up, in an almost upright position, except for those required to pack the bottom solid. For those grapes harvested into shallow trays and transported to the packing house, the sorting and packing procedure is similar, straight out of the field lugs. However, often the box is vibrated during packing to settle the fruits; this may help to prevent excessive shattering of berries from the clusters.

PACKAGING

Containers provide a means for efficiently handling small fruits during loading, shipping, unloading, and marketing. Ideally, they should protect the fruit from mechanical damage, excessive drying, contamination, and pilferage. Packages should also provide for rapid precooling, safe stacking, efficient palletization, and easy storage in the warehouse or home; and assist in display and sale of the fruits (Ryall and Pentzer, 1974). The small fruits should ideally be packed not too loosely, so that the individual fruits in top layers vibrate; nor so tightly that the stack weight rests on the fruit. The package and not the fruit should bear the load. Only top-quality fruit should be packaged since the fruit-to-package cost ratio is important to profits.

Blackberries, boysenberries, and other bramble fruits are harvested directly into pint containers. The shipping container is generally a 12-pint fiberboard flat. Raspberries and strawberries for fresh market are picked into ½ and one pint cups, respectively, which are packed 12 or 15 per shipping flat.

The standard blueberry consumer unit is a paper-pulp pint which has several openings near its base. Typically, a plastic sheet is placed over the top of the berries and is held in place with a rubber hand. Twelve pints are packed in a corrugated fiberboard shipping flat. These flats, until recently, were generally of the telescoping type. Today, however, there is a trend toward use of the 12-pint 'strawberry flat', which has wire handles at the ends for secure stacking of these flats and indentations along the tops of the sides which permit ready secure stacking of these flats and ready access of air. For faster rates of precooling, however, perhaps a more perforated or a 'net-like' soft plastic cap could be substituted for the present solid sheet of plastic that covers each pint. The use of the strawberry-flat and netted pint covering would permit a precooling rate nearly as fast as that for strawberries.

American and muscadine grapes for fresh marketing are packed in a variety of container types. European-type grapes are principally shipped in corrugated board, wooden, or laminated wood-veneer-kraft paper (wooden ends) lugs holding 18 to 28 lb of fruit each. Length of the lugs is standard for uniform stacking on pallets, but the other two dimensions vary. Some of the newer lugs have beveled corners to assist air circulation. Most lugs are closed with wooden or veneer lids which have end cleats to allow for a slight bulge of the packed fruit; this permits stacking of the lugs without undue compression damage to the berries (Ryall and Pentzer, 1974). Lugs lined with plastic film and containing one- or two-stage sulfur dioxide generator pads (Grapeguards) can be used for storage or export shipment of the table grapes. The generators evolve sulfur dioxide from time of cooling until 10 days (one-stage generator) or 10 weeks (two-stage generator). The system controls berry decay as well as stem and berry desiccation.

The few cranberries that are sent to market are packed in 1-lb perforated plastic bags or fiberboard, windowed boxes. These containers are in turn packed 24 per master shipping container of corrugated fiberboard.

About 6½ lb of kiwifruit of a given size are placed in a tray (Beutel et al., 1976). The tray is then enclosed in a perforated polyethylene bag before it is placed in a wooden or corrugated fiberboard shipping container, to minimize moisture loss by the fruit. Curtains of polyethylene sheeting may substitute for the polyethylene bag.

Gooseberries, currants, highbush cranberries, elderberries, and Juneberries are minor crops packed in a variety of types of containers for mostly local marketing.

PROTECTING AGAINST DETERIORATION

When handling fresh small fruits, one should be aware that they are living organisms. After harvest they continue to undergo respiration, which draws upon sugars and other substrates stored in the fruit during their development on the plant. Oxygen is taken up from the air and carbon dioxide is produced. The faster their rate of respiration, the more highly perishable are these fruits and the shorter is their postharvest life (Table 12-1). Therefore, speed in their handling is very important. However, one must also keep in mind that small fruits are easily damaged if they are mishandled. When they are damaged, their rate of respiration increases, thus decreasing their quality and shortening their market life.

Tips for minimizing fruit damage in pick-your-own operations are as follows: (1) provide wide, shallow containers so that dumping is eliminated; (2) advise

TABLE 12-1 RECOMMENDED TEMPERATURE AND RELATIVE HUMIDITY, APPROXIMATE STORAGE LIFE, AND HIGHEST FREEZING POINT OF FRESH FRUITS IN COMMERCIAL STORAGE

COMMODITY	TEMPERATURE [°F (°C)]	RELATIVE HUMIDITY (%)	APPROXIMATE STORAGE LIFE	HIGHEST FREEZING POINT [°F (°C)]
Blackberries	31–32 (−0.5 to 0)	90–95	2–3 days	30.5 (−0.7)
Blueberries	31–32 (−0.5 to 0)	90–95	2 weeks	29.7 (−1.2)
Cranberries	36–40 (2 to 4)	90–95	2–4 months	30.4 (−0.8)
Currants	31–32 (−0.5 to 0)	90–95	1–4 weeks	30.2 (−1.0)
Dewberries	31–32 (−0.5 to 0)	90–95	2–3 days	29.7 (−1.2)
Elderberries	31–32 (−0.5 to 0)	90–95	1–2 weeks	— —
Gooseberries	31–32 (−0.5 to 0)	90–95	3–4 weeks	30.0 (−1.0)
Grapes				
American	31–32 (−0.5 to 0)	85	2–8 weeks	29.7 (−1.2)
V. vinifera	30–31 (−1 to 0.5)	90–95	1–6 months	28.1 (−2.1)
Kiwifruit	31–32 (−0.5 to 0)	90–95	3–5 months	29.0 (−1.6)
Loganberries	31–32 (−0.5 to 0)	90–95	2–3 days	29.7 (−1.2)
Raspberries	31–32 (−0.5 to 0)	90–95	2–3 days	30.0 (−1.2)
Strawberries	32 (0)	90–95	5–7 days	30.6 (−0.7)

Protecting Against Deterioration

customers on gentle picking and handling; and (3) provide shade if possible and fast checkout service.

For processing fruit, utilize pallet bins, gondolas, tanks on trucks or trailers, and materials-handling equipment to reduce handling and to speed the harvested small fruits to the processor before undue deterioration occurs.

For shipment of highly perishable small fruits to fresh markets, consider hand harvesting, grading, and packing into consumer packages, all in one operation, in the field. On the farm, prepare and smooth roads as much as possible prior to the harvest season. For transport vehicles, use a balanced suspension system that carries an economical load, but yet offers a 'soft ride'. Reduce the speed of these vehicles appropriate to conditions of the roads and the economics of the distribution timetable.

Removing Field Heat (Precooling)

Respiration provides fruits with energy for their vital processes but simultaneously produces heat which can build up in poorly ventilated shipping containers. The rate of respiration and vital heat production of small fruits are dependent on fruit temperature and decrease by a factor of 2 to 4 for each 18°F (10°C) lowering of temperature. Since each fruit contains a fixed amount of respirable stored 'food' (sugars, starch, etc.) after harvest, the sooner the temperature of the fruit is lowered, the longer the postharvest life of that fruit. Except for cranberries, most small fruits can be cooled to as close to 32°F (0°C) as possible without danger of chilling injury. Cranberries should be cooled to a temperature no lower than 36°F (2°C) since cooler temperatures result in chilling injury (Lutz and Hardenburg, 1968).

Small fruits should be kept out of the sun during harvesting and postharvest operations, cooled as soon as possible after harvest, and kept cool [30 to 36°F (−1 to 2°C); Table 12–1] until consumed or processed. Even a delay of cooling by a few hours can significantly reduce the percentage of fruits that are of marketable quality upon delivery to retail stores. Perishable berries should be cooled within 2 hours of harvest (Ryall and Pentzer, 1974).

The fruits may be cooled immediately after harvest; prior to, during, or after packaging; or partially before grading and partially to final cooling temperature after packaging. Transport vehicles do not have the refrigeration capacity to cool rapidly. They only have the capacity to keep the fruits cool when the fruits have been precooled before loading and loaded while cool.

The most common medium for precooling small fruits is air. For best room cooling, containers should be stacked so that air can circulate among them; the containers should be well ventilated (a minimum of 5% of side areas open) (Mitchell et al., 1972). Heat passes from the fruit through the container walls and is picked up by the passing cool air (Mitchell et al., 1972). Room cooling was commonly used, but it has been replaced for the small fruits in many cases by faster cooling methods.

Forced-air cooling can be 5 to 10 times as fast as room cooling (Mitchell et al., 1972) and can cool berries in 2 hours. The system involves the production of a difference in air pressure on opposing sides of pallet loads or stacks of ventilated containers (Debney et al., 1980). This pressure differential causes cold air to be drawn through the holes in the container walls and past the warm fruit, from which it picks up heat. The greater the flow of air through the containers, the faster the rate of precooling. This more rapid cooling must be accompanied by a comparably greater refrigeration capacity of the facility. Room coolers can be reoriented to forced-air cooling, but this generally only speeds cooling by a factor of 2 to 3. Once the produce has been precooled, it should be moved to the temporary cold storage area since prolonged forced-air ventilation can cause excessive water loss from the fruits.

Hydrocooling, widely used for precooling crops such as peaches and sweet corn, is two to three times faster than forced-air cooling. However, it can be used only on those crops that can withstand wetting. Blueberries or cranberries might possibly be hydrocooled. However, a problem of subsequent drying (removal of excess surface moisture) before shipment to market then arises. Also, because of contamination by decay organisms and dirt, the precooler's water must be replaced with fresh water daily. Chlorine can be added to the water to destroy spores of decay organisms in the water. To be an efficient system, the water must pass over as much of the fruits' surface as possible. Shower systems are more efficient than submersion systems.

Once the small fruits have been precooled, they should be kept cool until consumption (fresh) or processing. Remember, temperature control is *the most important* way by which postharvest quality can be maintained. All other techniques are supplemental to, and mostly uneconomical without, proper temperature maintenance.

Decay Prevention

Postharvest losses of small fruits can be staggering. These highly perishable fruits are easily spoiled by fungi, bacteria, and yeasts, and can deteriorate in quality and nutritive value when improperly handled and stored (Fig. 12–10). For example, based on recent USDA surveys, the following percentages of strawberries are lost due to physical, physiological, and pathological factors: wholesale and storage, 25%; retail, 10%; in the kitchen, 15%; and during processing, 15%.

Major fruit rotting organisms of small fruits include species of *Alternaria, Botrytis, Colletotrichum,* and *Rhizopus.* These microorganisms cause decay when the crop is mechanically damaged, when the crop is not in a peak condition of maturity, when the temperature is not optimum, or when unsanitary conditions for infection are prevalent. Other sources of loss from postharvest decay include the production of ethylene by decay organisms. Ethylene speeds up deterioration processes such as softening and color changes of the fruit. Mycelia from decaying small fruits in a container can spread to other fruits and necessitate costly resorting and repacking, which result in lost postharvest life and reduced profits.

Infection of small fruits can occur before, during, or after harvest. It can occur on fruits as they ripen on the plant, or it can take place on young, developing fruits and then remain latent until the fruits ripen. For example, *Colletotrichum gloeosporioides,* the imperfect stage of *Glomerella cinqulata* (Ston.) Spauld, & Shrenk, infects highbush blueberry fruit soon after fruit set, remains latent, and

FIGURE 12-10 Pallet of California strawberries at wholesale market on electric-powered transporter with Tectrol wrap used to contain gases injected to modify atmosphere in transit to slow respiration.

then resumes development when the berries begin to ripen. Infection of fruits by decay organisms can occur by direct penetration of the cuticle or through natural openings of the fruit. Spores in the field originate from pathogens growing in the soil or from diseased parts of the plant on which the fruits are growing. Hail damage, water soaking, and surface cracks encourage inoculation and decay, which can be disastrous.

Control of latent and quiescent infections initiated in fruits before harvest is difficult to achieve after harvest. Therefore, the number of preharvest latent infections should be kept to a minimum. To accomplish this, the number of viable spores in the field should be controlled. Diseased parts of plants and decaying fruits should be removed from the ground. The surface of the fruits should be kept covered with a fungicide to prevent alighting spores from initiating infections.

Unclean packing houses, storage, and transport vehicles are also potential sources of inoculum. Removal of rotten fruits and plant parts in and around these areas reduces the source of spores and thus reduces the chances for inoculation of marketable fruits. Grading and packing lines should be cleaned regularly. Water used for grading or precooling should be changed regularly; chlorine added to the water can control the accumulation of viable spores in the water. Storage rooms and transport vehicles can be disinfected by the use of a 1% formaldehyde or a 5% sodium hypochlorite solution (Eckert, 1975).

Postharvest decay development can also be reduced or delayed by maintaining high concentrations of carbon dioxide in the atmosphere around the fruits. Strawberries and raspberries are often shipped with supplemental carbon dioxide (15 to 20%) in the atmosphere around them. There is also some evidence that carbon dioxide enrichment of the atmosphere around blueberries can be beneficial (Ceponis and Capellini, 1982).

In summary, decay of small fruits after harvest can reach devastating levels if the fruits are not harvested fairly free of infection, precooled within 2 hours after harvest, and kept cool until they are consumed or are processed; if sanitation is not exercised in and around the packing houses, precoolers, storage rooms, transport vehicles, stores, and kitchen; if the fruits are not handled gently to reduce injury to the fruit to a minimum; and if the fruits are not delivered as quickly as possible to the consumer. Keywords here are *sanitation* (before and after harvest), *careful and speedy handling,* and *temperature control.*

STORAGE

Refrigerated storage of small fruits, especially grapes, kiwifruit, and cranberries, extends their time of availability, tends to avert market glut at harvest, facilitates orderly marketing, and improves financial returns to the grower. As urbanization developed, precooling and refrigerated transport ('storage in motion') became essential for satisfactory distribution of all the many highly perishable small fruits.

Small fruits selected for storage should be handled carefully and should be free of bruises, skin breaks, compression injury, and abrasions. Damage to these delicate fruits increases their potential for invasion by decay organisms. Incipient decay infection can be predicted early in the storage period. Refrigerated storage does not kill most decay organisms. It merely slows their development. Subsequent warming results in a recurrence of rapid decay development. Physical damage to small fruits also detracts from their appearance, increases moisture loss, and by increasing respiration, increases their rate of senescence.

Maturity of these fruits at harvest affects their refrigerated storage life and their subsequent market quality (Anon., 1968). For each small fruit, there is a maturity that is best suited for refrigerated storage. Overmature fruits deteriorate too rapidly in storage; (immature) small fruits do not generally improve in quality during refrigerated storage. Therefore, only fruits of the highest quality should be placed in refrigerated storage, as soon as possible after harvest.

Temperature regulation is the most important factor in the control of postharvest quality of small fruits. Other factors, such as fumigation, modified atmospheres, and growth regulators, are merely supplements to temperature control. The postharvest life of these fruits is a function of temperature and time. Regardless of when the fruit is exposed to high temperatures, the longer the period of exposure, the greater the deterioration of the fruit. Therefore, successful protection of small fruits demands prompt and thorough precooling as soon after harvest as possible and strict temperature management throughout their postharvest life.

Since the physical makeup of small fruits predisposes them to loss of moisture after harvest, the relative humidity of the refrigerated storage room should be kept as high as possible without danger of moisture condensation on the fruits, which increases the potential for growth of decay organisms. The relative humidity of the storage can be kept high by providing an evaporator with a large cooling surface which provides a small temperature difference between the evaporator coil temperature and the air temperature. As this difference decreases, the relative humidity increases, and vice versa. Also, a tight, highly insulated storage room reduces leakage of heat into the storage room and thereby reduces the load on the refrigeration system; this facilitates operation of the evaporator at temperatures close to room temperature. Fluctuations in room temperature due to cycling of thermostats should be kept to a minimum by utilizing an adequate thermostat or by designing the system so that no cyclic fluctuations occur.

Storage Recommendations

Table 12-1 contains recommendations for the major environmental factors that must be controlled for optimum storage life and quality maintenance of various small fruit crops. Temperature and relative humidity within the storage are the two principal considerations.

Controlled-Atmosphere Storage

Addition or removal of gases resulting in an atmospheric composition different from that of normal air, such as in controlled-atmosphere (CA), modified-atmosphere (MA), or hypobaric (low-pressure) storage, has been employed to extend storage life of fruits, as an adjunct to low-temperature storage, or as a substitute for refrigeration. These methods aim at reduction in respiration and other metabolic reactions mainly due to increase in CO_2 and decrease in O_2 concentrations, reduction in the rate of natural ethylene production (as in the banana), and the reduced sensitivity of fruits to ethylene. Controlled atmospheres with high CO_2 inhibit breakdown of pectic substances and retain fruit texture and firmness for a longer period, and retention of flavor may also be improved. Modified atmospheres or controlled atmospheres involve the removal or addition of gases, resulting in an atmospheric composition surrounding the commodity that is different from that of air (78.08% N_2, 20.95% O_2, 0.03% CO_2). Usually, this involves reduction of oxygen (O_2) and/or elevation of carbon dioxide (CO_2) concentrations. For example, strawberry fruit may be stored or transported at 10% O_2 and 15 to 20% CO_2, while the kiwifruit atmosphere may be modified to 2% O_2 and 5% CO2.

REFERENCES

ANON. 1968. Fruits and vegetables. Chap. 29. In ASHRAE guide and data book. American Society of Heating, Refrigerating and Air Conditioning Engineers, Atlanta, Ga.

ANON. 1974. United States standards for grades of processed raisins. U.S. Dep. Agric. Fruit and Vegetables Division, Agricultural Marketing Service, Washington, D. C.

BALLINGER, W. E., AND L. J. KUSHMAN. 1970. Relationship of stage of ripeness to composition and keeping quality of highbush blueberries. J. Am. Soc. Hortic. Sci. 95:239–242.

BALLINGER, W. E., E. P. MANESS, AND W. F. MCCLURE. 1978. Postharvest decay of blueberries as influenced by stem attachment and ripening. Plant Dis. Rep. 62:316–319.

BEN-AIRE, R., J. GROSS, AND L. SONEGO. 1982. Changes in ripening parameters and pigments of the Chinese gooseberry (kiwi) during ripening and storage. Sci. Hortic. 18:65–70.

BEUTEL, J. A., F. H. WINTER, S. C. MANNERS, AND M. W. MILLER. 1976. A new crop for California-kiwifruit. Calif. Agric. 30:12–14.

BEUTEL, J. A., F. H. WINTER, S. C. MANNERS, AND M. W. MILLER. 1977. Growing, processing and marketing kiwifruit. Blue Anchor 54 (Jan./Feb.)

CEPONIS, M. J., AND R. A. CAPELLINI. 1982. Influence of cooling rates and carbon dioxide atmospheres on storage rots of blueberries. Phytopathology 72:258.

DEBNEY, H. G., K. J. BLACKER, B. J. REDDING, AND J. B. WATKINS. 1980. Handling and storage practices for fresh fruit vegetables. Product manual. Australian United Fresh Fruit and Vegetable Association.

ECKERT, J. W. 1975. Postharvest pathology. Chap. 19. In E. B. Pantastico (ed.). Physiology, handing and utilization of tropical and subtropical fruits and vegetables. AVI, Westport, Conn.

FLETCHER, W. A. 1970. Growing Chinese gooseberries. Bull. 349. New Zealand Ministry of Agriculture and Fisheries.

HARDENBURG, R. E., A. E. WATADA, AND C. Y. WANG. 1986. The commercial storage of fruits, vegetables, and florist and nursery stocks. U.S. Dep. Agric. Agric. Handb. 66.

HILL, R. G. 1958. Fruit development of the red raspberry. Ohio Agric. Exp. Stn. Res. Bull. 803.

HILL, R. S. 1942. Chlorophyll. p. 73–97. In M. Florkin and E. H. Stotz (eds.). Comprehensive biochemistry. Vol. 9, Elsevier, Amsterdam.

LUTZ, J. M., AND R. E. HARDENBURG. 1968. The commercial storage of fruits, vegetables, and florist and nursery stocks. U.S. Dep. Agric. Agric. Handb. 66.

MITCHELL, F. G., R. GUILLON, AND R. A. PARSONS. 1972. Commercial cooling of fruits and vegetables. Calif. Agric. Exp. Stn. Ext. Serv. Man. 43.

MORRIS, J. R. 1983. Influence of mechanical harvesting on quality of small fruits and grapes. HortScience 18:412–417.

MORRIS, J. R. 1984. Effects of mechanical harvesting on quality of small fruits and grapes. Fruit, Nut, and Vegetable Harvesting Mechanization. A.S.A.E. Publication 5–84:332–348.

MORRIS, J. R. 1984. Developing a mechanical harvesting system for blackberries. HortScience 19:188–190.

MORRIS, J. R. 1985. Approaches to more efficient vineyard management. HortScience. 20:1009–1013.

MORRIS, J. R., G. S. NELSON, AND A. A. KATTAN. 1984. Developing a mechanical harvesting and handling system for cane fruits and strawberrries. A.S.A.E. Publication 5–84:144–148.

NATIONAL CANNERS' ASSOCIATION. 1968. Laboratory manual for food canners and processors. Vol. 1. AVI, Westport, Conn.

PANTASTICO, E. B., T. K. CHATTOPADHYOY, AND H. SUBRAMANYAM. 1975. Storage and commercial storage operations. In Postharvest physiology, handling and utilization of tropical and subtropical fruits and vegetables. AVI, Westport, Conn.

References

RYALL, A. L., AND J. M. HARVEY. 1959. The cold storage of vinifera table grapes. U.S. Dep. Agric. Handb. 159.

RYALL, A. L., AND W. T. PENTZER. 1974. Handling, transportation and storage of fruits and vegetables. AVI, Westport, Conn.

SALUNKHE, D. K., AND B. B. DESAI. 1984. Postharvest biotechnology of fruits. CRC Press, Boca Raton, Fla.

SPAYD, S. E., AND J. R. MORRIS. 1981. Physical and chemical characteristics of puree from once-over harvested strawberries. J. Am. Soc. Hortic. Sci. 106:101–105.

WALLNER, S. J., AND P. A. FERRETTI. 1978. Postharvest handling and storage of vegetables and berries for fresh market. Penn State Univ. Spec. Circ. 247.

WEAVER, R. J. 1976. Grape growing. Wiley, New York.

WINKLER, A. J., J. A. COOK, W. M. KLIEWER, AND L. A. LIDER. 1974. General viticulture. University of California Press, Berkeley.

SUGGESTED READING

AMERINE, M. A., AND C. S. OUGH. 1980. Methods for analysis of musts and wines. Wiley, New York.

ARTHEY, V. D. 1975. Quality of horticultural products. Halstead Press, New York.

BARTSCH, J. A., AND G. D. BLANPIED. 1983. Refrigerated storage for horticultural crops. Dep. Agric. Eng. Cornell Univ. Ext. Bull. 448.

BARTSCH, J. A., AND G. D. BLANPIED. 1984. Refrigeration and controlled atmosphere storage for horticultural crops. Coop. Ext. RAES Publ. 22.

BONNER, J., AND J. E. VARNER (eds.). 1976. Plant biochemistry. Academic Press, New York.

FRANCIS, F. J., AND F. M. CLYDESDALE. 1975. Food colorimetry. AVI, Westport, Conn.

HARDENBURG, R. E., A. E. WATADA, AND C. Y. WANG. 1986. The commercial storage of fruits, vegetables, and florist and nursery stocks. U.S. Dep. Agric. Agric. Handb. 66.

HULME, A. C. (ed.). 1970. The biochemistry of fruits and their products. Vols. 1 and 2. Academic Press, New York.

KADER, A. A., R. F. KASMIRE, F. G. MITCHELL, M. S. REID, N. F. SOMMER, AND J. F. THOMPSON. 1985. Postharvest technology of horticultural crops. Univ. Calif. Spec. Publ. 3311.

NELSON, K. E. 1985. Harvesting and handling California table grapes for market. Univ. Calif. Bull. 1913.

O'BRIEN, M., B. F. CARGILL, AND R. B. FRIDLEY. 1983. Principles and practices for harvesting and handling fruits and nuts. AVI, Westport, Conn.

PATTEE, H. E. 1985. Evaluation of quality of fruits and vegetables. AVI, Westport, Conn.

PELEG, K. 1985. Produce handling, packaging and distribution. AVI, Westport, Conn.

RYALL, A. L., AND W. T. PENTZER. 1982. Handling, transportation and storage of fruits and vegetables. AVI, Westport, Conn.

SALUNKHE, D. K., AND B. B. DESAI. 1984. Postharvest biotechnology of fruits. CRC Press, Boca Raton, Fla.

SHOEMAKER, J. S. 1978. Small fruit culture. AVI, Westport, Conn.

WALLNER, S. J., AND P. A. FERRETTI. 1978. Postharvest handling and storage of vegetables and berries for fresh market. Penn State Univ. Spec. Circ. 247.

WILLS, R. H. H., T. H. LEE, D. GRAHAM, W. B. McGLASSON, AND E. G. HALL. 1981. Postharvest: an introduction to the physiology and handling of fruit and vegetables. AVI, Westport, Conn.

WOODROOF, J. G., AND B. S. LUH. 1986. Commercial fruit processing. AVI, Westport, Conn.

Suggested Reading

531

Chapter 13

Marketing Small Fruits

J. W. COURTER
R. B. HOW

INTRODUCTION

The marketing options open to growers of small fruits are many and varied but depend to a considerable extent on where they are located (Fig. 13–1). If growers farm in an area of intensive and specialized production, they may be largely limited to marketing large quantities through grower-shippers, cooperatives, or private shippers to distant receivers, or selling to processors for jams, jellies, frozen products, or wine. Some may be able to establish direct sales to nearby consumers of fresh or processed products, or wholesale to restaurants and institutions.

Outside the major producing regions, the sale of small fruit directly to consumers usually predominates. Many growers supplement direct sales with sales to local wholesalers or directly to operators of farm markets, retail stores, restaurants, and institutions. A few growers outside major regions have been able to develop shipping operations that serve distant markets, but this is not common. Each marketing channel has specific requirements that may be quite different.

Growers with only a few acres generally prefer to sell direct to consumers, as

532

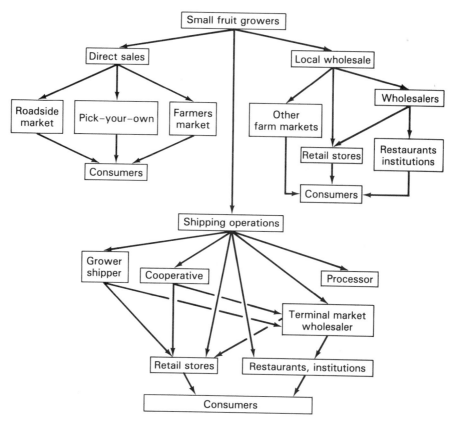

FIGURE 13-1 Major marketing channels for small fruits.

do some growers with large acreages. The principal means of selling direct is through a pick-your-own (PYO) operation, a farm roadside market, or a community retail farmers' market. Margins on direct sales are generally favorable and prices relatively stable. Growers must be aware of consumers' needs and preferences, and willing to deal with them daily. The volume of fruit that can be sold direct is often limited, however, and growers then must resort to wholesale exchange to move their total production.

There are many different types of wholesale outlets. Some wholesale buyers can handle fairly large volumes at short notice. Selling at wholesale involves dealing with only a few large buyers rather than coping with many consumers. Local wholesale buyers can be very demanding with respect to quality and packaging, wholesale prices can fluctuate in response to market conditions across the country, and the wholesale market tends to be highly competitive. Most wholesale buyers do not have the same degree of loyalty to their suppliers as do consumers. Growers who sell direct to consumers are often able to differentiate their products and services and so can set prices higher than their competitors. Growers who sell at wholesale usually must be price takers and have to accept the going market prices.

There are also significant differences between selling at wholesale for local

Introduction

consumption and selling in volume for shipment to distant markets. Growers outside the major production areas usually depend first on marketing direct to consumers, and then expand into local wholesale outlets. A few then may develop distant markets either directly or through a local wholesaler. Growers in major production areas can often ship fruit to distant markets themselves or market through grower-shippers, cooperatives, or private shippers. They often also sell to processors for freezing, jams and jellies, or wine making.

THE MARKETING PLAN

Before embarking on the commercial production of small fruits or making major changes in an existing operation, it is essential to prepare a detailed marketing plan. Seldom are there empty market niches just waiting to be filled. Your plan should include as a minimum the following information in fairly specific terms for the next marketing season and in general terms for the following three to five seasons:

1. The existing system, if any, for providing the kinds of fruit and the marketing services that you intend to offer to buyers and the impact that your production would have on the market.

2. The types of buyers with the names of actual firms, if possible, and the quantity of fruit and types of marketing services you intend to sell to each type of buyer.

3. The estimated prices, or range of prices, you expect to receive for each grade of fruit.

4. Means of keeping up with changing market conditions and of avoiding losses through slow payment or bad debts.

5. Your best estimates of your total costs of growing, harvesting, packing, cooling, advertising and promoting, selling, and shipping fruit to each type of buyer.

6. The net returns you may expect to receive based on conservative estimates of yields, sales, and prices.

It is not necessary to obtain this information in the foregoing sequence or focus on only one aspect at a time, although the final evaluation cannot be made until all the data are in. Much of this information will not be readily available. Ingenuity will be required to assemble as reliable information as possible, but rough estimates may have to suffice in some cases. Your situation is similar to that of a manufacturer introducing a new product, where the payoff for success is high but the risk of failure is great.

The outcome of such a marketing plan should give you greater confidence in whether you should go ahead with such a project. In addition, you may wish to estimate the risks involved by determining the effect on net returns that would result from changes in some of the important assumptions you have made in developing the plan. This might be approached by asking such 'What If?' questions as the impact of lower prices or yields or of higher costs than have been anticipated. This exercise should also help identify critical cost areas where reductions might be achieved.

Assessing the Existing System

Procedure to be followed to assess the existing system will depend on the type of market being contemplated. Planning for a direct marketing operation will require determining present operations in your marketing area, the population within the trading area, the effectiveness of the current marketers, and the impact that you would have on the market.

To find out what is going on in local wholesale markets will require direct observation, possibly with some degree of care not to reveal specific plans too far in advance. This could mean talking in general terms to prospective buyers, finding out present sources of supply, and observing the operations of wholesalers who provide the current supplies. If there is a regional wholesale market in the area, this could be the source of much useful information.

If considering supplying wholesale quantities to be shipped to distant markets from major production areas, the information on the current system is probably readily available. To set up a shipping operation where none presently exists represents a greater challenge. Again, interviews and observations of buyers and suppliers is essential, but must be conducted over a much wider territory than for local sale.

Prospective Buyers and Probable Sales

On the basis of your assessment of the current marketing system you need to develop a listing of the prospective customers for the fruit you intend to produce. If you are planning to sell direct to consumers, you need to have some idea of where they live and who they are in terms of their economic and socio-demographic characteristics. This will help you decide how to reach them and how much you may be able to sell to them.

In the case of wholesale buyers, they may be local independent stores, restaurants or institutions, or major buyers such as terminal wholesalers or chain store buyers. Some contact with these buyers prior to your first marketing season is almost essential. Such a contact should be in person, with as much information as possible on the product and services you intend to offer. Since it will not be possible to provide actual samples of your fruit during the off-season you should bring empty containers and pictures, if available, of the kind and quality of fruit you intend to supply. You should also indicate the period during which your fruit will be available, the quantities you can provide, and any other marketing services you can offer. A brochure on your farm operation to leave with the buyer could be very helpful.

Do not expect to obtain a firm commitment in advance from a wholesale buyer with respect to either the quantity of fruit that will be bought or the prices that will be paid. Buyers, of course, are anxious to have as many good sources of supply available as possible without being committed. Based on your conversations with buyers, you will have to determine how competitive your product is and the likelihood of making sales when the time comes. At least you will have made an initial contact prior to the marketing season.

Estimated Prices

Prices for small fruits sold on wholesale markets vary so much that they are difficult to predict for the coming season. Supermarket prices tend to follow wholesale prices to a degree, and set the tone for direct farmer-to-consumer sales. Prices for fruit sold on a pick-your-own basis do not vary as much from year to year, but can vary from one operation to another, depending on quality and location.

One important caution is not to base estimated prices for the coming season on those of the previous year but instead to look at trends and patterns over recent years. Short-run price changes from month to month or season to season tend to be the result of changes in supply due largely to weather or other unpredictable sources. Changes over a period of years are more influenced by changes in consumer demand, which in turn can be the result of changes in income, tastes and preferences, living and working habits, or other socioeconomic or demographic factors.

The Market News Service, a joint operation of the federal and state department of agriculture is an excellent source of information on prices and sales for major commodities such as strawberries and grapes in major market areas. Frequent daily reports are issued from major shipping areas during the marketing season and from major markets all year. Annual summaries are compiled that give an overview for the season or the year and that can be used to identify seasonal patterns and trends. For many minor crops and in many market areas, however, such information is not available.

Fortunately, prices of similar small fruits do tend to maintain a general relationship to each other when sold in different markets or through different types of outlets. When fruit is being shipped to deficit market areas, the prices on the market tend to be higher than those in the shipping areas by the cost of transporting and handling similar fruit between the two areas. Retail supermarket prices tend to exceed the local terminal wholesale price by only about 25 or 30% since supermarket chains usually seek a lower gross margin on small fruits than on most other fresh fruits and vegetables. Roadside market prices generally fluctuate with supermarket prices, sometimes above and sometimes below, depending on the product and the quality and reputation of the particular market. In most areas pick-your-own prices remain fairly stable from year to year and during the season, but reflect the lower costs of harvesting and packaging compared to wholesale prices.

If prices for strawberries on the nearby wholesale market, for example, are running about $7.50 per 12-pint flat or $0.62 per pint, they might be retailing at about $0.79 a pint in supermarkets, $1.40 to $1.50 a quart at roadside markets, and selling for $0.60 per pound or $0.75 per quart at pick-your-own operations. These price relationships will be somewhat different in different markets and can change from year to year, but the general pattern will be the same. In all price comparisons it is important also to recognize the effect of any differences in quality and packaging between different vendors.

In addition to random fluctuations in prices due largely to weather conditions, there are sometimes regular patterns of price changes that can be detected. Within each season, for example, prices often start out at relatively high levels as first supplies come on the market and then drop as supplies increase. Sometimes prices will recover at the end of the season as production dwindles. Such price patterns are not as evident as they once were, however, since plentiful supplies of most small fruits are available on many markets now all year. With grapes from Chile, strawberries from California, Florida and Mexico, and blueberries from New Zealand arriving during the winter, the prices do not exhibit the regular seasonal patterns they once did.

There are still, however, long-run fluctuations or cycles with which to contend. Many growers are apparently still influenced by immediate past prices. They consequently set out more plants following good years. When this added acreage comes into bearing, their markets become depressed. After a few seasons of depressed prices they cut back and move on to other enterprises. Prices then strengthen again and the cycle is repeated. Such cycles can be observed in the past, but unfortunately they are not regular and predictable, since they are influenced by exterior factors such as weather conditions, imports from other countries, competition from other fruits, and changes in consumer demand.

Keeping Up with Changing Market Conditions

When you take on the challenge of growing a different crop or marketing in a different way, you need to learn how to keep up with changing conditions in growing and marketing both locally and globally. This may require obtaining access to market news, subscribing to trade papers, joining commodity organizations, and keeping up with government services.

Most marketers keep up with changing market conditions in several ways. Observation and personal contact is probably the most important. In local markets the prices being charged by other growers, by retail supermarkets, or on local wholesale markets will reflect changing market conditions. The reasons for such changes may, however, not be apparent. Local receivers of shipped-in fruit will have definite ideas of market conditions in major producing areas, but may be reluctant to share this information. Direct contact with shippers in other areas and USDA Market News reports can add valuable information.

Federal–State Market News reporters cover major shipping areas and terminal markets, reporting shipments or arrivals, prices, and market conditions, not only for the market they cover but for other important markets across the country. Their reports can be obtained in person on the market as issued or by mail, by recorded telephone message, or by electronic distribution. Private companies also have established electronic networks to disseminate USDA market information, as well as information obtained from other sources.

The day-to-day information on markets and prices obtained from business contacts and Market News needs to be supplemented with information on developments that may affect the market in the future or that can explain past events. Subscribing to trade papers and magazines, joining trade associations and commodity organizations, obtaining USDA reports, and attending Cooperative Extension meetings can be helpful in this respect. Trade and commodity organizations, in addition to providing educational services, also often help protect and promote the interests of members through legislative activities. All growers, although mainly involved with immediate production and marketing operations, need to be aware of and concerned with matters of general interest.

Growers who aspire to, or already sell on, major wholesale markets need to be aware of the private and public services that facilitate the marketing system and protect against unfair or fraudulent practices. The Federal–State Inspection Service will, for a fee, certify as to the grade and condition of a wholesale lot of fruit according to established grade standards. Many states require those who deal in fresh produce within the state to be licensed and bonded. Under the federal Perishable Agricultural Commodities Act (PACA), those who deal in fresh produce in interstate commerce must be licensed under the PACA. The PACA also provides a mechanism by which disputes between shippers and receivers of fresh produce may be arbitrated, reparations determined, and penalties enforced. Withdrawal of a PACA license from a produce firm prohibits that firm from engaging in the produce business until the license is restored. Recent amendments to the PACA legislation have provided that under certain conditions receivers must establish trusts to protect the interest of shippers in the event of bankruptcy on the part of the receiver.

There are many firms in this country involved in the marketing of fresh produce, a few being quite large, but most being relatively small. Having a reliable source of information on the firms involved, and especially on their business practices and financial worth, can be very useful. There are two such services available, known from the color of their reference manuals as *The Blue Book* and *The Red Book*. These each provide information on names and addresses of principals, kind of business, volume of commodities handled, promptness of payment, business character, and financial worth for a large number of shippers, wholesalers, brokers, retailers, and other types of firms handling fresh produce. In addition, these reference manuals contain detailed information on trade practices and the text of important legislation and regulations affecting the produce industry.

Costs of Growing and Marketing

Your costs of growing and marketing small fruit in the future can only be estimated, but the closer your estimates are to actual experience, the more likely you will be to achieve financial success. Setting up a budget for the coming season should become a regular routine each year, but is especially important and also most difficult in the early stages of an enterprise.

Difficulty arises from the fact that costs differ from one grower to another and one year to the next. Some costs are easy to estimate, such as the costs per acre for materials such as fertilizer or plants, but these are generally not the most important costs. It is important not to neglect fixed or overhead costs. Fixed costs such as expense for regular labor or the use of equipment are more difficult to predict, but are often more important. Care should be taken not to overlook major costs such as the return to your own management and labor, or the costs of capital. An additional problem is that costs per quart or per carton depend not only on costs per acre but on how many quarts or cartons will actually be sold. This may be limited not only by production but by what can realistically be sold.

Average costs of growing, harvesting, and marketing small fruits may be available based on information gathered from other growers. Your local Cooperative Extension office may have helpful reports on costs. Information that reflects recent costs in your area is likely to be very limited. Cost data based on experience in other areas or for past years need to be adjusted for your current situation. Once the enterprise is launched, your own past costs will provide the best guide for the future and will provide a basis for the preparation of budgets each year.

Putting It All Together

As you explore each of the areas listed above, you will gradually come to have a better understanding of the potentials and problems of the enterprise you are contemplating. You may decide before the study is complete that the project has little chance of success and abandon further investigation, or you may find the potential is so exciting that you should drop everything else and forge ahead. More likely, however, you will discover that the proposal seems likely either to contribute a small net profit or incur a small loss.

An example of an operating statement for strawberries marketed in three different ways shows what is expected in terms of revenues and costs (Table 13-1). Revenues should be estimated conservatively. In this illustration the quantity of fruit sold per acre for PYO, roadside market, and wholesale sale is assumed to be the same, although yields are sometimes different for fruit sold PYO than for picked fruit. Variable marketing and harvesting costs are different for the three methods, but variable growing costs and fixed costs are presumed to be the same. Pick-your-own promises the greatest net returns in this illustration, followed by roadside sales. Sales at wholesale would cover all variable costs but fail to cover all overhead or fixed costs. Note what a major impact a few cents difference in average prices or a few quarts difference in sales per acre would have on net returns (Table 13-1).

Factors other than just the net return should be considered in making the decision to go ahead, especially if you are already involved in an ongoing farm business. How the proposed small fruit production and marketing project fits with your present activity should be considered carefully. Does it conflict with existing enterprises for your management or the labor of your employees during busy periods? Many of the expected benefits may be lost in this case. Or does it provide employment and require management attention during otherwise slack periods? If so, it may contribute sufficiently to overhead costs to warrant proceeding even though total costs are not covered. If direct variable costs such as materials and supplies are fully covered and there are no other alternative opportunities for management and regular labor during active periods of production and marketing, it may be wise to proceed. One should not forget, however, that a business cannot succeed unless fixed or overhead costs are completely covered by one means or another.

The exercise of assessing the existing market, deciding on the particular niche

TABLE 13-1 EXAMPLE COSTS AND RETURNS PER ACRE IN GROWING AND MARKETING STRAWBERRIES, NEW YORK, 1980

	PYO	ROADSIDE MARKET	LOCAL WHOLESALE
Returns			
Sales, quarts	6,000	6,000	6,000
Price per quart	$ 1.00	$ 1.60	$ 1.20
Total returns	$6,000	$9,600	$7,200
Variable costs			
Selling			
Direct labor	$ 400	$ 900	$ 150
Containers and supplies	50	200	600
Advertising	250	150	—
Buildings and equipment	100	900	350
Truck fuel, maintenance	—	—	250
Harvesting			
Direct labor	—	2,000	2,000
Tractor, wagon, fuel, maintenance	50	150	150
Growing			
Plants, fertilizer, pesticides, labor, fuel, equipment	2,500	2,500	2,500
Total variable costs	$3,350	$6,800	$6,000
Return over variable costs	$2,650	$2,800	$1,200
Fixed costs of land, buildings, and equipment	$1,500	$2,000	$1,500
Net return to management and capital	$1,150	$ 800	($300)

Source: Adapted from Phelps and How (1981).

one wishes to develop, projecting prices and returns, considering how to keep up with changing market conditions, determining current costs of operation, and looking at the enterprise in total is especially important at the beginning but needs to be a continuing process. In this ever-changing world of small fruit production and marketing, it is only in this way that one can hope to keep up with current developments and maintain a profitable business.

WHOLESALE MARKETING

Wholesaling for Local Consumption

There are many different types of wholesale buyers who purchase for local use, each with very specific needs (How, 1981). Growers who operate farm roadside markets but do not grow small fruit themselves or need to supplement their supplies are important buyers in many areas. Chain store produce buyers sometimes buy small fruit locally, but their requirements are usually very specific and this is a difficult, though not impossible market to penetrate. Some supermarket chains permit the direct delivery and sale of perishable small fruit such as raspberries and strawberries to individual stores near the growing area, but this practice is frowned upon by others. Locally owned supermarkets are more likely to buy locally and can be good market outlets.

Somewhere between 80 and 90% of the fresh fruits and vegetables sold at retail in most communities is bought at supermarkets, but there is a small but significant quantity sold through convenience stores. Most convenience stores depend heavily on the sale of beverages and grocery necessities, and limit their fresh produce to major items such as potatoes, lettuce, oranges, and apples. Some convenience stores are willing to experiment with specialty items such as small fruits, but this may require authorization from the chain management.

The eating out or away-from-home market is very important in some communities. It can also be financially profitable for growers of small fruit, but difficult to break into. Fast-food restaurants generally are required to purchase only from authorized suppliers who can meet rigid specifications, but locally owned full-service restaurants can develop into important customers. Although their quality requirements are usually very high, so also are the prices they are willing to pay. In many communities there are institutions such as colleges, hospitals, or nursing homes that can be persuaded to buy locally grown small fruits.

Growers who farm near major cities can often sell to wholesalers, who in turn service retail stores and institutions. Such wholesalers can often handle large volumes and sometimes are willing to accept fruit of less than top quality, especially if on consignment. Consignment sales, where the seller has to accept whatever the wholesaler can get for the product less the wholesaler's costs, often result in very low prices.

Buyers can be reached in different ways. Many communities have farmers' wholesale markets, and selling on these markets can enable growers to contact many potential customers (Fig. 13–2). Selling on wholesale markets is only economically feasible if the seller has sufficient variety and volume of product to warrant the time required and if the market is well attended by buyers. Otherwise, growers must make personal contact and be prepared to deliver at odd times as well as on a regular schedule.

Wholesaling for Shipping Operations

Marketing fresh fruit in quantity to be shipped to distant markets represents a greater challenge than does wholesale marketing for local consumption. Harvesting, packaging, and precooling requirements are generally more stringent, and a larger volume of production is usually necessary to attain profitability. In earlier days wholesalers would assemble sufficient volume for shipment by buying small quantities from many growers on auction markets or by private treaty. This practice continues in some localities but is not as common as it once was.

Growers outside the major production areas who wish to ship small fruit to distant markets often have to develop their own shipping operations, unless they have access to a wholesale shipper or another grower who is serving as grower-shipper. Grower-shippers ship to distant markets not only their own fruit but also that of neighboring growers, and are becoming an increasingly important link in the

FIGURE 13-2 Strawberry display showing typical means of selling at a wholesale market.

marketing chain (Fig. 13–3). Development of a grower-shipper operation today, however, requires considerable expertise in marketing.

In most major production areas there are already many established outlets for the shipment of fresh fruit or the purchase of fruit for processing. These include not only grower-shippers but also cooperative and proprietary shippers as well with facilities for precooling and temporary storage. Such shippers also make sales and arrange transportation, and may either buy fruit outright from growers to pay on a net return basis, depending on what the fruit brings in the marketplace. Some shippers may already have sufficient volume and not be willing to take on new growers, but others may have the capacity to handle additional fruit, especially if it is of good quality.

Wholesaling for Processing Markets

In some growing areas one or more major processing facilities may already be established. Processors of small fruits generally prefer to obtain their raw product from near at hand to reduce losses from damage and deterioration. The existence of a processing plant in the area will determine whether sales for processing is an option.

Processors make many different kinds of small fruit products, including unfermented items such as juices, jellies and jams, frozen berries, and mainly in the case of grapes, fermented beverages. Processors usually prefer a large volume of product delivered in bulk and, where possible, over as long a season as can be managed. Selling to processors is often quite competitive from the growers' standpoint, which results in relatively low prices. Quantities required and prices paid, however, tend to remain relatively stable from year to year compared to sales on the fresh market.

FIGURE 13-3 Many small fruits such as these California table grapes are shipped great distances for distribution at terminal markets like this one in Buffalo, New York.

The processing market can be attractive to those who wish to focus on their growing operations and minimize their immediate involvement in marketing. Growers who sell to processors do need to be aware of the changes taking place in the market for processed products, however, for these can have a major effect on the market for their products. For example, the U.S. markets for many processed products, such as frozen strawberries and wine, have been seriously affected in recent years by foreign competition.

INFORMATION SOURCES

Market News

The Market News Service on Fruits, Vegetables, Ornamentals and Specialty Crops, U.S. Department of Agriculture, Agricultural Marketing Service, Marketing Bulletin, contains useful information on the kinds of market news reports that are issued, the definitions of terms used to describe quality and condition as well as market activity, where to write for terminal and shipping point reports, and telephone numbers for recorded reports at terminal and shipping point offices. A list of the weekly, monthly, and annual reports and an address for the Washington, D.C.

Information Sources

office where they can be obtained is included. The taped telephone reports are a quick source of information. The telephone number and commodities covered are subject to change. At time of writing some of the shipping-point market news reports on small fruits were available as follows:

Plant City, Florida, January–June, (813) 754–2826

Fresno, California, all year, (209) 233–0341

Benton Harbor, Michigan, June–April, (616) 925–1096

ProNet

ProNet (The Packer Produce Network, 7950 College Boulevard, Overland Park, Kansas 66210) is an electronically based information and communications service designed specifically to serve the needs of the produce industry. Through the use of a telephone modem attached to a personal computer members of the produce industry are able to access a central mainframe to obtain late industry news, market information on individual commodities, the latest weather reports across the country, ratings on major produce firms in this country and in foreign countries, and newsletters and reports on the produce industry; to post or read buy/sell notices; and to send or receive electronic mail.

Trade Papers

The Packer	Vance Publishing Company 7950 College Boulevard Overland Park, Kansas 66210
The Produce News	The Produce News 2185 Lemoine Ave. Fort Lee, New Jersey 07024

Just about every member of the produce industry subscribes to a weekly trade newspaper. These papers provide current information and background on developments in the industry. *The Packer* has wide circulation, and in addition to the weekly paper publishes annually an availability and merchandising guide that lists firms supplying produce and information that is helpful in handling and merchandising. *The Produce News* is more regionally oriented toward the northeast.

Business Reference Books

The Red Book	Vance Publishing Corporation 7950 College Boulevard Overland Park, Kansas 66210
The Blue Book	Produce Reporter Company 315 West Wesley Street Wheaton, Illinois 60187

One or both of these excellent reference books, even though a subscription costs several hundred dollars, should be on the desk of everyone involved in the wholesale marketing of fresh produce. Each subscription covers a weekly newsletter, a weighty reference book issued every 6 months, and the opportunity to telephone for the latest information on potential customers or suppliers. The material in each book is similar. Most of each reference book is devoted to information on about 17,000 major produce firms in this country and in foreign countries. This includes the names and addresses of principals, the type of firm, the commodities handled, the volume of business, and the financial rating, paying practices, and business character. In addition, detailed information is included on customs and rules in the business, U.S. grade standards, USDA Inspection offices and Perishable Agricultural Commodities Act (PACA) regulatory branch offices, a summary of the PACA and Canada Agricultural Products Act, a trade association directory, information on Market News, chain stores, transportation, and truck brokers. Regular mail surveys are made to keep the information as current as possible.

Commodity Organizations

North American Blueberry Council
P. O. Box 166
Marmora, New Jersey 08223

North American Strawberry Growers Association
P.O. Box 1245
Tarpon Springs, Florida 34688

North American Bramble Growers Association
16022 Jerald St.
Laurel, Maryland 20707

In addition to these national organizations there are many state associations based either on individual commodities or for fruit in general.

INTRODUCTION TO DIRECT MARKETING

Direct marketing is covered in detail in the next portion of this chapter. Figure 13–4 shows the value of agricultural products sold directly to consumers in the United States in 1982. This includes the sales of products, such as fruit, vegetables, cattle, hogs, sheep, chickens, milk, and eggs. Sales from roadside stands, farmers' markets, pick-your-own activities, and so on, were included. Although this does not allow for the specific examination of small fruit crops, it does give a valuable indication of the geographical distribution of direct marketing activities around the country.

DIRECT MARKETING TO CONSUMERS

Small fruits are well adapted for direct marketing. Local consumers want high-quality berries for fresh table use and for home processing. Families who freeze or process the fruit buy large quantities and will drive to the farm or farm market to

FIGURE 13-4 Value of agricultural products sold directly to consumers for human consumption: 1982. (From U.S. Department of Commerce, Bureau of the Census.)

make their purchase. Strawberries have particular appeal because they are first to ripen in the spring, while other small fruits such as raspberries and blackberries are in demand because they are often unavailable in local stores and supermarkets. Home-grown blueberries and grapes also find good demand, depending on local availability.

Small fruits are relatively high income crops, and crops such as strawberries can provide a valuable source of early spring cash flow. Most berry crops, however, are labor intensive, especially at harvest time. This is one reason why small fruits have become popular for pick-your-own marketing. The consumer provides harvest labor and in return obtains a choice of vine-ripe quality, usually at a significant price savings. Pick-your-own has gained importance since the early 1970s, although individual farms have sold PYO for many years (Courter, 1979, 1985, 1987). Strawberry marketing trends for the past 20 years in Illinois have been typical for many other states in the midwest and northeast (Table 13-2).

Three kinds of markets are popular for selling small fruits directly to consumers. They are pick-your-own, farm markets or roadside stands, and community farmers' markets. The farm may also sell to local wholesale buyers or do some on-farm processing to add value for sales later in the year. The best marketing outlets vary and depend on the crop, season when ripe, and competition in the region.

PRIMARY OUTLET	1967	1971	1975	1979	1983	1987
Pick-your-own	23	41	88	96	92	86
Picked for retail sales	[a]	[a]	[a]	[a]	4	13
Wholesale to local roadside markets and stores	11	11	6	3	3	1
Ship wholesale	66[b]	48[b]	6	1	1	0

[a] Data not collected, but probably minor importance.

[b] In addition, most growers opened their fields to PYO customers at the end of the shipping season on a "cleanup" basis.

Pick-Your-Own

The principal market for many growers of small fruits is pick-your-own to consumers who live in nearby communities (Fig 13-5). Consumers come to PYO farms to obtain large quantities, better quality, and to save money. They will choose one farm over another for ease of picking, price, and efficiency of operation. The farm image — neatness, cleanliness, the logo, signs, personnel, quality of fruit, printed material, and access roads — are extremely important. City customers may especially value the farm outing for its recreational aspects. However, they may be critical of muddy or dusty roads, poor sign directions, weedy fields, and rude personnel.

Customers usually drive 20 miles (32 km) or less to PYO farms (Courter and Sabota, 1981). Although PYO sounds like a simple idea, the farms must be prepared to park cars and handle people with efficiency and courtesy. Some growers plant at

FIGURE 13-5 Pick-your-own marketing of small fruits such as strawberries has been successful in many areas.

Direct Marketing to Consumers

more than one location to provide picking fields closer to more customers in the surrounding population.

Each farm has a trading area where its customers live and this area may be defined geographically. The trading area will be delineated by the access roads, natural barriers (mountain, rivers, etc.), and location of competition. Poor and winding roads, limited travel routes, and long distances from populations deter PYO participation. The trade area is not a perfect circle surrounding the farm.

A survey in Illinois found that 7 out of 10 (71%) households bought fresh strawberries in 1985 (Courter, 1986a). Only one in seven (14%), however, picked their own. A higher percentage of households picked strawberries in rural areas than in heavily populated metropolitan areas. Of those who did not pick, more than one-half (53%) were not aware of PYO farms.

Estimating a Farm Trade Area

Studies at the University of Illinois have defined the primary trade area as the geographical area where 75% of all customers live (Courter, 1982). The farm depends on customers from the primary trade area for repeat business. For strawberries this has worked out, on average, to be a 20-mile (32-km) radius around the farm. Each farm situation will be unique, and small fruits other than strawberries have different yields, demand, and consumption patterns. However, this procedure helps provide preliminary estimates to establish a marketing plan.

On a map, draw an area of 20-mile (32-km) radius around the farm to include cities, towns, and rural populations that have direct and convenient access by car. Calculate the number of potential customers that live within this area. Determine the acreage of strawberries currently in production (including your own) within the area under study. Also note all acres outside of, but within, 5 miles (8 km) of the radius established on your study map. Remember that a city population may be within the primary trade areas of two or more PYO farms.

Estimating Potential Production

Using the data above, find the acreage potential from Table 13–3. Subtract the acres presently grown to obtain an estimate of additional acres that can be planted for PYO sales to this population.

The estimates given in Table 13–3 are conservative. Larger acreages *may* be sold when farms are located near very large populations with very little or no competition. These farms will have correspondingly larger trade areas, but they are *vulnerable* to competition. Larger acreages in rural areas than given in the table suggest a saturated PYO strawberry market. The PYO market is extremely competitive in some areas. Too many PYO farms competing for sales around a city will result in a shortage of pickers, cut-pricing, low profits, and ultimately a decline in acreage.

Four acres (1.6 ha) of strawberries require 1500 or more customer sales. This means participation by 20% or more of *all households* living within a primary trade area of 10,000 people. Limited populations will not, therefore, support a large PYO

TABLE 13-3 ESTIMATES OF STRAWBERRY ACRES FOR PICK-YOUR-OWN MARKETING

PRIMARY TRADE AREA POPULATION (THOUSANDS)	ACRES PRODUCING STRAWBERRIES FOR PYO	HECTARES PRODUCING STRAWBERRIES FOR PYO
2.5	1	0.4
5	2	0.8
10	4	1.6
20	8	3.2
30	11	4.4
40	15	6.0
50	18	7.2
60	21	8.4
70	24	9.6
80	27	10.8
100	30	12.0
150	37	14.8
200	44	17.6
250	51	20.4
300	58	23.2
400	64	25.6
500	70	28.0
600	75	30.0
700	81	32.4
800	86	34.4
900	92	36.8
1000	98	39.2

acreage. Landowners in these areas should consider PYO only as an opportunity to employ family labor and to supplement income.

A production unit of 5 acres (2 ha) of strawberries is probably the minimum size a farm can grow to justify specialized equipment (transplanter, sprayers, mulcher, irrigation, etc.). At this point investment reaches a level where the farmer can devote sufficient time to study the business, attend state and regional conferences, and learn how to produce the crop economically. A farm with 10 acres (4 ha) of strawberries requires a nearby population of approximately 30,000 people, with *no other competition,* to provide a suitable market.

Comparable data to estimate market potential have not been determined for small fruits other than strawberries. Limited studies, however, suggest that customers will drive greater distances to pick blueberries and raspberries when there are few farms growing these crops. A fruit farm may grow more than one small fruit to provide sales to farm customers throughout spring and summer months. The farm must carefully plan its marketing strategy to provide customers with adequate fruit, and, at the same time, sell a high percentage of its production (Table 13-4).

Advertising

The information contained in the trade area map will help you to plan your advertising program. Growers direct their advertising toward customers and poten-

CROP	YIELD [lb/ACRE (kg/ha)]	PYO AVERAGE SALE [lb (kg)]	APPROXIMATE NUMBER OF CUSTOMERS NEEDED [SALES/ACRE (SALES/ha)]
Strawberry	8000 (8960)	20 (0.91)	400 (100)
Raspberry			
Black	3000 (3360)	15 (0.68)	200 (50)
Red, purple	4000 (4480)	15 (0.68)	275 (65)
Blackberry			
Thorned	4000 (4480)	15 (0.68)	275 (65)
Thornless	8000 (8960)	20 (0.91)	400 (100)
Blueberry	6000 (6720)	12 (0.55)	500 (120)
Grape			
Table	8000 (8960)	10 (0.45)	800 (200)
Wine	8000 (8960)	100 (4.5)	80 (20)

tial new customers in the cities and town within that area. Advertising to customers living outside the 20-mile (32-km) radius must be judiciously planned.

Weekend days are usually the biggest picking days. Coordinating advertising and promotion with peak harvest is a challenge even for experienced growers. Pick-your-own farms advertise in many ways, but signs, newspaper, and radio are usually most important. Some use direct mail to alert regular customers to the start of the season. Recorded telephone messages provide up-to-date information on picking conditions. A farm that is fortunate enough to have a trade area that closely matches the population served by a newspaper, radio station, or TV station can use these media to greatest advantage. The University of Illinois has published clip art for direct marketers (Dahl and Courter, 1985).

Word of mouth is often reported to be the primary way that local consumers learn about PYO. Commonly, neighbors tell their friends about the delicious berries and the friendly farm experience. This explains why marketing begins with choosing the best cultivars, growing top-quality berries, and having clean weed-free fields and courteous friendly personnel on hand to supervise PYO customers. Also, most customers tend to tire quickly, so anything that makes the picking easier, such as high yields and convenient layout, will result in greater sales per customer. Happy customers are quick to tell their friends and neighbors about their recent experience.

Management

Pick-your-own is a people management business. Good organization is critical for success of large operations. Customers do not want to wait in line to check-in or check-out. Good farm layout is important, too, along with crop management to ensure that customers can pick a volume of good-quality fruit in a relatively short time. There is no one set of procedures for successful operation of PYO farms. The methods selected may work best for one farm and not another (Ginder and Hoecker, 1975).

Rules

The farm must establish rules that should be strictly followed. Rules are usually posted and may be printed in hand-out brochures that include fruit-handling tips, recipes, picking tips, and other farm information. Decisions to be made include day and hours the fields are open; minimum age of pickers (if any); prices; containers allowed; procedures for handling of checks, credit cards, and food stamps; and any safety considerations.

Parking

Visible access off and on the highway and ample parking are important. The parking areas may be located near the fields to be picked. The traffic flow should be carefully planned; one-way is advisable where traffic is heavy. Some farms transport customers to the fields on wagons, buses, trams, or trucks from central parking lots. Scenic rides provide recreational value for city customers.

Check-In, Check-Out

The first person to greet customers is usually at the check-in point. That person welcomes the customers, answers their questions, and directs them in a friendly, helpful manner. The check-in and check-out points may not be in the same location. Some farms are flexible and can quickly expand or reduce the number of check-in and check-out lanes to speed traffic flow. Growers should plan to avoid congestion and confusion, to provide security, and to have adequate communications. Usually, refreshments for sale and toilet facilities are located nearby.

Method of Sale

Berries are sold by volume (usually pints, quarts, 4-quart baskets) or by weight. Grapes may be sold in bushels for wine making. Most growers, however, sell small fruits by weighing them. Inspection of scales may be required by state law. Most growers provide containers either free or for sale, while others allow customers to bring their own containers.

Field Supervision

Pick-your-own customers like to pick bushes or rows that have not recently been picked. They appreciate supervisors in the field to show them how to pick, answer their questions, and provide extra containers. Some farms carry filled containers out of the field to shade at the check-out point.

Insurance

Growers should be careful, make the premises as safe as possible, and create a safety consciousness among all who work on the farm (Uchtmann, 1979, 1987). Liability

Direct Marketing to Consumers

for accidents occurs when crowds come to the farm. The normal farm insurance policy probably will not cover accident liability or the buildings used in the business. Growers should thoroughly discuss their operations with their insurance agent, especially in regard to premises liability coverage, products liability coverage, and worker's compensation coverage. Adequate insurance protection is essential.

Companion Crops

Many customers will buy other fruits or vegetables when they drive to the farm to pick small fruits. For example, strawberry farms may grow peas, asparagus, rhubarb, lettuce, radishes, cauliflower, cabbage, or broccoli for their customers. Growers of pick-your-own blueberries, blackberries, or raspberries often find good sales of melons, sweet corn, tomatoes, beans, cherries, and peaches. These crops may be PYO or available in retail containers at the check-out stand or in the farm market. The selection of crops will depend on your geographical location, soils, irrigation, and feasibility for other plantings in the farm operation. Day-neutral strawberries and everbearing raspberries may be planted for direct sales along with summer vegetables or fall apples and pumpkins. It is important to have an accurate estimate of the relative ripening times for the various crops which are to be grown so that appropriate labor, advertising, and marketing plans can be developed. The average ripening times at Geneva, New York, for many tree and small fruit crops are illustrated in Fig. 13-6.

Many enterprises are successful because the entire farm family works in the operation (Sullivan et al., 1981). Often, it is the wife who hires, trains, and supervises the help; handles the money and keeps records; helps in planning; prepares advertising; and meets customers on a daily basis; while other members of

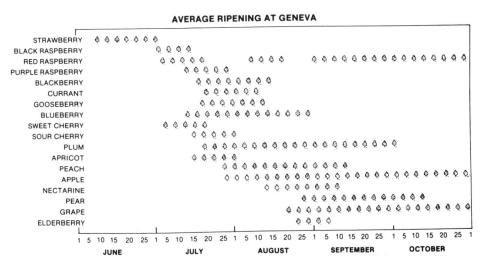

FIGURE 13-6 Relative ripening times for various small and tree fruits at Geneva, New York. (From *New and Noteworthy Fruits,* Courtesy of New York State Fruit Testing Cooperative Association.)

the family are involved in field operations. By meeting or exceeding customer expectations, local PYO marketing can be a successful enterprise. Growers can survey their customers to determine their attitudes and shopping habits (Courter et al., 1980). This information will help them plan production and marketing strategies.

Roadside Stands and Farm Markets

There is a trend toward increased sales of picked fruit (Courter, 1986b, 1987). Small fruit growers can take advantage of this and develop excellent outlets for their picked berries through roadside farm markets (Fig. 13-7). These roadside stands must be located close to customers, have good access roads, and offer top quality. Customers generally live within 10 miles (16 km), visit often, and make small purchases. A convenient location is critical for success. Markets that offer a wide variety of fruits and vegetables generally attract more customers than those that have a limited number of items for sale.

Farm stands can range widely in size and amount of investment. Temporary facilities such as inexpensive wagons, trailers, open sheds, and movable small buildings may be used for seasonal sales. At the other extreme the farm market might be an elaborate building with a full line of home-grown produce as well as items for year-round sales. Small fruits will fit nicely into any of these situations.

Small fruits must be picked, transported, and handled with care. They generally do not keep and must be sold quickly. Some market managers purchase fruit grown in other regions to supplement the home-grown supply. Today's marketing

FIGURE 13-7 Many small fruits are marketed directly to customers through roadside and farm markets.

Direct Marketing to Consumers

and transportation system allows markets to offer strawberries, kiwifruit, grapes, and blueberries over a long period. These and other home-grown fruits, however, will attract customers who believe them to be fresher and better quality than shipped produce. To compete, however, the farm must grow improved varieties, produce the best size and quality, do a good job advertising and be alert to changes in consumer demands.

Red raspberries, black raspberries, blackberries, and gooseberries are not often available in supermarkets. These fruits can become unique specialty items for the farm that can grow them. Harvest labor is one of the limiting factors that must be considered.

Small fruits are generally harvested by hand labor for fresh sales. The following pointers will aid growers who pick for sales through roadside stands or farmers' markets. The prices received and volume of sales will depend to a considerable extent on the care exercised in picking, handling, and displaying the fruit.

1. Instruct and supervise pickers. Pick directly into the retail containers whenever possible. Sorting is not desirable as berries are usually damaged. Place berries carefully into the containers and fill them properly. Do not drop or throw berries into containers.

2. Harvest the best eating quality for direct sales. Pick when the fruit is in prime condition. Pick firm fruit. Do not pick berries that are immature or overripe. Have pickers place overripes and inferior-quality berries into separate containers as they pick. These may be sold for jams, jellies, or other processing.

3. Use appropriate and clean containers for retail sales. Quarts, pints, and half-pint tills are commonly used, depending on the crop and the market.

4. Pick frequently. In hot weather it will be necessary to pick more often, perhaps every other day. Harvest during the coolest part of the day. Do not pick berries when they are wet.

5. Keep picked berries in the shade and out of the wind. A field shelter may be needed in large plantings.

6. Carefully transport the berries to the market as soon as possible. Avoid shaking and road vibration, which can settle and damage fruit.

7. Display berries for quick sales. Small fruits hold best in a refrigerated [40°F (4.4°C)] display case and most should be sold in 1 or 2 days. Do not wet or sprinkle water on the fruit. Blueberries and grapes cooled quickly after harvest can be held up to 1 week for retail sales.

8. Keep displays full. Provide recipes and consumer tips on how to use the berries properly. Remove decaying or spoiled fruit promptly.

Storage

Raspberries, blackberries, and strawberries are not adapted to storage (Hardenburg et al., 1986). They may be held satisfactorily for 1 to 3 days at 32°F (0°C) temperature and 90 to 95% relative humidity. Some growers prefer to hold strawberries at temperatures of 40 to 45°F (4 to 7°C). Blueberries, currants, gooseberries, and grapes in good condition may be held for 1 to 2 weeks at 31 to 32°F (-0.6 to 0°C) and high humidity. Loss in quality can be expected if the fruit is stored for longer periods or at warmer temperatures. Boxes of berries with mixtures of maturities decrease the storage potential for marketing.

Downtown Farmers' Markets

Farmers' markets are usually organized by a community group of business persons, civic leaders, or a church to bring farmers downtown. Such markets are located on the town square, in a vacant lot, in a park, or along closed streets. Communities may organize these markets as part of their revitalization program to attract more shoppers to the downtown area. Some cities and states provide permanent buildings for their markets. Although growers may organize farmers' markets on an individual or a cooperative basis, they are not common.

Consumers benefit by getting farm-fresh produce, high quality, and fair prices without traveling to the country. This especially attracts inner-city residents and workers, the elderly, and people without transportation. These consumers often feel that they get better value than in their local grocery stores (Sullivan et al., 1981).

Small fruits are usually popular and find plenty of buyers in farmers' markets. One of the reasons is that home-grown berries are not often available in supermarkets. Growers should pick their fruit fresh on the day of the market if this is possible. Handle with care, transport gently, keep out of the sun, and provide full measure. As customers get to know you, they will look for you to bring delicious high-quality berries, and other fruits or vegetables, to market each week. Farmers will require other market outlets because most community farmers' markets operate only one day a week. Small fruit growers will find it necessary to combine these sales with a farm stand, pick-your-own, or wholesale sales.

REFERENCES

COURTER, J. W. 1979. Pick-your-own marketing of fruits and vegetables. Univ. Ill. Coop. Ext. Serv. Dep. Hortic. Publ. HM–1.

COURTER, J. W. 1982. Estimating the trade area and potential sales for a pick-your-own strawberry farm. Univ. Ill. Coop. Ext. Serv. Dep. Hortic. Publ. HM–6.

COURTER, J. W. 1985. Pick-your-own: a growing farm market. Ext. Rev. 55(4):36–37.

COURTER, J. W. 1986a. Profile of the strawberry consumer in Illinois. ZapBerry News, Feb., p. 2–5.

COURTER, J. W. 1986b. Is your farm suited to pick-your-own? Proc. Successful Farming Adapt 100 Conference, Des Moines, Iowa. p. 152–154.

COURTER J. W. 1987. Trends in strawberry cultivars and marketing in Illinois. ZapBerry News, Apr., p. 2.

COURTER, J. W., AND C. M. SABOTA. 1981. Retail trade areas for pick-your-own strawberry farms in Illinois. p. 415–418. In N. F. Childers (ed.). The strawberry, Horticultural Publications, Gainesville, Fla.

COURTER J. W., C. M. SABOTA, AND J. C. O. NYANKORI. 1980. Methods of surveying direct market customers. HortScience 15(3):265–266.

DAHL, D. T., AND J. W. COURTER. 1985. Fruit and vegetable clip art for direct marketers. Univ. Ill. Coop. Ext. Serv. Dep. Hortic. Ser. 52.

GINDER, R. G., AND H. H. HOECKER. 1975. Management of pick-your-own marketing operations. University of Delaware Cooperative Extension Service, Newark, Del.

HARDENBURG, R. E., A. E. WATADA, AND C. Y. WANG. 1986. The commercial storage of fruits, vegetables, and florist and nursery stocks. U.S. Dep. Agric. Handb. 66.

HOW, R. B. 1981. Improving the wholesale marketing of locally grown vegetables in the Niagara Frontier region. A. E. Res. Publ. 81-4. Department of Agricultural Economics, Cornell University, Ithaca, N.Y.

PHELPS, J. B., AND R. B. HOW. 1981. Planning data for small scale commercial vegetable and strawberry production in New York. A. E. Res. Publ. 81-20. Department of Agricultural Economics, Cornell University, Ithaca, New York.

SULLIVAN, G. H., V. KULP, R. TREADWAY, AND P. KIRSCHLING. 1981. Direct farm to consumer marketing: a profitable alternative for family farm operations. Coop. Ext. Serv. Publ. HO-160, Purdue University, West Lafayette, Ind.

UCHTMANN, D. L. 1979. Liability and insurance for U-pick operations. Univ. Ill. Coop. Ext. Serv. Dep. Hortic. Publ. HM-2.

UCHTMANN. D. L. 1987. Liability issues facing fruit and vegetable growers. Proceedings of the 1987 Illinois Strawberry School. Univ. Ill. Coop. Ext. Serv. Dep. Hortic. Ser. 64:5–7.

SUGGESTED READING

ANTLE, G. G. 1978. Pick your own. Michigan State Univ. Extn. Bull. E-1246.

CARROL, F. Pick-your-own fruits and vegetables and more: a reference guide. Prosperity for Profit, Houston, Tex.

JACKSON, B., AND R. H. GRODER. 1978. Direct farm marketing. Oregon State Univ. Extn. Circ. 945.

Market News Service. USDA, AMS, F and V Division, Room 2503 – South Building, P.O. Box 96456, Washington, D.C. 20090.

SAMS, D. W., D. W. LOCKWOOD, AND A. D. RUTLEDGE, 1979. Pick your own fruits and vegetables. Univ. of Tennessee Agric. Extn. Serv. Pub. 801.

WAMPLER, R. L., AND J. E. MOTES. 1984. Pick-your-own farming: cash crops for small acreages. University of Oklahoma Press, Stillwater, Okla.

Chapter 14

Economics of Small Fruit Production

R. C. FUNT

INTRODUCTION

Small fruit crop culture offers an opportunity to extend and diversify agricultural operations and to provide additional income at a different time of year. A succession of small fruit crops alone, or combined with other produce and ornamental crops, has formed the basis for many successful family pick-your-own (PYO) and roadside marketing businesses. Small fruit specialty firms (producing fruit or nursery stock) require considerable technical expertise and equipment, and a good understanding of sound managerial, advertising, and marketing principles.

While small fruit production can be started or terminated relatively rapidly, returns to the growers fluctuate widely. There are basic differences in agricultural and industrial economics and management. An understanding of the production environment, labor requirements, length of production cycle, production costs, competition and pricing structure for a perishable product, and effect of supply on demand are necessary for continued success.

Returns for agricultural products vary in periods of inflation and deflation.

Imported fruit or fruit from other domestic production areas which have a more favorable growing environment may drastically alter marketing plans.

In the following discussion a list of factors to be considered before entering a small fruit production business is offered. Additionally, a method of examining the internal rate of return for estimating cost and returns of various fruit crops is discussed. These analyses will be an important aid in implementing business decisions on the fruit farm.

FARM BUSINESS MANAGEMENT

In the previous chapters, cultural practices that maximize production have been presented. However, management and marketing considerations are vital to the success of the farm. Management of people, money, and crops go hand in hand with marketing. Horticultural economics and management are more complex than other crops such as grain because more factors of production, management, and marketing are involved. For most small fruits the end product is perishable and must be sold or processed shortly after harvest.

Successful farming comes to those who recognize it as a business and prepare themselves in the skills of business management. Unlike other businesses, weather, climate, soil conditions, and diseases are factors over which managers have little or no control. Fixed costs are higher in farming because of large investments in land and machinery per unit of output. Farm work is less specialized because you are called upon to be a personnel manager, a production planner, and a horticulturist. The business risk (price changes, yield variation, technology changes, and changes in consumer preference) is much higher in farming than in other businesses (Calkins and DiPietre, 1983).

As in other businesses, however, the success of the farm business depends on efficiency. Carefully kept records are a prerequisite for determining efficiency, profitability, and future management decisions. Success requires an adequate volume of land or sales to have efficient use of labor and equipment. Finally, the farm business manager must have an eye on current events, sensitivity to consumer preference, and knowledge of the nonfarm business cycle. This information is needed in planning a year in advance and to be flexible in management and marketing.

Fruit production involves long-term commitment to land, labor, and capital. A mistake in site selection, cultivar, or plant spacing may not be evident for several years after heavy investment already has been made. Once a decision is made, it is revocable only with considerable loss. Cultural decisions are not the only factors that increase risk in fruit production. Waiting several years for a crop to come into production and then finding that consumer preference or the marketing system has changed can be equally costly.

Technology is knowledge applied by people to improve efficiency in production or marketing. Technology used in fruit production may include tractors, sprayers with computer-assisted output controls, improved cultivars and chemicals, automated computer-assisted irrigation systems, mechanical harvesters, and cultural practices such as raised-bed systems, new training systems, and close plant spacings. The objective of technology is to provide greater output from a given input of land, labor, and capital resources (efficiency).

The most important element contributing to technological advancement is improved communication. The flow of new technology into accepted practice is accelerated through computers, videotapes, television, commodity schools, specialized bulletins, and professional workers and consultants. In the near future, rapid electronic information exchange will be used to make information about fruit production, exports, and imports from all parts of the world available for use on farm computers. These developments will aid greatly to the decision-making process.

Technical and managerial knowledge are complementary. The use of a mechanical grape harvester requires not only a level or production in tons per acre for efficient use of equipment, but also necessitates the ability of a processor to handle larger volumes of a perishable crop. The processing plant may provide a market for certain cultivars of grapes. Thus the integration of all parts of production, harvesting, and marketing systems must be complete.

MAKING BUSINESS DECISIONS

Management is the human element in the production process, the element that initiates, modifies, and maintains the production process through decisions made regarding all the factors of production. Successful farm management involves the ability to plan, measure, and choose among the many options available. This understanding must be flexible, evolve and grow, and be capable of responding to a changing environment. The components of farm business management are:

1. Farm family goals
2. Economic principles
3. Records and budgets
4. Risk and government programs
5. Factors of production
6. Tax and business organizational structure

Decision making can be defined as the attainment of farm family goals by using economic principles to formulate and implement budgets. This process adjusts for risk and government programs, and combines the factors of production within suitable tax and business structure. Part of the decision-making process is learning to evaluate the compromises between the farm and family goals. Profit maximization, farm ownership, farm expansion, avoidance of risk, and an enjoyable standard of life are all worthy goals but may lead to serious conflicts. The wealthiest manager may not achieve the highest satisfaction. Once goals have been written, growers should compile data from farm records and experiment station or extension reports to assist in describing their current situation. With your goals, use economic principles to predict needed resources and prescribe the production alternatives that makes them efficient. Put the plan to work and go back and evaluate the steps that were effective. It is important to know why you did well, whether you could do better, and what options you have for the future (Calkins and DiPietre, 1983).

A potential small fruit grower, whether new or diversifying, usually has an objective of growing one or more crops for consumers in a given area. Site selection (including soil type), proximity to markets, amount of available labor, equipment dealers, weather patterns, water availability, and the use of capital (money) are important considerations before one enters the fruit business.

Farm size is of concern for equipment cost-efficiency and to produce sufficient income for the family. In many fruit producing areas, one manager and family labor will operate 40 to 80 acres of fruit production. This varies with the major fruit crops in the operation due to restraints of labor and marketing. Total farm size could be 100 or more acres because they contain nonproductive acres such as headlands, ponds, roads, forests, or meadows. In Arkansas, one set of equipment for blackberry production alone would be economically used on 13.4 to 53 acres of land (Price and Baldwin, 1980). If the objective of a grape producer is to own a mechanical harvester, 120 to 150 acres of grapes will need to be harvested for the machine cost to be equal or less than hand harvest. This means that the farmer must have this minimum number of acres in production on his own farm or supplement his smaller farm size by custom harvesting for other growers in his area. It is not uncommon for growers to own 200 acres of land and produce only 20 acres of fruit, vegetables, and grain crops on a diversified farm.

The median farm income (family of four) in 1987 was over $20,000 per year. With interest rates of 10 to 12% on an investment of $100,000, an annual net farm income of $30,000 to $32,000 would be necessary in 1987. For persons who own a few acres and only want to be involved part-time, small fruits offer one of the best ways to intensify production and receive a potentially large income on a few acres.

Next to the investment in land, equipment is one of the largest investments. Growers can purchase used equipment, borrow or hire custom operators, or rent equipment. However, when equipment is not owned, it may be difficult to accomplish the cultural requirements at the proper time. The type of equipment that is generally owned by growers includes tractors, sprayers, mowers, small trucks, and irrigation systems. Specialty equipment such as large trucks, rototillers, forklifts, plows, and harvesters may be rented or hired. Replacement and updating of equipment, due to changing technology, is one of the most important management decisions that has to be made.

Labor requirements are a component of farm size, type of crop and cropping system, and marketing. Production practices such as plowing, planting, and pruning can be done with owner-operator labor or additional family and hired labor. Harvest and supervising harvest labor may require additional off the farm seasonal labor. The amount of labor required in small fruit crop production and harvesting is more per area of land than for many other agricultural crops. Pruning and harvesting operations must be completed on a timely basis, and equipment for mechanizing these tasks is either not available or is too costly for small acreages.

Pruning raspberries, grapes, or thornless blackberries may require 30 to 100 labor hours per acre per year, and this may need to be accomplished in a relatively short time during late February or March. Weather will limit the number of hours per week. As plants begin to grow in April, pruning needs to be stopped so that other duties are completed. Thus managers must face the constraints of time, season, and weather.

In deciding the amount of acreage to plant, the types of fruit, and other crops, a grower must consider if sufficient labor is available during times of peak labor requirements (Figs. 14–1 and 14–2). For example, strawberries do not mix well with peaches, because a high labor requirement is needed for strawberry harvest at the same time that peaches need to be hand thinned. A month-to-month list of jobs and the amount of time needed for each job with reserved time for weather constraints is necessary for successful planning and management of more than one crop or additional acreage (Table 14–1).

Mechanical harvesting of small fruit crops reduces the number of people required for harvest. However, except for blueberries, the machine-harvested fruit are limited to the processed market, such as frozen berries, juice, or wine. Mechanical harvesters require sufficient acreage (50 to 150 acres per season) and above-average yields per acre to be efficient. Cultural practices and production systems may differ from hand harvesting for mechanical harvest in order to be cost-effective. In the case of blueberries or raspberries, the harvester must pass over the plants several times during the season, which adds to the total cost of production.

Pick-your-own retail or wholesale fresh marketing are alternatives in harvest labor requirements, but can be combined with hand harvest for increasing returns under adverse customer or weather conditions. A farm utilizing the PYO system of marketing usually has a number of fruit, vegetable, or other horticultural crops and/or a retail market to induce satisfied customers to return over an extended growing season. PYO farms must depend on the public to harvest the crop even under poor weather conditions.

BEGINNING THE BUSINESS

Before starting a small fruit enterprise it is important to consider some of the reasons why such businesses fail. Generally, 90% fail because of:

1. Lack of necessary skills for production, marketing, finance, personnel, and other management aspects
2. Poor record keeping
3. Poor cash management (flow)
4. Failure to plan
5. Misuse of time
6. Inattention to marketing
7. Ignoring the human factor
8. Failure to assume the proper management role

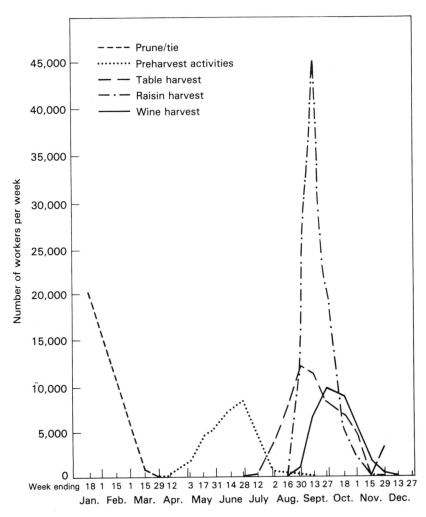

FIGURE 14-1 Employment of hired farm workers on grapes, southern San Joaquin Valley, 1975.

The need for a good accounting system frequently is overlooked. In some cases, where a grower may be unfamiliar with appropriate accounting procedure, a knowledgeable accountant should be hired. Decisions on cash flow and management should be based on accurate records. In new farms, undercapitalization (not enough capital) is a major problem. Planning for 1 or 2 years in advance can be done much better when budgeting and accounting procedures are followed. While there are presently few software programs available for horticultural crops, new software (data base management, spreadsheet analysis, etc.) programs will aid in using collected data for planning and management. In 1987, under the CASH program, the Ohio State University released software for horticulture called Market Model 2.

Fruit crops have very high initial investments and require 2 to 5 years before the volume of production creates an annual return higher than annual costs. The ability of the manager to make decisions at the correct time is critical to success. Decisions made prior to, or at planting, will affect income for 5 to 10 years. In general, high yields early in the life of the planting are an important management objective. Discounting methods of budgeting, such as the internal rate of return analysis (available with Lotus 1-2-3 or Supercalc 3 software), is the most preferred and practical way to assess decisions within fruit crop systems or between different crops.

The internal rate of return will provide an estimate, over time, of the potential earnings of a crop. It will indicate the highest rate of interest one could afford to pay for the investment. For example, the analysis may estimate a 15% return on investment over the 12-year life of a bramble planting. If you must borrow at 17%, at the end of 12 years, you have lost 2% on the investment. In contrast, if blueberries gave a 20% return on investment, a 3% return above borrowed capital rate would have been achieved.

The internal rate of return allows comparison of strawberries and blueberries, even though each has a different level of investment, a different production time period, and a different price per pound. Current prices for all inputs and reasonable labor requirements must be used from your records or from university data. A general conclusion, with regard to a single-crop enterprise, is that costs per acre are nearly the same each year and profit is made where yields are consistently high early

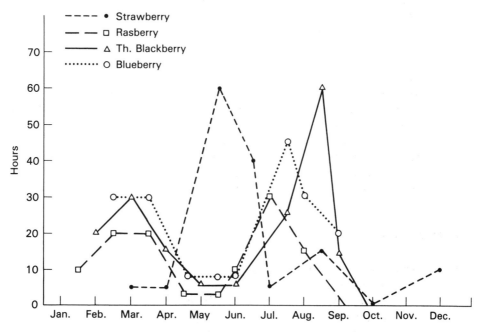

FIGURE 14-2 Man hours per acre for cultural practices and supervisory harvest labor for bearing strawberry, raspberry, and blueberry, in the eastern United States (assumes early, mid, late season cultivars). (From U.S. Department of Agriculture).

TABLE 14-1 ESTIMATED LABOR HOURS AVAILABLE FOR FIELD WORK PER MONTH[a]

MONTH	PERCENT WORK TIME[b]	AVAILABLE HOURS[c]		TOTAL AVAILABLE HOURS[d]
		Ordinary	Overtime	
January	50	74	28	102
February	50	67	33	100
March	60	89	69	158
April	65	90	86	176
May	70	106	110	216
June	75	112	112	224
July	75	118	113	231
August	75	112	104	216
September	70	106	82	188
October	65	99	63	162
November	50	72	26	98
December	50	67	25	92

Source: John Nix (1985).

[a]These values relate to medium land and these can be different on heavier or lighter soils, particularly if undrained. Indoor work can be continued over the full working week. These estimates will vary according to geographical regions but are typical of temperate fruit zones near 40°N. latitude.

[b]Forty-hour week, less public holidays.

[c]Adjusted for illness and nondelayable maintenance (½ hr/day). No overtime on weekdays or weekends is shown.

[d]Available days can be found by dividing 8 hours.

in the life of the planting and remain consistently high year after year. Average yields should be consistent with expected crop losses over time due to unfavorable weather. Inaccurate input information leads to inaccurate conclusions, particularly when several years are used in the calculations.

It is important to realize that all decisions on the farm are not made with respect to profit or loss. Some crops may be produced simply as a means of increasing the number of customers for a major crop. An example would be to grow peas to promote a large strawberry crop which will be available the following week.

MARKETING

Small fruits can be marketed as pick-your-own, hand harvested for retail or wholesale, and mechanically or hand harvested for processing. Each grower must determine which market or combination of markets are best, based on location, crop and weather conditions, economic advantage, and family goals. Management must be flexible in the decision of present and future markets for long-term returns on investment.

Sales are the secret to any business. The belief by some growers that their products will sell themselves is not true. An organized and rigorous marketing program is essential to build customer awareness. In PYO, the product must not only be of high quality, but also be promoted as the most desirable fresh fruit of the season and produced in clean fields with friendly people to assist the customer. Word of mouth is widely accepted as the best and least expensive advertisement. Radio, newspapers, and free television exposure can also be used effectively. Generally, 3 to 5% of the farm budget is used for promotion. Weather conditions can dramatically affect customer participation on pick-your-own operations. The use of automatic electronic devices to advise potential customers of field conditions and picking times can be of great use.

Advertising serves to keep you in the public eye. Without it there is a gradual decline in customers. Advertising maintains your sales and marketing position. Newspaper advertisements are most frequently used and they need to include name, address, telephone number, crops available, picking times, logo, and a map. It is important to remember that one of the best ways of upsetting customers is to advertise something that is not available. Location of the farm has an important impact on advertising and success of the enterprise. The less well situated the farm, the greater the advertising task. The proximity to a metropolitan area, location near a vacation (holiday) route, and the general beauty of the area are important. Advertising low prices makes customers suspicious of sensing inferior fruit or poor field conditions. Overall conclusions of one general report indicated that many growers failed to get feedback as to the effectiveness of advertising and lacked creative, distinguishable, and different advertising from that of their neighbor or similar PYO operations (Jackson and Nicholson, 1985).

Determining a fair price for the customer and for a return on investment requires a budget showing all costs. A fair return on investment is one equal to the interest rate for borrowed money. Reduced prices are not a substitute for a good location or other means of stimulating returns. Many growers who are not aware of their real cost of production believe that they only need to meet current expenses and fail to realize sufficient returns for inflation. Reduction in price requires considerable sales volume to make a profit (Table 14–2).

Retail, wholesale, and processing markets require various standards of quality, quantity, and packaging. These continue to change as buyers must meet competition in an environment of changing consumer preference. The ability of management to gain information as to future needs and address these to the current abilities of enterprise will become increasingly important in the future.

SUMMARY OF VARIOUS ECONOMIC REPORTS

Blackberry

In Maryland, thornless blackberry production for pick-your-own marketing and hand harvest for retail marketing was compared over a 12-year expected life for the planting (Funt, 1977). Costs and returns were based on 1975 prices. Estimated costs and returns were the highest of the small fruits that were compared. The internal rate of return was estimated to be 39% for hand-harvested and 56% for pick-your-

TABLE 14-2 INCREASED SALES REQUIRED TO EQUAL PRICE REDUCTION

PERCENT RETURN[a]	PERCENT PRICE REDUCED	PERCENT INCREASED SALES FOR ORIGINAL PERCENT RETURN
15	5	50
15	10	200
15	12.5	500
20	5	33
20	10	100
20	15	167
30	5	20
30	15	100
30	25	500
40	5	14
40	15	60
40	30	300

Source: North American Strawberry Growers Association, Inc. Newsletter, June 1984. Dryden Press, New York.

[a] Annual expected profit, not internal rate of return of total investment.

own. This assumed yields occurred for 11 years with no loss to low temperatures.

Erect blackberries generally have the same costs and yields as black raspberries and would be expected to have a similar rate of return. However, new cultivars have higher yield potential, according to reports from Arkansas, and thus will influence these figures.

In Arkansas, with yields of 2.46 tons/acre (5.5 MT/ha), net cash returns would be $615 per acre with a minimum acreage of 13.4 acres. Maximum acreage would be 54.6 acres but could be increased with a mechanical harvester (costs $36,000) to 109 acres (Price and Baldwin, 1980).

Blueberry

In North Carolina, the annual cost of blueberry production was $2000 per acre without irrigation and $2300 per acre with irrigation in 1980.Nearly 70% of cost not related to irrigation represents harvesting and packing (Johnson, 1980). A 50-acre blueberry planting was estimated to have a 15- to 20-year life expectancy. The cost would range from $135,000 to $214,000 for nonirrigated and irrigated systems, respectively. However, irrigation can nearly double the value of the planting (based on revenue from good soil), at $6640 per acre for irrigated versus $3486 for nonirrigated berries.

With good soil and irrigation, the rate of return was 28% and on marginal soil it was 18%. For nonirrigated production on good soil it was 24% and on marginal soil there was a deficit. Mechanical harvesting is not economical until fresh market prices and processing prices are within 20 cents per pound of one another (Johnson, 1980).

In Ohio in 1984, rates of return for pick-your-own irrigated highbush blueberries over a 12- or 18-year life at $0.70 to 0.80 per pound ranged from 16 to 26% (Table 14-3). Rate of return for hand-harvested irrigated blueberries at $1.00 to $1.10 per pound were 8 to 17%. Yield estimates averaged 7000 to 8000 pounds per acre (Funt, 1984).

The cost of different pruning procedures in lowbush blueberry production for 10, 100, and 1000 acres of blueberries ranged from $109 to $87 per acre for strawburning, which is best for small farms. Larger farms could afford the large investment for mechanical spreading of straw because the cost of equipment was much less when averaged over a large acreage. Flail mowing was the least expensive, ranging from $86 per acre (10 acres) to $21 per acre (100 acres) to $14 per acre (1000 acres), and had the lowest labor requirement. It works best on smooth soil. However, no attempt was made to compare expected yields from these systems (Hanson et al., 1982).

Currant, Gooseberry, and Elderberry

Commercial plantings of currants, gooseberries, and elderberries are limited. These winter-hardy plants have been grown in small commercial plantings in New York, Ohio, Michigan, and Oregon, where they are marketed mainly to processing plants for jam, jelly, pies, or wine. They are likely to be profitable if the market is prearranged or in a small pick-your-own planting as a test for consumer acceptance. Elderberries have serious virus, insect, and bird problems (Way, 1981). However, they can yield up to 3 to 4 tons/acre (6.7 to 9 MT/ha). In the past currants could not be planted in certain areas because they were an alternate host to white pine blister rust. Check with your state department of agriculture for laws that may prohibit currant plantings.

Grape

A 1980 economic study of a 25-acre 'Concord' vineyard that was mechanically harvested indicated a 4-year establishment cost of $4976 per acre, with revenues of $1400 or a net capital investment of $3576. The total cost for a mature vineyard was $1231 per acre per year. With receipts of $175 per ton and 8 tons/acre (18 MT/ha), net returns equaled $169 per acre. Based on these estimates, a 7-ton yield per acre (16 MT/ha) and a price of $175 per ton are needed to generate a positive return. At 4 tons/acre (9 MT/ha) and $175 per ton, the rate of return would be −8%, while a price of $200 per ton would equal −6% (Kirpes and Folwell, 1981).

In a similar study in 1980 in Ohio, a positive rate of return for 4-ton/acre production would occur at $400 per ton (20 cents per pound) for a vineyard having an 18-year life. However, actual prices were near $180 to $210/ton. Based on 100 hours of use per season and 1 acre/hour, mechanically harvested grapes had a higher rate of return per acre than hand-harvested grapes when labor was at $5.50/hour and harvested 1500 lb per 8 hours. Pull-type mechanical harvesters were more economical than self-propelled models for 50 acres or less; self-propelled harvesters were best for 150 or more acres (Funt, 1981). Table grapes yielded a 14.4 and 18.1% return at $0.45 and $0.35 per pound for hand-harvested and PYO, respectively,

TABLE 14-3 INTERNAL RATES OF RETURN FOR PYO OR HAND-HARVESTED SMALL FRUIT IN OHIO

CROP	YEAR OF ANALYSIS[a]	CROP LIFE (yrs)[b]	PERCENT RETURN[c]		PRICE/POUND		AVERAGE (lb/yr)
			Hand	PYO	Hand	PYO	
Blueberry	1984	12	12.3	17.9	$1.05	$0.75	6200
Blueberry	1984	18	15.6	25.6	1.05	0.75	6200
Grape (table)	1985	12	14.4	18.1	0.45	0.35	8120
Raspberries							
Red							
Fall[d]	1988	12	23.0	28.0	1.40	1.20	2000
Summer	1988	12	21.0	23.0	1.40	1.20	2000
Black	1988	12	21.0	23.0	1.40	1.20	2000
Purple	1988	12	21.0	23.0	1.40	1.20	2000
Blackberry (thornless)	1988	12	35.0	42.0	0.90	0.80	5000
Strawberry	1985	4	14.2	20.5	0.95	0.60	7000

[a]Rate of return will change as current costs change.
[b]Indicated crop life as used in analysis. Some crops will have a longer economic life.
[c]Rates of return based on the estimated yields and prices received, and may or may not be the average price received by growers.
[d]Heritage cultivar management system.

when the average yield was 4 tons/acre (9 MT/ha) per year (Funt, 1985) (Table 14–3).

In New York in 1978, 50 acres of 'Concord' single-curtain, Geneva double-curtain (GDC), and French hybrid production systems using machine harvest were compared with average yields of 4.3 tons/acre (9.6 MT/ha), 5.5 tons/acre (12.3 MT/ha), and 3.5 tons/acre (7.8 MT/ha), respectively, and 'Concords' at $190 per ton and French hybrids at $306 per ton. The total cost per ton was $250, $235, and $232, respectively. However, not all of the cost is a cash cost, such as operator labor, management, and annual depreciation. The grower, with 100% equity, no interest payments, and using operating funds without borrowing, will have about one-half of the total cost of a young grower with 50% of the equity in land, machinery, and buildings financed at 9% interest for 7 years. Established growers view rising costs and lower prices with less alarm than do new growers with lower equity. A new grower with 50% equity could have additional outlays per acre of $188, $241, and $223 for single-curtain, GDC, and French hybrids, respectively (White and Jordon, 1978).

In New York, 'Concord' grape growers were encouraged to retrain vines from an umbrella Kniffin (UK) system to a Geneva double-curtain system, which increased costs but created a greater increase in expected yields. A net present value (NPV) analysis using a 6% discounted cash flow (13% capital cost - 7% inflation) and a 2-year replacement cycle indicated a $3120 per acre increase over a 20-year life, with the best yields at 2.9 tons/acre (2.7 MT/ha) per year, 53% over the UK system. Only 7 out of 24 growers were capable of obtaining these yields. The yields during conversions dropped the first year but increased the following year. Growers who converted on hardpan soils reported the lowest yield increases, and those who overcropped did not market the crop, due to failure of the crop to ripen properly in some years. Further overcropping resulted in weak vines and lower yields in some years. More conversion to GDC would have occurred after 1980 had grape prices increased with the rate of inflation. Actually, prices fell, due to large supplies in Washington and California, and a strong dollar increased the import of grape products at low prices. However, a strong conclusion from this report is that conversion is a reasonable alternative where management skill is high and vineyard and soil conditions are favorable (Markin and White, 1982).

In California in 1972 a mechanical grape harvest of wine grapes showed an average rate of 0.7 acres per hour, operating 10.3 hours per day and 237 acres per season. At a farm price of $75 per ton for 'Thompson Seedless', financial losses occurred at the 8-ton yield regardless of farm size. At 10 tons/acre (22 MT/ha), the larger farms had positive net returns. The higher level of fixed costs made machine harvesting systems more costly per acre than hand systems on smaller farms. The break-even point at the 8-ton/acre (18 MT/ha) yield was reached at a farm size of 220 acres (Johnson, 1977). In Washington in 1971, at an average yield of 6 tons/acre (13.9 MT/ha) and a custom rate of $19 per ton, a machine needs to harvest 128 acres to break even with annual fixed costs of $10,000 and variable cost of $6.00 per ton (Dailey et al., 1971).

In the coastal counties of California in 1980, costs for cane-pruned cultivars for wine were determined to be $11,040 per acre, which included a land cost of

$6000. The cost for 3, 4 or 5 tons/acre were $1060, $813, and $650, respectively. For head-trained wine grapes, 3, 4, or 5 tons/acre, the costs were $676, $518, and $415 per ton. These costs include a land charge of 11% interest per year on an initial $6000 cost per acre (Bowers et al., 1980).

Profitability of wine operations was determined to cost $1.05 per fifth of pure Scuppernong wine for the small winery (20,000 gal) to $0.88 per fifth for medium (100,000 gal) to large (500,000 gal) wineries in 1976 (Mathia et al., 1977). Blending with bulk wines to double output lowered costs by $0.26 per fifth in small wineries but by only $0.13 per fifth in the large winery. The medium winery operated at lower costs, resulting from economies of size relative to the small winery and the tax advantages relative to the large winery. Internal rates of return did not have a position return for the small winery except for one option. The medium-sized winery had a positive return at $1.15 per fifth or higher. Blending increased rates before taxes by 4 to 5%. It is apparent that taxes are an important component in the costs of operating a winery (Bowers et al., 1980).

Raspberry

'Heritage', a fall-bearing red raspberry cultivar that can be mechanically pruned (rotary or flail mower), was compared to a hand-pruned Junebearing red raspberry for PYO marketing in Ohio in 1984 (Table 14–3). The Junebearing system (not the 'Heritage' cultivar) had higher costs due to pruning labor and had lower yields. The Junebearing system produced a 16.8% rate of return at $0.90 per pound, while the 'Heritage' system had 31.7% rate of return at $0.90 per pound when each was grown for 12 years (Funt, 1984).

PYO and hand-harvested black raspberries were compared in Ohio in 1984. At the suggested selling price of $1.10 per pound, the rate of return over a 12-year life was 13.2% for hand harvest and 22.8% for PYO (Funt, 1984).

'Brandywine', a promising vigorous, high-yielding purple raspberry, is grown in a manner similar to black raspberries, but berries mature after black raspberries and before blackberries. This is of benefit to PYO or retail markets because it extends the picking season. With yields averaging 3000 to 3400 lb/acre (6.7 to 7.6 MT/ha), rates of return ranged from 18.9 to 35.9% when price comparisons of $1.20 to $1.10 per pound for hand and PYO, respectively, were used (Table 14–3) (Funt, 1984).

In this study red, black, and purple raspberry systems were compared to an investment before planting of tile drainage, strip fumigation, and trickle irrigation. In general, a 15 to 20% yield increase plus a $0.10 per pound increase above the low investment was necessary to have an equal rate of return. In all of the studies above, expected yields were higher than those experienced during the early 1980s, due to cold winters and other weather conditions.

Strawberry

In New Jersey, Robson estimated costs of producing 7000 quarts of irrigated and fumigated strawberries for hand harvest at $2713 per acre (Robson, 1980). However, in Florida, the cost was $3000 per acre of fumigated and irrigated strawberries. The cost of producing 1400 (12 pint/flat) flats were $5.73, while 2000 flats cost $4.82 (Prevatt, 1980). Production costs in California were estimated in 1980 to be $3477 per acre, while harvest costs were $7351 (reflects high yields), making a total cost of $11,100 per acre. It was estimated that the returns would be $15,050 per acre or a cost of $3.17 and return of $4.30 per crate, to equal $1.13 per crate above costs (Seyman, 1980). Both Florida and California lead in total dollars received per acre for strawberries because of higher yields and price and wholesale marketing when other regions do not have a supply of berries. Overall, strawberry yields in California average 28 tons/acre (63 MT/ha), while Florida averages 10 tons/acre (22 MT/ha), and other states are in the range 4 ton/acre (9 MT/ha).

For small farms in Indiana which use small 12- to 16-horsepower tractors and frost protection, the total equipment investment was $12,000 to $14,000 even when plants were set by hand. This report concluded that yields for PYO marketing must be 8000 to 10,000 lb/acre (9 to 11 MT/ha) per year or higher at 50 cents per pound for small farms to realize positive returns (Kirschling and Sullivan, 1979). In Ohio in 1985, the estimated equipment investment for 5 acres of strawberries was $68,500 per small fruit farm, while in 1980 investment for the same equipment was $55,000 (Funt, 1985).

Two systems of strawberry production (3- and 5-year rotations) for PYO marketing and fresh sales were compared in Canada in 1981. Hand-harvested berries for 3 years required $0.68 to $0.80 per pound for positive returns for 4200 to 8300 lb/acre (4.7 to 9.3 MT/ha), while $0.40 to $0.48 per pound were needed for PYO marketing. The price range was nearly the same for 5 years, but yields were lower and ranged from 3750 to 7500 lb/acre (4.2 to 8.4 MT/ha) (Hanlon and Hamilton, 1981).

Strawberry growers in Ohio responded to increased costs and competition by using cultural methods to improve production. By using irrigation, fumigation, raised beds, and increasing the initial spacing from 20 in. (51 cm) to 5 in. (13 cm) apart in the row, growers increased their equipment and material (plants) cost per acre.

A comparison of various systems and their costs and returns over a 4-year period was conducted to indicate yield and price needed to obtain a fair return on their investment. The least expensive system with no fumigation, no irrigation, and plants at 20 in. (51 cm) by 38 in. (97 cm) had a cost of nearly $2000 per acre annually until the fourth year, when it was $800 (Table 14-4). The most expensive system, using fumigation, irrigation, raised beds, and high-density spacing at 5 in. (13 cm) by 38 in. (97 cm), had costs of $5892 the first year and $1072 the last year. Equipment costs were based on 5, 10, or 20 acres of production and were estimated to be $68,000, $85,000, and $102,000, respectively, with irrigation being responsible for the increased cost (cost/acre = $13,600, $8,500, and $5,100, respectively).

When 5 acres with no fumigation and irrigation is compared to 5 acres with fumigated and irrigated matted row systems, the fumigated and irrigated system requires 2000 lb more per acre average each year and $0.60 per pound than the low-cost system to cover increased costs. Further, if the grower decided to grow 5 acres of raised-bed, high-density (5 in by 3 ft), he or she would need 4000 lb per acre

TABLE 14-4 INTERNAL RATES OF RETURN FOR DIFFERENT STRAWBERRY SYSTEMS, OHIO, 1985[a]

SYSTEM	EQUIPMENT COST[b]	FIRST-YEAR COST PER ACRE[c]	PRICE PER POUND	YIELD (lb/ACRE)	RATE OF RETURN[d] (%)
Matted row—5A					
No irrigation, fumigation, tile drainage	$57,800	$2184	$0.60	4500	21.0
Irrigated, tile, and fumigated	68,500	3980	0.60	7000	20.5
High density—10A					
Raised bed, irrigated, fumigated	85,650	5891	0.60	9000	25.7

Source: Ohio Strawberry Manual.

[a] All systems show PYO system. Hand harvested systems were compared in original study.

[b] Does not include a 20-acre planting.

[c] Does not include land charge, interest, or tax on equipment.

[d] Based on four year life.

average per season more than the least expensive system, and 2000 lb per acre more than the fumigated and irrigated system to equal a 20% rate of return. Because the raised bed–high density system requires specialized equipment, 10 acres of raised bed–high density plants gave a higher rate of return than did 5 acres of the same system. A 10-acre planting yielding an average of 10,000 lb or more must have nearly 500 people per day to pick 10,000 lb per day over a 10-day harvest season. There are many rural areas, particularly in the midwest, where this type of production may not be completely harvested without strong promotion or advertising (Funt, 1985).

REFERENCES AND SUGGESTED READING

Blackberry

BURT, J. G., K. N., BROWN, AND T. L. CROSS. 1987. Enterprise cost study for Marion blackberries. Oregon State Univ. Extn. Serv. Special Rept. 792.

BUTT, L. A., M. E. WIRTH, AND L. S. BURT. 1981. Production, value, and cost trends of selected Pacific northwest berry crops. Wash. State Univ. Bull. 0899.

FUNT, R. C. 1977. An economic comparison of several small fruit production and harvest systems in Maryland, 1975. Md. Agric. Exp. Stn. Bull. MP 522:1–37.

PRICE, C., AND J. F. BALDWIN. 1980. Northwest Arkansas blackberry production: the relationship between machinery cost and acreage. Univ. Arkansas Agric. Exp. Stn. Spec. Rep. 88:12–19.

Blueberry

CARKNER, R. W., B. F. WOLFLEY, AND W. P. A. SHEER. 1981. Blueberry establishment and production costs and returns. Western Washington. Wash. State Univ. Ext. Bull. 0933.

DHILLON, P. S., AND R. G. LATIMER. 1987. Practices and estimated costs for producing blueberries in New Jersey, 1986. New Jersey Agric. Exper. Stn. Bull. P–02131–1–87.

FUNT, R. C. 1984. Rate of return for pick-your-own highbush blueberries in Ohio, 1984. Department of Horticulture, Ohio State University, Columbus, Ohio. p. 1–6.

HANSON, E. J., A. A. ISMAIL, AND H. B. METZER. 1982. A cost analysis of pruning procedures in lowbush blueberry production. Univ. of Maine Exp. Stn. Bull. 780:1–26.

JOHNSON, M. A. 1980. Profit or loss with blueberries. Proceedings Southeastern Blueberry Council. p. 41–51.

Cranberry

CARKNER, R. W., AND A. Y. SHAWA. 1984a. Cranberry establishment and production costs and returns, southwestern Washington, dry harvest. Wash. State Univ, Extn. Bull. 1295.

CARKNER, R. W., AND A. Y. SHAWA. 1984b. Cranberry establishment and production costs and returns, southwestern Washington, wet harvest. Wash. State Univ. Ext. Bull. 1296.

Currant, Gooseberry, and Elderberry

WAY, R. D. 1981. Elderberry culture in New York State. N.Y. State Agric. Exp. Stn. Food and Life Sci. Bull. 91:1–4.

Economics

CALKINS, P. H., AND D. D. DiPIETRE. 1983. Farm business management, Macmillan, New York. p. 3–18.

JACKSON, R., AND J. A. H. NICHOLSON. 1985. Advertising pick-your-own. Wye College (University of London), Wye, Ashford, Kent, England, EBU Pap. 11. Department of Agricultural Economics, p. 1–25.

NIX, J. 1985. Farm management pocketbook. 15th ed. Farm Business Unit, Wye College (University of London), Wye, Ashford, Kent, England.

SNODGRASS, M. M., AND L. T. WALLACE. 1970. Agriculture, economics and growth. Appleton-Century-Crofts, New York. p. 217–304.

STEGALL, D. P., L. L. STEINMETZ, AND J. B. KLINE. 1976. Managing the small business. Richard D. Irwin, Homewood, Ill. p. 9–18.

TOMEK, W. G., AND K. L. ROBINSON. 1972. Agricultural product price. Cornell University Press, Ithaca, N.Y. p. 10–106.

Grape

BOWERS, K. W., R. L. SISSON, B. E. BEARDEN, A. N. KASIMATIS, AND L. A. HOREL. 1980. Sample costs to establish and produce wine grapes in the north coast counties. Univ. of Calif. Coop. Ext. Spec. Publ. 3086:2–7.

DAILEY, R. T., R. J. FOLWELL, AND R. C. BEVAN. 1971. The economics of owning and operating mechanical grape harvesters in Washington. Wash. State Univ. Agric. Exp. Stn. Circ. 540:1–13.

FUNT, R. C. 1981. Economics of hand vs. mechanical harvested grapes in Ohio. Proceedings of Ohio grape-wine short course, Ohio State Univ. Hortic. Dep. Ser. 504:46–57.

FUNT, R. C. 1985. An economic comparison of pick-your-own and hand harvested table grapes, Ohio, 1985. Department of Horticulture, Ohio State University, Columbus.

JOHNSON, S. S. 1977. Mechanical harvesting of wine grapes. U.S. Dep. Agric. Agric. Econ. Rep. 385.

KIRCHNER, D. C., C. PRICE, AND J. MORRIS. 1987. Production guidelines for commercial Concord grapes in northwest Arkansas. Univ. Arkansas Spec. Rep. 125.

KIRPES, D. J., AND R. J. FOLWELL. 1981. Establishment and production costs in a 25-acre concord grape vineyard. Wash. State Univ. Coop. Ext. Bull. 0875:2–21.

LUTZ, S. M., R. J. FOLWELL, AND M. AHMEDULLA. 1986a. The economics of establishing a Concord grape vineyard in Washington. Wash. State Univ. Ext. Bull. 1415.

LUTZ, S. M., R. J. FOLWELL, AND M. A. CASTALDI. 1986b. Wine grape vineyard development in Washington: an economic perspective. Wash. State Univ. Ext. Bull. 1398.

MARKIN, A. R., AND G. B. WHITE. 1982. Economics of conversion to the Geneva double curtain training system of 'Concord' grapes. J. Am. Soc. Hortic. Sci. 107(6):1117–113.

MATHIA, G. A., A. BEALS, N. C. MILLER, AND D. E. CARROLL, JR. 1977. Economic opportunities for profitable winery operations in North Carolina. Dept. Econ. Bus. N.C. State Univ. Econ. Inf. Rep. 49:5–49.

McKibbon, E. B. 1981. The cost of establishing a vineyard in Ontario. Ontario Ministry of Agriculture and Food, Toronto, Ontario, Canada.

Putnam, J. D., G. B. White, and D. G. Himelrick. 1983. Grape farm business summary: Great Lakes region. Cornell Univ. Agric. Econ. Ext. Publ. 85–4.

Warner, M. E. 1985. Enterprise budget for table grapes on Long Island, New York. Cornell Univ. Agric. Econ. Res. Publ. 85–12.

White, G. B., and T. D. Jordan. 1978. Economics of grape production in the Great Lakes region of New York. Cornell Univ. Dept. of Agric. Econ. Ext. Bull. 78–36

Raspberry

Carkner, R. W., and W. P. A. Sheer. 1985. Red raspberry production costs and returns, western Washington, Wash. State, Univ. Ext. Bull. 0930.

Castaldi, M., et al. 1988. The cost of establishing and producing small fruits for pick-your-own and commercial harvest. Cornell University, Hudson Valley Laboratory, Highland, N.Y.

Funt, R. C. et al. 1988. Brambles: Production, management, and marketing. Ohio Coop. Extn, Bull. 783.

Funt, R. C. 1984. Rate of return of raspberries. Department of Horticulture, Ohio State University, Columbus, Ohio.

Funt. R.C. 1977. An economic comparison of several small fruit production and harvest systems in Maryland, 1975. Univ. Md. Agric. Exp. Stn. Bull. MP922:5–14.

Johnson, K. A., and G. K. Criner. 1985. Economic analysis of a pick-your-own raspberry operation in Maine. Dep. Agric. Resource Econ, Staff Pap. ARE 373.

Software

Lemon, J., R. C. Funt, and H. P. Willson. 1986. Market model 2. CASH project. Ohio Cooperative Extension Service, Columbus, Ohio.

Strawberry

Carkner, R. W., W. P. A. Sheer, and C. McConnell. 1982. Strawberry enterprise budget, western Washington. Wash. State Univ. Ext. Bull. 1077.

Funt. R. C. 1980. pp. 439–449. Costs and returns for pick-your-own strawberries, eastern United States. In N. F. Childers (ed.). The strawberry: cultivars to marketing. Horticultural Publications, Gainesville, Fla.

Funt, R. C. 1985. Ohio strawberry manual. Ohio Coop. Ext. Serv. Ohio State Univ. Bull. 436:21–43.

Hanlon, W. L., and A. Hamilton. 1981. Estimating production costs for Atlantic strawberry enterprises. Publ. A81–800. Agriculture Canada, Truro, Nova Scotia. p. 1–49.

Kelsey, M., and L. Bradford. 1985. Costs of strawberry production in northwestern Michigan. Mich. State Univ. Ext. Bull. E–1114.

Kirschling, P. J., and G. H. Sullivan. 1979. Small farm costs and returns: pick-your-own strawberries. Purdue Agric. Exp. Stn. Bull. 232:5–46.

OTTE, J. A., M. T. POSPICHAL, C. M. HOWARD, AND E. E. ALBREGTS. 1978. Estimated costs to grow strawberries in the Plant City area, 1977. Univ. Fla. Econ. Info. Rep. 86.

PREVATT, J. W. 1980. Florida strawberry production costs. p. 452–453. In N. F. Childers (ed.). The strawberry: cultivars to marketing. Horticultural Publications, Gainesville, Fla.

PREVATT, J. W. 1985. Florida strawberry budget. Bradenton GCREC Res. Rep. BRA 1985-1.

ROBSON, M. G. 1980. Estimated production costs of strawberries in New Jersey. p. 450–451. In N. F. Childers (ed.). The strawberry: cultivars to marketing, Horticultural Publications, Gainesville, Fla.

SAFLEY, C. D., AND E. B. POLING, 1985a. Strawberries, 'PYO': estimated cost per acre for a matted row system with a five acre irrigation system. Farm enterprise budget guidelines manual, N.C. Agric. Ext. Serv. Budget 80-4-7/85.

SAFLEY, C. D., AND E. B. POLING. 1985b. Strawberries, 'PYO': estimated net establishment costs per acre for an annual hill system with a five acre irrigation system. Farm enterprise budget guidelines manual, N.C. Agric. Ext. Serv. Budget 80-5-6/85.

SEYMAN, A. U. 1980. Cost and returns for strawberries, California. p. 454–455. In N. F. Childers (ed.). The strawberry: cultivars to marketing. Horticultural Publications, Gainesville, Fla.

WELCH, N. C., A. S. GREATHEAD, AND J. A. BUETEL. 1985. Strawberry production and costs in the central coast of California. Univ. Calif. Agric. Ext. Pub., Davis, Cal.

Appendix: Metric Conversion Chart

INTO METRIC			OUT OF METRIC		
If You Know:	Multiply By:	To Get:	If You Know:	Multiply By:	To Get:
Length					
inches	2.54	centimeters	millimeters	0.04	inches
feet	30	centimeters	centimeters	0.4	inches
feet	0.303	meters	meters	3.3	feet
yards	0.91	meters	kilometers	0.62	miles
miles	1.6	kilometers			
Area					
sq. inches	6.5	sq. centimeters	sq. centimeters	0.16	sq. inches
sq. feet	0.09	sq. meters	sq. meters	1.2	sq. yards
sq. yards	0.8	sq. meters	sq. kilometers	0.4	sq. miles
sq. miles	2.6	sq. kilometers	hectares	2.47	acres
acres	0.4	hectares			

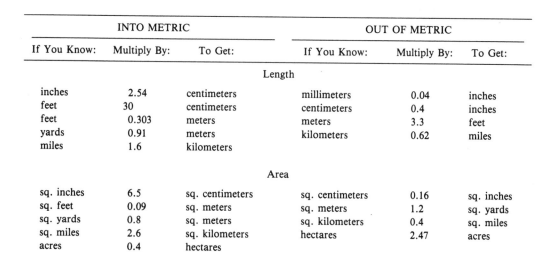

	INTO METRIC			OUT OF METRIC	
If You Know:	Multiply By:	To Get:	If You Know:	Multiply By:	To Get:
		Mass (weight)			
Ounces	28	grams	grams	0.035	ounces
pounds	0.45	kilograms	kilograms	2.2	pounds
short ton	0.9	metric tons	metric tons	1.1	short tons
		Volume			
teaspoons	5	milliliters	milliliters	0.03	fluid ounces
tablespoons	15	milliliters	liters	2.1	pints
fluid ounces	30	milliliters	liters	1.06	quarts
cups	0.24	liters	liters	0.26	gallons
pints	0.47	liters	cubic meters	35	cubic feet
quarts	0.95	liters	cubic meters	1.3	cubic yards
gallons	3.8	liters			
cubic feet	0.03	cubic meters			
cubic yards	0.76	cubic meters			
		Pressure			
lb/in^2	0.069	bars	bars	14.5	lbs/in^2
atmospheres	1.013	bars	bars	0.987	atmospheres
atmospheres	1.033	kg/cm^2	kg/cm^2	0.968	atmospheres
lb/in^2	0.07	kg/cm^2	kg/cm^2	14.22	lbs/in^2
		Rates			
lb/acre	1.12	kg/hectare	kg/hectare	0.892	lbs/acre
tons/acre	2.24	metric tons/hectare	metric tons/hectare	0.446	tons/acre
gal/acre	9.354	liters/hectare	liters/hectare	0.107	gal/acre
		Temperature			

$$°F = (°C \times 1.8) + 32 \qquad °C = 0.555 \times (°F - 32)$$

Glossary

F. E. LARSEN

Abscission zone: one or more layers of cells where transverse division occurs, resulting in separation of an organ from the plant (abscission).

Accessory fruit: a fruit having parts not entirely derived from the ovary; usually developed from an inferior ovary; with the floral tube constituting the accessory portion. In some fruits, a receptacle may be the accessory part.

Acclimation: the natural process of adapting to a climate; hardening.

Achene: a simple, dry, one-celled, one-seeded indehiscent fruit. Achenes are found on the surface of the strawberry receptacle and control its development into an edible "fruit."

Acropetal: moving or developing from base to apex.

Acuminate: having a long, slender sharp point with a terminal angle less than 45°; margins straight to convex.

Adnate: the union of unlike parts, organically united or fused with another dissimilar part (e.g., ovary to a calyx tube, or stamens to petals).

Adventitious: (buds, roots, shoots) plant organs produced in an unusual or irregular position, or at an unusual time of development.

Aggregate fruit: a fruit formed from a flower having several pistils, all of which ripen together in a single mass, as in blackberry and raspberry.

Alley: a narrow passageway left across rows (i.e., in a vineyard) to facilitate harvesting and cultural operations.

Allotetraploid: a polyploid having fours sets of chromosomes that are genetically different, resulting from hybridization between different species.

Ambient: relating to the environment at a particular time, as in ambient temperature.

Ampelographic: of or pertaining to the vine or the genus *Vitis.*

Anastomosing: an interconnecting network, having a net-like or basket-weave appearance.

Anlagen: undifferentiated tissue; primordium.

Anther: the pollen bearing part of the stamen.

Anthesis: the time at which a flower comes into full bloom and sheds pollen.

Anthocyanin: natural pigments of blue, purple, and red.

Apical dominance: the influence exerted by a terminal bud in suppressing the growth of lateral buds.

Apical meristem: a group of meristematic cells at the tip of the root or shoot from which all tissues of the mature axis are ultimately formed.

Apothecia (apothecium, pl): a fungal, spore-producing, fruiting body.

Arm: the main branch of a trunk.

Armed: having thorns, spines, prickles, or similar sharp projections.

Asexual (vegetative) propagation: propagation using plant parts other than seeds (leaves, stems, roots, etc.) such as budding, grafting, cuttings, and layers.

Astringency: a puckery taste sensation caused by tannins.

Autopolyploid: a plant, tissue, or cell having more than two complete sets of chromosomes, all of which came from the same original source.

Auxin: plant growth regulator that functions more by stimulation of cell elongation than through an effect on cell division. Stimulates root initiation. Important in development of fruit and apical dominance.

Axil: the angle between the stem axis and a leaf petiole, branch, or other appendage attached to it.

Bark: the tough, exterior covering of a woody stem or root outside the cambium.

Basipetal: moving or developing from tip to base.

Berry: a simple fruit with one or more carpels and having the entire pericarp fleshy. A true berry is derived from an ovary with no accessory parts (as in the grape) while a false berry is composed of parts in addition to the ovary (as in the strawberry or blueberry).

Bilateral cordon: training, as in grapes, where the trunk is divided into two branches extending horizontally on a supporting wire.

Blade: the expanded portion of a leaf; the lamina.

Bloom: the state of flowering; to yield or produce flowers; the delicate waxy or powdery substance on the surface of berries.

Bract: a modified, often very small leaf.

Bracteole: a small bract.

Bramble: a prickly shrub or vine, as raspberries or blackberries, in the genus *Rubus.*

Brush: detached vascular strands remaining on the pedicel of the grape after the berry is detached from the pedicel; sometimes also used to refer to the intact parts.

Bud: an undeveloped shoot, usually protected by scales. The concerned tissues are mainly meristematic.

Budding: production of a shoot from an underground stem; the new growth in the spring; a form of graftage using a single bud scion.

Bud scales: protective scale-like leaves which cover the shoot apex and embryonic leaves of a winter bud, preventing desiccation and injury.

Bunch grapes: grapes whose fruit is borne in relatively large clusters, as is characteristic of *vinifera* and *labrusca* cultivars, as opposed to fruit borne as single berries or small clusters which has been characteristic of muscadine grapes of the past.

Callose: a complex carbohydrate which is a common cell wall constituent associated with sieve elements of the phloem. May cause sieve blockages.

Callus: a tissue composed of large, thin-walled parenchyma cells which develop on or below a wound; undifferentiated tissue useful in tissue culture.

Calyptra: the fused petals of the grape that fall off the flower at anthesis (bloom).

Calyx: a collective term for all the sepals of the flower.

Cambium: a lateral meristem in vascular plants which produces increases in diameter of stems and roots through the production of xylem, phloem, and parenchyma cells.

Cane: a main stem of a small fruit plant. In grapes the term applies to new shoots after they have lost their leaves in the fall.

Canker: a necrotic symptom of disease in woody plant parts with the necrosis sharply limited to a definite area of cortical tissue and malformed bark that is surrounded with callus.

Canopy: the cover or horizontal projection of the vegetation of a plant formed by its leaves, branches, etc.

Cap: the fused petals (calyptra) of the grape that fall off the flower at bloom; the calyx and pedicel of the strawberry above which the fruit is born.

Capillary water: water held in the soil against the force of gravity by capillary force (i.e., adhesion and cohesion); the total amount of water available to the plant.

Cap stem: the pedicel; the stem of the individual flower or fruit of the grape.

Carpel: the unit of structure of a pistil. A simple pistil has a single carpel (ovule-bearing portion of the pistil), while a compound pistil has two or more units or carpels.

Catch wire: a wire that serves as an attachment for developing grape shoots or other plants with tendrils and similarly trellised; the movable wires on a bramble trellis.

Cation: a positively charged ion.

Centripetal: in inflorescences, differentiation or bloom from the outside inward, or from the base upward.

Certified plants: plants produced under strict guidelines and inspections controlled by a regulatory agency to ensure trueness to type and freedom from damage, insects, disease, etc. Usually distinguished by colored labels designated foundation, registered, or certified stock.

Chilling requirement: the number of hours at or below a certain maximum temperature that is necessary to produce internal changes in a plant that result in uniform budbreak and the normal sequence of growth following winter dormancy.

Chilling unit: a period of time (usually 1 hour) at or below a specified threshold temperature that has the maximum effect toward fulfilling the chilling requirement of a given plant.

Chimera: a plant having tissues of differing genetic composition growing adjacent to each other.

Chlorophyll: the green pigments found in chloroplasts which are essential for the utilization of light energy in photosynthesis.

Chlorosis: yellowing caused by loss of or reduced production of chlorophyll.

Clone: a group of genetically identical individuals, all having been vegetatively (asexually) propagated and having been ultimately derived from a single individual.

Colonize: to become established.

Compatibile, compatibility: lacking any condition that would prevent pollen grains from functioning properly on a pistil, or lacking any condition that would prevent formation of a normal graft union.

Complete flower: a flower having pistil(s), stamens, petals, and sepals.

Compote: fruits cooked in a sugar syrup in such a way as to retain their shape.

Compound leaf: a leaf composed of two or more leaflets.

Continental climate: a climate having large daily and annual ranges of temperature.

Corolla: a collective term for all petals of a flower.

Cortical cell: a cell of the cortex, the primary tissue (or ground tissue) of the stem or root, located between the primary phloem (or endodermis, if present) and the epidermis.

Corymbose: arranged in corymbs, a flat-topped or convex, indeterminate, racemose inflorescence (having individual flowers borne on pedicels attached to the main axis) having the lower or outer pedicel longer and opening first.

Cross-pollination: transfer of pollen from anther of one plant to the stigma of another plant (unless of the same clone).

Crown: the persistent base of perennial plant; the top of a tree; the junction between stem and root.

Culinary: suited for cooking or processing in some form.

Cultivar: a cultivated variety (as distinguished from a botanical variety). Refers to a plant type within a particular cultivated species that is distinguishable by one or more characters.

Cuticle: a noncellular layer of waxy or fatty materials on the outer walls of epidermal cells.

Cyme: a type of inflorescence consisting of a broad, more or less flat-topped, determinate flower cluster, with central flowers opening first.

Cytokinins: N^6-substituted adenine derivatives found in plants, such as zeatin, or synthetic compounds such as kinetin. These compounds promote such processes as cell division, branching, and bud initiation and retard abscission and senescence of flowers and fruits and may prevent root initiation.

Day-neutral plant: a plant that flowers independently of daylength, with flowering controlled by other factors.

Deacclimation: the loss of adaptation to a climate; dehardening.

Decaploid: a plant tissue or cell having 10 complete sets of homologous chromosomes.

Deciduous: the falling of parts at the end of a growing period; refers also to trees and shrubs that drop their leaves at the end of each growing season.

Decumbent: a growing habit in which the lower portions of the stems or shoots lie close to the ground, without rooting adventitiously, while the upper part is erect.

Degree day: a heat unit that represents one degree of temperature above a given mean daily-base value. This measure is used to determine how near a crop is to maturity or some other stage of development.

Degrees Brix: a measure of total soluble solids content which approximates the percentage of sugar found in juice or a fruit. Corresponds to degrees Balling.

Dehiscence: the process of opening of a fruit (seed pod), anther, or sporangium to discharge the contents.

Demographic: pertaining to the characteristics (e.g., where they live, age, marital status, health) of a human population.

Determinate: having defined growth limits; not continuing growth indefinitely in a particular fashion.

Dioecious: having staminate (male) and pistillate (female) flowers on different plants of the same species.

Diploid: a nucleus, organism, or generation that has two sets of chromosomes.

Disarticulating: to separate at a preexisting point.

Distal: opposite from the point of origin or attachment; toward the apex.

Dodecaploid: an organisim or cell which has 12 sets of chromosomes rather than the usual two sets (diploid).

Dormancy: the temporary suspension of visible growth of any plant structure containing a meristem.

Dorsal: the lower surface; abaxial.

Drupe: a simple, fleshy fruit, derived from a single carpel, consisting of three layers: (1) an outer skin, the exocarp (epidermis); (2) an inner fleshy mesocarp; and (3) a hard, stony, or woody endocarp (pit) which encloses the seed. Occurs in peach, olive, cherry, etc., and referred to as stonefruits.

Drupelet (drupet): a miniature drupe; found in fruit composed of an aggregate of tiny drupes, as in blackberries and raspberries.

Drying ratio: the pounds of fresh fruit required to make 1 pound of dried fruit, as in grapes and raisins.

Duff: the partially decomposed organic matter (e.g., leaves, flowers, fruits, etc.) found beneath plants, as on a forest floor; litter.

Elliptical: in the form of a flattened circle more than twice as long as broad.

Emasculate: removal of anthers from a bud or flower.

Endemic: native or confined naturally to a particular and usually very restricted geographic area.

Endocarp: the innermost differentiated layer of the pericarp; the stony part of a drupe or pome fruit.

Endogenous: originating from deep-seated tissue; from within.

Endosperm: in angiosperms, a triploid embryonic nutritive tissue formed during double fertilization by fusion of a sperm with the polar nuclei. In gymnosperms, a similar haploid tissue is formed from the megagametophyte.

Enology: the science and study of wine making.

Epidermis: the outer layer of cells of the primary tissues of a plant (e.g., of leaves, young stems, and young roots). Usually consists of one layer of cells.

Epigynous: a flower having an inferior ovary, with sepals, petals, and stamens attached at or above the top of the ovary.

Epinasty: the twisting and bending of stems; the downward bending of leaves in response to exposure to ethylene.

Episodic growth: growth occurring in spurts or flushes rather than in one continuous process.

Ethylene: a gas having a chemical structure of $CH_2{=}CH_2$, produced by many tissues in very small amounts; it affects many physiological reactions in plants (e.g., promotes fruit ripening, induces flowering in pineapple, inhibits cell elongation).

Etiolation: development of plants or plant parts in the absence of light resulting in small leaves, stem elongation, and lack of chlorophyll.

Evergreen: plants that have persistent green leaves for two or more growing seasons, with leaves usually shed over a long period.

Exocarp: the outermost layer of the pericarp or fruit wall, often the mere skin (epidermis) of the fruit.

Exogenous: produced externally or developing on the outside.

Exserted: projecting beyond, sticking out or protruding.

Eye: a common term for a bud.

Face-packed: a method of packing a container of fruit for market with the top layer artistically arranged and with the fruit below having no special orientation (and sometimes lower in quality).

Fastigiate: strictly erect and having more or less parallel branching.

Feeder roots: fine rootlets that form the ultimate branches of a root system and serve as the zone in which nutrients are absorbed.

Felting: a covering of intertwined hairs.

Fertilization: the union or fusion of two gametes to produce a zygote; the process of adding soil amendments to increase fertility.

Field capacity: the water content of a soil after the drainage of gravitational water is essentially complete and the water content is momentarily stable; the amount of water the soil will hold against the force of gravity.

Filament: the stalk of a stamen that supports the anther.

Fixed (overhead) costs: production costs that do not vary with changes in the amount of product output; costs that do not vary with the enterprise.

Floral tube: a tube or cup formed by the fused basal portions of the sepals, petals, and stamens that surround the ovary (often occurs in epigynous or perigynous flowers).

Floret: small, individual flowers that make up a very dense inflorescence, such as those on the head of a composite flower or the spikelet of a grass spike.

Floricane: a flowering and fruiting stem of a bramble the season after it was produced (in the season of production, it is called a primocane).

Floristically: concerned with or relating to flowers, floral emblems, or a flora; of or relating to floristics, which is a branch of phytogeography that deals with plants and plant groups from the numerical standpoint; pertaining to flower characteristics.

Footcandle: a measure of illumination that represents direct illumination 1 foot from a uniform light source of 1 international candle.

Foxy, foxiness: the unique smell and taste of grapes of the *labrusca* species.

Fruit: a ripened ovary or ovaries with or without accessory floral parts and/or seeds.

Fruit buds: buds containing undeveloped flowers; also referred to as flower buds.

Fruit set: persistence and development of an ovary and/or adjacent tissue following bloom.

Gamete: a mature haploid reproductive cell or nucleus which unites with another gamete to form a zygote in sexual reproduction.

Generic: relating to all members of a genus; common to or relating to a whole group or class of plants (or other objects) rather than particular subdivisions of the group (or brand names).

Genome: a complete haploid set of chromosomes, as is present in a gamete (egg or sperm). Two genomes are found in somatic cells of diploids, while more than two genomes occur in polyploids.

Genotype: the genetic constitution of an individual, in contrast to its appearance or phenotype.

Genus: a taxonomic subdivision between the family and the species which includes one or more closely related species.

Germplasm: the genetic material that provides the physical basis for heredity; a collection of genotypes of a particular organism.

Gibberellin(s): a group of plant hormones that affect many physiological processes, such as cell elongation, induction of parthenocarpy, promotion of seed germination, and flower induction. Analogs are referred to as GA_1, GA_2, etc. GA_4 and GA_7 are most commonly used in agriculture.

Girdling: the removal of a narrow ring of bark from a shoot, cane, spur, or trunk (e.g., in grapes to affect fruit set, size, and/or ripening).

Glabrous: without pubescence; not hairy.

Glandular: bearing or having glands.

Glaucous: covered with a removable, waxy coating which gives the surface a whitish or bluish cast.

Gondola: a low-profile, large-capacity (3 + tons), wheel-mounted, open tank-type carrier towed behind a motorized vehicle and used to transport produce in bulk from field to processor.

Grafting: the process of inserting a scion into (or onto) a rootstock in such a way that the two parts will unite and grow as one unit.

Green-manure crop: a crop, usually a small grain or a legume, plowed under while young and succulent in order to add organic matter and improve the soil.

Growth regulator: any of several classes of natural or synthetic chemicals that in some way regulate plant growth.

Guttation: an exudation of water through hydathodes from the tips of leaves.

Haploid: nucleus, cell, or entire organism in which only one member of each set of homologous chromosomes is present.

Hardpan: an extremely hard layer of soil through which plant roots, animals, and water will not penetrate.

Head: that portion of a trunk, as in a grapevine, where arms or cordons originate.

Headland: the unplanted space between the ends of rows and the field border that is left free of plants to facilitate cultural operations, turning of equipment, harvest, etc.

Heartwood: the inner layers of the xylem (wood) that are nonliving and nonfunctional.

Heeled-in: having the roots of a plant covered temporarily with soil or another moist medium to prevent drying until they can be planted in a permanent location. Plants are often stuck in at an angle rather than upright.

Herbaceous: a plant that forms little or no secondary thickening (woody tissue) in its stems, having the characteristics of an herb.

Herbicide: chemicals used to kill plants.

Hermaphrodite, Hermaphroditic: an organism or structure possessing both male and female reproductive organs [e.g., a flower with both stamens and pistil(s)]; also perfect.

Heteroploid: an individual or cell with uneven numbers of chromosomes in each set [i.e., one $(2n - 1)$ or both chromosomes of a pair may be lost or one or more chromosomes may be added to a set $(2n + 1, 2n + 2, $ etc.$)$].

Hill: a training system where plants are maintained as individuals with open space around each plant (e.g., the "hill" system in strawberries or raspberries). Ultimately plants may enlarge to fill the open space, but new plants are not allowed.

Homoploid species: a group of related species that all have the same chromosome number.

Hormone: an organic chemical, usually produced in very small amounts in one part of an organism and transported to another area of the same organism, where it affects growth and/or other functions.

Hybrid: an individual resulting from the union of gametes differing in one or more genes.

Hybridization: the process of crossing individuals with different genetic makeup.

Hydathode: a very small pore or specialized structure on a leaf (usually at the tip) which releases liquid by guttation.

Hydrometer: a floating device and graduated cylinder which are used together for measuring the specific gravity of liquids; a device used to determine soluble solids in a liquid, as with a brix hydrometer.

Hypertrophy: an excessive, abnormal, usually pathological enlargement of cell size in a tissue or organ.

Hyphae (plural of hypha): a single thread-like filament which is the structural unit of fungi. The hyphae together comprise the mycelium.

Imperfect flower: a flower that lacks either functional stamens or pistil.

Incompatability: a condition, controlled by a variety of factors, in which some otherwise normal pollen grains are unable to function properly on certain pistils; in grafting, the inability to form a successful, long-lived union.

Indehiscent: not dehiscent; remaining closed at maturity.

Indeterminate growth: unrestricted growth, as with a vegetative apical meristem capable of producing an unlimited number of lateral organs.

Indexing: determining the presence of disease or verifying the assumption of freedom from disease, such as a virus. Indexing usually involves placing scions of the test plant onto a sensitive indicator plant or may employ grafting runners together of a test plant and a sensitive indicator.

Inferior ovary: an ovary that is situated below the point of attachment of the other floral organs.

Infiltration rate (soil): rate of movement of water into the soil.

Inflorescence: the arrangement of flowers on a floral axis; a floral (flower) cluster.

Inoculum: a pathogen or its part which can infect a plant.

Integrated pest management (IPM): an approach to pest control using all possible methods but involving minimum use of chemicals and allowing natural forces to control pest populations until it is determined that populations will surpass intolerable levels without chemicals.

Interfertile: allowing union of male and female gametes of different individuals or groups.

Internal rate of return: a measure of profitability; for an investment, the return that equates the present value of annual net cash revenues with the project's cost.

Internode: the area of stem between nodes.

In vitro: has reference to reactions, responses observed, or experiments done in test tubes, petri dishes, etc., in isolation from the whole organism.

In vivo: biological processes that occur within the whole, living organism.

Isotherm: a line joining points on the earth's surface having the same temperature at a given time, or the same mean temperature for a given period.

Juvenile (plant): a young plant that has not yet gained the ability to flower, as opposed to a plant that is in the adult phase and possesses the ability to flower but is merely vegetative.

Knee roots: a root arising above ground level as a result of flooding or poor soil drainage.

Latent bud: a bud that does not grow in the season following its development. A shoot arising from such a bud is a latent shoot.

Lateral: a branch coming from the side of a main stem; a branch of the main axis of a fruit cluster.

Latitude: the distance measured in degrees north or south from the equator.

Leach, Leaching: the application of large amounts of water to the soil to remove excess salts or fertilizers; the natural downward movement of minerals through the soil by percolating water.

Leader: a main branch of a tree or shrub.

Leaf bud: a bud that produces only leaves.

Lenticils: spongy areas in the cork surfaces of stems, roots, some fruits, and other plant parts which allow interchange of gases between the tissue and atmosphere.

Locule: a compartment, chamber, or cavity in an ovary, anther, or fruit.

Long-day plant: a plant that flowers only after receiving illumination longer than a "critical photoperiod," which varies in length (11 to 14 hours) depending on the species.

Lug: a container for fruits and vegetables, normally holding 20 to 25 pounds of produce and made of wood, plastic, or cardboard and used in the past in the field and as a marketing container.

Lux: a metric unit of illumination equal to 0.0929 footcandle. One footcandle equals 10.76 lux.

Margin: difference between production or acquisition costs and selling price.

Maritime climate: climate influenced by the ocean (or other factors having the same influence), resulting in mild temperatures and small daily and annual ranges of temperature.

Maturation: differentiation or specialization of cells or tissues; in a fruit, the series of changes that occur in the period between the cessation of growth and the attainment of physiological maturity.

Meristem: a tissue region of mitotic cell division, such as the vascular cambium.

Meristematic: capable of cell division.

-Merous: a suffix indicating the number of parts, as in flowers "5-merous," in which each of the floral organs present are in groups of five (e.g., petals, stamens, or sepals).

Mesocarp: the middle layer of cells of the pericarp or fruit wall found between the endocarp and exocarp.

Mesophyll: the photosynthetic tissue between the upper and lower epidermis of a leaf.

Micropropagation: the production of plants from very small plant parts, tissues, or cells grown aseptically in a test tube or other container where the environment and nutrition can be rigidly controlled. The term "tissue culture" is often applied to this process.

Millerandage: a very loose fruit cluster condition in grapes caused by poor fruit set and large numbers of shot berries.

Mineral soils: soils with very low organic matter content, usually not more than 6% in the plow layer and lesser amounts in the remainder of the profile. Most agricultural soils are of this type.

Morphology: the study of the form, structure, and development of plants.

Mulch: soil, straw, peat, plastic, or any other loose or sheet material placed on the ground to conserve soil moisture, control weeds, promote early maturity, or prevent erosion; material, such as straw, placed over plants or plant parts to protect them from cold or heat.

Must: crushed berries and juice.

Mutation: an inheritable change in the genetic material of a cell.

Mycorrhiza: a symbiotic, nonpathogenic association between fungi and roots of many types of plants. Fungi may be superficial (ectotropic) or within the host cell (endotropic).

Nanometer: one millionth of a millimeter (formerly termed a millimicron).

Necrosis: the death of cells, resulting either from injury or normal senescence.

Nectary: any structure that secretes nectar, such as glands, trichomes, or stomata-like orifices.

Nematode (of plants): elongate, nonsegmented worms of the phylum *Nematoda*, which are important causative agents and vectors of many diseases.

Net assimilation rate: increase in dry matter during a particular time interval.

Net returns: the difference between gross returns (gross income) and the cost of doing business (expenses).

Node: an area on the stem where leaves are attached and shoots develop.

Noncount buds: buds on grape canes that are so close to the cane base that they are not included in the bud count used as the basis for balanced pruning.

Northern hemisphere: the half of the earth that is north of the equator.

Oblate: nearly spherical but compressed at the poles.

Obtuse: blunt or rounded at the apex, with the sides forming an angle of more than 90°, margins straight to convex.

On the flood: refers to the harvest of cranberries by flooding, including removal of berries with various devices and floating the berries for collection.

Ontogeny: the entire development of an organism (or part of it) from the zygote to maturity.

Open-pollination: the free exchange of pollen between flowers and plants regardless of flower type or cultivar.

Orbicular: more or less circular in outline or shape.

Organic soils: soils such as peats and mucks with a very high organic matter content (often 80% or more) not only in the plow layer but in the entire profile.

Outcrossing: the production of seed by crossing genetically different plants.

Ovary: the enlarged, basal portion of a pistil, which contains the ovules or seeds.

Ovule: the integumented megasporangium and enclosed structures which after fertilization become the seed.

Palmate: having lobes, veins, or divisions radiating from a common point, as in palmately-lobed, palmately-veined, or palmately-compound.

Papillae (plural of papilla): a soft nipple-shaped protuberance; a type of trichome.

Parenchyma cell: the most common plant cell type, occurring in stem and root cortex tissue, stem pith, leaf mesophyll, fruit flesh, etc. These cells are usually alive at maturity, are usually thin-walled, and have a variety of sizes and shapes. Functions include photosynthesis, storage, secretion, movement of water, and food transport.

Parthenocarpic (parthenocarpy): fruit developed naturally or artificially induced without sexual fertilization.

Parthenogenesis: the development of an unfertilized egg into an organism.

Pedicel: the stalk of an individual flower (or the resulting fruit) in an inflorescence.

Peduncle: the stalk of an inflorescence (or the resulting fruit cluster) or the stalk of a solitary flower.

Pendulous: suspended, nodding, or hanging down from a support.

Pentamerous: having parts in fives or multiples of five.

Pentaploid: a nucleus or organism that has five sets of chromosomes.

Penultimate: next to last.

Perfect (flower): a flower having both stamens and pistil(s).

Perianth: a collective term for the floral envelopes, usually the combined calyx (sepals) and corolla (petals).

Pericarp: the mature fruit wall that develops from the ovary wall, frequently divided into two or three distinct layers: exocarp, mesocarp, endocarp.

Pericycle: a layer of tissue located inside the endodermis which forms a cylinder around the vascular tissues. In seed plants, it is common in roots but infrequent in shoots. Branch roots arise from the pericycle.

Permanent wilting point: the soil moisture content at which the leaves on a plant wilt and do not recover when placed in a humid atmosphere.

Petiolar sinus: a cleft in the leaf margin in the area of attachment of the petiole.

Petiole: the stem of a leaf; the stalk attaching a leaf blade to a stem.

Phenotype: the external physical appearance of an organism resulting from an interactin between the genetic constitution (genotype) of the individual and the environment.

Phloem: the principal food-conducting tissue of the plant, composed of seive tubes, parenchyma cells, fibers, and sclereids.

Photoperiod: day length.

Phylloxera: a small, yellowish, aphid-like insect that attacks roots and/or leaves of grapes but does the most damage to the roots.

Pistil: the female reproductive organ of a flower, composed of a stigma, style, and ovary. It may consist of a single carpel or two or more fused carpels.

Pistillate flower: a flower having a pistil but no stamens.

Pith: the ground tissue that occupies the center of a stem or root inside the vascular cylinder. It usually consists of parenchyma cells.

Ploidy: refers to the number of chromosome sets in a cell, tissue, or organism.

Pneumatophores: vertical extensions of the buried roots of certain trees (i.e., mangroves) that exist in marsh or swamp habitats. They extend out of the mud or water and function as pathways for exchange of gases between the atmosphere and the submerged roots.

Pollinate, pollination: transfer of pollen from anther to stigma.

Pollinator: the agent of pollen transfer (i.e., insects or wind).

Pollinizer: the producer of pollen.

Polymorphic: having several to many variable forms within the same species.

Polyploid: a plant, tissue, or cell having more than two complete sets of homologous chromosomes.

Pomology: the science and art of fruit growing, usually now used in reference to temperate fruit and nut crops.

Positive rate of return: a return providing a net profit; where returns from resources used exceed the cost.

Primary flower, fruit: the flower that terminates the central axis of the flower or fruit cluster, as in the strawberry. This flower in the strawberry blooms first and produces the largest fruit.

Primocane: the first-year shoot or cane, as in brambles (raspberries, blackberries).

Primordia (plural of primordium): a cell, tissue, or organ in its earliest stage of differentiation.

Procumbent: trailing or lying on the ground without rooting at the nodes; prostrate.

Propagule: any structure, sexual or asexual, that becomes separated from the parental individual and serves as a means of propagation for that plant.

Proprietary shipper: a privately owned, usually nonproducing organization that ships produce under its own brand name(s), which are designed to develop brand recognition by consumers; a shipper having exclusive right or control of a commodity in a given area.

Prostrate: trailing or lying on the ground without rooting at the nodes; procumbent.

Protodermal: from primary meristematic tissue which differentiates into the epidermis.

Proximal: situated near the point of reference, usually the stem; next to the point of origin or attachment; away from the apex; opposite of distal.

Pubescent: covered with short, soft trichomes (hairs).

Pyrene: A hard, stony endocarp enclosing one or two seeds that is found in the center of each drupelet in a raspberry or blackberry fruit.

Quiescence: period of nonvisible growth controlled by external factors. Growth will proceed when environmental conditions are favorable. A new term proposed to describe this condition is *eco-dormancy.*

Raceme: an unbranched, indeterminate inflorescence, in which the individual flowers are borne on pedicels along the main axis.

Racemose: like a raceme; having flowers in raceme-like inflorescences that may or may not be true racemes.

Rachis: the axis of a compound leaf upon which the leaflets are attached; the major (central) axis of an inflorescence (or resulting fruit cluster).

Raphides: a needle-shaped crystal of calcium oxalate, usually occurring in bundles.

Receptacle: the portion of the axis of the flower stalk on which the flower is borne. It may become part of the fruit (i.e., in the blackberry) or may enlarge and become the entire fruit (strawberry).

Reflexed: abruptly bent or recurved downward or backward.

Rest: period of nonvisible growth of a plant structure that is controlled by internal factors. These factors usually originate within the structure and require a chilling period to overcome and would be considered a form of endodormancy.

Retail: Sales in relatively small quantities directly to consumers.

Return on the investment: the amount realized as profit from the use of capital; a measure of the profitability of the use of capital.

Rhizomatous: producing or bearing rhizomes which are root-like, usually horizontal, underground stems with roots forming on the lower side and shoots forming on ends or upper surfaces.

Ripening: composite changes that occur from the end of the maturation period to the beginning of senescence.

Roguing: the removal of undesirable individuals from a group of plants in order to maintain a high level of purity.

Rootings: newly rooted cuttings.

Runner: a specialized aboveground stem that develops from an axillary bud of the crown of the plant. It has long internodes and grows horizontally along the ground. It forms shoots and adventitious roots at some nodes.

Runnering: process of producing runners.

Sapwood: the outer portion of the wood (xylem) of a stem or trunk where active conduction of water occurs.

Schlereid: a schlerenchyma cell having a thick, lignified secondary cell wall with many pits. It may or may not be living at maturity and varies in form.

Scion (cion): the detached shoot containing one or more buds from a plant being propagated by grafting or budding; top part of the graft.

Secondary flower or fruit: the flower or fruit that terminates the two main subdivisions of the central axis of the flower or fruit cluster, as in the strawberry.

Self-compatible, self-fertile, self-fruitful, self-setting: a plant that is capable of reproducing sexually by itself; the ability to produce fruits with normal seeds which will germinate, following self-pollination.

Self-pollination: transfer of pollen from anther to stigma of the same flower, or of another flower on the same plant, or from one flower to another between plants of the same clone.

Self-sterile: incapable of reproducing sexually by self-fertilization.

Senescence: irreversible changes following ripening of a fruit which lead to death; the aging process of an organ or organism.

Sepal: one of the outermost, sterile appendages of a flower, which normally encloses the other floral parts in the bud; one of the separate parts of the calyx.

Serrate: having a sawtoothed margin with sharp teeth pointing forward or toward the apex.

Shatter: the loss of unfertilized or aborted berries (e.g., grape) in the field, or loss (drop) of berries at some subsequent stage of development or after harvest for a variety of reasons.

Shelter: a windbreak or plant growing structure.

Shoot: current season's stem growth prior to the time of loss of leaves in the fall. It may or may not produce flowers and fruits.

Short-day plant: a plant that flowers only after receiving illumination that is shorter than a "critical photoperiod," which varies in length (8 to 10 hours) depending on the species.

Shot berry: very small berries of the grape that fail to develop to normal size and are usually seedless.

Sieve element: a cell of the phloem concerned mainly with the longitudinal transport of food materials.

Simple fruit: a fruit produced from a mature, simple or compound pistil and having no other parts.

Sociodemographic characteristics: a description of a group of people in terms of social (race, religion, etc.) and population (age, sex, marital status, health, etc.) characteristics.

Socioeconomic characteristics: a description of a population in terms of social (race, religion, etc.) and monetary (income, spending habits, etc.) characteristics.

Soil fumigant: a pesticide that is usually a liquid at low temperature or when under pressure and will volatilize to form a gas when heated or released from pressure. When applied to the soil, a plastic cover may be required to retain the gas for a minimum time. Certain fumigants with low volatility may be formulated as granules and incorporated into the soil.

Southern hemisphere: the half of the earth south of the equator.

Spatulate: spoon or spatula-shaped.

Sporidia (plural of sporidium): basidiospores found in smuts and rusts.

Sport (bud sport): a plant or portion of a plant that arises by spontaneous mutation. It usually must be maintained by asexual propagation.

Sporulation: the process of spore production.

Stamen: the pollen producing structure of the flower of an angiosperm. It consists of an anther and filament.

Staminate flower: a flower with stamens but lacking or with a non-functional pistil.

Stellate: star-shaped hairs; plant hairs that have radiating branches.

Stenospermocarpy: a form of fruit set in grapes where fertilization occurs and seeds form but soon abort. Berries, however, continue to mature and usually contain only rudimentary seeds (e.g., in "Thompson Seedless").

Sterile: infertile; lacking functional reproductive structures or organs.

Stigma: the portion of the pistil upon which the pollen germinates.

Stipule: a small, leaf-like structure found at the base of some leaf petioles, usually found in pairs.

Stock (rootstock, understock): the root or the stem and associated root on to which a scion is grafted or budded.

Stoloniferous: producing or bearing stolons.

Stomata (plural of stomate): minute openings in the leaf or stem epidermis which function in gaseous exchange between the plant and its external environment. Stomata are bordered by guard cells which regulate the size of the opening.

Style: the slender stalk-like portion of the pistil between the ovary and stigma.

Suberized: having all walls impregnated with suberin; having cut surfaces heal by development of corky tissue.

Subtropical plant: plants grown in areas in which occasional light frosts occur. A period of dormancy induced by cool weather [temperatures below 50 to 55°F (10 to 13°C) for a month or more] is generally essential for proper flowering or best fruit quality.

Sucker: an adventitious shoot produced from a root. This term is also used to apply to shoots coming from the lower portion of the main stem or trunk.

Surfactant: material that favors or improves the emulsifying, dispersing, spreading, wetting, or other surface-modifying properties of a liquid used as a pesticide.

Sympodial: a zigzag or irregular form of growth.

Systemic: in reference to a pesticide, one that spreads throughout the vascular system of a plant; of or affecting the entire organism.

Tannin: a chemical compound of certain fruits, seeds, and wines that causes an astringent taste.

Teliospores: in some rust or smut fungi, a thick-walled spore in which fusion of two nucleii and meiosis takes place. It gives rise to a short tube (basidium) which bears basidiospores.

Temperate-zone plants: refers to woody plants that require a more or less extended chilling period for proper vegetative growth and flowering; plants that are usually grown in areas that have periods of prolonged cold weather, often below freezing.

Tendril: a long, slender, coiling structure (modified leaf or stem) on a stem that can coil around an object and help support a climbing plant.

Tetrad: a group of four spores derived from a spore mother cell as a result of meiosis. Some pollen grains are released in groups of four, maintaining the tetrad arrangement to the mature stage.

Tissue culture: the *in vitro,* aseptic system of maintaining and multiplying plant cells and tissues. *See* micropropagation.

Tomentose: covered with dense, matted, woolly hairs.

Torus: the receptacle of a flower. In blackberries it remains with the fruit after harvest, becoming an edible portion of the fruit.

Trailing: prostrate on the ground.

Transpiration: loss of water vapor from plant tissues primarily through stomata, but includes loss through the cuticle and lenticils.

Tropical plant: plants grown in areas free from frost, with growth ceasing in most crops at temperatures below about 68°F (20°C). Dormant periods controlled by moisture are essential for many crops of this group, but others do best with well-distributed rainfall.

Truss: flower or fruit cluster framework.

Turgid: swollen or inflated due to the uptake of water.

Turgor: the state of being turgid; the normal distension of plant cells resulting from internal pressure exerted when water is absorbed.

Tyloses (plural of tylose): a bubble-like outgrowth from a ray or axial parenchyma cell, which extends into the lumen of a vessel through a pit cavity. Such outgrowths may result in vessel blockages.

Unarmed: lacking any sharp projections such as thorns, prickles, or spines.

Variable costs: costs that vary in relation to the amount of product output or with the enterprise.

Variegation: a varied, somewhat mottled pattern of coloration in a leaf, flower, or other plant part because pigmentation is not uniform in density (e.g., chlorophyll in a leaf).

Variety: a subdivision of a species which differs as a group in some minor definable characteristic(s) from the rest of the species. This term should be used to refer to botanical varieties and the term cultivar should be used for cultivated (horticultural or agronomic) varieties.

Vascular tissue: the conducting tissues of a plant composed mainly of primary and/or secondary xylem and phloem and including procambium and/or vascular cambium.

Vector: a carrier; an organism, usually an insect, that carries a disease-causing organism from one plant to another.

Ventral: the upper surface; the inner surface of an organ; adaxial.

Veraison: the stage of development when grape berries begin to soften and/or color.

Viticulture: the art and science of grape growing.

Waterlogging: partial or complete submersion of roots in water as a result of a more-or-less permanent restriction of soil drainage.

Watersprout: a very vigorous shoot that arises from the lower trunk or large branch of a tree and grows rapidly straight up through the tree.

Wholesale: sales in relatively large quantities to jobbers or retailers rather than direct to consumers.

Xylem: the woody portion of the stem; the principal water- and mineral-conducting tissue in the plant.

PRIMARY REFERENCES

LITTLE, R. J., AND C. E. JONES. A dictionary of botany. Van Nostrand-Reinhold, New York.

SOULE, J. E. 1985. Glossary for horticultural terms. Wiley, New York.

Index

597

Blueberries, *continued.*
in Pennsylvania, 274
pest control and, 69, 71, 72, 74–76, 276, 288, 292–95, 306–309, 320, 325–27
planting/cultivation/harvesting/marketing of, 63, 65, 75, 285–96, 301–302, 304–10, 505, 506, 509, 517–18, 520, 522, 525–27, 546, 549, 552, 554–55, 561, 566–67
on Prince Edward Island, 302
in Quebec, 274, 310
rabbiteye, 2, 274–77, 279, 315, 317–28, 520
in Rhode Island, 275, 279
in Scotland, 275
soil and, 58, 274, 276, 277, 286, 289–91, 319–22, 327, 566
in South Carolina, 285, 315
in Tennessee, 318
in Texas, 275, 315, 318, 322
in United States, 12, 20, 276, 283, 289, 296, 301, 318, 320, 324, 327, 328
in Washington, 281, 283
in West Virginia, 274
in Wisconsin, 274
in Yugoslavia, 275
Boysenberries, 179–80, 215, 220, 522
Britain, 267
blackberries in, 219
blueberries in, 275, 285–86
currants in, 246, 254, 258, 259
gooseberries in, 247, 260
kiwifruit in, 472
raspberries in, 157, 174, 178
strawberries in, 85–88, 129
British Columbia:
blueberries in, 281
cranberries in, 335, 341, 347, 356–57, 371
raspberries in, 12, 157, 203
strawberries in, 130, 131

C

California, 22, 24–26
blackberries in, 229
grapes in, 12, 30, 383, 390, 409, 411, 415–17, 433, 436–38, 446, 448, 450, 512–14, 518, 569–70
kiwifruit in, 472, 474, 483–86, 488, 490, 491, 496, 499–501
raspberries in, 157, 180

strawberries in, 12, 14, 87, 103–104, 109–10, 113, 114, 126, 127, 129–31, 133–44, 146, 150, 151, 537, 571
Canada. *See* individual provinces and fruits
Chile:
grapes in, 537
kiwifruit in, 501
raspberries in, 157, 178–79
strawberries in, 87–88
China, 129, 472, 473, 475, 477, 483
Climate:
air movement and content, 16–19, 38, 51
altitude (elevation), 23–24, 28, 34–35, 43
blackberries and, 20, 47, 214, 220, 226, 229–30, 232, 235, 237, 238
blueberries and, 20, 35, 37, 40, 47, 274, 276, 285–86, 289, 317–19, 323–24
bodies of water, 44
continentality, 22–23
cranberries and, 20, 47, 334, 341, 342, 346–48, 352, 372
currants and, 47, 247, 252–54, 258, 259
elderberries and, 47, 364, 367
frost/freezing, 17, 26, 28, 30, 34–35, 37–42
gooseberries and, 40, 47, 246, 252–53
grapes and, 20, 23, 26, 30, 31, 35, 40, 45, 47, 73, 385, 387, 388, 392, 400, 410–14, 416, 418, 422, 428, 429, 438, 443, 444, 448, 450, 453
Juneberries and, 375, 377
kiwifruit and, 47, 477, 481–85
latitude, 20, 22
ocean currents, 23
mountain barriers, 23
precipitation, 18, 19, 22–23
raspberries and, 20, 47, 157–60, 164, 166–69, 171, 172, 174, 178, 180, 198
regions of United States, 24–26
soil flooding, 46–47
solar radiation, 18–20, 22, 32, 34
strawberries and, 20, 31, 39, 40, 47, 65–66, 96, 99, 100, 102, 105–6, 109–17, 129–32, 134, 139–42, 144–46
subdivisions of, 24

temperature, 16–19, 26, 28, 30–32, 34–35, 37–46
topography, 28, 34, 43–44
transpiration rate, 45–46
Colorado, 25, 66
Cranberries, 2, 4, 273
in Alaska, 336, 371
in British Columbia, 335, 341, 347, 356–57, 371
in Canada, 334, 335, 371, 372
climate and, 20, 47, 334, 341, 342, 346–48, 352, 372
in Europe, 336
fertilization of, 341, 344, 349–50, 373
highbush, 8, 363–64, 370–74, 523
irrigation of, 341–44, 346–48, 350, 352–54, 373
in Manitoba, 372
in Massachusetts, 334–35, 339–41, 347, 356–58, 372
in Michigan, 371
in Minnesota, 335, 372
in New Brunswick, 371
in Newfoundland, 335
in New Hampshire, 372
in New Jersey, 335, 349, 356–58
in New York, 371
in New Zealand, 12
in North America, 336
in North Carolina, 335
in Ontario, 335
in Oregon, 335, 340, 341, 347, 356–59, 371
origins/descriptions/types/uses of, 334–36, 338–40, 356, 363–64, 370–72
pest control and, 341, 342, 344, 351–52, 357–60, 372–73
planting/cultivation/harvesting/marketing of, 63, 340–44, 346–54, 356–61, 363–64, 372–74, 511, 520, 523, 524
in Quebec, 335
soil and, 340–42, 349, 372, 373
in South Dakota, 371
in United States, 12, 20, 334, 335, 339–40, 347, 356, 358, 363, 371–73
in Washington, 335, 339–41, 347, 356–59
in Wisconsin, 335, 338, 340, 341, 346–48, 356–60
Currants, 2, 3, 8, 12
black, 47, 245–48, 251–54, 258, 262–64, 266, 267
in Britain, 246, 254, 258, 259

600   Index